The Practical Guide to Wall Street

Founded in 1807, John Wiley & Sons is the oldest independent publishing company in the United States. With offices in North America, Europe, Australia, and Asia, Wiley is globally committed to developing and marketing print and electronic products and services for our customers' professional and personal knowledge and understanding.

The Wiley Finance series contains books written specifically for finance and investment professionals as well as sophisticated individual investors and their financial advisors. Book topics range from portfolio management to e-commerce, risk management, financial engineering, valuation, and financial instrument analysis, as well as much more.

For a list of available titles, visit our Web site at www.WileyFinance.com.

The Practical Guide to Wall Street

Equities and Derivatives

MATTHEW TAGLIANI

WILEY

John Wiley & Sons, Inc.

Published by John Wiley & Sons, Inc., Hoboken, New Jersey.
Published simultaneously in Canada.

For general information on our other products and services or for technical support, please contact our Customer Care Department within the United States at (800) 762-2974, outside the United States at (317) 572-3993 or fax (317) 572-4002.

Wiley also publishes its books in a variety of electronic formats. Some content that appears in print may not be available in electronic books. For more information about Wiley products, visit our web site at www.wiley.com.

Library of Congress Cataloging-in-Publication Data:

Tagliani, Matthew, 1974–
  The practical guide to Wall Street : equities and derivatives / Matthew Tagliani.
      p.   cm. – (Wiley finance series)
  Includes index.
  ISBN 978-0-470-38372-8 (cloth)
  1. Stocks.   2. Derivative securities.   I. Title.
  HG4661.T34 2009
  332.63′220973–dc22

                                                                    2008039517

Printed in the United States of America

10 9 8 7 6 5 4 3 2 1

To Nati, Sofía, and Cosmo

Contents

Preface

What makes a good Wall Street trader or salesperson?

There is no magic formula. Successful Wall Street professionals possess a mixture of intelligence, common sense, attention to detail, business savvy, wit, presence, energy, enthusiasm, interpersonal skills, self-confidence, as well as other attributes that are not only difficult to quantify, but that vary from one person to the next. Market conditions and client demands are constantly changing and success speaks as much to the person's ability to do a job well today as to the ability to adapt quickly and effectively to the ever-changing markets and the evolving requirements of the job.

In particular, success on "the Street" is not the result of a specific academic training. The men and women who work on the trading floor come from enormously varied backgrounds. In addition to the many MBAs and economics, finance, and business administration majors that one would expect to find, I have also worked with traders and salespeople who held degrees in English literature, art history, astrophysics, and everything in between, including a few (all senior to me, I should add) with no university education whatsoever.

Because the skills required for success on Wall Street are not easily defined, or correlated to strength in a particular academic area, trading floors have always operated on an apprenticeship model. Inexperienced hires (typically recent university graduates or newly-minted MBAs) are admitted to analyst and associate training programs based on an assessment of the quality of the "raw material" they offer as a potential employee—brains, personality, work ethic, and so on. They are then given a seat on a desk as either a trader or salesperson where they develop their knowledge and understanding of the business by actually doing the job.

Institutional finance is a broad and complex business and it takes years to develop a clear understanding of the activities and interactions of all the different groups around the trading floor, as well as the structure of markets, the dynamics of trading, the relationship with clients, and the unique language used among traders to communicate orders. The majority of this knowledge is not gained through formal training seminars or classes but through experience and informal explanations scribbled on napkins or scraps of paper by more senior coworkers.

Given the fact that almost every major investment bank and broker-dealer uses this approach to hiring and training, the apprenticeship model has clearly proven its merit. It is not, however, without its shortcomings and it was my own experience with the inefficiencies of this model and their consequences for both new hires and experienced traders and salespeople that motivated me to write this book.

NEW HIRES

Under this apprenticeship model, there is a tremendous information gap between those with actual business experience and outsiders: The only people who truly understand what happens on a trading floor are the ones who are already working there. How, then, are potential candidates to know whether a career in sales and trading would be interesting to them? The glamorized and greatly exaggerated image of Wall Street offered by Hollywood, or found in the gossipy, tabloid-style memoirs of some former industry employees, while certainly entertaining, does not accurately depict the day-to-day realities of a typical trader or salesperson in the equities division of an investment bank. The surprising fact is that the majority of applicants seeking jobs on Wall Street do so with as much, or more, misinformation about what they *think* the role will entail than concrete knowledge of what actually awaits them.

The information gap also makes the recruiting and hiring process inefficient. It is difficult to effectively interview someone who, in practice, does not speak your language and knows almost nothing about the job he is applying for. One of the reasons why Wall Street job interviews contain such notoriously obscure and seemingly random questions and requests as "Tell me how many ping-pong balls would fit inside a 747." or "Let me hear you shout." is that, if you cannot ask candidates questions specifically related to the role, then it is only possible to get a sense for their skills and qualifications in very roundabout ways.

Unfortunately, until now, even if new candidates have made a correct choice and the sales and trading business is the place for them, there is no way they can prepare in advance. Ask any trader or salesperson and you will get a similar response: The Harvard MBA, the Princeton economics major, the MIT physicist and every one of the other exceptionally bright, hardworking, and talented young people that come to Wall Street are, upon arrival on their first day of work, pretty much useless. It is not that they are not capable; they have simply studied the wrong things, and for the most part, lack applicable knowledge.

Without taking anything away from the enormous value of formal education, the fact is that the standard academic treatment of finance specifically removes from consideration most of the contribution provided by the sales and trading division. In order to model the complexities of real-world finance, certain simplifying assumptions are made: investors are assumed to be perfectly rational and markets are modelled as "efficient," meaning that the price of a stock incorporates all available information about the prospects for that company. If that were the case, there would be very little that a salesperson or trader could contribute to the investment process. What is more, the first assumption of virtually any stock valuation or derivative pricing model is that there are no trading frictions of execution costs. However, it is precisely these frictions that are the primary sources of revenue for the trading floor. The details academia excludes are actually the bread and butter of Wall Street.[1] While in recent years many universities have taken steps to give a more "real world" focus to their curriculum, this is still, in most cases, a nascent effort.

Perhaps the most glaring example of the inefficiency caused by outsiders' lack of basic trading floor knowledge comes from the experience of Wall Street's summer student interns. Summer internship programs are considered to be the highest-probability route to a Wall Street job for undergraduates and MBAs and admission is extremely competitive, with acceptance rates at tier-one institutions of as low as 2 to 3 percent. Students prepare intensely for their 10-week programs, during which they rotate through various desks on the trading floor, sitting beside the traders and salespeople, doing small jobs, and learning about the business in the hope of making a good enough impression to receive a job offer for the coming year. For students interested in a career in financial markets, there is really no better learning opportunity than to sit on the "front lines" of finance at a top tier investment bank and watch firsthand how the institutional traders and salespeople actually make it all happen.

Unfortunately, for many students, this opportunity is largely wasted. On arrival, the typical summer intern has so little idea of what happens on the trading floor that they spend most of their summer just trying to orient themselves. Their time with traders is squandered asking very basic questions that could be easily learned from a book, much to the frustration of busy front-office employees. Many interns finish their summer rotations with little more than some vague notions of what they have been told, a few notes or handouts, and the sense that something very important was going on, but that it was beyond their reach.

The logic behind the Wall Street apprenticeship model is that the subtleties and nuances of real-world finance can only be learned through experience. The inefficiency in the model is that, without an organized presentation to guide them, new hires and summer interns spend a great deal of time and effort learning basic concepts, and it is only after many months of working that the more refined understanding begins to develop.

In many ways, mastering the skills necessary for success in sales or trading is like learning to drive a car: there is simply no other option than to get behind the wheel and do it—slowly at first, and then gradually building up confidence, picking up speed, and taking on greater challenges. Where the problem lies, and what this book endeavors to solve, is that, if working in institutional trading and sales is like driving a car, historically there has been no driver's education course or handbook of road rules. New hires have been arriving on the job without knowing what the gas pedal, brake, or steering wheel are for and having never seen a street sign in their lives. What few books have been available were designed for experts and were as useful as a physics text on the thermodynamics of engine combustion would be to someone learning to drive.

EXPERIENCED PROFESSIONALS

Many firms provide employees with opportunities for additional professional development, though for the most part, beyond the initial training programs, learning is done on an ad hoc basis and in a fairly disorganized manner. Some traders and salespeople take it upon themselves to be a student of the business, and extend the breadth and depth of their understanding as far as possible. Most, however, assemble what can best be described as a "mosaic" understanding of the sales and trading business: based on the combination of a number of small pieces of information picked up from various places over time, they put together a broad picture of the activities on a trading floor which is fairly complete, but only from a certain distance. Drill down more closely and you will find that there are often significant holes in their comprehension and many areas are lacking in detail.

So long as a trader's or salesperson's activities remain limited to his or her primary area of expertise, this lack of a more granular understanding of other products is generally not a problem. In recent years, however, many of the traditional distinctions between groups within the equities division have been blurred or outright eliminated. Traders and salespeople whose experience had been limited to one area have to contend with the full spectrum of equity and derivative products including single stocks, portfolio trades, ETFs, futures, swaps, and options. This challenge is even more exaggerated for new transfers into the equities division from other asset classes who face a steep learning curve but lack a formal process by which to ascend it.

Buy-side traders working at hedge funds, mutual funds, pension funds, endowments, retail brokers, and investment advisors face a similar challenge. While many have ample experience and product knowledge, often obtained during previous careers as Wall Street traders or through a construction of their own mosaic, there are others who lack a detailed understanding of how the sales and trading business works. The lack of opportunity to obtain the "Wall Street Education" that comes from working on a trading floor means they often work at a significant informational disadvantage to their brokers, which can be a source of friction. Of particular importance are the cases where this lack of understanding manifests itself in a disagreement over how to calculate a fair price or what are reasonable expectations of the broker: It can be extremely difficult for parties with conflicting economic interests to come to an agreement without an independent reference.

WHY DO WE NEED ANOTHER FINANCE BOOK?

So clearly the way traders and salespeople acquire this large, unstructured body of knowledge is inefficient, but why do we need a new book? Don't the hundreds of existing finance books already explain everything a trader or salesperson needs to know? The answer is, strangely enough, *no*. While there exist books covering almost every aspect of academic and applied finance, the genre of "Introductory Institutional Finance," which best describes the contents of this book, has somehow not yet emerged.

In the existing finance literature, the words "introductory" and "institutional" have been treated as mutually exclusive. Books targeting the institutional (i.e., "professional") investor tend to focus on sophisticated pricing and risk management concepts appropriate only to those who are already experts in their field, while introductory texts provide personal financial planning advice or trading strategies ("How to Get Rich Trading XYZ") relevant only to the retail ("nonprofessional") investor.

A useful illustration of the dichotomy between the retail and institutional viewpoints comes from the concept of liquidity, which measures how many shares of a stock can be bought or sold in a given period of time without significant impact on the price. Due to the large size of institutional order flow, the concept of liquidity is ubiquitous in the activities of the professional trader and salesperson; it is the most fundamental factor in the analysis of risk and the first consideration in the execution of every client or proprietary order. For retail investors, on the other hand, liquidity is almost irrelevant due to the small size of their orders. However, despite its preeminent importance in institutional finance, liquidity considerations receive scarce attention in the existing literature because these books are written for professionals who, it is assumed, are already well versed in such a basic concept.

In writing this book, I have attempted to fill this gap in the literature. My intention is to provide the introductory explanation of the fundamental workings of the trading floor that I was looking for when I began my career, and that new hires have asked for on countless occasions since then (and continue to ask for). It is also meant to serve as a reference text for more senior traders and salespeople for those situations where they find it necessary to patch over a particular crack in their knowledge. This book does not pretend to be a substitute for what is learned through an apprenticeship on Wall Street. Success as a trader or salesperson requires an understanding of the subtleties of markets, risk management, and client relationships, which can only be learned through experience. My goal is to provide a logically structured and detailed presentation of the basic terminology and concepts of equities sales and trading so as to soften and shorten the steep learning curve that new arrivals to the equities division have traditionally encountered.

OVERVIEW OF CONTENTS

This book provides an overview of the front office sales and trading business of a typical Wall Street investment bank or broker-dealer. In selecting and structuring the material to include, and the level of detail to present, the primary criterion has been the probability that the reader would find the information useful in practice, either in a front-office environment or as a buy-side client. Anything I would not expect of the trader or salesperson sitting next to me on the trading desk, or that would not significantly benefit his or her job performance, has been omitted to ensure the reader is not distracted from the relevant material. The presentation and pace of the book are based on my own experience explaining this material to both junior and more senior professionals over many years.

Throughout the book I have made an effort to introduce, wherever possible, the language and terminology used by traders and salespeople in practice. Not only is there a great deal of vocabulary that is unique to the trading floor, but the correct use of that language, down to the trading-specific interpretations of the prepositions "for" and "at" is essential for such a fast-paced environment where it can easily mean the difference between a successful trade and an expensive error.

So that the book is accessible and useful to the broadest possible audience, the prerequisites have been kept to a minimum. The reader is assumed to have no particular familiarity with finance or economics beyond what could be considered the commonsense understanding of the dynamics of supply and demand. (Specifically, that an increase in demand, or scarcity of supply, for any good, tends to drive the price of that good up, while a decrease in demand, or excess supply, leads to lower prices.) However, because modern finance is inherently mathematical, it is necessary that the reader understand some of the basic concepts from calculus, probability, and statistics. Fortunately, our interest is only at the conceptual level: The reader must understand, to use one example, that the mathematical definition of the derivative measures a rate of change and can be interpreted as the slope of a line. It will not, however, be necessary that the reader be able to actually calculate the derivative. An appendix is included with a brief overview of the relevant mathematical concepts for those readers in need of a refresher.

A final observation is that, while the book is written from a U.S.-centric perspective, the structure of the equity sales and trading business globally is quite consistent and the concepts presented here can be easily extended to international markets, making the book relevant for both U.S. and international readers.

LAYOUT

The ordering of the material across the whole book has been carefully chosen so that, to the greatest degree possible, terminology and concepts are introduced with an appropriate motivation and readers with no previous experience will be best served by reading each chapter in sequence. At the same time, the structure of each chapter is designed to be a self-contained unit and readers with more experience can go directly to the chapters that interest them.

Part One: What Is a Stock?

The book begins by analyzing the most fundamental question about equities: what is a stock and what determines its price? We look at the first of these questions in Chapter 1, where we present the basics of financial accounting and the contents and structure of the standard financial disclosures made by companies (Balance Sheet, Income Statement, and Statement of Cash Flows). In Chapter 2 we look at various valuation methods used to determine the fair price to pay for a share of stock. While both of these subjects are amply covered in many other texts, the focus here has been to narrow the scope of the material down to those concepts and terminology of greatest practical use to the average trader or salesperson.

Part Two: Products and Services

The main body of the text, consisting of Chapters 3 through 11, covers all of the major equity and equity derivatives products. Each chapter focuses on a particular product or service (with the exception of Chapter 11, which summarizes several) and the ordering has been deliberately structured as a progression from simple to more complex products. The material can be divided into four sections, each of which centers on a particular concept:

1. *Single Stocks:* The first section (Chapter 3) focuses on the "cash" market for single stocks and provides a considerable amount of detail about market conventions and the relationship between salespeople and traders, much of which is directly applicable to the trading in other products.
2. *Multiple-Stock Products:* The next three chapters look at equity products that incorporate multiple underlying stocks. This includes equity indices (Chapter 4), program trading (Chapter 5), and exchange traded funds, or ETFs (Chapter 6).
3. *One-Delta Derivatives:* In this section, we encounter our first true derivatives, but restrict our focus to those that directly replicate exposure to the underlier (so called, one-delta derivatives): forwards and futures are covered in Chapter 7, and equity swaps in Chapter 8.
4. *Derivatives with Variable Delta:* In the last section (Chapters 9 and 10), we look at options, which have a varying sensitivity to the movements of the underlying stock (delta not equal to one).

The final chapter of Part Two is Chapter 11, which contains an overview of the various other groups that are either on, or interact with, the trading floor, and the services they offer.

Part Three: Economics

In the last section, we look at the interrelationships between economic data, market movements, and investor behavior from the point of view of the trader. Chapter 12 presents an overview of the structure of the economy and introduces some of the important terminology and concepts from macroeconomics. This then allows us to focus in Chapter 13 on what are some of the most important, market-moving data announcements—the daily economic data releases. We present an overview of all the major U.S. releases, their source, and what they tell us about the economy and an analysis of some of the factors that determine the market's reaction to these announcements. We then present a brief overview of the most salient data points for the rest of the globe. We end the chapter by reversing the direction of the inference to look at how certain market indicators can provide useful insights into the current state of the economy.

Appendix: Mathematical Review

The Appendix provides a brief review of the mathematical concepts necessary to understand the material in the book and relate intelligently to others on the trading floor. There is a common misperception, particularly among students, about the level of mathematical understanding relevant to a job on Wall Street. Because many of the most recent areas of development in finance have been mathematically complex, many applicants have the mistaken impression that by studying concepts such as stochastic calculus or probability theory, they will dramatically improve their chances of being hired. While more mathematics is never a bad thing—like speaking more languages or knowing more history—the effort expended to learn more esoteric concepts provides rapidly diminishing returns to the vast majority of trading and sales roles. In practice, the most useful mathematical skill is a facility with mental arithmetic: the ability to think clearly about numbers and quickly compute accurate approximations particularly under pressure. The job of a trader or salesperson much more often requires that they provide an "on the spot" estimate of, for example, how much 69,000 shares of an $84.10 stock is worth, or how much a 0.15 percent move equates to on an index level of 641.21, than virtually any other type of calculation.

Note: Throughout the text I use the terms *investment bank* and *broker-dealer* to refer to the financial services firms that provide equity and equity derivative sales and trading services to clients. In light of the sweeping changes in the industry that occurred in the latter part of 2008, many of these companies should be properly called "banks." Readers should interpret the words "investment bank" and "broker-dealer" as referring to those parts of banks that provide these services.

AN IMPORTANT CLARIFICATION: The contents of this book represent my own views of generally accepted market practices in the pricing, trading, and risk management of a variety of equity and equity derivative products, in the context of the institutional client's business. The information is a blend of objectively verifiable facts and subjective opinions that, while undoubtedly influenced by my professional experience, are entirely my own and should not be interpreted as representing the policies or practices of any of my employers, past or present.

I welcome any questions, comments, or feedback on the book. Readers can contact me at matthew.tagliani@gmail.com.

A Comment on the Events of 2008

The changes that have occurred in the global financial markets while this book was being written were unlike anything experienced since the Great Depression. The loss of confidence triggered by the deflation of a speculative housing bubble brought the market for short-term lending to a standstill, jeopardizing the solvency of financial institutions globally. Governments and central banks around the world took unprecedented actions including bailouts, nationalizations, and stimulus packages worth trillions of dollars. The consequences of these interventions will not be fully understood or appreciated for many years.

This uncertainty has raised many questions about the future of the financial services industry with gloom-and-doom prognostications of the end of Wall Street. While perhaps representative of the sentiment of the moment, these concerns are greatly exaggerated. The painful lessons learned about credit risk, leverage, and speculation will undoubtedly change the industry, but the recent market conditions are no more an indication of the end of financial services than the imploding of the technology bubble in 2000 spelled the end of the Internet. The industry will evolve and improve, but the trading, pricing, and risk management of the products described in this book will remain largely the same.

MATTHEW TAGLIANI, CFA
November 2008

Acknowledgments

There are countless individuals who have assisted me throughout my career and to whom I hold tremendous gratitude. While they have not been directly involved in the making of this book, which has been a rather solitary effort, they have helped to make it possible either by directly enhancing my understanding of the business or simply making the environment where I have worked and learned more enjoyable. Particular thanks go to Geoff Craig, Sam Kellie-Smith, David Russell, Craig Verdon, and Ben Walker, who provide me with my current opportunities to continue developing professionally, and to Guy Weyns, who kindly reviewed several chapters and made many helpful recommendations. Special thanks also go to Bill Gerace and Bill Leonard, who were instrumental in the development of my critical thinking skills.

I am greatly indebted to all the people at John Wiley & Sons who made this book possible, particularly Bill Falloon, Stacey Fischkelta, Emilie Herman, Joan O'Neil, Todd Tedesco, and Laura Walsh.

The writing of this book consumed most of my evenings, weekends, vacation time, and holidays over a period of slightly more than two years—the time and effort required to bring it to completion having far exceeded any of my initial estimates, which I now see were wildly overoptimistic. That I should, for so long, voluntarily sacrifice what little free time I am afforded outside of my day-to-day work as a trader to pursue this project could be considered somewhat deranged, certainly masochistic and, at the very least, a bit imbalanced.

However, that my wife Nati should not only tolerate such an extended period of my virtual nonexistence, but actively encourage, support, and motivate me along the way is simply beyond explanation. While I spent my time reclused in intellectual La-La Land, she brilliantly managed the very real-world responsibilities of raising a family and managing a home, while keeping me free from the distracting realities of daily life. This was no small feat, considering that between starting and finishing this book, we relocated to the United Kingdom and added a second child to our family roster. Hers has been a truly superhuman effort which, quite frankly, I haven't the vaguest idea how to repay.

I must also thank my daughter Sofía, who has accepted lame "Daddy can't play, he has to work." excuses on far too many sunny Saturday afternoons and yet somehow has still not given up on me, and my son Cosmo, who had the bad luck of arriving just as I immersed myself in the final intense push to complete this book. You have both given me far more than I ever had the right to ask of you.

PART One

What Is a Stock?

CHAPTER 1

Equity Fundamentals (Part 1)

Introduction to Financial Statements

INTRODUCTION

In this chapter and the next we lay out a general framework for answering the most fundamental question for anyone working in equities or equity derivatives: "What is a share of stock and how much is it worth?" The goal is to develop sufficient understanding of the relevant concepts and terminology from financial accounting to ensure that the reader can understand, participate in, and benefit from, the sort of general stock analysis and valuation discussions that are held on a trading floor.

The presentation of the material is deliberately of a general character—the focus is on developing a clear conceptual understanding without getting bogged down in the details that, while essential to the work of an equity research analyst, are unnecessary for our purposes. Readers interested in a more detailed presentation can consult any of the many well-written books available on equity analysis or financial accounting.

It is worth clarifying that while the material in the first two chapters is basic, that does not mean it is easy. Readers with no previous exposure to financial accounting or valuation may find the writing rather dense—many of new concepts are introduced in a small number of pages. Because the material is conceptually fundamental, it is presented at the beginning of the book. It is not, however, a prerequisite for understanding the contents of subsequent chapters and readers who find this first section challenging can jump straight to Chapter 3 and come back to these first two chapters either as a reference or for more careful study at a later time.

EQUITY AND CORPORATION

By definition, a share of *stock* is a unit of ownership in a corporation. This definition does not help us much unless we understand what a corporation is.[1] A *corporation* is actually a rather curious concept: It is an independent legal entity, with its own rights and responsibilities, but distinctly independent from the people who run and own it. In many ways a newly established corporation is like a new citizen born into the state in which it is incorporated. Like people, corporations have rights and responsibilities, and can be held legally liable for their actions. Whether the question is over the purchase of a piece of property, the payment of a tax, or the pollution of a river, the answers "Archibald Gricklegrass did it" or "XYZ Incorporated did it," while not identical, are similarly valid.

Although businesses may adopt any one of many different legal structures, there are two very important characteristics of corporations that make it by far the most popular option. The first is that a corporation can be divided into fractional units (*shares*) that can be owned by multiple parties and purchased or sold freely between them. These shares give ownership of the "equity" in the corporation—that is, the benefits that remain after paying off all debts, taxes, and other obligations, both now and for the indefinite future. They also give the holders a fractional say in the decisions of the corporation (*voting rights*). The holder of even one share of stock has the right to attend the annual shareholders' meeting and ask whatever questions they choose of the management and, if enough other shareholders agree, to replace the management or even dissolve the corporation and liquidate its assets. It is, in the truest sense, ownership of the corporation in fractional percentage with the number of shares held and the number of shares outstanding.

The second important concept is that the fractional owners—the shareholders—have *limited liability* in the event of financial or legal challenge to the corporation. While the holder of a share of stock is, in fact, a partial owner of the company, the most that he or she can lose in the event the company were sued or faced financial hardship is the value of the stock he holds. This makes stock ownership a remarkable concept: the holder of stock gets all the benefits of owning the company with no more risk than the invested capital. Once a stock's price has gone to zero, there is nothing more that can be done to reclaim additional responsibility from the shareholder—a stock price can never go *below* zero. Were this not the case, stock ownership would be significantly more risky and trading on the stock market would be considerably less active as investors would have to assess much more carefully the potential risks of association with the activities and management of the company in question.

While the owners of the corporation are actually the shareholders, the actual day-to-day running of the business is left in the hands of the officers of the corporation (from the President on down) whose actions are then supervised by an executive board whose job it is to insure that the actions of the corporation are in the best interest of the shareholders.

INTRODUCTION TO FINANCIAL STATEMENTS

For a potential investor to make an informed decision as to whether to purchase shares of a company, he or she needs some information about its internal operation and financial status. What does the company own? What does it owe to others? How much money is it making? How is it using that money? In the United States, publicly traded companies are required to publish, and make available to investors, a quarterly report summarizing all the financial details of the company. To ensure that this report is accurate and understandable to investors and can be compared with the equivalent disclosures by other firms, there is a set of *generally accepted accounting principles* (GAAP) that specify the definitions and conventions that must be adhered to in presenting the information. Because these quarterly public disclosures are generally the only information the public has about the internal operations of the company, they must be verified by an external independent auditor who verifies that the information is accurate and that there is no attempt by the management to deceive investors by manipulating the data.

There are three statements that provide the majority of the information in the quarterly financial disclosures, which we will examine in more detail here:

1. *Balance sheet:* Summarizes the assets (things owned) and liabilities (things owed) of the company and how they are financed through a mixture of debt (borrowed money) and equity (funds contributed by the shareholder owners).
2. *Income statement:* Summarizes the revenue, expenses, and resulting income in the period.
3. *Statement of cash flows:* Summarizes the sources and uses of cash.

In this chapter, samples of each of these three financial statements are presented, along with definitions and explanations of their contents.

Because all publicly traded companies in the United States must adhere to GAAP, the structure of the financial statements, and the definitions of the various components are deliberately general. This "one size fits all" approach facilitates the comparison of different companies but in doing so, removes a great deal of important detail. In practice, companies usually provide many clarifications and additional insights through footnotes to the statements and supplementary disclosures.

To maximize the comprehension and retention of the material, I would strongly recommend that readers choose a simple small business with which they feel comfortable and think about what the definition of each new concept would mean in this specific context. (Personally, I find a bakery a particularly useful example.) I have deliberately not provided my own example because it is the act of thinking about the meaning of each concept and applying it to the tangible example that actually leads to understanding and retention. Readers who make the effort should find that these first two chapters provide sufficient foundation in financial accounting and fundamental analysis (the subject of the next chapter) to be able to understand a typical analyst's research report or discuss investment ideas with coworkers.

THE BALANCE SHEET

The *balance sheet* summarizes the assets and liabilities of the company at the time of publication. Unlike the income statement and statement of cash flows, the balance sheet is a freeze-frame snapshot of the company, rather than an analysis of the performance over the period. The changes in the mix of assets and liabilities of the company can be seen by comparing the current composition of the balance sheet with that of previous periods. While these changes are not explicitly shown on the balance sheet, the previous quarter and one-year ago data are usually presented alongside for comparison.

The contents of a sample balance sheet for a hypothetical company, XYZ Inc., are shown in Exhibit 1.1. While our example is deliberately simple, the structure and layout of the balance sheet of even a large multinational corporation would be quite similar (which emphasizes the need for additional disclosures). To make the example as clear as possible, the formatting and notation are somewhat nonstandard and the potentially distracting previous period values have been excluded.

Balance Sheet Fundamentals

The balance sheet is structured with assets on the left-hand side and liabilities and shareholders' equity on the right. For an item to be considered an *asset*, it must have been acquired in the past and have the potential to generate a quantifiable economic benefit in the future. *Liabilities* are obligations

BALANCE SHEET (Figures in $mm)

ASSETS		LIABILITIES & SHAREHOLDERS' EQUITY	
Current Assets		Current Liabilities	
Cash and Mktable Securities	$2,400	Accounts Payable	$2,100
Accounts Receivable	$1,750	Short Term Financing (Notes Payable)	
Inventory	$7,350	+ Current Portion of Long-Term Debt	$4,750
Total Current Assets	**$11,500**	**Total Current Liabilities**	**$6,850**
Long-Term Assets (Fixed Assets)		Long Term Debt	
Plant, Property, and Equipment	$37,200	Long-Term Financing (Bonds Payable)	$36,350
Long Term Investments	$26,600	Deferred Income Tax Liability	$6,400
Intangible Assets	$5,350	**Total Long-Term Debt**	**$42,750**
Goodwill	$4,200		
Total Long-Term Assets	**$73,350**	Minority Interest	$1,500
TOTAL ASSETS	**$84,850**	**TOTAL LIABILITIES**	**$51,100**
		Shareholders' Equity	
		Preferred Stock	$2,500
		Common Shareholders' Equity	
		Retained Earnings	$21,650
		Paid-in Capital	$10,500
		Less: Treasury stock	($900)
		TOTAL SHAREHOLDERS' EQUITY	**$33,750**
		TOTAL LIABILITIES + SHAREHOLDERS' EQUITY	**$84,850**

EXHIBIT 1.1   Balance Sheet for XYZ Inc.

acquired in the past that require economic sacrifices in the future. The difference between the assets and liabilities of the company is what is left over for the owners (shareholders) of the company. This is called *shareholders' equity*. This leads us to one of the fundamental identities of accounting:

$$\text{Assets} = \text{Liabilities} + \text{Shareholders' equity}$$

That is, the things a company has (assets) are either paid for with borrowed money (liabilities) or belong to the owners (shareholders' equity). This identity means that the sum of the items on each side of the balance sheet must be the same—that's why it's called the "balance" sheet.

In order for the two sides of the balance sheet to remain equal, the assets and liabilities of the company must be recorded using a process called *double-entry bookkeeping*. A single item cannot be added to the balance sheet in isolation—there must always be an equal and offsetting adjustment somewhere else to keep things balanced. This offsetting entry can be an equivalent addition to the other side of the balance sheet, or a reduction in another item on the same side.

This is best illustrated by an example. Consider a brand new company that has yet to begin operation and whose only asset is $1,000 of cash invested by the founders. The company's balance sheet looks quite simple:

Assets		Liabilities + Shareholders' Equity	
Cash	$1,000	Liabilities	$0
Equipment	$0	Shareholders' Equity	$1,000
Total	$1,000	Total	$1,000

The company now purchases a piece of equipment for $600. The management has three ways to pay for it: they can spend the cash they have, they can buy it on credit (get a loan), or the owners of the company can contribute more capital to pay for it. The three approaches are recognized differently on the balance sheet, but each one requires two entries:

- *Pay with cash:* Two equal and offsetting adjustments are made to the left-hand side of the balance sheet. The Equipment line is increased by $600 while the Cash line is reduced by an equivalent amount. The assets of the company have simply changed shape from cash to machines.

Assets		Liabilities + Shareholders' Equity	
Cash	$400	Liabilities	$0
Equipment	$600	Shareholders' Equity	$1,000
Total	$1,000	Total	$1,000

- *Pay with borrowed funds:* If the machine is purchased with borrowed funds (credit), then the offsetting adjustment to the addition of $600 to the equipment line on the left-hand side would be an increase in the liabilities of the company (the borrowed funds) on the right-hand side. This has the additional effect of increasing the total size of the balance sheet from $1,000 on each side to $1,600. (The balance sheet is now *leveraged* by the addition of borrowed funds.)

Assets		Liabilities + Shareholders' Equity	
Cash	$1,000	Liabilities	$600
Equipment	$600	Shareholders' Equity	$1,000
Total	$1,600	Total	$1,600

■ *Owners contribute more capital:* The third option is that the owners of the company contribute additional capital to pay for the machine. In this case, the offsetting adjustment to the $600 addition to the equipment line is an addition of $600 to the shareholders' equity. The balance sheet increases in size from $1,000 to $1,600 but there is no leverage.

Assets		Liabilities + Shareholders' Equity	
Cash	$1,000	Liabilities	$0
Equipment	$600	Shareholders' Equity	$1,600
Total	$1,600	Total	$1,600

In all cases, there are two entries to the balance sheet—one to record the change in assets, the other to record how it was paid for—or alternatively, to whom it belongs (the owners of the company or the creditors).

Of the four items in this very simple balance sheet, three can be objectively measured: the cash holdings, the value of the equipment, and the amount of money the company owes. Shareholders' equity is effectively defined as everything that is left over. Suppose, for example, that during installation the newly purchased machinery is damaged and its value is reduced from $600 to $400. The asset side of the balance sheet is now reduced by $200 and there must be an equal and offsetting adjustment to the right-hand side. If the machine was paid for on credit, the debt does not change just because the machine is worth less than before. The only place where the loss of $200 on the asset side can be reflected is in the shareholders' equity line. The owners of the company take the loss, not the creditors.

In general, the shareholders' equity line is calculated as a "plug." That is, once all the assets and liabilities have been added up, the shareholders' equity is defined to be whatever value makes the two sides of the balance sheet equal.

Balance Sheet Contents

On both the asset and liability sides of the balance sheet, the contents are categorized as either *current*, consisting of liquid assets and short-term liabilities that will be used or paid off within one year, and *long term*, which includes everything else.

Left-Hand Side   Beginning on the asset side of the balance sheet, some of the standard items and their definitions are presented here. (*Note:* Not all items are included in the sample balance sheet in Exhibit 1.1.)

Current Assets
- *Cash and marketable securities:* Liquid short-term bank deposits and securities tradable in the market such as bonds or stocks. (Things that either are cash or could become cash quickly.)
- *Accounts receivable:* Money owed to the company for products or services that have been delivered but for which the company has not yet received payment.
- *Inventory:* Completed items ready for sale as well as the raw materials for production.
- *Prepaid expenses:* Cash that is "stored" in the form of prepayment of future obligations.

Long-Term Assets (also called *Fixed Assets*)
- *Plant, property and equipment:* The physical resources used in the running of the business.
- *Long-term investments:* Assets owned by the company that are not directly related to the functioning of the business (e.g., a piece of unused land).
- *Intangible assets:* Money paid by the company for rights, patents, trademarks, and the like, which can produce value but do not have a physical presence.

One particular intangible asset that is often given its own line on the balance sheet is *goodwill*. This is a slightly slippery accounting concept that requires a bit of explaining.

We first need to introduce the concept of *book value*. This is the simplest measure of the value of a company and is computed as the sum of the company's assets less its liabilities. The book value is the accounting-based measure of what the company is worth. Because of the way in which accounting standards require certain items to be recognized on the balance sheet, the book value is very different from the *liquidation value* of the company, which uses the market value of all assets and liabilities to determine what would be left if an investor bought the company, broke it up, and sold off all the buildings, inventory, and other "stuff" and paid off all the bills. In reality, however, the market value of a company, as determined by the total value of all outstanding shares, is many times (i.e., 10 to 20 times) both its book value and its liquidation value. The reason for this is because the benefit of owning shares of a company is not just the ownership of the equipment, inventory, and other "stuff," but the right to a proportional share of all the benefits that can be produced with those assets for the life of the company.

The concept of goodwill arises when one company acquires another for more than its book value. Let us assume Company X pays $10 billion in cash to acquire Company Y, which has $8 billion in assets and $5 billion in liabilities, for a book value of $3 billion. When Company X recognizes the purchase of Company Y on its balance sheet it will reflect both the cost—a decrease in cash assets of $10 billion—as well as what it has acquired for that price: $8 billion in assets and $5 billion in liabilities. The net effect will be a decrease in assets of $2 billion and an increase in liabilities of $5 billion for a net "loss" of $7 billion in shareholders' equity.

The problem is that the balance sheet knows nothing about the future economic opportunity presented by the ownership of Company Y; it just sees a $10 billion price tag on $3 billion of book value, which results in a $7 billion loss. To correct for this, a $7 billion intangible asset called "goodwill" is added to the asset side of the balance sheet. Goodwill is the accounting convention used to recognize the intangible benefit of owning all the future earnings that will be produced by Company Y. The standard accounting convention is that the value of the goodwill is retained on the balance sheet indefinitely but must be periodically tested by an auditor. If the value of the goodwill—the present value of all the benefits of owning the acquired assets—is judged to have decreased, then a *goodwill impairment* is recognized, in which the value of the goodwill is written down to its current value.

Right-Hand Side (Top)   The right-hand side of the balance sheet is divided into two parts: current and long-term liabilities on the top, followed by the details of the shareholders' equity. Standard classifications of liabilities and their definitions are as follows:

Current Liabilities
- *Short-term financing:* Notes payable, lines of credit, and other short-term debt obligations to be paid off within a year.
- *Accounts payable:* Money owed by the company for products or services that have already been received but for which it has not yet paid.
- *Current portion of long-term debt:* The portion of long-term debt obligations that is payable in the current period.

Long-Term Liabilities
- *Long-term debt:* Any long-term debt obligation of the company. For a smaller firm, this is likely to consist mostly of bank loans while for a larger company it can also include bonds and other debt obligations issued by the company itself.
- *Deferred income tax liability:* The method by which revenue and expenses are accounted for under GAAP is very different from what is required by the Internal Revenue Service (IRS). As a result, companies will usually show a larger profit on their accounting statements (where

it looks good) than on their income tax statements (where it means a higher tax bill). The difference between the two represents revenue that has not yet been taxed, but will be at some point. The deferred tax liability indicates the pending IRS bill that will need to be paid when this happens.

■ *Deferred pension obligations:* This is the present value of the expected future cost of the retirement benefits the firm has committed to provide to its employees.

Another liability that often appears on the balance sheet is something called *minority interest*. This entry appears on the balance sheet of a parent company that does not own 100 percent of one of its subsidiaries. When a company acquires a sufficiently large portion of another company (usually more than 50 percent), the full assets and liabilities of the acquired company are listed on the balance sheet of the acquiring (parent) company. An accounting adjustment is then necessary on the liabilities side since there is a portion of the subsidiary that is not owned by the parent.

As an example, assume that Company B has a book value of $100 consisting of $100 in assets and no debt and that Company A is able to purchase an 85 percent stake in Company B for $85. Because it owns a controlling stake, Company A will now add *all* the assets of Company B to its balance sheet. The purchase price for 85 percent of the company is equal to 85 percent of the book value so there is no goodwill adjustment to be made. However, when the full assets and liabilities of Company B are taken onto Company A's balance sheet, there will be a net increase of $15 in assets as the $100 of assets of Company B is added and the $85 reduction in cash is recognized. The imbalance comes from the fact that 100 percent of Company B has been added to the balance sheet but only 85 percent has been purchased. Company A would then recognize a $15 liability for minority interest to adjust for the 15 percent of the company that is still owned by the previous owners.

Right-Hand Side (Bottom)   The last section of the balance sheet contains the decomposition of shareholders' equity. Given the total assets and liabilities of the company, we already know what the total value of shareholders' equity must be, simply by rearranging the fundamental accounting relationship stated at the start of the section:

$$\text{Shareholders' equity} = \text{Assets} - \text{Liabilities}$$

In general terms, the shareholders' equity can come from two sources: either the money was put into the company by the owners or the company earned the money from its business activities but has not yet paid it out to the owners. These two forms of shareholders' equity appear on the balance sheet as follows:

1. *Paid-in capital:* This represents the money paid by investors in return for fractional ownership of the benefits of the company, through ownership of common shares, either purchased in an initial public offering or a secondary share issuance. If a company issues 1 million shares of stock and sells them in an initial public offering (IPO) at $25 each, then the company will have $25 million of common equity.
2. *Retained earnings:* Profits earned by the company that have not been distributed to the shareholders via dividends are recognized on the balance sheet as retained earnings. This entry is not actually calculated in the preparation of the balance sheet but is the "plug" value whose value is determined by the difference between the assets, liabilities, and the other elements of shareholders' equity whose value can be objectively determined.

Companies will sometimes repurchase their shares in the open market. When this occurs, the repurchased shares are represented on the balance sheet as *treasury stock* in the statement of shareholders' equity. The value assigned is the repurchase price of the shares and carries a negative sign as they are effectively an offset to the paid-in capital (they were sold and then bought back). These shares no longer represent an actual obligation since they are held by the company itself and not outside investors.

The sum of paid-in capital and retained earnings, less treasury stock, is the *common shareholders' equity.* In addition to common stock, some firms will also issue shares of *preferred stock.* This is a special type of non-voting stock that has priority over common shares in the event of a bankruptcy and liquidation of the company's assets. Preferred shares usually carry a fixed dividend that must be paid before any dividends are paid out on the common stock. Preferred dividends are similar to interest payments on debt but with the important caveat that, should the firm be unable to pay the dividend, this does not force it into bankruptcy—the dividend obligation simply accumulates and must be paid out in the next period. While preferred stock is, in many ways, more like a bond, it is recognized as an equity issuance and therefore shows up under the shareholders' equity rather than as part of long-term debt. The book value of preferred stocks is added to common shareholders' equity to arrive at the total value of shareholders' equity.

Some companies will provide an additional document called the *Statement of Shareholders' Equity,* which provides more complete detail of the composition of the shareholders' equity than what is shown on the balance sheet.

While it is not recognized as part of the shareholders' equity, a minority interest is technically a source of equity funding—it offsets the portion of the assets of the acquired company that are not owned by the parent but does not represent a debt obligation. The *total equity* of a firm is the sum of shareholders' equity and minority interest and can be thought of as the portion of the asset side of the balance sheet that can be associated to owners of the firm (parent and acquired subsidiaries), rather than creditors.

$$\text{Total equity} = \text{Shareholders' equity} + \text{Minority interest}$$

Capital

A firm's *capital* consists of the financial resources at its disposal that can be applied to the production of the goods or services it offers. There are two common definitions of capital derived from the balance sheet. The first of these is *working capital,* which measures the short-term liquidity of the company and is equal to the difference between the current assets and current liabilities. A company must maintain an adequate buffer of working capital to guarantee that current assets are enough to cover short-term liabilities and avoid an interruption in operations due to an inability to make payments on its obligations. This underscores the significance of "current," as it applies both to assets (they should be liquid and readily convertible into cash) and liabilities (anything that is coming due in the near term, including the current portion of long-term debt).

$$\text{Working capital} = \text{Current assets} - \text{Current liabilities}$$

A broader measurement of the resources a company has at its disposal is *total capital,* which is composed of all borrowed funds (short- and long-term) and cash supplied by the owners (shareholders' equity). The only item from the right-hand side of the balance sheet that is not included is Minority Interest, which is an accounting entry and does not represent an actual source of funds.

$$\text{Total capital} = \text{Current liabilities} + \text{Long-term debt}$$
$$+ \text{Shareholders' equity}$$

THE INCOME STATEMENT

The income statement summarizes the sources of revenue and expenses for the company during the period. It is the step-by-step reconciliation of the firm's books and records according to another fundamental accounting identity:

$$Income = Revenues - Expenses$$

The purpose of the income statement is to illustrate the conversion of the "top line" revenue, which represents the gross proceeds from the sale of the company's products, into a "bottom line" net income to the common shareholders. This is done through a series of intermediate sums, each of which shows the impact of a different category of expenses. A sample income statement for XYZ Inc. is shown in Exhibit 1.2.

The first step of the income statement is to convert the top line *net sales* number, which measures the gross proceeds from the sale of the primary product or service offered by the company (less an allowance for returns),

INCOME STATEMENT		Figures in $mm
Net sales		**$48,550**
Less: Operating expenses		$38,650
Cost of Goods Sold	$21,450	
Selling, Genl and Admin. Expenses	$8,850	
Depreciation and Amortization	$4,900	
Other	$3,450	
Operating Income		**$9,900**
Plus: Non-Operating Income		$550
Earnings before Interest and Taxes (EBIT)		**$10,450**
Less: Financing Costs / Interest Expense		$3,700
Pre-Tax Income		**$6,750**
Less: Provision for Taxes		$2,650
Net Income From Continued Operations		**$4,100**
Plus Income from Extraordinary Items		($250)
NET INCOME		**$3,850**
Less: Preferred Dividends		$250
NET INCOME TO COMMON EQUITY HOLDERS		**$3,600**

EXHIBIT 1.2 Income Statement

into the *operating income,* which represents the net revenue produced by the primary business of the company:

$$\text{Net sales} - \text{Operating expenses} = \text{Operating income}$$

Operating expenses are the recurring expenses related to the production, sale, and distribution of the products that constitute the primary business of the company, as well as the costs of the operation of the business itself. Operating expenses are decomposed into several important subcategories on the income statement depending on the nature of the expense:

■ *Cost of goods sold (COGS):* These are costs that are directly attributable to the production of the goods sold, including both raw materials and labor. The calculation of the cost of the raw materials of production requires an additional clarification. Most companies maintain an inventory of raw goods that are depleted and restocked according to the demands of production. In general, the items of inventory of a particular raw good are indifferentiable from each other (i.e., the screws, nuts, and bolts in inventory are identical to the new ones purchased) though the price the company pays for them may change over time (usually increasing). The difficulty comes in calculating the cost of the raw materials used in the production of the particular goods sold in the current period. If all the screws are identical, how do you know if you used the one that cost you $0.05 or $0.06? This problem of inventory accounting is solved by using one of three standard methods:

   1. *Last in, first out (LIFO):* As inventory is used in production, the assumption is that the most recently acquired inventory is consumed first. If the cost of the raw materials of production increases with time, this method will result in a higher cost of goods sold (and therefore lower profit).
   2. *First in, first out (FIFO):* The cost of the inventory consumed assumes the oldest inventory is used first. With increasing inventory prices, this will result in a lower cost of goods sold (and therefore higher profit).
   3. *Average price:* The cost of inventory is averaged between existing inventory and new purchases, resulting in a cost of goods sold that is usually somewhere between LIFO and FIFO.

   If there is significant variation in material costs, there can be substantial differences in the valuation of the consumed inventory under FIFO and LIFO methods. (These differences will also impact the balance sheet in the value of inventory.) To facilitate comparison between companies that use different inventory valuation methods, companies that use FIFO inventory valuation are required under GAAP to disclose a *LIFO Reserve* in a footnote on the balance sheet, which states the difference between the FIFO and LIFO valuations of inventory.

- *Selling, general, and administrative expenses (SG&A):* Costs associated with the running of the business but not directly attributable to the production of the product sold (i.e., salaries for Human Resources employees).
- *Depreciation and amortization:* Certain assets acquired for use in the production of the goods sold by the company have a long lifespan and their cost, rather than being written off as an expense in the accounting period when they were acquired, is recognized over multiple accounting periods. For example, it is not financially accurate to recognize in a single accounting period the entire cost of purchasing a piece of machinery with a 10-year lifespan. Not only would this result in dramatically lowered, or even negative, profits in one period, followed by 10 years of cost-free production from the paid-off machine, but it is inaccurate to write off the entire cost of the machine given that, at the end of the first year, the machine will likely have some resale value (it does not immediately become worthless).

  One of the principles of GAAP is the *matching principle*, which states that, whenever it is reasonable to do so, the recognition of revenues should be matched with the recognition of the associated expenses. An alternate approach would be to assess the resale (or scrap) value of all machinery at the end of each accounting period and mark the value of all assets to their market values. This would be an extraordinarily time-consuming task and, given the lack of any centralized secondary market to assess the true resale value of the assets, would be subject to manipulation and inaccuracies by companies looking to either over- or understate the value of their asset base.

  For this reason, the standard approach to recognizing the cost of a large purchase (i.e., the sort of things found under "Plant, Property, and Equipment" on the balance sheet) is to record it as an asset at the time of purchase (i.e., "I had $1 million in cash and now I have $400,000 in cash and a $600,000 piece of machinery.") and then recognize a fractional portion of the acquisition cost of the asset in each period over the life of the asset.[2] When the asset is physical, this process is called *depreciation*, while if it is an intangible asset (i.e., rights, patents, or goodwill) it is called *amortization*.

An even more basic measure of profitability than operating income is the *gross profit*, which is calculated simply as the difference between the revenue from net sales and the direct cost of producing the goods sold:

$$\text{Gross profit} = \text{Net sales} - \text{Cost of goods sold}$$

Gross profit measures the revenue from the primary business of the company without factoring in any indirect costs. While clearly it is impossible to run a company without incurring indirect costs, by comparing gross profit and operating profit between similar companies, it is possible to assess which company is running a "leaner" operation (though this is to some degree subject to each company's classification of expenses as either direct or indirect).

If the company has earned money from other sources not directly related to the operation of its business, this is added in as *non-operating income*. This allows for the distinction between how much the company earns from performing its core business (e.g., manufacturing and selling widgets) versus other sources of revenue that are not part of this core business (e.g., interest earned on credit extended to widget buyers).

The sum of the operating income and non-operating income represents the total earnings of the company from all sources, less the costs of production (operating expenses). This is referred to as the *earnings before interest and taxes* (EBIT) or *pretax operating profit* and is an important number because it isolates the revenues earned by the company from the impact of its choice of financing (the particular mixture of debt and equity used to fund its operations). This can be particularly interesting, for example, to an investor looking to potentially acquire the company since the financing and tax structure are likely to change after the purchase.

A common adjustment made to EBIT is to remove the accounting adjustments for *depreciation and amortization*, which do not represent real cash outlays in the period. This modified version is called EBITDA ("eebit-dah"), which, not surprisingly, stands for *earnings before interest, taxes, depreciation, and amortization* (EBITDA).

The *financing expenses*, which represent costs associated with borrowed funds, are subtracted from the EBIT to get the *pretax income*. From this we subtract the income taxes (either paid or provisioned for payment in the future) to arrive at the *net income from continued operations*. This measures the revenue generated by the firm from the pursuit of its business, after accounting for all costs (operational expenses, financing, and taxes).

We now add in any adjustments for *extraordinary items*. These are one-off occurrences that are not expected to repeat and can include anything from rebuilding costs after a hurricane to a favorable legal settlement. These extraordinary items are separated from the rest of the income statement so that, when making an assessment of the long-term potential for a company, investors can judge the firm's profitability based on its ordinary revenues.

Clearly, the definition of "extraordinary" is subjective and companies may attempt to classify certain events as extraordinary when in fact they are likely to recur. A Caribbean-based hotel chain can only write off so many "extraordinary" hurricanes before investors begin to view hurricane damage as a systematic risk to their business. Similarly, if a company loses a lawsuit and needs to pay money as part of the settlement, it may recognize this on the income statement as an extraordinary item if it is an isolated incident, but if there are hundreds more similar cases pending—for which this case may provide legal precedent—additional disclosures and *provisions* (money set aside from earnings in anticipation of future expenses) would be warranted.

After all these adjustments we now arrive at the *net income*—the total amount the company earned after all expenses, adjustments, extraordinary events, interest, and taxes. It is the final measure of the revenue of the company in the accounting period that can be transferred to retained earnings or paid out in dividends. If the company has preferred stock outstanding, where dividends are mandatory, the preferred dividends owed (both presently as well as any accumulated obligation from previous periods) may be subtracted as a separate line item to arrive at the *net income to common equity holders*.

When corporations announce their quarterly earnings, one of the most closely watched components is the *earnings per share (EPS)*, which is calculated as the net income to common equity holders, divided by the total shares of common stock outstanding. If 100 percent of net income was paid out via dividends, the EPS would measure the percentage return to the shareholder on the purchase price of a share of stock (ignoring changes in the stock price). In practice, only a portion of earnings (if any) are paid out in dividends. The EPS then represents the return to the investor based on the combination of dividends paid out and his proportional claim on the retained earnings of the firm.

MEASURES OF PROFITABILITY

The income statement is used to assess the profitability of a company. Of the four most commonly used profitability measures, two start from the "top line" (Net sales) number and subtract out unwanted items, and two start from the "bottom line" (Net income) and add back in items that should not have been removed.

(Continued)

(*Continued*)

Top-Down

> *Gross profit = Net sales – Cost of goods sold:* This is the most basic measurement of profitability: It tells for how much more than the cost of raw materials and production does the company sell its products.

> *Operating income = Net sales – Cost of goods sold – SG&A expenses:* Anything described as "operating" refers to the core business of the company, excluding income from other sources. Operating profit is the gross profit (how much was made by selling the product) less the selling, general, and administrative expenses (what it cost to run the business).

Bottom-Up

> *EBIT = Net income + Income taxes + Interest expense:* EBIT (earnings before interest and taxes) adds back to net income the income taxes and interest expense to give a measure of how profitable the company's business is, independent of the effects of how it is financed and how tax efficient it is.

> *EBITDA = EBIT + Depreciation and amortization:* Taking EBIT one step further, EBITDA adds back into EBIT the accounting adjustments for depreciation and amortization, which do not represent real cash outlays in the period.

STATEMENT OF CASH FLOWS

The third standard financial disclosure is the statement of cash flows, which, as its name implies, summarizes the sources and uses of cash during the period and computes the net change in the cash (and cash equivalents) of the firm. Each entry in the statement of cash flows is classified into one of three categories:

1. *Operating activities:* Cash flows related to the primary business function of the company.
2. *Investing activities:* Cash flows resulting from the purchase or sale of long-term assets (e.g. plant, property, equipment).

3. *Financing activities:* Cash flows related to the financing operations of the company (i.e., bank loans, bond issuances, sale or repurchase of stock, etc.).

The sum of the cash flows associated with these three sources, plus any adjustments due to changes in exchange rates, gives the net change in cash in the period.

The purpose of the statement of cash flows is to give investors an indication of the firm's *liquidity*, that is, its ability to meet its financial obligations, particularly in the short-term. While many of the items in the balance sheet and income statement are not "real" insofar as they represent additions or subtractions from income, assets, or liabilities stipulated by accounting conventions (e.g., depreciation and amortization) and not actual payments, the statement of cash flows focuses on the most liquid and tangible asset possible, the firm's cash position, and therefore provides a more accurate picture of the company's ability to continue operating. A sample statement of cash flows for XYZ Inc. is shown in Exhibit 1.3.

As we will see, many of the items in the statement of cash flows are either taken directly from the income statement and balance sheet, or can be derived by computing the changes to them between the previous period and the present.

Cash flows from operating activities: To calculate the cash flows from operating activities, we begin with the net income,[3] the final calculation of the money earned by the firm as computed on the income statement. Since our interest is in the operating activities only, the first step is to subtract from the net income, the non-operating income (also taken from the income statement) to isolate the net income from operating activities. (Because it is a source of cash for the firm, the non-operating income will be recognized elsewhere on the statement of cash flows, either in financing activities, investing activities, or partially in both.)

The next step is to convert the *net income from operating activities* into the *net cash flow from operating activities* by backing out all the noncash forms of revenue and expenses.

- *Depreciation and amortization:* There is no actual cash outflow associated with the depreciation of an aging asset or the amortization of the cost of an intangible asset. This is simply an accounting adjustment made to the income statement to align revenues with expenses. Therefore, the loss on the income statement from depreciation and amortization is added back in.
- *Changes in operating assets and liabilities:* The starting point for the statement of cash flows is the net income, taken from the income

STATEMENT OF CASH FLOWS	Figures in $mm	
CASH FLOWS FROM OPERATING ACTIVITIES		
Net income		**$3,850**
Less: Non-Operating Income		**$550**
Net Operating Income		**$3,300**
Plus: Depreciation and Amortization		**$4,900**
Plus: Other		$205
Plus: Changes in Operating Assets and Liabilities		**$3,350**
Decrease (Increase) in Accounts Receivable	$800	
Decrease (Increase) in Inventories	$1,200	
Increase (Decrease) in Accounts Payable	$1,900	
Decrease (Increase) in Other Current Assets	($450)	
Decrease (Increase) in Non-Current Assets	($100)	
Net Cash Provided by (Used in) Operating Activities		**$11,755**
CASH FLOWS FROM INVESTING ACTIVITIES		
Cash Used for Acquisition of Plant, Prop and Equip		($950)
Cash Used for Acquisition of Other Businesses		($7,800)
Other Sources (Uses) of Cash From Investing Activities		$50
Net Cash Provided by (Used in) Investing Activities		**($8,700)**
CASH FLOWS FROM FINANCING ACTIVITIES		
Proceeds From Issuance of Long-Term Debt		$4,600
Repayment of Long-Term Debt		($6,100)
Increase (Decrease) in Loans Payable		$200
Preferred Dividends		**($250)**
Dividends Paid on Common Equity		($1,250)
Net Cash Provided by (Used in) Financing Activities		**($2,800)**
CHANGES IN CASH AND CASH EQUIVALENTS		**$255**

EXHIBIT 1.3 Statement of Cash Flows
Note: The notation "Decrease (Increase) in Inventories" means that an increase in inventories would result in a negative number, shown in parentheses.

statement, which represents the total revenue of the company that can be transferred to shareholders' equity or paid out in dividends. By the balance sheet identity *Assets − Liabilities = Shareholders' equity*, the net income represents the change in the total assets and liabilities of the company. What it does not tell us is how the composition of the assets and liabilities has changed between cash and noncash items. In this section of the statement of cash flows, the cash balance of the firm is adjusted for changes in the composition of the current assets and liabilities. (Changes in non-current assets and liabilities are generally recognized in the cash flows from investing and financing activities, which we will see shortly.)

The general rules are that:

- A decrease in a noncash asset is a source of cash while an increase is a use of cash. For example, a decrease in accounts receivable implies that payment was received, which increases the cash balance.
- An increased liability is a source of cash while a decreased liability implies cash was used to pay down the obligation and therefore reduces the cash balance.

All of these changes in the current assets and liabilities can be computed by comparing the composition of the balance sheet to that of the previous accounting period.

Cash flows from investing activities: The cash flows classified as resulting from investing activities are those that relate to the acquisition or sale of long-term assets. These may be the sort of tangible assets classified under Plant, Property, and Equipment on the balance sheet, as well as the acquisition of other companies or any other long-term investment. Many of the major items here would be visible from the changes in long-term assets on the balance sheet from the previous period.

Cash flows from financing activities: The term *financing activities* broadly includes any of the interactions between a company and either its creditors or shareholders. This includes cash flows associated with the sale of shares to the public, a stock repurchase by the company, the issuance or repayment of debt, the receipt of a bank loan, or the payment of dividends on either preferred or common shares. Financing activities will often be visible from the changes in the composition of the shareholders' equity on the balance sheet.

Free Cash Flow

One of the most important values that is calculated from the statement of cash flows is the *free cash flow,* which measures the cash raised in the period that could either be retained by the company or paid out to shareholders as a dividend. It is calculated as the cash raised from the pursuit of the company's primary business, less what was actually spent on new fixed assets (actual expenditures, not depreciation and amortization) less what has already been paid out in the form of dividends to all holders of equities.

Free cash flow = Cash generated from operating activities

– Capital expenditures

Many analysts focus on free cash flow as a superior measure of economic performance to net income due to the fact that net income is more easily manipulated through accounting adjustments, while cash flow is more objective. While a company with strong free cash flow generation is in a position to expand their business without need for additional financing, this does not mean that significant positive cash flow is necessarily good or that low or negative free cash flow is bad. A company that generates a great deal of free cash flow but does not employ that cash to productive ends may be a much less attractive investment than a company with negative free cash flow due to large investments in capital goods that will produce significant returns in the future.

SUMMARY

A corporation is the legal structure that is most appropriate for publicly traded companies for two principal reasons. The first is that a corporation can be divided into fractional units (shares), which can be owned by multiple parties and bought and sold freely between them. The second is the limited liability that comes from stock ownership; while the shareholders are the owners of the corporation, in the event of a bankruptcy they cannot be held liable for losses beyond the value of their investment.

There are three financial statements that must be provided by publicly traded corporations so that existing and potential shareholders can assess the financial state of the company. The definitions of all items are based on the generally accepted accounting principles (GAAP):

- The balance sheet provides a snapshot of the assets (things owned) and liabilities (things owed) by the corporation at a particular point in time and is constructed based on the method of double-entry bookkeeping. The information in the balance sheet can be summed up in the fundamental accounting identity *Assets = Liabilities + Shareholders' equity,* where shareholders' equity is the sum of funds invested in the corporation (through share issuance) and retained earnings.
- The income statement shows how the "top line" *net sales* of the corporation is distilled down into a "bottom line" *net income* after subtracting off both the tangible expenses of running the business (cost of goods, taxes, financing costs) as well as the intangible costs of depreciation and amortization.

- The statement of cash flows analyzes the sources and uses of cash during the accounting period and classifies them according to whether they relate to the primary business of the company, its financing expenses, or its investing activities. The statement of cash flows allows us to compute one of the most important measures of economic performance: the free cash flow, which measures the available cash generated that could be paid out as dividends.

CHAPTER 2

Equity Fundamentals (Part 2)

Financial Ratios, Valuation, and Corporate Actions

INTRODUCTION

Companies are required to disclose their financial statements to the public to ensure that existing and potential investors have sufficiently detailed and reliable information to make an informed decision whether they want to invest. However, for the most part, the individual numbers provided in each of the three statements are of limited value on their own. Is a net sales of $10 billion per year good? That depends. It certainly isn't if the cost of goods sold is $11 billion. What about $10 billion of net sales and $1 billion of net profit? Well, maybe... unless there are other similar companies that earn the same $1 billion of net profit with only $5 billion of net sales, in which case the company in question would appear to be poorly run compared to its peers. The answers to these questions are important not only for present and future investors, but for the management of the company itself who are responsible for maximizing the profitability of the company for the shareholders.

Rather than examining individual data points, it is often more illustrative to compute the ratios between various elements of the financial statements. There are a number of standardized financial ratios that are used to assess factors such as the profitability, efficiency, liquidity, growth potential, and riskiness of a company. Ratios provide useful information about an individual company and facilitate comparisons between companies of different sizes.

While there are very many potentially interesting ratios, we focus here on introducing the most salient examples from each category. It should be observed that, while the definitions of these ratios presented here are standard, there is not universal agreement as to the specific definitions of many ratios (what is included, and what is not). Each analyst must make a decision based on the characteristics of a given industry, as well as the idiosyncrasies of the company in question and the specific choices made by the management in preparing their financial statements.

While some of the ratios have intuitive definitions that are readily remembered, this is not always the case and it is easy to become bogged down trying to memorize what to include or exclude from each calculation. Fortunately, our goal is not to produce a rigorous analysis but to develop a big-picture understanding of what information the ratios give us about the state of the company and what makes one ratio different from other similar measurements. It is therefore not particularly important that the reader memorize the formulas presented.

It is also important to keep in mind that there is no "right" value for any of these ratios. While a range of generally acceptable values can be determined by the characteristics of the industry in general, the value of any ratio must be considered in the context of the specific circumstances of the company.

FINANCIAL RATIOS

Liquidity Ratios

Liquidity ratios (also known as *solvency ratios*) provide information about the company's ability to meet short-term financial obligations. Regardless of the quality of the product or service provided, or the long-term potential for the company, if it does not have the resources to make payments on the outstanding debts in the short term, the company's ability to continue functioning (and avoid bankruptcy) is jeopardized.

There are three common measurements of liquidity. The most commonly used is the *current ratio*, which, as its name suggests, is a comparison of the current assets to current liabilities from the balance sheet. This is the simplest and broadest measure of the company's ability to meet its short-term debts with liquid assets.

$$\text{Current ratio} = \frac{\text{Current assets}}{\text{Current liabilities}}$$

A slightly more demanding measurement of liquidity is the *quick ratio* (also called the *acid test ratio*), which removes inventories from current assets. Not all companies can easily convert inventories to cash, making the current ratio an overstatement of their actual liquidity position.

$$\text{Quick ratio} = \frac{\text{Cash} + \text{Marketable securities} + \text{Accounts receivable}}{\text{Current liabilities}}$$

The quick ratio implicitly assumes that marketable securities can be liquidated at something close to the prices at which they are marked, and that accounts receivable can be collected quickly (and will not default).

The most conservative measurement of solvency is the *cash ratio*, which only includes cash and marketable securities (i.e., cash equivalents) from the asset side of the balance sheet.

$$\text{Cash ratio} = \frac{\text{Cash} + \text{Marketable securities}}{\text{Current liabilities}}$$

If the firm's cash ratio is greater than one, there is little solvency risk since all pending liabilities can be covered by existing liquid assets. While in a difficult economic environment a high cash ratio is a strong signal of financial strength, in a robust market this high level of cash may indicate that the firm is managing its finances excessively conservatively and missing opportunities for growth.

Activity Ratios

The other commonly used measurements of liquidity relate to turnover, which can be thought of as the speed with which goods and payments flow into and out of the company or, alternatively, a measurement of how quickly noncash assets are converted into cash.

Inventory turnover measures how many times the inventory is depleted and restocked in the process of producing the goods sold by the firm during the period. It compares the average amount of inventory held[1] to the total amount of raw materials consumed in the course of one period (COGS).

$$\text{Inventory turnover} = \frac{\text{Cost of goods sold}}{\text{Average inventory}}$$

If we assume the inventory turnover data is calculated as a yearly figure, then by dividing it into 365 days per year we can measure how many days' worth of production demand are stored as inventory (or equivalently, how long an average item remains in inventory). This is called the *days in inventory*.

$$\text{Days in inventory} = \frac{365}{\text{Inventory turnover}}$$

There are two similar ratios dealing with financial turnover. *Payables turnover* measures how long the company is taking to pay off the accounts payable (in fractions of a year), with *days in accounts payable* the corresponding number of days:

$$\text{Payables turnover} = \frac{\text{Cost of goods sold}}{\text{Average accounts payable}}$$

$$\text{Days in accounts payable} = \frac{365}{\text{Payables turnover}}$$

Receivables turnover measures how long customers are taking to pay the company in fractional years and *days in accounts receivable* the corresponding number of days:

$$\text{Receivables turnover} = \frac{\text{Net sales}}{\text{Average receivables}}$$

$$\text{Days in accounts receivable} = \frac{365}{\text{Receivables turnover}}$$

Risk/Leverage Ratios

The next set of ratios explores the impact of leverage (also known as *gearing*) on the risk of a company. Borrowing funds increases the firm's potential returns but also increases the riskiness of the enterprise and the potential volatility in earnings from one period to the next.

The most commonly used measurement of leverage is the *debt-to-equity* ratio, which compares the relative weights of the top and bottom of the right-hand side of the balance sheet. The standard calculation uses only the long-term debt in the numerator but both the common and preferred equity in the denominator.

$$\text{Debt-to-equity} = \frac{\text{Long-term debt}}{\text{Total equity}}$$

The specific items to include in the measure of long-term debt and equity that provide the most accurate picture of the risk profile of the company will depend on the firm's business activity and capital structure (i.e., the particular mix of debt and common and preferred equity used to finance its operations).

The broadest measure of the firm's *financial leverage* is the ratio of the total assets to total equity. This compares the entire asset base on the left-hand side of the balance sheet with only that portion of shareholders' equity (on the bottom right-hand side) that belongs to the common shareholders. From the perspective of the common shareholders, the firm's financial leverage measures how much "stuff" the company owns as compared to how much money they've put in.

$$\text{Financial leverage} = \frac{\text{Total assets}}{\text{Total common equity}}$$

If the firm has leveraged its shareholder capital by borrowing, it must pay interest on the borrowed funds. The *interest coverage ratio* (also known as the *times interest earned ratio*) measures the firm's ability to meet existing debt payments given the current level of earnings. The relevant measure of income for calculating the interest coverage is earnings before interest and taxes (EBIT) since interest payments are themselves a tax-deductible expense.

$$\text{Interest coverage} = \frac{\text{EBIT}}{\text{Interest expense}}$$

Profitability Ratios

Profitability ratios measure one of two characteristics of a company:

1. *Margins:* The difference between what a company spends to manufacture its products and what it makes from selling them.
2. *Returns:* The amount of money a company makes compared to its size.

Margins Based on the various measures of profitability in the income statement—gross profit, operating profit, and net profit—we define three progressively more conservative profitability ratios by comparing each of these to net sales.

- *Gross profit margin* is simply the mark-up on the company's products, exclusive of any indirect costs of production.

$$\text{Gross profit margin} = \frac{\text{Gross profit}}{\text{Net sales}} = \frac{\text{Net sales} - \text{Cost of goods sold}}{\text{Net sales}}$$

- *Operating profit margin* includes both direct and indirect costs, as well as accounting adjustments, but before taxes and financing expenses.

$$\text{Operating profit margin} = \frac{\text{Operating profit}}{\text{Net sales}}$$

$$= \frac{\text{Net sales} - \text{COGS} - \text{SG\&A expense} - \text{D\&A}}{\text{Net sales}}$$

- *Net profit margin*, which compares the top and bottom lines of the income statement, is the most conservative measurement of profitability:

$$\text{Net profit margin} = \frac{\text{Net income}}{\text{Net sales}}$$

To provide an improved assessment of long-term profitability, the net profit margin may be adjusted to remove the effects of extraordinary items.

Return   Most financial considerations boil down, in one way or another, to an assessment of the return on a particular investment, and the risks associated with achieving it. The most general definition of financial return is the *return on investment (ROI)* which measures the gain from an investment as a percentage of the amount invested:

$$\text{Return on investment} = \frac{\text{Gain from investment}}{\text{Invested capital}}$$

While this calculation is quite straightforward for a simple product (such as a plain-vanilla government bond) the estimation of the return on an equity investment is much more complicated given the idiosyncratic nature of each company and its operations. Due to the vast differences between companies in different industries, there is no single set of metrics that allows for comparison between all companies. Instead there are many different measurements of return, each of which gives a slightly different view on the company's performance. Not all metrics are relevant to all companies and within each industry, analysts will focus on those metrics that are most indicative of the actual performance of the companies in that sector. It is only through the analysis of different measures of return and their comparison with industry norms, as well as the specific considerations of the stock in question, that an accurate assessment of profitability can be made.

The most commonly used measurements of return are as follows:

- *Return on (common) equity (ROE):* This is the most relevant measure of return to the holders of common stock and one of the most important of all financial ratios. ROE measures how much the company is earning relative to the total amount of money left with it by common shareholders (either as paid-in capital from previous share issuances or retained earnings from prior periods).

$$\text{Return on equity} = \frac{\text{Net income} - \text{Preferred Dividends}}{\text{Average common equity}}$$

  If common equity measures all the funds given to the company to work with by its owners, then ROE measures the rate of return the management has been able to produce on those funds in the period after all costs are accounted for (including preferred dividends, which are obligatory and therefore, from the perspective of the common equity holders, similar to an interest payment on debt).

- *Return on assets (ROA):* The ROA compares the firm's net income to its total asset base (the entire left side of the balance sheet).

$$\text{Return on assets} = \frac{\text{Net income}}{\text{Average total assets}}$$

  Instead of thinking in terms of assets, we can think in terms of the right-hand side of the balance sheet and view this as the net income generated from all short- and long-term borrowed funds as well as minority interest and preferred and common equity. This measures the firm's total ability to generate returns with the capital it has been given.

THE DUPONT DECOMPOSITION

The *DuPont model,* so named because it was developed by Donaldson Brown while working in the accounting department of the DuPont Chemical Company, provides an interesting decomposition of ROE and ROA that highlights the relationship between the two.

We first define *Asset turnover = Sales/Total assets,* which measures sales produced by the company as a function of the size of its asset

(Continued)

(*Continued*)

base. Given our definition of ROA = Net income/Total assets, we can rewrite this as:

$$ROA = \left(\frac{\text{Net income}}{\text{Sales}} \right) \left(\frac{\text{Sales}}{\text{Total assets}} \right)$$

$$= (\text{Net margin}) \, (\text{Asset turnover})$$

The return on assets is therefore the product of the firm's ability to generate sales given its asset base—the asset turnover—and the net margin produced on those sales. Management can improve ROA either by increasing the sales generated on the current asset base, or improving the net margin realized on sales. (Either sell more or make more per sale.)

The extension of this decomposition to the calculation of return on equity produces:

$$ROE = \left(\frac{\text{Net income}}{\text{Sales}} \right) \left(\frac{\text{Sales}}{\text{Total assets}} \right) \left(\frac{\text{Total assets}}{\text{Avg. common equity}} \right)$$

$$= (\text{Net margin})(\text{Asset turnover})(\text{Financial leverage})$$

ROE can therefore be improved by either of the methods for improving ROA, or by increasing leverage. This decomposition highlights the fact that:

$$ROE = ROA \times \text{Leverage}$$

The return generated on common equity is the product of the return generated on assets and the degree to which shareholder equity is leveraged up to increase the size of that asset base.

- *Return on capital employed (ROCE)*: The capital employed by a company is everything on the right side of the balance sheet except for the current liabilities. This includes all long-term financing, minority interest, and shareholders' equity. The convention is to use the left side of the balance sheet as the reference (since the two sides must be equal) and define capital employed as:

$$\text{Capital employed} = \text{Total assets} - \text{Current liabilities}$$

The measurement of profit used in ROCE is the pretax operating profit (the EBIT) which, as observed previously, isolates revenue earned from the mix of debt and equity used to finance it.

$$\text{ROCE} = \frac{\text{EBIT}}{\text{Capital employed}}$$

Non-GAAP Measures of Profitability   The generally accepted accounting principles govern the structure and contents of the financial disclosures of U.S. companies. The goal, however, is transparency and insight and while GAAP is a framework for analysis, it has many shortcomings. In analyzing companies for the purpose of making an investment decision—whether from the perspective of an outside investor or the management of the company—adherence to GAAP is not the primary concern, finding value is. For this reason, there have emerged several non-GAAP measurements of return that have gained popularity in recent years and are now presented on the financial statements of many companies. We will look briefly at two of the most common.

1. *Economic value added (EVA®):* Originally developed and promoted by the management consultancy of Stern, Stewart & Co., EVA measures the excess return on capital invested, above the cost of raising that capital. In general terms it can be expressed as

$$\text{EVA} = (\text{Return produced} - \text{Cost of capital}) \times \text{Invested capital}$$

The *invested capital* is the total cash investment made by shareholders and debt holders and includes all entries on the right-hand side of the balance sheet that expect a return (i.e., does not include accounts payable, which are generally free of interest charges). Observe that EVA is *not* a ratio but a measurement of the excess dollar return produced (i.e., EVA will be something like $7 million, not 12 percent). EVA is a flexible tool and can be used to analyze the company as a whole or applied by company management to assess the profitability of individual projects or divisions.

When calculating the EVA for an entire company, the measure of the return used is the *return on invested capital* (ROIC) while the measure of the cost of capital is the *weighted average cost of capital* (WACC):

$$\text{EVA}_{\text{Firm}} = (\text{ROIC} - \text{WACC}) \times \text{Invested capital}$$

The ROIC measures how effectively a company uses the capital invested in its operations to generate returns. It is defined as the ratio of the tax-adjusted operating profit to the invested capital:

$$ROIC = \frac{\text{Operating profit } (1 - \text{Tax rate})}{\text{Invested capital}}$$

The numerator is referred to as the *net operating profit after taxes* (NOPAT). It measures the potential earning ability of the company if it had no debt (i.e., no leverage).

The *weighted average cost of capital* (WACC) measures the average rate of return that the firm pays on funds raised from all sources (debt, common and preferred equity). It is calculated as:

$$WACC = [\%\text{Debt} \times \text{Cost}_{\text{Debt}} \times (1 - \text{Tax rate})] +$$
$$[\%\text{Equity} \times \text{Cost}_{\text{Equity}}] + [\%\text{Pref} \times \text{Cost}_{\text{Pref}}]$$

The percentage weight applied to each type of financing is computed based on the market value of each type of long-term financing. For publicly traded assets, such as bonds or common or preferred shares, the market value is simply the number of shares (or bonds) outstanding multiplied by their market price.

The "cost" of each type of financing is the required yield on each type of security offered by the firm. The cost of debt is scaled by (1 − Tax rate) to account for the fact that interest expenses are tax deductible so the effective interest cost of debt payments is less than their nominal cost. From the perspective of the management of the company, the WACC measures the hurdle rate for return from all projects. If a project produces a return lower than the WACC then the company loses money by pursuing it since the average cost of the funds it devotes to is higher than what it earns from the effort.

2. *Cash flow return on investment (CFROI®):* The measurement of CFROI was originally developed by HOLT Value Associates (now Credit Suisse HOLT) and gained popularity in the 1990s as a more accurate measurement of return, either for an individual project or for the company as a whole. The actual calculation of CFROI involves significant adjustments to GAAP-based accounting values, the details of which are beyond the scope of this book. For our purposes it is sufficient to understand that CFROI, as its name suggests, calculates the return on the capital invested in the company in terms of the cash flow generated.

$$CFROI = \frac{\text{Cash flow generated by company}}{\text{Total capital employed}}$$

Where CFROI differs from other measures of profitability is that it computes an inflation-adjusted internal rate of return generated by the company on its assets and includes adjustments for the expected lifespan and salvage value of its physical assets.

Dividend Ratios

When a company pays out a cash dividend, it is returning to the owners (shareholders) some of the earnings it has produced, rather than retaining them for future projects. The *payout ratio* measures the portion of available income paid out to holders of common equity.

$$\text{Payout ratio} = \frac{\text{Common dividends declared}}{\text{Net income to common shareholders}}$$

where

Net income to common shareholders = Net income − Preferred dividends

We can also express the payout ratio based on a per-share calculation using the *earnings per share* (EPS).

$$\text{Payout ratio} = \frac{\text{Dividends per share}}{\text{Earnings per common share}}$$

The sister concept to the payout ratio is the *retention ratio*, which measures the portion of eligible earnings retained by the company for reinvestment into its business. (Retention ratio = 1 − Payout ratio).

Investors looking for steady income from their investments often look at dividends in terms of the stock's *dividend yield,* which is simply the annual dividend divided by the current stock price.

$$\text{Dividend yield} = \frac{\text{Annual dividends per share}}{\text{Stock price}}$$

The firm's return on equity is a key determinant of what its dividend policy should be. If ROE is high, the company is generating attractive returns on the capital left with it by investors and should therefore retain that capital and continue to dedicate it to high-yielding projects that will promote the growth of the company. If ROE is low, the company is not making enough of the capital it has, and equity holders would be better off receiving a dividend, which could be invested elsewhere to receive a higher return. Smaller, younger companies will generally pay out little or no dividends as the funds are needed for the development and growth of the business. More mature companies, with less dramatic growth profiles and more excess capital are more likely to pay out some of that capital in the form of dividends.

While the dividend yield is, in some ways, an analogous measurement to the yield earned on a corporate bond, this comparison should be used with caution. A corporation is legally obligated to pay the annual coupon on its bonds while the dividends paid to common equity shareholders are entirely at the discretion of the firm. Additionally, in a bankruptcy scenario, in which the firm's assets are liquidated, bondholders have first claim and recovery rates (the amount of the initial face value of the bonds that can be recovered) are frequently in the 30 to 60 percent range. The equity shareholders, on the other hand, are the last in line and in most cases lose their entire investment. Companies that appear to pay an unusually high dividend yield relative to the average for their sector should be viewed with caution as it is more likely that the dividend yield appears high due to a recent drop in the share price (lower denominator) rather than to a high dividend payout (higher numerator).

All things being equal, the sustainable long-term growth rate of a company is given by the product of its ROE and the retention ratio. At one extreme, if the payout ratio is zero and all earnings are retained and reinvested, then the company will grow at the rate determined by its ROE; at the other extreme, the firm pays out all earnings as dividends and cannot grow at all.

GROWTH AND VALUE

At the start of this chapter, we commented that there is no "correct" value for any of these ratios. The specific characteristics of the company in question, and of the industry in which it operates, determine a range of generally acceptable values for any given ratio. The classification of stocks as either *growth* or *value* provides a simple example of how companies with very different values for the same financial ratio can provide attractive investment opportunities.

As the name would suggest, *growth stocks* are those of companies that are experiencing above-average rates of expansion in their business activities, as measured by the rate of growth in EPS or sales per share. These stocks are valued based on what the company will become, not what it is today. As a result, their valuations, as measured by the price-to-earnings or price-to-sales ratio, appear rich because these metrics are based on their current earnings or sales. Due to the rapidly increasing rate of return of the companies, investors are willing to pay a premium for participation in an enterprise that is expected to grow significantly in the future. Because their internal rate of return is much higher than the market average, growth stocks will generally not pay dividends but retain all earnings for reinvestment into the business. The returns from growth stocks come in the form of capital appreciation—an increase in the stock price—rather than from the dividend yield.

At the other end of the spectrum are *value stocks,* which are those that appear "cheap" when analyzed according to price-to-earnings, price-to-book, or price-to-sales ratios. Value stocks generally have more bond-like qualities, including a higher dividend yield, and represent established companies with stable businesses that are not expected to become something very different in the future than they are today.

The classification of stocks as either growth or value is not intended to be mutually exclusive—many stocks display characteristics of both; growth and value should be viewed as two ends of a spectrum along which stocks can be classified. The classification also depends on the stage in the company's life cycle. Most value stocks were growth stocks at some point: The stocks of small startup companies are almost always purchased for their growth potential and not for their valuation as a mature business. Similarly, since no company can continue at a faster rate than the market indefinitely, the rate of expansion of a successful growth company will eventually slow to a levels more consistent with the market as a whole, and take on more value characteristics. (There is also a percentage of growth companies that will be unsuccessful as the anticipated rates of future growth in sales or earnings fail to materialize.)

The classification of stocks according to the growth and value characteristics is commonly referred to as a classification by *style.*

BLOOMBERG

Thus far, we have looked at the contents of the three principal financial disclosures provided by public companies and how the ratios between different items in these statements can provide insight into their risk and return characteristics. Professionals working in financial services have various tools at their disposal with which they can access and analyze this information. First among these is their *Bloomberg.*

A Bloomberg® terminal is arguably the single most useful tool available to a financial professional (challenged only by Microsoft Excel in terms of its indispensability for most traders and salespeople). Given the incredible range of functionality offered, (and the not insignificant cost[2]), one of the most important first steps for new arrivals to Wall Street is to familiarize themselves with as much of the functionality of their Bloomberg as possible.

To facilitate this process, throughout the book we will include references to Bloomberg functions relevant to the material presented.

There is an enormous amount of fundamental information available on Bloomberg including both current and historical company data as well as useful tools for comparing the financial characteristics of different companies. A few of the more commonly used functions are listed here.

- **DES** *(Description):* An excellent starting point for fundamental information on any company. The **DES** function includes up to 10 screens of information including a summary of recent price performance, all commonly used security identifiers, management profiles, financial ratios, revenue and earnings-per-share information, indicies of which it is a member, product and geographic segmentation, and summaries of the three primary financial statements. The **DES** function can also be used with other product types (indices, ETFs, futures, options) and contains similarly useful information.
- **RV** *(Relative Value):* Compares companies according to a wide variety of fundamental characteristics, which can be chosen by the user. The comparison can be global or limited by region or sector.
- **ERN** *(Earnings):* Provides historical earnings-per-share data as well as next-period analyst estimates. Each historical value is accompanied by the percentage change versus the same period value from the previous year as well as the percentage out- or underperformance versus analysts' expectations.
- **REQ** *(Related Equities):* Provides information on the existence of alternate classes of stock (voting and nonvoting shares or preferred stocks) as well as listings on other exchanges (particularly useful for international stocks).
- **FA** *(Financial Analysis):* Provides an extensive selection of tools for analyzing fundamental data with the ability to make comparisons to other companies.
- **CN** *(Corporate News):* News stories related to the company.

VALUATION

In what we have presented so far, we have focused on the analysis of financial statements and the calculation of financial ratios for the purpose of assessing how well a company is run (its efficiency, profitability, degree of risk) using data taken from the financial disclosures of the company itself. This analysis is useful to both the internal audience of firm management, who must assess the company's financial condition and performance, as well as to the external audience of creditors, investors, and ratings agencies wanting to analyze the future prospects of the company.

However, we have not yet considered the most important question to a common equity investor: given what is known from the company's financial disclosures, how much should he be willing to pay to participate in the revenues of the company as a shareholder? What is the "correct" price for a share of the company's common stock and how does this compare with the current market price?

The process by which an analyst or investor endeavors to determine the fair price for a stock based on its financial data is called *fundamental analysis.* The central assumption of fundamental analysis is that it is possible to incorporate all available information about the company's current state and future prospects into a valuation model to produce an objective price for the company. There are two primary approaches to fundamental valuation:

1. *Discounted cash flow (DCF) valuation:* In a discounted cash flow valuation, the analyst estimates the magnitude and timing of all future cash flows produced by the company and discounts these to the present. This is the "purest" form of valuation as it bases itself on a generalized theoretical framework that is valid for any financial asset.
2. *Relative valuation:* A more common (and much easier) form of valuation is relative valuation, which assumes that the market prices companies correctly *in general,* but can make mistakes in its valuation of individual companies. By comparing the financial ratios of different companies (both the internal ratios covered previously as well as others that incorporate the market price of the stock) the analyst seeks to identify companies with superior (inferior) financial characteristics that are undervalued (overvalued) relative to their peers.

DCF Valuation

The fundamental axiom in all of valuation is that the value of a financial asset is equal to the present value of all the future cash flows it will generate, with each one discounted at a rate of return that incorporates both the timing and riskiness of that cash flow. Assuming we know the n cash flows $CF_1, CF_2, \ldots CF_n$ that will be produced by the asset at times $t_1, t_2, \ldots t_n$ and the relevant discount rates for each $r_1, r_2, \ldots r_n$, then the present value of the asset can be expressed as:

$$V = \sum_{i=1}^{n} \frac{CF_i}{(1+r_i)^{t_i}} = \frac{CF_1}{(1+r_1)^{t_1}} + \frac{CF_2}{(1+r_2)^{t_2}} + \cdots + \frac{CF_n}{(1+r_n)^{t_n}}$$

While this general valuation expression is relevant for any financial asset, our interest is in applying it to the specific case of valuing an equity security. Due to the complexity of real-world finance, it will be necessary to make a few assumptions about these cash flows and discount rates. While, for any particular valuation scenario, these assumptions may not be appropriate and adjustments will need to be made to accommodate the idiosyncrasies of the particular company under analysis, in the development of a general valuation framework, they are reasonable and allow us to produce much more compact and insightful expressions for the value of a company.

- Assume that cash flows occur at regular intervals (i.e., quarterly, annually, etc.). We can then define the interval of time between cash flows as "1" and write $t = 1, 2, \ldots n$.
- In general, the specific discount rates r_1 for payments occurring at different times in the future will vary because a different rate of return is required on investments of different maturities. However, for our purposes, we will assume that we can use a single blended rate of return r for all maturities.
- While other financial assets, such as bonds, have a clearly defined maturity, a corporation is considered a "going concern" and assumed to operate indefinitely. Therefore there will not be n cash flows but an infinite number. (This may appear to make the situation more complex but, as we will see shortly, this is not the case.)

Our general valuation formula is now:

$$V = \sum_{i=1}^{n} \frac{CF_i}{(1+r)^i} = \frac{CF_1}{(1+r)} + \frac{CF_2}{(1+r)^2} + \cdots + \frac{CF_n}{(1+r)^n} + \cdots$$

Questions About Valuation

While valuation is a broad and rich area of study, no one on a trading floor is actually going to perform a discounted cash flow valuation so we have little to gain by going into the specifics in great detail. We will therefore focus our analysis on answering three relatively high-level questions about valuation, the first and third being relatively more conceptual while the second is quite practical:

1. What cash flows should I discount and at what rate?
2. How do we sum up an infinite stream of payments?
3. How do I account for the changing character of the business over time?

Question 1: Which cash flows?   The correct answers to the question of "What cash flows and what rates?" is, of course, "All those that matter" and "At the rates that the market requires." This may be a uselessly vague response but it is, nonetheless, the correct one. In reading through the explanation of the valuation models presented below, it is important to remember that, while these models provide a conceptual framework for determining the fair price to pay for a stock, they are only a starting point. The role of the financial analyst is to use his understanding of the specific details of the company to produce a valuation that incorporates judicious estimates of the magnitude and timing of all future cash flows, their probabilities, and the appropriate discount rates to apply to each one. Each company is unique, and what matters is that the valuation makes sense and provides insight, not that it adheres to some standardized model.

Our goal in this section is significantly more modest: we are not looking to actually perform a discounted cash flow analysis but simply to understand enough about how one is done to be able to speak intelligently about valuation with colleagues and understand an analyst's research report. Given these objectives, a general understanding of these standard models will suffice.

> *Dividend discount model (DDM):* The only cash flows that are actually received by the common shareholder are dividends. Therefore, the simplest answer to the question "What will I get for owning this stock?" is to compute all future dividend payments Div_i and then discount them to the present at the *cost of equity*. The cost of equity, r_{CE}, is equal to the sum of the risk-free rate of interest (r_f), which can be taken as the return on a riskless government bond of similar maturity, and the *equity risk premium* (ERP), which is the additional amount required by investors to compensate for the riskiness associated with an equity investment. The value of the firm under the Dividend Discount Model is then:

$$V_{DDM} = \sum_{i=1}^{\infty} \frac{Div_i}{(1 + r_{CE})^i}$$

where

$$r_{CE} = r_f + ERP$$

While it is commonly spoken of as though it were a single number, the equity risk premium required to value any particular stock will depend on the riskiness of the company, particularly given that dividends are paid at the discretion of the company and may be canceled at any time. The equity risk premium associated with large, stable companies with long dividend histories will be very different than that applied to a smaller, younger company with more uncertain future prospects.

Free cash flow: The obvious problem with the dividend discount model is that it will not work if the company does not pay a regular dividend. A growing company with an above-average ROE would be expected to retain its earnings and channel them back into the business where they can earn an attractive return and promote growth—this hardly makes the company worthless. However, since the common stock is a claim on the present and future benefits of the company, it should not matter whether profits are paid out as dividends or retained by the company—share ownership entitles the investor to their proportional share of those profits, wherever they are. An alternate approach is therefore to value a company based on how much money it generates, regardless of whether that money is returned to investors or reinvested in the business.

A free cash flow valuation can be done in two ways: by valuing only the equity portion of the firm using the *free cash flow to equity* (FCFE), or valuing the entire firm using the *free cash flow to the firm* (FCFF). Both are measures of free cash flow (i.e., net income adjusted for mandatory expenses, depreciation, and amortization, working capital needs, etc.) with the difference that the free cash flow to equity includes only that free cash that is available for payment to equity holders as dividends, while free cash flow to the firm includes all cash available before payments on borrowed funds.

The discounting rates applied to the two types of cash flows are different. For the free cash flow to equity, the relevant discount rate is the cost of equity (r_{CE}), the same as was used in the Dividend Discount Model. In reality, the only difference between the models is that in the FCFE model, we are valuing the company based on the cash *available* to pay out as dividends while in the DDM the valuation is based on the cash *actually* paid as dividends. If the firm paid out all free cash flow as dividends, the DDM and FCFE valuations would be the same. In the Free Cash Flow to the Firm model, the discounting rate must incorporate the different rates of return required on equity, debt, and preferred stock, in proportion to the weight of each in the firm's financing mix. This is precisely what the *weighted average cost of capital* (WACC), defined previously in the context of EVA analysis, tells us. The two valuation models can be expressed by the following formulas:

$$V_{FCFE} = \sum_{i=1}^{\infty} \frac{FCFE_i}{(1 + r_{CE})^i}$$

$$V_{FCFF} = \sum_{i=1}^{\infty} \frac{FCFF_i}{(1 + WACC)^i}$$

It is important to realize that the two models are valuing different things. The FCFE valuation gives the present value of that portion of the firm's earnings that is available to the common equity holders. The FCFF model values the entire company, including its debt and will therefore produce a higher value than valuation of only the equity. In using the WACC as a discount rate, there is also the implicit assumption that the firm's blend of debt and equity financing will be constant forever.

Question 2: Infinite Sums   One sticking point in all these valuation formulas is that they contain infinite sums. While at first consideration this might seem to cause problems—if we add up an infinite sum of numbers won't our valuation become ridiculously large or even infinite itself? In reality, there is actually quite a simple mathematical solution to these problems that produces very "nice" prices (i.e., not infinite), so long as certain criteria are met.

The easiest way to see that these infinite sums will not cause problems is to consider the following series, which most of us learned in a pre-calculus class (and then quickly forgot):

$$\sum_{n=1}^{\infty} \left(\frac{1}{2}\right)^n = \frac{1}{2} + \frac{1}{4} + \frac{1}{8} + \frac{1}{16} + \cdots = 1$$

Calculating a few terms it quickly becomes clear that the sum of the infinite series is equal to one. This particular series is the basis for the riddle about the man who wants to walk out of the room and decides to do it in pieces: he first walks halfway to the door ($\frac{1}{2}$), then half of the remaining distance ($\frac{1}{4}$), then half of the remaining distance ($\frac{1}{8}$), and so on. How does he ever get out of the room?

So long as the number that is being raised to successive powers is less than one, this particular infinite series converges to a finite limit. The formula for the sum of the infinite series is:

$$\sum_{n=1}^{\infty} \left(\frac{a}{b}\right)^n = \frac{a}{b-a}$$

You can check that it works with $a = 1$ and $b = 2$. The key is that this formula only works when a and b are both positive and $a < b$. When the fraction a/b is less than one, each successive term smaller becomes smaller at a sufficiently rapid rate such that the sum of the terms converges to a finite number. If the fraction is greater than or equal to one, the sum diverges (i.e., grows infinitely large) because each successive term is either the same size or larger than the previous one.

We can now illustrate how this formula is applied to our valuation models. As an example, we will use the *Gordon Growth Model* (GGM), which is a specific case of the standard dividend discount model in which the company is assumed to pay an annual dividend that grows at a constant rate, g, indefinitely. If the current year ($t = 0$) dividend is Div_0, then the dividend Div_1 in year one will be $Div_1 = Div_0(1 + g)$ and the dividend Div_n in year n will be equal to $Div_n = Div_0(1 + g)^n$. Applying this to our DDM model we get:

$$V_{GGM} = \sum_{i=1}^{\infty} \frac{Div_0(1 + g)^i}{(1 + r_{CE})^i}$$

Pulling the constant term Div_0 out of the sum we can fit this formula to the structure of the general formula for the infinite series where $a = 1 + g$ and $b = 1 + r_{CE}$.

$$V_{GGM} = Div_0 \sum_{i=1}^{\infty} \left(\frac{1+g}{1+r_{CE}}\right)^i$$

To use our formula, we need the growth rate g of the dividend to be less than the cost of equity r_{CE}. Not only is this necessary from a mathematical perspective but it makes sense intuitively—a company could not possibly keep increasing its dividend at a greater rate than the rate of return required of it or it would attract an unending amount of investment and therefore grow infinitely large. Making use of the fact that $Div_1 = Div_0(1 + g)$ we can apply the formula for the infinite sum to this last equation to produce a general pricing formula for the Gordon Growth model:

$$V_{GGM} = Div_0 \left(\frac{1+g}{(1+r_{CE}) - (1+g)} \right) = \frac{Div_1}{r_{CE} - g}$$

The formulas for the other valuation methodologies are derived similarly.

Question 3: Changing Character of the Company   An obvious limitation of the single stage model is that it requires that the growth rate of the company (either measured by the dividend or free cash flow) must be constant for the life of the company and that it cannot exceed the required rate of return on equity, r_{CE}. While this may work for a mature company with limited plans for expansion, clearly during some finite period of time, a given company can (and some companies must) grow at a much faster rate than is required by the return on equity.[3]

Fortunately these limitations on the growth rate are only necessary for the "from here to infinity" portion of the calculation. Our solution, therefore, is to divide the life of the company into different stages. During the immediate future of the company, where an analyst has more visibility and can make more informed predictions, the returns can be calculated on a year-by-year basis with different rates of growth applicable during different periods. The stable long-term growth assumption is then only applied to the "everything after that" portion (the infinite part) which can calculated using the previously introduced formulas.

The result is the multistage versions of the DDM and FCF models. A two-stage model, for example, will have an initial period of rapid growth that is followed by an eternity of stable growth. Three stage models could include a rapid growth phase, followed by a steadily declining phase in which the growth rate drops down to the long-term market average, followed by the long-term stable growth phase. In terms of the calculation, it simply means summing a few terms manually before applying the formula to the long-term result.

As an example, we calculate a two-stage Gordon Growth model based on an assumption of five years of a high dividend growth rate g_{HI} followed by a long-term growth rate g_{LT}. The general formula would look like the following:

$$V_{GGM2} = Div_0 \left(\sum_{i=1}^{5} \left(\frac{1+g_{HI}}{1+r_{CE}} \right)^i + \sum_{i=6}^{\infty} \left(\frac{1+g_{LT}}{1+r_{CE}} \right)^i \right)$$

The first term (years 1 through 5) we calculate on a period-by-period basis and the second term uses the infinite series formula.

$$V_{GGM2} = Div_0 \sum_{i=1}^{5} \left(\frac{1 + g_{HI}}{1 + r_{CE}} \right)^i + \frac{1}{(1 + r_{CE})^5} \left(\frac{Div_6}{r_{CE} - g_{LT}} \right)$$

While the formula looks messy, it can be expressed quite easily in words:

Value under 2-stage GGM = (The sum of the first 5 years' cash flows)

+ The present value of (the cash flows for the rest of time)

Similar multistage extensions can be constructed for the free cash flow to equity, free cash flow to the firm, and other discounted cash flow valuation models.

Relative Valuation

While discounted cash flow analysis forms the foundation of valuation it is, undoubtedly, a challenging and time-consuming process involving many highly subjective assumptions. Small adjustments to the long-run growth prospects of a company or the required return on equity can result in large changes in the valuation. The magnitude and timing of the cash flows themselves can also be extremely difficult to predict. And even if the analyst is highly confident of the estimations used in his analysis, what should he do if he arrives at a "correct" price for the company stock of $25 per share and then observes that the stock is currently trading in the market at $40? Is it likely that *everyone else* in the market is mispricing the stock and only he knows the correct price? And even if this were the case—is there any reason the market must move to the "right" price? If it is wrong now, could it get "wronger"? While extraordinarily important for establishing the conceptual foundation for valuation in general, because of the many challenges it presents, it is rare to find anyone other than a research analyst, investment banker, or particularly diligent proprietary trader actually producing a discounted cash flow valuation.

In practice, the majority of actual valuation discussions center on the question of *relative valuation*. In a relative valuation, the market prices of the shares of different companies are compared with their underlying financial characteristics to identify those companies whose shares prices are out of line with their economic fundamentals and therefore represent either over- or underpriced securities. The question is not whether the price of the security is correct in absolute terms, but whether a company with superior fundamentals is trading at a price that is below that of a company with inferior fundamentals. Regardless of what the theoretically correct price is for a security, investors should be able to produce a profit by purchasing superior fundamentals at low prices and selling stocks with higher prices than their fundamentals would justify.

Multiples

To assess the relative valuations of different companies, analysts frequently use financial ratios called *price multiples*. These compare the market price of the stock to the value of different fundamental metrics such as earnings, book value, or sales.

> *Price-to-earnings (PE):* The most commonly used price multiple is the *price-to-earnings ratio* (PE ratio), which is the ratio of the market price of the stock to the earnings per share generated by the company.

$$\text{PE ratio} = \frac{\text{Market price per common share}}{\text{Earnings per common share}}$$

The PE ratio can be thought of as the price paid per units of earnings—that is, a PE ratio of $15\times$ indicates[4] that purchasers of the stock are paying \$15 for every \$1 of earnings produced per share. While PE ratios will vary greatly between companies and industries depending on risk, growth prospects, and other factors, they generally fall in the range of $10\times$ to $25\times$. The inverse of the PE ratio (the *earnings-to-price ratio*) is called the *earnings yield* and measures the return on an investment in a stock in terms of the per-share earnings generated. PE ratios of $10\times$ to $25\times$ would correspond to earnings yields of between 10 percent and 4 percent respectively.

It is important to specify whether the PE ratio is calculated on a forward or historical basis. A historical PE compares the previous period's earnings (either the annualized one-quarter earnings or the sum of the previous four quarters) to the current market price, while a forward PE compares the expected earnings in the next period (or year) to the current price. If earnings are expected to increase, then the forward PE will be lower than the historical. While forward earnings are generally of more interest, they implicitly include the analyst's expectations of future growth and are therefore more subjective than historical earnings, which can be computed objectively from a firm's financial disclosures.

While in general, lower values indicate a better value (earnings that can be acquired more cheaply), in practice, the PE ratio at which a given stock trades is a function of many factors. A stock with a historical PE ratio of $20\times$ but whose earnings are expected to double would be "cheap" compared with a company with a PE of $12\times$ whose earnings are not expected to grow at all. The risk associated with the actual production of future earnings will also affect the PE as more volatile or uncertain earnings streams command a lower PE (higher earnings yield) than more stable earnings.

One way to more explicitly factor a company's expected growth rate into the historical PE ratio is to calculate the *PEG ratio*, which is the PE ratio divided by the expected growth rate.

$$\text{PEG ratio} = \frac{\text{PE}}{\text{Expected\% annual growth}}$$

PEG ratios below two are generally considered attractive. (The expected annual growth is expressed as an integer rather than a percentage (i.e., 20 instead of 20 percent). The combination of the historical PE and forward-looking PEG ratio gives a more complete picture of the stock's price based on both the present and future earnings generation ability (though adjustments for risk are still necessary).

Enterprise Value to EBITDA Ratio: A limitation of the PE ratio is that it only values the equity portion of a company. An alternative is the ratio of the *enterprise value* (EV) of the firm to its EBITDA. The enterprise value is the sum of the market values of all existing sources of capital: common equity, preferred equity, debt, and minority interest, less cash, and cash equivalents. Computation of the enterprise value consists effectively of the marking-to-market of all of the major components of the right-hand side of the balance sheet and can be thought of as an estimate of the cost to acquire the whole firm. (An acquirer would need to purchase all outstanding shares and assume existing debt, but would get the cash the firm holds.) The inverse ratio, EBITDA/EV, can therefore be seen as the measure of the return on investment to the acquirer.

Price-to-book (PB): An alternative measure of the value inherent in the stock price is the *price-to-book-value-ratio* (PB).

$$\text{PB ratio} = \frac{\text{Market price per common share}}{\text{Book value per common share}}$$

The book value ignores the earnings potential of the company and focuses primarily on what has already been done—the retained earnings and paid-in capital that belongs to the common equity holders.

Price-to-sales (PS): Within a given industry, where products and margins are relatively homogeneous, it can be useful to compare stocks based on a *price-to-sales-ratio* (PS).

$$\text{PS ratio} = \frac{\text{Market price per common share}}{\text{Sales per common share}}$$

Dividing the PS ratio by the *Net profit margin = Net income/Sales* gives the PE ratio. This separation of the PE ratio into the combination of sales and margins can be useful in situations where margins are an exogenous factor (e.g., sectors highly sensitive to commodity prices) or as a means of isolating the sales-producing ability of the company from the efficiency of its production.

Price-to-cash-flow (PCF): A final measure of profitability uses the all-important free cash flow. The PCF ratio compares the stock price to the per-share operating cash flow.

$$\text{PCF ratio} = \frac{\text{Market price per common share}}{\text{Free cash flow per common share}}$$

The inverse of the PCF ratio is the *free cash flow yield*, which measures the return on an investment in the stock in terms of free cash flow generation.

TECHNICAL ANALYSIS

The determination of the "correct" price for a stock, based on the methods that we have sketched in these first two chapters is called *fundamental analysis* and is the primary role of the research division of a Wall Street investment bank. It is, unquestionably, a time-consuming and mentally demanding approach and requires the careful analysis of objectively verifiable information as well as the judicious estimation of many subjective factors. In theory the efforts should be well rewarded. The methods of fundamental analysis allow the investor to identify mispriced securities in which he can take positions that will produce a profit as the stocks correct toward their "right" price. The frustrating reality for the fundamentally driven investor is that, no matter how correct the valuation model, there is nothing that forces mispriced stocks to move toward their "fair" price. Markets can remain oblivious to fundamental considerations and sustain irrational valuations for very long periods of time. Many mispriced stocks become much more mispriced as investors focus on the "bigger fool" theory, which says that the "right" price of a stock is irrelevant so long as there is a bigger fool who is willing to buy the stock off you when you want to sell.

An alternative approach to determining the likely future direction of stock prices is *technical analysis,* which makes little or no reference to the fundamental characteristics of the company but focuses instead on the analysis of the historical movements of the stock price. Despite its popularity and widespread use in the sales and trading business, we will limit ourselves to only a cursory overview of the subject. There are several reasons for this, but the most important is the fact that technical analysis is popular precisely because most people find it quite intuitive. While an understanding of the more esoteric aspects may require more significant study, the basics are both widely available quickly understood and we add little value by including them here. We therefore limit ourselves to a few quick observations on the general character of technical analysis and leave it to the interested reader to pursue the subject in more detail elsewhere.

The underlying concept of technical analysis is that certain patterns of price movements in financial assets repeat in predictable ways, and that these patterns can be identified by analyzing the graph of the evolution of the asset price over time (technical analysis is sometimes called *charting*). Many of the most popular indicators can be distilled down into the concepts of support and resistance levels. A *support level* is a price below which a stock is unlikely to fall while a *resistance level* is a price above which the stock has difficulty rallying. A support (or resistance) level can be thought of as a floor (or ceiling) on the level of the stock price. The movement of a stock price through a support or resistance level is considered to be a significant indicator of the strength of the directional movement. Once broken, a previous resistance level often becomes a support level going forward and vice versa.

While the concepts of support and resistance levels are quite simple, the determination of the location of these levels is where the complexity of technical analysis lies. In some cases the establishment of a technical level can be very simplistic—psychological barriers such as the Dow Jones Industrial Average breaking 10,000 or the observation that the stock price has, on several occasions, reached a certain level without going through it. Other times, a technical level may be determined by the presence of one of many established patters in the graph of the stock price, such as a "pendant," "channel," or "head and shoulders" formation.

The desire to find order and determinism in the randomness of stock price fluctuations has motivated the development of many other, far more elaborate technical indicators. These include the analysis of the percentage retracement of previous price movements, comparisons of the stock price with its multiday moving averages, or supposedly significant ratios based on the Fibonacci number sequence. There exist entire schools of technical analysis, such as the Elliott Wave Theory, which provide a framework for analyzing daily stock price movements in the context of larger trends over multiple months or years. Technicians (as they are often called) will use other corroborating technical indicators to determine the significance of a particular movement including the volume of shares traded, the breadth of the market move, and whether a particular technical breach occurred on an intraday basis or closing basis (particularly if this occurs on a Friday, as this sets the tone for investor ruminations over the weekend).

There is a great deal of disagreement between industry and academia as to the validity of technical analysis as a tool for accurately predicting future price movements. Among industry professionals, it is a commonly used tool in market analysis; within the academic community, it is almost universally condemned as meaningless pseudoscience. While there are many strong opinions on both sides of the argument, for the pragmatic objectives of this book, there is no need to either prove or refute the validity of technical analysis as a tool for forecasting markets. With die-hard chartists and pure fundamental analysts on each side, most Wall Street professionals (myself included) stick to a healthily agnostic middle ground regarding the study and use of technical analysis, which can be summarized in three points:

1. *Self-fulfilling prophecy:* Regardless of the validity of its underlying assumptions, technical analysis will have some predictive power if a large number of market participants believe it to be true and trade accordingly. An awareness of the significance of certain technical levels can be a useful tool in understanding and anticipating the likely actions of those investors that adhere closely to technical indicators.
2. *Language:* It is a practical reality that many market practitioners use technical analysis and it is necessary to have at least some familiarity with the language and concepts in order to communicate effectively.
3. *Simplicity:* The most meaningful technical indicators are usually the simplest ones. Where investors make trading decisions by looking at the graph of the stock, the eye will perceive the most obvious patterns first and these will have the greatest likelihood of motivating trading decisions. The more esoteric and obscure the technique (i.e., the more it sounds like witchcraft), the less likely it is to be important or useful.

The best technical analysis is generally that which corroborates (or is corroborated by) other fundamental, or economic indicators. Investors should always be aware that our human brains are poorly wired to deal with randomness and we tend to look for patterns and assume they will repeat. This gives us a natural predisposition to want to believe in technical analysis and be influenced by graphical patterns in our trading. To offset this, it is wise to keep a somewhat skeptical view and utilize technical indicators only within the larger context of economic, fundamental, and trading flow analysis.

Bloomberg offers an extensive selection of tools for graphical analysis of stock price movements. Some of the more popular functions are:

- **GIP** *(Graph of Intraday Price)*: A graph of the intraday price history of a stock (or other asset), which updates in real time (subject to relevant market data permissions). The graph may be extended over multiple (up to 31) trading sessions by appending the desired number of days to the function (e.g., **GIP5** graphs the last five days of trading).
- **GP** *(Graph Price)*: A graph of the historical price of the stock (default setting provides six months of daily closing data) with the option to select specific date ranges and pricing frequency (daily, weekly, monthly, and so on). This function also provides a number of tools for performing technical analysis on historical price performance including trend lines, moving averages, percentage change, volume data, and many others.
- **GPO** *(Hi-Lo Graph)*: Enhances the **GP** with the addition of indicators of the high and low price during the day (or other chosen period). The **GPC** *(Candlestick Graph)* further enriches the **GPO** through the use of a *candlestick* charting method, which indicates not only the high and low but also the opening and closing prices on each date.
- **G** *(Graph)*: Allows users to create custom chart types with the function. Graph types are stored under consecutive names **G1, G2, G3**, and so on.
- **COMP** *(Comparison)*: Works similarly to the **GP** but allows for the comparison of the performance of up to three securities.
- **HP** *(Historical Price)* function gives historical closing price and volume data in a tabular, rather than graphical format, while the **HCP** *(Historical Change in Price)* provides the historical closing price and the percentage change from the previous day's close.

CORPORATE ACTIONS

In this last section, we look at a few of the more common types of corporate activity and how they impact the trading in the stocks of the companies involved. While the analysis of the benefits, risks, and financial consider-ations that motivate companies to undertake different types of corporate activity is primarily the responsibility of those in the investment banking or capital markets divisions, a trader or salesperson should have a general sense of how the most common corporate actions impact investors and some of the important factors to consider in determining how the affected stocks' share prices will react. Details of all types of corporate actions for most publicly traded companies, both historical as well as those future events that have been publicly disclosed can be found on Bloomberg using the **CACS** (*Corporate Actions*) function.

Stock Split

The simplest corporate action is a stock split, in which a company issues new shares of stock and gives them, free of charge, to all existing shareholders in proportion to the number of shares they currently hold. For example, in a two-for-one split, the number of shares outstanding is doubled and all current shareholders will receive an additional share for each share held. A stock split does not create or destroy value and the firm's market capital-ization, which measures the market value of all outstanding shares, must be the same before and after the split.

Market capitalization = Total shares outstanding × Market price per share

Therefore, as soon as the new shares are issued, the stock price will decrease by the inverse of the split ratio such that the market capitalization of the company remains constant. In a two-for-one split, for example, the stock price would halve.

There is no economic impact to a share split. The issuance of the new shares is not dilutive to the existing shareholders (i.e., their fractional own-ership of the company and its earnings is the same) because while the com-pany's earnings are now divided up among a larger number of shares, they still hold the same fractional percentage of the outstanding shares. Depend-ing on the degree to which the level of the share price is to be reduced, the split can be done in any proportion (3-for-2, 4-for-1, etc.). Where fractional shares occur, investors are usually given a cash payment equivalent to the value of the fractional share on the split date. The only effect of a split is to change the price of the share and the number of shares available for trading in the market.

It is reasonable to ask why, if there is no economic impact, would a company bother to split its shares just to reduce the share price?[5] When asked, most companies will justify a share split by saying something to the effect that they want to put the stock price at an accessible level for small investors. This is generally a nice sounding but rather weak justification. The main reasons are to do with optics and psychology. If a company's share price is much higher than that of its competitors in nominal terms, particularly where this is the result of a recent rise in the price of the stock, there is a psychological tendency to perceive the share price as expensive, irrespective of any measurement of fundamental value (such as the PE or PB ratio). Though we prefer to believe otherwise, when it comes to financial decision making, we are remarkably simplistic creatures, as research in the field of behavioral economics has shown. Particularly at the retail level, an investor will usually prefer to buy 100 shares of a $50 stock than 10 shares of a $500 stock both because of the perceived valuation difference and because of the tendency to think of share price movements in nominal amounts ("if my $50 stock goes up $1.00, I'll make $100 while with the $500 stock I'll only make $10"), without adjusting for the dramatically different percentage change this represents for each security.

For stocks that look "too cheap," companies can perform a *reverse split* in which the number of outstanding shares is reduced. For example, in a 1-for-2 reverse split, the number of shares is reduced by half, which would lead to a doubling of the stock price. Just as stocks whose prices are too high compared to their competitors' can be perceived as "expensive" on a valuation basis, stocks that are too cheap can sometimes be perceived as lower quality or risky, particularly when the low share price is the result of a recent slide in the stock price. A company that has fallen precipitously and finds the share price at an uncomfortably low level can use a reverse split to prop the price back up to a more "eye-pleasing" level. There is also the hope that the new higher stock price may strike some investors as indicative of a rebound in the company performance, making the stock more attractive. Stock splits are, for the most part, a meaningless exercise intended primarily to encourage retail interest in the stock on the basis of nonfinancial factors.

It is telling that Warren Buffett, one of the greatest investors of all time and a strong advocate of corporate responsibility and shareholder protection, has never split the shares of his investment holding company, Berkshire Hathaway, which, in early 2008, traded as high as $150,000 per share.

Dividends

When a company pays a cash dividend, it gives to the shareholders a portion of the earnings it has accumulated during the current and prior periods. The share price of a company generally reacts favorably to the announcement of an increase in the dividend amount or the issuance of a new dividend if there was not one previously. There are several reasons for this. The first is that investors tend to like dividend payments, which give the shares of common stock some of the steady, coupon-like income of a bond. Second, the ability to pay out cash to investors makes a positive statement about the liquidity position of the company—the company must have the cash to pay out in the first place. Third, by returning some portion of earnings to shareholders, the company allows investors to choose where they want to invest their cash, rather than making that decision for them by retaining the earnings.

From an economic perspective, investors' love of dividends is not entirely rational given that, by returning cash to shareholders, the management of the company is suggesting that it is not confident it can employ that money to produce above-average returns. For a growth company, the announcement of a dividend can actually be perceived as a negative, particularly since growth stocks are valued at higher PE ratios on the assumption that future growth and revenue generation will be high.

There are four dates associated with the payment of a dividend. The first is the *announcement date*, which is the day the company discloses to the public the timing and amount of the dividend. The dividend is then paid to the owners of the stock as of a specific date, called the *record date*. The determination of the ownership of the shares is determined based on *settlement* of a trade—the actual delivery of shares versus payment—which occurs three days after the trade is executed on the exchange. (This is called a T + 3 settlement cycle: Monday's trades settle on Thursday; Friday's trades settle the following Wednesday, and so forth.) The specification of the record date therefore determines an earlier date after which a buyer of the stock will not have been able to settle the trade before the record date, and will therefore not be the considered the owner of the shares for the purposes for payment of the dividend. This date, two business days prior to the record date, is called the *ex-dividend date* (colloquially referred to as the *ex-div date* or *ex-date*). On this day, the stock begins trading at a price that assumes that the buyer will not receive the dividend.[6] Lastly there is the *pay date*, which is the day that the owner of the security as of the record date actually receives the dividend. In order to allow time for the processing of the payments, the pay date can be several weeks after the record date. The details of both announced upcoming as well as historical dividends for stocks are available on Bloomberg using the **DVD** (*Dividend*) function.

On a stock's ex-dividend date the share price will drop by the amount of the dividend to adjust for the fact that the share purchased the day before came with the dividend while today's shares do not. For example, if a stock closed at $24 and went ex-dividend ("ex-div") on a $1 dividend, all other things being equal, the stock price should open the next morning at $23. On Bloomberg, the calculation of the percentage change in the stock price on the ex-date will automatically adjust such that, if the stock price drops by exactly the amount of the dividend, the percentage change on the day will show as zero, regardless of the size of the dividend.

Companies will sometime perform a stock split via a *stock dividend* in which additional shares are paid out to all shareholders in the form of a dividend. While the payment is in the form of shares rather than cash, the economic impact is the same (i.e., proportional reduction in the stock price on ex-date based on the dollar value of stock distributed).

An important consideration for investors purchasing a stock outside of their home country is the rate of withholding tax on dividends. In general, corporate profits are taxed twice: first through corporate taxes paid by the company, and then again through the income tax assessed on the share-holders when those profits are paid out as dividends. When the holder of a share of stock is a foreign resident, however, the tax authority of the country where the company is domiciled loses out on the second of these two taxes because a foreign resident will only pay tax in his home country, not in every country in which he invests. To compensate for this, there is usually a withholding tax assessed on dividends paid to foreign shareholders. For each dividend there is a *gross dividend* amount, which is paid to local residents and a few foreign investors where specific tax treaties have been negotiated, and a *net dividend*, which is paid to all other foreign investors. Depending on the country in which the company is based, and the domicile of the investor, this dividend withholding will generally range between 15 percent and 30 percent.

Spin-Offs

In a spin-off, a company decides to separate a particular subset of its operations into an independently listed corporation. The specific reasons for spinning off a portion of a company can be quite varied though in general, it indicates that the activities of the particular division or business line that is to be spun off are significantly differentiated from those of the parent company and that the management feels that it is in the best interests of the shareholders that they focus on their primary line of business and separate off the subcompany under an independent management. Depending on the specific circumstance of the spin-off, there can be radically different views of the new entity. A large, diversified company with a strong "value" profile may feel that a particularly dynamic, growing portion of its operations is undervalued when viewed as a division of the parent and will be more highly valued in isolation. In this case, the parent will often retain a substantial ownership in the spun-off entity in order to benefit from the revaluation of the high-growth business. The scenario can also be played out in reverse—a large dynamic parent that feels its valuation is unfairly dragged down by the presence of a low-growth division. Spinning off the division as a private company extracts the cash value of the spun-off division, which can then be devoted to higher-ROE projects. The performance of the spun-off entity will depend on investors' perception of whether it represents the liberation of a high-growth business or the shaking off of unwanted baggage by the parent.

Rights Offering

When a corporation wants to raise additional equity capital, it issues new shares and sells them to the public in a *secondary offering*, usually at a discount to the current market price. This is often viewed negatively by existing shareholders as it directly dilutes their holdings: By increasing the shares outstanding, the fractional ownership of each share is reduced. Particularly when the newly issued shares are offered to investors at a discount, existing shareholders can view this as unfair; if the market consensus is that the shares are worth a certain price, why should new investors be given the opportunity to buy them for less?

One way of resolving this is through a rights offering. The company issues to all existing shareholders a new security, called a *right*, which entitles them to purchase their fractional allocation of the newly issued shares at the discounted price. These rights are then listed on an exchange so that shareholders who do not wish to increase their holdings can sell the rights in an open market and realize their cash value as though they were a dividend. Rights that are neither sold nor exercised will expire worthless.

There is a natural *arbitrage* opportunity (a means of realizing a riskless profit) that frequently arises in rights offerings. Investors who do not wish to subscribe to the rights offering and purchase additional shares must sell their rights in the market. If many investors attempt to sell their rights, there can accumulate a substantial excess supply of rights from sellers who are, in some sense, captive, as rights not exercised expire worthless. If a trader can buy rights in the market at a price below the fair price determined by the terms of the rights offering, and simultaneously sell the underlying shares to hedge (i.e., to offset the risk of the shares he has implicitly purchased via the rights), he can lock in a riskless profit.

Mergers, Acquisitions, and Tender Offers

When two companies combine to form a single entity, a large amount of trading activity is generated, often accompanied by significant price movements in the stocks of both companies involved. The dynamics of trading in these stocks is entirely different than that of other stocks. In general, stock price movements are driven by a combination of company-specific news and broader market trends. For stocks involved in mergers or acquisitions, the sensitivity of the stock prices to all but the most significant outside news is greatly reduced as investors focus closely on those news announcements related to the transaction. For this reason, the market-making in *deal names* (stocks involved in a merger or acquisition or other substantial corporate restructuring) is often transferred from the trader who would usually handle flows in the relevant sector to a separate group of *special situations* traders and salespeople whose responsibility it is to develop the specialized knowledge required to properly risk manage trading in these names.

It is worth clarifying the difference between the three ways companies can combine. In a *merger,* two companies agree to fuse with no hierarchical distinction between the two; the businesses join to form a new entity that combines the operations of the independent companies into a single unit. There is often even an effort to combine the names of the two companies to reflect the equality of the participants. In an *acquisition,* there is a clearly defined acquirer and target and the name of the acquired company is commonly dropped. In many cases the difference between an acquisition and a merger is purely semantic—there is a clearly stronger firm in the negotiations and the term "merger" is used primarily to allow the management of the acquired firm to save face. In a friendly acquisition the management of the target company is amenable to being acquired.

If the management of the target company does not agree to the transaction, the acquisition is considered hostile and referred to as a *takeover*. One of the common ways in which this is done is through a *tender offer* in which the acquiring company communicates directly to the target company's shareholders, via a public announcement, its interest in purchasing the target company's shares. The public announcement will state the terms of the offer, a period of time during which it is valid, and a minimum and maximum number of shares that will be purchased. If the number of shares tendered is below the minimum, the offer is cancelled and no shares are acquired, while if more than the maximum number of shares are tendered, there will be a pro-rata percentage accepted from each investor.

There are three common ways in which one company will offer to pay for the shares of another company: with cash, with stock, or with a combination of cash and stock. It is generally the case that on the announcement date, the price (whether all in cash or including shares) will represent a significant premium to the current share price of the target company, to incentivize the existing shareholders to sell their shares.

From the perspective of the sales and trading operation of a Wall Street investment bank, the difference between a friendly merger or acquisition and a hostile takeover is primarily related to the uncertainty of the outcome. With the exception of mergers between very large corporations, where antitrust concerns may arise requiring approval by both U.S. and foreign regulatory bodies, there is a higher degree of certainty that a friendly transaction will be successfully completed. In a hostile takeover, the risk is much higher that the transaction fails or is completed under different conditions than were initially planned. The target company may invoke defensive measures (sometimes referred to as a *poison pill* strategy) or seek out other companies to make a more attractive counteroffer (a *white knight*).

Regardless of the degree of goodwill or animosity between the managements of the companies involved in the transaction, from the perspective of the trading in the shares of the companies involved, the three cases are quite similar. In a merger the shares of both companies cease to exist and shares of the merged company are distributed to the shareholders of both companies. In an acquisition, the holdings of existing shareholders of the acquiring company are not changed (though their value may change) and it is only the holders of the target company whose holdings are replaced either with acquirer shares, cash, or both.

There is a significant impact on the trading of the companies involved in a merger that is best understood through an example. Consider a hypothetical acquisition of MiniMart, a chain of small 24-hour convenience stores, by MacroMart, a large national supermarket chain. On the day prior to the announcement, MiniMart stock closes at $24 per share and MacroMart stock closes at $40. After the close of trading, MacroMart announces a hostile bid for all outstanding shares of MiniMart consisting of a combined stock and cash payment of 0.4 shares of MacroMart plus $14 in cash. Based on the closing share prices of each company, the MacroMart offer is worth $30 per share, which represents a 25 percent premium to the closing price of MiniMart:

$$0.4 \times \text{MacroMart} + \$14 = 0.4 \times \$40 + \$14 = \$30$$

The market's reaction to the news of the takeover depends on the characteristics of the companies themselves. Specific considerations might include:

- Will the addition of the local MiniMarts to MacroMart's existing chain of shops add value to MacroMart? Will the combination of the two companies result in increased efficiencies (lower costs, greater pricing power, etc.) or is it simply a matter of two companies running under the same name? With such similar businesses, operational synergies would seem likely. If MacroMart had instead acquired a company in a completely different sector—a ball-bearing manufacturer, for example—the synergies of combining the companies would be less apparent.

- How will MacroMart pay for the acquisition? The impact on the share price of MacroMart will be very different if the cash and shares used to purchase MiniMart are sitting in the corporate treasury than if they must be raised through borrowing or a dilutive secondary share issuance.
- What is the likelihood of the shareholders of MiniMart accepting the offer? Are there any other companies that might perceive the acquisition of MiniMart as a threat and be in a position to launch a counteroffer (presumably at a higher price) and acquire MiniMart themselves? If this happens, what would be the impact on MacroMart?
- Are there any legal or regulatory impediments that might prevent the acquisition? Might a MiniMart–MacroMart merger make a market monopoly?

Regardless of the specific circumstances of acquisition, one thing is certain: There will be significant trading activity and rapid price moves in both stocks as soon as the markets resume trading the next day. The most common reaction to news of an acquisition is that the shares of the acquiring company drop in price as investors factor in the costs of the transaction into the valuation of the company, while the shares of the target company rise to slightly below the acquisition price implied by the current share price of the acquirer.

In our example, we assume the shares of MacroMart drop 5 percent on the news to $38; the new implied share price offered for MiniMart is now $0.4 \times \$38 + \$14 = \$29.20$, which implies a 21.7 percent premium over the closing price of MiniMart. We might expect to see the MiniMart share price rise to $28.80, a 20 percent increase over the prior close.

The fact that MiniMart's share price is still 1.4 percent below the tender price of $29.20 creates the opportunity for an arbitrage profit. An investor could purchase MiniMart shares for $28.80 and simultaneously sell 0.4 shares[7] of MacroMart at $29.20. The investor pays out $28.80 on the purchase and receives $0.4 \times \$38 = \$15.20$ from the sale for a net investment of $13.60. If the investor then accepts the MacroMart offer of 0.4 shares + $14, he would receive, upon the completion of the tender, 0.4 shares of MacroMart with which to cover the shares he sold, plus $14 that covers the $13.60 cost of entering the trade and leaves him with a riskless profit of $0.40. This type of trade, in which the shares of merging companies are bought and sold against each other, is called *risk arbitrage*.

If this is, in fact, a riskless profit, then investors should quickly buy up shares of MiniMart and sell shares of MacroMart to capture the arbitrage and, in the process, drive the prices toward an equilibrium level where the implied price of MiniMart, based on the terms of the acquisition, matches the market price of the stock.

There are, however, a few additional factors that must be considered. The first is the cost of financing the arbitrage. The simultaneous purchase and sale of MiniMart and MacroMart shares resulted in a net investment of $13.60. Assuming the risk arbitrageur borrows this cash there will be an interest charge which will erode part of the profit. For example, assuming the arbitrageur can borrow at the risk-free rate of interest rates of 4 percent, if it took two months to complete the transaction, the financing cost on the borrowed funds would be $13.60 × 4% × 60/365 = $0.089, which reduces the profitability of the trade by roughly 22 percent to $0.31. There are also borrow costs associated with shorting the MacroMart shares that can further erode the profitability or the trade, potentially significantly, depending on the availability of shares in the stock loan market. (More on stock loan in Chapter 11.) The arbitrageur must also assess the risk that there are delays in completing the transaction because these will increase his financing and borrow costs and further deteriorate his return.

The second, and most important factor, is the likelihood that the trade will be successfully completed at all. If the acquisition fails, it is likely that the shares of both stocks will return to something close to their preannouncement levels of $24 and $40. For the arbitrageur who has purchased MiniMart shares at $28.80 and sold MacroMart shares at $38, this would result in substantial loss. The initial investment in the trade was $13.60 in the hope of realizing a $0.31 profit (after funding costs), or approximately 2.3 percent return in 2 months.[8] If the deal is canceled and the stocks return to their original levels, the arbitrageur would lose $4.80 (= $24 – $28.80) per share on the MicroMart leg and $0.80 [= 0.4 × ($38 – $40)] on the MacroMart leg. Ignoring financing, stock borrowing and transaction costs, the total loss is $5.60 on an investment of $13.60, or 42 percent. For an arbitrageur who has borrowed heavily to leverage up an apparently low-risk arbitrage strategy, this loss could be devastating.

One of the most memorable cases in recent years where a merger was cancelled late in the game was the acquisition of Honeywell by General Electric in July 2001. Risk arbitrage desks across Wall Street had bet hugely on the successful completion of the acquisition, which carried a larger risk premium than usual due to the concerns about the ability to successfully complete a $42 billion merger. When the European Commission eventually blocked the deal due to antitrust concerns, Honeywell stock plummeted more than 25 percent as traders around the street frantically unwound hundreds of millions of dollars of positions at huge losses.

In general, the spread between the market price of the shares of the target company and the price of those shares implied by the terms of the acquisition (after adjusting for financing, borrowing, and transaction costs) represents a premium for risk determined by the arbitrage community. In a deal that is perceived as having a very high degree of certainty, the spread will be small as traders are happy to make a small, but virtually riskless profit. As the uncertainty about the likelihood of success of the merger or acquisition increases, the spread that arbitrageurs require, in return for the risk of the deal failing increases.

While the standard reaction to the announcement of a merger is that the stock of the acquiring company drops in price while that of the target rises, there are other possibilities. For a merger that is perceived as creating significant value for the acquiring company it is possible that the negative impact on the share price from the acquisition costs is more than compensated by the positive impact of the value added by the acquisition and the share prices of both companies rise. Consider, for example, a company sitting on a large hoard of cash that it then employs to purchase the target company. If the expected ROI of the acquisition is greater than the return earned on the cash, then the acquisition could provide a substantial boost to the shares of the acquiring company. In some cases the shares of the target stock will rally to a price above that implied by the terms of the acquisition because investors believe that either the offer will be improved or that another company may make a higher counteroffer. On the other hand, an acquisition that is very negatively perceived by the market can result in such significant price depreciation in the acquiring company shares that, if the terms of the offer are primarily in shares, the implied price offered for the target is actually lower than the market price.

SUMMARY

One of the most useful ways of analyzing the data provided in the standard financial disclosures of a public corporation (balance sheet, income statement, and statement of cash flows) is by computing ratios between different items in these statements. This has the benefit of allowing comparisons between differently sized companies and provides a great deal of insight into a firm's liquidity, leverage, risk, profitability, and other characteristics.

While financial ratios provide useful information on the quality of a company's performance and its level of risk, there remains the question of what price an investor should be willing to pay to participate in the benefits of that company as an owner (shareholder). The two general approaches to answering this question are:

1. *Discounted cash flow valuation:* The timing and magnitude of all future cash flows that will be produced by an investment are estimated and then converted to their present value by applying a discounting rate that incorporates both the timing and the riskiness of those cash flows. While this is the "purest" form of valuation, it is very labor intensive and requires the subjective estimation of many factors that can be extremely hard to assess.

2. *Relative valuation:* A company can be determined to be either cheap, expensive, or fairly priced, through the analysis of financial ratios that compare the market price of its shares with various underlying measures of financial strength (price-to-earnings, price-to-sales). While these ratios do not produce a concrete price at which the shares should be trading, their comparison between different companies allows the analyst to identify assets that represent better value (i.e., a cheaper price for better fundamentals).

Where fundamental valuation attempts to derive the "right" price for the security, which can then be compared to the market price to determine if the stock is over- or underpriced, relative valuation takes the view that the market prices assets correctly in general, but can make mistakes with regard to individual securities.

An alternate method for determining the future direction of a stock price is through technical analysis, which analyzes historical trends in the chart of the stock price to identify recognizable patterns. While this approach is popular among market practitioners, it is generally viewed with skepticism by the academic community.

There are many different types of corporate activity that have a direct impact on the share price. For some actions, such as the payment of a dividend or share split, the impact is quite deterministic and easy to anticipate. Others, such as mergers, acquisitions, rights offerings, and spin-offs, are more complex and the impact on common shareholders can only be estimated after performing a detailed analysis of the specific terms of the transaction, the companies involved, the relevant legal and regulatory framework, and market conditions in general.

Products and Services

Cash Market

INTRODUCTION

The *cash market* refers to the buying and selling of stocks either on an exchange or in "upstairs" transactions negotiated directly between brokers and clients. Regardless of his or her area of specialization, every member of the sales and trading division must have a detailed understanding of how the underlying cash market functions. The practical knowledge of how the markets work, and the ability to use that knowledge to service client requests, is an important part of the value salespeople and traders add.

In this chapter we look first at the structure of the market and how buyers and sellers are matched off to complete trades, and then examine the various roles within the equities sales and trading business and how they work together to service the customer business. While our focus here is on single stocks, the market structure, as well as the division of responsibility between traders and salespeople, is similar across all equity products and the concepts presented here are applicable to the sales and trading of derivatives as well.

HOW A STOCK EXCHANGE FUNCTIONS

The concept of a stock exchange is the same as that of any other market—it is a place where buyers and sellers come together to trade. In this case, the goods traded are financial assets: the shares of public companies. However, due to the central importance of a smoothly functioning stock market for the health of the national financial system, there are some important characteristics that make a stock exchange very different from, for example, your local antiques fair.

The most important of these is the fact that, rather than simply providing a central location where buyers and sellers trade among themselves, the exchange acts as an intermediary: after pairing up a buy and sell order, the exchange acts as the counterparty to both trades. In this way, each market participant must only establish a settlement procedure with a single counterparty (the exchange) rather than setting up individual relationships with every other participant. This not only greatly simplifies the clearing and settlements of trades but ensures that buyers and sellers are indifferent to the identity of the counterparty of a transaction (if they are even aware of who it is), which increases the ease and fluidity of trading.

The centralization of all clearing and settlement through the exchange gives it a tremendous amount of power to regulate the activities of market participants to promote fair dealing by all parties involved. In order to trade directly on the exchange, a firm must become a member (which will require payment of a fee). The stock exchange also can require that member firms maintain certain minimum standards for financial stability, internal controls, and legal compliance. If a member firm is found to employ unfair practices or attempt to manipulate the market, the exchange can simply revoke their membership, effectively shutting down their business. (While most trading is centralized through a single primary exchange, the existence of several alternative exchanges prevents the abuse of this sort of power or the establishment of monopolistic control of trading.)

Investor confidence is extraordinarily important in financial markets and exchanges make great efforts to encourage investors to perceive the stock market as a safe place to invest their money. A key component of this is the establishment by the stock exchange of listing requirements for companies wishing to have their shares traded on the exchange. These may include minimum levels of earnings, market capitalization or trading volume and are designed to ensure that the stocks traded on the exchange represent ownership in legitimate businesses with sound financial characteristics. Companies that do not meet these requirements cannot trade their shares on the exchange and those companies that are listed on the exchange must maintain their status or risk a delisting (i.e., have their shares removed from trading on the exchange). While exchange-listed companies can and do go bankrupt and equity share ownership always implies a level of risk, exchange listing provides an implicit "stamp of approval" and prevents the listing of phony shell companies for the purpose of defrauding investors.

Centralization of Orders

In assuming the role of intermediary to all trades, the exchange guarantees that there is a fair process for matching up buyers and sellers to complete orders. While the process is quite simple—priority of execution is given based on price and, where orders have the same price, on order of arrival—we will walk through it in some detail to illustrate the concepts and simultaneously introduce the particular language used on the trading floor to communicate orders and market information.

An investor who has purchased shares of stock is said to be *long* the shares. When he sells them he is selling out of a long position or *selling from long*. Many financial assets also admit the possibility of selling a position before buying it. In this case the seller borrows shares from a long holder and *sells them short,* on the agreement that at some future point, he will buy back the shares (*cover his short*) and return the shares to the lender. The specific mechanics of how the market for borrowing and lending shares works is provided in Chapter 11.

Short sales are perceived somewhat differently by market participants than long sales. A long seller, by eliminating his long exposure to the stock, will no longer make money as the stock rallies. In so doing, he is expressing a view that the balance of probabilities between the stock going up and going down are equal or perhaps skewed in favor of a downward move. Whether he is right or wrong, it is only an opportunity cost that is lost—the investor is out of the position and can, for all intents and purposes, forget about the stock. A short-seller, however, is expressing a much clearer view in favor of a downward move. If the stock rallies, his loss is not merely the missed opportunity of the premature long seller, but an actual economic loss, as the proceeds needed to repurchase the stock will exceed those raised by the initial sale. Additionally, there is a fee that must be paid to the lender of the shares for facilitating the short sale. In this way, the act of shorting implies a significantly more negative assessment of the future prospects for a stock than does a long sale.

Bids and Offers

Market participants submit *orders* to the exchange, which consist of four elements:

1. *Side:* Indicates whether they want to buy or sell
2. *Stock identifier:* A code which specifies the company whose shares are to be bought or sold
3. *Quantity:* The number of shares desired
4. *Limit:* The price where they are willing to buy or sell the shares (Orders can be submitted to the exchange without a limit, as we will see later.)

An order to buy shares of stock is called a *bid*, while an order to sell is called an *offer*. (The *offer price* is also known as the *ask price*.) One of the primary responsibilities of the exchange is to organize the bids and offers in a stock and disseminate them so that investors can make informed decisions based on the current state of the market. At any point in time there may be hundreds of different orders to buy and sell a given security at dozens of different prices. However, what most traders and salespeople will watch on their screens is a one-line summary of the *inside quote* and *last trade*. The inside quote summarizes the highest bid price (*best bid*) and lowest offer price (*best offer*) and the number of shares for which those bids and offers are valid. (The best bid and offer may actually be the aggregation of several individual orders that have the same limit price.) The last trade information simply indicates the last price at which the stock traded and the number of shares executed at that price.

We refer to the combination of the inside quote and last sale information as simply *the quote*. For shares of our hypothetical company XYZ Inc. the quote that would be displayed on a trader's screen might look like the following:

Ticker[1]	Last	Last Size	Bid-Ask	Bid-Ask Size	Prior Close	% Chg
XYZ	25.41	12	25.40/ 25.42	45 × 61	25.2	0.83%

The last traded price in XYZ is $25.41 and the current *best bid* is $25.40 and the *best offer* is $25.42. In the United States, share quantities are indicated in *round lots* of 100 shares,[2] so the quote indicates that the last trade was for 1,200 shares executed at $25.41 and that the current $25.40 bid is good for 4,500 shares and the offer for 6,100. The *bid-offer spread* (also known as the *bid-ask spread*) is the price difference between the best bid and offer and can either be quoted in cents per share (cps) or in basis points (bps—pronounced "beeps" or "bips") relative to the midpoint of the inside quote. For XYZ, the bid-ask spread is 2 cps (= $25.42 – $25.40) or $0.02/$25.41 = 0.08% or 8 bps. A basis point quotation is generally preferable as a cents-per-share quotation is only meaningful if the stock price is known. (A 2 cps spread means much more in a $1 stock than a $100 stock.)

The measure of the amount of stock that can be easily bought or sold in the market without excessive price impact, usually measured in terms of shares, is called the *liquidity*. A liquid stock is one where lots of buyers and sellers transact or, even if trading volume is small, where the bids and offers in the market provide ample opportunity to trade at prices close to the current market price. An illiquid stock is one where trading is infrequent, occurs in small size, and the available shares on the bid or offer are small.

Traders also refer to the shares available to be traded as the liquidity of the stock. In our example we would say there is greater liquidity on the offer side (6,100 shares) than on the bid side (4,500 shares).

It is market convention to always list bids on the left and offers on the right. In addition to the inside quote and last sale, traders and salespeople will generally watch the change in the stock price on the day, computed as the difference between the last sale price and the prior night's closing price, to get a sense of the stock's performance on the day. (In our example, this is equal to $25.41 − $25.20 = 21$ cps or $0.21/$25.20 = 83$bps.) The Bloomberg **Q** (*Quote*) function provides precisely this one-line summary, along with a few other useful facts such as the intraday high, low, and opening prices and the notional value traded on the day (i.e., the total dollar value of all shares traded).

Most of the time, there are multiple bids below and offers above the inside quote. In many markets it is possible to see the whole *book,* that is, the summary of all bids and offers. This is also called *market depth* and for our sample case might look like the following:

Ticker	Last	Last Size
XYZ	25.41	12

Bid Size	Bid	Ask	Ask Size
45	25.40	25.42	61
112	25.38	25.45	100
95	25.30	25.47	82

There are two bids below the best bid of $25.40: a $25.38 bid for 11,200 shares and a $25.30 bid for 9,500 shares, and two offers above the best offer of 6,100 shares at $25.42: 10,000 shares at $25.45 and 8,200 shares at $25.47. The number of shares available on the best bid or offer is often referred to as the size available *at the touch.*

Subject to appropriate market data permissions, the Bloomberg **BBO** (*Best Bid and Offer*) function allows the user to see the entire depth of the order book (all bids and offers and sizes) updating in real time.

Order Matching

When an order to buy or sell shares is submitted, the exchange will determine whether that order can be matched against an existing bid or offer in the market to complete a trade. If it cannot, it will be added to the order book for that stock and remain unexecuted. In our example of stock XYZ, if an order to pay $25.42 for 2,000 shares is submitted it will be filled immediately against the offer of 6,100 shares and the quote in the stock will change to:

Ticker	Last	Last Size	Bid-Ask	Bid-Ask Size	Prior Close	% Chg
XYZ	25.42	20	25.40 / 25.42	45 × 41	25.2	0.87%

The size of the offer has been reduced to 4,100 shares and the last trade price has changed to $25.42. The execution of 2,000 shares would be automatically recorded by the exchange and disseminated via market data providers so that all investors are made aware of the most recent activity in the stock. When this happens a trade is said to have printed *to the tape,* a linguistic remnant of the days when trade prices were communicated to brokerage houses by the exchange via ticker tape (which is also why stock symbols are referred to as "tickers").

The minimum increment by which the price can move is called the *tick* size, and is equal to $0.01 for most stocks. Traders will commonly describe a stock as "ticking up" (rallying) or "ticking off" (going down). The word "tick" is also used to classify stock trades into one of four types, depending on how the trade price compares to those that came before it:

1. *Plus-tick* (also an *uptick*): The trade price is higher than the price of the last trade that occurred.
2. *Zero plus-tick:* The trade price is equal to the last traded price but higher than the most recent trade that occurred at a different price.
3. *Minus-tick* (or *downtick*): The trade price is lower than the price of the last trade that occurred.
4. *Zero minus-tick:* The trade price is equal to the last traded price but lower than the most recent trade that occurred at a different price.

As mentioned, the best offer of $25.42 may be composed of several individual orders; for example, 800 shares from one seller and 5,300 from another. The question of who will make the sale to the buyer of 2,000 shares depends on which of the two orders was submitted first. Where there are multiple orders to trade at a particular price, a queue is formed based on time of arrival. If the 5,100 share order arrived first, that seller will sell 2,000, leaving 3,100 shares unexecuted, while the seller of 800 shares will sell nothing. However, if the 800 share offer was placed first, that order will be completed and the seller of 5,300 shares will only sell 1,200. In either case, the buyer pays $25.42 for 2,000 shares and, as this trade is settled versus the exchange, can remain happily indifferent to the identities of the sellers or how many of them there are.

The results would be exactly the same if the buyer had used a limit of $25.43 rather than $25.42. The fact that the buyer was willing to pay a higher price than what was offered in the market does not mean that she has to. Orders *on the book* are always filled at their limit prices while new orders submitted to the exchange are filled against the existing orders on the book and may receive better prices than their limit. It is also possible to submit a *market order* in which a share quantity is specified but no limit price. A market order will be filled immediately against existing orders in the market at their limit prices. Using the original summary of market depth for stock XYZ, an order to buy 20,000 shares of XYZ at market would be filled in three pieces: 6,100 shares at $25.42, 10,000 shares at $25.45, and 3,900 shares at $25.47. The last traded price would update three times though in such rapid succession that an observer would see only a flicker and then a final inside quote of:

Ticker	Last	Last Size	Bid-Ask	Bid-Ask Size	Prior Close	% Chg
XYZ	25.47	39	25.40/ 25.47	45 × 43	25.2	1.07%

While three individual trades will be recognized by the exchange and need to be settled, it would be inconvenient for investors to have to deal with all of the individual executions, particularly when working large orders that may be broken up into hundreds of individual trades. To simplify customer bookings (i.e., the recognition of the transactions in the customer's account), brokers use a special structure called a *wash account* (also called an *average price account*), which allows them to book the multiple individual executions versus the exchange but then settle versus the customer at a single average price, in this case, of $25.4448. (Average execution prices are usually computed to four decimal places.)

Once an order has been submitted to the exchange, it can be amended by the broker who submitted it. Each order is assigned a unique order ID by the exchange and the broker retains the right to cancel, replace, or amend that order as they wish. However, in most cases, an amendment to an order (change of limit price or share quantity) is treated as a cancellation and replacement of the existing order and will therefore cause the order to lose its priority in the order book.

For example, using the market depth example just presented, let us assume that the $25.38 bid for 11,200 shares is composed of one order for

1,000 shares, followed by 10,200 shares that arrived later. If the owner of the 1,000 share bid wishes to increase the quantity to 1,500, he would cancel-and-replace his order with a $25.38 bid for 1,500 shares, which would then sit behind the other 10,200 shares in the queue. Alternatively, if the bid price were increased to match the best bid of $25.40, the existing order would be cancelled and the new order would be placed behind the 4,500 shares already on the best bid. The exception to this is in the case of a reduction in the order size. Because a reduction in the share quantity of an order is already implicitly yielding to other orders by taking less of the available liquidity from the market, the order retains its priority in the order book.

Conceptually, the priority rules of the order book are the same as waiting in line at the supermarket checkout counter. You pick a checkout lane (price) and get in line behind the other customers (orders) who were there first. If you want to buy something more than what's in your shopping cart (increase the order size), you need to get out of line and go get the other items, which causes you to lose your place in line (lose priority in the order book). If you decide not to buy a few of your items (reduced order size), you're only speeding up the process for everyone else behind you so you can leave them with the cashier and stay where you are (no loss of priority in the order book). If you change lanes (new limit price) because you think you can check out more quickly in another (get your order filled), you have to go to the back of the line (lose your place in the order book) in the new lane, regardless of how long you've been waiting.

The summary of all executed trades and the time each one took place (*"time and sales"*) is available on Bloomberg via the **QR** (*Quote Recap*) function. The **QRM** (*Quote Recap & Market)* function provides a recap not only of trades but of every change of the inside quote (best bid and offer and size).

There are two other functions that provide very useful summaries of trading activity as well as a graph of price performance and other information about a stock: **BQ** (*Block Quote*), provides a large amount of fundamental and historical data, while **EQ** (*Equity Quote*) features a more prominent graph and can be used as a an alternative to **GIP** for monitoring intraday price action.

EXCHANGE STRUCTURE

Though the specific rules and regulations of each stock exchange are unique, the overall structure of the exchange can be generally described as following one of three general models (or a combination thereof) based on the number of participant firms that are designated as *market makers* in each particular stock on the exchange. Market makers act as continuous participants in the trading of a stock by displaying at all times a bid and offer price against which other market participants can trade (this is called *making a market*). In return for providing liquidity, market makers receive reduced transaction costs and other benefits from the exchange. On some exchanges there are predefined minimum sizes for bids and offers and maximum bid-offer spreads that the market maker can show, while on others the guidelines are more subjective. The presence of a market maker is intended to give potential investors confidence to trade on the exchange by guaranteeing that, when they want to trade, whether to open a new position or close out an existing one, they will always find a bid or offer against which to transact.

The Specialist System (A Single Market Maker)

The New York Stock Exchange (NYSE) is one of the few stock exchanges left in the world that still uses a single market maker, or *specialist* system, as well as a physical trading floor staffed by floor brokers. Over time, the role of the specialist has been diminished as technological alternatives have proven more efficient. However, the general model of a single market maker still exists and continues to provide certain unique benefits.

Under the specialist system, a single broker (a physical person), called the *specialist*, working for an independent company is selected by the exchange to act as the center point for all flow in a particular stock. All orders must be routed through him (or her) and it is his responsibility to maintain a "fair and orderly" market. Where the bids and offers in the market are sufficient to meet investor demand, the specialist simply matches buyers and sellers on the book against each other according to the standard priority of price and time. However, whenever there is no bid or offer, or when the inside market created by the bids and offers available on the book is too wide, the specialist is obligated to show a bid and/or offer price at which he is willing to trade. The specialist is also required to take the other side of any market order where the liquidity on the book is insufficient to complete it.

By agreeing to provide a bid or offer where none is available the specialist puts himself in a compromised position. The most obvious example is when important news comes out during the trading session, which then causes a sudden flood of orders on one side of the market. For example, consider a pharmaceutical company that receives FDA approval to sell a new drug, which will significantly improve earnings in the future. Where this result was not expected previously, and is therefore not already factored into in the stock price, the news should result in a substantial revaluation for the stock and an increase in the "fair" price for the shares, triggering a significant inflow of orders, many of which will be market orders and expect an immediate fill. While the first orders are paired off against existing offers on the book, these offers will quickly be filled or pulled out of the market by the sellers as they decide they either do not want to sell the stock, or see the opportunity to sell at much higher prices.

The specialist is now left as the only seller into a crowd of buyers. On the stock exchange floor, where brokers stand at the post and verbally communicate orders with the specialist, it can in fact be a crowd of people shouting orders at the specialist, who must then decide on the appropriate level at which to fill these orders against his own book. What no one else wants to sell, he must sell short and will need to buy back later. The question is, at what price? As he fills each new order at successively higher prices, the sales made at previous (lower) prices become more and more costly. When other sellers arrive in the market they will require still higher prices creating even greater losses for the specialist. The specialist must make a rapid judgment as to the appropriate level at which to sell short shares to facilitate the buyers.

In the case of very significant news announcements that result in particularly violent price action, the specialist can request that the exchange halt trading in the stock temporarily to allow buyers and sellers to digest the news and submit their orders more calmly, rather than in the frenzied rush to jump in first. During the halt, the specialist will disseminate an indicative level at which the stock will reopen. In our pharmaceutical company example, a temporary halt of 10 or 15 minutes would give time for buyers to more accurately assess the true impact on the company's earnings to determine a new price (as opposed to just submitting a market order) and also for potential sellers or short-term traders to put in offers at levels where they consider the stock price to have overreacted to the news.

The decision as to the appropriate price at which to fill orders is a function of the specialist's view on what is the equilibrium level for the stock and where he thinks he can likely get out of the position. In an actively traded stock, the specialist may have confidence that new orders will be received quickly enough that only a few cents cushion is necessary to ensure that he can unwind the position profitably (or at least breakeven). In a thinly traded stock, where the specialist will likely take a long time to get out of the position, he may offer liquidity only at a significant spread (discount or premium) to the current market, even for reasonably small size. He must adhere at all times to the "fair and orderly market" guidelines and, were a complaint to be raised to the exchange that markets were unfairly wide, he could be called upon to justify his pricing. If it is found that the specialist is failing to provide appropriate liquidity by taking unduly large spreads and then subsequently trading out of the position at a significant profit, the exchange may judge that he is not fulfilling his responsibilities and either sanction him or, in an extreme case, remove his right to act as specialist in the stock.

As described so far, it is hard to see why anyone would *want* to be the specialist in a stock. There is, however, a flipside to the responsibilities and risks. The specialist is allowed to trade in the shares of the stock for his own account, and does so at a tremendous informational advantage to other market participants. While his actions are governed by strict rules that prevent him from unfairly using this knowledge to the detriment of other members, there are significant opportunities to make a profit based on the short-term mismatches between buyers and sellers. The simplest example is simply capturing the bid-offer spread. Where the bid and offer prices belong to the specialist, he fills market buy orders at the offer price and sellers on the bid and captures the spread between them as profit. The specialist sees all market orders before they are filled and can decide at what level to facilitate liquidity based on his knowledge of what other market participants are likely to do. Until only a few years ago, the full order book was visible only to the specialist while outsiders relied on the limited information available from the inside quote and last sale price. Historically, this informational advantage has been sufficient to provide substantial profits to the specialist firms whose business it is to take on this role, though recent technological advances and the move toward greater transparency by the exchanges have diminished this opportunity.

It should be noted that while the specialist system evolved from a face-to-face verbal dialog between brokers and the specialist, the NYSE currently employs a hybrid system which allows for direct electronic trading with the specialist's book as well as intermediation by a broker physically located on the floor of the exchange.

The Multiple Market Maker Electronic Exchange

A far more common model globally for structuring an exchange is via a multiple market maker model in which the exchange is electronic and functions primarily as a regulated communication network between participants, some of whom (the number depends on the exchange structure) are designated as market makers. This is the model of the NASDAQ market in the United States and most European exchanges.

In a multiple market maker model, each market maker is required to continuously post a bid and offer of a minimum size and maximum spread in the stock, which they must then update continually as the market moves. When an order is executed against the market maker's quote, he is momentarily relieved of his obligation to quote on that side of the market to give him an opportunity to adjust his quote and hedge or trade out of the position as necessary.

Compared with the specialist model, there are advantages and disadvantages to a multiple market maker model. For each individual market maker, the risks are far smaller—in the event of a sudden move in a stock, each market maker can pull back their quote to the minimum size and widest spread possible to reduce the risk of losses. There is, however, a commensurate decrease in the informational advantage and the opportunities it provides. In general, the trade-off for each individual market maker is the reward of continually capturing the bid-offer spread versus the risk of being caught in a sudden market movement. In recent years, as the speed and sophistication of electronic market-making technology has eclipsed that of humans, many brokers have drastically reduced their staff of market makers and rely primarily on electronic algorithms.

For the individual buyer or seller submitting an order to the market, the benefits of the multiple market maker model are generally positive. The distribution of risk among many market makers tends to reduce the bid-offer spread as each participating broker takes only a small portion of the risk. However, when news is released that impacts the stock price, the absence of a centralized ownership for maintaining the orderliness of the market can result in greater price volatility. To counteract this, many electronic exchanges establish automatic triggers that temporarily halt trading in a stock that has experienced excessive price volatility. These may also be supplemented by manual halts by the exchange regulators in the event of pending news to ensure all interested parties have had an opportunity to hear and digest the news and provide a more orderly mechanism for finding the new equilibrium price in the stock.

A Pure Electronic Exchange (No Market Makers)

The third option for structuring an exchange is a flat playing field, in which there are no market makers. In the United States, the pure electronic exchanges are not generally thought of as proper exchanges (though legally they may be registered as such) but referred to under the general description of *electronic communication networks* (ECN). In this model, the exchange is simply a venue where buyers and sellers meet and, where no counterparty exists to an order, the order is simply left unexecuted. (Each exchange determines its own rules regarding the treatment of market orders where no other side exists.)

One particularly interesting type of purely electronic network is what is referred to as a *dark pools*, which are crossing networks in which all parties remain anonymous and all bids and offers hidden. Limit orders can be submitted into a dark pool and, if there exists an offsetting order in the pool, the two are paired off and a trade is completed. It is not, however, possible to see what is in the pool, which can be a very attractive feature for traders looking to execute illiquid orders (i.e., orders that are large relative to the typical trading volume in that stock). In a transparent market, traders must be very careful about the size orders they display because of the risk that other market participants will see a big order on the screen and either jump in front of it (if they are on the same side of the market) or back away (if they are on the other side). In an opaque and anonymous dark pool, traders can submit their entire order to try to find the other side of the trade without disclosing any information to the market about their intentions and possibly jeopardizing their execution.

Some European exchanges use a combination of models in which the stocks where trading is most active (and the natural liquidity is sufficient to ensure a smoothly functioning market) are left to operate without market makers while those where liquidity is less consistently available are facilitated by market makers. In the United States, the pure electronic exchanges have historically been perceived as secondary venues for trading in stocks that are already listed on other exchanges. In recent years, however, many ECNs have begun to show levels of trading activity that are comparable with the primary exchanges.

Competition between Models

The specialist system is a natural means of centralizing order flow and ensuring fair dealing in a market where orders are transmitted verbally and documented on paper trade tickets. As such, most of the oldest stock exchanges began with this model. However, with the passage of time and the evolution of technology, the specialist model—particularly where this represents a physical person who manually oversees the order book—has given way to formats in which the centralization of order flow is electronic and the rules for fair dealing are monitored via sophisticated trade surveillance systems. Additionally, the massive increases in trading volume caused by electronic trading have simply overwhelmed the old manual order pairing and trade entry models of the specialist system of the past. Even the NYSE, the last major market in the world to use both a specialist system and a physical trading floor, has begun to make the transition to electronic making as underscored by the purchase, in 2006, of Archipelago Holdings, one of the largest ECNs.

ORDER TYPES

Regardless of the exchange structure, when investors wish to trade they must communicate the order to the exchange in some way. Investment banks and broker-dealers establish the necessary connections with the exchange and then offer their services as intermediary, taking client orders and submitting them to the exchange for execution. Trades executed by a broker are classified into one of three types: *agency, principal,* or *proprietary,* which is indicated on the order when submitted to the exchange (though not disclosed to other market participants).

Agency

An agency order is one in which the broker buys or sells shares on behalf of a client, in return for a commission. The broker takes no risk in executing the trade but is required to adhere to *best execution* guidelines, which are designed to guarantee that the broker works in the client's best interests to achieve the highest quality execution possible. An important characteristic of an agency execution is that the client receives exactly the price executed by the broker—the trades are effectively cleared directly between the client account and the exchange. In the event that the client is dissatisfied with the execution, the broker cannot amend the price other than to reduce the commission rate. By the same token, if the broker achieves a far superior execution price to what the client has requested, the broker cannot keep any of the outperformance. The trade belongs to the client.

The only situation in which the broker can give the client a different price from his execution is in the event of a legitimate execution error. For example, a broker forgets to submit an order where the execution was to be spread out over the day and instead executes the entire order in the last few minutes of trading. If the execution price is as good as or significantly better than what would likely have been achieved by working the order over the entire day, the client will be given the superior fill. (The *fill* is the price at which a trade is executed.) However, if the execution is significantly worse, the broker will book the exchange executions into a specially designated *error account* and then book the customer trade versus that account at a fair price given the instructions. Commonly, when a trade is run through an error account, an error form must be completed providing an explanation of the error, the trader and client involved, and the amount of the loss. This form is retained to provide an audit trail in the event of an inquiry by the exchange. (Stock exchanges will occasionally perform random screening of broker trades to ensure compliance with the exchange rules.)

While it is a requirement that the economics of an agency order be passed directly to the end client, this does not mean that the client has to receive every execution from the exchange. The wash account structure allows the broker to greatly simplify the booking process for clients by first taking all of the "street side" executions versus the exchange into a firm account and then booking these shares to the client at the realized average price. While technically the executions are booked versus a broker account and not the client's account, the structure of a wash account is such that it cannot hold a position or earn a profit or loss. The precise economics of what is booked into the account must be booked out as to do otherwise would create either a position or price break (discrepancy) in the account that would need to be corrected. Aside from the operational simplicity, the use of a wash account is also beneficial to clients because it allows them to submit a single order and then allocate the total shares executed between multiple accounts, with each account receiving the same average price. Particularly where the client is managing funds for multiple investors, the allocation of a single execution price across multiple accounts prevents questions from arising as to whether the client is providing preferential treatment to one of her investors over another.

An alternate means of executing an agency order is via *direct market access* (DMA). Many brokers provide electronic platforms through which clients can use the broker's connections to the exchange to execute their own orders directly. While most brokers will provide a trading interface that can be installed on the client's computer, this may prove insufficient where clients require a greater degree of integration with their own internal systems or use specially-designed algorithmic strategies, which generate high order volumes. In these cases clients may have the option to establish a direct electronic connection to the broker's infrastructure and route orders straight to the exchange from their own systems, but via the brokers "pipes." As DMA trades require no direct involvement by the broker (other than to keep the systems running properly and the clearing and settlement of executed trades) they generally carry much lower commission costs.

Although in an agency execution the broker is working purely on the behalf of the end client, this does not exonerate the broker from all responsibility. If the strict adherence to the instructions given by the client would significantly disrupt the market or if the order has been given for the purposes of manipulating the stock price, the broker must refuse to execute the order as directed. If not, both the client and the broker can potentially be held liable for improper trading. The same applies to DMA flow and brokers have thresholds and checks that prevent abusive trading practices by clients.

Types of Agency Orders When a client gives an order to a broker, she must provide instructions as to how she wants that order to be executed. This is a delicate point because it is impossible for the client to specify a particular action the broker should take in each of the infinite possible scenarios that could occur. The client must choose between giving rigid instructions, which may or may not achieve her desired goal, or providing general guidance regarding those objectives and relying on the discretion of the trader to execute the order in the best way possible. Clearly there is a certain risk of misunderstanding when using loosely defined, qualitative instructions. To minimize this, traders and salespeople have developed a number of standardized execution instructions used for communicating orders that have well-defined meanings. While this does not entirely eliminate disagreements, it plays an essential role in reducing them and one of the first requirements of a new trader is to learn this rather particular vocabulary. What follows is an explanation of some of the most commonly used instructions with examples of how they are communicated in real-life situations. Commonly used written abbreviations for some of the trading instructions are included for reference.

- *Market (MKT) or limit (LMT):* As discussed previously, an order submitted with a *market* instruction will be filled at whatever price is available in the market while a limit order can only be filled at the limit price or better. Buy limits are often referred to as having a "top" while sell limits have a "low." Example: "Sell 25,000 XYZ with a 22.50 low." "Buy 10,000 ABC with a $14.10 top." "Sell 5,000 PQR at market."
- *Not held (NH):* Most orders are given to brokers on a *not held* basis, which means that the broker is given discretion in how to best execute. If the order is submitted as *held*, the broker must exactly represent the client's instructions in the market. A simple example is a market order to buy shares. If the instruction is *market, not held* (MNH), the client is indicating that they are willing to pay as high a price as necessary to complete the order but give the broker permission to use his discretion as to how to achieve the best price. If the order is large, the broker might execute only a portion at current prices and then wait to see how the market reacts, looking for additional sellers to arrive to reduce the impact he has on the price. Clients will sometimes include qualitative instructions such as *careful discretion* to indicate that, while the order is a market order, the trader is expected to work the order carefully and not just "bang it out" all at once. By comparison, if the order is given as *market, held,* the broker has no choice but to submit the entire order to the exchange at market, regardless of the advisability of that decision (so long as it would not be disruptive to the market). Held orders are very rare and all of the subsequent order types are assumed to be not held.
- *Percentage of volume (POV):* Rather than decide a priori the time interval over which the order is to be executed, a client may instruct the

broker to participate with trading at a certain percentage of the volume. In this case, the broker will not buy shares unless others are buying shares and will do so only in the percentage specified by the client. Percentage-of-volume orders generally range from a conservative 10 percent to a relatively aggressive 33 percent of the volume. As the broker has no ability to guarantee participation in all trading activity that occurs on the exchange, the percentage of volume can only be taken as a target, subject to the broker's best efforts.

- *In line*: An instruction to execute an order *in line* indicates that the client is happy to complete the order at current market levels—effectively a loosely defined limit order. If the broker cannot complete the order at the levels prevalent at the time the order is submitted (or better) the order will remain incomplete and unless specified otherwise, the broker will not participate in trading at less attractive prices.

- *Work*: To *work* an order means to spread out the execution over a period of time and can be loosely interpreted to mean participation at around 25 percent of the volume. A limit order with a *work* instruction indicates that the client does not want the order immediately completed simply because the price is better than the limit. For example, if the instructions are to "Buy 25,000 XYZ with a $25.10 top, work," the broker will not pay above $25.10 for stock and, when the price is below that limit, will not look to immediately complete the entire order but to participate at approximately 25 percent of the volume. In this way, if the stock price is moving lower the buyer will participate in the progressively lower prices rather than being "plugged" at the $25.10 limit. The risk is that the stock trades back through the limit and only part of the order is completed due to the lower participation percentage.

  A client may also instruct a broker to work an order with an *ultimate* limit. The addition of the word "ultimate" indicates that the client considers the limit to be fairly far away from the current levels and does not expect that, by executing his order, the broker will push the stock to that price. Traders eager to complete an executable order sometimes need to be reminded that, as the saying goes, "It's a limit, not a goal."

- *Would*: "Would" indicates a willingness to complete the entire order at a given level. For example, if the client submits an order to "Buy 25,000 XYZ with an $18.50 top, would" he is indicating that if the entire order could be completed at the limit price, he would be willing. If the stock then subsequently trades lower, the broker cannot be held accountable for not participating in the lower prices because the instruction was that the client "would" at the limit, and not to "work" the order.

- *Combinations*: It is common to combine the above instructions in a single order. For example, a client might instruct the broker to "Buy

25,000 XYZ—would in line, otherwise work." In this case, the client would be happy to complete the entire order at current levels if possible but, if not, would like to participate at approximately 25 percent of the volume at higher levels.

- *Descriptive:* Depending on the relationship and the level of confidence between the client and broker, it may sometimes be more effective to simply describe the situation and leave the specific trading decisions to the broker. A useful example is the trade-out (liquidation) of a position that results from a broker error. Every trader has made errors and understands the sensitivities associated with trading out of the position. There is the well-established Wall Street protocol that "You don't trade an error," which is to say, a position that results from an error is an unintended and uncalculated risk and should be closed out as quickly as possible. No one will ever be commended or receive a bigger bonus because they made money on an error, and a large profit serves only to underline the magnitude of the risk taken. However, as adverse moves in the stock price will result in losses to the broker, the person unwinding the position will want to make every effort to minimize any loss.

- *Volume-weighted average price (VWAP—"vee-wop"):* Rather than specify a particular level at which to trade, many clients will request that their order be worked targeting the average trading price during a given time period, often over the full day. The instruction is equivalent to asking that the broker "trade when everyone else trades" and is common for investors who do not have a strong view on the market direction themselves and do not want to give discretion to the broker to try to add value through subjective judgments about when to trade. VWAP is a particularly popular instruction for overnight orders from clients in other regions who will be sleeping while their trade is executed.

The *VWAP* computes the average of all executed trades during a period of time applying a weighting factor to each trade based on the number of shares exchanged. This is done by first computing the notional amount of every trade during the time period by multiplying the shares traded by the trade price. The sum of these is equal to the total notional traded in the period, which is then divided by the total number of shares executed to arrive at an average price at which all shares traded, weighted by the quantity executed at each price. If we number the trades from 1 to n, the VWAP would be calculated as:

$$VWAP = \frac{\sum_{i=1}^{n} Shares_i \times Price_i}{\sum_{i=1}^{n} Shares_i}$$

The VWAP serves as a guideline for the execution level that can be expected from participating with volume during the entire day. It is not, however, an easy thing to match or, as clients often request, beat the VWAP. The difficulty comes from two facts. The first is that it is not possible to know at what times and price levels more or less volume will trade. While brokers will generally use statistical analysis of historical volume data in order to identify general patterns and bias their trading accordingly, this is only an estimate and the actual percentage of the total day's volume that is traded at any particular price can only be known once the day's trading is complete. Particularly when important news arrives late in the day, causing significant price movements on heavy volume, the broker is often unable to replicate the VWAP very closely because, by that point in the day, he has already executed too much of the order and is left with insufficient ammunition to participate in the late day moves in the proper proportion.

Abnormal volume profiles can either help or hurt the broker. For example, if a negative announcement is made late in the day that causes a stock to trade down on heavy volume, this will pull the VWAP significantly lower. In this case a seller targeting VWAP will tend to outperform the benchmark since, relative to the actual day's trading volume, he will have sold proportionally more of the order at the more attractive levels early in the day. While this may be entirely due to chance, as the old Wall Street maxim says, "Better lucky than good." However, if the broker is buying stock targeting VWAP he will perform poorly since he will, on a relative basis, have traded too much early in the day at the higher prices. In absolute terms, the client benefits from the late-day sell-off as this produces a lower execution price (he bought stock cheaper). However, because the amount purchased at the lower levels is insufficient when compared with the day's trading pattern, the performance versus VWAP looks poor and the client is likely to be disappointed.

The second challenge in meeting (or beating) VWAP is the fact that the VWAP is a function of all trades during that period, some of which will occur on the bid side of the market, some in the middle, and some on the offer. The average execution is therefore likely to sit somewhere near the middle of the bid-offer spread. However, when the broker goes to the market with an order, the only price at which he can be guaranteed an execution (and a partial one at that) is the far side of the market—the offer side if he is a buyer and the bid side if he is a seller. As a result, even if the broker matches the intraday volume profile perfectly, if he only uses market orders, he will on average miss the VWAP by one-half the bid-offer spread. Depending on the particular stock, this can be a significant amount. In targeting the VWAP benchmark, the broker must balance the dual objectives of completing a certain amount of the order during each time interval, and having the patience to sit on the near side of the market (buying on the bid, selling on the offer) to avoid paying away the bid-offer spread.

The choice of VWAP as a benchmark is, in many ways, an expression of view that markets are efficient and that the broker cannot add value by making subjective assessments of when and how to execute the order. While this may often be the case, it is important to recognize that VWAP is a relative benchmark for assessing the quality of the broker's execution, but not a measure of any real economic benefit that has been captured. Investors make money by buying low and selling high, not by beating VWAP.

The VWAP data are available on Bloomberg using the **AQR** (*Average Quote Recap*) and **VAP** (*Volume At Price*) functions. To better understand the relationship between the traded price of the stock and the volume profile through the day, the **IGPO** (*Intraday Hi-Lo Graph*) function provides an enhanced intraday **GIP** graph with an associated graph of the traded volume during each five minute (or other customizable) time interval.

■ *Time-weighted average price (TWAP):* The alternative to the VWAP is the *TWAP* ("*tee-wop*") in which the average is computed by snapping prices at regular time intervals over the time period and taking a simple average of those prices, irrespective of the number of shares traded at each price. While not a particularly sophisticated strategy—the broker trades the same number of shares in each time interval—the TWAP has the appealing characteristic that the client can quickly judge the quality of the execution by "eyeballing" the graph of the stock price and estimating an "average" level at which the stock traded during the time period. VWAP can be a difficult benchmark for clients to "see" on the graph because it requires the simultaneous consideration of both the price at which the stock traded and the shares that traded at that price.

■ *Course of day (COD):* Orders are sometimes submitted with a *course of day* instruction that sits somewhere between a "market, not held" and a TWAP instruction. The client is indicating that they do not have a clear view on the direction of the stock over the session and therefore do not want to complete the order at current levels since there is the possibility that more attractive levels present themselves later in the day. However, by not specifically referencing the TWAP or VWAP, the client is giving a certain amount of discretion to the broker to choose how much of the order to execute at different times of the day. While the expectation is that the broker will not simply punt the entire order in one go and hope to have picked a good time, there is room to add value through timing decisions rather than being forced into a slavish adherence to a time-slicing model for a TWAP or VWAP. It is, however, common for clients to compare a course of day order to the VWAP to get a sense of performance.

- *Stop* or *stop-limit:* A *stop order* (short for *stop loss*) is used to limit the potential loss of an existing position by setting a trigger price at which the position is closed out. Particularly when a position cannot be watched as closely as is desired, stops are used both to protect against large losses as well as to enforce good trading discipline. The trader takes a position with the expectation of making a profit but also specifies a level at which they must concede that the view was wrong and the trade should be cut before additional losses are incurred. It is human nature to hold onto losing positions for far too long because of our unwillingness to admit we are wrong and the hope that it will turn around and we will recuperate our loss. Everyone does it; smart traders realize it and set stops accordingly.

  As an example, let us assume a trader pays $25 for 10,000 shares of stock on the view that the stock can easily go to $30, a 20 percent rally. However, the trader also submits a sell stop order 5 percent below the market, at $24. If the stock price drops to $24 the trigger is hit and the shares are sold at market. To ensure that the liquidation of the position is not overly costly, a *stop-limit* order can be submitted in which two prices are specified, a trigger price for the stop, and a limit price for the subsequent liquidation order. Using our example, once the $24 stop is triggered, the order submitted could be a limit order with a $23.75 low. If there are bids in the market between $23.75 and $24, the order will be executed. Any residual balance will remain as an offer at $23.75. It is important not to set the limit of the stop loss order too close to the trigger price as this increases the probability that the trigger price is hit, but the stock is not executed due to the close limit, effectively undoing the loss-limiting benefits of the stop order.

- *Good till canceled (GTC):* The default is that all client orders are cancelled at the end of the trading session. If a client wishes for an order (usually a limit or stop) to be left in the market for multiple sessions the order is flagged as a *good till canceled* order and will be resubmitted each session until cancelled. In some markets the GTC order can be submitted to the exchange while in others the broker takes on the responsibility of resubmitting the order each session. When he does this, it is important that he check all GTC orders for corporate actions, which may require changes to the order instructions. For example, with shares of XYZ stock trading at $26, a client submits a GTC order to pay $25 for 10,000 shares. If shares of XYZ were to split 2-for-1, the stock price would immediately drop to $13. If the GTC limit order is not updated to the equivalent post-split terms (a $12.50 bid for 20,000 shares), the order would be executed as soon as the stock began trading but would not represent the same economics as the original order. This would also occur with a sufficiently large dividend. In general, GTC orders are cancelled and given back to the customer to be updated when a corporate action occurs.

Two special types of agency orders are those that target the opening and closing prices, referred to as a *market-on-open* (MOO) and *market-on-close* (MOC), respectively.[3]

- *Market-on-close (MOC):* The closing price of the trading session has particular importance because it serves as the day's final reference price for the stock and is used for all end-of-day position marking and profit and loss (*p&l* or *pnl*) calculations, margin adjustments, collateral valuations, and the like. For mutual funds, pension funds, and other collective investment vehicles, the closing price is the point at which the customer deposits received on the day are invested into the fund (or removed from the fund, in the event of a withdrawal). Under *mark-to-market accounting* (which is what all investment banks and broker-dealers use to monitor the value of trading positions), the profit or loss from a position is computed as though it had been liquidated at the closing price and the day's performance is recognized as though it were an actual gain or loss.

  In order to ensure fair treatment for all investors, the official closing price of a stock is not determined in the regular trading session but through a closing auction in which all participants receive the same price. An investor who wishes to execute an order in the closing auction can attach the "close only" condition to their order. Regardless of the time the order is sent, the participation is limited exclusively to the closing auction. A market-on-close order will be executed in the closing auction, regardless of price, while a *limit-on-close* (LOC) order will only be executed if the closing auction price is better than the limit.

  While the specific mechanism of the closing auction differs from one market to another, the general structure is similar. At the end of the session, an auction period begins during which regular trading may or may not be halted. During this time, all market-on-close orders are pooled together to determine a net buy or sell, which is then matched up against buy and sell orders on the book from the regular trading session, as well as any limit-on-close orders, to determine an equilibrium liquidating price at which all market-on-close orders can be completed.

In some markets, prior to completing the closing auction an indicative closing price is disseminated. This is particularly useful in cases where there is a large imbalance between orders to buy and sell on the close and the resultant equilibrium price is at a significant premium or discount to the last traded price before the auction. By advertising this information, the exchange invites offsetting orders to be submitted to reduce the imbalance and therefore minimize the price deviation necessary to complete all orders. In some markets (NYSE, for one) there is a cut-off time well after which on-close orders are no longer accepted. When a significant imbalance is published, however, this reopens a window of opportunity for the submission of offsetting orders. A trader looking to sell stock who sees a significant buy imbalance may want to take advantage of the opportunity to make a sale by submitting an offsetting limit on close order at a level he considers attractive.

- *Market-on-open (MOO):* The functioning of the market-on-open order is structurally similar to that of the closing auction except for two points. The first is that, with the exception of those days where significant overnight news events or the expiration of derivatives at the opening price results in heavy trading activity, there is generally much less focus on the opening auction than on the close. The second is that the urgency to participate in the opening print is smaller because there is still the entire trading day ahead and excessively large movements on the open are likely to correct themselves in subsequent trading. There is also much greater flexibility to delay the opening print, sometimes for hours, to allow for additional orders to be submitted in the event of a large order imbalance in the opening auction.

Auctions and Exchange Structure

The handling of the opening and closing auctions provides a useful framework for comparing the benefits of different exchange structures. Looking specifically at the closing auction, the two principal concerns of most participants is that their order be completed—as a residual position would create unwanted risk overnight—and that where imbalances exist between buyers and sellers, the auction price does not represent an excessive dislocation from where the market was trading immediately prior to the closing auction.

Specialist: Under a single market maker specialist system, all market-on-open and market-on-close orders are guaranteed to be completed because it is the specialist's obligation to take the other side of any order imbalance. While this completely satisfies the first requirement, the model can come up somewhat short in regard to the second. Many specialist firms are small operations with limited capital, and taking the other side of a large closing imbalance can often represent an investment of a significant portion of the firm's assets. As a result, specialists needed to balance the exchange requirement to make a "fair and orderly" market with the need to protect their businesses interests by pricing the risk conservatively—that is, buying (selling) at a significant discount (premium) to the last traded price in order to have a sufficient cushion to trade out of the position the next day and hopefully make a profit or, at the very least, not suffer a loss.

While the facilitation of the closing auction imbalance creates a risk for the specialist, it is also an opportunity, particularly considering that, within reason, the specialist has discretion to fill the order wherever he likes. In order to reduce both the risk to the specialist and the potential for abuse, the NYSE requires that whenever the imbalance between buy and sell orders exceeds 50,000 shares, an "MOC Auction Imbalance" alert be disseminated to advise potentially interested traders of the possibility of a disconnect in the closing auction and give them the chance to participate.

Multiple market maker: In a multiple market maker system there is no single person responsible for guaranteeing that all orders in the closing auction are completed and there exists the possibility that market-on-close orders are left incomplete. In practice, however, this rarely occurs because, where the indicated auction price is at a sufficient premium (discount) to the current price level, traders will see the opportunity to sell (buy) stock at an attractive spread to current market levels and will usually provide the necessary liquidity. This system allows multiple parties to take a piece of what would, under the specialist system, be the responsibility of a single person. This broader distribution of the risk among multiple parties would theoretically tend to reduce the spread at which the auction is priced since the smaller size of the position taken by each individual requires a smaller risk premium.

No market maker: The functioning of a purely electronic exchange is similar to that of the multiple market maker model. While execution is not guaranteed, the existence of countless broker-dealers, hedge fund traders, arbitrageurs, and day traders looking to take advantage of a short-term liquidity mismatch means that, in general, there will be sufficient liquidity to complete most orders. While the pure electronic venues in the United States (ECNs) do not generally have closing auction facilities, this model does operate in other countries, though it works best in stocks where trading is quite active and the risk of either a major dislocation or incomplete auction (i.e., not all orders completed) is low.

Principal Trade

The other type of client order, called a *principal trade,* is one in which, rather than executing on the client's behalf, the broker acts as counterparty, buying from, or selling to the customer at an agreed-upon price. In doing this, the client transfers the entire execution risk to the broker who must then attempt to achieve an equal or better price in the market himself or, as is more commonly the case, minimize the shortfall of the actual execution versus the price traded with the client. In practice, a principal order actually results in two trades being executed: the broker's trade versus the client, which must be reported to the exchange as an *upstairs* execution (i.e., not through the exchange floor), and then the broker's trade-out in the market. Because they are the direct consequence of a client order, principal trades are often referred to as *customer facilitation* trades.

> *Risk price:* In the simplest case, the client wishes to buy or sell a particular number of shares and asks the broker for the price at which he is willing to take the other side of the trade. The broker quotes a price and the client has a couple of seconds to either accept the price or refuse. This is generally a very quick process and, in the case that the client is slow to respond, the broker will likely inform him that the price is now *subject,* meaning that the broker reserves the right to quote a new price if the market has moved while waiting for the client to respond. In general, risk prices are always executed *on the wire,* meaning that the client is on the phone while the price is being made.
>
> The client may indicate which side of the market he is on by requesting either a *risk bid* (if he is selling) or a *risk offer* (if he is buying). Alternatively, a more aggressive approach is for the client to ask the broker to make a *two-way market* in the stock for an indicated size. In this case the broker must provide both a bid and offer price at which he is willing to deal and the client can then decide, subject to the same few seconds of validity, whether he wants to trade at the indicated price. If so, he tells the broker that he agrees to trade and indicates whether he is a buyer or a seller.
>
> Many clients are highly sensitive to divulging any information about their positions or intentions for fear that the broker might use

that information against them. The advantage of a two-way price is that, in the event that he decides not to trade, the client discloses much less information and the broker has no knowledge of what his intention was (i.e., opening a new long or short position or either adding to, or closing out of, an existing position). There is also a perception that by requesting a two-way market, the client pushes the broker to be more aggressive in his pricing. By showing both bid and offer prices, the broker implies a bid-offer spread that he considers appropriate for the given size. If the broker prices his bid and offer too conservatively, the spread will be very wide making the broker look uncommercial.

It is common for brokers to provide clients with more aggressive risk prices than what they are actually able to achieve in the market and to take a small loss on the trade-out of the position. While brokers will closely monitor the profitability of trading with a particular client, some amount of loss on risk trading is considered acceptable and assumed as part of the service provided. In exchange for providing aggressive risk pricing when necessary, clients will pass a certain amount of riskless, agency execution business to the broker, effectively paying the broker back for the service. The percentage of total commission dollars lost through risk trading is called the *loss ratio* and, depending on the client, commonly ranges somewhere between 5 and 25 percent, with extreme cases of negative ratios—representing the very rare case where the broker has actually made money through risk pricing—to greater than 100 percent—where the broker is losing more on trading than the sum of all commissions paid. Clients often request a risk price with the agreement that there is additional agency flow behind it. For example, a client might ask for "a bid on 100,000 to work 100,000," meaning he wants the broker to buy the first 100,000 shares on risk with the agreement that, once the broker has traded out of the position, the client will leave another 100,000 to sell as an agency order. The fact that a riskless agency order is explicitly offered behind the risk order will often encourage the broker to be more aggressive in his risk pricing.

When a risk price is agreed between a broker and the client, the trade does not need to pass through the centralized order book of the exchange because the buyer and seller have already found each other. This type of off-exchange trade is called a *cross*. So that all market participants can trade based on the same information, in most countries the cross must be *printed* or *reported to the tape*; the details of the trade are sent to the exchange and disseminated publicly like any other trade, though often with an indicator showing that the trade was executed off-exchange.

The specific rules for printing cross trades differ by country; there are some more lenient markets where a print is not required at all, while others have an outright prohibition of off-exchange executions. In some cases, the cross can only be executed if it is inside the bid-offer spread on the screen at the time of the trade. There is also a general prohibition in all markets against *"painting the tape,"* which is the act of printing trades to the tape for the purpose of creating the impression of trading activity when there is in fact none. When a trade is printed it must represent a true change of beneficial ownership (i.e., a transfer of a position between two trading books at the same broker dealer would not be printed.) Back and forth trading between two brokers ("I'll buy it from you and then you buy it from me") to manipulate the price or create a false perception of activity is also prohibited.

Block trading: While many risk trades are priced "on the wire," there are some cases where the quantity of shares for which a client wants a bid is so large, either in absolute notional or in comparison to the average daily volume in the stock, that the trader will make a price based less on the liquidity available in the market (how long it will take to trade out of the position and how much impact will be had in the execution) than on the firm's ability to utilize its network of clients and contacts to find buyers that would be interested in the opportunity to purchase shares, particularly if they were offered at an attractive discount to the current market price. This type of trade, called a *block trade* can come from an institutional client, a large private holder, or, as is often the case, from a corporate seller, often the company itself. Block trades are almost exclusively bids—most clients tend to build up into positions slowly and then ask for a bid on the way out.

Block trades can be extremely large, frequently into the hundreds of millions of dollars, and the specific pricing of any trade is a function of many different factors including the relationship with the client, the size of the block, the recent performance of the stock, the identity of the seller and his motivation (if it is disclosed), the current market environment, and whether there have been other recent blocks, particularly from the same sector, which may have exhausted the risk appetite of potentially interested clients.

In general, the broker will guarantee a price to the seller and then take one of two approaches to selling that stock to their clients. One option is for the firm to offer the stock to its clients at a specific price, usually a significant discount to the current market price to entice buyers to participate, on a first-come, first-served basis. For an attractive deal, this creates a certain sense of urgency with clients and trades can often be completed very quickly. Another option is to set a range in which the stock will be sold and offer clients the opportunity to participate on a *book-build* basis. In a book-build, clients submit nonbinding indications of interest in the stock—how many shares they would be willing to buy and at what price—but do not receive an immediate fill. Rather, the broker gives all clients the opportunity to submit their orders, subject a specified cut-off time and then prices the trade based on the level of demand. A highly attractive block (either because the stock is well-liked or the discount is significant) may be oversubscribed (more demand than shares) and priced at the top end of the range with clients receiving a fractional allocation of their desired size.

The important fact in both cases is that, if client demand is insufficient to place the entire block, the broker will end up owning the stock—the client, who is selling, is always given a fill. The substantial risk in a block trade is that, unlike a typical risk bid, where only the seller knows that the broker is long the stock, in a block trade, the broker has advertised to all its clients that they are offering stock. If the trade goes poorly, the entire street knows the broker is stuck long a huge block of shares and will need to sell. This puts the broker in a very uncomfortable position. Given the enormous risks involved, the pricing of a large block will be escalated to the most senior traders and risk managers of the equities division to ensure that the trade is priced appropriately.

Guaranteed VWAP (GVWAP): Another type of principal trade is a *guaranteed VWAP*, in which the broker gives the client an execution price equal to the VWAP over a previously defined time period, regardless of his actual execution. Unlike a risk bid or offer, the specific price at which the broker agrees to fill the client order is not agreed upon prior to the trade, since it cannot be known. Instead the broker and client agree on the characteristics of the fill that will be received—the volume weighted average price of all trades between a preset start and end time, usually including only those trades that occur on the primary exchange where the stock is listed—and then once the time period is passed, provide the numerical fill.

"Beat the close": Mutual fund inflows (outflows) are added to (removed from) the fund's assets at the closing price of the day. As a result there are substantial flows that target this price and it is common to ask brokers to guarantee that the execution will match the closing price. While an MOC execution is guaranteed by the exchange and the broker can execute as agent, if the order is particularly large, or the stock illiquid, sending the whole order MOC could have significant impact on the market. One way to reduce this impact, and simultaneously improve the execution, is to trade a portion of the order early, prior to sending the remainder of the order MOC. The portion of the order traded early will depend on the relative size of the order and the liquidity in the stock and can range from a few shares to the majority of the order. By trading early, the broker takes advantage of liquidity other than just that available at the close, and also reduces the size of the market-on-close order—both of which benefit the customer. He must, however, be careful to leave enough stock for the MOC order to ensure that his average execution price is better than the close or he will end up taking a loss on the trade. Because the order is a guaranteed MOC the broker must trade as principal since he is assuming the risk of underperforming the close.

Exhibit 3.1 shows a hypothetical example of how working a portion of a large buy order early can not only reduce the total impact on the closing print (the stock closes at $40.36 as opposed to $40.73), but also achieve a better execution price than the close due to the participation in trading prior to the close (average price of the execution is even lower at $40.23, which is $0.13 or 32 bps better than the close).

It is important to be aware that a "beat the close" order, even if well-executed is by no means a sure winner. The trade is a bet on a short-term liquidity imbalance and corresponding price impact. It is not a directional view on the market and abrupt changes in overall market conditions can easily overwhelm the effects of market impact. There is always the risk of a larger order on the opposite side of the market in the same stock at another broker, which results in the stock price moving in the opposite direction to what was expected, precisely in the closing auction. In the context of Exhibit 3.1, this would mean the stock price, instead of spiking upward in the closing auction, would actually drop sharply. If the closing price were $39.80, the broker would have achieved an average execution of $39.90 (or so) on his purchases. However, since the client is guaranteed the closing price or better, the broker would

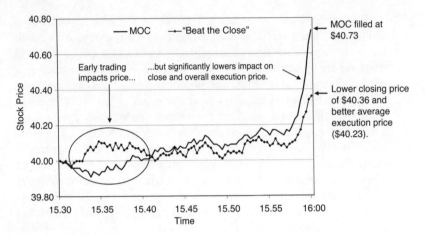

EXHIBIT 3.1   Stock Price Movement Associated with a Large Buy Order
Executed as MOC and "Beat the Close"

then have to sell the stock to the client at the closing price of $39.80 for a $0.10 loss per share.

Limit-price stop order: When requesting a principal bid or offer, the client transfers to the broker all the risk associated with the ability to achieve that price in the market. Compared with the agency execution, this transfer of risk benefits the client whenever the execution price achieved by the broker is worse than the price given to the client. However, if the market moves in the broker's favor and he gets a better price in the market than the risk price shown, the client would have been better off with an agency execution. This is the trade-off between risk and agency executions; the person taking the risk has the upside as well as the downside.

An alternative is a *limit-price stop* order (not to be confused with a stop-loss order), in which the broker guarantees that the client's fill will be no worse than a particular price. In this case the broker works the trade in his own account but agrees to pass on the realized execution directly to the client so long as it is better than the price at which he has "stopped" the client. In this case, the client gets the best of both worlds—protection in the event the price achieved by the broker is worse than the limit price, and full participation if the stock acts well and the execution is better than the limit. For the broker there is no upside; the client receives the better price in all cases. With a stop order, the broker takes on risk but receives only the execution commission and has no opportunity for trading profits.

It is important to distinguish between the pricing of a risk bid or offer and a stop. When quoting a risk price to a client, a broker will make his best estimate of where he can trade out in the market and then, depending on how commercial he wishes to be, quote a risk price somewhere around this level. The expectation is that, while on any individual trade he may make or lose money, the average over time will result in an acceptable loss ratio. With a stop order, however, the broker can only lose money; the upside of any execution price better than the limit is given to the client while the loss from any price worse than the limit is worn by the broker. Due to the asymmetric payoff caused by stopping the client, the limit price offered as a stop will generally be further from the current market price than would the equivalent risk price. It is a common mistake for salespeople and clients alike to ask for a risk price and then assume that it can be converted to a limit-price stop, as though this were a minor detail. This indicates a lack of understanding of the asymmetry of the risks posed by stopping a client order and is a great way to irritate traders.

Agency versus Principal An important distinction between agency and principal orders is that, while they are both executed in response to a client request, in the agency case the orders are represented on the exchange as "client" while a principal order is represented as "firm." The difference is not merely semantic; where two equivalent orders arrive simultaneously to the market, a client order will receive precedence over a firm order. A consequence of this is that, where a client's agency order can be better serviced via a principal execution, the broker must first obtain the client's permission to do so as the conversion of the order type identifier from "agency" to "firm" would technically disadvantage the client's execution. For example, an agency MOC order cannot be traded as a beat-the-close principal order without client consent.

Proprietary

The last type of trade is a proprietary trade, which is an order executed by the firm for its own benefit and with its own capital and is not related to any client order. It is common for most large firms to have a dedicated proprietary trading division, separate from the client business, which invests the firm's capital. Because of the responsibility entrusted to these groups to invest the firm's capital, "prop" desks are generally perceived as somewhat exclusive as the traders are freed from the day-to-day work of servicing client requests and can focus exclusively on trading "for the house."

In recent years, however, there has been a significant push across most Wall Street firms to increase the amount of proprietary trading done by the client traders, in an effort to monetize the knowledge gained through client interaction. The logic is simple—a trader who spends his day studying the *price action* (stock price movements), news flow, and published research of a small universe of stocks and who, in addition, sees the trading flows of many different, highly educated clients, is likely to develop a far more educated view on the direction of future price movements in those stocks. If the trader is allowed to take positions for his own account, he should be able to convert this informational advantage into a trading profit.

When this trend began, there was a considerable amount of skepticism and concern expressed by clients, many of whom felt they would in some way be disadvantaged if the client facilitation traders were also executing for their own books. Concerns typically centered around the idea of *front-running*, in which a trader has received a client order and, based on an expectation that the execution of that order will have significant market impact, trades shares for his own account first in order to capture a profit from the market movement he himself is about to create. Not surprisingly, this is illegal.

In reality, the concerns about client traders also taking positions for their own accounts have been dramatically overblown. Speaking from personal experience, in more than a decade of trading, I have never seen a trader deliberately take a position in front of a client order or otherwise disadvantage an agency execution for his own benefit. Aside from the fact that most strategies for benefiting from prior knowledge of a client trade are illegal, it is also an extraordinarily stupid trade from a business perspective as the risk/reward balance is simply not attractive. An investment bank caught front-running client orders would suffer a massive loss of client trust which would jeopardize the entire client business. The small profits that can be gained from stepping in front of a client order are no compensation for the massive reputational and franchise risks taken. As an additional safeguard, to ensure that the pressure put on traders to earn profits does not result in behavior that is inconsistent with firm policy on best execution and fair order handling, firms closely monitor proprietary trading and cross-check proprietary activity against client activity and investigate any abnormal patterns.

While concerns about improper broker activity were overblown, even more confused was the view, frequently espoused by retail investors, that clients were somehow disadvantaged if their broker was trading "against" them—that is, selling when the client was buying, or vice versa. Some smaller brokers went so far as to claim that they provided a superior service because they "never trade against your order." This argument does not make sense. If the broker wishes to take the other side of a client agency order (i.e., trade "against" the client) he must do so according to the "best execution" guidelines that require him to provide a price that is as good, or better, than what is available in the market—it can only benefit the customer.

Algorithmic Execution and Electronic Trading

A significant advance in cash trading in recent years has been the development and implementation of sophisticated electronic algorithms for executing many types of trades. The underlying concept is that many of the standard trading strategies used by brokers can be reduced to a simple set of trading rules, which can be codified into a well-defined series of instructions and implemented by a computer. The massive increases in trading volumes since the late 1990s, and the corresponding decrease in trading costs, have been possible because many types of orders can now be managed as well, or better, by a computer than by a human trader.

A simple example is an order to work a trade over the day targeting VWAP. Barring specific indications to the contrary, such as a major overnight event or an impending intraday news release, the best approach to working a VWAP order is to spread the execution over the entire session, in line with the volume "smile" that is typical of U.S. stocks.[4] A typical VWAP algorithm will begin with a statistically-determined volume profile and then apply an implementation strategy that attempts to balance the costs of crossing the bid-offer spread with the risks of deviating too significantly from the target volume profile. For example, the algorithm may initially submit orders on the same side of the market (i.e., buying on the bid/selling on the offer) and leave them there for a given period of time before becoming more aggressive to avoid lagging behind on volume. Smarter algorithms may include more sophisticated monitoring logic that looks to see how the market is trading and become more aggressive where stocks are moving in the wrong direction and less aggressive when stocks move favorably. While monitoring the costs associated with doing so, trading engines may submit, cancel, amend, and execute hundreds or even thousands of individual executions throughout the day on a single trade.

If the trader decides to work the order manually, he will need to constantly monitor the stock and trade many small orders throughout the day in order to reduce the risk of realizing a significantly different price than the VWAP. This is a time-consuming process and, particularly in the case of large, actively traded stocks, the value added by active trader involvement is limited, particularly when the higher costs of broker involvement are factored in. Additionally, it is physically impossible for a human trader to make the number of small adjustments of which a computerized algorithm is capable.

Another reason for the popularity of algorithmic strategies among clients is that, compared with the more subjective approaches used by traders, electronic algorithms tend to have much less variation in their performance versus the VWAP. While some traders may be able to add value by calling the market direction and appropriately skewing the volume profile of the execution, the results of deviating significantly from the historically defined volume profile is that the performance versus VWAP is likely to be much more broadly distributed, beating by a large amount on some days and missing by a mile on others. Even where the trader, on average, adds value, many clients give a significant premium to the consistency of the performance and are actually more comfortable with an electronic system whose average performance versus VWAP is less impressive, but whose distribution of performance is narrow.

Execution targeting a VWAP benchmark is only one of the many strategies where electronic algorithms can produce equivalent or superior performance to human traders. Other common trading instructions, such as targeting the TWAP, working as a percentage of volume or even minimizing the implementation shortfall from the time the order is received, can be codified into a series of trading rules and implemented en masse across thousands of securities simultaneously. The speed, scalability, and low cost of electronic execution have all contributed to the dramatic decreases in the number of physical traders required on a trading floor, despite the massive increases in trading volumes.

This does not mean that traders have become obsolete. What has changed is that the responsibility of the trader has shifted as the more mechanistic portions of the job have been solved through technology, allowing the trader to focus on the subjective, circumstance, and client-dependent scenario analyses that cannot be decomposed into a series of "if X then Y" trading rules. In the extreme volatility that surrounds a major news announcement in a stock, no computer will ever be able to make the nuanced decisions between protecting the firm's interests in the short term (not taking a trading loss) and the long term (maintaining a relationship with an important client) that are required of a trader. There are also many circumstances, such as trading in highly illiquid stocks, where the outcome achieved through active involvement by the trader is significantly superior to what can be achieved with a machine.

HOW THE CASH TRADING BUSINESS WORKS

Given the basic understanding of the functioning of the cash market developed so far, we can now examine how the sales and trading business of a typical large investment bank is structured in order to best respond to client demands for information, execution services, and capital commitment.

Exhibit 3.2 shows a schematic diagram of the life cycle of a typical client order. In recognition of the fact that different steps in the investment process require very different skill sets, investment banks divide the responsibility for servicing clients between three distinct groups: *sales, sales-trading,* and *trading.* Our goal in this section will be to understand the roles and responsibilities of each of these groups and how they interact to service the client business.

Sales

In broad terms, equity salespeople are responsible for delivering the firm's knowledge, insight, and services to external clients. This can mean many different things, depending on the specific characteristics of each client. Some may want little more than a quick summary e-mail or voice mail each morning to update them on any interesting insights on the market or newly published research. Other clients will expect their sales coverage to maintain a much more active dialog about market conditions and trading ideas, as well as providing other services such as arranging meetings with analysts, traders, and corporate management, assisting with quantitative analyses or the opportunity to participate in *initial public offerings* (IPOs) of stock. A good salesperson not only knows which clients want a bullet-point e-mail summary and which prefer to chat about markets on the phone for hours, but can provide them both with what they need.

The objective of a salesperson is, of course, to bring the client's business into the firm. In some cases a particular broker may offer a product or service no other firm can provide (such as access to an IPO or a particularly innovative trade idea) and will receive orders based on the attractiveness of the investment opportunity or quality of the product or service provided. However, in highly commoditized offerings such as agency stock execution, the ability of the broker to differentiate itself is limited and what often leads a client to direct orders to one broker over another is the quality of the sales coverage provided.

A challenge arises when dealing with clients who have very narrowly focused interests, for example, a fund that only invests in utility companies, or specializes in trading "special situation" arbitrage relationships. A salesperson responsible for covering a wide variety of different clients (often referred to as *generalist salesperson*) cannot possibly provide the detailed knowledge necessary to properly service this type of investor. As a result, many firms have *specialist salespeople* who focus exclusively on a particular sector or group of stocks.

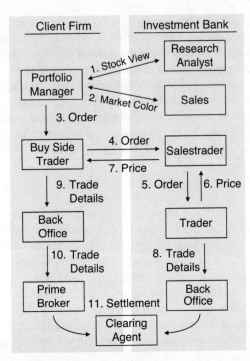

1. The portfolio manager (PM) discusses a stock view with the research analyst.
2. The salesperson, either generalist of specialist, can add additional insight as well as market color from the trading floor.
3. Having decided on an investment, the PM passes the order to his dealer who is responsible for managing the broker relationship.
4. The dealer passes the order to the sales-trader along with his instructions for how it is to be executed, either as agency or risk.
5. The sales-trader passes the instructions to the trader and puts the details of the order (ticker, side, shares, client name, commission rate) order into the firm's order management system.
6. Once executed, the trader puts the fill price on the order ticket for the sales-trader.
7. Sales-trader reports the execution price to the client
8. The trader's system will automatically pass the trade downstream to the back office for booking. If all details provided by the sales-trader are correct, and match what is booked by the client, the trade should clear with no additional manual involvement.
9. The buy side trader passes the details of the order to his back office.
10. Details of the trades are passed to the prime broker who maintains the client's positions and insures proper settlement of all trades.
11. The prime broker settles the trades for the client account with the clearing agent, who will have received the details of the trade from the broker back office and be looking to settle these against the prime broker firm.

EXHIBIT 3.2   Life Cycle of a Client Order: The Broker-Client Relationship

The specialist salesperson acts as a trading floor authority in the stocks in her sector. Where these are covered by the firm's Research division, he will have a detailed knowledge of the analyst's recommendations and views on the stocks. However, the universe of stocks covered by a specialist salesperson is not limited to those stocks covered by the research analysts and an important contribution of the specialist sales team is their knowledge of those stocks where the firm does not have a published view. Additionally, a salesperson sits on the trading floor and is in constant contact with both clients and the firm's own traders and combines her fundamental understanding of the companies with information on the price action in the stocks, client sentiment, and trading flows.

In addition to an external client base of sector-specific and general funds that they cover, specialist salespeople also service the internal audience of traders and sales-traders by providing information on upcoming events of significance as well as analysis of news announcements and their likely impact on the stock price. Because of their detailed knowledge of the companies in the sector and the most active investors in those stocks, specialist salespeople are sometimes brought "over the wall"[5] and consulted by the investment banking arm of the firm for their opinion on the appropriate pricing for corporate deals (secondary share issuances, IPOs, etc.).

Sales-Trading

Exhibit 3.2 shows how the investment process at a typical buy-side[6] firm is divided between two distinct roles. A *portfolio manager* (PM) makes the investment decisions for the fund based on his views on the market, which he develops through independent research as well as conversations with research analysts and salespeople. The PM then passes the instructions to a *dealer*, also known as a *buy-side trader*, who is responsible for executing the trades required to express the view. This distinction between idea generation and trade execution is reflected within the sales and trading business of the broker as well. The salesperson, as we have discussed, provides information and opinion to the PM to assist in the development of the investment thesis. There is then a *sales-trader* who, as the name would imply, sits between the salesperson and the traders and is there to coordinate the practical aspects of executing the trade.

While distinct, these roles are not mutually exclusive; in practice, the best salespeople are those that have an understanding of how the trade can be implemented (since there's no use in pitching an idea if you can't actually execute on it), and the best sales-traders are those who understand the investment thesis.

The sales-trader manages the execution of the client's trade from start to finish, a process that involves a number of different responsibilities. One of the most important of these is to act as an intermediary between the client dealer and the internal trader, representing the interests of each to the other so that, insofar as possible, both parties come away satisfied with the results of the trade. This can be particularly challenging when the broker is asked to commit capital by providing a risk price for stock as the economic interests of the two parties are then directly opposed. Once the trade is executed, the sales-trader is also responsible for coordinating the efforts of the various groups involved in the downstream processing and settlement. This includes checking that the client's account is set up properly, that the trade is booked with the correct details (price, commission rate, allocation between subaccounts) and that any post-trade settlement issues are resolved quickly.

Just as important as the sales-trader's skill in executing an order is his ability to bring in new orders. While the PM may direct the dealer to trade with a particular broker to compensate them for sales coverage and research services, in many cases, it is left to the discretion of the dealer to decide with which counterparty to execute a trade. A sales-trader's responsibility, therefore, is not simply to wait for the phone to ring with an order, but to make sure the phone *does* ring by staying constantly in front of his clients, providing them with market color and updates on trading activity in stocks where they have an interest.

The responsibility of a sales-trader to provide his clients with information is taken very seriously. When there is a sudden move in the market, a good sales-trader will find out the reason (if there is one) and then proactively call his clients with a quick "Hey, market just ticked lower because XYZ said holiday sales were weaker than expected." If the move cannot be attributed to a particular piece of news, he may still acknowledge the movement and the client's potential interest in an explanation with a call saying, "The market's ticking lower here but we're not seeing any reason for it—flows are light and we're actually a better buyer into this weakness." This shows the client that his sales-trader is "all over" the market and wants to keep his client informed because he values his business. If the client doesn't receive a phone call and has to dial the broker and ask if there is any news out (and worse yet, if the broker doesn't know), it shows a lack of attention to markets and a poor level of service.

Sales-traders are rewarded, in the end, for "hustle"—being very quick to get things done and thinking about their client's needs. A good sales-trader knows his client's interests and will selectively advertise to him activity and trading opportunities in those names where he would want to be kept informed. It is important that the sales-trader use good judgment in selecting what information to reflect to the client. While it would be poor sales trading to not advise a client of an important news announcement or trading opportunity in a stock of interest, it is just as bad to inundate a client with lots of irrelevant information as this not only wastes time and causes annoyance, but dilutes the value of the service.

In addition to providing color on what is happening in the market, dealers will expect to be made aware if one of their brokers is going to make a large trade in a stock where they have an interest, and, where possible, to be given the opportunity to participate. For example, if the client has been buying a stock, then the sales-trader should know that if a significant sell order is received, before selling those shares to anonymous strangers in the market, this particular client should first be given the opportunity to take the other side. If the client trades, this is a triple win: the seller gets his trade done quickly and with little impact, the buyer takes advantage of the opportunity to purchase more stock at an attractive price and feels well-serviced by the broker, and the broker gets a commission on both sides of the trade.

At the other end of the spectrum is the worst-case scenario where the sales-trader is unaware of the sell order, which is then executed in the market with sufficient impact to draw an incoming call from the client asking for color on why a stock he owns is trading lower. In this case, the sales-trader responds initially with "I don't know, let me find out" and then has to call back with "Oh, it was us selling it." The triple-win is now a quadruple-loss as the execution price for the seller was worse than could have been achieved, the buyer missed the opportunity to participate and a commission-paying ticket was lost, the sales-trader looks sloppy, uninvolved, and unaware of what is going on in his own firm (much less the market in general) and the client feels under-serviced and is likely to direct flow to other more attentive brokers. The difference between the triple-win and quadruple-loss outcomes all hinge on the sales-trader simply being aware of what was going on around him. There is much to be gained through good sales trading, and even more to be lost.

Trading

While many people use the word "trader" to describe their work, the word means very different things in different contexts. The word can be used to describe the most senior risk-taker at a multibillion-dollar hedge fund who actively takes large directional bets on the market and moves in and out of positions in an effort to achieve superior returns. Alternatively, it can refer to low-level order processing clerk who simply pushes client trades into the electronic trading engines, taking no risk on the execution and having no input in the decision of what is bought or sold.

In the context presented here we will focus on the role of an institutional *flow trader,* who is the person ultimately responsible for executing orders in the market, determining the appropriate price at which to commit capital in principal trades, and managing the risk associated with trading out of the positions taken. A flow trader may also take on a significant amount of proprietary risk in order to extract further value from his knowledge of the markets though, for our purposes here, this will be a secondary responsibility.

When working orders, either on behalf of a client or trading out of risk for his own book, a flow trader utilizes two types of knowledge: precise, factual information about the stocks he trades, and a subtle, intuitive understanding of how markets work and the unwritten rules of the client service business.

The first of these is quite straightforward and is the part that a new trader can most quickly acquire. Most traders will usually focus on stocks from one or two sectors and, in order to properly understand the drivers of daily price movements, will develop a detailed knowledge of all aspects of those stocks. This includes details of the company's business activity, financial ratios, timing of dividends and earnings announcements, recent price movements, and historical performance as well as any unique issues or circumstances faced by particular companies (pending lawsuits, new drug approvals, and the like). In addition to the stock-specific information, the trader must also have a complete understanding of the relevant laws, exchange regulations and firm policies that govern the behavior of traders servicing client orders and how those orders can be executed.

The second type of knowledge is more nuanced and takes time and experience to develop. By actively participating in the markets day after day, traders develop a "feel" for how stocks trade, which greatly improves their ability to determine the best way to work an order. One of the reasons clients utilize the full-service trading model, as opposed to the low-cost DMA approach, is because they can benefit from the trader's knowledge and experience to improve the quality of the execution. Specifically, a trader uses his experience as a guide to strike a delicate balance between the two primary risks associated with a stock execution: market risk and market impact.

Market risk refers to the possibility of adverse market movements occurring prior to an order being completed, where those movements are unrelated to the act of executing the shares. For example, if a client submits an order to buy a single share of stock at market when the offer price is $22.35 and, by the time the order has been sent to the exchange and executed the offer side has moved to $22.45, the clients fill will be $0.10 higher than expected. The change in market conditions between the time the decision was made to take a position and the time it is actually executed—in this case the move of $0.10 against the client—represents the market risk. Market risk is symmetric—the stock price could move favorably during the time period (for example, if the offer price had decreased to $22.30 resulting in an execution price $0.05 better than expected).

The degree of adverse price movement that is actually created by the act of executing the shares is called *market impact,* and is, by definition, always negative. While conceptually simple, it can be difficult to accurately assess the market impact of a trade because it requires the distinction between price movements in the stock caused by the execution from what the market would have done had the order not been there. If the order is executed in a very short period of time, it is often reasonable to assume that the stock price would have remained roughly constant over that time and therefore the market impact can be measured as the deviation of the execution price from the last sale (or alternatively, the midpoint of the bid-offer at the time the trade was submitted).

For example, using the screen market in XYZ stock from earlier in the chapter, if a client were to submit a "held" market order to buy 20,000 shares, the order goes directly to market and is executed at an average price of $25.4448. In this case, it is clear that the entire price movement is due to the act of purchasing the shares since the market order was executed immediately and went through three levels of market depth to be completed. The entire deviation between the market price and the execution price is therefore due to market impact, which can be calculated as $0.0348 = $25.4448 – $25.41, or roughly 14 bps.

Ticker	Last	Last Size
XYZ	25.41	12

Bid Size	Bid	Ask	Ask Size
45	25.40	25.42	61
112	25.38	25.45	100
95	25.30	25.47	82

Where market impact becomes more nebulous is when an order is executed over a longer period of time. In this case, in order to differentiate market risk from market impact, there must be an estimation of what the stock price would have done had the order not been in the market. A common method for doing this is to use the performance of a benchmark equity index, such as the S&P 500 or an index of stocks from the relevant sector of the market, as a proxy for what the stock would have done during the time period. For example, if a relatively large buy order is worked over an hour during which time the stock price rises 50 bps while the relevant sector index rises only 20 bps, the estimate of the impact of the execution would be 30 bps. The market impact would be the same if the stock price remained flat during the time period while the relevant sector index fell by 30 bps. In both cases, the estimation is that, were it not for the presence of the buyer, the stock would have been 30 bps lower at the end of the time period than it was.

Another means of determining the degree of market impact of a trade is to compare the total number of shares traded during the time period the order was executed and compute the percentage of the traded volume the order comprised. For example, if an order to buy 50,000 shares is executed over an hour in a highly liquid stock that trades two million shares in that time period, it is likely that the 50,000-share order had little or no market impact given that it was only 2.5 percent of the traded volume in the time period. However, if the same 50,000 shares were executed during a time period in which only 100,000 shares traded, the executed order would represent 50 percent of the traded volume and would likely have had significantly more impact.

To estimate the likely impact of a planned stock trade, the shares to be executed are compared to the *average daily volume* (ADV) in the stock, which measures the average number of shares of the stock that have traded each day over a given number of trading sessions. For example, the 30-day ADV would measure the average number of shares traded during the last six weeks of trading. While ADV can be calculated over any number of sessions it is common to use calculation based on the 20- or 30-day average as this will generally give the best estimate of current conditions as well as capturing seasonal effects. Assuming the trading volume in the session is similar to recent levels, an order that is a small percentage of the 30d ADV will likely be able to be executed quite quickly. An order of greater than 25 or 30 percent of ADV will likely have some amount of impact even if it is executed over the entire session.[7] Orders for very large percentages of ADV (i.e., >100%) can certainly be executed but will need special attention and can have more significant impact unless an investor interested in taking the other side of the trade can be found.

Given the client's instructions, it is the trader's responsibility to determine the appropriate balance between trading aggressively to complete the order quickly, which will imply greater market impact but less market risk, and working the order over a longer period of time to reduce impact but exposing the client to adverse market movements. The trader must also understand the characteristics of the stock in question to determine the best method of executing the shares with the lowest impact. Two stocks may be similarly liquid but trade very differently. In some very liquid stocks, many small orders trade with very high frequency but the bid and offer size showing in the market remain quite small. In this type of stock, even an order that is a small percentage of ADV can have significant impact if the entire size is shown in the market because it stands out from the crowd and advertises the presence of a buyer or seller of larger size than what is typically shown. Alternatively, in a relatively low-priced stock very large size may be shown on the inside quote, both because a larger number of shares of a low-priced stock is necessary to achieve the same notional value, and because the minimum price increment (the tick size) of \$0.01 represents a significantly larger percentage move in the price.

For example, a broker working an order to purchase \$1 million of a \$100 stock only needs to execute a total of 10,000 shares and may do so by placing many small orders at multiple limits in order to achieve an execution price that is within, say, 20 bps of where the stock was when received. The same order in a \$5 stock requires that 200,000 shares be traded, and due to the low price of the stock, a single tick represents a 20 bps move. The lower price stock is likely to show a much larger bid and offer size and the broker will need to decide whether to cross the bid-offer spread and pay the 20 bps to complete the order, or place the 200,000 at the back of the queue on the bid side and take the market risk that the stock price moves up and the order remains unexecuted. If both the bid and offer move up by \$0.01 then the new offer side will be 40 bps away.

While a cash trader's primary responsibilities are to execute trades, price principal orders, and work out of risk positions, equity sales and trading is a client service business and traders must balance the short-term requirement to protect firm capital by pricing risk appropriately with the long-term need to ensure that clients are happy with the service they receive and keep giving business to the firm. While different roles within the organization may be more focused on the internal risk management and pricing issues, every employee contributes to the commercial success of the business.

This requirement to focus on client service manifests itself in many ways. For example, when pricing a risk trade, many times the trader will know the "right" price to quote, given the liquidity of the stock and the market conditions, but offer the client something much more aggressive to ensure he feels well treated. Particularly in the case of the larger, more important clients of the firm, it is often necessary to knowingly take a loss on a particular trade in order to preserve or potentially strengthen the client relationship.

Traders must also be aware of how their actions affect clients and, whenever possible, advise the sales-traders of opportunities in which their clients might have an interest to participate. While essential to the client business, this cooperation between traders and sales-traders is not always easy. For example, if the trader has a large sell order, sales-traders will expect to be given the opportunity to reflect that information to other clients who may have an interest in buying stock before the trader executes. While pairing off with another client is the optimal situation for the trader as well, in giving the sales-traders the time to "shop the order" to get to the other side, he deliberately holds back on executing and in doing so takes on market risk that the stock price moves lower without his participating. While individual situations can cause friction and encourage the stereotype of traders and sales-traders at each others' throats, in practice, it is extremely important for traders and sales-traders to work together amicably. The success of the business depends on striking the proper balance between the conflicting goals of maintaining and strengthening the client relationship and running a profitable business within appropriate risk limits.

COMMUNICATION

In the fast-paced world of a trading floor, clear communication and efficiency are essential. As a result, certain linguistic standards have evolved to which all trading floor personnel must adhere to avoid confusion. Provided here is a list of some of the most commonly used expressions along with translations and examples. In all cases, we reference the following screen quote in stock XYZ.

Ticker	Last	Last Size	Bid-Ask	Bid-Ask Size
XYZ	25.09	12	25.08 / 25.12	45 × 41

Bid for/Offer at: The prepositions *for* and *at* are inextricably linked with the buy and sell side of the market, respectively. Whether communicating an order to buy, or reflecting a risk bid to a client, the language is always the same: you *"Bid $X for Y shares."* Similarly, with a sell order or risk offer: you *"Offer Y shares at $X."* While other verbs are sometimes used besides "bid" or "offer," or sometimes omitted altogether, the prepositions remain constant. A few examples will illustrate this. (*Note:* Each bullet-point is an independent comment or dialog.)

- *Trader:* "I'll bid you $25.10 for 35,000 shares."
- *Sales-trader:* "Can you offer me 10,000 XYZ at $25.12?"
- *Sales-trader:* "Where can I buy 15,000 XYZ?"
  Trader: "At $25.12."
- *Sales-trader:* "In XYZ—can I pay $25.12 for 25,000?"

Make a market for X shares: When "making a market," the sales-trader (or client) is requesting an indication of the price at which he could buy or sell X shares. Where the number of shares is not specified the trader may ask for clarification or simply choose a number he considers commercial. If the bid and offer sizes are the same, this is indicated by saying *"up."* Another way of requesting a market is to ask the trader "where he is" for a given size.

- *Sales-trader:* "Can I get a market in 100,000 XYZ?"
  Trader: "$25.07 at 14." (Understood to mean $25.14.)
- *Sales-trader:* "Can you show me a market in 50,000 XYZ?"
  Trader: "The touch" (i.e., the screen bid and offer, in this case $25.08 at $25.12).
- *Sales-trader:* "Where are you in XYZ?"
  Trader: "$25.07 at 14; 100,000 up."

Decimal quoting: Particularly where both trader and sales-trader (or client) are looking at the screen quote in a stock, it is usually not necessary to specify the integer value when quoting a stock price, and only the decimal is used. Where it requires specification, the integer value is often referred to as the *"big figure."* Alternatively, *the figure* is used to refer to the nearest whole integer value (since there is nothing after the decimal place to quote).

- *Sales-trader:* "Where can I buy 50,000 XYZ?"
  Trader: "At 14."
- *Sales-trader:* "What's the big figure?"
  Trader: "25—I'll sell you 50 at $25.14."
- "I'm a figure bid for 250,000 XYZ." (In this case, a "figure" bid would imply a bid price of $25.00.)

Hit and lift: A bid is always *"hit"* and an offer is always *"lifted."* If a client has just "hit" the trader, the trader is now long. If the trader has just been lifted, he is short.

A senior prop trader with whom I worked some years ago described himself as a "hit 'em and lift 'em kinda guy." That is to say, rather than working an order to try to get a price that was a few cents better on the execution, he preferred to simply get the trade done quickly (hit bids and lift offers) and then move on to the next thing. An analogous expression is the trader admonition "Don't be a dick for a tick" which is a reminder to traders to keep perspective. In general, traders tend to be extremely focused on the minute price fluctuations intraday and, particularly with proprietary trades, want to see the market "come to them" rather than just lifting offers or hitting bids. However, an order submitted at a limit runs the risk of not being executed. Traders too often make the right call on a movement in a stock and then end up not participating in that movement because they tried to be a bit too clever and refused to cross the bid-offer spread to get the trade done. The excessive focus on the value of one "tick" means they have missed out on an opportunity to capture a big move.

Mine, yours, sold, done: When a broker is asked to quote a market, various expressions are used to indicate that the client wishes to trade at the indicated price. Where the broker has communicated a two-way price, the response must indicate not only that the client wants to trade, but whether the client has bought or sold at the indicated price. Assuming the trader is asked to make a market in 100,000 shares of XYZ and quotes a price of "$25.05 bid, at $25.15," the sales-trader, speaking from the perspective of the client, might respond with any of the following:

Client Buys/Broker Sells 100,000 Shares at $25.15

- "I buy 'em."
- "Mine." (From the client's perspective, the shares are now "his"—bought from the broker.)
- "I'll lift you."

Client Sells/Broker Buys 100,000 shares paying $25.05

- "Sold."
- "Yours." (From the client's perspective, the shares are now "yours"—sold to the broker.)
- "I'll hit you."

If the broker has quoted a one-sided market, the sales-trader needs only to say *"Done"* to indicate that the client wishes to deal at the quoted price for the indicated size.

Subject: The trader will announce that a price has become *"subject"* if the client takes too long to decide whether to trade. A price being subject indicates that the broker reserves the right to not trade at the price indicated to the client. If the broker wants to make clear that the previously quoted price is no longer valid he can simply say he's *"off"* the price and if the client wishes to trade, he must re-quote.

- "$25.10 bid for 100,000 XYZ." <5 seconds pass> "That's subject." <The stock now drops to $25.02 offer.> "I'm off that. Figure bid for 100."

Choice price/Locked market: When a broker quotes a *choice* price, he indicates a single price at which he is willing to buy or sell. This is also called a *locked* market and is the most aggressive price a trader can show—he makes no bid-offer spread for taking the risk and relies entirely on the commission to cover any losses on the trade-out of the position.

- *Sales-trader:* "Where are you in XYZ in 100?"
  Trader: "$25.10 lock on 100." (assumed 100,000)

An axe: When a broker is in a position to provide superior price, liquidity, or both in a particular trade, as compared with what would likely be available from another broker, he is said to "*have an axe*" or to "*be axed*" in the name. This is frequently the result of the broker having taken on a position as part of a risk trade.

- *Trader:* "I'm axed to sell XYZ—I can offer 250,000 mid-market."

Cans: If a sales-trader is working an order in a particular stock with the trader and giving him multiple orders, it must be made clear whether the new orders are in addition to existing orders or replace them. For example, if the sales-trader has instructed the trader to bid $25.05 for 10,000 XYZ and then says "Bid 10 cents for 10,000," he should specify whether this order cancels the existing $25.05 bid he is already working or if it should be submitted in addition to that (i.e., pay $25.10 for 10,000 *and* keep bidding $25.10 for another 10,000). This would usually be said either as "*10 cents cans the nickel bid,*" which means to move the $25.05 bid up to 25.10 and continue to work a total of 10,000 shares, or "*$25.10 bid for 10,000, no can,*" which means that the existing order is still in effect and the trader should put another 10,000 share bid into the market with a $25.10 top.

As a final observation about communication, it should be observed that, while *instant messaging* (IM) applications have greatly increased the ability of traders to quickly communicate with large numbers of clients, live markets are traded on the phone. IM chats lack the immediacy and clarity of a real-time phone conversation and introduce too many possible additional sources of error and miscommunication (typos, overlooked messages, computer hanging). Where a trader has quoted a live price, the latency associated with anything other than a live phone conversation is too great: a market sent via IM is almost by definition, subject.

PURCHASING A STOCK IN A FOREIGN CURRENCY

When buying and selling securities denominated in a currency other than their home currency, investors assume additional risk related to exchange rate movements that, depending on how the purchase or sale is financed, can be relatively small or quite significant. Surprisingly, despite their central role in international investing, the currency considerations of a foreign security purchase are widely misunderstood.

The two ways to pay for a stock denominated in a foreign currency are either by borrowing the foreign currency or by purchasing it. The exposure to exchange rate fluctuations in the two scenarios is very different and is best be demonstrated through a concrete example.

Funding in the Foreign Currency

Let us assume a U.S. dollar (USD)–based investor borrows 1 million euros (EUR) and uses them to purchase 10,000 shares of XYZ for a price of 100 EUR per share. Assuming that there are no other positions in the account, the investor's holdings are summarized in the table that follows. There are two positions: a long equity position and a short currency position, each worth 1 million EUR. The initial exchange rate is assumed to be 1.5 USD/EUR.[8]

Asset	Position	EUR Price	EUR Value	USD/EUR	USD Value
XYZ	10,000	100.00	1,000,000	1.50	1,500,000
EUR	−1,000,000	1.00	−1,000,000	1.50	−1,500,000

We will now consider what happens when the stock price moves, when the exchange rate moves, and when both of them move. We begin by assuming that the stock price moves from 100 to 110 EUR per share. Since the client is holding a long position of 10,000 shares, he earns a profit of 10,000 shares × 10 EUR/share = 100,000 EUR, which, at current FX rates, is equal to $150,000. The movement in the equity price does not affect the short currency position. Absent any movement in the exchange rate, the USD value of the position has experienced exactly the 10 percent return of the underlying equity.

Asset	Position	EUR Price	EUR Value	USD/EUR	USD Value
XYZ	10,000	110.00	1,100,000	1.50	1,650,000
EUR	−1,000,000	1.00	−1,000,000	1.50	−1,500,000
		EUR P&L =	100,000	USD P&L =	150,000

In the case where the stock price remains constant at 100 EUR but the EUR weakens against the USD, dropping from 1.5 USD/EUR to 1.4

USD/EUR (it takes fewer USD to buy a EUR). The currency move impacts the USD value of the long stock position, causing it to drop by $100,000 despite the fact that the stock price has not moved from its initial value of 100 EUR. However, the USD value of the short currency position of 1 million EUR has also decreased by an equivalent amount (the borrowed EUR that must be returned are now worth less in USD terms than they were when borrowed). The currency move impacts the long and short sides equally, resulting in no net gain or loss.

Asset	Position	EUR Price	EUR Value	USD/EUR	USD Value
XYZ	10,000	100.00	1,000,000	1.40	1,400,000
EUR	−1,000,000	1.00	−1,000,000	1.40	−1,400,000
		EUR P&L =	0	USD P&L =	0

Let us now examine the impact of a combination of a stock price appreciation from 100 EUR to 110 EUR and a simultaneous weakening of the EUR from 1.5 USD/EUR to 1.4 USD/EUR. In this case, the weakening of the EUR impacts the long and short positions equally on a percentage basis, but because the long equity position has generated a profit, the long and short positions are no longer the same size and therefore the equal percentage moves do not result in equal and offsetting profits or losses. The investor has earned a profit of 100,000 EUR and, until the position is closed out and these euros converted back to USD, he will have currency exposure on that profit. In this case, the weakening of the currency has reduced the USD profit from the rally in the stock price from $150,000 to $140,000. (A 9.4 percent return in USD instead of 10 percent.)

Asset	Position	EUR Price	EUR Value	USD/EUR	USD Value
XYZ	10,000	110.00	1,100,000	1.40	1,540,000
EUR	−1,000,000	1.00	−1,000,000	1.40	−1,400,000
		EUR P&L =	100,000	USD P&L =	140,000

An easy way to visualize this is to think of the investor as holding a long position in a combined equity-and-currency asset (the foreign stock) and a short position in a pure currency asset. The investor has complete equity exposure but the long currency exposure is offset by the short currency exposure in the amount of the initial purchase price of the stock. The only currency exposure on the position arises when the long and short notional values differ—that is, when there is a profit or loss on the equity: a profit on the foreign equity position produces a long position in the EUR while a loss on the equity leaves him short the EUR.

Funding in the Home Currency

The other alternative is for the client to borrow USD and use these USD to purchase EUR, which can then be used to pay for the long stock position. In this case, the client will have a long position in the equity but no offsetting short position in the EUR. The positions in the investor's account are then:

Asset	Position	EUR Price	EUR Value	USD/EUR	USD Value
XYZ	10,000	100.00	1,000,000	1.50	1,500,000
USD	−1,500,000				−1,500,000

The difference is that to a USD investor the value in USD of a USD position is constant and will not be affected by movements in either the currency or stock prices. If we now consider the same three cases—an equity move, a currency move and a combined equity and currency move, the results are very different from what we saw in the previous section in those cases where the currency moves because the offset that was previously provided by the short currency position is no longer there.

In the case of an equity move with no currency movement, the result is the same. This is hardly surprising—if the exchange rate does not move then it does not really matter that the trade was in a foreign currency. The investor makes a profit of 100,000 EUR that, at current rates, is worth $150,000.

Asset	Position	EUR Price	EUR Value	USD/EUR	USD Value
XYZ	10,000	110.00	1,100,000	1.50	1,650,000
USD	−1,500,000				−1,500,000
		EUR P&L =	100,000	USD P&L =	150,000

The difference between funding in the local currency, and funding in the home currency, is clearest in the case where the stock price is constant and the currency weakens from 1.5 USD/EUR to 1.4 USD/EUR. If the position is funded in the local currency, as shown in the previous example, there is no exposure to the movement in the currency. By funding in the home currency, the investor takes on currency exposure on the entire notional value of the position which, in the case of a weakening of the foreign currency, results in a $100,000 loss.

Asset	Position	EUR Price	EUR Value	USD/EUR	USD Value
XYZ	10,000	100.00	1,000,000	1.40	1,400,000
USD	−1,500,000				−1,500,000
		EUR P&L =	0	USD P&L =	−100,000

In the third case, the combination of a favorable equity movement and an adverse currency movement, what was previously a small loss due to currency exposure on the profit on the trade is now a significant offset of the equity profit with a currency loss, resulting in a net profit of $40,000, versus the previous gain of $140,000.

Asset	Position	EUR Price	EUR Value	USD/EUR	USD Value
XYZ	10,000	110.00	1,100,000	1.40	1,540,000
USD	−1,500,000				−1,500,000
		EUR P&L =	100,000	USD P&L =	40,000

There is not a "correct" answer to whether positions should be funded in the local currency or the home currency of the investor. In the previous example, the weakening euro produced a loss for the USD-based investor, but it could just as easily have been a gain. The key point to understand is that by funding in the local currency of the stock, the investor limits his exchange rate exposure to the profit or loss on the trade, while by funding in his home currency he is expressing a double-barreled bet on both the equity performance and the exchange rate. An easy way to remember this is that, when funding in the home currency, the first thing the investor did was buy EUR to pay for the stock—the investor is now long EUR for the full notional amount of the trade.

Currencies

For reference, Exhibit 3.3 contains a list of some of the most actively traded currencies. All currencies globally are quoted against the USD using a three letter symbol. The majority of foreign currencies are quoted as the number of foreign currency units per USD (e.g., 110 JPY per USD). However, a few

Americas		Europe, Africa and Middle East		Asia	
USD	U.S. dollar	EUR*	Euro	JPY	Japanese yen
CAN	Canadian dollar	GBP*	British pound	AUD*	Australian dollar
MXN	Mexican peso	CHF	Swiss franc	CNY	Chinese renminbi
BRL	Brazilian real	SEK	Swedish krona	HKD	Hong Kong dollar
ARS	Argentine peso	NOK	Norwegian krone	KRW	South Korean won
Middle East and Africa		DKK	Danish krone	INR	Indian rupee
AED	UAE dirham	ISK	Icelandic krona	SGD	Singapore dollar
QAR	Qatari riyals	RUB	Russian rouble	TWD	Taiwan dollar
KWD	Kuwaiti dinar	PLN	Polish zloty	NZD	New Zealand dollar
EGP	Egyptian pound	CZN	Czech koruna	THB	Thai baht
ZAR	South African rand	TRY	Turkish lira	MYR	Malaysian ringgit

EXHIBIT 3.3 Global Currencies

Note: Currencies indicated with an ∗ are quoted in units of USD/Foreign.

of the most important currency rates—euros, British pounds, and Australian dollars—are quoted as the number of USD per foreign currency unit (i.e., 1.55 USD per EUR).

ADRs and Dual-Listed Securities

Investors are naturally inclined toward trading in their home currency and on their domestic exchange—it is easier, more familiar, and usually less expensive, and the market is open during hours when they are awake. However, there are significant benefits to international diversification in an investment portfolio and many foreign companies provide attractive investment opportunities. For investors in the United States, *American depositary receipts* (ADRs) provide an attractive solution to this problem: they are U.S.-listed securities that trade in U.S. dollars on a U.S. exchange but represent claims on shares of foreign stocks.

The structure of an ADR is simple: a depositary bank purchases shares of a foreign stock and then issues receipts (claims of ownership) against those shares, which are then listed. The holder of an ADR has the option of exercising this claim and delivering ADRs to the depositary bank and receiving in return the equivalent number of foreign securities, subject to a nominal ADR conversion fee. The ADR issuance process is open ended—new ADRs can be created almost without limit to meet the demands of investors (subject only to the availability of local shares). If the foreign security has a very low price in USD terms, ADRs will sometimes be constructed such that one ADR represents a claim on several shares of the foreign security.

ADRs are an extremely popular way to invest in foreign equities without ever leaving the comfort of the U.S. markets and exchanges. In many cases, because of the enormous liquidity of the U.S. markets, the ADR actually has superior liquidity to the local share, particularly where trading in the local markets is hampered by currency restrictions or, as is the case for ADRs on Asian stocks, occurs at inconvenient hours for U.S. investors. The easy convertibility between ADRs and local shares guarantees that ADRs rarely trade at a significant premium or discount to the local shares because traders with the ability to trade both ADRs and local shares can easily trade one against the other. Because ADRs provide easy access to foreign markets for U.S. investors, they frequently trade at a slight premium to the *parity value* implied by the local share price and FX rate, even after factoring in the frictional costs of the execution costs in both regions, bid-offer in the FX and ADR conversion fees. In the cases where there is a significant gap in the exchange hours of the local share and the ADR, the arbitrage can be more difficult to capture without a significant amount of market risk and the ADR price can deviate more significantly from its parity value.

In terms of the exposure to the exchange rate, an ADR is equivalent to purchasing the foreign security directly and funding in USD. An investor can pay USD to buy an ADR and then convert the ADR into local shares, which leaves him long the foreign stock and short USD.

An alternative to issuing an ADR is to actually list the local security on a U.S. exchange. This is particularly popular with many Canadian stocks that trade on both the Toronto Stock Exchange, in CAD, and the NYSE or NASDAQ, in USD. The important feature of a dually listed security is that it is *fungible* which means that the only difference between the local shares and the U.S. listing is the currency of settlement; a share purchased on Toronto can be sold in New York with no additional processing fees. As a consequence, the arbitrage opportunity, should the relative prices of the two listings get out of line with the exchange rate, is even easier to capture than with an ADR, and therefore appears less frequently (particularly since Canada and the United States have the same trading hours.) In stock where there is a significant level of interest in a Canadian company by U.S. investors, the U.S. listing can actually have superior liquidity to the Canadian listing.

SUMMARY

An understanding of the structure and functioning of the markets for trading in individual stocks is the most basic part of the knowledge set required of a trader or salesperson working in the equities or equity derivatives business. Stocks in publicly listed companies are traded on an exchange, which serves not only to centralize, organize, and match up orders to buy and sell individual stocks, but also acts as the counterparty to all orders, which greatly facilitates the booking and clearing of trades. In fulfilling this role, stock exchanges can be structured according to several models, depending on the number of market makers (traders obligated to provide continuous liquidity) that exist in each name.

Orders submitted to the exchange are classified as one of three broad types:

1. *Agency:* The broker acts purely on the customer's behalf and all fills are passed directly to the client (often via a wash account).
2. *Principal:* The order is executed for an account belong to the broker but in response to a client order that has already occurred (a risk bid or offer) or will occur (guaranteed VWAP). Very large principal trades are called *blocks*.
3. *Proprietary:* A trade executed for the broker's own account based on a view in the underlying stock and not in relation to any client inquiry.

The instructions given by the client to direct the broker's actions in executing the trade must be clear enough to ensure that the trader acts according to the client's wishes, but general enough to allow the broker to react to the ever-changing conditions of the market. The result is a variety of standardized terminology, some of which have precise definitions (MOC, MOO, VWAP), and others that are more qualitative ("would," "work," "in line"), which are used to quickly communicate trading instructions with as little ambiguity as possible. There are also a number of very specific linguistic conventions (e.g., "bid for" and "offer at") to which traders and salespeople adhere strictly when communicating orders with each other.

The investment process involves the interaction of three different groups within the equity sales and trading division. Salespeople (generalist and specialist) focus on delivering the best ideas of the firm to its clients and assisting in the development of the investment thesis. Sales-traders manage the trade execution process and act as the primary point of contact for the client dealer. Traders are the ones ultimately responsible for executing orders, pricing principal trades, and managing the associated risk.

When a stock is denominated in a currency other than the home currency of the investor, there is an additional risk from holding the position related to exchange rate movements. The magnitude of this risk depends on whether the investor borrows or buys the foreign currency needed to purchase the shares.

CHAPTER 4

Equity Indices

INTRODUCTION

"How'd the market do today?" is quite possibly the most commonly asked finance question in the world. For those who work in the financial markets and are expected to have a ready answer to this question at all times, it can be a frustrating one given its ambiguity. An emerging market bonds trader will have a very different definition of "the market" than a floor broker on the New York Mercantile Exchange in the crude oil futures pit. What is more, it is unlikely that the person asking is interested in what either of these people have to say about their markets because "How did the market do today?" is usually intended as a shorthand way of asking "Give me a five-second summary of how the U.S. equity market performed today." Equity indices give us the best way of answering this question.

An equity index is a weighted average of a selected group of stocks' prices, which is designed to summarize the performance of all or part of the equity market. Equity indices are useful because they synthesize the massive amounts of stock price data in the marketplace into more readily understandable aggregates. Most of us are familiar with several, particularly the Dow Jones Industrial Average (DJIA), which, despite its flaws, has a special place in the hearts of U.S. retail investors due to its longevity, having been calculated continuously, in various forms, since 1896.

Strangely, many people have difficulty understanding what an index really is and how one works. In the most general terms, an index is nothing more than a number calculated by applying a mathematical formula to the prices of a group of stocks. While in practice virtually all indices are simple weighted averages, any mathematical formula that results in a number could be considered an *index level* and the percentage change in that level from one time to another constitutes the return on the index. However, only those stock selection criteria and index calculation methodologies with some logical basis and whose returns can be replicated by investors will receive interest.

The question is then, what makes a good index? For an index to be of interest it must accomplish several objectives.

- It must provide some useful information about the market that is not already available from existing indices.
- It must use logical stock selection criteria and an intuitive weighting scheme such that the index level has some significance.
- If the goal of the index is to promote trading in related products it must be replicable. Investors must be able to reproduce the returns of the index almost perfectly through buying and selling of existing products in the market. (As we will see, this issue of replicability of returns is extremely important and pervades many areas of finance.)

Developing and maintaining an index is a significant undertaking. Apart from the creation of a novel stock selection and/or weighting methodology and the continuous calculation and dissemination of the index level, the index provider must keep the index updated. This is done through regular (usually quarterly) rebalances in which the selection methodology is reapplied based on current market conditions and the constituent stocks and weightings are updated accordingly. In addition, the index provider must monitor for corporate actions in any of the component stocks and update the weightings to reflect them. All adjustments must be publicly announced in advance of the change taking effect so that investors attempting to replicate the index return have sufficient notice to appropriately adjust their holdings.

Given the considerable work involved, it is clear that there must be a significant benefit to creating and maintaining an index. While some sell-side institutions develop indices as a part of their research product, and are compensated through commission revenue from clients in related derivatives, in most cases the reward for creating an index comes through licensing fees. An index that performs well will generate investor interest in products that provide exposure to its returns. Investment companies that wish to offer funds tracking the index or broker-dealers that want to use the index as the basis for derivative products must pay a licensing fee to the index provider for permission to reference the name of the index in their products.

INDEX CONSTRUCTION

Composition

Putting the specific stock selection methodologies and weighting schemes aside for the moment, we can break down the universe of equity indices into three broad categories based on their goals:

1. *Broad market:* Broad market indices provide a picture of equity market activity across all industries. They are usually structured in such a way that the weighting of each market sector (pharmaceuticals, technology, finance, oil, and so forth) are represented in proportion to their weight in the composition of the economy as a whole. These indices can be divided into two categories:

   ■ *Total market:* As the name suggests, total market indices give the broadest possible picture of market activity by measuring the performance of all, or nearly all, publicly listed companies. While this may be interesting conceptually, in practice, total market indices are not very popular because they are very hard to replicate. A fund or broker looking to reproduce the index returns would need to purchase shares in all of the constituent stocks, many of which are small and illiquid. Additionally, because these indices generally utilize a weighting scheme in which a stock's weight in the index is based on the size of the company (more on weighting schemes shortly), the contribution to the index performance of the hundreds of tiny companies is minimal.

   ■ *Capitalization range:* To create a more tradable alternative to a total market index without losing the breadth of representation, we can limit our stock universe to only the largest companies in each market sector. This dramatically reduces the number of stocks in the index without a significant loss of informational content given that, in a total market index, these small stocks have a very small weight and make only a minimal contribution to the index performance. Our measurement of the size of a company is based on its market capitalization ("*market cap*"), which we defined in Chapter 2 as the total value of all of its outstanding shares (Market cap = Total shares outstanding × Market price). Based on their market capitalization, stocks can be classified as either large cap (market cap greater than $5 billion), mid cap (between $2 billion and $5 billion), or small cap (less than $2 billion)—though these cutoff points are not rigidly defined. Because of their greater informational content, the most popular broad index benchmarks globally are large cap indices. There also exist broad market indices that limit their constituents to the mid cap and small cap ranges, allowing investors to monitor the relative performance of smaller companies.

2. *Sector indices:* These are smaller indices, usually containing between 15 and 75 members, which restrict the universe of potential constituent stocks to those of companies active in a particular line of business (e.g., pharmaceuticals, utilities, oil companies). Sector indices may be defined as the subset of a larger, well-known index (e.g., all the financial stocks in the S&P 500) or constructed independently.

3. *Concept-based:* This is an extremely broad category and includes indices constructed based on many different selection criteria. Examples include:

   ▪ *Style:* Stock selection and weighting based on growth and value characteristics

   ▪ *Economic sensitivity:* Indices of cyclical stocks (those that are significantly exposed to movements in the economic cycle) and defensive stocks (those which are less sensitive to economic cycles and therefore tend to perform well in an economic downturn).

   ▪ *Fundamental factors:* Stocks with particularly high or low scores based on various fundamental metrics such as dividend yield or price-to-earnings ratio.

   ▪ *Thematic:* Many recently-created indices fall into this category and consist of stocks chosen based on selection criteria which do not line up cleanly with traditional sector, market cap, or style classifications. Examples include indices of companies with exposure to increased demand for clean energy and biofuels ("green" indices), exposure to emerging market growth, or Shariah-compliant businesses.

All of these types of indices can be constructed on a single-country, regional, or global basis. As global markets have become progressively more interconnected, the differentiation of companies according to the country where they are incorporated has become less significant, making global benchmark indices progressively more interesting to investors. In certain industries, such as steel, oil, and mining, the operations of the major companies are so globally diversified that the country of domicile has become all but irrelevant.

Selection Criteria

The specific selection criteria for inclusion in an index can be extremely simple or quite complicated. In general, the creators of the index want to produce a high quality product that will differentiate itself from other indices and hopefully attract customer interest and subsequent licensing revenues. In addition to the specific characteristics that the index is intended to isolate (e.g., stocks from a certain sector or related to a particular theme) criteria for inclusion also frequently include specifications of a minimum (and sometimes maximum) market capitalization, average daily trading volume, or a minimum percentage of shares in *free float*. (The free float measures the number of shares available for purchase by investors and not tied up in corporate cross-holdings, government stakes, treasury stock, etc.).[1] Some index providers seek to construct a higher quality index through the application of additional selection criteria, which they believe will isolate higher quality companies (e.g., stocks must have positive earnings). Others take the view that the market has already decided which companies are higher quality through the stock price and therefore keep selection criteria to a minimum to avoid introducing additional, unwanted biases.

Weighting Schemes

An equity index can be thought of as a measure of the value of a portfolio of stock holdings. While the selection criteria can be extremely diverse, the weighting schemes—the methodology used to determine the number of shares of each constituent stock to put in our hypothetical portfolio—generally fall into one of four categories:

- *Market capitalization: Market-cap-weighted* indices include a number of shares per constituent stock equal to the total outstanding shares of the company. As a result, the value of the total portfolio is a measure of the total market capitalization of all the companies in the index, and the percentage weight of each stock is determined by its fractional contribution to that total. For broad market or sector indices, which are intended to measure the performance of a particular part of the economy, this is the most common, and most intuitive, methodology because the contribution of each stock to the index performance mirrors that company's significance in the specific industry or the market as a whole. Often, the number of shares included in the index weighting is not the total shares outstanding but the free float shares, which give a more accurate picture of the size of the company that is actually available to investors.

  It is sometimes the case with market-cap-weighted indices that one or two individual stocks make up an unacceptably large fraction of the total weight of the index. The existence of one very large constituent can result in an index which, while providing an accurate measurement of the relative significance of the constituent stocks in that industry, becomes so sensitive to the idiosyncratic risks of the single stock that it is no longer an attractive investment tool. In these situations it is common to use a *modified market capitalization weighting* in which the stocks are weighted based on their market cap but with a limit on the percentage of the total index that can be concentrated in a single constituent. Where a given stock exceeds this maximum, its share quantity is reduced to decrease its contribution to the index and at the same time, increase the contribution of each of the other stocks on a pro rata basis.

- *Price:* A *price-weighted* index is calculated based on an equal number of shares of each constituent stock. The percentage weight of each stock, and therefore its contribution to the movement of the index, is a direct function of the stock price. This is a rather crude methodology and few new indices are constructed in this manner. One particularly well-known example of a price-weighted index is the DJIA. There are two specific drawbacks of a price-weighting:

  - *The absolute price of the stock has no relevance to the importance of a company:* Large companies with many shares can have low prices and small companies with few shares can have high prices. Due to its high stock price, IBM is the largest constituent of the DJIA with a weight of 9.2 percent. While clearly an important contributor to the U.S. economy, it does not make sense that the weight of IBM is greater than the weights of General Motors, Citigroup, Pfizer, Intel, Home Depot and Microsoft *combined*,[2] particularly where Microsoft is the third-largest stock in the United States by market capitalization.

  - *Stock splits:* As discussed in Chapter 2, a stock split is a relatively meaningless exercise. New shares are issued for the sole purpose of reducing the stock price to a more "eye-pleasing" level for investors. There is no change in the company's underlying fundamentals. However, while a stock split has no economic significance, in a price-weighted index the stock's percentage weight would be dramatically changed. For example, in a two-for-one split, the stock price halves and so too does the weighting of the stock in the index. For funds replicating the index, the additional shares received in a split must be sold and the cash raised is then reinvested across all the constituent stocks.[3] As an extreme example, if IBM were to perform a 1-for-10 reverse split, causing the price to increase 10 times, it would then make up more than 50 percent of the weighting of the DJIA.

- *Equal-weighted:* An *equal-weighted* index (also referred to in the United States as a *dollar-weighted* index) assigns, on a specified start date, an equal percentage weight to each share (i.e., in a 20-stock index, each stock has a weight of 5 percent). This is done by assigning a share weight to each stock that is inversely proportional to its price. The name is a bit of a misnomer since, as soon as the stocks' prices begin to move the percentage weights of each name change—those that rally increase in weight while those that sell off decrease. The share weights of these indices are therefore re-calculated regularly (usually quarterly) and the index rebalanced to insure that the percentage weights do not get too far out of line.

As compared with a market-cap weighting, where the overweighting of larger capitalization stocks serves to underscore their greater significance in the particular sector of the economy, equal-dollar weighting is popular in thematic indices and other situations where constituent stocks are selected because of their sensitivity to a particular trend in the market but where there is no clear reason to overweight one stock versus another. A difficulty with equal-dollar weightings is they assign the same percentage weight to an easily tradable, large-cap stock and an illiquid small-cap name, which can make the index difficult to replicate for investors. An alternative is a *modified equal-dollar weighted* index where stocks are given one of several weights (e.g., 5, 10, or 15 percent) depending on their liquidity or other factors.

▪ *Other weighting*: While the majority of popular indices use either a market cap, price, or equal weighting, it is possible to weight an index based on almost any criteria. For example, in a thematic index of U.S. stocks with significant exposure to growth in China, we might weight the index according to the percentage of each company's total earnings derived from China, potentially with a secondary criteria based on the liquidity of the stock. This would have the effect of skewing the weight of the index toward those stocks with greatest exposure to the theme while still maintaining tradability.

WHAT AN INDEX DOESN'T TELL US

By aggregating large amounts of data into a single number, equity indices provide a convenient summary of market conditions. However, this reduction in complexity has its cost: A given change in the overall index level can be the product of innumerable changes in the constituent stocks whose internal trends and shifts can contain a great deal of valuable information that is lost in the aggregation. It is important to be cognizant of what an index level does and does not tell us, and specifically the biases inherent in a calculation of any average.

What can an investor conclude if the index level of a broad, large-cap index benchmark remains generally unchanged from one day to the next? One possibility is that the price of most stocks in the index stayed more or less the same. In statistical language, the dispersion of returns was low—in colloquial language, it was a boring day in the markets. Another possibility is that stocks were very active—some individual stocks rallying strongly and others selling off dramatically—but with the winners and losers roughly "balanced."[4] If there is a consistent theme that relates the members of the winning and losing groups then there is a lot of information in the movement *within* the index that is not visible from the surface. A major "market moving" announcement can actually have a negligible net impact on a broad index if its effect is not universally positive or negative but differs across the various types of companies in the index.

As an example, imagine the impact on a hypothetical broad market index of an announcement by the U.S. Department of Energy that it expects the long-term price of oil to be higher than it had previously estimated. This is very positive news for oil companies, which make up 25 percent of the index, and their stock prices rise an average of 3 percent. The higher oil price, however, is expected to act as a drag on consumer spending which is negative for the rest of the market and causes the other 75 percent of the index to sell off by 1 percent. The net impact on these movements on the index is zero—the oil stock rally exactly off-sets the rest of the market's sell-off. However, one would hardly say that nothing had happened. (This is another reason why many experienced market practitioners often dislike the general "How'd the market do?" question.)

Some important internal features of the market not visible from the change of a broad index level from one day's close until the next include:

- *Internal movements:* Shifts associated with certain classes of stocks based on other criteria (sector rotation, cyclical vs. defensive, commodity related, interest rate sensitivity, etc.).
- *Dispersion of returns:* How widely dispersed are the returns of individual stocks? Did most stocks move in the same direction or were returns highly scattered? How many stocks advanced versus how many declined?
- *Significant one-off events in large-weight stocks:* This is particularly a problem for indices with few constituents, such as the DJIA where a specific event in one stock can have a major impact on the index as a whole without being indicative of the performance of the market in general.
- *Intraday volatility:* An unchanged index level says that the market ended more or less where it started but tells us nothing about how it got there. Large intraday price swings can be very important to the traders (particularly options traders as we will see in Chapters 9 and 10) and have significant impact on the "feel" of the trading in the market as a whole but be lost in a close-to-close comparison of the index.

VALUATION AND CALCULATION

The easiest way to understand how an index works, and how the individual members contribute to the overall performance, is to actually compute one. Like most things, we learn best by doing. We will consider a hypothetical example of a four-stock, market-cap-weighted index, which we will define as being equal to 100 USD at an initial reference point in time (t_1). We will then compute the index level at a later time (t_2) based on the individual stock prices at that time. Exhibit 4.1 shows a snapshot of an Excel spreadsheet which has been built to calculate the index level. Since we cannot see the formulas, we will walk through the calculations.

- *Index data:* In the left-most section of the spreadsheet, labeled "INDEX DATA" we have, for each constituent stock, the total number of shares that will be used in the index definition. In this case, we are using a free-float market capitalization weighting and the *share weighting* of each component in the index is equal to the number of shares (in millions) of that company's stock that are currently in free float (e.g., there are 594.5 million shares of NTI).

  Observe that the definition of the index is not in terms of a specific percentage weight in each stock, but in terms of a specific number of shares of each constituent, called the *index shares*. The percentage weight will be a function of the number of index shares, and the market price of the stock. If we think of a market-cap-weighted index as measuring the total size of an industry or some part of the economy, then it is intuitive that the percentage weights fluctuate. If a company performs well it will grow and in so doing, take on a larger portion of the industry while a company that performs poorly will decrease in weight, eventually reaching zero if it were to go bankrupt.

- *Time_1:* The second section contains the individual share prices in U.S. dollars at time t_1 and the calculations of the initial index definition. In

INDEX DATA		TIME_1			TIME_2			T_1 vs T_2
Ticker	**Float Shs**	**Price_1**	**MktCap_1**	**%Wgt_1**	**Price_2**	**MktCap_2**	**%Wgt_2**	**Px Chg**
NTI	594.50	76.25	45,331	35.36%	79.70	47,382	36.20%	4.52%
SOF	1,032.34	35.64	36,793	28.70%	35.75	36,906	28.20%	0.31%
CSM	494.40	52.25	25,832	20.15%	53.35	26,376	20.15%	2.11%
MTT	317.51	63.70	20,225	15.78%	63.70	20,225	15.45%	0.00%
		Σ Mkt Cap_1		128,181.01	Σ Mkt Cap_2		130,889.43	
		Divisor		1,281.81	Divisor		1,281.81	
		Index_1		100.00	Index_2		102.11	
					Change (bps)		211	

EXHIBIT 4.1 Sample Index Level Calculation

the second column, we use the share quantities and prices to compute the (free float) market capitalizations of each of the individual stocks at that time. For example, the market capitalization of NTI is equal to $594.50 \times \$76.25 = \$45,331$.[5] Summing the values in the second column gives us the aggregate market cap of the entire index—the total value of all the companies—equal to $128,181.01. Given this, we then compute in the third column, the percentage weight of each stock in the index (based on the initial t_1 prices) as the percentage of the total market capitalization that it contributes. The percentage weight of NTI is therefore equal to $\$45,331 / \$128,181 = 35.36\%$.

We stated previously that we wanted our initial index level at time t_1 to be equal to 100 USD. We therefore define a *divisor* that will be used to scale the level of the index from the rather cumbersome value of 128,181.01 to our target index level of 100.00. This divisor, which in this case is equal to 1,281.81, is a constant and acts as a scaling factor, which allows us to put the index in more comfortable terms. To get our index level to the "comfortable" value of 100, we could simply divide the share quantities of each constituent stock by this amount and not utilize a divisor (similar to the way we divided all the share quantities by a million). However, as we will see later, when index constituents change, the divisor provides an easy way to adjust the overall index level in order to ensure continuity between the index level under the old and new constituent definitions. For now, it is just a constant that we use to make our lives easier.

■ *Time 2:* We have defined the constituent stocks in the index and, based on their initial prices and our initial index level of 100, computed a divisor and determined each stock's percentage weight. We can now look at calculating the index level based on the underlying stock prices at a future point in time t_2. The calculations are done in exactly the same way as before. As shown in the third section of Exhibit 4.1, the new stock prices are multiplied by the share quantities to derive the t_2 market capitalizations, which are then summed to produce a new aggregate market capitalization of the index. The percentage weights at t_2 are computed based on each stock's contribution to the new aggregate market capitalization. To compute the new index level we apply the same scaling factor—the divisor—to the new aggregate market capitalization. The percentage change in the index is then calculated as the change in the index level divided by the initial index level, resulting in a 2.11/100.00 = 2.11% (211 bps) increase in the index between t_1 and t_2. Observe that this same result would be derived by measuring the change in the total market capitalization 130,889.43 − 128,181.01 = 2,708.42 and dividing this by the t_1 aggregate market cap of 128,181.01. Applying the same multiplier to the market capitalization at both times has no effect on the percentage change in the index level.

- *Time_1 versus Time_2:* The last section of Exhibit 4.1 shows the percentage change in the prices of each of the individual constituent stocks between t_1 and t_2, computed in the same way as the percentage change in the index. If we look at the individual share performances, and compare this to the change in the percentage weight of each of the stocks, we see that the change in the percentage weight of each stock in the index between t_1 and t_2 depends on the relative performance of the individual stock versus the index as a whole. Stocks outperforming the index (NTI) increase in weight while those underperforming the index (SOF and MTT) decrease in weight. CSM's weight remains exactly the same because its return is the same return as that of the index (+211 bps). Notice that SOF decreases in weight from 28.7 percent to 28.2 percent despite the fact that the stock price increased by 31 bps—what matters is the relative performance and relative to the index SOF went down (i.e., didn't go up enough).[6]

Virtually every equity index is computed according to this simple methodology, with only small variations necessary for alternate weighting schemes. The three key facts to take away from the example are:

1. The weighting scheme of the index is determined by the number of index shares applied to each stock. The index shares determine the weighting that is applied to each stock's price and can have an economic meaning (like the free float shares used in our example) or be determined according to other factors (in a price weighted index they would all be equal to one).
2. The divisor is a scaling factor that is used to set the initial index level to an attractive level and to simplify the adjustment of the index shares for corporate actions and rebalances (more on this later).
3. The percentage weight gives the fraction of the total portfolio value invested in each stock and is constantly changing as the prices of the individual stocks move. Changes in the percentage weight of each stock are a function of the *relative* performance of the stock in question as compared with the index.

A calculation that is not included in the figure (but that the reader can easily check) is that the performance of the basket (+211 bps) can also be computed as the weighted average of the individual stock performances (from the last column) using the percentage weights of each stock from time t_1. ($2.11\% = 35.36\% \times 4.52\% + 28.70\% \times 0.31\% + \cdots$)

REPLICATING PORTFOLIO

A replicating portfolio is a basket of stocks whose returns match those of the index. It should not be surprising that the way to do this is to buy the constituent stocks of the index in quantities proportional to the index share weights used in its calculation.

Given the instruction to build a $20 million basket of our index from Exhibit 4.1, we need to determine the specific quantity of each stock that must be purchased such that (1) we invest the full $20 million and (2) the returns generated on the stock portfolio exactly reproduce those of the index. The calculation of the replicating portfolio, using the stock prices at time t_1 is shown in Exhibit 4.2.

The data in the first five columns of Exhibit 4.2 are identical to Exhibit 4.1. The calculation of the replicating basket is in the section below the words "Target Value."

To calculate the replicating basket, we multiply the target dollar amount of the basket by the percentage weight of each stock to get the notional amount to be invested in each security. For example, NTI carries a 35.36 percent weighting in the index, so we need to invest 35.36% * $20 million = $7,072,908 in NTI. Dividing this notional by the share price of the stock we get the required number of shares ($7,072,908 / $76.25 = 92,759 shares). As a double check of our work, we compute the market value of our replicating basket by taking the product of the share quantity and stock price in each of the constituents and summing them. The $34 slippage between the Actual Value and Target Value is due to rounding error on the share quantities (there are no fractional shares).

While in this case we have the index definition at hand, in general this is not the case. For most popular indices, however, this information can be downloaded from Bloomberg, either alphabetically, using the **MEMB** (*Member*) function, or in descending order by percentage weight using the **WGT** (*Weight*) function. (The **WGT** function can be used on an index

INDEX DATA   Target Value $20,000,000

Ticker	Float Shs	Price_1	MktCap_1	%Wgt_1	$ / Stock	Basket Shs
NTI	594.50	76.25	45,331	35.36%	$7,072,908	92,759
SOF	1,032.34	35.64	36,793	28.70%	$5,740,725	161,075
CSM	494.40	52.25	25,832	20.15%	$4,030,613	77,141
MTT	317.51	63.70	20,225	15.78%	$3,155,754	49,541

Σ Mkt Cap   128,181.01   Actual Value $19,999,966

EXHIBIT 4.2   Calculating a Replicating Index Basket

ticker, to get the index composition, or on an equity ticker, to get that stock's percentage weight in all of the indices of which it is a constituent.) Both these functions offer a convenient "Export to Excel" option that dumps the data into a spreadsheet. With this information we can calculate the market cap and percentage weights for any index in the same way we did in Exhibit 4.1.

A common error when calculating replicating baskets is to use stale price data. While the share quantities in the index definition are constant, the share quantities in a $20 million basket will depend on the current price of the constituent stocks. As the stock prices rise, and with it the index level, the number of shares of each stock in the replicating portfolio will decrease proportionally—you need fewer shares of higher priced stocks to get the same dollar notional. If the prices used to calculate the share quantities of the replicating basket are not kept current, the dollar value of the basket when executed can deviate substantially from the target dollar value. If the basket created in Exhibit 4.2 using t_1 prices is revalued using t_2 prices it is worth $20.4 million or 211 bps more, consistent with the change in the index. In practice, it is possible to create real-time data links from Bloomberg into an Excel spreadsheet such that, as each constituent stock's price changes, the number of shares in the replicating portfolio updates automatically.

Another common mistake when constructing a replicating portfolio is to forget that the percentage weights fluctuate with the prices of the individual stocks. When using the percentage weights to compute a replicating basket, as in Exhibit 4.2, it is important that the prices used to compute the number of shares of each stock in the replicating portfolio (based on the target notional investment in each stock) are the same as those used to derive the percentage weight of each component. If these are different, the share quantities in each constituent will be incorrect and the replicating portfolio will not exactly reproduce the index returns.

We can now introduce an alternate method for computing the replicating portfolio. If we play around with the index calculation a bit in Excel, we will eventually notice that the ratio of the number of shares of each stock in the $20 million replicating basket to the index shares in the second column is a constant, in this case equal to 156.03. This is precisely equal to $20 million divided by the sum of the market caps, $128,181.01. We can think of the index share weights as defining a single *unit of index*, worth $128,181.01 and all replicating portfolios will then be a multiple of this. (This is independent of the weighting scheme chosen.) Another way to see this is to create a $128,181.01 stock basket at t_1 and observe that the shares in the hedge basket are exactly the same as the index share weights. This is most obvious in a price-weighted basket in which the share weights are all equal to one and, as a result, any replicating basket will hold an equal number of shares of each stock.

INDEX DATA

Ticker	Float Shs	Price	MktCap	Basket Shs
NTI	594.50	76.25	45,331	92,759
SOF	1,032.34	35.64	36,793	161,075
CSM	494.40	52.25	25,832	77,141
MTT	317.51	63.70	20,225	49,541

Σ Mkt Cap = Value of 1 index unit   128,181.01
Target Basket Value   20,000,000
Number of Baskets   156.03

EXHIBIT 4.3 Calculating a Replicating Index Basket—
The Shortcut Method

This leads us to a quicker, but initially less intuitive, way to calculate a replicating portfolio. Given the value of one index unit (excluding the divisor)—in this case $128,181.01—we simply divide this amount into the target portfolio value of $20 million to get the desired number of units. The number of shares of each stock in the index definition is then multiplied by this number to create the replicating portfolio. This is shown in Exhibit 4.3.

TRADING AN INDEX PORTFOLIO

As we will see in later sections, there are a great number of derivative products whose values are based on the performance of an underlying equity index. There is not, however, a way to buy or sell an index—it is not a "thing" that trades. An index is a number on the screen, computed as the weighted average of a series of stock prices: when those prices change, the index changes. For a broker to "buy the index" to hedge a derivative that is based on it, he must purchase the entire replicating stock portfolio and then apply his realized execution prices to the defined index weights to compute an implied index level.[7] He will also need to update his portfolio holdings whenever there is a change in the constituents of the index, or their index share weightings.

The practical realities of trading a stock basket and computing an implied index price can be the source of a tremendous amount of confusion and contention between brokers and clients. It is a common misperception that the index level on the screen can be captured in the market in the same way as what can be done for a stock—you see the stock price on the screen and you buy the stock at that level, perhaps with a small bid/offer spread around it. This is not the case for indices. While in general, the implied index level achieved on a replicating stock portfolio will correspond closely to the index calculation on the screen, they are, in reality, quite distinct and can be surprisingly different.

Throughout the day, market data providers disseminate real-time calculations of the index level, based on the last traded price in each security, usually updated every 15 seconds. This is very different from a single stock for two reasons. First, in a stock, every trade is disseminated and can be seen on the graph of the stock price while for an index, large amounts of trading activity in the constituent stocks can be lost in the space between index calculations. The second point is that with a single stock, any move in the price on the screen indicates a buyer and seller matching off to complete a trade. If nothing trades, the graph doesn't update and nothing shows on the screen. An index level, on the other hand, is computed every 15 seconds whether there has been trading or not—every 15 seconds there will be a price. A *print* in a stock tells you where the stock is now—a print in the index only tells you where we last saw the stock.

For these reasons, changes in the index level are somewhat deceptive. In order for the index level to change, all that is required is that a single constituent trades at a different price from its last sale. This is frequently misinterpreted as indicating that the index "traded" there—that the whole index level could have been realized at that price level—and it is assumed that the broker had the opportunity to participate in that price. In reality, it is possible that almost none of the stocks actually traded. In multicurrency indices (described at the end of the chapter) where there are currency effects, it is possible for the index level to change based purely on currency movements with no equity trading whatsoever.

Buying the Basket above the High of the Day (Really, Your Broker *Is* Honest!)

For investors accustomed to trading stocks, a particularly common problem arises when trying to reconcile the implied level on a basket whose execution is spread over an extended period of time with the level of the index shown on the screen. Each index price that appears on the screen is based on a snapshot of the last traded prices in all securities at a particular instant. However, if an execution is spread over a period of time, not all of the stocks in the replicating basket are executed at the same time and the implied level is therefore based on a large number of noncoincident single stock prices. This can result in implied index levels that differ substantially from what appears on the screen.

A simple situation where this occurs is the execution of a market-on-open order in an index. Most indices begin publishing as soon as the market opens and, where a stock has not yet traded, the prior night's closing price is used in the index calculation. This is apparent from the fact that the first disseminated price of most indices, which is published as soon as the market opens, is frequently equal, or very close, to the prior night's closing index level, since no new trading data have yet been recorded in many of the constituent stocks. The true "opening price of the index"—by which we mean the index level computed from the opening prices of each of the index members—cannot be calculated until all constituent stocks have opened, which can easily take 10 or 15 minutes in an index containing a large number of stocks (particularly less liquid mid- and small caps).[8]

The example in Exhibit 4.4 illustrates clearly the problems this can cause. A customer wishes to purchase one unit of a derivative product which is based on a three-stock, price-weighted index, and he would like the broker to execute his hedge at the market open and use this opening index price to compute the execution price of the derivative. The broker correctly sends orders pre-open to the exchange to purchase one share each of the three stocks market-on-open. As it turns out, the customer is not alone in wanting to buy these stocks at the open: due to unusually high demand, all three stocks open at a premium (between 1.1 percent and 2.8 percent) to the prior night's closing levels and two stocks (MNO and XYZ) do not open until several minutes after the start of the trading session. After opening on their highs, the prices of all three stocks drift back down toward their previous closing levels. Exhibit 4.4 shows the graph of the evolution of the stock prices and of index levels from the open until 9:50 A.M. along with individual index level computations for the first 10 minutes.

Time and Price Data: Minute Intervals

Ticker	Prior	9:30	9:31	9:32	9:33	9:34	9:35	9:36	9:37	9:38	9:39	9:40
ABC	33.10	34.04	33.99	33.96	33.90	33.84	33.68	33.61	33.56	33.52	33.50	33.43
MNO	33.50	-	-	-	-	-	33.89	33.87	33.84	33.75	33.66	33.55
XYZ	33.40	-	-	-	-	-	-	-	-	-	-	33.94
Index	100.00	100.94	100.89	100.86	100.80	100.74	100.97	100.88	100.80	100.67	100.56	100.92

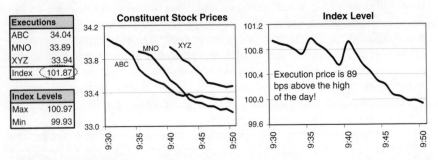

Executions	
ABC	34.04
MNO	33.89
XYZ	33.94
Index	101.87

Index Levels	
Max	100.97
Min	99.93

Execution price is 89 bps above the high of the day!

EXHIBIT 4.4   Executing a Basket Outside Market Levels

The first observation is that, while the index level was quoted continually from 9:30 A.M. to 9:39 A.M., none of those index prices could be achieved via a replicating stock portfolio because stock XYZ did not open until 9:40 A.M. The second is that, unfortunately for the client, the opening print was the high of the day in all three stocks. Where the problem is likely to arise is when the broker gives his client a fill at an implied index level of 101.82, which is 89 bps above the high print in the index over the first 20 minutes of trading. The broker followed the client's instructions exactly and, in doing so, achieved an implied index level on his stock hedge that is wildly outside of what the client will be expecting. The problem is not with the broker's execution but with the misleading impression that graph gives and the expectations that it creates. Of course, if this had been a sale, the broker would like a hero (more of a magician really) and the customer would be confused but happy to accept the fill. As is often the case, bread falls butter-side down, Murphy's Law prevails, and the order is a buy and the salesperson has some explaining to do.

Ironically, if the client had traded three MOO orders in the individual stocks, he might have been irritated to have paid the high of the day, but would have had no argument with the quality of the broker's execution, since the opening prints are all quite clear. It is only when those prints are combined into an index that is then compared against the graph that confusion arises.

INDEX CHANGES

There are many events that require changes in the constituent stocks and their weights in an index. These include mergers, acquisitions, spin-offs, stock splits, corporate stock repurchases (which decrease the float shares), secondary share issuances (which increase the shares outstanding), special dividends, failure of a company to meet the index inclusion criteria, IPO of a new company that meets the inclusion criteria, and other changes in the composition of the market. These changes can occur as part of a quarterly rebalancing of the index or, where the change is significant enough to warrant it (e.g., a stock is acquired and needs to be removed from the index), during the period between rebalances.

The specific methodology for deciding when and how to add or delete stocks or adjust the weights of the existing stocks varies from one index to another. While the specific trades necessary to rebalance the portfolio will be unique to the particular details of both the index and the reason for the rebalance, for the purposes of understanding the add-delete and reweighting process, a single example will suffice to demonstrate the logic and

INDEX DATA		OLD INDEX DATA				NEW INDEX DATA				TRADE DETAILS			
Ticker	Price	Float Shs	Mkt Cap	%Wgt		Float Shs	Mkt Cap	%Wgt		Portfolio Shs	Tgt Posn	Trade Shs	Trade ($)
NTI	79.70	594.50	47,382	36.20%		594.50	47,382	38.65%		92,759	99,028	6,269	$499,639
SOF	35.75	1,032.34	36,906	28.20%		1,032.34	36,906	30.10%		161,076	171,961	10,885	$389,139
CSM	53.35	494.40	26,376	20.15%		494.40	26,376	21.51%		77,141	82,354	5,213	$278,114
MTT	63.70	317.51	20,225	15.45%		-	-	-		49,541	-	(49,541)	($3,155,762)
LNA	20.70	-	-	-		576.80	11,940	9.74%			96,080	96,080	$1,988,856

Mkt Cap	130,889.43	
Divisor	1,281.81	
Index Lvl	102.11	

Mkt Cap	122,603.81	
Divisor	1,200.70	
Index Lvl	102.11	

Curr Portfolio Val	$20,422,593
Tgt Basket Val	$20,422,579
Total Trade	($14)

EXHIBIT 4.5 Computing an Index Rebalance

methodology. If the concepts behind the calculations are well understood, the reader should have little difficulty applying them to particular situations that may arise. Exhibit 4.5 demonstrates the calculation of the hedge portfolio rebalance for a simple index change consisting of the addition of one stock and deletion of another.

Before looking at the hedge portfolio rebalance, we must first understand how the definition of the index changes with the modification to the constituent stocks. Using the basket created in our first example, the decision is made at time t_2 to replace MTT in the index with a new stock, LNA. The sample spreadsheet shows all five securities and their prices at t_2 along with the relevant float shares for use in the definition of the "old" and "new" indices.

The calculation of the new index is identical to what we have done previously. Using the t_2 prices and the float shares for the new set of constituent stocks (NTI, SOF, CSM, and LNA) we compute the aggregate free float market capitalization of the new index, equal to $122,603.81. We then define a new index divisor such that, when we divide the new capitalization by this divisor we get the same index level, 102.11, that we had prior to the rebalance (i.e., the divisor is equal to the new market capitalization divided by the old index price).

Divisor Adjustment

The adjustment to the divisor raises a number of questions. Why do we need to change it in the first place? We did not change it when we calculated the index level at t_2 as compared to t_1. And if we are going to change it, can we make it whatever we want? When we first created the index we chose a divisor such that the initial index level was equal to something "nice"—in our case 100, though 250, 1,000, or any other number would have worked as well. What is different now?

The key fact here is that, because the constituents have changed, the market capitalization of the index has changed—it has been reduced from $130,889.43 to $122,603.81 due to the smaller market capitalization of

LNA as compared to MTT. If we do not adjust the divisor, the decrease in capitalization between the old and new constituents will be recognized in the performance of the index—as though a sudden downward move in the stock prices had caused the market capitalizations of the original index constituents to drop. For our specific example, the index level computed with the original divisor would be $122,603.81/12,81.81 = 95.65$—a 6.3% decrease from the prerebalance level of 102.11.

Clearly this is not correct. Changing the constituents of the index will alter the behavior of the index going forward by shifting its focus such that it is sensitive to movements in LNA and unaffected by MTT. It should not, however, change the index level, as this should represent the economic performance of the constituent stocks, none of which have dropped by 6.3 percent. Since everything is being calculated using t_2 prices, there is no economic performance to measure and the index level should remain the same. We therefore must define our new divisor to be precisely the number that, when divided into the new index market capitalization, gives the old index level; in this case this is equal to $122,603.81/102.11 = 1,200.70$.

Hedge Portfolio Rebalance

In addition to redefining the index with its new constituents, we also wish to rebalance the $20 million replicating portfolio constructed at t_1 to reflect the new index constituents. To do this we first calculate the portfolio value at the t_2 prices, in this case equal to $20.42 million. This notional amount is then used as the basis for computing a new target hedge portfolio based on the revised constituents and weights (i.e., including LNA in place of MTT). The new portfolio is then subtracted from the old portfolio to derive the number of shares of each stock that need to be traded, where positive quantities indicate additional shares to be purchased and negative share quantities indicate sales. For example, the entire position in MTT must be sold, and a large amount of LNA must be purchased. In order for returns of the replicating portfolio to precisely mirror those of the index, these rebalance trades must be executed in the market at the t_2 prices. The prices at which the stock is added to or subtracted from the hedge portfolio must exactly match the prices at which these stocks are added or removed from the index. Any deviation between the two will result in a difference in the returns generated on the hedge portfolio and the index.[9]

The correct adjustment of the divisor is particularly important for traders who have sold derivatives based on the performance of the index. If the divisor adjustment were done incorrectly and caused the index level to change, this would result in a gain or loss on the derivative which would not be offset by a gain or loss on the hedge portfolio, resulting in a profit or loss for the broker. Since an index will only be used as the basis for derivatives if its returns can be precisely reproduced, index providers are careful to insure that their rebalance methodology can be replicated in practice with very low tracking error if they hope to attract any interest in the index and licensing revenues.

Observations

Many assume that an add or delete simply requires that the shares of the deleted stock be sold and shares of the newly-included stock be purchased with the proceeds. However, in Exhibit 4.5 we see that we need to trade *all* the stocks in the index to correctly rebalance the portfolio. Why? The reason for this is that the market cap of LNA is significantly smaller than that of MTT (by about 40 percent) and therefore its weight in the index is smaller: 9.74 percent versus 15.45 percent. If we sell 15.45 percent of the portfolio assets and only reinvest 9.74 percent, the remaining 5.71 percent must then be distributed across all the index constituents to "top up" these holdings whose weights have now grown, in aggregate, by 5.71 percent. As we can see from the last column, the total trade is dollar neutral—no additional cash raised or spent in the rebalancing process (minor slippage of $14 is due to rounding errors).

In the parlance of Wall Street it would be said that this index change resulted in "$1 million of index to buy." While a rebalance is, by defini-tion, dollar neutral, what is meant by this comment is that, apart from the purchase and sale of the two stocks specifically involved (LNA and MTT), there is roughly $1 million of cash that will be invested across the balance of the index due to the market cap difference of the two stocks. The notional value of the trading in the other stocks can be estimated as the difference in the percentage weights of the added and deleted stocks (in this case, 5.71 percent) multiplied by the indexed assets ($20.42 million).

Index rebalances are big business for Wall Street because of the massive flows that result from the rebalancing trades of the investors who maintain replicating portfolios for the major equity indices. In a significant rebalance in a popular benchmark, the trading in the added and deleted names will be completely dominated by rebalance flows on the date of the index change. When there is a large market cap differential between these two names, the rest of the index can be significantly impacted as well.

INDEX DIVIDEND POINTS

There are two sources of return that must be considered when computing the performance of an investment in a single stock: the change in the price of the stock (the *price return*) and the dividends. The sum of these two is called the *total return*. Since the performance of an index is just the weighted average of the single stock returns of its constituents, the same must also be true when computing the return on an index. The index calculation methodology described thus far does not incorporate dividends—the percentage change in the index measures only the price return of the underlying stock portfolio. However, when a constituent stock pays a dividend the drop in the stock price on ex-date will produce a corresponding drop in the index level, in proportion to the size of the dividend and the weight of the stock in the index.

In order to properly measure the total return of an index it is therefore necessary to compute the index dividend points—that is, the changes in the index level caused by the dividends of the constituent stocks. One way to visualize how this is done is to imagine that we hold the prices of all constituent stocks constant with the exception of the stock paying a dividend, whose price drops by exactly the dividend amount (as it does on the ex-div date). The change in the index level is then equal to the change in the stock price, multiplied by the number of shares of that stock in the index, divided by the index divisor. This change in the index level measures the performance of the index, which is produced by the dividend yield of the underlying stocks, and is called the *index dividend points*.

$$\text{Index dividend points} = \frac{\text{Div per share} \times \text{Index shares}}{\text{Divisor}}$$

If there are multiple stocks going ex-dividend on the same day, the index dividend impact is simply the sum of the individual contributions.

Using the data in Exhibit 4.1 as an example, assume that NTI pays a $0.50 dividend; the index shares of NTI are 5,944.60 and the index divisor is 1,281.81. On the ex-dividend date the price of NTI will drop from $76.25 to $75.75. Holding all other stock prices constant, the change in the index level caused by the $0.50 drop in NTI would be 0.2319 index points based on:

$$\frac{594.50 \times 0.50}{1,281.81} = 0.2319$$

If we do not know the index shares and divisor,[10] we can calculate the index impact of the NTI dividend in percentage terms by multiplying the percentage change in NTI (= 0.5/76.25 = 0.6557%) by the weight of NTI in the index at t_1 (35.36%) to get 0.2319%, which is the same result given our t_1 index level of 100.00.

TOTAL RETURN INDEX CALCULATION

Because it excludes the dividend yield, the price return index gives an incomplete picture of the performance of the index constituents. While over short time frames this may not be a significant shortcoming, over a longer period, and particularly in indices with high dividend yields (such as those focused on value stocks), the price return index can understate the actual constituent stock performance by several percent per year.

For this reason, many popular indices are also computed on a total return basis. In a total return index calculation, the daily index performance is computed as the sum of the price return of the index plus the dividends. Let us denote by TR_1 and PR_1, the closing levels of the total return and price return indices on day 1. We have already seen in Exhibit 4.1 how to compute the day 2 closing level of the price return index, PR_2 based on the closing levels in the individual stocks. We now assume that there is an amount Div_2 of index dividend points whose ex-date is day 2. The percentage change in the total return index between day 1 and day 2 is then calculated as:

$$\frac{TR_2}{TR_1} = \left(\frac{PR_2 + Div_2}{PR_1} \right)$$

The numerator in the second term, $PR_2 + Div_2$, tells us where the price return index *would have been* at the close of day 2 if the stocks had not gone ex-dividend. Separating the right-hand side of this equation we see how the total return index can also be thought of as the sum of the one-day return of the price return index PR_2/PR_1 plus the one-day dividend yield Div_2/PR_1.

$$\frac{TR_2}{TR_1} = \frac{PR_2}{PR_1} + \frac{Div_2}{PR_1}$$

In the hypothetical case where all stock prices remain constant except for those that go ex-dividend, which decrease by exactly the amount of the dividend, then PR_2 would be exactly equal to $PR_1 - Div_2$. In this case, the economic reality is that nothing has happened—a portion of the index has been converted to cash and paid out to shareholders and the stock prices have adjusted to reflect this. However, in the price return calculation, the index level would drop by the amount of the index dividend points. Substituting $PR_1 - Div_2$ for PR_2 in the first formula for the total return index we can see that in the total return calculation, TR_2 would be exactly equal to TR_1, which accurately reflects the economic reality.

An important point comes when we calculate the next day's index return. As compared with a price return calculation, in which dividends simply fall out of the index and sit as cash, the total return index calculation implicitly reinvests the dividends in the index as of the close of business on the ex-date. Because the total return index level at the close of day 2 includes the amount of the dividend, the index performance on day 3 is applied to the base amount of the index as well as the accrued dividends. This is very important to a trader who must reproduce the return of a total return index as part of a derivative because it means he must monitor the notional amount of dividends paid out on index constituents each day and reinvest this amount into the entire index at the close of business.

The **TRA** (*Total Return Analysis*) function on Bloomberg compares the total return of an index under three different calculation methodologies: as the sum of the price return plus dividends, as a total return index where dividends are continuously reinvested, and as the sum of the price return plus the dividends but assuming that dividends sitting as cash are invested and return a fixed rate of interest defined by the user. The historical returns under each methodology are computed and graphed and the user can page forward through the historical data to see the daily index dividend points.

MULTICURRENCY INDICES

The calculation of an index level is more complex when the index constituents are in multiple currencies. In what we have covered so far, we have not referenced a particular currency when referring to the level of the index. In keeping with market convention, we have used the terms of "index points" which obscures the fact that the index level has always been denominated in U.S. dollars (USD) as it is effectively a calculation of the value of a portfolio of stocks, which are themselves denominated in USD. The slightly careless treatment of the currency is not unintentional: most investors do not think of the currency of an index until they first consider an index with constituents in multiple currencies, and so we have not either.

In reality, every index is computed in a currency, and the same constituent stocks and share weights can be used as the basis for the computation of the same index in many different currencies. In dealing with a multicurrency index, the understanding of the currency effects is clearer if we think of the index as a portfolio of stocks that have been paid for in a single currency (the currency of the index). As an example, Exhibit 4.6 shows the calculation of an index in USD which contains four stocks, three of which are quoted in currencies other than USD. Not surprisingly, to compute an index in USD, we need to value all of our constituent stocks in USD (otherwise the sum of the market caps would be a sum of amounts in four different currencies which is meaningless). Our index computation now has three additional columns: the local currency of each underlying stock, the exchange rate between that currency and the USD, and the USD equivalent to the local share price.

Some care must be taken in computing the USD equivalent to the local currency stock prices. The first point that must be checked is the quotation convention for the particular currency. The Canadian dollar (CAD) is quoted as CAD/USD while the euro (EUR) and British pound (GBP) are quoted as the number of USD/EUR and USD/GBP respectively. In the case of the shares of ELI, we have the additional complicating factor that UK-listed stocks trade in pence (GBp), not pounds (1 GBp = 0.01 GBP) which means that the local price of 2,540 GBp must first be divided by 100 to get a GBP price of 25.40 and then converted to USD.

The other complexity in dealing with multicurrency indices comes when hedging them. As we discussed in the previous chapter, there are two ways to finance the purchase of a foreign security, in local currency or in the home currency of the investor. When financing in the local currency, the investor was only exposed to moves in the currency once there was a profit or loss on the position, while if the position was financed in the home currency, the investor had full currency exposure on the notional amount of the trade right from the start.

Looking at our index calculation it is apparent that, when hedging a multiple currency index, we are funding in the currency in which the index is calculated. This is apparent from the fact that each of the non-USD stock prices is being converted at the spot exchange rate into a USD price, which is then being used to compute the index level. If any of those exchange rates move, the USD price of the stock will change and the index will change with it. The currency exposure between the local currency and the USD is implicit in the index calculation.

Therefore, the execution of a replicating portfolio for our index in Exhibit 4.6 would require not only the four equity trades, but three currency trades as well. Assuming we were purchasing the portfolio, we would

INDEX DATA

Ticker	Float Shs	Local Px	Curncy	FX Rate	USD Px	MktCap (USD)	Wgt %
NTI	594.50	76.25	USD	1.00	76.250	45,331	35.16%
QUI	941.01	35.64	CAD	0.95	37.516	35,303	27.38%
JUA	345.22	52.25	EUR	1.55	80.988	27,959	21.69%
ELI	410.45	2,540.00	GBp	1.95	49.530	20,330	15.77%

					Σ Mkt Cap	128,921.45
					Divisor	1,289.21
					Index Level	100.00

EXHIBIT 4.6   Multicurrency Index Calculation

need to buy CAD, EUR, and GBP versus selling USD, and then use these currency positions to pay for the purchase of the foreign stocks, resulting in a net position of long stock, short USD. This means that the returns of the index are driven not only by the equity movement but have a significant exposure to exchange rates as well. If the CAD were to strengthen 1 percent against the USD, this would cause the USD value of QUI to increase by 1 percent which would have an impact of 27.4 bps on the index as a whole. When investing in derivative products based on multicurrency indices, investors can partially neutralize the implicit FX exposure of the index by entering into separate offsetting FX transactions.

The confusion that can result from the misinterpretation of the persistent dissemination of an index level, regardless of trading in the underlying constituents, is even greater in multicurrency indices where the index level is driven by both equity and exchange rate movements. Currency movements also exacerbate the disconnect between the implied execution level of a basket executed over a period of time and the published level of the index during that time. Equity investors who are accustomed to watching only the stock price are often surprised by the amount of impact, currency movements can have on a multicurrency index.

EQUITY INDICES IN PRACTICE

Given the size and breadth of the U.S. equity market, with thousands of publicly-traded companies across every sector and industry, the availability of equity indices to aggregate and summarize the mass of information into digestible pieces is extremely important. However, the existence of thousands of indices covering every imaginable subset and cross-section of the market means that there is still more narrowing that must be done to find those indices of greatest value and broadest use.

In practice, there are a small handful of indices that receives the lion's share of investors' attention and on which the majority of derivative activity is based. This section presents a summary of the most closely watched equity indices in the United States, how they are constructed, and what they tell us, and then expands this analysis to look at the most popular indices internationally.

Broad Indices

The four principal providers of broad indices in the United States are Standard and Poor's, NASDAQ, Russell, and Dow Jones. While all four of these providers offer a wide variety of products, each has one index that receives particular attention.

Standard & Poor's (S&P)[11]   Far and away the most closely watched and widely used index benchmark for the U.S. equity markets is the Standard & Poor's 500 Index, better known as the S&P 500 or by its ticker symbol, SPX. With an aggregate market capitalization of $11.2 trillion, the SPX covers approximately 75 percent of the U.S. equity market.

Stock selection for inclusion in the SPX is done by the S&P Index Committee. To be eligible for inclusion, a company must be domiciled and listed in the United States, have a market capitalization greater than $5 billion, at least 50 percent of all outstanding shares in free public float, positive earnings during the past four quarters, and maintain a minimum average daily trading volume (volume depends on the size of the company). The members of the Index Committee then select the stocks for inclusion from the universe of eligible candidates based on a more subjective analysis of the current constituents and the structure of the equity market as a whole. The goal is to produce an index that is the best possible indicator of the performance of the U.S. equity market as a whole and at the same time easily tradable for index fund managers and broker-dealers who need to replicate its returns.

SPX constituents are weighted by free float market capitalization as calculated by S&P's own methodology for determining float shares. Constituents are monitored constantly to insure continued adherence to the inclusion criteria and the entire index is rebalanced on a quarterly basis at the close of business on the third Friday of March, June, September, and December. Standard & Poor's also makes adjustments to the constituent stocks and their weightings during the quarter whenever there is a material change in the characteristics of one of the members.

The S&P 500 is one of the most widely followed index benchmarks in the world with an estimated $1.53 trillion in indexed assets. Comparing this to the total market capitalization of the index we can conclude that approximately 14 percent of all outstanding shares in SPX constituents are held by index fund managers who will adjust their holdings whenever there is a change in the index composition. This massive base of indexers means that the announcement of additions, deletions, and reweights of the SPX can cause sudden, large price movements in the affected stocks. These announcements are made at several times through the day via S&P's "Index Alert" service which keeps the investment community informed of upcoming index changes to all S&P indices.

The SPX is part of a much larger family of indices published by S&P. Its most well-known siblings are:

- *S&P100 (OEX):* Defined as the top 100 stocks in the SPX, the OEX measures the performance of the *mega-cap* sector of the market. The market capitalization of the constituent stocks ranges between $10 billion and $430 billion[12] and makes up 58 percent of the weight of the SPX.
- *S&P MidCap 400 (MID):* Employs a similar methodology to the SPX but applied to midsized companies, which is defined by S&P as those with a market cap of between $1.5 billion and $5.5 billion. The MID covers approximately 7 percent of the total U.S. equity market.
- *S&P SmallCap 600 (SML):* An index of small-cap stocks with market capitalization between $300 million to $2.0 billion, covering between 3 percent and 4 percent of the total U.S. equity market.
- *S&P1500 Composite index (SPR):* Constructed as the sum of the SPX, MID, and SML indices, the composite is rarely used as an index benchmark on its own due to the predominance of the SPX constituents, which make up nearly 90 percent of the index. Its most popular use is as the basis for the construction of broad market sector indices.
- There is also a total return version of the SPX published under the ticker SPTR.

The SPX covers most of the largest and most actively traded stocks in the U.S. equity market. New arrivals to Wall Street are strongly recommended to invest the time to memorize the ticker symbols for the 500 constituent stocks and, for those with longer commutes during which to occupy their time, the sector or general business activity of each (at two stocks each way, it only takes six months of commuting). The ability to alternate between ticker symbols and company names is an essential skill for traders and salespeople and is what allow an experienced trader to look at a list like "AYE, D, EIX, MRO, TEG, XTO" and say immediately "It's a bunch of energy companies and utilities." It's a simple matter of memorization and especially for new hires, there's no excuse for not learning it before showing up for the first day of work.

NASDAQ[13]   The next most important index benchmark in the United States is the *NASDAQ-100* or NDX. This includes the largest 100 stocks (excluding financials) that trade on the NASDAQ marketplace, subject to certain selection criteria. To prevent the index from becoming too concentrated in any single stock, the NDX utilizes a modified market-cap weighting in which no stock can exceed 24 percent of the total index. This weighting cap is not currently a limitation as no stock comprises more than 14 percent of the index. While the index is composed of stocks across many sectors, it is heavily weighted in technology, which, due to the higher volatility and cyclicality of these stocks, makes the performance of the NDX a useful proxy for investors' appetite for risk.

The NASDAQ also publishes the *NASDAQ Composite Index* (CCMP), a market-cap-weighted average of all stocks trading on the NASDAQ marketplace. While this index receives a fair amount of attention from retail investors and in the popular press, it is almost completely ignored by the institutional investment community due to the fact that, with nearly 3,000 constituents, many of which are extremely small and illiquid, it is an incredibly difficult index to replicate. Given that the 100 stocks in the NDX comprise nearly 60 percent of the market capitalization of the CCMP, it is not surprising that the correlation of the CCMP return with that of the NDX is high (R^2 of approximately 0.96) and that, given the option, investors tend to lean toward the NDX.

Russell[14]　　There are several important indices published by Russell Investments that are notable, among other reasons, for their very straightforward construction methodology. Rather than select index constituents through an elaborate methodology that can potentially introduce subjective biases, Russell takes the stance that, through market capitalization, investors have already expressed their view of relative importance. Therefore, subject to a few very minimal admission criteria (i.e., domiciled in the United States and listed on a U.S. exchange, free float greater than 1 percent), Russell produces a market-cap-weighted index of the top 3,000 stocks in the U.S. market. It is called, intuitively enough, the *Russell 3000 Index* (RAY). This index is then divided into two sub-indices: the *Russell 1000* (RIY), which consists of the top 1,000 companies and comprises approximately 91 percent of the total market cap of the index, and the *Russell 2000* (RTY), which contains the smaller 2,000 constituents.

The last of these, the Russell 2000 index of small-cap stocks, is by far the most important of the three and serves as the standard benchmark for measuring the performance of the small-cap marketplace. The constituents of the R2000 (as it is commonly abbreviated) range in market capitalization from $3.8 billion—roughly the middle of the mid-cap range—down to as small as just $56 million. Given the higher risk-return profile of small-cap stocks, and their tendency to outperform in rising markets and underperform in falling markets, the performance of the RTY plays a similar role to the NDX as an indicator of investors' risk appetite.

Another important fact about the Russell indices is that they only rebalance once a year, at the close of business on the last Friday of June (new IPOs are added to the index quarterly). The *Russell rebalance* trade is one of the biggest events of the year for program trading desks (explained in Chapter 5), which start planning technological developments, risk analytics, and trading strategies early in the year and often begin building up rebalance-related trading positions early in the second quarter. Although the value of assets benchmarked to the R2000, and therefore the notional size of the rebalance flows, is much smaller than that of the SPX, the Russell rebalance is by far the most closely watched index rebalance of the year due to the tremendous trading opportunities (and risks) provided by the illiquidity and wide bid-offer spreads that are common to small-cap stocks.

The other important fact about the Russell rebalance is operational—portfolio trades of thousands of stocks are extremely unwieldy and the strain on system capacity is tremendous as trading volumes on all exchanges on the rebalance date surge to several times their normal levels. So great are the demands on the exchanges that in 2001, the NASDAQ market was forced to extend the close of trading by one hour because the massive intraday volumes had caused the network to fail, leaving brokers for several hours with no way to execute billions of dollars of rebalance orders.

THE RUSSELL REBALANCE

The flows related to the reconstitution of the Russell indices each June creates attractive trading opportunities for institutional traders. On the rebalance date, and in the days leading up to it, as index funds adjust their holdings to reflect the new index constituents, there is significant demand for the stocks that are added to the index (or whose weightings increase in the rebalance) and selling pressure in the deletions (or weighting decreases). Based on estimates of the total assets indexed to the Russell indices, traders can estimate the size of the inflows (share purchases) and outflows (share sales) for each of the constituent stocks in the index. In situations where these flows are large relative to the average daily traded volume in the stock, traders will take positions—buying the stocks where large inflows are expected and shorting (taking a short position) in those that will experience significant outflows.

(Continued)

(*Continued*)

On the rebalance date, traders holding rebalance positions are able to profit from these flows by offering liquidity (selling their long positions) to other buyers at higher levels in the additions and bidding for stock in the deletions (to cover their shorts) at lower levels. If the rebalance-related flows have sufficient market impact, the trader willing to hold the portfolio of additions and deletions for several days or even weeks prior to the rebalance (it can take a long time to build up a position in many of the smaller stocks which can have poor liquidity) is rewarded with a profit. For index fund managers looking to trade on the rebalance date, these traders provide bids and offers in highly illiquid stocks which reduces the impact of their trading.

The risk in the rebalance trade is that the volume of orders from traders who have put on the trade early and are looking to unwind it into the close on the rebalance date ("wrong-way flow") is greater than the "right way" flow from the index rebalancers. In this case, the prices of the stocks experiencing inflows (the new additions and weighting increases in the index), which should be pushed higher toward the close of trading as index fund demand picks up, actually sell off while the stocks experiencing outflows (deletions and weighting decreases) rally. The art of successfully trading the rebalance is in the analysis of the excess trading volume and price action in the affected stocks in the days leading up to the rebalance date and the careful assessment of the balance between risk and opportunity in positions taken early. While the Russell rebalance is generally an attractive and profitable trading opportunity, Wall Street program trading desks are also full of Russell rebalance horror stories where trading desks have seen previously profitable positions drop millions (or tens of millions) of dollars in the last hour of trading on the rebalance date.

Dow Jones   It is not unintentional that the publisher of what is by far the most widely recognized equity index in the world has been left for last. The reason is that, while the *Dow Jones Industrial Average* (INDU though often abbreviated as DJIA) holds a special place in the hearts of retail investors due to its long history, it is a poor benchmark for U.S. equity performance given its crude construction methodology (price weighting), narrow focus, and few constituents. As a result, the institutional finance community pays relatively little attention to the Dow beyond the short-term trading impact of the most significant levels of interest (Dow 10,000!), which can attract attention and trading activity from retail investors due to their psychological effects.

Others There are many other companies that create, calculate, and disseminate indices for the U.S. markets in the hope that they will attract interest and with that, licensing fees as investment products are developed based on them. These include the NYSE, Bloomberg, Wilshire, ValueLine, and MSCI Barra as well as well-established European index providers such as STOXX and FTSE and many others. While these companies produce many well-constructed, high-quality indices, the battle for investor attention is a case of "winner takes all" and these indices receive a tiny fraction of the attention that is paid to the primary benchmarks we have discussed.

Style Indices

Market capitalization is only one of many possible criteria by which to divide a universe of stocks. Another commonly used metric, which is the basis for several popular subdivisions of the indices just presented, is the separation of stocks according to their growth and value characteristics. Many institutional money managers classify their investment style as having either a growth or value focus and it is important to have standardized index benchmarks against which to measure the performance of individual asset managers. The most commonly used of these are the *S&P 500 Growth* (SPG) and *Value* (SPV) indices, which divide the constituents of the SPX according to these characteristics. There are also growth and value versions of the MID and SML as well as the Russell 1000, 2000, and 3000.

It is an oversimplification to suggest that every stock can be classified as either a growth or value stock: clearly many stocks share some characteristics of both. As a result, the methodology used by both S&P and Russell for the construction of the growth and value subindices does not assume the two groups are mutually exclusive. Instead, the universe of stocks is divided into three, roughly equal-sized groups based on each stock's score on a series of fundamental metrics: pure growth, pure value, and mixed growth-and-value. The growth index then consists of all of the pure growth stocks plus a fraction of the market cap of each of the mixed growth-and-value stocks. The value index consists of the sum of the pure value stocks, with their full market cap, and the portion of the market cap of the mixed growth-and-value stocks that was not allocated to the growth index. In this way, the sum of the market caps of the growth and value subindices is equal to the market cap of the full index, though the number of stocks in each of the style indices is significantly greater than one-half of the total. For example, the growth subindex of the S&P 500 has 306 constituents, while the Value index with 349. However, the sum of the market caps of the growth and value subindices is equal to that of the SPX, with each style index occupying approximately one-half of the total.

Sectors

Although broad market indices provide a very useful synthesis of overall market activity, there is a limit to how much information a single number can provide. The change in the level of a broad index can be caused by innumerable combinations of individual price changes in the constituent stocks and while a name-by-name analysis would be excessively time-consuming and risk losing the big picture amid the details, there is clearly value to be added from a smaller-scale analysis of activity.

Sector indices fill this gap between single stock and broad index data by reducing the mass of individual stock performances into aggregates across companies engaged in similar types of business. Depending on the desired level of specificity, these classifications can cover a range of industries under a broad heading such as "consumer discretionary," or they can be much more narrowly focused and divide "consumer discretionary" into specific subgroups such as "manufacturers of tires and rubber," "photography products," or "casinos and gaming."

One of the most widely used methodologies for decomposing broad indices into sectors is the *Global Industry Classification System* (GICS), which was developed jointly by MSCI Barra and Standard & Poor's. The GICS consists of four classification levels of increasing granularity. At the highest level, each company is assigned to 1 of 10 possible sectors; these sectors are then broken down into 24 industry groups, 67 industries, and 147 subindustries.

Applying the GICS to a broad index such as the SPX (or the S&P 1500 Composite), we can construct a total of 248 possible indices consisting of the companies in each sector, industry group, industry, and subindustry. The weighting of each of these subindices within the broad index gives insight into the index's relative sensitivity to movements in different parts of the market, and says a lot about the structure of the economy as a whole. (This will be particularly true when we look at international indices.) Exhibit 4.7 shows the decomposition of the SPX into its sectors and industry groups with the percentage weights of each and the Bloomberg ticker for each one.[15]

Bloomberg has several functions for analyzing broad indices and comparing the relative weights and performance of each sector and their contributions to the overall performance of the index.

- **MOV** *(Movers):* Decomposes the index performance into the individual stock contributions (how much has the move in XYZ impacted the index level).

Sector	(GICS Level 1)			Industry Group	(GICS Level 2)	
S5COND	Consumer Discretionary	8.10%	S5AUCO	Automobiles & Components	0.40%
			S5CODU	Consumer Durables & Apparel	1.00%
			S5HOTR	Consumer Services	1.40%
			S5MEDA	Media	2.70%
			S5RETL	Retailing	2.60%
S5CONS	Consumer Staples	11.30%	S5FDSR	Food & Staples Retailing	2.70%
			S5FDBT	Food Beverage & Tobacco	5.90%
			S5HOPR	Household & Pers. Products	2.60%
S5ENRS	Energy	14.10%	S5ENRS	Energy	14.10%
S5FINL	Financials	15.50%	S5BANKX	Banks	3.10%
			S5DIVF	Diversified Financials	7.80%
			S5INSU	Insurance	3.40%
			S5REAL	Real Estate	1.20%
S5HLTH	Health Care	12.60%	S5HCES	Health Care Equipment & Svc	4.20%
			S5PHRM	Pharmaceuticals & Biotech	8.40%
S5INDU	Industrials	11.40%	S5CPGS	Capital Goods	8.70%
			S5COMS	Commercial Svc & Supplies	0.50%
			S5TRAN	Transportation	2.20%
S5INFT	Information Technology	16.50%	S5SECO	Semiconductors & Semi Equip	2.50%
			S5SFTW	Software & Services	6.20%
			S5TECH	Technology Hardware & Equip	7.90%
S5MATR	Materials	3.70%	S5MATRX	Materials	3.70%
S5TELS	Telecommunication Svc	3.10%	S5TELSX	Telecommunication Svc	3.10%
S5UTIL	Utilities	3.70%	S5UTILX	Utilities	3.70%

EXHIBIT 4.7 SPX Decomposition into Sectors and Industry Groups
Source: Bloomberg, weights as of July 31, 2008.

- **GMOV** *(Group Movers):* Decomposes the index performance into the individual contributions of each sub-sector (GICS level 4).
- **GRPS** *(Groups):* Lists all subgroup-level indices with direct links to popular functions for each (MOV, DES, TRA).
- **IMAP** *(Index Map):* Provides a multilevel decomposition of index performance at each of the GICS levels using a color-coded "heatmap" to indicate relative performance. (A personal favorite.)

Decomposition of a broad index according to GICS is not the only means of creating a sector index. There are many other popular sector indices which are created by independent analysis and not restricted to the constituents of any particular broad index. In many cases these indices are more attractive because the deliberate choice of constituents and weightings produces a more balanced index than the formulaic GICS-based indices, which adhere strictly to the market-cap weighting of the broad index and

Ticker	Name	Ticker	Name
BKX	KBW Banks Index	MVRX	Morgan Stanley Retail Index
BTK	AMEX Biotech Index	OIX	CBOE Oil Index
CMR	Morgan Stanley Consumer Index	OSX	PHLX Oil Service Sector
CRX	Morgan Stanley Commodities Index	SOX	PHLX Semiconductor Sector
CYC	Morgan Stanley Cyclicals Index	UTY	PHLX Utility Sector
DRG	AMEX Pharmaceutical Index	XAU	PHLX Gold/Silver Sector
HUI	AMEX Gold BUGS Index	XBD	AMEX Securities Broker/Dealers Index
MSH	Morgan Stanley Technology Index	XNG	AMEX Natural Gas Index

EXHIBIT 4.8   Other Sector Indices
Source: Bloomberg.

sometimes result in indices with excessively large concentrations in a one or two stocks, Some of the most popular independently-developed sector indices are listed in Exhibit 4.8.

INTERNATIONAL INDICES

Global Indices

While the indices covered so far provide a comprehensive picture of U.S. trading activity, these are inadequate for investors with a global focus. The local indices of foreign countries can be used to judge the performance of specific markets, but this is only a partial solution as there is still the question of the relative weightings of each country in a global portfolio. For monitoring equity market activity as well as benchmarking performance, consolidated global index benchmarks are needed.

By far, the most popular international index provider is MSCI Barra with more than 90 percent of all foreign-indexed assets in the United States, and over $3 trillion globally, benchmarked to MSCI indices.[16] Their comprehensive global index framework is extraordinarily complete with thousands of global, regional, and individual country indices, as well as sector, style, and thematic variants. To provide an appropriate benchmark for different types of investors, MSCI calculates their indices according to several different methodologies: a local currency version, in which the index is calculated as though all positions were funded in the local currency; a standard single currency index calculation in both EUR and USD; and two different dividends-reinvested total return versions, one based on gross dividends and one based on net dividends. The gross dividends reinvested total return index establishes the "best case scenario" of a hypothetical investor who is not withheld on any dividends, while the net dividends reinvested index is calculated based on the "worst case scenario" (a Luxembourg-based investor) who is subjected to the highest withholding in each market.

The distinction between gross and net dividend reinvestment is an important one as a portfolio manager attempting to track a global index will be subjected to withholding taxes on dividends on most of his foreign stock holdings. This makes the gross-dividend-reinvested total return index an unattainable benchmark against which the manager will almost always underperform. The net dividend reinvested index is a more appropriate benchmark and, given that most investors receive somewhat better dividend treatment than the worst-case Luxembourg-domiciled investor, the manager actually has the chance to outperform, even with a passive index replication strategy (i.e., the exact replication of the index holdings with no subjective under- or overweightings). For the total-return indices, MSCI does not disseminate real-time values throughout the day but publishes a single end-of-day price once the U.S. markets have closed.

Some of the most popular MSCI global and regional indices are listed in Exhibit 4.9. (All indices are weighted by free-float market capitalization.)

U.S. investors looking to add global diversification to their portfolios usually prefer to use the familiar U.S. benchmarks (SPX, NDX, RTY) for their domestic holdings and a global benchmark for "everything else." For this reason, while the *MSCI World Index* provides the most comprehensive picture of global developed market activity, investors generally prefer to use

Index Name	Description
World	23 developed markets globally.
Emerging Markets	25 emerging markets globally.
All Country World	World Index + Emerging Markets Index (48 countries).
EAFE (Europe, Australasia, and Far East)	Equal to the World Index ex-U.S. and Canada; the most popular international benchmark for U.S. investors.
Europe	16 developed markets in Europe.
Pan-Euro	A subset of the Europe index designed for ease of trading; contains about half the members and 90% of the market cap.
KOKUSAI	MSCI World ex-Japan (22 developed markets); popular for Japanese investors.

EXHIBIT 4.9 Selected MSCI Global Indices
Source: MSCIBarra data (www.mscibarra.com) as of July 14, 2008.

the *MSCI EAFE*[17] *Index* which is equal to the *MSCI World* but excluding the United States and Canada.

Other Americas Indices

In terms of investor perception, the equity markets of Canada and Brazil are somewhat unfairly overshadowed by the size and liquidity of the U.S. equity market. The economies of Canada and Brazil are each about one-tenth the size of the United States, and on a global comparison, rank 9th and 10th respectively: right after Spain and above Russia (though admittedly if California were an independent country it would be slightly larger than both of them).[18]

- *Canada*: The primary index benchmark for Canadian equities is the *S&P/TSE 60 Index (SPTSX60)*, a market-cap-weighted index of 60 stocks which is particularly concentrated in the energy (30 percent), basic resources (19 percent), and financial (20 percent) sectors. The Canadian economy benefited significantly from the extended bull market in oil and other commodities, which began in earnest in 2002.
- *Brazil*: Brazil is by far the most active equity market in Central or South America and one of the most developed of the emerging markets. In recent years it has received particular attention in the context of the "*BRIC*" countries of Brazil, Russia, India, and China, which have been highlighted as the markets with the greatest growth potential in the next 40 to 50 years.

  The primary index benchmark for Brazil is the *Bovespa Index* (IBOV) which consists of the most actively traded stocks on the Bovespa stock exchange weighted by trading activity. Due to this rather unusual construction methodology, many investors prefer to use the *MSCI Brazil* as a benchmark, which has a more standard process for the selection of constituents and their weighting. The Brazilian economy is highly leveraged to basic materials (27 percent) and energy (16 percent) sectors and, like Canada, has benefited from the extended bull market in commodity prices.

  Even among emerging markets the performance of the Bovespa Index over the last decade has been extraordinary; from a low of 8,370.88 in October 2002, the Bovespa rallied to a high of 73,516.81 in May 2008 for a cumulative return over five and a half years of 878 percent—an annually compounded 47.5 percent return. Over the same period the Brazilian real (BRL) strengthened from 3.87 to 1.65 BRL/USD, resulting in a compound return to a USD-denominated investor of 2,063 percent (annually compounded return of 71.8 percent). While much of this exceptional market performance was lost in the global market sell-off in the fall of 2008, the changes in the Brazilian economy in the last decade have been striking.

European Indices

The establishment of the European Union and the introduction of the euro as the common currency for much of the continent was a powerful catalyst for a shift in the dynamics of European trading which began in earnest in the late 1990s. As the degree of homogeneity in economic and monetary policy across Europe increased, and stock exchanges became more open, integrated and electronic (and in many cases merged), the focus of European trading shifted from a country-specific viewpoint to a regional and sector-based perspective. This in turn stimulated the development of pan-European indices, which have, in the span of 10 years, become the standard framework through which European market movements are viewed. European integration not only encouraged investors to *look* at Europe as a whole, but it greatly facilitated the development of the tools with which to *trade* Europe as a whole, both on a broad and sector level.

The two most popular index providers for pan-European benchmarks are STOXX, a joint venture between Dow Jones and the German and Swiss stock exchanges, and MSCI Barra. While the MSCI indices, and their associated style, size, and sector indices are popular among so-called *real money* investors (such as mutual funds, pension funds, endowments) that use the MSCI index framework to structure their equity investments globally, the trading activity is heavily concentrated in the STOXX indices, which are more popular with hedge funds and other *fast money* accounts.

STOXX The framework for understanding the STOXX European indices begins with the *STOXX 600* (SXXP), a modified[19] free-float market-cap-weighted index of 600 of the largest stocks from across Europe.[20] While there is relatively little trading in derivative products that track the STOXX 600, it provides the framework for the construction of the indices that underlie many of the most actively traded products.

- *Eurozone:* The *Euro-STOXX* (SXXE) index consists of the subset of stocks from the SXXP that are traded in euros. As the constituents of the SXXE are derived formulaically from the constituents of the STOXX 600, the number of constituent stocks can vary, though it is generally around 320.

- *Size:* The STOXX 600 is divided into three subindices based on market capitalization, each with 200 stocks: the *Large-Cap Index* (LCXP), consisting of the top 200 and approximately 82 percent of the total market cap, the *Mid-Cap Index* (MCXP) made up of the middle 200 and about 12 percent of the market cap, and the *Small-Cap Index* (SCXP) of the bottom 200, which makes up the remaining 6 percent of the market cap of the STOXX 600. The corresponding *Euro Large-Cap* (LCXE), *Euro Mid-Cap* (MCXE), and *Euro Small-Cap* (SCXE) indices, each having roughly 100 to 110 constituents, are created from the Euro-STOXX index.

- *The "50s":* The largest 50 stocks in the STOXX 600 index are used to create the *STOXX-50 Index* (SX5P). Applying the same process to the Euro-STOXX index produces the *Euro-STOXX 50 Index* (SX5E). Despite its narrow scope, it is the last of these, the SX5E, which is by far the most commonly-used benchmark for active traders and the basis for many of the most actively traded index products in Europe.

- *Sectors and ICB:* The STOXX 600 and Euro-STOXX indices are decomposed into sector indices according to the *Industry Classification Benchmark* (ICB) system, a stock classification methodology developed jointly by STOXX and FTSE (the primary UK index provider) which is structurally similar to the GICS introduced previously. Stocks are classified into four progressively more granular categories—10 industries, 19 supersectors, 41 sectors, and 114 subsectors. Based on the ICB structure, STOXX constructs indices at both the industry and supersector level for the STOXX 600 and Euro-STOXX indices. The 18 supersector indices (usually just referred to as "sectors") of the SXXP are by far the most actively traded sector products in Europe. Equivalent Eurozone sector indices based on the SXXE exist, though these are less popular due to their narrower focus and tendency to be heavily concentrated in just a few names. (While they are the only STOXX indices we have covered where it would be relevant, unlike the rest of the STOXX indices, the sector indices do not apply a cap to the percentage weighting of any constituents stocks.) Exhibit 4.10 provides a summary of the sector indices of the SXXP. Their Eurozone equivalents would be the same tickers but ending in "E" (i.e., SX3E).

Local Indices Economic integration allowed investors to look at Europe as a whole, but it did not result in a single homogeneous economy across the continent. There remain vast differences in the economies, cultures, and markets of the European nations and as a result, there continues to be a significant level of attention paid to the local indices of the various countries.

Ticker	Sector	Ticker	Sector	Ticker	Sector
SX3P	Food & Beverage	SXDP	Healthcare	SXNP	Industrial Goods
SX4P	Chemicals	SXEP	Oil & Gas	SXOP	Construction & Materials
SX6P	Utilities	SXFP	Financial Services	SXPP	Basic Resources
SX7P	Banks	SXIP	Insurance	SXQP	Personal & Household Goods
SX8P	Technology	SXKP	Telecommunications	SXRP	Retail
SXAP	Automobiles & Parts	SXMP	Media	SXTP	Travel & Leisure

EXHIBIT 4.10 STOXX 600 Sector Indices

The Bloomberg **WEI** (*World Equity Index*) function provides a useful summary of the performance of the most significant regional and local-country index benchmarks globally. Users can then dig deeper into the Americas, Europe, and Asia to get a more detailed listing of the regional and country indices and their performance.

While there are national benchmark indices for each European country, from a trading perspective, only the larger, more liquid indices from the primary European economies receive significant attention. Using trading activity in associated derivatives as a measurement of investor interest, the two most important markets are by far Germany and the United Kingdom (the two largest economies in Europe), followed by a second tier consisting of France, Italy, Spain, Switzerland, and Sweden. The rest of the European national indices, while undoubtedly very important to local investors, receive relatively little international attention due to their small size, illiquidity, and the limited degree to which the performance of the index indicates anything broader than the local economic conditions.

Another reason why many of the smaller national benchmark indices are less attractive to international investors is that they are often highly concentrated in only a few names. In most countries there is usually at least one, and perhaps several companies that have grown large enough to a take on a global significance. In a small economy, the capitalization disparity between one of these international contenders and the rest of the local players is more extreme and makes the indices very imbalanced. There is also the fact that the sector weightings of a small national index are frequently dominated by the staple industries of utilities, banking, and energy and lack more interesting diversification.

For these reasons, and to avoid distracting the reader from the more meaningful information with too much minutiae, we will limit the observations in this section to the main characteristics of the most popular European contracts. (A more complete listing of the national benchmark indices for all of the major Western European countries, as well as the rest of the major developed markets globally, is provided in Exhibit 7.2 at the end of Chapter 7.)

- *Germany:* The *German Stock Index* (DAX) is a market-cap weighted index of 30 of the largest stocks in Germany. The constituents of the DAX are heavily concentrated in highly cyclical industrial sectors[21] such as automobiles (14 percent), capital goods (12 percent), and materials (10 percent), giving a relatively high volatility when compared with the broader European market. There is also a much less liquid *German DAX Mid-Cap Index* (MDAX), which contains the next 50 largest stocks after the DAX. Notably, both the DAX and the MDAX are calculated as total return indices.

- *United Kingdom:* The *FTSE-100* (UKX)—pronounced "footsie"—is the primary index reference for the United Kingdom. It is a highly liquid, market-cap weighted index of 100 of the largest companies in the United Kingdom, which includes many of the largest companies in Europe. Like the DAX, the UKX is highly cyclical due to heavy sector concentrations in energy (20 percent), financials (17 percent), and basic materials (12 percent). For the small- and midcap sectors, there is the *FTSE-250 Mid-Cap Index* (MCX) which consists of the 250 largest UK stocks outside of the UKX. It is also market-cap weighted and is one of the more popular small-midcap benchmarks in Europe. Combining these two indices on a market-cap basis (approximately 92 percent UKX and 8 percent MCX) we get the *FTSE-350 index* (NMX), which is not a widely used benchmark in its own right but provides the basis for the FTSE-350 sector indices, which are popular with investors looking for a more detailed picture of specific segments of the U.K. market.

- *France:* The *CAC-40 Index* (CAC) is a modified market-cap-weighted index of 40 large-cap French companies. Though not as liquid as the German or UK markets, the French economy is quite diversified and the CAC-40 constituents are spread widely across many sectors with no noteworthy sector concentrations.

- *Spain:* The primary Spanish index, the *IBEX-35* (IBEX), is a typical case of the national index of a smaller economy that we described previously; the three largest-weight sectors—banks (33 percent), telecom (21 percent, made up entirely by one company), and utilities (18 percent)—make up 72 percent of the index with the top three stocks alone—two banks (Santander and BBVA) and a telecom company (Telefónica)—comprising 50 percent of the index. Spain's economy is also heavily leveraged to the construction sector and homebuilders and infrastructure providers carry significant weight in the index.

- *Italy:* The *S&P/MIB Index* (SPMIB) is a market-cap-weighted index of 40 of the largest stocks in Italy and an even more exaggerated example of a highly concentrated and narrowly focused national index than the IBEX. More than 80 percent of the total market capitalization of the SPMIB is concentrated in financials (banks and insurance making up 50 percent), energy (21 percent), and utilities (12 percent).
- *Switzerland:* The *Swiss Market Index* (SMI) is a bit of an anomaly among European indices in terms of its sector weights. Despite its small size, Switzerland has a surprising number of very large, internationally recognized companies in many sectors. As a result, the sector weightings of the SMI are unusual with pharmaceuticals (34 percent; Novartis, Roche Holdings), food and beverage (21 percent—entirely Nestlé), and a mixture of banks and financials (23 percent; UBS, Credit Suisse) taking the top spots.
- *Sweden:* The most liquid of the Scandinavian markets, the *OMX Stockholm 30* (OMX), is very well diversified across sectors (though most sectors are dominated by one or two stocks) and includes significant weights in retail, banks, telecom, technology, capital goods, and pharmaceuticals.

While still an emerging market, it is worthwhile to mention Russia, another of the BRIC countries and a massive beneficiary of the bull market in commodities of recent years. The *Russian Trading Systems Index* (RTSI) contains 50 stocks, the top 16 of which are all in the energy, banks, and materials sectors. These three sectors make up 84 percent of the total index, with the energy sector alone accounting for 54 percent of the total market cap of the index.

Japan

There are two primary benchmark indices in Japan. The *Nikkei-225* (NKY), which is a price-weighted index of 225 large-cap stocks, and the *TOPIX Index* (TPX), which is a market-cap-weighted index of roughly 1,720 stocks across all market capitalizations. While derivative trading activity is more active in products based on the Nikkei, the sector indices are constructed based on the larger, more diverse and more appropriately weighted TOPIX.

Non-Japan Asia (NJA)

Due to the general lack of homogeneity or integration among the different markets, the focus in non-Japan Asia—also referred to as Asia ex-Japan (AeJ)—is still on a country-specific basis. The two most popular pan-regional

Country	Index Name	Ticker	# Stocks	Sector Concentrations
Australia	S&P/ASX 200	AS51	200	Materials (28%)
China	Shanghai A-Share	SHCOMP	893	Banks (21%), Energy (29%), Materials (10%)
Hong Kong	Hang Seng	HSI	43	Banks (36%), Telecom (14%), Real Estate (13%)
	Hang Seng China Enterprises *	HSCEI	42	Banks (40%), Energy (24%), Insurance (13%)
India	Nifty 50	NIFTY	50	Energy (25%), Banks, Software, Telecom and Utilities (10% each)
Malaysia	Kuala Lumpur Exch Comp.	KLCI	100	Banks (21%), Capital Goods (13%), Food, Beverage and Tobacco (12%) Utilities (12%)
New Zealand	NZSE 15 Gross	NZSH15G	15	Telecom (29%), Materials (16%)
Singapore	Staights Times	FSSTI	30	Banks (30%), Capital Goods (20%), Real Estate (17%), Telecom (12%)
South Korea	KOSPI 200	KOSPI2	200	Semiconductors (15%), Materials (16%), Capital Goods (20%), Banks (12%).
Taiwan	TWSE (Taiex)	TWSE	690	Technology Hardware & Equipment (27%), Semiconductors (18%), Materials (15%)
Thailand	SET 50	SET50	50	Energy (39%), Banks (20%)

EXHIBIT 4.11   Non-Japan Asia Country Indices
*There are three primary types of share listing for Chinese companies. On the continental exchanges (Shanghai and Shenzhen), there are usually two types: *A-shares* trade in local currency—the Chinese *renminbi* (CNY) or *yuan*—and are generally only available to domestic Chinese investors. The other are the *B-shares*, which are available to both domestic and foreign investors and trade in currencies other than the CNY. Foreign investors, however, generally find it easier to trade a third share class, called *H-shares*, which are listed on the Hong Kong stock exchange. The *Hang Seng China H-Shares Index* (HSCEI) is a free-float capitalization weighted index of Chinese H-Shares listed on the Hang Seng exchange and, despite its association with Hong Kong, is really a benchmark for the Chinese market.

benchmarks are the *MSCI Pacific ex-Japan Index,* which consists of the four developed markets in AeJ (Australia, Hong Kong, New Zealand, and Singapore) and the expanded *All-Country Pacific ex-Japan Index,* which adds to this the seven largest emerging markets (China, Indonesia, South Korea, Malaysia, Philippines, Taiwan, and Thailand). For single country exposures, investors based outside the region tend to focus on the MSCI country indices, while local investors focus primarily on the most liquid national indices, particularly those with active derivatives markets. Though still very much emerging economies, the markets of China and India, the last two of the BRICs, receive particular attention due to their massive size and rapid rate of growth.

There is a great deal of diversity in the sector concentrations of the various benchmark national indices of Southeast Asia, though there is a clear tendency toward export-driven, cyclical industries. Listed in Exhibit 4.11 are the primary indices for each of the developed and several of the more popular emerging economies along with an indication of the most significant sector weights in each.

SUMMARY

Equity indices provide the best way of measuring the aggregate performance of the broad equity market or a specific subset of it. While the stock selection criteria depend on the objectives of the index and the universe of stocks from which the constituents are chosen, the weighting scheme usually follows one of three standard methodologies: market-capitalization weighted (sometimes adjusted for the shares in free float), equally weighed, or price weighted. Although the performance of an index is a useful indicator, it is also important to be aware that there can be a great deal of information in the internal movements of the index constituents which is not apparent at the surface.

The actual calculation of an index level is quite simple. Given the number of shares of each constituent stock in the index definition and their current prices, the total value of the stocks in the index is computed and then scaled by a divisor, which has the dual purpose of allowing us to assign an "eye-pleasing" level to the index as well as facilitating the reweighting of the index in the event of a change to the member stocks or a reweighting of an existing constituent.

The computation of a replicating stock portfolio can be accomplished in two ways. The more intuitive approach is to multiply the percentage weights of each stock by the target notional of the portfolio to get a notional investment in each stock; this is then divided by the market price of the stock to get a number of shares of the particular stock. An alternative approach is to divide the target notional amount by the value of the index stock portfolio (before applying the divisor) and then multiplying the index shares of each stock by this number. Rebalancing a hedge portfolio consists of computing the replicating portfolio under the new weightings which has the same notional value as the existing portfolio and subtracting one from the other. Portfolio rebalances should always be dollar neutral (same value of buys and sells).

The most popular broad index benchmarks in the United States are created by Standard and Poors (SPX, MID, SML), NASDAQ (NDX), Russell Investments (R1000, R2000, R3000), and Dow Jones (DJIA). In addition to the S&P and Russell growth and value style indices, there are also a number of popular sector indices, some of which are derived formulaically from broad indices and some that are original constructions. In Europe, interest in broad indices is focused primarily on the STOXX and MSCI indices, both of which are broken down into sector subindices, with secondary focus on the national benchmark indices. Interest in Asia is primarily country specific with the Nikkei and Topix in Japan and individual country indices in each of the smaller countries in NJA (non-Japan Asia). MSCI-Barra provides the most popular and comprehensive collection of global benchmark indices.

CHAPTER 5

Program Trading

INTRODUCTION

Program trading[1] is unquestionably one of the most misunderstood and unfairly vilified businesses on Wall Street. The popular perception is of unsupervised decision making and high-velocity trading by computers using sophisticated models to pick the pockets of unsuspecting investors who just want to buy a few shares to tuck away something for retirement or their kids' education.

It is certainly a colorful image but, fortunately, it is also wholly inaccurate. While there do exist so-called "statistical arbitrage" traders that use computer models to detect and profit from anomalous trading patterns in the market, they make up a small fraction of the total traded volume and, more importantly, have nothing whatsoever to do with the program trading business of a typical Wall Street investment bank.

The question then is, what exactly is program trading? At the risk of completely disappointing those readers who found the previous characterization of program trading appealing, we can use as a starting point the definition provided by the NYSE.

> **Program trading** is defined as a wide range of portfolio trading strategies involving the purchase or sale of 15 or more stocks having a total market value of $1 million or more.
> —New York Stock Exchange, July 31, 2008

It is a remarkably simple definition—15 names and a million dollars—and, admittedly, not particularly useful. In practical terms, *program trading* is the simultaneous execution of a portfolio of stocks in which the individual details of the securities take secondary importance to the analysis of the characteristics and performance of the portfolio as a whole. It is the trading approach that has evolved to meet the needs of those investors whose holdings are either too numerous to examine on a case-by-case basis, or whose strategy is focused on portfolio level aggregates. While the actual execution of a basket of stocks always comes down to the name-by-name purchase and sale of the constituent stocks, portfolio traders have specially designed trading applications that allow them to analyze and execute whole portfolios using a single-stock-like approach.

Why the Bad Rap?

Given such an apparently innocuous definition, it is reasonable to ask how program trading got such a bad reputation? In the end, a program trade is simply a coordinated execution of single stock trades—as though a single broker were conducting an army of single-stock traders—and contains nothing inherently violent or destabilizing to the market. The "bad boy" image is a primarily a result of three factors:

- *Ignorance:* There is a general misperception and lack of understanding of what program trading involves among both retail investors and government regulators. This is not helped by the misleading name, which is frequently substituted by the more appropriate term *portfolio trading*.
- *Old school:* Program trading leveraged the technological advances of the 1980s and 1990s to increase efficiency and decrease costs, making it an attractive means of executing trades for many established customers. As a result, program trading desks cannibalized much of the business previously directed to single-stock traders. In the days when it was still a relatively new product, many among Wall Street's "old guard" attempted to defend their way of doing business by laying blame for many of the world's evils at the feet of program trading.
- *Brady Commission Report:* The Brady Commission was established by President Reagan to investigate the causes of the stock market crash of October 19, 1987. In their final report, a significant portion of the responsibility for the precipitous drop in the market (approximately 25 percent in one day) was incorrectly attributed to program trading. In particular the Brady Report focused on index arbitrage, a trading strategy that captures mispricings between the stock market and the market for futures contracts on equity indices. As we will see in the next chapter, when we examine this strategy in more detail, index arbitrage is a market-neutral strategy involving the simultaneous purchase and sale of two different assets—an index futures contract and a replicating stock portfolio—each of which provides exposure to the same underlying

index. By buying the one that provides cheaper exposure to the index, and selling the one that is more expensive, a trader can capture a profit between the two. However, because both assets provide exposure to the same underlying index, and the dollar value of the purchase is the same as what is sold, the strategy is "market neutral" and cannot produce a directional move in the market as a whole (viewing "the market" as inclusive of both the stock market and the index futures market). On the day of the crash, futures were trading at a much lower price than the equivalent stock portfolio and arbitrageurs were buying futures and selling stock to bring the two prices in line (and capture the difference as profit). The Brady Commission only saw the selling in the stock market and erroneously blamed index arbitrage for the crash.

Regulations

In response to the market crash of 1987, and the misappropriation of blame to index arbitrage and portfolio trading strategies in general, several new exchange rules were established. The first of these, New York Stock Exchange Rule 80A, established the *index arbitrage collars*, an investor protection measure that went into effect any time the market moved by more than 2 percent. (In this case, the definition of "the market" was the NYSE Composite Index, a market-capitalization weighted average of all NYSE listed common stocks.) When the collars were "on," program trade orders submitted as part of an index arbitrage strategy were required to be *stabilizing*, which meant that sell orders had to be submitted with a *sell-plus* trade instruction (which specifies that the order can only be executed at a price that is a plus-tick), while buy orders had to be submitted with a *buy-minus* instruction (meaning they could only be executed on a minus-tick). These order types prevented the arbitrageur from "going to where the liquidity is," by hitting bids or lifting offers, as this would potentially exaggerate the directional move in the market. Instead, he was required to wait for the market to come to him—effectively giving precedence to all non-arbitrage orders. The collars were removed only once the market had come back to less than a 1 percent move.

For example, if the arbitrageur wanted to sell the replicating stock basket, once the collars have been switched on, his market order in each stock in the portfolio would need to be assigned a sell-plus instruction. A sell-plus order is unlikely to be executed so long as there are other more aggressive sellers in the market who are willing to hit the bid as these sales would create down-ticks in the stock price and the sell-plus order cannot be executed on a down-tick. Until the other sellers either complete, or cancel, their orders and a buyer arrives who is willing to "pay-up" for stocks thereby creating an up-tick, the arbitrageur would be unable to sell his shares.

The "tick" requirement makes the arbitrage much more difficult to capture. Because of their ease of trading, futures markets generally react more quickly than the underlying cash markets. In a sudden downward move, the futures will go down further, and do so more quickly, than the stocks. As a result, an index arbitrageur would need to sell the more expensive of the two (the stock) and purchase the futures contract. However, when the collars were on, he could only sell stock on an uptick, which is unlikely to occur when the market is dropping rapidly. As a result, while the purchase in the futures market was easy (buying futures in a falling market), the offsetting sale of the stock portfolio was very difficult, making the arbitrage opportunity almost impossible to capture. The situation was reversed in the event of a sudden market spike—the stock prices reacted more slowly than the futures and the arbitrageur would need to buy the stock basket versus selling futures. However, the stock purchase can only occur on a down-tick in the stock prices, which was similarly hard to come by.

Rule 80A displays a fundamentally flawed logic. Index arbitrage is not a directional strategy but rather acts as a messenger, communicating price information between the cash and futures markets to ensure that the prices of equivalent assets in the two markets are consistent. When the index arbitrage collars are on, the stock market is effectively saying that, because it doesn't like what the futures market is saying, it will silence the messenger. Additionally, the very tight trigger level—a 2 percent move in either direction—means that in volatile markets, the collars are turned on frequently. In 1998, Rule 80A was triggered 366 times on 227 different days (out of a total of approximately 255 trading days in the year).

In the end, logic prevailed and Rule 80A was eventually repealed, though not until 2007. Interestingly, around the same time, a similarly misguided piece of regulation introduced in the aftermath of a market crash, this one dating back more than 70 years, was also repealed. Rule 10a-1 of the Securities and Exchange Act of 1934 stipulated that short sales could only be executed on an up-tick. This resulted in an asymmetry in trading as positive views on a stock could be expressed freely, while negative views, where these implied a short position, were subject to restrictions. The approach was the same as with Rule 80A: The market doesn't like the message that the short-sellers are expressing, so it silences them. After years of traders struggling to "get the tick" on short sales, the uptick rule was gradually removed in 2007 as part of the Regulation SHO, thereby allowing for more symmetric expression of stock views.

Ironically, little more than one year after the elimination of the "tick rule" on short sales, the Securities and Exchange Commission (SEC), together with the U.K.'s Financial Services Authority (FSA) and securities market regulators of other European countries, temporarily imposed a much more severe limitation on short sales.

In the weeks following the bankruptcy of Lehman Brothers in early September of 2008, the shares of financial stocks came under extraordinary pressure. The aggressive short selling of financials by speculators, fueled by unfounded rumors about other impending bankruptcies, pushed share prices to extremely low levels, with many stocks dropping 20 and 30 percent in a single session. Plummeting stock prices were seen by many as indicative of a fundamental underlying problem (the view that "the market knows best") and investors and lenders refused to do business with those perceived as most vulnerable. This destructive cycle continued to accelerate to such a point that there was a real risk that short-sellers could actually *cause* the bankruptcy of perfectly sound businesses through a combination of speculation, fear, and rumor.

Given the extraordinary circumstances, and the potential consequences for the economy as a whole of the failure of another financial institution, the decision was made to temporarily ban all short-selling in select financial stocks in order to restore a more fair and orderly market. The measure was broadly successful in halting the downward spiral of many firms and giving investors a moment to breathe and more rationally assess the risks of each institution. While some investors commented that this situation would never have happened had Rule 80A not been repealed, the tactical application of a regulation on a temporary basis to prevent a market abuse, is unquestionably superior to the blanket application of a flawed rule.

A second piece of regulation that remains in effect is NYSE Rule 80B, which established specific percentage movements downward in the DJIA—called *circuit breakers*—that trigger trading halts on the exchange. The length of the trading halt depends on the size of the movement and the time at which it occurs.

10% decline		20% decline		30% decline	
Before 2:00	1 hour Halt	Before 1:00	2 hour Halt	Anytime	Market Closes
2:00–2:30	30-min Halt	1:00–2:00	1 hour Halt		
After 2:30	No Halt	After 2:00	Market Closes		

Source: New York Stock Exchange data (www.nyse.com) as of July 28, 2008.

The 80B circuit breakers are far less controversial than the 80A index arbitrage triggers for two reasons. First, the circuit breakers are symmetric and halt all trading to allow market participants to take a breath and make a more considered assessment of the true market conditions, while the index arbitrage collars are asymmetric and apply only to one side of a market-neutral trade. Second, unlike Rule 80A, which has at times been triggered multiple times per day, the large moves required to trigger the circuit breakers have made trading halts extremely infrequent events. Since its inception, Rule 80B has only been triggered twice, both times on October 27, 1997 resulting in the market closing 30 minutes early.

The Irony of the Little Guy

The irony of program trading, and its demonization in the popular imagination, is that the greatest beneficiary of the reduced costs and operational efficiency of program trading is in fact, the small, retail investor. The primary client base of program trading desks consists of large mutual and pension funds that specialize in the low-cost, highly-diversified index replication strategies that are the most appropriate investment vehicles for the small, individual investor. There are very few hedge funds that trade through program trading desks, as these funds tend to focus on adding value through deliberate stock selection, not adherence to an index benchmark. While a sophisticated investor with a large amount to invest may be willing to take the greater risks, and pay the higher fees (usually a 2 percent annual management fee plus 20 percent of profits) and invest in a hedge fund, the average man-on-the-street is much better off with the 10 to 20 bps annual management fees of a passive replication strategy of a diversified benchmark index. These low-cost funds can only exist because there are program trading desks to service them.

In spite of many areas of resistance, the benefits of portfolio trading as a means of trading have been too great to ignore and use of the product has grown dramatically with the percentage of total NYSE volume executed via program trades currently averaging approximately 30 percent. The NYSE monitors program trading activity closely and since 1988 has required all member firms to submit a *daily program trading report* (DPTR) with details of all orders executed as part of a program trade, and a description of the intent of the trade (agency order, customer facilitation, principal trade, index arbitrage). Individual member submissions are then aggregated into a weekly DPTR summary report containing details of overall program trading activity on the exchange with specific details about the share volumes traded by the 15 most active program trading firms. This report is available from the NYSE web site.

Exhibit 5.1 contains the 52-week averages of selected volume data taken from the July 31, 2008 DPTR report with comparisons to the previous two years. Trading volumes reported here refer only to program trading in NYSE-listed stocks. Observe that, not only has there been a large increase in trading volumes over the period (up 62 percent from 1.67 billion to 2.70 billion shares per day), but there has been a dramatic shift of venue. In the 2005–2006 period, the split between the percentage of NYSE-listed stocks traded on the exchange and via alternate liquidity venues (ECNs,

NYSE Program Trading Summary			
52wk Averages (as of July 31)	2008	2007	2006
Average Daily Volume (MM S	**2,703.00**	**2,178.20**	**1,664.90**
NYSE	40.10%	47.40%	58.00%
Other	59.90%	52.60%	42.00%
% Total NYSE Volume	27.70%	31.90%	29.10%
Breakdown by Strategy			
Agency	63.80%	59.70%	55.80%
Customer Facilitation	5.60%	6.50%	5.20%
Principal (ex-Index Arb)	27.10%	28.80%	31.30%
Index Arbitrage	3.40%	5.00%	7.70%

EXHIBIT 5.1 One-Year Average DPTR Statistics
Source: New York Stock Exchange data (www.nyse.com) as of July 31, 2008.

broker liquidity pools, etc.) was roughly 60/40. Just two years later, this split has reversed, with 60 percent of volumes now traded off-exchange.

EXPLANATION OF A SAMPLE TRADE

Because program trading is a service and not a traded product like a stock or option—the best way to understand how a program trading desk works comes from sitting beside the trader and watching what he or she does. The closest approximation we can manage here is to walk through the life cycle of a hypothetical client order, describing the various steps and providing examples of trade details and typical dialogue. To facilitate the explanation, I have included a simplified mock-up of a typical program trading order management system, shown in Exhibit 5.2. A close examination of the tools used by a program trader can provide valuable insight into what he does and what is important to his business.

Step 1: Trade Initiation

The process begins when the client informs the sales-trader that he will be sending over an order and provides preliminary details of what it contains and how he wants to execute it. At this point, no specific details of the constituent securities are provided, only gross portfolio characteristics, which are used primarily to ensure that the full order has been transmitted successfully. The sales-trader gives the trader a heads-up that the client is about to send over the details of the trade.

Sales-trader to Trader: "Hey—Onceler Investments sending over a trade—it's 62 buys, 85 sells for a total of 1,220,100 shares, worth about $35 million. He wants to work it over the day VWAP-style but he's willing to skew it a bit if you have a view and think you can do better. He'll be FIX-ing it over in the next couple of minutes. Once I get it in and have confirmed details can you give him a call to discuss execution strategy?"

Step 2: Order Transmission and Upload

The trading desk may receive the order either via an e-mailed spreadsheet or text file or, as is now the standard, via a *FIX* connection. FIX, an acronym for Financial Information eXchange, is a series of messaging specifications for communicating trade and execution information between brokers and clients—almost like a programming language. Clients establish electronic connections with a broker and use the FIX protocol to transmit orders directly to the trading desks. Compared with e-mailed spreadsheets, the straight-through processing and lack of manual intervention greatly speeds up the process and reduces errors.

Regardless of how it is communicated, the order will contain some type of security identifier (ticker, RIC, CUSIP, Sedol), the share quantity to be executed and an indication of the side (buy, sell, or sell short). Some clients may indicate a buy to cover (i.e., a purchase that covers a short, rather than initiating a new long) though this is primarily for their own benefit as a buy to cover is treated identically to a buy from a trading perspective. The trade direction will sometimes be indicated by assigning to the shares either a positive or negative share quantity. In this case, however, it is important to confirm whether a positive quantity is a buy (i.e., I want to end up with 10,000 shares) or a sale (I have 10,000 shares and want to liquidate them). There may also be an indication of the client account to which the executions should be booked, though this is sometimes provided later.

The Order Management System The order is loaded into the program trading order management system, as shown in Exhibit 5.2. The system will first check to confirm that all identifiers submitted by the client are valid (i.e., they represent real securities) by confirming versus the internal product databases. The portfolio order is given a name, *Onceler_310808*, by the trader and the basic details of the total portfolio, including the number of stocks, total shares, and an estimated notional value of the whole portfolio in USD (in this case $35,761,131), are then displayed in the uppermost grid on the screen (the *Portfolio List*). Share quantity and notional value details are first provided in aggregate for the whole portfolio and then broken

PROGRAM TRADING ORDER MANAGEMENT SYSTEM

31 Aug, 2008   11:19:48

PORTFOLIO LIST:

Portfolio Name	Tickers	Shares	Total $	Buys	Buy Shs	Buy $	% Exec	Sells	Sell Shs	Sell $	% Exec
VWAP_Risk_310808	145	2,844,300	91,358,916	85	1,223,049	51,160,993	25.0%	60	1,621,251	40,197,923	28.4%
→ Onceler_310808	147	1,220,100	35,761,131	62	448,500	15,616,697	43.4%	85	771,600	20,144,434	31.4%
Tech_Rebal_310808	41	338,700	9,452,114	10	83,400	2,327,801	0.0%	31	255,300	7,124,313	0.0%
...											

NEW   IMPORT FIX / REPORTS / SEND FILLS

STOCK DETAILS: Onceler_310808

SIDE: B/S [O] B [●] S [O]   VIEW BY: STOCK [●] SECTOR [O]

Ticker	Name	Side	Total Shs	% Portfolio	Total $	% ADV ▽	Shs Exec	% COMP	Shs UnEx	Avg Px	Vwap	Perf (bps)
ENRG	Popular Energy	B	24,100	6.84%	1,068,112	30.58%	7,150	29.7%	16,950	44.220	44.312	41.4
SSG	Simon Signal Group	B	12,100	4.19%	655,033	13.84%	5,410	44.7%	6,690	15.899	15.885	(8.7)
ITI	IT Technonlogy	B	25,000	3.07%	479,500	12.49%	11,000	44.0%	14,000	19.296	19.319	11.6
MNET	Micronet Software	B	10,400	2.01%	313,976	2.10%	4,700	45.2%	5,700	30.561	30.337	(73.9)
GEE	Giant Oil	B	112,400	3.00%	468,224	1.88%	52,300	46.5%	60,100	37.866	37.923	15.1
WBP	Warjason Badpuns	B	3,500	1.49%	232,015	1.54%	1,485	42.4%	2,015	66.557	66.432	(18.7)
CAR	Carlauto	B	8,700	1.43%	223,068	1.34%	4,050	46.6%	4,650	25.705	25.793	34.1
TOTAL			**448,500**		**15,616,697**		**194,515**	**43.4%**	**253,985**			**4.4**

CREATE % WAVE / SNG STK ORDER

WAVE DETAILS: Onceler_310808

Basket Name	Side	Wave #	State	% Portfolio	Tickers	Total Shs	$ Value	Resid Shs	UnEx $	% Exec	Instrux	Time Sent
Onceler_310808	Buy	4	Working	5.0%	62	22,425	780,835	7,310	254,533	67.4%	Last	11:05:55
Onceler_310808	Buy	3	Cancelled	5.0%	62	22,425	780,835	-	-	100.0%	Last	10:30:25
Onceler_310808	Buy	2	Working	6.8%	1	24,100	1,068,112	16,950	751,224	29.7%	Cash Desk	9:22:25
Onceler_310808	Buy	1	Complete	23.2%	61	106,100	3,637,146	-	-	100.0%	MOO	8:59:22

UPDATE WAVE / CANCEL WAVE / VIEW WAVE DETAILS

EXHIBIT 5.2 Program Trading Order Management System

down between buys and sells. We also find an indication of what percentage of how much of the portfolio has already been executed. In Exhibit 5.2, for example, the snapshot of the Onceler_310808 is taken when 43.4 percent of the buy side of the portfolio is completed, and 31.4 percent of the sell side. Portfolio-level actions such as uploading a new trade or importing an order via a FIX connection, generating execution reports (more on this later) or sending *fills* (execution prices) back to the client via FIX can be done using the buttons attached to the bottom right of the grid. The details of all orders that have been loaded into the system will be visible by scrolling through the Portfolio List. (The arrow indicates the Onceler order.)

When the order is uploaded, the order management system queries the firm's market data systems for details on each of the individual securities (last price, currency, average daily trading volume, etc.). Selecting on the portfolio in the Portfolio List causes the details of the individual orders in the portfolio to be displayed in the *Stock Details* grid, in the middle of the screen. Details will include ticker, company name, side (buy or sell), shares, the percentage weight of that order in the portfolio, the notional value of the order, and an estimate of the liquidity of the order (i.e., what percentage of the *average daily traded volume* (%ADV) does the particular order comprise). This Stock Details grid will continually update each order in real time with the number of shares executed, both in absolute terms and as a percentage of the whole order, the residual shares still unexecuted, and the average execution price. The benchmark price for the portfolio (in this case, the VWAP) is shown to the far right along with the relative performance of the actual execution versus that benchmark. Aggregate details for the portfolio are also shown in a *Total* row at the bottom of the Stock Details.

To allow the trader to analyze the portfolio from different perspectives, there are several different sorting and filtering options for the Stock Details window. The order management system shown in Exhibit 5.2 includes toggles (just above the middle of the grid) that allow the trader to choose between viewing the entire portfolio or just the buy or sell side, as well as the option to view all individual stock-level details or aggregated information by sector. The Stock Details grid can also be sorted by clicking on the column headings. (It is sorted in descending order by %ADV in the figure.)

Step 3: Pre-Trade Analysis and Strategy

Prior to executing the order, the trader will examine the portfolio to familiarize himself with its general characteristics as well as to understand any particular sensitivities that might influence the execution. His goal is to understand the composition of the portfolio so that he can determine the best trading strategy to achieve the customer's objectives, as well as to be able to advise the client of any particular characteristics of the portfolio that might require special attention (such as a single stock that comprises a very large portion of the order or a particularly illiquid stock that might be difficult to trade). The pre-trade analysis allows the trader to determine if the client's desired trading approach is consistent with the portfolio's characteristics and, if not, to propose an alternative approach. While clients frequently calculate their own portfolio analytics, many rely on the trader for guidance and it is his responsibility to make sure that the trading approach does not jeopardize the client's interests or cause unnecessary market volatility or disruptions.

For most situations, a quick examination of the largest weights in the portfolio and any liquidity issues directly from the program trading order management system is sufficient to guide the execution. However, for larger, more complicated or more sensitive trades, it is often necessary to perform much more detailed portfolio analytics. Most firms will offer a *pre-trade tool*, usually either Excel, or web-based, that produces more complete portfolio analytics including more refined sector decomposition, breakdown by market capitalization, country, and currency (for international portfolios), as well as historical performance, correlation versus a benchmark, and anticipated execution impact analysis.

The particular client in our example has indicated that he wants to spread the execution of the basket, targeting VWAP but has expressed a willingness to take some risk in an effort to outperform the benchmark and has asked the trader for guidance and any views he might have.

> Trader to Client: "Overall the portfolio is very liquid large-cap names with the exception of a couple of names where you're over 10 percent of the volume. Popular Energy's really the only one where we might have difficulties because it's a thin stock and you've got a third of a day's volume. Sector-wise you've got a lot of energy—about a quarter of your basket—which we'll watch closely: there was OPEC news overnight and it looks like energy stocks will be opening lower. Otherwise the market looks strong. I'd suggest overweighting the open a bit on your buy side to take advantage of weakness there and hold back a bit on your sales."

The specification of a benchmark, be it VWAP or any other, is intended, in a program trading context, to apply to the aggregate performance of the whole order. Even if some of the individual executions are far from VWAP, the client will most likely be satisfied if, on average across the whole portfolio, the execution is better than the VWAP. The client may choose to drill down into the individual stock details to see if any particular orders were particularly well or poorly executed but, in principle at least, the broker's goal is to provide an execution that compares favorably against the chosen benchmark in aggregate for the entire portfolio.

Step 4: Execution

An execution strategy, no matter how clever or appropriate, cannot be agreed upon if the tools do not exist to implement it. Over the years progressively more sophisticated strategies and techniques for executing large stock portfolios have been developed to meet the ever more complex requirements of clients and traders.

Trading a portfolio is conceptually very similar to trading a single stock. The difference is that, rather than speaking in concrete share numbers and prices ("I have 100,000 XYZ to sell and I am going to offer 10,000 shares at 47.25"), we speak in *percentage terms* and *descriptive prices.* ("I'm going to offer a 10 percent slice of the basket at last sale.") It is important to remember that the stock exchange understands single stocks only—there is no concept of linking orders together or using some sort of combined price. It is the job of the program trading tools to convert the "10 percent at last sale" portfolio-level instruction into a *wave* of single stock orders, each for 10 percent of the respective share quantity, with a limit price equal to the last sale price in each stock.

In the program trading tools this wave is then monitored and treated like a mini portfolio. The program trading software keeps track of each of the individual order numbers of the single stock trades and aggregates the results into a wave detail. The waves that have been sent to market in the hypothetical trading system are shown in the *Wave Detail* at the bottom of the screen in Exhibit 5.2.

Depending on the characteristics of the portfolio and the objectives of the client, the trader will choose from a number of possible approaches to executing the basket. The specific functionality available will vary from one trading system to another, but the general concepts are consistent and correspond to the various trading instructions that clients or traders might request. The essential specifications are the stocks to include in the wave, the share quantities of each, and the trading instruction that goes with them.

- **Waves:** The shares of each individual stock included in the wave may be based on:
  - *Percent of total:* A percentage slice of the total order in each stock (e.g., "10 percent of the total order").

- *Percent of residual:* A percentage of the shares of each stock not already allocated to another wave order (e.g., "half of what's left").
- *Percent of a subset:* A percentage, either of the total or residual amount, of a subset of the total order. This can be selected based on predefined characteristic such as sector, market capitalization or liquidity, or manually chosen by the trader according to other criteria (e.g., orders that can be paired off internally against other client flows and do not need to be executed in the market).
- *Single stock:* A specific number of shares of a single stock.

- **Trading instructions:** The trading instructions for a wave may be described in terms of a reference price or a particular approach, such as a VWAP target:
  - *Exchange orders:* For orders sent directly to the exchange, the instruction can be a market order, either for continuous trading or limited to one of the auctions (MOC or MOO) or a limit order based on any readily available reference price (bid, ask, last, prior close, etc.). At the time the wave is sent, the reference price is snapped and applied as a numerical limit to each individual stock order. The limit price may also be adjusted by a given number of cents per share, ticks, or basis points (e.g., a wave of sell orders sent with a limit equal to the offer side less one tick: This would establish a new best offer in each stock which puts the order at the front of the queue).
  - *Automated execution:* For many "plain vanilla" orders there is little value to be added through active management of the trade. These orders are best executed via the algorithmic trading engines.[2] Automated trading engines are even more appropriate for program trading due to the natural averaging effect of a portfolio trade. Algorithmic strategies must, by necessity, make assumptions about the "normal" trading patterns of stocks and will use statistical analysis of stock price movements to determine this. In any given situation, due to the idiosyncratic movements of a particular stock, the algorithmic approach may produce good or bad results. However, if the system is well designed and produces, on average, a good execution, then the application of the algorithm to a portfolio consisting of many securities will tend to perform well as the individual good and bad performances net off.
  - *Direct to cash desk:* Orders that require special attention or that match off against other cash desk client flows can be given a trading instruction and sent to the cash desk traders for execution. Where there is significant news or a particular situation in a stock, or for very illiquid names, this is often the best alternative.

■ *Single-name order:* If the wave only contains a single name, then a specific numerical price limit may be specified as well as any of the above instructions.

The responsibility of the trader is then to monitor the execution of each wave order and how the combination of the waves contributes to the aggregate portfolio execution. However, unlike a cash trader, who immediately looks into the details of each single stock order, the program trader works first with high-level summary information about each wave and then, when he suspects that there may be an issue with a particular stock, he can drill down into the wave details to analyze the specific situation more closely.

A program trader may, for example, send a 10 percent slice of a buy portfolio with a limit of "last sale" and leave the orders in the market for a few minutes. He is likely to get a portion of the wave, say 20 to 30 percent, done quite quickly because in many stocks the "last" trade will have occurred on the offer side and the instruction to "pay last" will therefore be equivalent to "pay the offer." If not enough shares are available on the offer side to complete the individual order, the balance remains in the market as the new best bid. For the rest of the basket, where the "last" occurred either on the bid or midmarket between the bid and offer, he will need to wait to see if a seller hits his bid.

By watching the percent complete the trader can monitor how many of his orders are being completed. If he sees a steady increase in the percentage of the wave that is executed, this would indicate that the market is "coming in to him" (i.e., his bids in the market are, bit by bit, being hit). If he sees that the wave stagnates at a certain percentage completion, he may choose to update the limits on his unexecuted orders to the current "last" in each stock. Alternatively, he could choose to pay the offer side or change from a limit to a market order to complete the balance of the wave more quickly. These decisions depend on how wide the bid-offer spread is in the portfolio constituents (how much will it cost to cross the spread), the liquidity of the portfolio, the general trend of the market, and many other subjective factors. If there are particular stocks in the portfolio that are proving problematic, the program trader will address these individually, particularly where they have a significant weight in the portfolio and are likely to have a noticeable impact on the aggregate basket-level performance versus the benchmark.

This last point is an important one. While program trading focuses on the aggregate performance of the portfolio, this does not mean that program traders are uninterested in specific stock details. In a large, diversified portfolio, the intraday movements of many stocks will be very similar to that of the broad market as a whole, and a program trader can make intelligent decisions about when to be more or less aggressive in his trading using a broad market index for guidance. However, there will also be some outlier stocks whose price action is driven by company-specific news and therefore very different to that of the market as a whole. While statistical averages and historical volume distributions are appropriate for the management of most orders, it is the appropriate management of the outlier stocks that often determines the performance versus the benchmark.

Even stocks with small weights in the portfolio can require significant attention if their percentage deviation from the benchmark is large. Missing by 10 bps on an order that is 10 percent of the basket will have the same impact on the total portfolio as missing by 100 bps on an order that has only a 1 percent weight. While the focus is naturally concentrated on the largest constituents, a poor execution in illiquid or highly volatile "tails" of the portfolio can have a very detrimental impact on the aggregate portfolio performance.

Step 5: Feedback

The interaction between customers and traders (or sales-traders) depends very much on the personality of the client and the characteristics of the portfolio. While some prefer to leave the order in the hands of the broker and wait for an end-of-day e-mail with details of their performance, other clients prefer to be much more involved, in some cases to the point of specifically directing the execution. ("Put out a 10 percent slice of the buy side right now—bid side plus a tick.... How much am I done? Move the balance to last sale. Market's coming off here, cancel the balance! How much have I done? Put another 10 percent out bid side less two ticks ...")

In general, small, highly liquid portfolios to be executed at market require little, if any, feedback since there is really not much to say other than "you're done" and send back the fills. Customers executing large or illiquid portfolios or trading strategies that depend on the evolution of market conditions will more often require intraday feedback. It is common for the trader or sales-trader to provide one or more intraday updates on the progress of the execution, the performance versus the benchmark and any particular drivers of the returns that may require attention.

> Trader to Client: "We're about 40 percent done right here—a bit ahead on the buys and holding off some on the sales as the market rallies. So far we're doing well—we're beating VWAP by about 4.5 bps. The majority of that is coming from the energy stocks where we took advantage of the opening sell-off to get ahead on volume. The Micronet news is hurting us—we're missing VWAP there by about 74 bps, but fortunately it's only 2 percent of the portfolio. The one

particularly illiquid name—Popular Energy—I'm working with the cash trader. We're a bit behind on volume because we're trying to be delicate and pick our spots but it's going very well—we're beating VWAP by quite a bit. Overall liquidity is pretty good and I don't see any difficulties in completing the order today."

Step 6: Trade Reporting, Post-Trade Analysis, and Booking

When the trade is completed, the client will require execution details for each of the individual orders including the shares traded, the average price, details of any commissions, fees, or taxes, the net price after factoring in these costs and the trade and settlement dates. Customers with a FIX connection can receive all this information directly from the execution systems (sometimes in real-time through the day), while others will require an execution summary report. Some customers may specify a custom execution report format that they require for their orders.

It is also common for clients to request a post-trade *performance analysis report,* which provides a comparison of the portfolio execution to the benchmark at the aggregate level as well as a line-by-line analysis of each individual order and the fractional contribution to the overall performance contributed by each stock. (More on this shortly.)

Trades are then booked at the net execution prices (gross prices adjusted up or down for commission) into the customer's accounts. As discussed in Chapter 3, the thousands of individual executions against the exchange are booked versus a wash account and each of the client's accounts receives a single execution in each stock at the average price (adjusted for commissions and exchange fees). In order for a program trading desk to function effectively, the booking process must be completely automated as the volumes are simply too large to handle any other way. If nothing goes wrong, the booking and settlement process should require relatively little manual intervention by traders, salespeople, or back-office support staff.

WHEN IS PROGRAM TRADING MORE BENEFICIAL?

The explosive growth of portfolio trading over the last 20 years has demonstrated that this alternative approach to trading has merit and is attractive to many clients. Its popularity is due in part to practical considerations: With commission rates usually of one-half to one-third of the cash business, program trading offers a flexible, low-cost alternative to the high-touch service provided by a single-stock trader.

There are also enormous operational advantages to program trading. For index fund managers who replicate highly diversified broad-market indices, the only economically or operationally feasible means of managing cash inflows and outflows, index constituent rebalances, or reallocations of assets between funds is via program trades. Portfolio trading is also an attractive means of execution for investment managers who do not replicate indices but who prefer to look at their positions from a portfolio perspective rather than a single-stock viewpoint. A particular examples would be managers of *quant funds,* which select stocks according to certain fundamental or technical criteria and use large, diversified portfolios to eliminate (or at least minimize) the single stock risks, These funds can hold hundreds or even thousands of positions that are rebalanced frequently, making the low cost, highly-automated service of program trading attractive.

The growth of program trading also benefited from timing; the technological advances that allowed program trading to flourish coincided with (and facilitated) the explosion in popularity of broad index-replication strategies by institutional investors. In the 1960s and early 1970s, concepts such as the *Efficient Market Hypothesis* and *Modern Portfolio Theory,* which eschews single stock selection in favor of a broadly diversified "market portfolio," were widely accepted in academic circles, but mostly ignored in industry where they were not only heretical to the stock-picker culture of the time, but also virtually impossible to implement. It was not until the late 1970s and early 1980s, just as the computing power needed to execute and risk manage portfolios of hundreds of stocks was being developed, that buy side investors began to see the appeal of passive, broadly diversified investment strategies. In a sense, Modern Portfolio Theory made investors want index funds, and program trading allowed them to have them.

International Program Trading

Many large investment banks have portfolio trading desks not only in New York, but in London, Tokyo, and Hong Kong. This international offering is particularly attractive to clients looking to execute global portfolios that require coordination across multiple regions. Due to the specialized knowledge of global markets (and the unique trading and settlement issues of each) that is required to properly manage this process, these trades will usually be handled by a dedicated group of *global portfolio sales-traders.*

The role of the global portfolio sales-trader is to coordinate the local traders in each region so that the portfolio is executed in accordance with the client's instructions. While the experts on executing in any region are always the local traders, the global portfolio sales trading team will have sufficient understanding of the details of each foreign market to ensure that clients are advised prior to execution of any potential issues with their order (global holidays, settlement cycles, exchange rules). Global portfolio sales-traders are also closely involved with settlement issues, which can be considerably more complex in international markets, and managing any currency transactions related to the trade.

PORTFOLIO ANALYTICS

A distinguishing characteristic of program trading is the focus on high-level portfolio aggregates, in lieu of single stock details. In order to understand program trading, it is therefore necessary to have a sense for what kinds of statistics are important, what they tell us, and how they are calculated. We will use the performance analysis report for a simplified four name hypothetical portfolio in Exhibit 5.3 as a reference to guide the explanations.

Execution Data The information in the first section of the report is mostly self-explanatory: the list of individual stocks, the share quantities executed and the average price of execution, and the percentage weight of each stock in the portfolio, computed using the execution prices. The execution price shown is the gross price, exclusive of commissions, fees, taxes, or other costs, rather than the net price. The goal of the report is to measure the quality of the execution; the cost of obtaining that execution is a separate matter. Where part of the order is unexecuted, the performance analysis will usually only reference the executed portion of the portfolio.

The *Totals* row at the bottom contains the sum of the data in the share quantity and percentage weight columns. For the *Exec Price* column, the sum of the prices paid for each stock is meaningless and is therefore replaced by the value of the entire portfolio at the executed prices (i.e., the amount paid for the entire portfolio).

Execution Data				Side: BUY Performance versus Benchmark				Perf Attribution	
Ticker	Shares	Exec Price	% Wgt	VWAP	$	cps	bps	cps	bps
BRLN	108,220	79.7185	27.8%	79.8019	9,026	0.083	10.5	0.015	2.9
FFT	245,100	35.7584	28.3%	35.8012	10,490	0.043	12.0	0.018	3.4
MUN	132,770	53.3595	22.9%	53.3072	(6,944)	(0.052)	(9.8)	(0.012)	(2.2)
DUS	102,000	63.7375	21.0%	63.7242	(1,357)	(0.013)	(2.1)	(0.002)	(0.4)
Totals	588,090	30,977,286	100.0%	30,988,501	11,215	0.019	3.6	0.019	3.6

EXHIBIT 5.3 Performance Analysis Report

Performance versus Benchmark   The second section of the report provides the details of the quality of the execution versus the benchmark for each of the individual stocks, as well as for the portfolio as a whole. In our example, the benchmark was the VWAP and the individual VWAP prices are provided in the first column. As with the *Exec Price* column in the previous section, the sum of the individual benchmark prices is meaningless and is replaced by the value of the entire portfolio at the VWAP prices.

The performance versus the benchmark for each constituent stock is expressed in three different ways: total dollars, cents per share (*cps*), and basis points (*bps*). It is easiest to begin with the second of these—the cents-per-share calculation, which is simply the difference between the execution price and the VWAP. Because this is a performance metric, an outperformance is always a positive while an underperformance is negative. The correct formula therefore depends on whether the order is buy or a sale. In the example of Exhibit 5.3, all orders are buys and the calculation is *Performance = Benchmark – Execution* such that an execution price that is lower than the benchmark produces a positive result (bought it for less). For sales the formula would be reversed (*Performance = Execution – Benchmark*). For portfolios containing both buy and sell orders, the out- or underperformance of each side would be computed separately and then summed in the portfolio-level calculation. In keeping with a slightly sloppy but nevertheless common market practice, the column heading is labeled "cps" but the value shown for each stock is actually a dollar difference in the execution price per share (e.g., $0.083) rather than a true cents-per-share value (e.g., 8.3 cents).

This cents-per-share performance then can be easily converted to our other two measurements ($ and bps). In the column labeled "bps," we divide the cps deviation by the benchmark price to get a measure of the percentage difference between the executed and benchmark prices, which is then expressed in basis points. For example, in BRLN, the outperformance of $0.083 is divided by the VWAP price of $79.8019, which gives 0.00105 or 10.5 bps.

To compute the dollar deviation, we multiply the cps slippage between each execution from the benchmark by the number of shares executed. This gives the total dollar difference between the executed value of the traded shares and the value of those shares at the VWAP price.

There are two ways to calculate the total dollar deviation of the entire portfolio from the benchmark: either as the difference of the portfolio value at the executed prices and the value at the benchmark prices, or as the sum of the individual dollar deviations in column two. Both methods produce the same result, a $11,215 outperformance. For the cps and bps columns, however, the totals at the bottom of the columns are not equal to the sum of the data in the columns because the cents per share and basis point performances are not additive—each of the individual cps (bps) performances is applied to a different number of shares (notional value) and therefore does not have an equal weight in the portfolio. To compute the portfolio-level performance in cents-per-share, we divide the aggregate dollar outperformance on the whole trade by the total number of shares traded ($11,215/588,090 = 0.019cps). For the basis point performance we divide the aggregate dollar out- or underperformance by the value of the portfolio at the VWAP ($11,215 / $30,988,501 = 0.036% = 3.6 bps).

Performance Attribution   The last section of the performance analysis report attributes to each constituent stock, its fractional contribution to the performance of the portfolio as a whole. The data in this section answer the question: "How much of the total performance is due to the execution in this particular stock?" This is done by combining into a single statistic the quality of the individual stock execution against its benchmark and the weight of the individual stock in the portfolio. As we have mentioned previously, the individual stock's performance is only relevant insofar as it contributes to the aggregate portfolio performance; the performance attribution tells us by how much each stock matters.

For the cents-per-share performance attribution, we divide the dollar value of the deviation in the individual stock by the total number of shares in the portfolio. For example, the $9,026 outperformance in the execution of BRLN contributed $0.015 per share to the overall performance of the trade ($9,026 / $588,090 = $0.015).

The basis point attribution is computed by dividing the dollar value of the deviation in the individual stock by the notional value of the total portfolio at the benchmark prices. For example, the $9,026 outperformance in the execution of BRLN contributed 2.9 bps to the overall performance of the trade ($9,026 / $30,988,501 = 2.9bps)

Because these values are the *basket-level* contributions of each individual stock to the aggregate portfolio performance, the totals for each of these columns can be computed as the sums of the individual elements, which add up the same values that were previously computed.

Implied Index Level   Another way of viewing the economics of a portfolio trade is to convert the execution price into an implied level in a benchmark index. This is a particularly common calculation for investors attempting to replicate a particular index or whose performance is measured versus an index benchmark. To calculate the implied index level, the executed level of the basket is compared to a fixed reference point at which both the value of the stock basket and the level of the benchmark index can be determined (often that day's, or the previous day's, closing price). The percentage change in the value of the portfolio between the reference point and the executed prices is then computed. The value of the index at the reference price is then adjusted by this same percentage to produce the implied index level corresponding to the executed portfolio value. The implied index level calculation tells us where the index would have been if it had moved by the same percentage amount as the portfolio did.

As an example, we consider a portfolio manager running an index tracking fund who receives a new cash inflow of $2 million to be invested as of the close of business that day. Due to a complication, the money is not invested and needs to be held in cash overnight. The market closes with the index at 1,250.00. The next morning, the portfolio manager buys the basket of stock as soon as the market opens, and pays a total of $1,992,000 for it. This $8,000 outperformance versus his benchmark (the close) is equal to 20 bps on the total portfolio value ($8,000 / $2,000,000 = 20 bps.) By applying the same 20 bps move to the closing index level, we can view the purchase price of the stock portfolio as being equivalent to having purchased exposure to the index at an implied index level of 1,247.50.

Implementation Shortfall   While VWAP has historically been one of the most popular benchmarks for performance analyses, its shortcoming is that it only measures the quality of the broker's execution, not the economic performance of the trade. A broker's execution can be exactly in line with VWAP and the trade can still be economically disastrous for the client—all the performance versus VWAP says is that the broker didn't trade the stock any worse than the average broker would have. In fact, there are many situations where the trading approach most likely to produce a good performance versus the VWAP will not be the approach that minimizes the market impact of the execution. Particularly where there are performance-dependent commission structures or a policy of allocating business based on the broker's ability to outperform the benchmark, the instruction to execute with a "beat the VWAP," target can produce a situation where the broker and the client have misaligned goals.

In recent years, as investors have recognized the limitations of VWAP as a measure of performance, many clients have begun to focus on *implementation shortfall,* which measures the total change in portfolio value from *all* sources relative to a specified price level, often referred to as a *strike price.*[3] This is usually either the prior night's close or a snap of the price level at the time the order was given to the broker. It is important that the strike price be in the past so that it is not something that will be affected by the broker's actions. Rather than deciding a priori how the stock should be traded, the client gives the broker discretion to use whatever approach he believes is best to minimize the shortfall, taking into consideration both the market impact of the trading and the market risk of delaying execution. This fully aligns the broker's goals with the client's interests and allows the broker to make use of all the information available to him at the time of trading to provide the best possible execution.

The same methods for measuring market impact that were discussed in the chapter on cash trading are applicable to portfolios, though there are some additional considerations. For example, a single-stock trader can compare the price movement of a stock he is trading to the relevant sector index as a means of estimating the degree of market impact attributable to his trading. For a program trader, the determination of the benchmark can be more complex. While a large diversified portfolio can be comfortably compared to a broad index benchmark, a portfolio that is heavily concentrated into a small number of sectors should be compared to the performance of these sectors. However, depending on the size of the portfolio being executed and the number of constituent stocks of the index present in the portfolio, the index itself may be significantly impacted by the trading and no longer provide an objective reference.

The analysis of implementation shortfall, and the determination of the optimal trading strategies for mitigating it, becomes progressively more complicated as the execution of the portfolio is spread over longer periods of time. Even on a portfolio of moderate size that can be executed in a single day there are many interrelated factors that must be taken into consideration:

- *Dollar balance:* If the buy and sell sides of the portfolio are not of roughly similar size then the portfolio has a directional bias and will be sensitive to the direction of the market. How does the buy/sell imbalance in the portfolio change when we adjust for the differing sensitivities of the individual stocks on each side of the portfolio to movements in the market? (The stocks' beta, as defined in Chapter 12.)
- *Sectors, market capitalization, style:* Are there significant differences in the composition of each side of the portfolio when broken down by sector, market capitalization, or style (value versus growth)?
- *Liquidity:* How liquid are the stocks? How long will it take to trade them without significant impact? How much impact is acceptable in order to complete quickly? Is one side much more liquid than the other such that, if each side is traded with volume, the portfolio will develop a dollar imbalance? Do some liquid stocks need to be traded more slowly than their own liquidity would allow to prevent the development of sector, market cap, or style biases in the unexecuted portion of the portfolio?

- *Idiosyncratic risks:* Are there any stocks with news out on them? If we have a very illiquid position that will take a long time to trade, do we maintain an offsetting position in a more liquid name to keep the portfolio balanced or is the correlation so low that the additional position creates more risk than it reduces?

If we now consider the execution of a very large portfolio over multiple days, the process becomes significantly more complex—particularly if the portfolio stocks are in multiple currencies or across several regions. The management of liquidity issues and the balance between getting stock executed and having impact take on much greater importance, as it is presumably the lack of liquidity that makes it necessary to execute the portfolio over several days in the first place. Sector, capitalization, and style biases that might be left unaddressed on a one-day trade become much more significant when the trade is going to be executed over multiple days. It also becomes necessary to monitor the constituents for corporate actions (stock splits, spin-offs, etc.) that may change the share quantities of constituents of the portfolio from one day to the next.

TRANSITION MANAGEMENT

One of the situations in which these sorts of large portfolio trades arise is in *transition trades,* a general category describing many types of large-scale portfolio restructurings by investment managers. The transition may be due to changes in asset allocation, investment style, benchmark, portfolio managers, or other reasons. In all cases, the common characteristic is that, when compared with the typical trades made by the fund, either to adjust portfolio weights or accommodate investor cash flows, transition trades are much larger (anywhere from a few hundred million to tens of billions of dollars) and involve a greater percentage of the fund's assets. The focus in these trades is on the preservation of capital as it is transferred from one set of investments to another. Transition trades are usually subjected to tremendous scrutiny by the client as the slippages involved in the execution can have a noticeable impact on the fund's performance.

Another common characteristic of transition trades is operational complexity. It is frequently the case that the transitioned assets come from, and are going to, multiple funds. The specific allocation to each fund will be different and each fund's trade may be subject to cash constraints (for example, the purchases must be funded by the proceeds from the sales). These cash constraints impose trading restrictions on the broker because the execution of a highly liquid order on one side of the portfolio may be contingent on the execution of a highly illiquid order on the other side. Many transition trades will also involve both equity and fixed income products and therefore require the coordination of execution across different divisions within the executing broker firm.

In very large transitions there is also an extreme sensitivity to the confidentiality of the information. For example, the news that a large fund is making a shift in its equity allocation out of the United States and into Europe sends a strong message to the market about that fund's expectation for the future performance of each region. If the news leaks out before the trade is completed (or even initiated), other market participants are likely to put on the same trade, pushing Europe higher and the United States lower before the fund has had the opportunity to make its transition.

Because of the high degree of sensitivity, scrutiny, and operational complexity of transition trades, many large investment banks employ specialized groups that focus exclusively on *transition management*. To ensure confidentiality and client confidence, these groups are generally somewhat separated from the client-facing sales and trading desks.

Broadly speaking, the transition management process consists of three steps:

1. *Pre-trade:* Transition managers provide extensive pre-trade analysis and develop a plan of implementation across all asset classes involved to minimize the risks during the period when the portfolio is being executed. The *legacy* and *target* portfolios (i.e., the current holdings and the holdings they want to get to) are compared to determine any overlap and reduce the amount of actual trading necessary (called *in-kind crossing*). Transition managers can also help to coordinate the legal and operational aspects of the trade.

2. *Execution:* Given the size of the portfolios in question there is a significant focus on reducing market impact. One of the most important tools for limiting impact is *crossing*. Rather than simply executing in the market, the transition manager works with the program trading desk to find natural flows from other customers that can be paired off against the transition portfolio—the greater the amount of crossing, the lower the impact on the market. As a result, the program trading houses with the greatest amount of customer flow often have the most active transition management groups. (As the Wall Street maxim says: "flow begets flow.") Whatever cannot be crossed is traded in the market. Additional hedging transactions that are not part of the original portfolio may be executed to adjust the level of market exposure during the trading period.

3. *Post-trade:* Transition managers are expected to perform extensive post-trade analysis for their clients. In many cases the clients themselves are required to present a formal review of the success of the transition process to the senior management or trustees of the fund. A typical analysis includes an explanation of the transition plan that was followed and of its execution including details of the sources of liquidity used (crosses versus market), cost analysis (the implementation shortfall as well as specific commissions paid), market conditions during the trade, and any other factors that were relevant to the overall performance of the transition.

The analysis of implementation shortfall, and the decomposition of that shortfall into exogenous market movements, market impact, commissions, and fees, is particularly important in a transition. In the case of a transition of funds between managers, the shortfall may be measured versus a reference date several weeks prior to the execution of the portfolio, when the new fund managers were first advised of the new assets they would be managing and required to produce their target holdings. The shortfall can then be decomposed into market movements that occurred in the pre-trade period, during which the legal and operational issues involved in the transition were being resolved, plus the costs related to the actual act of transitioning the portfolio. In this way, the total performance of the fund at year-end can be calculated as the sum of the performance of the old portfolio (attributable to the previous managers), the performance of the new portfolio from the time of implementation, and the shortfall due to the transition. This allows the fund to appropriately measure the asset management skills of the new managers and not reward or punish them for portfolio movements due to the transition.

PRINCIPAL TRADES

Thus far we have looked at agency orders only which, as we can see from Exhibit 5.1, make up the majority of program trading volume. However, there is also a significant amount of *client facilitation* flow that requires that the broker take some amount of risk, either by guaranteeing a price to a client that he himself may not be able to obtain, or by taking the other side of the customer order. Two of the most common program trading principal trades—guaranteed VWAP and "beat the close"—have already been discussed in the section on cash trading. There are, however, a few additional considerations when applying these strategies to a portfolio trade:

- *Guaranteed VWAP:* It is generally less risky to guarantee VWAP on a portfolio trade than on a single name. When guaranteeing the VWAP on a single name, the broker takes on all the idiosyncratic risks of the individual stock and while execution through an automated trading engine is an option, these algorithms are based on statistically derived volume profiles that may prove highly inaccurate for the particular stock in question on the given day. When trading a portfolio of stocks, the natural averaging properties of diversification significantly reduce the risk associated with the trade. Additionally, a portfolio may include both buys and sells, such that, in the event of a significant directional move or abnormal volume distribution in the market as a whole, the underperformance on one side will be offset by an outperformance on the other. The risk in guaranteeing VWAP on a portfolio comes largely from the fact that the absolute size of the trade, which can comfortably be in the hundreds of millions of dollars, is much larger for a portfolio than for a single stock.
- *Beat the close:* The primary client base of program trading desks are index funds whose investor deposits and redemptions are recognized at the close of business. As a result, there is a significant amount of program trading flow that is benchmarked to the close. When targeting the close on a portfolio, the trader will divide the orders up by liquidity and trade early only in those names where the order represents a significant portion of the average daily volume. The highly liquid names will be sent directly to the closing auction as there is no need to work these early.

An important source of "beat the close" orders for program trading desks are index rebalances. As we saw in the previous chapter, index add-deletes or constituent re-weightings result in buy and sell orders across all index constituents, with large orders in a few names. When there is a change to the constituent stocks of the index, the entire community of funds that replicate that index must rebalance their portfolio holdings at the close of business on the day the change is made. In popular indices, these rebalance flows can be the equivalent of several days' trading volume and result in very large market movements around the close. Much of this flow is routed through program trading desks, which compete aggressively for these trades.

Blind Risk Bids

Of the many different types of trades in which the broker is required to put capital at risk for a client, perhaps the most exciting and challenging of all is a *blind risk bid*, a trade that is absolutely unique to the program trading desk.

In a blind bid, the client provides the broker with a special type of pre-trade analysis, called a *bid sheet*, for a portfolio he wishes to execute. The bid sheet contains aggregate portfolio characteristics—such as the dollar value of the trade, sector breakdown, and liquidity information—but none of the specific details of the individual stocks. Based on this high-level information, the broker quotes a price—expressed as either a cents-per-share or basis point commission rate—for which he would be willing to buy the entire portfolio from the client, *without knowing the actual stocks it contains*. If the price quoted by the broker is agreeable to the client, the prices of the constituent stocks are snapped at an agreed-upon time and all portfolio holdings are crossed at these prices from the client to the broker. It is only after the trade has been agreed and the prices captured that the trader gets to see exactly what it is he has purchased and start to think about how best to trade out of the risk.

The language of risk bids can be a bit confusing. A client's portfolio can contain both buy and sell orders to which the broker will be the counterparty, selling what the client buys and buying what the client sells. Nevertheless, the broker is still asked to make a "bid" for the portfolio. To avoid the clumsy and repetitive use of "buys or sells," throughout this section we will utilize this same one-sided language and describe the client as selling the portfolio and the broker as buying it.

The risk management and trade-out of positions acquired through risk program trades is unique. Each new portfolio that is acquired is folded into a trading book containing all the residual positions from previous trades. The *risk trader* (the program trader who runs the risk book) focuses first and foremost on the aggregate performance of the entire book, and then drills down into the specific details of individual stocks as necessary. In the language of Wall Street, he "trades the book" rather than trading each individual position.

This is very different from the way a single stock trader looks at risk. When asked to quote a risk price a cash trader will consider the specific characteristics of the stock (its liquidity, volatility, bid-ask spread, any recent news or upcoming announcements, etc.) and use all of this to determine the price at which he is willing to trade with the client. Once the trade is completed, he will work out of the position as quickly as possible without having undue impact on the price. A program trader, on the other hand, could end up taking on exactly the same position in a blind bid, for a very different price, without ever knowing the stock was in the portfolio or anything about the company, and then hold the position for several days before trading out because it offsets other exposures in the book.

Because of the risk-reduction that comes through portfolio diversification, particularly in two-sided portfolios, blind risk bids can be very large; trades with notional values in the hundreds of millions of dollars are common and larger brokers will occasionally be asked to bid on trades over a billion dollars. Most risk bids are done *in competition* with multiple brokers pricing the trade at the same time. Brokers will usually be told that they are in competition and possibly with how many brokers.

The level of granularity in the portfolio analytics provided in the bid sheet depends on both the client and the size of the trade. For a small and relatively liquid portfolio, a few high-level characteristics may be sufficient, while for illiquid or very large portfolios the broker's pricing will differ significantly depending on the level of detail he is provided. Because the actual constituents are never disclosed, there is an additional risk premium attached to a blind bid as compared with an equivalent bid on a known portfolio. The larger or more complex the trade, the greater the risk premium associated with not knowing the actual constituents. If the client provides only rudimentary analytics, the risk will be large while if more detail is provided, the broker can make a more informed assessment and bid more aggressively for the portfolio.

The Client Relationship   In pricing a risk bid, the broker is placing a significant amount of trust in the client. So long as the portfolio analytics are correct, the broker has no recourse to turn around and refuse to accept the trade once the price has been agreed. This provides the client with a potentially attractive opportunity to surreptitiously offload highly illiquid positions onto the broker, knowing that they will be very difficult, and potentially costly, to trade out of without significant impact. By hiding these stocks in a large, relatively diversified portfolio, the client can stick the broker with these "toxic" positions at a much lower cost than what he would be charged if he were to ask for a risk price in these names directly from the cash desk. However, while the client can argue that the broker priced the trade based on accurate portfolio analytics, the broker will perceive this as unfair dealing (risk traders tend to use slightly more colorful language) and will provide much less aggressive pricing to the client in the future. If the trades consistently lose money, the broker will eventually stop trading on risk with that client. A client cannot afford to "pick off" too many brokers or she will eventually find herself unable to trade on risk with anyone.

As a result, while their economic interests in the pricing of a blind risk bid are contrary, the broker and client must still work in a semi-partnership.

The broker accepts that portfolio analytics cannot tell the whole story and that he will occasionally be stuck with difficult and costly positions to trade out of. The client, on the other hand, accepts that the broker will only provide risk capital if the loss ratio is acceptable and, in order to continue trading blind bids with that broker, she must be careful not to take excessive liberties with what she puts in the portfolio or, at a minimum, to provide sufficient information so that the broker can price the risk fairly.

One of the protection mechanisms that brokers will frequently require of a client is a *force majeure* agreement (usually just verbally agreed) stating that, in the event of a significant outlier event in one of the stocks immediately after the trade is struck, that stock is removed from the basket. For example, on a trade that is struck off the closing prices, the broker and client might agree to a 5 percent, news-based force majeure based on the next morning's opening prices. If any stock opens more than 5 percent away from the prior night's close *and* that movement is attributable to a news announcement in the stock, then it is automatically removed from the portfolio. The broker will agree with the client whether the removal of stocks is one-sided (i.e., only the stocks that move adversely for the broker are removed) or applied symmetrically to all news-based moves over 5 percent. The movement may also be measured relative to the performance of a reference index (i.e., if the index is down 2 percent then the stock would need to be down 7 percent, or up 3 percent, to be removed.)

Risk Bid Analytics We will now consider some of the standard portfolio analytics that would be provided on a bid sheet for a blind risk trade, along with the reasons these factors would be relevant to the broker. In the case of a two-way portfolio, all of the following characteristics would be provided independently for each side of the trade.

- *Side:* The broker must know whether the client is a buyer or seller of the portfolio, though the client will occasionally withhold this information and ask for a two-way price. While this makes the pricing more difficult for the broker, the client benefits from the fact that the brokers who quoted on the portfolio and did not win, will not know which way the client is positioned. This is particularly important if the client does not receive a sufficiently aggressive price and decides to work out of the positions as an agency trade or not to trade at all.
- *Size:* The client will usually provide the number of stocks in the portfolio along with the number of shares and total notional value. The risk in a blind bid is computed in percentage terms based on statistical assumptions about the likelihood of certain events. Actual profits and losses, however, are in real dollars. The broker may assign a very low probability to an event but, as the notional value of the trade gets

larger, the consequences of that event actually occurring become more significant. In a small trade, a multiple-standard deviation move might wipe out a significant portion of the trader's profits for the year and with that, a large part of his bonus. That same unlikely event, if it occurs in a large portfolio, could significantly impact the revenues of the entire division. While the likelihood remains small, the size of the portfolio makes consequences of a mispricing greater and pricing must be considered more carefully.

- *Beta:* In order to accurately hedge the market exposure of the portfolio it is necessary to know not only how big the portfolio is, but whether the stocks it contains tend to move more or less than the market in general. Beta, which is defined more precisely in Chapter 12, is a measure of the likely magnitude of the move in a stock for a given move in the broader market. If a stock has a beta >1, it will tend to move more than the market while stocks with betas <1 tend to move less. Negative betas have the same interpretation except that the direction of the stock move tends to be opposite the direction of the market. Even in a dollar-balanced portfolio, if there is a significant difference in the betas of each side, the portfolio can be exposed to directional moves in the market and it may be necessary to add to the exposure of the lower-beta side to neutralize the market risk.[4]

- *Tracking:* When a program trader buys a one-sided portfolio from a client, he will usually hedge the market exposure with a broad index future or other index product. The question remains as to how much risk is there in the combined position. The *tracking risk* is a measurement of expected magnitude of the slippage between the return of the portfolio and that of the index. It can be thought of as the volatility[5] of a combined position in the portfolio and an offsetting position in the index. In a two-sided portfolio, the tracking is measured as the volatility of the combination of the long and short sides. Particularly in the case of a one-sided portfolio, tracking risk is a more useful statistic than the absolute volatility of the portfolio because it takes into account the offsetting effect of the market hedge—a volatile portfolio is only a risk if its movements cannot be hedged. A perfect replicating portfolio of a benchmark index will still show a significant amount of volatility, but will represent a virtually riskless trade for a blind bid since all of the risk of the portfolio can be neutralized through a hedge in a broad index future.

- *Liquidity:* After size and side, the liquidity of the stocks in the portfolio is probably the most important information in a blind bid. A bid sheet will generally contain the weighted average of the liquidity of the stocks in the portfolio, calculated as the percentage of the average daily trading volume of each stock. There will also usually be a breakdown of the portfolio into liquidity "buckets" based on the percentage of ADV. For example, "less than 2 percent," "between 2 percent and 5 percent," "from 5 percent to 10 percent" and so forth up to a final "greater than 100 percent" bucket. This gives much more detail to the broker and allows him to differentiate a portfolio of moderately liquid positions all averaging around 10 percent of ADV, from a basket of mostly highly liquid stocks plus several days' volume in one toxic position. Where the ">100% ADV" bucket contains a significant percentage of the portfolio, the client may also provide a measurement of the most illiquid position in the portfolio.

- *Sector composition:* Providing the sector breakdown of the portfolio allows the broker to compare the exposures created by the trade with the existing exposures on his book from other business that has not yet been unwound as well as his own views on the market. If the broker's risk book has a net long position in energy stocks (that he does not want) and he is presented with a portfolio that would give him the opportunity to sell energy stocks, he will bid more aggressively since, even if the stocks are different, he can neutralize his sector exposure and be paid a commission to do so. Particularly where the client is requesting quotes from several brokers, disclosing the sector composition to the broker increases the probability of matching off against natural exposures held by one of them and receiving a more aggressive price.

- *Bid-offer spread:* A commonly included measure of liquidity and tradability is the average size of the bid-offer spread, usually computed as the average of intraday observations over a given number of trading days in a similar way to the computation of the ADV. The narrower the bid-offer spread, the less the broker can expect the portfolio to move when he attempts to trade out of it. A wide bid-offer spread is also generally indicative of poor liquidity in the underlying stocks.

The price quoted to the client for the portfolio is expressed either as a basis-point or cents-per-share commission relative to their desired strike price. Once the deadline has arrived for brokers to submit bids, the client will either decide not to trade (if all bids are unsatisfactory), or else take the most aggressive price and inform the winning broker. If the trade was quoted without an indication of direction, he will tell the broker whether he is a buyer or seller so that the broker can execute any necessary market hedges at the time of the trade. The client will often tell the broker what the *cover* was. For the winning broker, this means by how much his winning price beat the next best price (i.e., how much more could he have charged and still have won). For a losing broker, this means by how much the winning price beat his price. Some clients will provide more detail regarding the different prices received while others will provide none. For the trader this information is extremely valuable because it gives useful information about where other brokers are pricing the same business and what sorts of prices he needs to show in the future to remain competitive.

When the trades are crossed between the broker and the client, the commission that has been agreed can be either explicitly or implicitly applied to the trade. If the commission is explicit, the trades are crossed on the tape at the reference prices and the commission is charged separately. If the commission is implicit, the reference prices will be marked up or down by the relevant amount and the trades crossed at those prices, and no commission is charged. Some clients require the explicit commission to be the same as their standard agency rate and that the rest be implied via a markup or markdown. This will vary from client to client and depend on how the specific client firm prefers to recognize transaction costs. To the broker, the economics are the same.

Risk Bid Pricing   The pricing of a risk trade is part art and part science. The goal is to derive as much insight as possible into the actual contents of the portfolio so as to make the most accurate and objective assessment of the actual risks of the trade, and the fair price to show a client for it. The difficultly comes from the fact that both the information about the portfolio, and the time given to analyze it, are extremely limited. When the client sends a bid sheet to the broker, he will usually indicate (if it is not already understood) by what time he expects the broker to produce a price. While very large trades may require more than an hour to price, an "average" sized trade will usually need to be priced within a couple of minutes.

The pricing of each portfolio is a unique challenge and will be heavily influenced by the idiosyncratic characteristics of the particular portfolio—"chunky" concentrated positions, highly illiquid stocks, significant sector biases, and so on—as well as the relationship and historical experience with the particular client, the current composition of the risk book, and overall market conditions (volatility, directional trend, level of activity, etc.). There can be no universally applicable pricing formula for all trades. There is, however, a general methodology that is used as a starting point for consideration, which we'll sketch qualitatively.

The first question is, how long will it take to trade out of the position? Based on the liquidity of the portfolio and a target participation rate on the trade-out (i.e., 20 percent of ADV) the trader makes an estimate of how many days it will take him to completely unwind the entire trade (assuming he were to do so). Because he will be unwinding the position over this time, on average he will only be holding half of the position for this amount of time. For example, if the trader sells out of the portfolio evenly over two days, then by the end of the first day, he will have liquidated half of the position, which gives an average exposure during the first day of only three-quarters of the portfolio. On the second day he starts with half of the portfolio and liquidates it down to zero, giving an average day-two holding of one-quarter of the portfolio. The average over the two days is therefore only one-half of the portfolio.

Given this, the trader now must estimate how far the portfolio, whether as a combination of a one-sided portfolio and a market hedge or a combined long-short portfolio, can be expected to move in that time. This is exactly what is measured by the tracking risk, which is defined as the annualized standard deviation of the difference in the two portfolios' returns (or the long and short legs of the portfolio against each other). For example, a tracking risk of 4 percent means that roughly two-thirds of the time (the percentage of observations within 1 standard deviation of the mean), the difference between the annual return of the portfolio and that of the benchmark index will be less than 4 percent.

As we will see when we discuss options pricing, this annualized tracking can be converted to an equivalent estimate of slippage over a shorter period (in our case, the time required to trade out of the portfolio) by dividing the annual number by the square root of the number of periods per year. For example, the standard deviation over a one-day period is computed by dividing by the square root of the number of trading days per year, which is equal to approximately 16 (there are on average, 255 trading days per year).

An initial estimate of the risk in a portfolio can then be computed by combining the average time during which the portfolio will be held, based on our trade-out assumption, and the expected tracking over that time, with an additional adjustment for the anticipated cost of crossing half of the bid-offer spread on trade-out.

In practice, this estimate of the tracking risk plus trading slippage during the trade-out period serves only as a starting point for pricing the portfolio. Even after making the necessary adjustments for the unique characteristics of the portfolio, the specific client, the state of the risk book, and the broader market conditions, there is still a final, highly subjective assessment that must be made. Given what the trader knows about the market for blind risk bids, where does he think the trade will actually be priced? While the assessment of the risk characteristics of the portfolio will suggest a "fair" price for the portfolio, actual business usually trades significantly inside this (i.e., at cheaper prices). An important part of the value added by a risk trader is in knowing where a portfolio with particular characteristics is likely to be priced by other brokers. Pricing is then guided by the combination of the trader's assessment of the actual risk in the trade and his knowledge of what price it takes to actually win a piece of business.

Risk pricing is a delicate game. A trader who is too conservative, and becomes perceived as uncommercial, may be cut off by clients and not provided the opportunity to participate in future bids, while a trader who prices too aggressively is likely to discover that there is a good reason why other brokers are pricing the business wider than he is, and may suffer significant trading losses.

Why on Earth Would Anyone Do This? Trading blind risk bids is an extremely challenging, high-risk business and very few brokers have been able to consistently make money trading risk programs year after year. While there are "gentlemen's rules" about fair dealing, there is little a broker can do to hold clients to them. A client can divide a portfolio into slices and trade on risk with multiple brokers simultaneously, each one thinking he is pricing risk in isolation when, in fact, there will be several other brokers looking to sell the same positions he is selling and buy the same stocks he is short. Alternatively, a client can sell half a portfolio to one broker and work the balance of the trade as an agency order with another, pushing down the very same stocks that he has just sold to the first broker. Clients can hide highly illiquid positions in risk portfolios. If a broker suspects a client of using any of these tricks he will likely refuse to do business with him in the future. However, on the trade that is already completed, the damage is done and the broker is at risk for significant losses.

With all the possible risks, it is reasonable to ask why any broker would trade risk programs in the first place. There are several reasons.

- *Client expectations:* The willingness to price blind risk business is part of the suite of products that clients will expect from a top-tier broker-dealer.
- *Market information:* There is a tremendous amount of information that can be derived from pricing risk programs. The risk trader will often be the first to perceive trends in institutional investor positioning between sectors, styles, or capitalization ranges and this can provide important information about future market direction, investor risk appetite, and opinion. Once positions are on the book, the daily profit or loss from those positions also gives an extremely accurate indicator of trends in the market that can be difficult to detect otherwise.
- *Feeds agency business:* Many large institutions will reward the firms that most aggressively price risk business with a larger share of their riskless agency orders. The agency flow, which could be directed to any firm, serves as a kind of compensation to the broker for putting his neck on the line with risk programs.
- *Attracts flow:* As mentioned in the section on transition management, "flow begets flow." Even clients who are not interested in trading on

risk will often give agency orders to a broker with an active risk book due to the possibility of reducing the market impact of trades through crossing. A large and active risk book also provides an opportunity for cash traders to pair off orders and advertise trading opportunities to the market.

- *Knowledge:* Any trader will tell you that the best and probably only way to understand a stock and the idiosyncrasies of how it trades is to have a position in it. An experienced risk trader will have, at one point or another, traded, risk managed, or hedged a position in almost every stock, and through this develops an encyclopedic knowledge of the markets. This understanding of stocks, sectors, indices, and the risk management of large, diversified portfolios is a tremendous asset to the trading floor.

From the investor's perspective, there are many reasons why a risk program trade might be preferable to an agency execution. In an agency execution, the client pays a lower commission rate but retains the risk of the portfolio until it is completely executed, making the outcome of the trade much less predictable. Once a client decides to trade, he will generally want to complete the trade as quickly as possible to reduce market risk, while at the same time minimizing market impact. These are two contrary goals and many clients find it extremely frustrating to watch a trade drag on due to lack of liquidity as the market moves adversely. There can also be internal operational challenges when large or illiquid trades are worked over multiple days, particularly when the trades are allocated between multiple accounts with cash constraints.

By trading on risk, the client is able to execute the entire portfolio immediately for a fixed cost. In return for paying a higher commission, all of the risk associated with the trade-out of the positions is passed to the broker, making it an extremely clean way to trade large portfolios. There is, however, a trade-off—the broker is taking on risk and must be paid for that. Brokers would not price blind risk bids if they consistently lost money doing so. Therefore, on average, the client should expect to pay more for risk programs than what the sum of the market impact and commissions would be for an agency execution. The benefits of operational ease, immediate completion, and predictable results of a risk program do not come for free.

SUMMARY

Despite popular and professional misunderstanding and skepticism about program trading, the portfolio-level approach to trading large baskets of stocks has persistently grown in popularity since its introduction and regularly comprises upwards of 30 percent of NYSE volume.

The program trading process begins with the transmission of the client's order, usually via FIX, to the broker and a pre-trade analysis and development of a trading strategy of how to execute the order given the client's benchmark. The execution of a portfolio order is done through the creation of "waves" of orders in the individual stocks that are sent to the exchange with a trading instruction. While these waves are treated as a single unit by the program trading systems, they are not viewed this way by the exchange and each order is managed independently. Unlike a single stock order, where the quantity of shares and limit price are explicitly stated, portfolio wave orders are constructed based on percentage share quantities (e.g., a 10 percent slice of every order) and descriptive limits (e.g., bid side plus one tick). Traders and sales-traders will provide the client with intraday updates on the performance of the order and any issues that may require attention, followed by more complete post-trade reporting once the execution is complete.

Many clients will require a post-trade analysis that provides a detailed comparison of the performance of the execution to the client's benchmark including both aggregate portfolio-level comparisons, as well as stock by stock performance and details of the marginal contribution of each stock to the overall performance of the trade. The careful analysis of implementation shortfall (how much the portfolio moved from a fixed strike point prior to trading) and the decomposition into market impact and market risk, while generally important in post-trade analyses, is a particular focus in the management of large transition trades, where the post-trade scrutiny is great.

Clients unwilling to take the market risk of a portfolio trade-out can pay a broker to take the entire portfolio from them in a blind risk bid. In a blind bid, the trader quotes a price at which he will take the other side of the portfolio based on a series of high-level portfolio aggregates (liquidity, sector composition, beta, etc.), without ever knowing the actual constituents. The client exchanges the uncertainty of the market trade-out for the fixed cost of the risk price. This type of "blind" risk pricing is unique to the program trading risk book and requires a combination of objective risk analysis, subjective market "sense," trading skill, and a high tolerance for risk.

CHAPTER 6

Exchange-Traded Funds (ETFs)

INTRODUCTION

An *exchange-traded fund* (ETF) is a type of open-ended investment company that uses the money deposited with it to purchase a portfolio of stocks (or bonds) that replicates the returns of a reference index. The ownership of the assets of the fund is recognized through the issuance of shares. The term *open-ended* indicates that the number of shares of the fund is variable—as new money is deposited, new assets are purchased and new shares are issued, without limit. The notional amount of new shares issued is always strictly equal to the money deposited with the fund and therefore is not dilutive to the holdings of existing shareholders. The initials "ETF" are generally used to refer to the shares of an ETF, while the actual entity that issues them is referred to as the fund or the ETF sponsor. In terms of their investment objectives and structure, exchange-traded funds are very similar to passive index funds. There are, however, several important differences between the two products, and it is precisely these differences that have made ETFs so popular.

The first is that ETFs trade like stocks. In a traditional fund, all purchases and sales of fund shares must be made with the fund itself, and this can only be done at the closing *net asset value* (NAV)[1] of the fund on the day of the trade. All orders submitted during the day receive the same execution price at the close. Funds only publish a single valuation of the fund shares each day and this is generally only available on a $T + 1$ basis (i.e., you can find out today where the fund closed yesterday). As a result, the traditional fund structure is most appropriate to investors with a longer-term, buy-and-hold strategy.

While the structure of an ETF is similar to that of an index fund—both the ETF sponsor and the index fund manager replicate a benchmark index and charge a small annual management fee for the service[2]—trading in an ETF differs in that it is virtually indistinguishable from stock trading. ETFs can be purchased and sold multiple times per day on an exchange and trades and crosses in fund shares print to the tape and are disseminated in real time. Like stocks, ETFs pay dividends, can be purchased on margin,[3] and can be borrowed and shorted. It should be emphasized that ETFs are not the same stocks as they do not represent ownership in a publicly traded company but legal claims on the assets held by a fund. (The nature of the relationship between the ETF investor and the holdings of the fund is determined by the legal structure of the ETF, which varies between products. Specific details can be obtained from the fund prospectus.).

The second characteristic that makes ETFs unique is that the investment strategy of the fund—the way in which it attempts to replicate the returns of the benchmark index—is defined formulaically through an equivalence between a given number of ETF shares (called a *creation unit*) and a specific basket of stocks (plus possibly a small cash amount, which will be discussed later), as shown in Exhibit 6.1. This rigid definition and total transparency regarding the underlying holdings of the fund is unique to ETFs. Most investment funds, including those that passively replicate a benchmark index, provide a snapshot of their holdings only on a quarterly basis: At any given point in time, an outside investor cannot know the precise holdings of the fund. The formulaic definition of the assets held by the ETF sponsor allows investors to accurately calculate a continuously-updating intraday NAV of the assets of the fund. This real-time NAV tells investors what the "fair" price for an ETF share is, based on the current prices of the underlying stocks held by the fund. For many ETFs this value is calculated and disseminated in real time by market data providers.

While direct purchases of ETFs from the fund sponsor are limited to multiples of the creation unit, which usually ranges from 25,000 to 600,000 shares, once created, the shares can be traded on the exchange in lots as small as a single share.

A third important feature of ETFs is that the fund sponsor allows certain *authorized participants,* usually large investment banks or broker-dealers, to exchange a replicating stock basket for fund shares and vice-versa. These

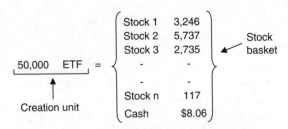

EXHIBIT 8.1 ETF Creation Unit Definition

exchanges are referred to as either a creation or a redemption. In a *creation,* the authorized participant delivers a multiple of the underlying basket of stock to the ETF sponsor and receives in return the corresponding number of fund shares (thus the name "creation unit"). In a *redemption,* a block of ETF shares (in multiples of creation units) is delivered to the fund sponsor in exchange for the corresponding basket of stock.

Creations and redemptions are performed at the closing prices of all stocks in the replicating portfolio (versus the closing NAV of the fund) and can be done on any business day. A nominal processing cost is assessed by the fund sponsor and there is a late afternoon cutoff after which requests for that day's closing NAV are no longer accepted. An important feature of ETFs is that creations and redemptions are considered *in-kind transfers* (an exchange of equivalent assets and not a separate purchase and sale) and therefore do not create a taxable event, which makes the ETF structure highly tax efficient.

TRADING MECHANICS

These latter two characteristics—the complete transparency regarding the fund's holdings and the ability to create and redeem fund shares versus a basket of replicating shares—combine to make trading in ETFs fundamentally different from normal stock trading. By providing a mechanism by which the underlying portfolio can be exchanged for fund shares, the liquidity of that underlying stock basket is transferred to the shares of the ETF itself. So long as there is an authorized participant willing to create or redeem shares with the fund sponsor, the ETF shares are immediately as liquid as the underlying stock portfolio, even if there is no trading activity in the ETF shares themselves.

The mechanism by which ETFs acquire the liquidity of the underlying portfolio is relatively simple but it is so fundamental to the popularity and success of ETFs that we will walk through it in some detail to ensure it is well understood. The underlying idea is that a creation unit of shares is exchangeable for—and therefore equivalent to—the underlying hedge basket. Therefore, an authorized participant with sufficient infrastructure to manage the execution of a program trade in the underlying basket should be indifferent to trading one or the other. What's more, the equivalence is not just theoretical but can be realized on the very same trading day through a creation or redemption.

Consider the case of an investor who wishes to purchase shares of an ETF in which there is very little trading activity with small quantities on the bid and offer and a wide spread. If the broker tries to buy the ETF shares directly, he will have considerable market impact due to the lack of liquidity. This will raise his execution price in the ETF shares above the current net asset value of the fund, which means he will be paying more for the ETF than what it is actually worth.

While a small deviation from net asset value is common (and probably unavoidable), there will be a point beyond which it will be attractive for the broker to facilitate the order via the replicating portfolio. To do this, the broker computes the appropriate replicating stock basket for the number of ETF shares in the client's order and purchases it in the market. Given the execution prices on his individual stock trades, he uses the definition of the creation unit to compute the ETF price that corresponds to the execution of his stock basket. He then fills the client's ETF order against his own book (he shorts the ETF shares to the client from his trading account) based on the implied ETF price.

Due to the superior liquidity of this underlying stock basket, the broker is able to provide the client with a fill on his order that is far superior to what could have been achieved directly in the market for the ETF shares. The broker is then left with a pair of perfectly matched positions: long the replicating stock portfolio and short the ETF shares. To flatten out this position, he can submit a creation request to the fund sponsor and, after the close of business, deliver the replicating portfolio he has purchased and receive in return the equivalent number of ETF shares. This now completely flattens his position and leaves him as he was before the trade. Because he has created new ETF shares on the same day that he shorted them to the client, there is no need to bring in borrowed shares to cover the short sale of the ETF. (The broker can sell short the ETF even if no borrowable shares can be located.) So long as the ETF creation is settled on time, the broker can deliver the shares he receives from the fund sponsor to cover the short sale.

The reverse case—in which the client wishes to sell the ETF—is analogous. The broker facilitates the trade by selling short the more liquid underlying portfolio and purchases the ETF shares from the client. He then performs a redemption on the same day, delivering the ETF shares to the sponsor in return for a stock portfolio, which will be used to cover his short positions in the underlying stocks, leaving him flat. In both cases, the client is able to trade based on the liquidity in the underlying stock portfolio rather than that of the ETF itself because the broker is able to convert one into the other.

Compared with a single stock execution in the ETF itself, there is clearly a significantly greater operational complexity to trading the underlying portfolio, computing the ETF price implied by the stock execution, crossing the ETF to the client, and then creating or redeeming shares with the fund sponsor to flatten out the position. In the end, the client will generally pay the same commission whether the broker trades the basket or trades the ETF directly. Why then, would the broker bother—much less set up an entire trading desk devoted exclusively to ETF trading—since, in the end, it is much more work for the same commission? The primary reason is competition: If the broker is unwilling to facilitate, someone else will and the broker will lose the trade entirely. The second reason is the opportunity for profit. The broker will offer a price that is acceptable to the client but which represents a greater deviation from the NAV than what he expects to realize on his stock hedge. If his portfolio execution implies a better ETF price than what was given to the client, the spread between the two will produce a trading profit in his book.

In the more liquid ETFs, the spread between the bid or offer and the net asset value rarely becomes very large and trading in moderate size is easily executed in the ETF shares directly. In less liquid products, however, particularly those where the underlying basket can be difficult to trade (e.g., large global indices) where there are fewer market makers with sufficient infrastructure to facilitate client orders, the spread around the NAV can become quite wide. While the broker would ideally want to capture the entire spread between the screen bid or offer and the level at which he can execute his hedge, in practice, the ETF market is highly competitive and if the spread is excessively wide, the broker will often need to give the client a fill inside the best bid and offer showing on the screen.

NET ASSET VALUE (NAV)

As mentioned previously, the net asset value (NAV) of an ETF is the total value of all assets held by the fund. These assets are the property of the shareholders (either directly or indirectly, depending on the structure of the fund) and can be acquired by an investor through a redemption of fund shares. The NAV is based on the value of all stock holdings, as well as accumulated cash from dividends received, stock loan revenue, and interest earned on cash positions held in the fund (less the management fee charged by the fund sponsor).[4] This cash amount is not something that can be computed independently but must be obtained from the fund sponsor, who disseminates it on a daily basis. ETFs commonly pay a quarterly (or at least yearly) dividend in which most of this accumulated cash is paid out to fund shareholders.

An important characteristic of the creation and redemption process is that it must not affect the value of the holdings of other fund investors. The basket delivered to the fund provider in a creation must contain precisely the combination of stocks and cash that is currently held by the fund since this defines what the existing fund shares are worth and, therefore, what the new shares must be worth since all ETF shares are identical. Likewise, in a redemption, the fund sponsor gives to the broker a perfect "slice" of every asset held by the fund, in proportion to the number of units redeemed. If a broker were to redeem all outstanding shares, he would take delivery of all the fund assets. If he redeems half the outstanding shares, he would receive one-half of every position, and so on.

The issuance of new shares is neither dilutive nor does it change the mix of cash and equity held by the previously existing investors, as the following example illustrates. Assume that the fund sponsor for an ETF holds a stock portfolio worth $100 million and has accumulated an additional $1 million in cash from dividends and stock lending revenue (after subtracting off management fees). This $101 million in assets corresponds to 1 million ETF shares with a per share NAV of $101. In a creation of 10,000 shares, the creating broker would deliver the specified basket, worth $1 million as well as an additional $10,000 in cash. The fund now holds a pool of $102.01 million in assets—a $101 million stock portfolio plus $1.01 million in cash. While the total NAV of the fund has increased, the per-share NAV is still exactly the same (= $102.01 million/1,010,000 = $101.00), and has exactly the same composition of $100 in stock and $1 in cash.

In addition to the standard descriptive and performance data provided for all stocks, the Bloomberg **DES** function provides a great deal of useful information specific to ETFs. This includes the number of units outstanding, market capitalization of the fund, ticker symbol for the intraday NAV, details of the management fees, creation unit size, the cash component of the creation unit, and current holdings of the fund as well as a graph showing the relative performance of the ETF versus the relevant index benchmark.

POPULARITY

The unique structure of ETFs, and its consequences, makes them a highly attractive investment tool for both institutional and retail investors and has led to the explosive growth of the ETF marketplace. The first ETF was the SPDR® on the S&P 500, which was introduced in 1993 under the ticker SPY. The success of the SPY, which has more than $74 billion in assets under management,[5] has led to the creation of hundreds of new funds offering exposure to every imaginable cross-section of the equity market. More sophisticated recent developments include leveraged funds, which use derivatives to produce returns that are as much as two times that of the index; inverse funds, which pay the negative of the index return (they go up when the index goes down); and ETFs on other asset classes including bond indices, currencies, and commodities.[6]

There are presently more than \$600 billion in ETF assets under management in the United States alone, with average daily trading volumes of more than \$80 billion across nearly 700 funds. Exhibit 6.2 shows the spectacular growth in both the assets under management (which have nearly quadrupled in five years) and the number of funds available (more than half of which have been launched since 2006).

Despite this rapid growth, the ETF market remains highly concentrated with the top 50 funds controlling over 70 percent of all assets under management and the top 20 funds accounting for 85 percent of daily trading volume. The table on the left of Exhibit 6.2 shows the breakdown of assets under management by fund objective, with equity large-cap, international, and sector index products accounting for nearly 70 percent of *assets under management* (AUM).

For retail investors, the appeal of ETFs is readily apparent: ETFs combine the diversification and low cost of index mutual funds with the intraday liquidity, flexibility, and familiarity of stock trading. The low management fees and diversification of ETFs benchmarked to broad indices (both domestic and international) make ETFs an appropriate choice for the buy-and-hold investor. At the same time, the ability to buy, sell, and sell short funds tracking sectors, market capitalization ranges, countries (including emerging markets), and even non-equity asset classes (commodities, interest rates) makes ETFs the product of choice for the active investor.

Among institutional investors, the greatest interest has been in the broad index and sector ETFs, which have proven to be extremely useful tools for dealing with many different trading, risk management, and liquidity issues of both buy- and sell-side investors. A few concrete examples of particularly popular application of ETFs are listed here:

- *Sector trading:* One of the most significant changes made possible by the invention of ETFs has been the ability to trade sectors quickly and easily. There are many situations in which an investor may want to express a view on the performance of a particular sector, either in absolute terms or relative to the market as a whole or another sector. Examples include:
  - Funds that focus on top-down macroeconomic analysis of the market.
  - Portfolio managers looking to tactically over- or underweight a particular sector as an overlay to existing positions.
  - Program traders who need an easy way to offset sector exposures acquired through a risk trade.
  - Equity long/short traders who want a more focused hedge for a single-stock position.

Fund Objective	# Funds	Assets ($mm)	Market Share (%)
Broad-Market	16	16,841	2.7%
Large-Cap	43	173,496	28.3%
Mid-Cap	30	32,675	5.3%
Small-Cap	27	24,309	4.0%
Sector & Industry	175	71,926	11.7%
International	168	181,534	29.6%
Dividend Income	14	8,130	1.3%
Leveraged	68	17,558	2.9%
Custom	52	7,904	1.3%
Fixed Income	59	43,763	7.1%
Commodity	18	30,376	4.9%
Currency	15	4,921	0.8%
Other	3	389	0.1%
Total	**688**	**613,822**	**100.0%**

EXHIBIT 6.2 ETF Assets Under Management and Breakdown by Fund Objective

Source: Morgan Stanley data as of May 20, 2008.

Prior to ETFs, an investor looking to express a sector view without taking on significant single-stock risk needed to execute a portfolio trade. Those investors without the infrastructure to maintain large portfolios had no other option than to pick a few names in each sector and take on the significantly more stock-specific risk.

■ *Cash-drag and equitization:* Mutual funds need to hold a certain portion of assets in cash in order to meet redemption requests (i.e., investors removing assets from the fund).[7] In a rallying market this uninvested cash creates a drag on the performance of the fund, known as *cash drag*. As the cash balance in the fund rises above or falls below the target level, the fund managers need to make small trades to either equitize (i.e., invest into equity) excess cash or sell off fund assets to raise cash. Holding a small portion of assets in an ETF with a similar composition to the fund's target holdings provides an easy tool for managing the residual cash balance and maintaining the highest possible amount of the fund assets invested at all times.

■ *International diversification:* Many investors find direct investment in foreign markets difficult both because of the time differences in market hours as well as the challenges of maintaining a multicurrency portfolio and the greater complexity of corporate actions in foreign markets. For all but the most sophisticated investors, a much more attractive option is to utilize any of the liquid, U.S. dollar-denominated ETFs that replicate diversified foreign indices and can be traded during U.S. market hours. While historically there have been few investors with sufficient infrastructure to express a global equity market view to "buy Brazil versus selling Malaysia," with ETFs, this type of trade can be easily implemented by even a small retail investor.

■ *Complex index replication:* While there is much focus on the use of ETFs as trading vehicles, for many institutional investors on both the buy and sell side, ETFs provide a convenient and inexpensive means of replicating large and complex indices with very low tracking error. (More on this in the next section.)

Another historical reason for the popularity of ETFs was that the SEC provided an exemption for ETFs to the tick-test rule for short sales that was required under rule 10a-1 of the Securities Act of 1934. The logic behind this exemption was that, since the price of the ETF is a direct function of the price of the underlying basket of securities, all of which are themselves subject to the tick test, there was no need for an additional test on the ETF. While the tick test has subsequently been revoked by Regulation SHO, this was a particularly attractive feature of ETFs for many years.

TRADING VERSUS HOLDING

The work required to perform many of the operational aspects of managing an index fund—the processing of dividends, monitoring corporate actions, calculating and trading portfolio rebalances—is relatively independent of the size of the fund. The fees earned by a fund, however, are a fixed percentage of the assets under management. This means that a fund with $5 billion under management earns 100 times the fees of a fund managing $50 million, for doing much of the same work. The result is that, as the fund grows, the work required to manage and maintain the fund holdings stays relatively constant while the revenues from the management fees increase.

Some costs can actually go down as the size of the fund increases. For example, when the underlying index rebalances, brokers will generally offer more aggressive commission rates to clients with larger trades. Particularly where these trades are benchmarked to the close (as most rebalances are), the larger trade is more likely to be worked early to reduce market impact and hopefully achieve a better price than the close. Part of this outperformance is kept by the broker for taking the risk (the client will be guaranteed the closing price or better) and managing the rebalance process. A large portion, however, is passed back to the client, which either reduces the cost of managing the fund or improves performance, depending on how it is recognized.

As a result, there are massive economies of scale in the management of index funds (particularly very large and international indices). For many small and medium-sized portfolio managers it is often more cost-effective, and unquestionably simpler, to outsource the entire index maintenance responsibility to the fund provider by purchasing the ETF. For precisely this reason one of the three most popular ETFs on the market is the EFA, one of the iShares® products sponsored by Barclays Global Investors (BGI).[8] The EFA tracks the MSCI EAFE index, the most popular benchmark for international (non-U.S.) market performance. Exhibit 6.3 compares a replicating portfolio of EAFE versus a position in the EFA.

Given the complexities and costs associated with replicating an index like the EAFE, it is not surprising that many investors would trade the ETF instead. As a result, the EFA is one of the most popular ETFs in the world, with more than $40 billion dollars in assets under management.

We can get a sense for whether an ETF is used primarily as a trading vehicle or for index replication purposes by comparing the total assets under management in the fund with the average daily turnover, as shown in Exhibit 6.4. ETFs used primarily as trading tools—such as those on sectors—have high rates of turnover relative to the total assets under management, while funds held primarily for index replication can have billions of dollars in assets but only turn that over a couple times per year.

	MSCI EAFE Portfolio	EFA
Trading	Over 800 stocks across 21 countries requiring 10 currency hedges into USD.	One NYSE-listed stock trading in USD with average daily trading volume of over 12 million shares (~$800 million).
Rebalances	Annual index rebalance plus frequent portfolio adjustments due to corporate actions. (Commission charged on all rebalance trades.)	None.
Execution Commission (Agency)	8–10 bps average commission rate for small portfolios, decreasing down to 2 bps for large size.	An average of 3 cps (approx 5 bps) commission for ETF execution with lower rates for large orders.
Corporate Actions	Accurate index tracking requires the reinvestment of all dividend income as well as correct response in the case of all mergers, tenders, spin-offs.	A quarterly dividend in USD. One corporate action in 7 years (3-for-1 share split in 2003).
Fees	More significant prime brokerage or custodian fees required for the maintenance of all stock positions.	One position to maintain. ETF annual management fee of 35 bps implied in the price.
Stock Loan	Hedge portfolio consists primarily of large, liquid names globally with little loan value.	Due to the complexity of replicating an EAFE basket and the difficulty of shorting in many countries, EFA shares carry a higher-than-average lending rate.
Tracking	Depends on the ability of the portfolio manager to maintain an accurate hedge and limit cash drag. Most portfolio managers use optimized tracking portfolios for small inflows/outflows which can increase slippage.	Inclusive of management fee, average annual tracking since inception (17 August, 2001) has been 15 bps underperformance (implying a 20 bps outperformance on a pre-fee basis).
Minimum Trade Size	Portfolios of $5–10 million are generally considered too small to track the index.	1 share (approx $66 as of July 2008) Note that the creation unit size is 600,000 shares (~$40 millon).

EXHIBIT 6.3   Comparison of MSCI EAFE Replicating Portfolio versus EFA
Source: MSCI-Barra and iShares data as of July 31, 2008.

Ticker	Name	Average Daily Trading ($mm)	Assets Under Mgmt	% Daily Turnover
Most Popular Overall				
SPY	SPDR Trust Series 1	39,188	73,931	53%
QQQQ	PowerShares QQQ	8,009	16,801	48%
IWM	iShares Russell 2000	8,293	9,944	83%
Trading Funds				
XLE	Energy Select Sector SPDR	2,789	5,971	47%
XLF	Financial Select Sector SPDR	5,072	7,138	71%
OIH	Oil Service HOLDRs Trust	1,785	2,202	81%
Index Replication				
EFA	iShares MSCI EAFE	976	39,928	2%
IWO	iShares Russell 2000 Growth	258	3,092	8%
IWN	iShares Russell 2000 Value	199	3,521	6%

EXHIBIT 6.4   ETFs—Trading versus Passive Replication
Source: Bloomberg data as of July 31, 2008.

ETFS IN PRACTICE

Exhibit 6.5 provides a summary of the most actively traded U.S.-listed ETFs. The median daily traded notional across all products is $197 million (minimum is $10 million) and assets under management is $2.0 billion (minimum of $500 million). The ETFs based on style indices, while not actively traded, are included here for completeness.

SUMMARY

Exchange-traded funds (ETFs) combine the diversification and low cost of index mutual funds with the ease of trading, intraday liquidity, and familiarity of stocks, making them enormously popular products with institutional and retail investors alike. In just over 15 years since their introduction, the market for ETFs has grown exponentially with more than $600 billion in assets currently under management and $80 billion in daily trading volumes across nearly 700 products in the United States alone.

While there are many attractive features to ETFs, the two most directly responsible for their extraordinary success are the formulaic method of index replication and the ability to create and redeem new ETF shares with the

Broad		Styles	
DIA	Diamond Trust Series 1	IVW	iShares S&P 500 Growth Index
OEF	iShares S&P 100	IVE	iShares S&P 500 Value Index
SPY	SPDR Trust Series 1	IJK	iShares S&P MidCap 400 Growth
MDY	MidCap SPDR Trust Series 1	IJJ	iShares S&P MidCap 400 Value
IJR	iShares S&P SmallCap 600	IJT	iShares S&P SmallCap 600 Growth
QQQQ	PowerShares QQQ	IJS	iShares S&P SmallCap 600 Value
IWB	iShares Russell 1000	IWF	iShares Russell 1000 Growth
IWM	iShares Russell 2000	IWD	iShares Russell 1000 Value
IWV	iShares Russell 3000	IWO	iShares Russell 2000 Growth
Sector		IWN	iShares Russell 2000 Value
IBB	iShares Nasdaq Biotech Index	IWZ	iShares Russell 3000 Growth
IYE	iShares DJ US Energy Sector	IWW	iShares Russell 3000 Value
IYF	iShares DJ US Financial Sector	**International**	
IYR	iShares DJ US Real Estate	EEM	iShares MSCI Emerging Markets
IYT	iShares DJ US Transport	EFA	iShares MSCI EAFE
KBE	KBW Bank	EWA	iShares MSCI Australia
KRE	KBW Regional Banking	EWC	iShares MSCI Canada
OIH	Oil Service HOLDRs Trust	EWG	iShares MSCI Germany
RKH	Regional Bank HOLDRs Trust	EWH	iShares MSCI Hong Kong
RTH	Retail HOLDRs Trust	EWJ	iShares MSCI Japan
SMH	Semiconductor HOLDRs Trust	EWM	iShares MSCI Malaysia
XLB	Materials Select Sector SPDR	EWP	iShares MSCI Spain
XLE	Energy Select Sector SPDR	EWS	iShares MSCI Singapore
XLF	Financial Select Sector SPDR	EWT	iShares MSCI Taiwan
XLI	Industrial Select Sector SPDR	EWU	iShares MSCI United Kingdom
XLK	Technology Select Sector SPDR	EWW	iShares MSCI Mexico
XLP	Consumer Staples Select SPDR	EWY	iShares MSCI South Korea
XLU	Utilities Select Sector SPDR	EWZ	iShares MSCI Brazil
XLV	Health Care Select Sector SPDR	EZA	iShares MSCI South Africa
XLY	Consumer Disc. Select SPDR	FXI	iShares FTSE/Xinhua China 25
XHB	SPDR S&P Homebuilders	**Fixed Income**	
XME	SPDR Metals and Mining	AGG	iShares Lehman Aggregate Bond
XRT	SPDR S&P Retail	SHY	iShares Lehman 1-3 Year Treasury
Commodity (ETCs)		IEF	iShares Lehman 7-10 Year Treasury
USO	United States Oil Fund	TLT	iShares Lehman 20+ Year Treasury
GLD	streetTRACKS Gold Trust	TIP	iShares Lehman Treasury Inflation
SLV	iShares Silver Trust	LQD	iBoxx $ Investment Grade Corporate

EXHIBIT 6.5 Summary of Most Popular ETFs

fund sponsor by delivering the underlying stock portfolio. The combination of these two features allows market makers to execute portfolio trades in the underlying stocks and pass through this liquidity to the ETF, making an ETF instantly as liquid as the portfolio that defines it.

ETFs are used by the institutional investment community for many purposes including sector trading, cash equitization, international diversification and as an easy tool for replicating complex indices. The massive economies of scale in index fund management mean that, for many small- to medium-sized portfolios, it is more cost-effective (and unquestionably easier) to replicate a large index (particularly total return and multicountry indices) by purchasing the ETF rather than through a replicating stock portfolio.

One way to determine whether an ETF is used primarily for passive index replication or active trading is by comparing the assets under management with the average daily trading volume. Whereas one of the very popular and actively traded ETFs may turn over 50 percent or more of the total AUM each day, an ETF held primarily as a means of index replication can have billions of dollars in assets and only turn those assets over once every couple of months.

CHAPTER 7

Forwards and Futures

INTRODUCTION

As the name would suggest, a *derivative* is a financial instrument whose value is derived from the level of an underlying asset. In this chapter we introduce our first derivative: a *forward contract,* in which a buyer and seller of a given asset agree to trade based on current prices but with settlement of the trade—that is, the actual exchange of the asset for payment—delayed until a time in the future (anywhere from a few days to several years away). While a forward contract may be written on virtually any type of asset, we will focus primarily on forwards with equity underliers, either single stocks, baskets of stocks, or indices.

To price a forward fairly, we need to determine how the act of delaying the settlement changes the economics of the transaction for both parties. Using the current price as a reference, our goal is to calculate the "fair price" to pay for the asset such that the economics of the forward-settled transaction are identical to those of the equivalent *spot market* trade. (The spot market, refers to the trading of the underlier for standard settlement [i.e., T+3] and can, in the case of equity underliers, be replaced by "cash market." I use the more general term "spot" in this chapter because of its common use with futures, which can have many non-equity underliers.)

Before deriving the exact formula for the fair price of a forward, we need to develop some intuition about what it tells us and where it comes from. Let us assume we have two rational investors with the following characteristics:

- Investor A wants to buy one share of stock XYZ, which is currently trading in the market at $100.
- Investor B has a share of XYZ stock that she is willing to sell at current market levels.

Investor A wants to buy the stock from Investor B (who is happy to sell it), but does not want to pay for it, or take delivery of it, for three months

(90 days). Investor B must decide what additional premium (if any) to charge Investor A to compensate for the delayed settlement. The question is: What does Investor B gain or lose by delaying settlement?

The clearest way to see this is to view the two scenarios from the perspective of where they will leave each investor in three months' time. Were the trade to settle today, Investor B would receive $100 in cash that could be invested in a riskless asset (e.g., a government bond) for three months, to generate interest. By delaying settlement, Investor B loses this interest income and will need to be compensated accordingly. However, because the delivery of the shares is also delayed, Investor B will be holding the physical stock position for an additional three months and will receive all the dividends paid out during that time. This represents a benefit to the seller (disadvantage to the buyer) that must also be incorporated into the forward price.

The fair price that Investor B should charge Investor A to compensate for the delayed settlement would therefore be the market price of the asset *plus* the interest income on $1 million for three months (what she loses by delaying settlement), *less* the dividends paid out on the stock basket over that time (what she gains). At this price, the economics of forward settlement are identical to the economics of regular settlement and, barring specific benefits related to physical ownership of the stock (for example, voting rights), both parties should be indifferent between executing the trade at current market prices for regular way settlement, or at the fair forward price for settlement in three months. This is called the *fair value* of a forward:

Fair value = $100 for one share of XYZ

+ Interest on $100 for 3 months

− Stock dividends on one share of XYZ for 3 months

The difference between the price of the forward and the market price of the stock is called the *basis*. Based on the previous formula, we can now express the *fair value of the basis* (or *fair basis*) as:

Fair basis = Interest on $100 for 3 months

− Stock dividends for 3 months

Depending on whether the interest that can be earned is greater or less than the dividend income on XYZ over the next three months, the fair value of the basis[1] may be positive or negative, indicating a higher or lower value of the forward as compared to the spot price of XYZ.

CALCULATION OF FAIR VALUE

The calculation of fair value requires the specification of four parameters:

- S current price of the stock
- d days until settlement of the contract
- r simple interest rate over that period
- div dividends per share that will be paid out during the period

Given these parameters, we can now express the fair value (FV) of the forward as the sum of the spot price of the stock, plus the simple interest earned on a cash amount equal to the stock price, less the dividends paid out per share.

$$FV = S + S\frac{rd}{365} - divs$$

Or equivalently:

$$FV = S\left(1 + \frac{rd}{365}\right) - divs$$

While the formula is simple, care must be taken to ensure the inputs are correct.

- *Day count:* Because the forward price is intended to replicate the economics of an actual stock transaction, the days d of financing must be calculated based on the number of days between when the cash would be received in a spot-market transaction and when it will be received in the forward-settled trade. The *maturity date* of a forward (also called the *expiry* or *expiration*) represents the day until which the spot transaction is being delayed; the actual delivery of the shares for payment would then take place three business days after this date. Therefore, the number of days of financing is not computed between the trade date and maturity date, but between their respective settlement dates. This is an important distinction because interest is accrued on a calendar day basis, not a business day basis and, due to the effect of weekends, the settlement-date to settlement-date day count is often different than the trade-date to maturity-date computation. For example, a forward priced on Tuesday that matures one day later, on Wednesday, would actually require three days of financing because the trade executed Tuesday would settle on Friday, while the trade executed on Wednesday would not settle until the following Monday. Care must also be taken to factor in settlement holidays (the Bloomberg **CDR** *(Calendar)* function provides information on exchange holidays globally.

■ *Dividends:* In order for a dividend to be included in the computation of fair value, the ex-dividend date must fall after the trade date and on or before the maturity date of the contract. Because dividends are paid out at the discretion of the firm management, and usually only announced a few weeks in advance of the record date, it can be difficult to accurately estimate the dividend amounts that should be included in the pricing of a forward. Even companies with a historically steady dividend payment can increase, decrease or suspend their payments at any time as circumstances change. Where the underlier of the forward is an index with many constituents, the computation of the appropriate dividend amount is significantly more difficult, particularly in the case of longer dated trades due to the impossibility of estimating the impact of future index constituent changes on the dividend stream.

■ *Interest rate:* Our formula for fair value assumes simple interest is received on the notional amount of the trade over the full life of the contract. While the rate that is used in a theoretical calculation would be the relevant risk-free rate of interest for the given time period, in practice each investor will compute their own fair value based on the particular rate at which they can borrow or lend money.

Subtracting the value of the stock price S from our expression for the fair value of the future, we get the fair value of the basis:

$$\text{Fair basis} = S\frac{rd}{365} - divs$$

It is important to recognize that the fair value of the basis is not a fixed number but a constantly moving function of the price of the underlier, dividends, interest rates, and the time remaining to maturity. Two of these—the interest rate and the dividend estimates—may also differ from one investor to the next, resulting in different values for fair value depending on who calculates it.

While the formulas that have been presented so far focus on the case of a forward contract on a single share of a stock, the extension of the logic to the pricing of forwards on baskets of stock, indices, or other underliers is straightforward. The stock price is replaced with the index level or portfolio value and the dividend term is expressed either in terms of index points or a notional amount of dividends to be paid out on the basket. The extension to nonequity products requires some additional and more complex adjustments. For example, in the pricing of forward contracts on commodities, while there are no dividends to consider, there are costs associated with the storage of the physical asset. The fair premium to pay for delaying the delivery of a few thousand live pigs or a million gallons of oil must incorporate the expenses associated with keeping the asset somewhere until delivery.

For completeness, it should be noted that the interest carry costs for the computation of futures fair value are also sometimes calculated based on a daily compounded overnight rate, rather than a simple interest rate. This results in a slightly more complex formula for fair value:

$$FV = S(1 + r)^{\frac{d}{365}} - divs$$

In this calculation, the funding rate, r, is an average overnight rate which is different from the simple interest rate used in our previously derived formula. So long as the interest rates are properly derived, neither formula can be considered "more correct." However, in the discussion that follows, we will use exclusively the simple interest calculation as this is more commonly used in practice.

Convergence to Spot

With the passage of each day, both the financing costs until maturity and the dividends left to be paid decrease. This causes the value of the basis to decrease until, at maturity, the forward price and the spot price are equal. Intuitively this makes sense because the adjustments necessary to account for the delayed settlement should reduce as the amount by which settlement is delayed goes to zero. It is also apparent from the formula as both the number of days d and the dividends $divs$ reduce to zero at maturity and the formula becomes simply $FV = S$.

Observe, however, that the basis does not converge smoothly and uniformly to zero. Depending on whether the financing costs are higher or lower than the dividend yield, the basis may be positive or negative. The reduction in the financing costs with the passage of time always pushes the basis downward, though in the case of a negative basis, this may actually mean an increase in the absolute value of the basis (it becomes a larger negative number). Dividends, on the other hand, are subtracted from the basis, so the arrival of the ex-dividend date of an underlying stock (which reduces the *divs* term) has the opposite effect, causing the basis to increase in value. This can mean either a larger positive basis or a less negative basis. These movements can occasionally cause confusion as it is assumed by many that the absolute value of the basis only decreases with time. While convergence of the forward price to the spot price is guaranteed at maturity, the path from start to finish is by no means straight or one-directional and the sign of the basis can change back and forth between positive and negative over the life of the contract.

The Trouble with Forwards

A forward contract is an independently negotiated *over-the-counter* (OTC)[2] agreement between a single buyer and seller and can be specified with whatever combination of terms suits the parties involved. The problem with this sort of custom-tailored contract occurs when one side of the trade wants to get out of the position prior to maturity. Unless the contract specifically includes early termination agreements, the party looking to unwind will need to negotiate an unwind price with the counterparty, who is under no obligation to provide one.

If the unwind price offered is unattractive, the investor will need to look for a third party to whom the position can be sold. However, because the forward is an over-the-counter agreement, the specific parties involved in the transaction are written into the terms of the contract and even if a buyer for the position can be found, the counterparty to the trade would need to approve the transfer (called a *novation*) as this would involve a rewrite of the contract. The particular issue here is counterparty credit risk; if the investor looking to get out of the trade is a large, stable, multibillion dollar bank and the new party is a small, highly leveraged hedge fund, the counterparty to the trade would be assuming a much greater risk of default were he to allow the transfer of ownership.

In the event that the counterparty does not allow the transfer of the position, the party looking to get out would have to strike an equal and opposite trade with the new counterparty, paying to one what he receives from the other. While this flattens out the exposure, he is now locked into two separate trades which together produce no net return but expose him to counterparty credit risk and may require him to tie up funds unnecessarily by posting collateral.

Forwards are therefore an appropriate tool for structured transactions where a very specific payoff is needed. However, as a tool for active trading, where positions will be opened and closed frequently, the highly customized terms become a liability, making the forward difficult and potentially costly to unwind. In order to stimulate the development of an active secondary market (i.e., somewhere buyers and sellers of forwards can meet to trade in and out of positions) there are two changes that need to be made. The first is to agree on a set of standardization terms for trading in a particular underlier, so as to reduce the number of different products and channel liquidity into a more manageable universe of contracts. The second is exchange intermediation, which removes the rigidity of contracts where the names of the parties are written into the terms, making them readily transferrable between parties. This leads us to the concept of a futures contract, which will be the subject of the rest of this chapter.

FUTURES

Definition of a Futures Contract

A *futures contract* is an exchange-listed forward with standardized terms. The futures exchange defines a set of generally agreeable contract specifications for delayed-settlement trading in each underlier including a series of fixed settlement dates at which the contracts expire, the price at which the expiry occurs (for example, the opening or closing price of the underlier on the expiration date), the form of payment acceptable at settlement, and any other details relevant to the particular asset that underlies the contract. Trading in these futures contracts is then centralized on an exchange, which acts as counterparty to both the buyer and seller.

Futures contracts are also generally assigned a *multiplier,* which determines the number of shares of the underlying stock (or units of index or other asset) per contract. For example, the underlier of each S&P e-Mini contract is 50 units of the SPX index. The price of the future is still quoted on a per-share or index unit basis and it is the trader's responsibility to know how many contracts to execute to get the appropriate exposure. (The multiplier of the contract can be found on the **DES** page for the futures contract on Bloomberg.) For example, if the level of the index is 1,000 and the basis is 10, the future will be quoted at 1,010, even though the actual price paid per contract would be $50 \times 1,010 = \$50,500$.

This standardization of terms makes futures contracts an extremely attractive investment vehicle. The homogeneity of terms across all contracts in a given underlier greatly increases the liquidity and ease of trading since all contracts are identical. When compared with a customized forward contract, an investor may find the standardized definition to be more or less appropriate to their specific needs. However, in return for conforming to the established terms, the investor benefits from the greatly increased liquidity and ease of trading of the centralized market. Trading on an exchange also reduces the counterparty credit risk as all of the U.S. futures exchanges have extremely high credit ratings making them virtually free from default risk. As a result, while there is still a significant market for OTC forwards on equity underliers, the volume of trading in listed futures is far greater.

As an aside, the standardization of terms is of particular importance in the markets for commodity futures. While two shares of stock or "units" of an equity index are identical, this is not the case for two bushels of wheat, lengths of lumber, or gallons of orange juice (all of which are traded as commodity futures). Where the delivered asset does not conform to the minimum established terms, the exchange may specify price adjustments that compensate the buyer for the lower quality of the product.

For a given underlier, there will usually be futures contracts with several different maturities trading at any point in time, with the majority of trading activity concentrated in the nearest-to-expire (*front month*). In the United States, most equity futures have quarterly maturities, though in international and non-equity markets there are many products that expire on a monthly cycle.

Unlike shares of stock, there is not a fixed number of futures contracts in existence—new contracts are created and destroyed as necessary to meet demand. For example, if a buyer establishes a long position by purchasing a contract from an existing long holder, then ownership of an existing contract changes hands and the total number of outstanding contracts (the *open interest*) remains constant. However, if the buyer purchases from a seller who is initiating a short position, then a new contract will be created and the open interest will increase by the number of contracts traded. Short sellers of futures contracts do not need to locate because the contracts they short are created automatically by the exchange should it be necessary.

The open interest is monitored by the exchange which requires that all futures trades must be designated as either *opening* or *closing* depending on whether the transaction creates a new position or unwinds an existing one. The initiation of a new long is a *buy to open* and the closing out of that position is a *sell to close* while a new short is indicated as a *sell to open*, which is then closed out with a *buy to close*. The opening and closing indications determine how each trade affects the open interest: When an opening buy is paired off with an opening sale, the open interest increases; when two closing trades are matched, the open interest is reduced; when an opening and closing trade are paired off, the open interest remains unchanged.

Physical Settlement versus Cash Settlement

One of the most important properties of a futures contract is the type of settlement required. While in commodity futures, the typical means of settlement is physical delivery of the asset, futures contracts on financial assets are usually *cash settled*, meaning that, rather than delivering the underlying asset, the futures position is closed out (a short position is bought back and a long position sold) at the spot price at maturity.

For example, the most actively traded equity futures contract in the United States is the S&P e-Mini futures contract, whose underlier is 50 units of the SPX index. As we saw in Chapter 4, an index is equal to the weighted average of the prices of a group of stocks—it is not a "thing" that can be bought and sold, much less physically delivered. While it would be conceptually possible to deliver a replicating portfolio of the underlying constituents of the index, the practical logistics are so complex that this solution causes more problems than it resolves. Therefore, the S&P e-Mini future is cash settled. On the expiration of the contract, long futures holders automatically sell their contracts, and short futures holders buy back their position, at a specially-calculated expiration price of the SPX index. The economics of the replicating portfolio are used to derive the fair price of the futures contract, and play an integral part in the arbitrage relationships that we will discuss shortly, but the futures contract itself is a pure cash product whose only direct link to the level of the index is the cash value paid to holders at maturity.

A key difference between a physically settled and a cash-settled future is that, when the contract expires, the holder of a physically settled future takes delivery of the underlier and therefore retains his economic exposure to the price movements of that asset. With a cash-settled contract, the investor's exposure to the underlier terminates precisely at the expiration price, as though they had closed out the position. This is of particular importance in those situations in which a trader simultaneously holds equal and off-setting positions in a futures contract and the underlying asset. As part of arbitrage strategies employed to exploit price discrepancies between the prices of the underlying stock and the futures contract, a trader may hold billions of dollars of perfectly matched positions on which he expects to capture only a few basis points of profit. If the futures contracts were physically settled, there would be no risk in the unwind of these positions at maturity. If the trader is long the underlier and short the future, he would simply deliver the assets held to settle the contract, leaving him with no position. Similarly, if he were short the underlier and long the future, he would take delivery of the assets to cover his short and again, end up with no position.

However, when the contracts are cash settled (as all equity index futures are), the trader must understand the mechanics of the calculation of the expiration price precisely because it is at this price that the futures side of his arbitrage position will be liquidated. Given the small profit margins on this sort of trade, the trader must make sure that he can close out the physical position at exactly the price at which the futures expire. If this price cannot be achieved with certainty, the trader takes the risk of slippage between the unwind price of the two legs of his position, which could wipe out the entire profit on the trade.

For our example of the S&P e-Mini futures contract, the expiration price of the futures is equal to the SPX level computed using the opening print of every stock in the index on the day of expiration. This is a price that *can* be guaranteed on the hedge portfolio because both stock exchanges (NYSE and NASDAQ) provide a market-on-open auction facility in which all orders receive the same execution price. This allows the trader to unwind very large stock positions held against futures at precisely the expiration prices of those contracts. In some contracts (particularly in Europe) the expiration of the futures is based on a more complex benchmark (for example, a 10-minute intraday TWAP calculation based on snapshots of the index level every 15 seconds). In this case, there is no way for the trader to guarantee that the stock hedge will be liquidated at precisely the same level as the futures. The trader must "trade the print" and can only hope that the slippage on the stock unwind versus the futures expiration is small. The inability to risklessly unwind a stock hedge at the expiration print makes it more difficult for traders to implement some of the arbitrage trades that we will discuss later, and can result in less efficient trading in the futures market.

Uses of Futures

This ability to buy and sell exposure to units of an index as though it were a tangible asset has been one of the most attractive features of futures for equity investors and the majority of futures traded in the equity market have an index as their underlier.[3] In fact, with the exception of a few highly liquid ETFs that make it into the top rankings, all of the most liquid equity products globally are index futures. For this reason, in the rest of the chapter, we assume that all futures contracts are cash-settled equity index futures, unless otherwise specified.

While we have specified various details about the mechanics of forwards and futures, we have not yet given any indication of how investors use them. Trading in futures contracts can be loosely classified as falling into two broad categories—hedging and speculating.

Hedging   The use of futures as a hedging tool can be viewed in two ways. Where the futures contract is identical to the asset being hedged, the combination of the two positions eliminates the investor's exposure to the movements of the underlier. This is a "perfect" hedge. The easiest example of this comes from commodity futures. Assume a wheat farmer estimates that, in six months' time, he will have 50,000 bushels of wheat to sell. While the current price for wheat is attractive, he is concerned about the risk that the price will be lower by harvest time. In order to protect himself against a drop in the price, he can sell short futures contracts expiring in six months, on 50,000 bushels of wheat. By doing so, he locks in a price today for the wheat he will be prepared to deliver in the future. This completely removes his exposure (aside from mark-to-market requirements on the margin amount posted with the exchange which we will discuss later) to the price of wheat. At the maturity of the contracts (which are physically settled) he can simply deliver the 50,000 bushels of wheat he harvests to fulfill the contract.

Depending on whether the spot price of wheat at the maturity of the futures contract is lower or higher than the implied price (after adjusting for the implied carry and financing costs) from the futures contract, the farmer will have made or lost money through the hedge. Even if the decision to hedge results in a loss (the price of wheat is higher at harvest time than it was when he sold the futures, and he loses money on the futures position), it is often the preferable approach because, by hedging, the farmer has removed his exposure to the movements of the grain market and made his cash flows more predictable over the period. This gives him greater stability in his business and allows for more effective business planning (and a better night's sleep).

More commonly for equities investors, the underlier of the future is not identical to the asset being hedged and the position is no longer riskless, but instead retains some exposure to the performance of the asset. Usually, the futures position is used to hedge out a portion of the risk of the asset so as to isolate those exposures that the investor wishes to retain. Clearly, if the underlier of the futures contract and the long asset have nothing in common, then the addition of the offsetting futures position is not really a hedge because it does not actually reduce the risk to the investor (and possibly increases it).

For example, an investor might short a broad index future to hedge a long position in a single stock. In this case, the hedge acts to remove the overall market risk of the long stock position and converts the bet from a pure directional view on the long stock to a bet on the *relative* performance of the stock compared with that of the market in general. An outright stock purchase will only make money if the stock price goes up and there is the risk that, even if the company in question performs well, the stock price may go down due to exogenous factors (a downturn in general market conditions). If the long position is hedged with a short position in a broad index future, the investor is now expressing the view that the performance of the long stock will be superior to that of the broad market—even if both are negative. If both the stock and the market in general go down, the position will return a profit so long as the stock goes down less than the market (outperforms relatively). The futures hedge removes the exposure to the movements of the market in general and isolates the idiosyncratic risks of the single stock. The flipside to this is that, if the stock price goes up, the investor is not guaranteed a profit and can, if the index price rises more than the stock, actually suffer a loss.

Speculation   The other broad classification of investors in the futures market is as speculators. While our focus so far has been on taking positions in futures for the purpose of holding the contract until maturity, the vast majority of positions taken in futures contracts are liquidated prior to expiration and the existence of an active secondary market is one of the most attractive characteristics of futures as compared to OTC forwards. Speculators buy and sell futures contracts as a "synthetic" means of trading in the underlying asset—that is, a way of taking long or short exposure to the underlier without actually trading it.

There are several advantages to using futures as opposed to a direct purchase or sale in the underlying spot market.

- *Leverage:* Because the contract does not require payment until the future, only the posting of an initial margin amount, the futures position is highly leveraged. For a given amount of investable capital, the investor can take on much greater exposure to the asset than what would be possible in the underlying spot market.
- *Convenience:* An equity index future can give instant exposure to a portfolio of hundreds or even thousands of stocks in a single security. Commodity futures allow investors to buy and sell everything from live hogs to crude oil to gold without having to work out the logistics of where to store them (assuming the position is unwound before maturity as commodity futures are physically settled).
- *Liquidity:* While many investors may have a view on the price of the assets underlying commodity and equity index futures, only a fraction of these are in a position to actually trade in the spot market. As a result, the liquidity of many futures contracts is significantly greater than that of the underlying spot asset.
- *Centralization:* The vast majority of futures trading is concentrated on a few primary exchanges, while the trading in many of the underliers— particularly in the case of commodity futures—may be spread out across the country or the globe.

Secondary Trading

When compared with a direct purchase or sale of the underlying asset in the spot market, there are some very different risks that must be taken into consideration when trading futures.

Unlike any of the products we have looked at in previous chapters, the current price of a futures contract (or forward) is based not only on the market price of the underlying asset, but also incorporates information and assumptions about events that will occur in the future.[4] In more formal language, the value of a futures contract is the *net present value* (NPV) of the cost of delivering the underlying asset at the future settlement date. In computing the net present value, the interest rate over the relevant period must be determined along with the value of all dividends that will be paid out on the underlying stocks during that time. Even in the absence of any movement in the underlying asset, a change in either the interest rate or dividends will cause an immediate movement in the price of the future as this information is incorporated into the new assessment of fair value. Where dividends to maturity are not known with certainty (as is generally the case with index futures and with longer-dated futures contracts in general), the market price of a futures contract will react to a change in the *expectation* of what dividends will be, even in the absence of any real information.

For the investor who holds the contract to maturity, these changes matter little. The financing expense and dividends priced into the contract at the time of purchase are what will be realized in aggregate over the life of the contract. When information or expectations change, there will be a mark-to-market gain or loss, as the new information is factored into the price. However, if the contract is held until it expires, this profit or loss will be reversed and the financing and dividend costs priced into the contract at the time of the initial trade will be realized.

Let us assume that stock XYZ is trading at $100 in the spot market and we purchase a futures contract expiring in 90 days. (We will use a single stock future to make the language simpler: the logic is identical for index products.) The market rate of interest is 10 percent and the stock is expected to pay a $1 dividend in 60 days, though this is yet to be confirmed. The price of the future is equal to the spot price ($100), plus 10 percent interest over three months (= $2.50) minus the dividend ($1) for a total price of $100 + $2.50 − $1.00 = $101.50. An investor who pays $101.50 in the market for one contract and holds it to maturity will expect to make a profit equal to the movement in the underlying stock price between $100 and the contract's maturity, less $1.50 as the basis converges to zero. If the stock price is $110 at maturity, the investor will make $8.50; this can be viewed as a $1.50 net loss between financing and dividends plus a $10 price appreciation in the underlier, or alternatively as the difference between the $101.50 futures price paid and the futures price at maturity, which equals the spot price, of $110.

Assume now that the instant after the future is purchased, it is announced that XYZ will pay a dividend of $2.00, rather than the expected $1.00 dividend. Assuming that the stock price does not move, the market price of the future will immediately drop to $100 + $2.50 − $2.00 = $100.50, for a mark-to-market loss on the position equal to the $1.00 increase in the dividend. When the investor bought the futures contract he was given a credit of $1.00 for the dividend. Now, based on the new information, if he was to try to sell the contract in the market, it would be worth less than he paid just moments ago because market participants would require a credit of $2.00 for the dividend.

If the investor intends to hold the future until maturity and is satisfied with the economics priced in at the time of the initial trade, the mark-to-market loss is not necessarily of particular concern (other than the frustration of having missed an opportunity to buy the future cheaper). If the stock price is $110 at maturity, the profit on the futures contract, relative to the current market price of $100.50, will be $9.50. The $1 drop in the price of the future is made up by the fact that, on ex-date of the dividend, the basis will now increase by $2, rather than $1, due to the larger dividend. For the holder to maturity, the dividend was locked in at the time of the trade and while subsequent information may move the current market, the economics do not change.

It is, however, crucial that an investor who buys and sells futures contracts as a synthetic version of the underlying asset be aware of the fact that the futures price is a function not just of the underlying asset price, but of the interest rate and dividend estimates in the computation of fair value. If the price of XYZ rises $2 on the news of the increased dividend, the holder of the physical shares would experience a 2 percent profit on a $100 position. The holder of a future would only recognize a profit of slightly less than 1 percent: The $2 stock price gain is offset by a $1 loss due to the increase in the dividend, for a net profit of $1 on an investment value of $101.50.

A change in the market level of interest rates will also impact the price of a futures contract due to the impact on the funding costs that must be implied in the basis. Where the size of the position is sufficiently large to warrant doing so, it is possible to hedge out the interest rate exposure on the futures contract through derivatives in the fixed income market.

Dividend Trades   A consequence of the sensitivity of the futures price to the expected future dividend payments is that a combined long and short position in an asset and a forward or future on that asset can be used to express a view on the level of dividends. The holder of a physical position in a stock receives the actual dividends paid out by the company, while the holder of a futures contract will price in an implied dividend at the time of the trade. If a trader has the view that the market price of the dividend (as implied from the pricing of futures) is below the actual dividend that will be paid out, he can make a bet on the value of the dividend by purchasing shares of the stock and simultaneously selling an equivalent position via futures. The combination of the long physical and short synthetic positions removes his exposure to movements in the stock price. However, on his long position, he will receive actual dividends, while on the short position, he has paid an implied dividend. If the actual dividend announced is greater than what was priced into the future, the position will produce a profit as soon as the market price of the future adjusts to reflect the new fair basis. If the actual dividend is the same as what was implied in the future, the positions will likely show a small loss from transaction cost (bid-offer spread, financing costs, etc.).

Margin Requirements

By acting as counterparty to all trades, the futures exchange greatly simplifies the booking and settlement process for all investors, and removes the need for each investor to assess the credit risk of the counterparty to each trade. In doing this, the exchange takes on the credit risk of all investors because it guarantees payment to holders of profitable positions regardless of whether the investors with losing positions settle their debts with the exchange on time.

A futures exchange takes on a far greater amount of credit risk than a stock exchange does. The settlement of a purchase or sale of stock takes place three business days after the trade date and requires payment in full by the buyer and delivery by the seller. By the very definition of a futures contract, the payment does not need to be made until some point much further in the future. An investor who purchases a futures contract takes on full exposure to the movement of the underlying asset without having to make payment up front (subject to some adjustments that we will clarify in a moment). Even an investor with only a small amount of money can take very large positions, achieving a high degree of leverage on his investment. If the market moves adversely, the highly leveraged investor may find the loss on the futures position to be greater than the capital he has to invest and be unable to cover the payment of the loss. If the exchange is guaranteeing the payment to the holder (or holders) of the offsetting positions (who have made money), it must have a means for guaranteeing that the holder of the losing position does not accumulate a debt larger than what he can pay.

The way the exchange does this is by requiring that each investor deposit a small percentage of the notional amount of the contract value—called *margin*—in an account with the exchange. The exchange then marks the value of the investor's position to market each day and makes a cash adjustment in the margin account to reflect the daily profit or loss on the position.

Where the position has proven profitable, the investor can remove the additional cash credited to his account, so long as the initial margin level is maintained. Where there is a loss on the position, the investor's margin deposit is debited by the amount of the loss. If the margin in the account drops below a predefined *maintenance margin* level, the exchange considers the cash on deposit to be insufficient protection against the possibility that the investor accumulates additional losses that he is unable to pay. In this case, the investor will receive a *margin call* requiring that additional funds be deposited in the account. If the investor fails to make the deposit in a timely manner, his position may be closed out by the exchange to protect against additional losses.

In order to guarantee the stability of the futures market (and in today's highly interconnected market, the financial system as a whole), the exchange must take a conservative approach to extending credit to investors. This is done by minimizing the number of times where investors have an actual net debt to the exchange. Positions are marked-to-market each day and, so long as the loss on the day does not exceed the margin in the account, the investor will retain a positive cash balance with the exchange, which is sufficient to settle all payments (for that day at least). The requirement of a minimum margin amount ensures that, while it is always possible that a large, one-day, adverse move in the contract will wipe out the margin balance in an investor's account, the number of cases where this occurs is limited. Finally, the centralization of futures trading gives the exchange the power, through the threat of revocation of the right to trade, to make sure investors cover any payments quickly. As a result of the diligent implementation of the margin system, the credit rating on U.S. exchanges is very high and no U.S. exchange has ever failed.

To give a sense of scale, the most liquid U.S. equity index future, the SPX e-Mini future, traded on the Chicago Mercantile Exchange, has an initial and maintenance margin requirement of $3,600 on a contract value approximately $66,000 or roughly 5.5 percent.[5]

In light of the margin structure of the futures exchanges, a clarification is necessary regarding the previous comment that, for an investor planning on holding a futures contract to maturity, the movements caused by changes in interest rates and dividends were not of particular importance because the entire economics of the trade were locked in on trade date. This is not entirely correct: Because margin requirements are recalculated on a daily basis, even if an investor holds a position that will, over time, produce a guaranteed arbitrage profit, he must be able to meet the short-term margin requirements or risk having the position closed out against him by the exchange.

The collapse in 1998 of the hedge fund Long-Term Capital Management (LTCM) was, in many ways, the result of precisely this problem. In the case of LTCM, the products traded were over-the-counter derivatives and the margin calls came not from the exchanges but from the investment banks that were the counterparties to the fund's trades. As a result of the extraordinary events in the fixed income markets that year, theoretically low-risk arbitrage strategies that would have produced an almost guaranteed profit over the lifetime of the trade suddenly experienced huge adverse movements that, according to the statistical models of the fund, were so improbable as to be safely ignored. These movements triggered margin calls that the fund was unable to meet, due to the tremendous leverage on LTCM's positions (estimated in some cases to have reached 100 times). In order to prevent the forced liquidation of the fund's assets, which posed the risk of triggering a snowball effect and destabilizing global financial markets, the Fed made the controversial decision to organize a bailout of the fund by the investment banks that were its counterparties.

INDEX ARBITRAGE

We will now focus our attention on certain types of trades and arbitrage relationships involving both index futures and the underlying replicating stock portfolio. As there is a bit more mathematics in the next few sections let us first define the notation we will use. We will denote by F the price of a futures contract on an equity index with price S. The calendar days between trade date and the expiration of the future, calculated on a settlement-date to settlement-date basis, will be denoted by d, and r will be the risk-free rate of simple interest over that period. We denote by $divs$, the index dividend points whose ex-dates fall between the trade date and the maturity date of the contract. The formula for the fair value of the futures contract, F_{FV}, as derived earlier in the chapter, is then:

$$F_{FV} = S\left(1 + \frac{rd}{365}\right) - divs$$

Alternatively we can express the fair basis B_{FV} as:

$$B_{FV} = S\frac{rd}{365} - divs$$

To most closely replicate the standard practice in equity index futures, we assume that the futures contract is cash settled and that the expiration of the futures contract occurs at a price that can be risklessly achieved on the stock hedge portfolio (for example, the opening print).

Deviation from Fair Value

Given our derivation of the theoretical fair value for a futures contract, it is worth asking whether the contract trades at or near this level in the market and, if so, why? The answer to the first question is that yes, futures contracts do generally trade at or close to fair value. As for the "why," there is nothing inherent to the futures contract that requires that it trade at fair value. However, there are market forces—specifically, the opportunity for risk-free profits—that work to prevent the basis from getting too rich or too cheap.

In the chapter on program trading, we briefly discussed the concept of *index arbitrage*, which involves the simultaneous purchase and sale of a futures contract and the underlying hedge basket to capture the difference in the index level implied by each. We will now walk through the two possible arbitrage scenarios (futures trading above fair value and futures trading below fair value) in more detail as they provide a convenient framework for introducing some of the practical considerations of real-life trading. We take an informal and intuitive approach to understanding the arbitrage in the first scenario and then present a more mathematically formal argument in the second scenario.

We will assume the dividend yield on the underlying index to be less than the risk-free interest rate, resulting in a positive basis. While this is not always the case, it is a convenient simplifying assumption and makes the explanation much easier. All the results presented are equally valid for the case of a negative basis.

Futures Trading above Fair Value

When futures are trading above fair value (trading *rich*), the premium over the spot price paid by the buyer for delaying settlement—the basis—is greater than the actual cost to hold a long position in the underlier until maturity. If this is the case, an investor should be able to earn a riskless profit by borrowing money and purchasing the replicating stock portfolio (becoming a long holder of the physical stock) and simultaneously selling it for delayed settlement, via a futures contract. By buying the stock basket and selling the future, the investor eliminates his exposure to movements in the underlier and instead establishes a financing trade.

The trade is closed out by selling the stock basket on expiry and allowing the futures contracts to expire (which, for a cash settled contract, is identical to selling them on the expiration print). Because the two positions are unwound at the same price, and provide the same exposure to the equity underlier, the investor will have no profit or loss from the movement of the underlying index—the stock and futures perfectly offset. His costs to maintain the long physical position are equal to the interest charges on the borrowed funds less any dividends paid out on the shares. This is precisely the definition of fair value—the investor's cost to hold the physical position is equal to the fair value of the basis. The short position in the future generates a profit through the convergence of the basis implied in the actual futures purchase to zero. However, since the basis received on the sale of the futures is, by assumption, greater than the fair basis, the strategy produces a profit, which is therefore equal to:

$$\text{P\&L}_{\text{Total}} = \text{Actual basis} - \text{Fair basis}$$

Index arbitrage traders monitor the spread between the futures and the underlying index (the *cash index*) constantly and will trade futures contracts against rapidly executed program trades in a replicating portfolio of the underlying index to capture these profit opportunities between the two. In most developed markets, these opportunities are small and last only briefly, and the profit opportunity is generally only available to the first trader to get his order in the market. As soon as one trader begins to sell futures versus buying the stock basket, the price of the futures is pushed downward while the level of the cash index is pushed upward until the actual basis is brought in line with fair value. The act of capturing the arbitrage also acts to eliminate it.

Futures Trading below Fair Value

We now assume that futures are trading below fair value, or in the language of Wall Street, the futures are trading "*cheap.*" This means that with the underlying index at price S_1, the futures price F_1 is less than the sum of the index and the fair value of the basis B_{FV_1}:

$$F_1 < S_1 + B_{\text{FV}_1}$$

where

$$B_{\text{FV}_1} = S_1 \frac{rd}{365} - divs$$

The riskless profit opportunity between the forms of the index (stock basket and futures contract) is always captured by buying the cheaper version and selling the expensive version. In this case, the investor would purchase the futures contract at price F_1 and simultaneously sell short the replicating portfolio of stock[6] at a price S_1. Selling short the portfolio of stocks raises an amount of cash S_1, which can be invested to earn the risk-free rate of return r. However the holder of a short position in a stock is required to pay to the lender of the shares any dividends *divs* that occur on the underlying stocks during the period that the stock is borrowed. At maturity, the short position in the stock basket is covered in the market at the expiration price and the futures contract expires, both at the same price $S_2 = F_2$.

We can now work out the profit or loss on each leg of the trade. On the short position in the stock basket the p&l is based on the difference between the index price when the trade was put on and unwound, which equals $S_1 - S_2$ (a loss if the price has gone up and a profit if the price has gone down). To this we add the interest earned on the cash raised less any dividends paid out on the stock basket. Together this gives a p&l on the stock leg of:

$$
\begin{aligned}
\text{P\&L}_{\text{Stock}} &= (S_1 - S_2) + S_1 \frac{rd}{365} - divs \\
&= (S_1 - S_2) + B_{F_1}
\end{aligned}
$$

This says that by replicating a short position in the index through a stock basket, the investor realizes a gain or loss equal to the short return on the basket plus the fair basis.

On the futures leg, the p&l is simply the difference between the purchase and sale prices of the futures contract:

$$
\text{P\&L}_{\text{Futures}} = F_2 - F_1
$$

The total p&l on the trade is therefore:

$$
\begin{aligned}
\text{P\&L}_{\text{Total}} &= \text{P\&L}_{\text{Stock}} + \text{P\&L}_{\text{Futures}} \\
&= (S_1 - S_2 + B_1) + (F_2 - F_1)
\end{aligned}
$$

However, because at maturity the futures price F_2 is the same as the stock price S_2, we can rewrite this as:

$$
\begin{aligned}
\text{P\&L}_{\text{Total}} &= (S_1 - S_2 + B_1) + (S_2 - F_1) \\
&= S_1 + B_1 - F_1
\end{aligned}
$$

By assumption, the futures were trading at a discount to fair value when the trade was initiated:

$$F_1 < S_1 + B_1$$

This implies that the right-hand side of the equation is a profit, equal to the difference between the fair basis and the actual basis.

$$P\&L_{Total} = B_1 - (F_1 - S_1)$$
$$= \text{Fair basis} - \text{Actual basis}$$

As with the first scenario, the act of buying futures versus selling the stock basket will capture the profit opportunity presented by an underpriced basis, but also eliminate that cheapness by pushing the futures price up and the index price down until the actual basis is in line with its fair value.

With many "index arb" traders watching the futures basis, it is rare that it deviates substantially from fair value. One exception would be in the case of a major news event, where the futures market will react much more quickly to new information than the cash market due to the greater ease of trading a single futures contract as compared with large baskets of stock. In this case, the basis may deviate significantly from fair, though usually only for a short period of time. Sustained deviations from fair value are generally due to structural issues in the market that prevent the effective implementation of an index arbitrage strategy.

The Bloomberg **FVD** *(Fair Value Detail)* function allows the user to compute fair value and compare this to the current market price of the future to determine the degree of deviation. While all fields (interest rate, dividends, days to maturity, index level) are automatically populated with Bloomberg-calculated values, these can all be overridden by the user.

Practical Considerations

Given an understanding of the mechanism that keeps futures trading in line with fair value, we can now look at some of the practical issues related to actually implementing a cash versus futures (also called a *cash and carry*) index arbitrage to understand when, and why, the actual futures basis can differ from fair value, often for long periods of time.

The first point of clarification is the fact that, as observed previously, the fair price for the basis is a function of the specific funding and dividend assumptions of each investor. From the perspective of a small investor with limited access to capital and high funding costs, futures may always appear to be cheap because the market price of futures will reflect an average interest rate assumption for all participants, which is much lower that what a small investor might pay. By comparison, a large retail bank takes in deposits at interest rates well below the market rates (through customer savings and checking account deposits) and may perceive the market price of futures as persistently rich.

Another consideration is the rate of withholding tax charged on dividends. As discussed previously, any dividends paid out to a foreign investor on a U.S. stock would be subjected to a withholding tax of up to 30 percent, which would not be assessed on a U.S.-domiciled investor. On a futures contract, there is no dividend payment—the market price of the contract implies a consensus view of the expected dividend payment via the basis but there is no actual dividend and therefore no withholding. Because the majority of index futures are traded by local investors for whom the dividend taxation is not an issue, 100 percent the dividend amount will be implied in the basis. Therefore, for a foreign investor calculating fair value based on the withheld dividend amounts, the futures may appear consistently cheap.

In terms of actually implementing an index arbitrage trade, there are several points that must be taken into consideration:

- *Transaction costs:* Commissions must be paid to execute both the futures and stock portfolio trades, including both the initial trade implementation as well as the unwind of the stock position at expiration.
- *Bid/Offer:* If a trader wishes to capture an index arbitrage opportunity, he must do so quickly, or risk executing one leg of the trade and then having the market move before the other is completed. This means that on whichever of the two legs (cash or futures) is purchased, he will generally pay the offer while on the other leg he will hit the bid. The calculation of the index level is based off last sale, which will, on average, represent something close to the midpoint of the bid-offer spread. The last traded price in the futures could be bid-side, offer-side, somewhere mid-market, or, if the futures trade infrequently, outside of the bid-offer spread completely. In order for an arbitrage opportunity to be most easily captured, it must exist between the bid on one leg and the offer on the other. Depending on how wide the bid-offer spread is in each leg, this defines a range of prices that are different from fair value but cannot be captured via an index arbitrage trade.
- *Liquidity:* Even in cases where the arbitrage opportunity still works after crossing the bid-offer spread in both legs, there is the question of liquidity. If the futures are very illiquid and the size available "at the touch" (the best bid or offer) is small, the potential revenue opportunity from capturing the arbitrage may be too small to be worthwhile. In

the execution of the replicating portfolio there must be sufficient shares available—based on the number of shares that are required in each stock—for a perfect basket to be executed. If only a partial execution is accomplished, the trader will be at risk on the balance of the basket which may be completed at less favorable prices.

- *Dividends:* As explained before, one important difference between the stock basket and the futures contract is that the stock basket receives (or pays, if short) the actual dividends while the futures position locks in an implied dividend at the time of trade. If there is significant uncertainty around the dividends that will be paid out on the index during the life of the contract, it may be necessary to price in a bid-offer spread in the dividend term. The lower dividend estimate (which implies a smaller basis and higher futures fair value) would determine the futures price above which a long stock/short futures arbitrage spread would become attractive. (The trader receives actual dividends on the physical stock and has paid out the futures-implied dividend.) The higher dividend estimate (resulting in a smaller basis and lower futures fair value) would be used to determine the threshold price in the futures for opening a long futures/short stock arbitrage. (The trader will receive the futures implied dividend and pay out actual dividends on the borrowed stock.)

- *Stock loan costs and availability:* If futures are trading cheap relative to fair value, the arbitrage opportunity requires that the replicating portfolio of stock be sold short. A short sale of stock requires a loan of shares from a long holder of each constituent stock in the replicating portfolio. (Stock loan is covered in more detail in Chapter 11.) Depending on the number of lenders in the market and the demand for borrow, this cost, quoted as an annualized fee, can range anywhere from as low as 40 to 50 bps per year, for an *easy* name, to several percent for a *hard* name or even no availability at all. The weighted average borrow cost for the portfolio must be known in order to assess how cheap to fair value the futures must trade in order for the arbitrage to be viable. Where there is no borrow in a particular name, an assessment of the potential tracking error between the futures contract and the imperfect stock basket must be made and, until the theoretical profit from the arbitrage opportunity exceeds that, the futures will continue to trade below fair value. In many emerging markets stock lending is not permitted, which causes a disconnect between the futures and the underlying cash market, allowing futures to trade persistently cheap to fair value with no arbitrage to push them back in line with the cash index level.

- *Ability to unwind at expiration:* Where the expiration of the futures contract is not based on a readily replicable price in the underlying stock basket, index arbitrageurs must factor in an assessment of the

likely slippage versus the unwind benchmark to the minimum spread
necessary for a trade to be considered attractive.

- *Associated costs:* Index arbitrage is usually only executed by large institutions with well-developed back office infrastructure. Once the position
  is established, the replicating portfolio must be adjusted for corporate
  actions (mergers, splits, acquisitions), dividends must be monitored, and
  any rebalances of the index must be hedged. As discussed in the previous chapter on ETFs, there are enormous economies of scale in these
  tasks as the effort required to maintain a small position and a very large
  one is very similar. For small trades and small firms, the narrow arbitrage opportunities provided by the market may simply not be worth
  the effort.

THE FUTURES ROLL

There are two ways to look at the futures basis. The first is in terms of the
premium (or discount) at which futures are trading relative to fair value.
For example, if the fair value of the basis is $4.50 and the actual basis is
$5.10, then the futures are trading $0.60 rich. The other approach is to
determine the financing rate that would result in a calculated fair value
equal to the current basis. Given the level of the underlying index and a
particular assumption about dividends, every value of the basis corresponds
to a particular funding rate. For example, if fair value is $4.50 based on a
funding rate of 3.50 percent and futures are trading $5.10 over cash, one
can reverse the fair value calculation (as we will show later) to solve for the
funding rate and conclude, for example, that futures are trading based on
an implied rate of 4.05 percent, which is then quoted as 55 bps rich relative
to the market rate of interest.

To derive an expression for the implied rate of a futures price we begin
with the expression for fair value we have previously derived:

$$FV = S\left(1 + \frac{rd}{365}\right) - divs$$

In computing fair value, we assumed that S, r, d, and $divs$ were all known
(or observable in the market). The knowns on the right-hand side of the
equation allowed us to solve for the unknown on the left-hand side. If we
solve this formula for the interest rate, r, we get the following expression:

$$r_{imp} = \frac{365}{d}\left(\frac{F + divs}{S} - 1\right)$$

Observe that we have changed notation from *FV*, the fair value of the future, to *F*, the market price of the future and *r*, the risk free rate to r_{imp}, the futures-implied interest rate. The formula expresses a general relationship between the five variables and we can input any four to solve for the fifth. When we input *S*, *r*, *d*, and *divs* the formula produces the fair price for *F*, which we denote by *FV*. When we input *S*, *F*, *d*, and *divs*, the formula solves for the interest rate implied by the market price of the futures, which we then denote by r_{imp}.

This approach to quoting the futures basis is not often used in intraday trading as it is much more difficult to compute than the dollar value deviation from fair value (e.g., the futures are $0.60 rich) which can be done instantly. This is, however, the most common way of analyzing the futures roll, which will be our focus in this section. It should also be observed that quoting the richness or cheapness of the basis in terms of an interest rate is purely a linguistic convention and does not imply that the market is actually mispricing the interest rate, which is an objectively observable variable in the marketplace.

Definition of the Roll

As the expiration of a futures contract approaches, the holder of a position in the expiring contract must decide whether or not he wants to retain the exposure to the underlier past expiration. If so, he needs to close out the soon-to-expire *front-month* contract and open an equivalent position in the *deferred-month* (the next-to-expire) contract. This process of "rolling" a futures position forward is called the *futures roll,* or alternatively the *calendar spread*. During the weeks prior to expiration, the roll trades independently separate from standard buying and selling of the two individual futures contracts, and is quoted as a single price, equal to the spread between the front and deferred month contracts. A trader who executes a roll will receive one contract and make delivery of the other.

The convention for what "buying the roll" means differs depending on the contract and market. We will use the convention that the word "buying" or "selling" refers to what is done in the deferred month contract. For example, the holder of a long futures position who wants to roll them forward will need to buy the roll—buy the deferred month contract versus selling the front month—to maintain the long exposure. Due to the differing linguistic conventions in different markets, however, it is best practice to always clarify at least once what is being done in each leg. For example, a trader looking to extend a long position in soon-to-expire September futures might submit an order to "buy the roll" but also specify "selling Sep and buying Dec."

The difference between the fair values for the front-month and deferred-month contracts implies a fair value for the roll. When traders compare where the futures roll is trading relative to this fair value, the standard quotation is in terms of the financing rate over the period between expirations that is implied by the market price of the roll. An advantage of quoting the roll as an implied interest rate is that it allows the richness or cheapness of different contracts to be compared. The absolute price of the roll depends on the level of the particular index and the amount of dividends and is therefore not comparable between different indices—there is no way to know whether rolls trading $3.50 above fair in one contract are richer, in real economic terms, than rolls trading $0.50 over fair in another. By converting the price of the roll into an implied interest rate, the deviation from fair value can be compared easily between different indices—even when those indices are denominated in different currencies.

The calculation of the implied rate of the roll requires a bit of algebra so we will first develop a conceptual understanding of what it means. The fair value of the basis for the deferred month contract can be thought of as the sum of the *carry costs* (interest charged less dividends earned) on the underlying equity index until the maturity of the front month contract plus the additional costs to hold the position from the front month contract's maturity until the expiration of the deferred month contract. For example, if in February we were to calculate the fair value of an equity index future expiring in June, we could decompose this into the fair price to delay the settlement until the expiration date of the March contract, plus the additional costs of further delaying settlement until the June futures expiry. The price of the roll is effectively the cost of the forward-starting future that "comes to life" at the March expiry, when the front month rolls off, and matures at the June expiry.

We can express the value of the roll as the difference of the values of the front and deferred month contracts (indicated by the subscripts F_1 and F_2 respectively):

$$\text{Roll} = F_2 - F_1$$

This expression can be expanded using the definition of fair value and, applying the subscripts 1 and 2 to both the relevant interest rate and the number of days until maturity for each contract we get:

$$
\begin{aligned}
\text{Roll} &= \left[S\left(1 + \frac{r_2 d_2}{365}\right) - divs_2 \right] - \left[S\left(1 + \frac{r_1 d_1}{365}\right) - divs_1 \right] \\
&= S\left(\frac{r_2 d_2}{365} - \frac{r_1 d_1}{365} \right) - (divs_2 - divs_1)
\end{aligned}
$$

The second term is equal to the dividend index points whose ex-dates fall between the maturity dates of the two contracts. The first term is the financing cost on the position until the expiry of the deferred contract less the financing until the front month expiration. We can decompose the financing costs until the maturity of the deferred contract into the sum of the financing costs until the near expiry and the subsequent financing costs until the deferred expiration. Using the subscript *fwd* to indicate the period between the expirations we can rewrite the above as:

$$\text{Roll} = S\left(\frac{r_1 d_1}{365} + \frac{r_{fwd}d_{fwd}}{365} - \frac{r_1 d_1}{365}\right) - divs_{fwd}$$

$$= S\frac{r_{fwd}d_{fwd}}{365} - divs_{fwd}$$

We now have the expression for the price of the roll based on the interest rate, days, and dividends between the two maturities. If we input our own values for the forward dividends and rates, this formula gives us the fair value of the roll. However, as we encountered previously, the expression describes a more general relationship and, given the values of any two of the three variables around which there may be doubt (assuming S and d_{fwd} are unambiguous), we can express the third in terms of the other two. The most common case of this is to assume the dividends are known with certainty and to express the market price of the roll in terms of an implied financing rate r_{fwd}:

$$r_{fwd} = 365\frac{(\text{Roll} + divs_{fwd})}{Sd_{fwd}}$$

We can compare this implied forward rate to the actual interest rate in the market for the inter-maturity period and express the richness or cheapness of the roll in terms of a basis-point spread versus fair value.

This means of expressing the market price of the roll may initially appear somewhat obscure but is particularly useful to those investors who use futures as an alternative means of maintaining long index exposure to the purchase of a replicating portfolio. As compared with the purchase of a replicating stock portfolio, which must be paid in full, the purchase of futures contracts does not require an initial outlay of cash (other than a small amount of margin). Implicitly, via the futures basis, the investor is paying someone else to finance the long position in the underlying stock basket. Using the interest rate that can be earned on his cash position as the reference rate of interest, the investor can determine the implied richness or cheapness of the futures roll to assess how much additional cost is incurred by maintaining index exposure via futures. For example, if the implied rate of the roll is 40 bps above the interest rate that can be earned on his cash, the index manager will be implicitly paying 10 bps per quarter to maintain the index exposure (in addition to a small commission cost to execute the futures rolls). This can then be compared versus the costs per quarter of maintaining the replicating portfolio to determine which option is economically preferable.

Expressing the costs as an interest rate differential rather than a fixed expense has the additional advantage of scalability. The cost, expressed as a rate differential, can be applied equally to any futures position—regardless of size—to determine the costs of maintaining the position.[7]

Deviations of the Roll from Fair Value

The same index arbitrage opportunities that exist in the futures market exist in the futures roll market, subject to slight modifications in terms of hedging. The key fact to remember is that, at the time of execution, buying or selling a roll does not create a net exposure to the market as the roll is by definition composed of offsetting long and short positions in contracts of different maturities.[8] Buying or selling rolls creates a market exposure at the moment the front month future expires, at which point the arbitrageur must replace the expiring exposure with a stock hedge or be left with an unhedged position in the deferred month contract.

If, for example, the roll trades below fair value, the appropriate trade is to buy cheap rolls—that is, buy the deferred contract and sell the front contract. This requires that a replicating portfolio of the underlying stocks be sold at the time the front month contract expires, in order to maintain an offset to the long position in the deferred contract. As with the previous discussion of index arbitrage, high costs or lack of availability in the stock loan market can result in futures rolls trading persistently cheap as the arbitrage hedge cannot be executed. If the roll trades above fair value the trade is reversed—rich rolls are sold, leaving the investor short the deferred contract and long the front month. This long front month exposure must be replaced through the purchase of the underlying stock portfolio at expiry.

It is common in futures contracts on popular benchmark indices (such as the SPX) for the roll to trade slightly rich. This comes from the fact that the operational simplicity and low transaction costs of index futures (as compared with full index replication via stock baskets) is such that many institutional buy-side investors (pension funds, mutual funds, etc.) are willing to pay a small premium over fair value for the convenience of holding futures to hedge their index exposure. In economic terms, the demand on the long side is less *elastic* than that of the short side and therefore, the roll trades above fair value until such a point that the index arbitrageurs find the richness of the roll is sufficient to make the trade attractive.

EXCHANGE FOR PHYSICAL (EFP)

In an *exchange for physical* (EFP) trade, a block of futures is exchanged for a perfect replicating stock basket of the underlying index in an upstairs transaction either between two brokers or between a broker and client. For investors with sufficient infrastructure to handle the management of futures positions and the replicating stock baskets, EFPs provide a mechanism for moving between stock and futures positions at a price close to fair value (plus or minus a small premium) without taking the risk associated with trading out of the positions in the open market (called *basis risk*).

There are many reasons investors would want to trade an EFP. For an index arbitrageur who has captured a deviation in the basis via a cash-versus-futures arbitrage spread, the EFP provides a means of locking in a profit and unwinding the position without having to wait for the eventual convergence of the futures and cash at maturity. (Closing out the position also removes the risk that the actual dividends paid on the stock basket are different than what was implied in the futures basis.) Index funds often utilize futures as a liquid tool for balancing short-term cash flow needs caused by investor deposits and redemptions. The majority of the fund's assets are invested in the replicating portfolio and futures are used to fine-tune the holdings (similar to what is done with ETFs). If the number of futures held becomes either excessive or insufficient, the fund can use an EFP to switch between stock and futures without taking on market risk.

The EFP is quoted as a bid and offer for the futures, expressed in terms of the basis. For example, a quote of "7.45 at 7.65 for $100 million" means a customer can sell a $100 million replicating portfolio of stock and buy the equivalent exposure in futures by paying $7.65 over the level of the index for the futures ("7.65 over cash"). If the customer wants to sell futures and buy stock, he can do so at $7.45 over the cash level. Fair value will generally sit somewhere in the middle of this spread.

Once an EFP is agreed between two parties, each side must notify the futures exchange of their side of the trade along with the name of the counterparty. The exchange will then look to clear the trades versus each party, acting, as always, as the central clearing point for all futures transactions. Because futures can only be crossed in certain defined increments, (the minimum tick size is different for each contract) the agreed-upon average price for the block of futures must be decomposed into the closest approximation possible by dividing the total number of contracts between two nearest available execution prices. (For example, if a block of 1,000 futures is to be crossed at an average price of 761.243, with a tick size of 0.10, this would be executed as 430 contracts at 761.30 and 570 contracts at 761.20.)

The individual stock trades that make up the replicating basket are crossed separately on the relevant stock exchange, usually at the closing prices of the day. Most EFPs are executed after the close of business based on the closing prices of the index constituents.

Delta Adjustment

The fair value of the basis is determined by the financing costs and dividends on the underlying index. As the level of the index changes, so too does the cost of financing and with it, the basis. This dependence of the basis on the level of the index level S, is apparent from our formula for the basis derived previously:

$$B_{FV} = S\frac{rd}{365} - divs$$

Because the fair basis changes continuously through the day, the EFP market is quoted relative to the prior night's closing level in the index for convenience and consistency.[9] However, the stock basket for an EFP trade agreed today will be crossed at today's closing prices, which correspond to a different index level. There is therefore a need to make an adjustment to the agreed-upon basis, which was referenced the prior night's index level, to produce the economically equivalent value, based on today's closing index level.

To derive the adjustment factor that must be applied to the basis, we begin with our general expression for the value of a futures contract as a function of the underlying stock price:

$$F = S\left(1 + \frac{rd}{365}\right) - divs$$

If the underlying index moves from S_1 to S_2 during the course of the day, the r, d, and $divs$ terms all remain constant and the corresponding change in the value of the futures will be:

$$F_2 - F_1 = \left[S_2\left(1 + \frac{rd}{365}\right) - divs\right] - \left[S_1\left(1 + \frac{rd}{365}\right) - divs\right]$$

which reduces to

$$F_2 - F_1 = (S_2 - S_1)\left(1 + \frac{rd}{365}\right)$$

The change in the value of the futures contract, $F_2 - F_1$, is therefore equal to $\left(1 + \frac{rd}{365}\right)$ times the change in the index level, $S_2 - S_1$. Since the price of a future is equal to the underlying index level plus the basis, $(F = S + B)$, the change in the futures level is then equal to the sum of the change in the underlying index plus the change in the basis:

$$F_2 - F_1 = (S_2 - S_1) + (B_2 - B_1)$$

Combining this with the last equation we can express the change basis for a given intra-day change in the level of the index as:

$$B_2 - B_1 = (S_2 - S_1)\left(\frac{rd}{365}\right)$$

The formula says that for a given change in the level of the index, the change in the basis is equal to the financing costs on the difference between the new and old index levels.

This factor $\left(\frac{rd}{365}\right)$ is called the *delta* (Δ) of the futures contract and determines the change in value of the future for a given movement in the underlying index. The delta can be thought of as measuring the *excess* movement in the futures for a given movement in the index. It is also exactly the adjustment factor we were looking for to convert the agreed-upon basis, which was computed using last night's closing index price, to an economically equivalent basis relative to tonight's closing index price.

$$B_2 = B_1 + \Delta(S_2 - S_1)$$

This is called *delta adjusting* the futures basis.

The term "delta" is used in several different contexts in finance to describe the change in a derivative for a given change in the value of the underlying asset. Relating to futures, traders will sometimes refer to the entire $\left(1 + \frac{rd}{365}\right)$ term, as "delta" as well. In Chapter 9 we will encounter the definition of delta relating to options, which is a similar concept but very differently defined.

Tailing Futures

A second question that must be considered in an EFP is the appropriate number of futures contracts to trade to produce an equivalent futures position to a given notional of stock. We have just shown that the change in the value of a futures contract for a given change in the underlying stock can be written as:

$$F_2 - F_1 = (S_2 - S_1)(1 + \Delta)$$

The equation shows that the change in the value of a futures contract is equal to $1 + \Delta$ times the change in the underlying index. Effectively, the future has a beta (a sensitivity to the underlying index) of $1 + \Delta$, which is slightly greater than one. This means that, for a given number of index units of exposure to the underlying index, the number of futures contracts necessary to hedge the position is less than what would be implied by a one-for-one hedge by a factor of $1/_{1+\Delta}$. The act of adjusting the number of contracts traded to accommodate the higher beta is called *tailing the futures.*

The tailing of futures on an EFP illustrates the important distinction between positions that are notionally equivalent (the same size) and those that provide equivalent exposure (the same gain or loss for a given movement). This is a common stumbling block for new arrivals to Wall Street in the analysis and understanding of risk and has much broader application than just the computation of an EFP. To clarify the point, we present a more careful analysis of the precise calculation of the futures tail, and some of the most common errors in Exhibit 7.1. Because futures contracts are almost always defined with a multiplier, we will assume a multiplier of 50 in our example to make the computations more consistent with real-life practice.[10]

Exhibit 7.1 shows the slippage between a position in the index, via a replicating portfolio of stock, and three different futures hedges. Each of the hedge quantities is computed using a different method, all of which are quite common. In working through each calculation we can see that the first two of these methods are incorrect and, in the process, gain considerable insight into the hedging process. The exhibit is divided into four parts:

1. A list of the assumptions used in the calculations.
2. Calculation of the fair value of the futures under the initial and final index level assumptions (all other variables held constant for simplicity— we are assuming an instantaneous jump in the index) as well as the calculation of the delta.

1. Assumptions		2. Calc of Futures Fair Value	
Initial Index	1,250.00	Initial FV	1,260.82
Final Index	1,400.00	Final FV	1,414.52
Interest Rate	10.0%	Delta	0.0247
Days	90		
Div Points	20.00		
Multiplier	50		
Portfolio ($)	100,000,000		

3. Change in Value of Index and Hedge Positions

	1-for-1 Futures	$ / Futures	Tailed	*Stock Basket*
Units/Contracts	1,600	1,586	1,561	*80,000*
Initial Value ($)	100,865,753	100,000,000	98,438,503	*100,000,000*
Final Value ($)	113,161,644	112,190,352	110,438,503	*112,000,000*
Change ($)	12,295,890	12,190,352	12,000,000	*12,000,000*

4. P&L on Combined Long Stock / Short Futures Position

	1-for-1 Futures	$ / Futures	Tailed
Initial $ Exposure	(865,753)	0	1,561,497
PnL ($)	(295,890)	(190,352)	0
PnL (bps)	−0.30%	−0.19%	0.00%

EXHIBIT 7.1 Calculations of Future Tail under Two Incorrect and One Correct Methodology

3. Under each of the three methodologies, we calculate the number of futures contracts that would be held to hedge the indicated notional stock position.
4. We calculate the initial delta exposure between the long and short positions and then examine how well each hedge works for the given movement in the index.

The results of the analysis are summarized in the exhibit and explained in more detail here:

- *One-for-one index unit matching:* In the first case, 1,600 futures contracts are held, which, applying the multiplier of 50, gives an index exposure of 80,000 units, which exactly matches the stock position. Because the fair value of the futures is greater than the spot price (positive basis), the combined long stock / short futures position results in a net short exposure of $865,000 (short futures are worth more than the long stock). Since we are net short, we would expect a loss on in a market rally. However, when the index rallies, the higher beta of the futures contract results in a loss on the position of $295,000, which is significantly larger than the $104,000 loss that would be expected based on a 12 percent rally on an $854,000 short position. The mis-hedge (wrong number of futures) results in approximately 30 bps of slippage on the full notional.

- *Matched stock and futures notional:* Another common, but similarly incorrect, hedging technique is to hold an equivalent notional value of futures and stock—that is, dividing the stock notional by the futures price to get the number of contracts to hedge. This has the attractive feature of showing a flat delta at the start of the trade but is incorrect because, while the futures price does contain the necessary $(1 + \Delta)$ term used to tail the futures, the price also incorporates an adjustment for dividends that introduces an error.

   In this case, using a fair value of $1,260.82 and a target notional of $100 million, we get 1,586.27 contracts (before rounding), or 79,313 index units of exposure. While this results in zero net exposure at the time the trade is initiated, there is still a loss of –$190,000 or 19 bps after the move in the index.

   The fact that this is slightly better than the previous case is entirely due to luck. If we were to recompute Exhibit 7.1 assuming 40 index points of dividends, in which case the basis would be negative and the initial fair value drops to 1,240.82, the number of contracts computed by matching the notional amount of the stock and futures positions would be 1,611, which is even less accurate than the 1,600 futures computed in the 1-for-1 case previously described. The only case where dividing by the futures price will produce the correct futures hedge is when the dividend term is zero, in which case the fair value of the future is given by $F = S(1 + \Delta)$ and dividing by the futures price produces the same result as dividing by the index price S and then tailing the futures (dividing by $(1 + \Delta)$).

- *Correctly tailed futures:* Given the computed delta of 0.0247, the beta of a futures contract is therefore 1.0247 and the correct number of futures to hedge the $100 million long position is 1,600/1.0247 = 1,561.50. The notional value of this futures position is smaller than that of the long stock position, resulting in a net long exposure of $1.56 million or 1.56 percent of the total notional. Without factoring in the higher beta of the futures we would expect there to be slippage between the futures and stock positions due to the long market exposure of the position. However, due to the futures contract's greater sensitivity to movements in the underlier, the position is actually hedged on a beta-adjusted basis. We can see this when the index moves and the gain on the long stock position is exactly offset by the loss on the short futures position indicating zero net exposure to movements in the underlier—a perfect hedge. Observe as well that calculation of the futures tail was independent of the size of the market move, which implies that the position will be hedged for any size move in the index.

The beta of a futures contract is greater than one because when the index level changes, so too does the cost to finance that index position to maturity, and the two move in the same direction (both increasing or decreasing.) The amount by which the beta of the futures is greater than that of the stock is given by Δ, which is a function of the time to maturity and the level of interest rates. An important consequence of this is that, as time passes, or interest rates change, the value of the delta will also change, eventually converging to zero at expiration. Therefore, the appropriate number of contracts by which to tail the futures position will change with each passing day until expiration. A hedged book of stock versus futures will not remain hedged but must be continually updated to account for the decreasing beta of the futures.

In practice, it is common to see traders tail their futures by multiplying the un-tailed number of futures by Δ and then subtracting this amount from the number of futures to be traded (i.e., subtracting $1,600 \times 0.0247 = 39.45$ contracts from the 1,600 contracts in a one-for-one hedge). While not precisely correct, the error from this approximation is quite small—in the example of Exhibit 7.1, the difference is only about 1/20th of a contract. Interested readers can see why in the *Technical Comment* at the end of this chapter.

It is important to have some perspective on the significance of the adjustments described earlier. An EFP is intended to be a like-for-like exchange of futures and stock—a riskless trade used to manage inventory positions that is traded off-exchange at a mutually agreed price. In this case, there is no reason *not* to be precise in computing the number of contracts since it is in both parties' interest to minimize unnecessary slippages. Particularly for traders who manage large positions and need to trade EFPs frequently, an understanding of the details is important.

However, the tailing adjustment is usually relatively small. In our example using 90 days to maturity (i.e., a full quarter) and high interest rates (10 percent) and we still only get a tail adjustment of 2.47 percent or 39 contracts on 1,600. Under more "normal" conditions, for example a 4 percent interest rate and 45 days to maturity (i.e., halfway through a quarterly cycle) the adjustment is only 0.5 percent or a mere eight futures on 1,600. In the context of actual trading in fast and volatile markets, this represents a second-order consideration. If asked to hedge $100 million of market exposure by selling futures, a trader will focus first on "the big picture"—cutting market exposure and reducing risk—and execute something close to 1,600 futures. Once this is complete, if he wanted to be particularly diligent, he might tail the number of contracts. In the fast-paced environment of a trading floor, where time and resources are almost always constrained, it is important to have a clear understanding of the magnitudes of different types of risks and construct priorities accordingly.

EFP SUMMARY

To execute an EFP, a customer must agree to a *basis* and a *delta*. Given the closing level of the index the pricing of the trade is as follows:

$$\text{Futures} = \text{Index close} + \text{Basic} + \text{Delta} \times \text{Change in index}$$

$$F = S_2 + B_1 + \Delta(S_2 - S_1)$$

Where $\Delta = \frac{rd}{365}$. The number of futures to trade is based on the traded notional, the multiplier of the futures contract and the index level.

$$\text{Untailed futures} = \frac{\$\text{Notional}}{\text{Index level} \times \text{Multiplier}}$$

This number is then "tailed" by dividing by $1 + \Delta$ to account for the higher beta of the futures contract. This can be done in two nearly identical ways (the first being slightly more accurate):

$$\text{Tailed futures} = \frac{\text{Untailed futures}}{(1 + \Delta)} \approx \text{Untailed futures}(1 - \Delta)$$

When Fair Value Lies Outside the EFP Market

The forces that tend to keep the futures trading in line with fair value have a similar influence on the EFP market. In fact, a mispriced EFP market can be arbitraged away even more easily than futures trading in the market since the stock and futures trades are executed risklessly in an upstairs transaction against the other broker or client, as opposed to in the volatile world of on-exchange trading.

It is interesting to note, then, that it is not uncommon for fair value to often lie outside the bid-ask spread of EFP markets quoted by brokers to potential counterparties (clients or other brokers). There are many different reasons why this can occur based on imbalances in the supply and demand dynamics among "index arb" traders and index fund managers, limitations on balance sheet usage by brokers, the availability of capital, market events, the time of the year and uncertainty around the future level of dividends.

We will consider one example for illustrative purposes. Assume that a positive news announcement (e.g., surprise Fed rate cut) causes a sudden, large market movement to the upside. The greater liquidity and ease of trading in the futures market allows it to react much more quickly to news events than the underlying cash index. In this case, the sudden spike in the futures price, as market participants respond to the news, results in the futures trading substantially rich (say $6 above fair value). Index arb traders react by aggressively selling the rallying futures and buying stock to lock in the rich basis. Having done this, these index arb traders are now long a lot of stock and short futures and will look to unwind their position and lock in the profit by "EFP-ing" out of the position (selling stock, buying futures). Since they shorted the futures $6 rich, they are likely to be willing to pay above fair value in the EFP market to lock in the arbitrage profit today rather than waiting until expiration, which may be a couple months away. Effectively, because the broker has already made an attractive profit on the position, he is willing to pay someone else to take it off his books by paying slightly above fair value to unwind. The combination of increased demand and decreased price sensitivity is likely to cause the EFP market bid to be above fair value until arbitrageurs have managed to unwind positions.

Risk EFP

Sometimes customers want to exchange an imperfect index basket for futures. This is called a *risk EFP* because the broker takes on the tracking risk between the stock portfolio and the underlying index. In some markets, where there are limits on the ability to trade futures "upstairs" (off exchange), there may be requirements as to the types of baskets and the minimum degree of tracking required in order to trade a risk EFP.

Obviously, the pricing of a risk EFP would depend on whether the client disclosed the contents of the index portfolio in advance, giving the broker the opportunity to compute the rebalance of the imperfections in the portfolio. If so, then it is an easy trade to execute the rebalance on the close and convert the tracking basket into a perfect hedge (particularly if the EFP is executed at the close). If there is not, the broker is effectively pricing a blind risk bid in which the client provides the broker with the necessary futures hedge for the position. Pricing of the risk EFP in this case would be identical to what has already been discussed in risk program trading.

Interdealer Brokers (IDBs)

Brokers looking to trade an EFP will generally prefer to do so with a client, where the trade is not only useful in terms of inventory management but builds the relationship. If no clients have interest, an alternative is to trade with another broker who, despite being a competitor, might have an interest in trading an EFP at a price that would be attractive. The question is how these people can find each other: Brokers are reluctant to disclose any information about their positions or trading interests that could potentially be used against them. They will also be suspicious of the intentions of another broker who comes "sniffing around" looking for prices. Without a means of anonymously finding each other, two brokers can have perfectly matched interests and never trade because neither one will want to "show his hand" to the other.

This is where the *interdealer broker* (IDB)—also known as a *"broker's broker"*—comes in. Interdealer brokers act as matchmakers, calling around to get as many brokers' indications of interest in the EFP market and trying to pair off trades, for which they receive a fee. The interdealer broker will show around his best prices to all potential counterparties without giving any indication of where those prices come from. It is only once the trade has been agreed that they will disclose to each party who the counterparty to the trade is. The anonymity of information makes the IDB an essential intermediary between brokers, many of whom would not speak openly to each other.

BASIS TRADES

A basis trade is a stock-only transaction between the customer and the broker with no exchange of futures. There is, however, a futures transaction executed by the broker for his own account, which establishes a reference futures level that is then used to compute the prices at which the stock basket is crossed to the client. Because the broker and client have previously agreed to the fair basis and delta that will be used to convert the futures execution into an index price, the broker is indifferent to the specific execution level of the futures as the stock trade will be exactly matched to it. In cases where the stock basket is not a perfect replicating portfolio of the index the broker will also price in an additional risk premium to the basis.

For a client looking to execute a stock portfolio with little or no tracking error versus the index, a basis trade provides a way to take advantage of the liquidity and simplicity of trading in the futures market to facilitate the stock trade. Basis trades can also be attractive if futures are trading persistently rich or cheap (depending on whether the client is a seller or a buyer) to the client's measure of fair value. If the broker's EFP market represents a basis that the client considers advantageous, he can capture this mispricing (relative to his own calculation of fair value) via a stock-only execution, without ever having to take delivery of futures himself.

How Is a Basis Trade Priced?   There are three steps in executing a basis trade:

1. Executing the appropriate number of futures and computing the average execution price.
2. Pricing the stock portfolio by calculating the implied index level that corresponds to the futures execution.
3. Computing the percentage difference between the implied index level and a fixed reference point and crossing the stocks to the client at the reference point prices adjusted by this percentage.

Let us now examine each of these steps.

Step 1. Given the notional value of the basket that the client wishes to execute, and the agreed-upon basis and delta, the broker computes the equivalent (tailed) number of futures that must be traded. Since the futures execution is what will determine the execution prices on the stock portfolio the client is frequently given a significant amount of discretion to direct the futures execution.

Step 2. The second step, while conceptually straightforward, requires a bit of work. What needs to be done is effectively the reverse of the calculation that we did in the delta-adjusting of an EFP. In an EFP, we agree to a basis which references the prior night's closing index level and then delta-adjust to find the equivalent value of the basis using the new closing index level (or whatever prices are to be used to cross the stock portfolio). In a basis trade, we start with the futures price and must reverse-engineer the stock execution level that it implies.

- **The Direct Method.** Going back to the calculation for an EFP in the previous section, given the index level on trade date, S_2, we calculated the fair price F at which to cross futures in terms of the reference index level S_1, the agreed-upon basis relative to that index level, B_1, and the delta Δ:

$$F = S_2 + B_1 + \Delta(S_2 - S_1)$$

In a basis trade we have F, S_1, and B_1 and need to solve for S_2. In this case it, is not the closing index level but the implied cash level corresponding to the futures execution. Rearranging terms in the formula we get:

$$F = S_2(1 + \Delta) + B_1 - \Delta S_1$$

From which we can easily solve for S_2:

$$S_2 = \frac{F - B_1 + \Delta S_1}{1 + \Delta}$$

We now have a formula for computing the implied index level corresponding to the futures execution price, given a previously agreed basis and delta. Unfortunately, while the formula is mathematically correct, it is not easily decomposed into individual steps with some intuitive significance and feels a bit like a "black box" to many clients. As a result, brokers often use an alternative highly accurate approximation that can be broken down into intuitive steps in a similar manner to the EFP calculation and is generally more easily understood and explained.

- **The EFP-Based Method.** When pricing an EFP, we computed a delta-adjusted basis B_2 based on the initial basis B_1, the stock price movement and the delta according to:

$$B_2 = B_1 + \Delta(S_2 - S_1)$$

We then added this delta-adjusted basis to the closing price of the index on the trade date to get the futures execution level:

$$F = S_2 + B_1 + \Delta(S_2 - S_1)$$

We can rewrite this expression more descriptively in terms of the delta-adjusted basis:

$$\text{Futures} = \text{Index} + \Delta\text{AdjBasis}$$

where

$$\Delta\text{AdjBasis} = \text{Basis} + \text{Delta} \times (\text{Index} - \text{Prior close})$$

We use the word *Index* rather than *Close* to denote the reference index level S_2) since, in the case of a basis trade, the level is not equal to the closing index level.

For the computation of the implied index level in a basis trade, it would appear from this first descriptive formula that, given the futures execution, we could arrive at the implied index level by simply subtracting from it the delta-adjusted basis.

$$\text{Index} = \text{Futures} - \Delta\text{AdjBasis}$$

The problem with this, as the expression for ΔAdjBasis shows, is that the computation of the delta-adjusted basis itself includes the value of the index level—which is precisely the thing we do not know and are trying to derive.

To get around this obstacle, we compute an *approximation* to the implied index level by simply subtracting the agreed-upon basis (not delta adjusted) from the executed futures level.

$$\text{Index}_{\text{Approx}} = \text{Futures} - \text{Basis}$$

While this is not the actual implied index level, because the basis has not been delta-adjusted, it is a reasonable approximation. We can then plug this approximate index level into the calculation of the delta-adjusted basis to get:

$$\Delta\text{AdjBasis}_{\text{Approx}} = \text{Basis} + \text{Delta} \times (\text{Index}_{\text{Approx}} - \text{Prior close})$$

Given this approximation to the delta-adjusted basis, we can now compute the implied execution level.

$$\text{Implied Index} = \text{Futures} - \Delta\text{AdjBasis}_{\text{Approx}}$$

While this formula is not as mathematically precise as the previously derived expression for the implied index level corresponding to the futures execution, it has the benefit of being able to be broken down into intuitive steps in a manner similar to the calculation of an EFP. In the *Technical Comment* at the end of this section we show that the errors in the approximation are negligible.

We can rewrite these formulas in more standard notation (using the "$\sim$" to indicate approximate values) in the following way:

Approx. to the futures-implied index level: $S_{\sim 2} = F - B_1$

Approx. to the Δ-adjusted basis: $\qquad B_{\sim 2} = B_1 + \Delta(S_{\sim 2} - S_1)$

Final index level using Δ-adjusted basis: $\quad S_2 = F - B_{\sim 2}$

Combining these three formulas we arrive at an expression for the implied index level under our approximated approach:

$$S_2 = F - [B_1 + \Delta(F - B_1) - S_1)]$$

Step 3. Having established, by either of the two methods, an implied index level corresponding to the futures execution price, we must now cross the stock portfolio to the client at prices that correspond to this index level. To do this, we first compute an adjustment factor that measures the percentage difference between the implied execution level and a fixed reference point (usually the close). For example, if the implied cash level is 1,227.74 and the closing index level is 1,214.45, then the implied index level of the futures execution is 109.4bps (= 1227.74 / 1214.45 − 1) over the close.

Each stock in the replicating stock basket is then crossed with the client at a price equal to the closing price of the stock, adjusted by the percentage difference between the implied index level and the close. In the case of our example, all stocks would be crossed with the client at a price 109.4 bps above their closing price. In this way, the implied cash level of the stock basket corresponds to the economics of the futures execution.

BASIS TRADE SUMMARY

STEP 1

As with an EFP, the customer first agrees to a basis and delta. The number of futures to be executed is calculated in the same way as an EFP.

$$\text{Untailed futures} = \frac{\$\text{Notional}}{\text{Index level} \times \text{Multiplier}}$$

$$\text{Tailed futures} = \frac{\text{Untailed futures}}{1 + \Delta} \approx \text{Untailed futures}(1 - \Delta)$$

STEP 2

Once the futures order is executed, the corresponding cash level is calculated according to either:

Method 1: Precise but Opaque

$$S_2 = \frac{F - B_1 + \Delta S_1}{1 + \Delta}$$

Method 2: **Transparent but with Negligible Errors**

(a) $Index_{Approx} = Futures - Basis$

(b) $\Delta AdjBasis_{Approx} = Basis + Delta \times (Index_{Approx} - Prior\ close)$

(c) $Implied\ Index = Futures - \Delta AdjBasis_{Approx}$

Or putting it all together:

$Index_{Approx} = Futures - [Basis + Delta((Futures - Basis) - Prior\ close)]$

STEP 3

Given the implied index level, compute a factor by which to adjust the closing price (or other reference price) in each stock:

$$Adjustment\ factor = \frac{Implied\ index\ level}{Index\ close}$$

The closing prices of the stocks in the basket are then multiplied by this factor and crossed with the client.

FUTURES CONTRACTS IN PRACTICE

Exhibit 7.2 contains a list of all the major equity index futures globally. In addition to descriptive information on the futures contract itself (multiplier, currency, expiration cycle) and the underlying index (ticker, members), there is an indication of the average daily traded notional and open interest (in $ millions) of each contract. While these last two items are only current at the time of writing and will change over time, they serve as a useful indicator for the liquidity and level of interest in each contract.

Symbology

The ticker symbol for each futures contract is composed of a two letter prefix, followed by a single letter indicating the month in which the contract expires and a number indicating the year. For example, the S&P 500 future that matures in September 2009 has the symbol SPU9, where the prefix "SP" indicates the specific contract on the SPX, followed by the letter "U" for September and the number 9 for 2009. The NASDAQ-100

Country	Underlying Index	Index Ticker	Memb	Fut. Code	Crncy	Mult	Cycle	ADV ($mm)	Open Int. ($mm)
United States	S&P500	SPX	500	SP	USD	250	Q	12,088	176,963
	S&P500 (e-mini)	SPX	500	ES	USD	50	Q	141,997	156,157
	Nasdaq-100	NDX	100	ND	USD	100	Q	840	5,604
	Nasdaq-100 (e-mini)	NDX	100	NQ	USD	20	Q	15,771	11,999
	Russell 2000	RTY	1976	RL	USD	500	Q	554	11,303
	Russell 2000 (e-mini)	RTY	1976	RR	USD	100	Q	17,608	42,805
Europe	EuroSTOXX 50	SX5E	50	VG	EUR	10	Q	84,322	145,068
	MSCI Pan-Euro	MSPE	227	MP	EUR	20	Q	45	948
Austria	Austrian Traded	ATX	20	AX	EUR	10	Q	20	703
Belgium	BEL 20	BEL20	20	BE	EUR	10	M	16	1,080
Denmark	OMX Copenhagen 20	KFX	20	KX	DKK	100	M	16	142
Finland	OMX Helsinki 25	HEX25	25	OT	EUR	10	Q	39	499
France	CAC-40	CAC	40	CF	EUR	10	M	3,677	34,873
Germany	DAX	DAX	30	GX	EUR	25	Q	45,466	55,791
	DAX Mid-Cap	MDAX	50	MF	EUR	5	Q	119	1,148
Greece	FTSE/ASE 20	FTASE	20	AJ	EUR	5	M	169	480
Italy	S&P/MIB	SPMIB	40	ST	EUR	5	Q	3,846	8,020
Netherlands	Amsterdam Exchange	AEX	21	EO	EUR	200	M	1,648	11,262
Norway	OBX	OBX	25	OI	NOK	100	M	91	1,247
Portugal	PSI-20	PSI20	20	PP	EUR	1	Q	3	85
Spain	IBEX 35	IBEX	35	IB	EUR	10	M	1,900	15,825
Sweden	OMX Stockholm 30	OMX	30	QC	SEK	100	M	679	7,739
Switzerland	Swiss Market	SMI	20	SM	CHF	10	Q	4,096	21,671
U.K.	FTSE 100	UKX	100	Z_	GBP	10	Q	12,431	52,137
	FTSE 250	MCX	250	Y_	GBP	10	Q	37	2,353
S. Africa	FTSE/JSE TOP 40	TOP40	40	AI	ZAR	10	Q	1,611	7,797
Japan	Nikkei 225 (Osaka)	NKY	225	NK	JPY	100	Q	14,600	45,221
	Nikkei 225 (Simex)	NKY	225	NI	JPY	500	Q	6,024	12,307
	Nikkei 225 (CME $)	NKY	225	NX	USD*	5	Q	990	5,118
	Nikkei 225 (CME JPY)	NKY	225	NH	JPY	500	Q	946	3,625
	TOPIX	TPX	1719	TP	JPY	10,000	Q	5,757	44,408
Australia	S&P/ASX 200	AS51	200	XP	AUD	25	Q	294	28,680
Hong Kong	Hang Seng	HSI	43	HI	HKD	50	M	3,323	14,817
	China Enterprises	HSCEI	42	HC	HKD	50	M	1,467	6,872
India	Nifty 50 (India)	NIFTY	50	NZ	INR	200	M	2,212	1,499
	Nifty 50 (Singapore)	NIFTY	50	IH	USD*	20	M	215	2,859
Malaysia	KLX Composite	KLCI	100	IK	MYR	25	M	89	487
Singapore	MSCI Singapore	SGY	-	QZ	SGD	200	M	216	3,265
S. Korea	KOSPI 200	KOSPI2	200	KM	KRW	500,000	Q	21,510	10,239
Taiwan	TWSE (Taiex)	TWSE	690	FT	TWD	200	M	3,306	2,253
	MSCI Taiwan	TWY	-	TW	USD*	100	M	482	4,904
Thailand	Thailand SET 50	THB	50	BC	THB	1,000	Q	105	246

EXHIBIT 7.2 Global Equity Index Futures

Note: Cycle: M = monthly, Q = quarterly. *Contracts listed in a currency other than that of the underlying index of quantos, which are explained in detail in Chapter 8.

Source: Bloomberg. 30-day average trading volume and open interest are calculated as of July 31, 2008.

future expiring in December 2009 would be NDZ9. The month codes do not correspond to the name of the month but are alphabetically arranged.

January	F	February	G	March	H
April	J	May	K	June	M
July	N	August	Q	September	U
October	V	November	X	December	Z

While at any point in time there will generally be futures with several different maturities trading, the greatest liquidity is found in the front month contract. About one week prior to expiration, the "front month" designation is transferred to the next-to-mature contract as liquidity drops off in the last few days of a future's existence as there is little point in buying a contract that will immediately need to be rolled. On Bloomberg it is possible to designate the front month future generically by replacing the month and year indicator with either the letter A or the number 1. For example, the front-month SPX future can be represented by either SPA or SP1.

There is an important difference between these two generic identifiers. The "A" ticker is a shortcut way of identifying the current front month contract and is converted into the correct letter and number combination by Bloomberg. The "1" ticker, however, indicates the *rolling* front month contract and the price shown on any historical date will be the value of the contract that was the front month *at that time*. Using the rolling front month ticker, it is possible to analyze historical futures price data over longer periods of time than any particular contract has been in existence.

A subtle point to be aware of regarding the rolling front month ticker is that when the front month contract changes, the difference in the basis between the old and new contracts will cause a jump in the graph of the rolling front month contract that is not indicative of a movement in the underlying index. If the difference in the basis between the front and deferred month contracts is significant, this can be a slightly misleading indication on the graph.

Information on the contracts currently trading, the volumes and open interest, as well as whether the contract expires on a monthly or quarterly cycle, are available on Bloomberg by using the **CT** (*Contract Table*) function.

Expiration

The expiration for all major equity index futures in the United States takes place at the official opening price of the index on the third Friday of the months of March, June, September, and December. These are generally the most active trading days of each quarter and are referred to as the *triple witching* days due to the simultaneous expiration of index futures and index options, on the open, and single-name options at the close. This is also the date on which the majority of indices rebalance, including all of the S&P indices.

Electronic versus Floor Trading

For each of the U.S. futures contracts there are two versions: a "big" contract, which is traded on the floor of the Chicago Mercantile Exchange (CME) and an *e-Mini* contract that is one-fifth the size and trades electronically, around the clock (23.25 hours per day) from Monday to Friday, on the CME's Globex platform.

In all cases, the liquidity in the e-mini contract is far superior. This is a relatively new phenomenon; as recently as 2003 the trading in index futures was still primarily centered in the open-outcry "pits" on the floor of the CME. In the open-outcry market, orders to buy or sell futures contracts were passed to a broker working on the floor of the exchange who would execute the trade by literally shouting the order into the crowd to find someone willing to take the other side. The number of contracts, the price and whether the order was a buy or sell was communicated via a complicated system of hand signals and traders knew with whom they were trading by the badges and colored vests each trader wore. When a trade was agreed between brokers—through some combination of eye contact, shouting, and pointing—each side would write the details of the trade on a paper trade ticket that was then passed (or thrown) to a clerk in the center of the pit who would record the trade electronically. Due to the size and chaotic nature of the trading floor, at times of heavy activity futures would occasionally be trading at different prices on opposite sides of the pit.

Trading alongside the brokers who executed orders for large investment houses were floor *locals* who bought and sold for their own accounts. These traders paid a fee for the right to trade on the floor and were there to add liquidity to the marketplace. In general they made their money as flow traders, moving in and out of positions through the day and going home flat (with no position) and hopefully with a profit. Many of the locals were extremely colorful characters and there are countless stories—both true and apocryphal—of the adventures of men (and a few women) who made and lost fortunes by reading other traders' body language, understanding the psychology of the crowd, and taking extraordinary risks.

In the end, it was inevitable that the speed and accuracy of electronic trading would supplant the excitement and pageantry of floor trading and become the primary source for liquidity in futures trading. The electronic-only e-Mini contracts were introduced in 1998 and by 2003 daily traded notional had surpassed the floor traded contracts, which had been trading since 1982. In Exhibit 7.2 we can see that today, the volumes in the E-mini contracts are between 10 and 30 times their floor-traded equivalents.

TECHNICAL COMMENT ON THE
ACCURACY OF APPROXIMATIONS

Tailing Futures

When we tail the number of futures in an EFP, we first compute the equivalent number of contracts N for a given notional on a one-for-one basis and then divide by $1 + \Delta$ (see Exhibit 7.1). We commented that many traders will simply subtract ΔN contracts from N to get a "highly accurate" approximation. What we are saying is:

$$\frac{N}{1 + \Delta} \approx N(1 - \Delta)$$

When we discussed valuation in Chapter 2, we introduced the following expression for the sum of the infinite series:

$$\sum_{n=1}^{\infty} \left(\frac{a}{b}\right)^n = \frac{a}{b - a}$$

If we extend the sum to include the $n = 0$ term and reverse the order of the equality the expression becomes:

$$\frac{b}{b - a} = \sum_{n=0}^{\infty} \left(\frac{a}{b}\right)^n$$

We can now make the substitutions $b = 1$ and $a = -\Delta$. Expanding out the first few terms on the right-hand side we get the following expression:

$$\frac{1}{1 + \Delta} = 1 - \Delta + \Delta^2 - \Delta^3 + \ldots$$

Our approximation therefore consists in dropping off all terms from the right-hand side of the order is Δ^2 or higher and multiplying both sides by N. The question is: how much error does this introduce? In practice, Δ is quite small, on the order of 0.01, and the terms of order Δ^2 are therefore very small, (on the order of 0.0001). This implies a mishedge of approximately one contract per 10,000, which, in the context of the rounding errors and other slippages of trading, is small enough as to be comfortably ignored.

Basis Trade Approximation

The second method of calculating the implied index level in a basis trade makes use of the same approximation. The precise formula for computing the implied index level in a basis trade was given as:

$$S_2 = \frac{F - B_1 + \Delta S_1}{1 + \Delta}$$

Using the approximation above, we can rewrite this as:

$$S_2 \approx (F - B_1 + \Delta S_1)(1 - \Delta)$$

Multiplying out the two terms and dropping the $\Delta^2 S_1$ term for the same reasons described above, we can arrive at the following expression:

$$S_2 \approx F - [B_1 + \Delta((F - B_1) - S_1)]$$

This is precisely the formula derived under the second basis calculation methodology. The error in this approximation is therefore on the order of Δ^2 and can be safely ignored.

SUMMARY

A forward contract is an agreement to purchase an asset based on today's prices, but with settlement delayed until a time in the future. The fair value of the forward is the price at which the economics of the contract for delayed settlement exactly match those of the spot transaction. The difference between the two, called the basis, is equal to the interest costs from the trade date until maturity (calculated on a settlement day basis) less the dividends paid on the underlier (on an ex-date basis). As the maturity of the forward approaches, the basis decreases to zero until expiration, when the forward and spot prices converge. Forwards are over-the-counter agreements between individuals and may be constructed with any combination of mutually agreeable terms.

Futures contracts are exchange-traded forwards with standardized terms (maturity date, underlier, form of payment). While the investor loses the "custom tailoring" of an OTC forward, the standardized terms and exchange listing mean that futures are readily transferable between parties (investors can trade in and out with ease) and therefore much more liquid. The most actively traded equity futures contracts are those on indices. Because an index is not a "thing" that can be delivered, index futures are settled at maturity against a cash payment of the expiration price.

Equity futures are used both for hedging purposes—to remove part of all of an investor's exposure to an equity underlier, as well as for speculation on the market direction. Unlike shares of stock, the number of futures contracts in the market (the open interest) is a function of supply and demand and fluctuates continually.

Because the price of a futures contract is a function of funding costs and dividends that will occur in the future, investors using futures contracts as a "synthetic" version of the underlying equity take on additional risks (changes in dividends or interest rates) that a holder of the underlier would not experience.

In addition to the purchase and sale of index futures for trading purposes, there are several special trades involving futures contracts that either explicitly involve, or are priced based on, the replication of a futures position via a stock portfolio.

- *Index arbitrage:* By simultaneously executing a buy and sell trade in a futures contract and a replicating stock basket, it is possible to capture the deviation of the basis from its fair value, subject to the execution costs, trading slippages, and liquidity constraints of the market.
- *Exchange for Physical (EFP):* An off-exchange trade executed either between two brokers or between a broker and a client in which a replicating stock portfolio is exchanged for an equivalent number of futures at an agreed-upon basis. The two key points to consider when pricing and trading an EFP are the computation of the appropriate number of futures contracts to trade for a given notional of stock (tailing the futures) and the adjustment of the agreed-upon basis, which is quoted based on the prior night's closing index level, to an economically equivalent level based on today's closing index price (delta-adjusting the basis).
- *Rolls:* When the front-month futures contract approaches expiry, futures holders that wish to retain their exposure must roll their positions forward to the next contract. The futures roll trades separately from the standard buying and selling of futures so that traders can trade both contracts simultaneously without taking execution risk on each leg. Any deviation between the market price for the roll and the fair

price is quoted in terms of a spread between the interest rate implied by the market price of the roll, and the prevailing level of interest rates for the same maturity. The ability to execute a replicating basket at the maturity of the front month contract to monetize any mispricing of the roll and keeps it trading generally in line with fair value.

- *Basis trades:* A basis trade is an upstairs cross of a stock portfolio between the client and broker where the prices of the individual stocks in the portfolio are derived from the execution price of an offsetting futures hedge. The broker first agrees a fair basis and delta with the client and then executes the futures hedge often with significant input and direction from the client. An implied index level corresponding to the average price of the futures execution is computed and, by comparing this index level to a fixed reference point (usually the closing price), a scaling factor is computed, which is applied to all the prices of the stocks in the portfolio, which are then crossed between the broker and the client.

Exhibit 7.2 contains a summary of the most actively traded equity index futures globally including the futures ticker, multiplier, settlement cycle, currency, and indicative open interest and liquidity, as well as the ticker name and number of members in the underlying index.

CHAPTER 8

Swaps

INTRODUCTION

Within equity derivatives, equity swaps has been an area of considerable growth in recent years, with many firms setting up new swaps trading desks or expanding their existing businesses. Surprisingly, while other recent areas of growth on Wall Street—such as credit, energy, and weather derivatives—involve esoteric structures that require sophisticated mathematical models for valuation and risk management, an equity swap is perhaps the simplest equity derivative available. Stranger still is the fact that, despite being such a simple product, it is also one of the more widely misunderstood. The reasons for this are many but generally center on the fact that, unlike other equity products, whose appeal for clients is readily apparent from their structure, an equity swap is so simple that it is not immediately apparent what benefit there would be for a client in using one. As we will see, the appeal of swaps is not in the structure itself but in the applications of that structure, some of which are quite obvious while others can only be properly appreciated by those with a more detailed understanding of finance.

Because it is such a flexible tool with so many different applications, a general definition of an equity swap is so broad as to be almost useless. We therefore take a different approach to this chapter and focus first on a particular use of an equity swap in order to clearly establish *why* an investor would use a swap in the first place. This, then, leads us to expand our discussion to consider more general applications.

MOTIVATION FOR A SWAP

We begin with the observation that all investors are not equal. By this we mean that two different investors can experience very different costs and benefits from holding identical positions. This can be due to differences in many factors including:

- *Financing abilities:* If the purchase is financed with borrowed funds, how much does it cost to gain that leverage? The cost of borrowing funds is very different for banks, broker dealers, hedge funds, and private investors.
- *Infrastructure:* There are significant economies of scale in the management of broad indices, particularly total return indices (dividends reinvested) or those that involve multiple countries and currencies.
- *Market access:* Many countries have expensive, complicated, and time-consuming registration procedures that make it very difficult for foreign investors to obtain access to their local markets. Only those investors that anticipate a large amount of activity will find it economical to set up direct local connectivity.
- *Execution costs:* Trading costs can vary dramatically between investors. Market makers, for example, are often subject to much lower exchange fees.
- *Stock loan:* In markets that do not allow stock lending, or where it is not possible to locate shares to borrow, the only investor who can take a short position is one who has a natural reason why he must be long. For example, a fund manager who holds shares as part of a replicating portfolio to a benchmark index can express a short view by holding fewer long shares than their index exposure requires. If the replicating portfolio requires a long position of 10,000 shares and the fund manager chooses to only hold 6,000, he is implicitly short 4,000 shares.
- *Everything else:* Country of incorporation, legal structure of the investment vehicle, tax domicile, regulatory environment, and virtually anything else that makes one investor different from another.

As a result of these differences, with respect to any given position, potential holders can be divided into *advantaged* and *disadvantaged* groups.[1] As we will see, swaps provide a bridge between the advantaged and disadvantaged groups. To illustrate this we first present a specific application of swaps that will, for the moment, serve as a "predefinition" of a swap.

> An **equity swap** is a tool that allows an investor holding an equity position to pass the economic benefits and risks of that position to a third party.

We can now see a use for swaps: An advantaged investor can hold a position and then enter into a swap contract to pass those advantaged economics to a disadvantaged party. The advantaged party can charge a fee for the service and, so long as the fee does not exceed the improvement in the economics, the disadvantaged party will find the trade attractive. We have already encountered this concept in Chapter 6 where we saw that, for small- and medium-sized index portfolios, it can be more cost-effective to leverage the economies of scale available to the largest fund sponsors and simply buy an ETF than to attempt to replicate the index independently. Swaps generalize this concept allowing virtually any position to be transferred to the party that can extract the greatest economic benefit from it, and then pass that benefit back to the intended holder.

A LONG EQUITY SWAP EXAMPLE

We will illustrate the structure of a long equity swap and the associated stock trades and financing transactions through an example.

An investor wishes to purchase 100,000 shares of stock XYZ but is, in some way, disadvantaged relative to his broker in terms of the economic benefits he will receive on this position. The broker and client therefore execute the following trade: the broker pays $10 for 100,000 shares of XYZ in the market and holds the shares in her own account. She then enters into a *long equity swap* with the client in which she agrees to pay to the client the full economics of the position—paying positive returns plus dividends (money she makes) and charging the client negative returns (money she loses). In doing this, the broker eliminates her economic exposure to the stock and passes her advantaged economics to the client. Because the broker has purchased the shares with her own money, the client agrees to pay the broker interest on the $1 million, as well as an execution commission for the service (which is generally slightly higher than what he would pay for the stock execution in recognition of the additional work incurred in the swap trade).

The interest rate charged to the client on an equity swap is generally quoted as a fixed spread (i.e., a given number of basis points) over a floating rate of interest. The floating rate is set at the time of the trade and then up-dated at regular intervals over the lifetime of the swap. The most commonly used reference rates for U.S. dollar-denominated swaps are the one-month and three-month LIBOR rates and the Fed Funds Overnight Rate.

- *LIBOR* stands for the London Inter-Bank Offer Rate and represents an average of the rates at which 16 major UK banks are willing to loan each other U.S. dollars for a given period of time. This average is computed and published shortly after 11:00 A.M. London time each weekday by the British Bankers' Association (BBA). Rates are published for maturities from overnight to one year and can be found on Bloomberg by typing **BBAM**. (Rates are also published for several other currencies that are frequently used as the reference for non-USD swaps.)

- The *Fed Funds Overnight Rate* represents the price at which deposits at the Federal Reserve are loaned between banks on an overnight basis. This rate is generally in line with the target Fed Funds rate set by the Federal Open Market Committee (FOMC) at its regular meetings. This is explained in more detail in Chapter 12.

The structure of the swap trade, and the associated hedging transactions, are shown in Exhibit 8.1. We will walk through the trade step-by-step:

1. The broker borrows $1 million and agrees to pay an interest rate equal to 25 bps over the one-month LIBOR rate in return.[2]
2. The broker uses the borrowed funds to purchase 100,000 shares of XYZ stock for $10 per share in the marketplace.
3. A swap is written between the broker and the client in which the broker pays to the client the profit or loss on 100,000 shares of XYZ starting at $10. In return, the client agrees to pay to the broker a funding rate of one-month LIBOR plus 50 bps as well as an execution commission.

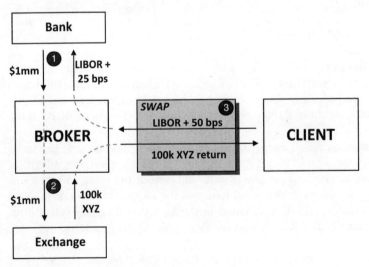

EXHIBIT 8.1 Long Equity Swap

We can now examine the positions held by each party. For the client they are quite simple since his only exposures are via the swap. He receives (is long) the return on 100,000 shares of XYZ with the advantaged economics that can be provided him by his broker and in return pays (is short) an interest payment of 50 bps over the one-month USD LIBOR rate on the $1 million notional of the swap. The position is structurally identical to borrowing money at LIBOR + 50 bps and purchasing the shares himself, with the exception that, by gaining long exposure to the stock "synthetically" via his broker, he is able to capture the advantaged economics.

On the broker's side of the figure there are many more arrows, but as we can see, the positions net nicely, leaving her with no equity exposure, an execution commission on the trade, and an interest rate spread in her favor that will generate a small amount of financing profit so long as the swap is active. (Remember that the 25 bps spread between what is earned via the swap and what is paid to the bank is an annual number—the broker earns approximately 2 bps per month for holding the trade, or $200 per $1 million notional of positions.)

Steps	Asset	Broker's Net Position
1 → **2**	**Cash**: $1 million borrowed from bank and used to purchase securities in the market.	Zero
2 → **3**	**XYZ stock**: The broker is physically long 100,000 shares of XYZ but pays all upside returns and dividends, and charging all losses, to the client via the swap.	No stock exposure. Receives an execution commission
3 → **1**	**Interest Rate**: Receiving 1 month LIBOR + 50 bps from the client versus paying 1 month LIBOR + 25 bps to the bank.	Financing spread of 25 bps in broker's favor

While the broker is the counterparty to the swap—and therefore short the stock's return to the client—her net exposure to the stock is flat because of the offsetting position in the physical stock. The broker's role is to facilitate the client swap in return for a commission and funding spread. However, a broker will not, in general, take the other side of a customer order unless she can hedge herself.

It is worth observing that, compared with a trade in a stock, ETF or futures contract, where the "fill" reported to the client consists simply of the execution price of the asset and the commission rate that will be charged, with an equity swap there are at least two more pieces of information that must be specified: the reference rate for interest calculations and the spread over that rate. As we will see in the next section, there are actually several other details that must be specified.

THE SWAP IN DETAIL: DEFINITIONS AND TERMINOLOGY

Having provided a big picture overview of the swap structure and a motivation for why an investor might use one, we will now analyze the product in more detail. We begin by presenting a general definition of a swap:

> An **equity swap** is an over-the-counter contract in which two parties agree to make a payment, or series of payments, based on the performance of an underlying equity reference.

A swap is a legal contract, signed by both the broker and client. In it, the two parties specify precisely what payments will be made, how they will be calculated, when they will occur, how they will be settled, and all other details regarding their respective obligations under the agreement. Each swap is a unique over-the-counter transaction with none of the standardized terms of an exchange-traded contract.[3] The terms of the trade are documented in an official swap confirmation, which is produced by the middle-office (see Chapter 11) and sent to the front-office trader for approval. Only once the trader has reviewed and agreed to the terms will the confirmation be sent to the client for approval and signing.

The swap confirmation is the final word on the obligations of each party under all possible eventualities. As a result, a full *long-form confirmation* may run over 20 pages and take several days to produce. This is particularly the case where the swap incorporates novel terms or conditions that fall outside the standard templates used by the middle office and requires guidance from the legal department to be properly documented.

As a result, it is not uncommon for the broker to provide the customer, at the time of trade, with a much-reduced *term sheet* specifying the basic conditions of the swap to make sure all parties are in agreement. Clients sometimes request one to ensure that the details they pass to their own back office for booking match what the broker will be expecting. While for the sake of professionalism, broker term sheets generally look somewhat formal, they are not in any way legally binding—a term sheet is purely indicative (effectively a fancy-looking e-mail) and in the event of a discrepancy between the term sheet and the official swap confirmation, the confirmation always takes precedence.

A sample term sheet for Example 1 is presented in Exhibit 8.2 and provides a useful framework to introduce some important concepts and terminology. With none of the standardization of exchange-listed products to fall back on, there are many details that need to be specified in order for both parties to say "I do" to the trade. As a result, even in the much-reduced form of the term sheet, there is a bit of new vocabulary that needs defining. Some terms may seem redundant or so obvious that they could be readily excluded with no loss of clarity. While this may be true in our example, due to the incredible flexibility of swaps, there are times and

EQUITY SWAP TERMSHEET

Date:	08 Feb, 2007	Trade Date:	Thu, Feb 08, 2007
To:	*Customer Name*	Effective Date:	Thu, Feb 08, 2007
From:	*Broker Name*	Maturity Date:	Fri, Feb 08, 2008
Subject:	Equity swap on XYZ	Termination Date:	Wed, Feb 13, 2008

EQUITY LEG		**FLOATING LEG**	
Payer:	Broker	Payer:	Customer
Equity:	XYZ Inc.	Reference Rate:	3M USD Libor
Underlier (RIC):	XYZ.N	Initial Notional:	$1,000,000.00
Shares / Units:	100,000	Spread:	+ 0.50%
Initial Price:	$10.02 (= 10.00 + 0.02)	Day Count:	Actual/365
Initial Notional	$1,000,000.00	Initial Rate:	TBD
Currency:	USD	Valuation Dates:	Quarterly
Valuation Dates (Resets):	Quarterly	Rate Fixing:	Next business day following valuation dates
Payment Dates:	3 business days following valuation dates	Payment Dates:	Equity Payment Dates
Return:	Total (Price + 100% divs)		
Unwind Price:	MOC on Maturity Date		

COMMENTS:

Mutual right of early termination (subject to 3 business days notice). This termsheet is not legally binding and all terms and conditions are superceded by the official confirm which will follow.

EXHIBIT 8.2   Equity Swap Term Sheet

circumstances in which, in order to reproduce a particular exposure, these terms may be assigned unexpected values and therefore, the standard is to include them.

■ *Dates:* The *trade date* of the swap is the day the terms are finalized and both parties are effectively "locked in" to the trade. For equity swaps this is usually the same date as the *effective date,* when the hedge would be executed and the swap begins to create an economic exposure for each counterparty, although they can differ. The *maturity date* is the date when the swap terminates (i.e., when the hedge would be unwound), with final payments taking place on the *termination date* (usually three days after maturity).

If the client wishes to continue the swap for longer than the initially stated maturity, the trade can be *rolled*. A new swap is initiated on the maturity date of the first swap and using the final price of the first swap. In this case, the broker simply retains his hedge and the swap carries on.

■ *Legs:* The swap is generally considered to have two "legs," corresponding to the two arrows in the diagram between the client and the broker. The *equity leg* contains all payments related to the movement of the underlying equity or dividends while the *floating leg* contains all interest rate-related payments. (If the interest rate is fixed then this would be called the *fixed leg*.)

■ *Notional:* This is the dollar value on which the interest payments will be calculated and is equal to the initial gross price of the underlier (exclusive of commissions) multiplied by the number of units.

■ *Currency:* The currency in which all swap payments will be calculated. If this is different from the home currency of the client, a spot currency transaction can be executed when payments are settled to convert this to the investor's desired currency.

■ *Resets:* Most equity swaps are structured with regularly scheduled *resets* at which the broker and client make the necessary cash payments to flatten any obligations accumulated to that point. Economically, a reset is like a termination of the existing swap and an initiation of a new swap at the same underlying equity level. If a swap has no resets before maturity it is called a *bullet swap*.

There are two important steps to a reset. First, on the *valuation date,* the reference equity price is measured and the liabilities of each party to the other under both legs of the swap contract are computed. These payments are then exchanged on the *payment date,* usually three days later. At this point, the accumulated obligations of each party to the other have been settled and the credit exposure on the performance of the trade since the last reset—the risk that the counterparty does not pay what is owed—is reduced to zero. The swap, however, continues in effect.

The second step is the *rate reset*. In the term sheet you can see that the swap has a maturity of one year, but the reference interest rate is only a three-month LIBOR rate. At each quarterly reset, the current value of the three-month LIBOR rate will be observed and this rate (plus the agreed-upon *spread*) will be used in the financing calculations for the next quarter. It is not uncommon for a bullet swap to have floating leg resets that do not pay out—the rate is updated, but there is not an actual reset payment. Similarly, the swap can reset with one frequency but update the interest rate with another. This is the case with swaps where the floating leg is referenced to the overnight Fed Funds rate. The daily rates are captured and averaged to come up with a blended rate that is used for calculating the floating rate payment at the next reset.

You may notice from the term sheet that the initial rate has not been determined yet while the equity leg details are complete. This is because the settlement convention for interest rate products is T + 2, versus the T + 3 standard for equities. To adjust for this, the rate is chosen the next business day after the initial equity leg fixing (and similarly for all subsequent valuation dates) such that, if the interest rate exposure on the floating leg needs to be hedged, payments will settle on the same day.

■ *Return:* Like indices, swaps can be either *total return* or *price return*. In a *total return swap*, the change in the value of the stock position from all sources is paid out to the client, including price appreciation as well as any dividends, special distributions or other payments. Note that dividends are paid out as part of the reset, not when they occur on the underlying stock. Not all investors are entitled to 100 percent of the dividend and the specific amount paid out will depend on both the domicile of the client as well as what the broker's firm is able to achieve, as it may be subject to withholdings and be unable to pay 100 percent). The vast majority of swaps are *total rate of return* (TROR) swaps.

Occasionally, a client may wish to trade a *price return swap*, in which only the change in the stock price is paid out to the client, and any dividends or other distributions received are kept by the broker. For example, the reconciliation of payments on a swap with an index underlier requires the computation of the index dividend points over the life of the contract. If the client does not have appropriate staffing or infrastructure to confirm that the payments from the broker are correct, he may find it preferable to remove the dividends from the swap contract altogether.

Clearly the client is not going to give away the dividends for free and will expect compensation. To do this, the broker calculates the expected dividends between trade date and maturity and converts it into a dividend yield that is then subtracted from the interest rate he will charge. For example, if stock XYZ has a dividend yield of 300 bps per annum, a long total return swap that trades at LIBOR+40 bps (often abbreviated as simply L + 40), would be equivalent to a price return swap trading at L − 260. If the dividend yield is greater than the interest rate plus the spread (i.e., if L < 260 bps in this example), then the net interest rate may become negative and the direction of the interest payments switches (in this case, the broker would pay interest to the client). This means that dividends paid out on the underlier are sufficient to cover all the broker's interest charges (so he does not need to charge anything for the trade) and still have some left over to give back to the client.

Price return swaps are infrequent and usually a bit more expensive since the broker must add an extra premium for the risk that the anticipated dividend yield differs from what is actually paid out. The broker must also be mindful of the fact that, by factoring the dividend yield into the interest rate, he is implying that dividends are paid out evenly throughout the year. In reality dividends are lumpy and occur at discrete times, particularly in Europe where many stocks only pay dividends once a year, usually between April and June. Should the client decide to terminate the swap early, the difference between the dividend yield originally priced into the trade and the actual dividends paid out on the underlier since the swap's inception would need to be computed and factored in to the unwind price.

■ *Day count:* This is the convention that is used for calculating the interest costs. Different fixed income products use different day count conventions. The Actual/365 means that the actual number of days from reset-to-reset are calculated and divided by 365 (even in a leap year) to calculate the percentage of a year over which the interest rate is calculated. Other options are Actual/Actual, Actual/360 (assuming all years have 360 days) and 360/360 (all months have 30 days and all years 360).

■ *Unwind price:* A swap will specify not only the termination date (when the equity exposure ends) but also the price at which the trade will be unwound. Clearly a specific numerical price cannot be given but rather a reference level is used such as MOO, MOC, or VWAP. In general, the broker will try to contact the client prior to maturity to ask whether to let the swap expire or roll the expiring contract into a new swap to extend the position for an additional period of time. However, in the event that the client cannot be contacted or does not provide a timely response, the broker will have to terminate the swap according to the terms of the confirmation. By specifying in advance the price at which the swap is to be unwound, the broker insures that there is no ambiguity or opportunity for dispute if the client is unhappy with the unwind price.

▪ *Mutual right of early termination:* It is standard practice to give both parties the right to terminate the swap transaction early, subject to sufficient advance notice (usually two or three days). This is really only a protection for the broker. In practice, almost all swaps are unwound early at the request and specific direction of the client and the broker does not require advance notice to do so. Investors use swaps as a tool for expressing views on the underlying stocks and the decision to hold or unwind the position is based on their view of the underlying stock, not the maturity of the contract.

In very rare cases, however, the broker will require an early termination of a swap against the wishes of the client. While a broker is always reluctant to do so, he will usually retain the right to early terminate in the event that circumstances necessitate it. One such situation would be if the broker lost the ability to hedge the swap position—he must either terminate the swap or take the other side of the trade unhedged. A very different scenario would be where the client has failed to return signed confirmations or settle payments in a timely fashion and is perceived as an excessively risky counterparty. While brokers will be very reluctant to exercise this right to early terminate, and make efforts to avoid it, it is an important safeguard to ensure that the client cannot force the broker to continue to take the other side of a position he does not want.

CALCULATION OF PAYMENTS

Let us now briefly look at how to calculate payments on the plain vanilla equity swap in our example in Exhibit 8.1 to illustrate the terminology just introduced. The calculations are the same whether it is a reset or the swap maturity; variables with subscript "0" refer to the beginning of the period value (trade initiation or previous reset) and "1" refer to the end of the period (termination or current reset). The "0 − 1" subscript refers to events that occur during the period.

Equity Leg Payment

$$(\text{Price}_1 - \text{Price}_0 + \text{Divs per share}_{0-1}) \times \text{Units}$$

The payment on the equity leg is the sum of the change in the price per share of XYZ between observations, plus any dividends that have gone ex-div during that time, multiplied by the number of shares specified in the swap. A positive amount indicates a payment by the broker to the client (broker is the equity leg payer) while a negative amount indicates a payment by the client to the broker.

Floating Leg Payment

$$\text{Notional}_0 \times (\text{Rate}_0 + \text{Spread}) \times \frac{\text{Days}_{0-1}}{365}$$

The floating leg payment is equal to the annual rate of interest specified at the beginning of the period, plus the agreed-upon spread, applied to the notional value of the underlying position as computed at the beginning of the period ($= \text{Price}_0 \times \text{Units}$), for a time equal to the fraction of a year that has passed between observations (computed on a settlement-date to settlement-date basis).

For clarity, we will run through a sample calculation to illustrate the precise calculations. Using the trade from Exhibit 8.1, we add the following information:

- Reference interest rate taken on February 9 was 3.5215 percent.
- It is now Tuesday, May 8 and the first reset is being calculated.
- Stock price at the close of business (taken as the reference value) is $10.26.
- XYZ pays a cash dividend of $0.12 per share: the ex-dividend date was April 21 and the payment date will be June 4.

The payments would then be calculated as follows:

Equity Leg $= (10.26 - 10.02 + 0.12) \times 100,000 = \$36,000$

Floating Leg $= \$1,000,000 \times (0.035215 + 0.0050) \times 87/365 = \$9,585.49$

Net Payment $= \$26,414.51$ (from broker to client)

A few observations on our calculations:

- *Day count:* Because the swap was initiated on Thursday February 8, the initial trade did not settle until Tuesday, February 13 (trade date plus three business days that carry over a weekend). While the reset date of May 8 is exactly three months (90 days) from trade date, because it falls on a Tuesday, payments settle on Friday, May 11. As a result, there are only 87 days for interest rate calculation purposes.
- *Dividends:* Dividends on the underlier are accrued to the swap on the stock's ex-dividend date and paid out at the next reset, based on the agreed-upon percentage participation (100 percent in this example). The cash dividend that went ex on April 21 is paid out to the client at

the reset, despite the fact that the actual dividend payment date is not until June 4 and therefore has not yet been received by the broker. The treatment of dividends in an equity swap is generally quite simplistic and it is not common practice to accrue interest on dividends already received but not paid out on the swap, or to charge interest on dividends paid out on the swap before their actual pay date. While these adjustments are, strictly speaking, economically "fair," the impact is simply too small to justify the effort.

- *Middle office:* The calculation and settlement of payments is managed by the middle office—the front office traders would only be involved if there were a dispute. Clients holding multiple swaps with the same counterparty will often request that all reset on the same date with one netted payment across all swaps to reduce paperwork and operational hassles.

SHORT SWAP

Having covered in detail the structure of the long swap, we can now introduce a *short swap*—in which the client gains short exposure to the underlier—quite concisely.

The mechanics of the trade are shown in Exhibit 8.3. The structure is very similar to a long swap except that in this case, the trade begins with

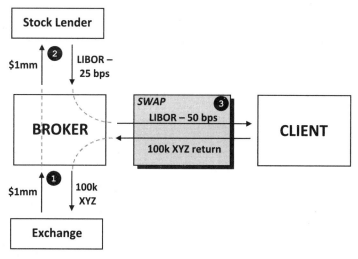

EXHIBIT 8.3 A Short Swap

the broker borrowing shares from a long holder of the stock and selling them short in the market. The economics of this short position are then passed to the client via the swap with the client now receiving the downside performance of the stock (what the broker earns on his short position) and paying the positive return (what the broker loses) plus any dividends (which are owed to the lender). The funding leg is also reversed; the broker earns interest on the cash raised from the short sale, which is paid to the client, minus a small spread.[4]

As with the long swap, the client's position is very simple—he has only the swap. The broker's position is more complicated but, as before, nets down nicely.

Steps	Asset	Broker's Net Position
Pre-trade	In order to sell short, the broker must borrow 100,000 shares of XYZ from a long holder. Because the shares are borrowed, as opposed to being purchased in the market, the long holder retains all economic exposure.	Zero
①→②	**Cash**: The 100,000 borrowed shares of XYZ are sold in the market raising $1 million of cash. Since the broker is no longer holding the physical shares he posts the cash raised to the lender as collateral until the shares are returned.	Zero
②→③	**Interest**: The stock lender pays the broker L-25 bps on the cash collateral, 25 bps being his compensation for lending the stock. The broker passes a reduced rate of L-50 to the client.	Funding spread of 25 bps in the broker's favor
③→①	**XYZ**: The client pays the broker the return on XYZ stock, offsetting his exposure from the short sale. The convention in the stock loan market is that 100% of dividends are charged to the borrower. The client will therefore pay 100% of dividends to the broker via the swap.	No stock exposure. Receives an execution commission

BACK-TO-BACK SWAPS

A *back-to-back*, in the context of equity swaps, is the situation where a broker holds two equal and offsetting swap transactions on the same underlier. In this case, the broker has no stock hedge or financing commitments and the payments made by one client directly offset the obligations to the other. In an active swaps trading book, back-to-backs occasionally occur naturally—one client takes a long position in XYZ on swap and, at some later time, another client shorts it. While this happy circumstance lasts, the

EXHIBIT 8.4 Back-to-Back Swaps

broker earns a much higher return on the position: using our long and short swap examples, it would be a spread of 100 bps *through the middle* as he would receive L+50 bps on the long swap and pay out only L–50 bps on the short. At any point, however, one party or the other can unwind their position and the broker will need to reestablish the necessary hedges and see his 100 bps pick-up will drop back to 25 bps on the one-sided trade.

There are also situations where the only option is a back-to-back swap. For example, there are some emerging markets that are completely closed to outside investors—only the local residents can trade. If a client wants to gain long exposure to a stock in one of these markets and contacts his broker to see if it can be traded on swap, the broker's options are limited. In this case, the client and the broker are both absolutely disadvantaged with respect to trading in this particular stock since neither one is allowed to purchase the underlying shares. One possible solution is if the broker can find another investor who wants to go short the same stock. In this case he can act as a matchmaker and trade equal and offsetting long and short swaps with the two counterparties, filling both orders without ever touching the actual stock.

An important caveat in this type of back-to-back swap is that the terms under which each party can unwind the swap must be symmetric. The broker cannot allow a situation where one client can unwind one and he cannot unwind the other, as this would leave him with an unhedgeable risk.

The structure of a back-to-back swap is shown in Exhibit 8.4.

SWAPS AS A TRADING TOOL

As mentioned at the beginning of the chapter, the complexity in the swaps trading business does not come from the structure of an equity swap, which is quite simple. Rather, it comes from the extraordinarily broad range of applications of that simple structure and the fact that, in many cases, the difference between a physical holding in the underlier and a synthetic exposure via a swap come down to nuanced financial details that are well beyond the scope of this book.

For most traders and salespeople, however, the majority of their interaction with swaps does not come from complex structured transactions dreamed up by bald lawyers tucked away in windowless offices, but from their use by clients as a *flow* product—that is, as a trading tool for expressing views on the market, in the same way they trade stock, futures, ETFs, or options. In this section we will explore several of the more common uses of swaps, and their motivations.

Leverage

One of the most attractive features of swaps is the leverage they offer. In the United States, when a client purchasing securities for his own account, the Federal Reserve Board's *Regulation T* limits the amount of credit that may be extended to him by the broker to 50 percent of the purchase price of the securities. This restriction applies to all investors, from retail clients to large institutions, and prevents investors from leveraging positions more than two times. For many sophisticated investors this degree of leverage is insufficient to achieve their desired returns.

However, if the same securities are purchased via a swap, Regulation T no longer applies[5]; the amount of leverage is determined by the amount of collateral the broker requires the client to post, which will depend on that broker's assessment of the riskiness of the position and the credit risk of the client. For established clients, where the risk of the swap can be offset by other positions held with the broker (whether swaps, equities, or other asset classes), the potential leverage can be significantly greater (from three times to as much as 10 times).

Index Replication

Another common use of equity swaps is as a mechanism for replicating the return of an index. The broker buys (or sells, in a short swap) the underlying stock portfolio and then enters into a total return swap on the index with the client. We have already discussed in several contexts how the economies of scale in index replication make it both easier and more cost-effective for larger institutions with more robust infrastructure to manage large and complex indices. However, even when compared with the alternative forms of index exposure—ETFs or futures—index swaps offer some special features that make them attractive to investors:

- *Broader offering:* While many popular benchmark indices have ETFs or futures contracts that track them, this only covers a small fraction of the thousands of indices that are published. In many cases, the only ways to gain exposure to an index are to either replicate the index returns via a stock portfolio, or to use an index swap and leave the index replication to the broker.

- *Zero tracking risk:* Because the swap contract references are written on the index itself, the swap pays out precisely the returns of the index. Any slippage between the underlying hedge portfolio and the index sits with the broker.
- *Cost:* Compared with ETF management fees, index swaps are often less expensive.
- *Long maturity:* Investors holding futures contracts must roll their positions each quarter (or monthly in some cases) and are at a risk that the futures roll trades significantly away from fair value. In a swap, the financing spread is locked in for the life of the trade, making funding costs more predictable.
- *Leverage:* ETFs are listed securities and therefore subject to Regulation T margin requirements. (Futures, it should be noted, are not and will often offer even higher leverage than swaps.)

The low cost, perfect tracking, and predictable cost structure of index swaps makes them a very attractive tool for investment companies looking to reproduce index returns—particularly when index replication is not their area of expertise. Consider a fixed-income fund that specializes in managing bond portfolios but whose investors are asking for the ability to diversify their holdings into equities. To prevent investors from taking assets away, the fund decides to launch an S&P 500 index tracking fund for which it receives an initial inflow of funds of $100 million. Given that they have no in-house infrastructure for maintaining equity portfolios, much less a 500-name index, the fund decides to outsource the entire index replication responsibility to a broker. The fund enters into a $100 million long swap on the SPTR (the total return version of the SPX with dividends reinvested) at a financing rate of one-month LIBOR + 10 bps.[6] The fund posts 20 percent of the notional in a collateral account with the broker on which they receive interest at one-month LIBOR flat (no spread). With the other $80 million the fund purchases a portfolio of corporate bonds that generates a yield of 50 bps over the average one-month LIBOR rate.

At the end of the year, the fund has generated an average return on their cash—between the bond portfolio and the collateral account of L + 40 bps (L+50 bps on 80 percent and L–flat on 20 percent) while on the swap, they have paid L + 10 bps to receive the total return of the SPX with perfect tracking. All together, the net return of the fund (before fees) in its first year is an attractive 30 bps outperformance versus the index benchmark. This strategy—which falls under the broad category of *enhanced indexing*—is popular because it allows a fund manager to outsource to the broker the work of replicating the index returns while the fund focuses on what it does best, in this case, trading bonds.

Customized Baskets

One application of swaps that has been the focus of a great deal of attention in recent years is swaps on customized baskets of stocks. The broker creates a custom-tailored portfolio of stocks for the client, which is then treated as a single unit (like an index) and serves as the underlier to the swap. The customer defines what is in the basket once and from that point on can simply buy and sell units of the basket on swap. Customized baskets fill the gap between a portfolio of individual stocks, which gives complete flexibility but can be cumbersome to work with, and an index product, which provides broad diversification in a single security, but lacks flexibility.

One of the more popular uses for swaps on customized baskets[7] is in the construction of hedges. Many funds use index products—futures, ETFs, and index swaps—to hedge out the market risk of concentrated long stock positions. One of the difficulties for fund managers is to find the appropriate index product to appropriately hedge out their exposures. If the long positions are concentrated in a few sectors (say, energy and utilities), a broad index product may not be appropriate since it will create "offsetting" short exposures in many sectors where the fund has no long exposure, resulting in multiple implied sector bets (long energy and utilities versus short tech, media, health care, etc.). An alternative is to use a sector-specific hedge such as a sector ETF. However, in many cases, the very stocks that are being hedged will occupy a significant weight in the sector index, resulting in partial cancellation of the long stock exposure.

As a simple example, an investor looking to hedge a long position in Exxon Mobil (XOM) with any U.S. oil sector index product will find that the largest constituent in virtually all of these indices, which are usually market cap weighted, is XOM itself, which is the largest company in the United States. If the weight of XOM in the chosen index is 25 percent, then hedging a $10 million long position in XOM with a short position in the index will result in an implied $7.5 million position in XOM versus the rest of the sector and a $2.5 million position in XOM against itself. The overlap between the long and short holdings not only needlessly ties up investable capital but, due to the difference between the financing rates charged on a leveraged long position (i.e., the cost of borrowed funds) and the rebate received on an identical short (the borrow rebate), the $2.5 million long-short position in XOM will actually "bleed" money.

What the investor really wants to do is short "the rest of the sector," excluding their long stocks. This can be done via a portfolio trade in the individual stocks. For many clients, however, this can be a cumbersome option as the combination of all of these positions in their portfolio can make it very difficult to see their actual exposure. A concentrated portfolio of a handful of long positions in two or three sectors can become lost when mixed in with a hedge basket of 50 or 100 short positions in stocks about which the client has no particular opinion.

A far simpler alternative would be to create a customized basket consisting of the stocks in each sector index that he wants to short (i.e., excluding those that are held as long positions). This customized sector basket can then be shorted on swap and appears as a one-line entry in the client's positions, making it much easier to focus on the long exposures (which are his primary interest). It is also greatly simplifies the adjustment of the hedge if the client trades around his long position actively. Each time he makes a trade in one of the longs, he can add or subtract the relevant number of units of the custom basket from his swap, rather than trading a small number of shares of many individual stocks. (He passes this responsibility to the broker.)

Emerging Market Access

As mentioned at the beginning of the chapter, many emerging markets monitor closely the investment activity of foreigners and impose significant restrictions to protect local companies and investors. *Foreign ownership limits* (FOL), which apply to the aggregate shares of ownership by all foreigners and range anywhere from 0 percent to 49 percent, are established to insure that local companies are not at risk of hostile takeover by foreign competitors. Once a stock has reached its FOL, all foreigners are prevented from purchasing shares.

In developed markets, a broker registered with the exchange can buy and sell securities freely for the account of any client; the exchange only cares whether the trade is for the broker or a client (principal or agency). In many emerging markets, the end client itself must obtain a *national investor number* (NIN) such that, when the broker buys shares, the exchange knows not only who is the executing broker but for whose account those shares are purchased (and specifically, whether that investor is local or foreign).

While for a broker with an active business in emerging markets it may be worthwhile to go through the complicated and time-consuming registration process to obtain a NIN, for all but the largest and most active clients, it is simply not worth the effort. Instead, an unregistered foreign investor can gain access to the local market via swaps with a registered broker. The broker purchases shares for his own account and then passes the economic exposure to the local share to the client via the swap. Because the executing broker firm itself is registered as a foreign investor, the local exchange is still able to accurately monitor the aggregate exposure by foreigners.

Most emerging markets with restrictions on foreign investment do not allow stocks to be lent as this would greatly complicate the process of monitoring foreign ownership. However, once a broker has built up sufficient inventory of local shares in a particular emerging market, he can then offer clients the ability to take short positions in that market by selling against his long inventory. By selling against natural long inventory, the broker can provide short access to the local market, without ever actually going net short of shares. Short swaps facilitated by existing inventory are effectively back-to-backs against the long swap holders. As a result, the short swap will carry the condition that the broker is allowed to immediately terminate the short swap should he lose the long inventory that was used to facilitate it. Additionally, the broker will monitor foreign ownership limits closely since, if he has sold out of long inventory to facilitate a short swap, when the client comes back to cover their short exposure, there is the risk that the stock has hit FOL and the broker is unable to close out the swap because he is unable to buy the shares back.

A COMMENT ON HEDGING

Clients using swaps as a flow product will usually think, and provide trading instructions, in terms of the underlying stock basket. This is natural given that, in general, the economics of the swap are replicated by an equivalent hedge position in the underlier. Clients are therefore apt to use the very same trading language and instructions used for stock orders, as covered in Chapter 3, for orders on swap. A client might give an order to execute a swap and instruct the broker to work the order VWAP over the day, or ask for a risk price or guaranteed market-on-close.

While this language is a convenient market convention for instructing how the client would like the broker to execute the underlying stock hedge, it is important to understand that there is a clear legal distinction between any hedge transactions made by the broker and the swap with the client. A swap is an over-the-counter derivative in which the two parties agree to make a series of payments *based on the performance of an underlying reference equity*; it does not represent a claim on any position held by the broker and there is no pass-through of economics from the broker's hedge position to the client.

In fact, there is no obligation on the broker's part to hedge the position at all. The colloquial trading language used in flow swaps is a very efficient means of communication between the broker and the client, but it is also very misleading. Take, for example, a client who wants to enter into a $10 million long swap on an index and instructs the broker to "Work it agency over the next hour." While this would be considered a perfectly normal trading instruction and is unlikely to cause any problems, there are several implications of this instruction that are not correct and can potentially lead to confusion.

The first is the use of the word "agency." An *agency order* has a very strict definition, particularly in the United States: it implies a direct pass-through of the executed prices to the client. This is impossible with a swap because there is no market where swaps trade—the broker cannot go out and "buy a swap" in the market. The trading instructions provided by the client are guidelines for how the client would like the broker to determine the fill price on the swap. If the client is dissatisfied with the fill, he cannot demand to "see his executions" as he would with an agency cash order since, not only are they not "his" executions, but there may not be any executions at all.

While the use of "agency" is incorrect even in a single stock swap, it is even more so with respect to an index swap. Not only is the swap not an exchange-listed product, but the underlying index is not a tradable product, either. If the broker agrees to pay the return of an index to the client via a swap, he must then decide how to go about replicating those returns himself. He may hedge his position with a replicating stock portfolio or choose to use an ETF or futures contract on the index. Depending on the liquidity of the underlier and the existing exposures on his book, he may hedge with another index and take the tracking risk between the two. Even in the execution of a perfect replicating portfolio, there may be some stocks that the broker is unable to execute due to restrictions, lack of borrow, or limited market access. (In multicurrency indices there is the additional complicating factor of the necessary FX hedges.)

While the use of cash-trading language is convenient and therefore unlikely to change, it is important to understand the differences between exchange-listed and over-the-counter products. Swaps are OTC derivatives and all swap orders, by definition, receive a risk price from the broker. The distinction between an "agency" and "risk" price on a swap is more accurately expressed as whether or not the client allows the broker to *pre-hedge* (execute his hedge before giving the client a price) or if he requires a price "on the wire" (i.e., while the broker and client are still on the phone) and leaves it to the broker to sort his hedge out later.

SWAP VALUATION: ACCRUAL VERSUS NPV

Despite their very different legal interpretations, equity swaps are viewed by many investors as a "synthetic" version of a position in the underlying stock. Particularly with swaps on single names, investors tend to think of their swap as a cash equivalent—something that is not actually a stock, but looks and feels like one. For the broker, who is in most cases hedging the swap exposure with a position in the underlying equity, the greater the similarity in the economics of the swap and stock ownership, the more accurately he can hedge himself.

For this reason, the daily mark-to-market of swap positions is usually done by the *accrual method,* which is the method by which physical positions are valued. Each day, the performance of the underlying equity position, whether due to price movements or dividends, is added to the accumulated obligation on the equity leg, and one day's financing is added to the financing leg. The two legs are then summed to determine the net change in the accumulated obligation between the two parties, which will be paid out at the next reset. The valuation is entirely "backward-looking" and only factors in those events that have already occurred.

Swaps are rather unique among equity derivatives in their use of accrual valuation. Virtually all other products, both equity and fixed income, are valued according to their *net present value* (NPV), which is the general framework for the valuation of all financial assets. The NPV methodology measures the value of a financial asset as the sum of all the cash flows that it will produce in the future, discounted to the present at a rate that incorporates both the timing and riskiness of each cash flow. This is precisely the same logic we saw applied in the fundamental valuation methodologies discussed in Chapter 2.

A simple example of a derivative that uses NPV valuation is a futures contract. As we have already seen, the market price of a future is a function of the anticipated carry costs and dividend income associated with holding the underlier until maturity, both of which are locked in at the time of purchase. If the contract is held until it expires, the purchaser of the future will realize precisely those economics (the implied carry and dividends) that were priced in at the time of the trade. Where the accrual method takes a "you'll get whatever happens, when it happens," the NPV method guarantees future economics today.

The important difference between the two valuation methodologies comes when the trade is unwound early. In an equity swap valued by the accrual method, nothing has been guaranteed about the future and therefore the client's economics at unwind are unaffected by events that have not yet occurred. In a product valued using an NPV valuation, specific future economics were locked in at the time of the trade, but the market price at which the trade can be unwound is based on the current expectations of those future events. Insofar as those expectations have changed, the unwind price of the contract will be a combination of the life-to-date movement in the underlying equity, plus the change in the forward-looking expectations of future events. As discussed in Chapter 7, the value of a futures contract can move based on a change in dividend or interest rate expectations, even if the underlying equity prices are constant. By contrast, in a swap valued by the accrual method, nothing that happens in the future can affect the swap value today.

Swaps can also be valued on an NPV basis. The initial value of the swap, instead of being just the spot price of the underlying asset multiplied by the number of units, is computed as the sum of all expected future dividends plus the entire cost of financing the position to maturity, with the relevant discounting factors applied to each one. While for flow-style swaps NPV valuation is uncommon, in more structured transactions it can often be preferable. As an example, consider a single stock, long swap written as a two-year bullet with no interest rate resets. Because the funding costs on the underlying stock hedge will most likely be assessed on an overnight basis, the broker now has a substantially mismatched interest rate exposure—he is receiving a two-year rate and paying overnight. This can easily be hedged in the fixed income market via an interest rate swap, which will be marked-to-market on an NPV basis. However, if the swap is marked-to-market based on an accrual valuation, the broker will see significant swings in his P&L as the changes in the market's expectations of two year interest rates affect his interest rate hedge, but are not factored into the mark-to-market of the equity swap. The broker must also be careful if the client wants to unwind his equity swap early. An unwind price computed on an accrual basis will not incorporate any potential loss taken on an interest rate hedge that is valued on an NPV basis.

CURRENCY EXPOSURE

In Chapter 3 we looked at two different ways to finance a foreign stock position: by borrowing the foreign currency or by purchasing it. When borrowing the foreign currency, the investor limited his exchange rate exposure to only the profit or loss caused by the equity movement; the initial notional amount of the position was unexposed. By purchasing the foreign currency, the investor took the double-barreled bet: long the foreign equity and long the foreign currency, both on the full notional amount of the position.

These two possibilities are mirrored in swaps, which economically behave like a physical position in the underlier, purchased with borrowed funds. If the swap is denominated in the currency of the foreign underlier, then via the swap, the investor has a long position in the underlying equity and a short position in the currency, which is exactly the same exposure as when the position was purchased directly with borrowed foreign currency.

Alternatively the swap can be denominated in the investor's home currency, which we will assume to be USD. The swap will now be booked in USD, versus a USD interest rate. This has two implications. The first is that, because the swap is denominated in USD, the local price of the stock must be converted into USD by multiplying by the spot exchange rate. To continue with our example from the last section of Chapter 3, the underlier of the swap is now the product of the XYZ stock price and the USD/EUR rate. This underscores the fact that the currency exposure is on the total notional amount of the swap since the movements of this hybrid underlier are equally determined by the equity and currency moves. The swap is said to have *composite* currency exposure.

Secondly, since the client will be paying a USD-based interest rate, the broker must replace his foreign currency debt (the money he paid to buy the stock) with a USD debt. This means that the broker will sell USD versus buying the foreign currency. This leaves him long the foreign stock and short USD, which is precisely the position from Chapter 3 when we considered funding in the home currency of the investor.

With swaps, and other derivatives, there is also a third option, called a *quanto,* in which the broker removes *all* currency exposure by guaranteeing the client a fixed exchange rate over the life of the transactions.

In a quanto, the client looks at the price on the screen and says "I want that many dollars" and ignores the fact that the asset is denominated in another currency. The quantoed swap is denominated in USD and the level of the swap is determined by the level of the foreign asset but without multiplying by the spot exchange rate to convert the foreign price into dollars—the local price is taken to be a dollar price. Using our example from Chapter 3, if the client were to enter into a quantoed swap on XYZ for $1.5 million, it would be documented as a swap on a dollar amount equal to 15,000 times the market price of XYZ, with an initial reference share price of $100. If the price of XYZ rises from 100 EUR to 110 EUR, the profit on the swap will be equal to 10 USD on 15,000 units or $150,000, regardless of what the currency may have done. While the swap references 15,000 units of the XYZ stock price, it is not a swap on 15,000 shares of XYZ as this would be worth 1.5 million EUR or $2.25 million. The appropriate stock hedge is still 10,000 shares of XYZ since this is what will produce the notional exposure of $1.5 million.

The challenge in hedging a quanto comes from the fact that exchange rates actually do move. A price movement in a foreign stock produces a profit or loss in the foreign currency, which, depending on the movement of the foreign currency versus the dollar, can be worth more or less in dollar terms. In our example, we considered two scenarios in which the investor earned a profit of 100,000 EUR based on a 10 percent movement in the underlying stock. In the first case, the currency remained unchanged and the USD profit was equal to 10 percent of the initial USD investment, or \$150,000. In the second case, the USD return on the position was reduced to 9.3 percent (\$140,000) due to a weakening of the EUR versus the USD. In a quanto, the broker would owe the client a 10 percent return (=\$150,000) in both of these cases.

In order to hedge the currency exposure of a quanto, the broker must try to eliminate his exposure to the exchange rate by dynamically hedging the profit or loss on the foreign asset back into dollars. If he makes a profit in EUR, he must sell EUR and buy USD since what he owes the client is a dollar return. However, if the stock price then swings back to its original level, the broker must buy back the EUR and sell the USD since, if the stock price is unchanged, the client will expect no payment and the broker has no need for USD. In this case the broker will have done two equal and offsetting currency transactions that, in the end, were unnecessary. Depending on the change in the exchange rate during that time, the trades may produce a profit or a loss.

The broker's risk can be broken down into an exposure to:

- *The volatility of the underlier:* Because the broker cannot hedge continually, he will set a threshold movement in the stock price, which corresponds to a profit or loss of a given magnitude, above which he will hedge his currency exposure. The greater the volatility of the stock price, the more frequently he will need to hedge and the larger the notional amount of each hedge, implying a greater risk.

- *The volatility of the exchange rate:* The broker's risk is that, given a movement in the underlier (which produces a EUR gain or loss) that the USD/EUR rate moves against him before he can hedge. Currency moves that occur when there is no movement in the equity price do not affect him. His risk is only when the currency moves at a time when he has an unhedged profit or loss in the EUR. If the exchange rate is very stable, then he is unlikely to suffer a significant adverse movement on his local currency exposure, while a very volatile exchange rate will mean a much larger risk.

- *The correlation between the stock price and the exchange rate:* If, when the broker earns a profit in EUR, this tends to coincide with a strengthening of the EUR against the USD, then the USD amount he will receive when he sells the EUR to hedge his gains will be more than what he owes the client, resulting in a profit. Alternatively, if the times when the broker has a loss on the underlying stock position, the EUR tends to weaken, then the USD value of the loss on the stock position will be less than what the client will pay to the broker via the swap, which also results in a profit. The reverse situation, where profits on the underlying equity position tend to be reduced by a weakening exchange rate and losses magnified, will result in losses to the broker each time he rehedges his currency exposure.

As it turns out, in the mathematical derivation of the price of a quanto (which we will not include here) a term emerges that is exactly the product of the volatility of the stock, the volatility of the exchange rate, and the correlation between the movements of the two. The larger the magnitude of each of these variables, the greater the adjustment that will be made to the price of the swap in order to account for the quanto.

Care must be taken in determining the sign of this adjustment. A historical correlation analysis only says whether the movements in the stock price and the exchange rate are positively or negatively related. For pricing the trade, the correlation that matters is between the broker earning a *profit* (loss) on the foreign equity position, and the *strengthening* (weakening) of that currency versus the dollar. A positive correlation will result in a reduced price for the quanto because the broker will tend to earn an additional return through his currency hedging. If this correlation between profits and strengthening is negative, then the quanto will be more expensive.

There are three factors that must be considered in order to determine the correlation between "profits" and "strengthening" and with it, whether the price for the quanto:

1. *Long or short swap:* Does the broker make a profit when the stock price rises or falls?
2. *Sign of the correlation coefficient:* The coefficient of correlation can be determined from a historical regression of the stock price and the exchange rate. The magnitude of the correlation determines the degree to which the movements of the two assets are related. The sign determines whether the changes in the two numbers tend to be in the same direction (either both increasing or both decreasing) or in opposite directions.[8]
3. *Currency quotation convention:* An increase in the numerical value of the currency rate must be converted into an underlying economic significance of whether the currency is strengthening or weakening. If the currency is quoted as the number of USD per foreign currency unit (as is the case for EUR and GBP) then an increase in the numerical value of the currency (EUR going from 1.5 to 1.6) indicates a strengthening of the EUR versus the dollar (it takes more dollars to buy a EUR). However, as mentioned in Chapter 3, most currencies are quoted as the number of foreign currency units per dollar (110 JPY/USD) in which case an increase in the numerical value of the currency quotation indicates a weakening of the foreign currency against the dollar (takes more JPY to buy a USD).

ISDA

Despite the simplicity of the swap structure, because it is an over-the-counter product, trading swaps requires significantly more documentation than what would be necessary to trade a listed product. While a swap can be fully documented in a single contract, if a client intends to trade swaps regularly, the process can be greatly simplified by establishing a set of standardized terms and definitions to which both parties agree to adhere. This then reduces the amount of documentation necessary for each subsequent trade.

Rather than each broker establishing their own set of unique terms, an industry standard has been established, called an *ISDA Master Agreement,* and most brokers will require their client to have a signed ISDA in place in order to trade over-the-counter products. *ISDA* ("Izz-duh") is the International Swaps and Derivatives Association, a professional body made up of over 825 member institutions that participate in the over-the-counter derivatives market. The ISDA Master Agreement, most recently revised in 2002, acts as an umbrella contract that is signed by both the broker and the client, and thereafter provides a framework for subsequent contracts entered into between the two parties. The broker will also require that the client sign a *Credit Support Annex* (CSA), which specifies the terms for posting of collateral by each party to cover mark-to-market exposures.

The ISDA provides a complete framework for brokers and clients to transact in a wide variety of over-the-counter derivatives. While many of the definitions are simply legal formalizations of the language used by market practitioners, the ISDA Master Agreement, and accompanying definitions, also provide clarity on many "what if?" scenarios that could result in disputes between counterparties. While some of these are quite straightforward (What if a regularly scheduled reset falls on a weekend; do we reset Friday or Monday?) there is also a great deal of consideration given to the more extreme situations such as: What if a stock underlying a swap is nationalized by the government and can no longer be traded? What if the currency becomes restricted and payments can no longer be converted from the underlying currency to the client's home currency? What if the exchange on which the stock trades is destroyed and trading is halted for the foreseeable future—how do we determine the unwind price?

While clearly improbable, the risks to both the broker and client in these extreme situations is great and unless the responses to them are agreed before the fact, there is the risk that the parties will end up fighting time-consuming and costly legal battles because of different interpretations of what is the "fair" response.

As a tangible example, what would be the fair price at which to unwind a swap that was set to expire on September 11, 2001? The exchange was closed for four days and reopened significantly lower on the following Monday. Is the client entitled to unwind at the last price on September 10 or is he forced to retain his long exposure until the market reopens and take the loss? If the position is retained until the market reopens, at what price should the swap be unwound? If the original contract specified an unwind price of market on close does the broker wait the entire session before unwinding the position of does he close out the swap before that? Since the broker will not be able to unwind the position for six additional days, does he charge the additional interest costs to the client (adding insult to injury)? The ISDA is there to ensure that the answers to all of these questions are clear to both parties from the outset of the trade.

RISKS AND OTHER CONSIDERATIONS

While ostensibly a simple product, the trading and risk management of a swaps book requires careful consideration of many factors, even within the relatively simplistic framework of nonstructured, flow-type swaps. Without going into any of them in particular detail, we will give a short list of some of the more noteworthy risks in order to give the reader some appreciation for how the trader views his positions and what factors are taken into consideration in pricing a new piece of business.

- *Stock borrow:* The broker must carefully monitor what he is charged on all his short stock positions to ensure that, if a previously easy-to-borrow stock suddenly becomes more expensive, that the client swap rate will need to be adjusted accordingly. In general, clients are willing (if perhaps a bit begrudgingly) to accept the re-rate of the swap as part of the cost of doing business. If a client were to refuse to allow the rate to be changed, the broker would always have the option of calling for an early termination of the trade, though this would be an extreme measure and only invoked if no other solution could be found.
- *Dividends:* When hedging a total return swap with a physical position in the underlying equity, there is no dividend risk—both positions are valued on an accrual basis and whatever dividend the broker gets is passed on to the client. However, if the broker trades price-return swaps, or uses product that is valued based on an NPV basis, such as a futures contract, to hedge an accrual based swap, he will develop an exposure to differences between the actual dividend paid out and what was priced into the swap or future.

- *Index replication:* In an index swap, the broker guarantees the client the exact index return and must then find a way to replicate those returns himself. If he chooses to trade a replicating stock portfolio he must insure that the portfolio is updated for all corporate actions, rebalances, and additions or deletions from the index. The broker needs to make sure he finds out about all index changes before they occur so that he can update his hedge position in time. Particularly with respect to the more complex corporate actions that are found in foreign markets, the broker always has the risk that the index provider accounts for an index change in a manner that the broker is unable to replicate, resulting in slippage.

- *Tracking risk:* If the broker decides to hedge an index position with something other than a replicating portfolio—such as a futures contract, ETF, or optimized hedge basket, he takes on the tracking risk between the hedge and the index. In hedging an index with futures contracts on the index, the tracking risk comes from the possibility of differences between actual and implied dividends, and mispricing of the futures roll. This can also apply to foreign stock positions hedged with ADRs or alternate listings (e.g., Chinese H-shares versus A-shares).

- *Execution risk:* As with a stock trade, the client may ask for a guaranteed price on the execution of a swap position that the broker may not be able to achieve on his hedge—such as a guaranteed VWAP.

- *Roll risk:* Index swaps lock in a financing spread versus the reference rate for the life of the contract. Futures must be rolled quarterly (and in some cases monthly) and will only lock in a spread (as implied by the basis) for the period until the next maturity, leaving the broker exposed to an unanticipated mispricing of the basis.

- *Interest rates:* Physical stock positions, whether long or short, are usually funded based on an overnight rate. The reference interest rate used on client swaps may be overnight, monthly, quarterly, or longer-dated. All these rates are different and changes in the interest rate market do not affect all of them equally. In a large swaps book, these interest rate exposures can become a significant risk.

- *Balance sheet:* The majority of equity swap positions are hedged with a physical position in the underlier. Anytime the broker buys an asset for his own account, that asset sits on the balance sheet and ties up some of the firm's capital. The trader on a swaps book will need to ensure that positions that utilize balance sheet meet the firms required hurdle-rates for profitability. Even if a trade is profitable, if the return generated is insufficient for the capital utilized the trader may be asked to unwind it or find a more efficient way to structure it.

■ *Credit risk:* With any over-the-counter transaction, there is always the risk that the client fails to make good on a payment owed to the broker. To ensure that the risk of non-payment is appropriately managed, the counterparty credit risk assessment is not left with the trader—who might be tempted to enter into attractive trades with excessively risky counterparties—but is managed by a separate group within the risk management division.

SUMMARY

Due to the extraordinarily simple structure of an equity swap, it is often unclear from a general definition why an investor would find this particular derivative useful. One of the most common reasons clients choose to use swaps is that, with respect to any given equity position, the economic benefits received by holding that position are not the same for all investors, due to any number of possible differences (access to restricted markets, financing costs, infrastructure, execution costs, etc.). A swap is a derivative tool that allows the owner of an asset to transfer to another party the economic exposure to the movements of that asset, thus acting as a bridge between advantaged and disadvantaged investors.

In more general terms, an equity swap is an over-the-counter contract in which two parties agree to make a payment, or series of payments, based on the performance of an underlying equity reference. Swaps are structured with two legs: the equity leg contains payments related to the movements of the underlier, while the floating leg contains financing payments (usually referenced to either LIBOR or the Fed Funds Target Rate for USD swaps) associated with the financing of the position.

Because they are over-the-counter transactions, and not subject to the standardization of exchange-listed products, there is a large amount of detail that must be specified in each swap transaction. While an individual swap agreement can be documented and executed in isolation, clients who trade actively will usually sign an ISDA Master Agreement with the broker that defines standardized terms for all transactions and greatly simplifies the documentation and trade confirmation processes.

In a long swap, the client receives the long exposure to the underlier (receives upside versus paying downside) and in return pays a floating rate of interest. In a short swap, the client receives short exposure to the underlier (paying upside versus receiving downside) and earns an interest payment on the notional amount of the swap. When a broker holds equal and offsetting long and short swaps with two different clients (and therefore has no need to hedge as the payments made to one client are covered by the payments received from the other) he is said to have "back-to-back" swaps. In all these cases, the broker's profit on the trade comes from the execution commission plus a small funding spread on the floating rate leg.

Payments on the swap are made at regularly-scheduled resets at which the broker and client make the necessary cash payments to flatten any obligations accumulated to that point. Economically the reset acts like a termination of the swap and an initiation of a new swap. Swaps are unique among equity derivatives in that they are valued on an accrual basis as opposed to an NPV calculation. This makes them economically most similar to a physical stock position and means that they have no sensitivity to future events (changes in dividends or interest rates) the way a forward or futures contract does.

Swaps are popular for many reasons. Their flexibility makes them a natural tool in more complex, structured transactions where highly specific payoffs are needed. However, they are also popular as a trading tool for expressing views on the market (flow product). Specific benefits and applications of swaps include their high degree of leverage, the ability to gain exposure to indices with no tracking risk, the construction of customized baskets, and access to emerging markets.

Because of their stock-like characteristics, swaps are often treated as though they provided a direct pass-through of the economics of the broker's hedge positions. While this is a convenient framework in which to communicate orders, it is important to distinguish between the swap contract, which stipulates payments based on a reference underlier, and any hedging transactions the broker may or may not choose to make.

Although the swap structure is simple, the risk management of a swaps trading book requires the careful consideration of many different factors including the availability and cost of stock borrow, dividend reinvestment, tracking risk on index positions, interest rate exposure, credit risk, and other factors.

CHAPTER 9

Options (Part 1)

INTRODUCTION

Options are the first thing many people think of when they hear the word "derivatives." Compared with what we have done so far, they are a much more technical product and, done properly, even a general overview of their structure, pricing, and risk management will involve a certain amount of mathematics. While some may prefer a purely qualitative treatment, it is neither worthwhile nor admirable to attempt a presentation of options that is devoid of any mathematical content. Mathematics is an inescapable part of many areas of finance and the analysis of options is one of them.

In order for the concepts presented to have the highest probability of being both understood and retained by the greatest number of readers, I have kept the mathematics to a level that can reasonably be expected of a recent university graduate or a professional in the financial services industry. Readers whose mathematical skills are a bit rusty should refer to the Appendix for a brief refresher. I would actually recommend a quick read through of this appendix for most readers who do not have a natural predisposition for (or interest in) mathematics; the presentation focuses on understanding, rather than computation, and the material covered is generally elementary—basic ideas from algebra, calculus, probability, and statistics that should be understood by any educated adult.

Throughout this chapter and the next, wherever possible, concepts are illustrated via graphical interpretations rather than algebraic formulae. This is the way my own understanding is structured and, as our focus is conceptual understanding, and not calculation, I believe the visual presentations are more intuitive, less intimidating, and provide greater insight.

In what follows we will examine how options work, the factors that influence their price, and how changes in those factors interact. For an options trader, the products, concepts, terminology, and relationships presented would be considered "core" knowledge—things so well understood they are immediately apparent and no longer require thought. For sales-people, the more "automatic" these things become, the service provided to customers will be.

DEFINITIONS AND TERMINOLOGY

In order to begin our discussion of derivatives, we first need to acquaint ourselves with a bit of vocabulary, some of which will be familiar from our discussion on futures and swaps.

The holder of an *option contract* has the right, but not the obligation, to buy or sell an asset (the *underlier*) at a previously agreed upon price (the *strike* price), on or before the expiration date of the option (the *maturity*). If the holder of the contract does not *exercise* the right to buy or sell, the option *expires* worthless.

A *call* option gives the right to buy the underlier while a *put* option gives the right to sell it. The price paid to the *writer* of the contract (the person who sells the option) is called the option *premium*. The purchaser of the option is said to be long the option, and the writer of the option is short, regardless of whether it is a call or put. The distinction between long and short depends on the ownership of optionality and not on the directional view that may be implied by the position in the underlier. This should be distinguished from traders who say they are long or short "via options," in which case they are describing their directional position in the underlier and simply adding the clarification that the exposure comes from an option position.

As our focus is equity derivatives, we assume that all options are writ-ten on shares of stock and that at maturity, if the owner of the option exercises the contract, the writer of the option makes physical delivery of the required shares.[1] Options are much broader than this and can be written on equity indices as well as bonds, currencies, commodities, and most any asset that can be valued. Fortunately, the general characteristics of options and the methods for valuing them are similar across different asset classes and a familiarity with how equity options work goes a long way toward understanding options on other underliers.

As with futures, it is standard practice for options contracts to contain a *multiplier* such that a single contract gives the right to purchase or sell a number of shares greater than 1. The option, however, is still quoted on a per-share basis. For simplicity, in the discussion of options pricing that follows, we will not include a multiplier. However, I deliberately mention it here because it is a fundamental detail in the practical reality of trading op-tions (as well as futures) and the source of many painful and costly "rookie" errors.

One way of classifying options is by when you can exercise them. A *European option* only allows the holder to exercise the right to buy or sell stock at the option's maturity while an *American option* allows the holder to exercise at any point up to and including the maturity of the option.[2] Prior to maturity, an investor holding a European call can only choose between selling the option or holding on to it, while the holder of an American option has the additional possibility of exercising it and taking delivery of the stock. In the United States, all index options have European exercise, while single stock options, where physical delivery is possible, have American exercise. As we will see later, outside of very specific circumstances, it is rarely advantageous to exercise an American option prior to maturity.

Like forwards and futures, options can be traded over-the-counter or on an exchange. (Unlike forwards and futures, there is no difference in terminology between listed and OTC options.) In listed trading, the options exchange acts as intermediary to all transactions and guarantees settlement of all trades, removing the need for individual counterparty risk assessments by each participant. It also enforces its trading rules as well as the margin and collateral requirements of participants. As with futures contracts, the exchange records whether trades are opening (establishing a new position) or closing (unwinding an existing position) and monitors and disseminates the open interest in each contract.

In our discussion going forward all options are assumed to be exchange-listed contracts on a single-stock underlier with European-style exercise and physical delivery unless otherwise specified.

PAYOFF STRUCTURE

As a first step toward understanding the behavior of option prices, we will examine the value of the contract at maturity, at which time the only variables that impact the value of the option are the stock price and the strike price. The more complex question of the correct price today for an option expiring in the future will be discussed later.

Calls

The holder of a call option has the right, when the contract expires, to purchase a share of stock at the strike price. If the market price for the stock is below the strike price, then the option expires worthless since the stock can be purchased more cheaply in the market, and there is no value in a contract that gives the holder the right to pay more than the market price. If the market price for the stock is above the strike price of the call, the option has value because it allows the holder to buy a share of stock at a below-market price. The value of the option is determined by how much below the market price the holder is entitled to pay. If S_T is the underlying stock price at maturity (time $=T$), and the strike price is K, then if $S_T > K$, the value of the option is $S_T - K$ while if $S_T \leq K$, the value of the call is zero. We can express the value of the call option C at maturity for all values of S_T as:

$$C = Max(S_T - K, 0)$$

The lower bound on the option price is zero. Because it is always an option to buy or sell, not an obligation, the contract can never be worth less than zero.

> *Example:* An investor holds a $100-strike call option on one share of
> XYZ stock. If the market price of the stock at maturity is $98, the
> investor will make a decision about whether he wants to own the
> stock, and then either buy the stock in the market at $98, or let
> the option expire worthless and do nothing. Either way, he would
> not exercise the option to buy at $100 given a cheaper price in the
> market. However, if the market price were $104, then the investor
> would exercise the option *regardless of whether he wants to be long
> the stock or not.* If he wants to own shares, he would exercise the
> option and purchase them for a below-market price of $100 and
> immediately show a mark-to-market profit of $4. However, even if
> he does not want the shares, he should still exercise the option to
> buy at $100 and then immediately sell those shares in the market
> at $104 and lock in the $4 per share profit. If the option is not
> exercised, he is simply throwing away the $4 value of the contract.

The graph in Exhibit 9.1 shows the value of a $100-strike call option at maturity as a function of the underlying stock price S_T. For $S_T < K$, the call option is worthless, while starting for $S_T = K$, and for all $S_T > K$, the call option value increases in values one-for-one with S_T. (The graph rises at a 45° angle.)

Puts

The holder of a put option has the right to sell the underlying stock at the strike price when the contract expires. The option to sell is only valuable if it gives the right to sell the stock at a price that is higher than the market price. Therefore, the value of a put option is determined by how far the stock price

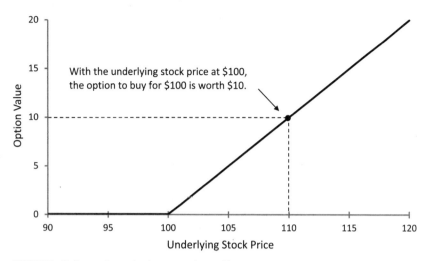

With the underlying stock price at $100, the option to buy for $100 is worth $10.

EXHIBIT 9.1 Value of a $100-Strike Call at Maturity

is *below* the strike price at maturity—that is, for how much more than the market price of the stock can the holder of the put sell the shares? Using the same notation as with the call option, the payoff at maturity of a put, P, is given by:

$$P = Max(K - S_T, 0)$$

As with a call option, the payoff of the put can never be negative.

> *Example:* An investor holds the $100-strike put on stock XYZ. If, at maturity, the stock price is above $100, the investor can either choose to do nothing and let the put expire worthless, or sell the stock in the market at a better price. If the stock price is below $100, the investor will exercise the put and sell stock at an above-market price. The value of owning the put will be the difference between the actual sale price and where the stock could have been sold without the put. If the market price of the stock is $95, the option gives the holder the right to sell stock at a price $5 per share higher than market, and is therefore worth $5 itself. If the investor no longer wants to sell the stock, he would still exercise the put but simultaneously buy the shares back in the market at a lower price to capture a profit. Either way, if the market price of the stock is below the strike, the options should be exercised, regardless of whether the investor wants to sell the stock.

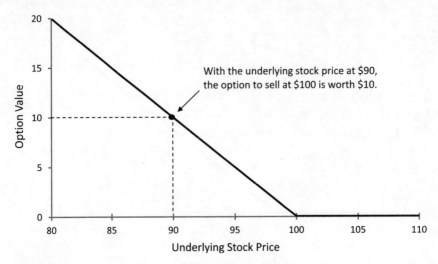

EXHIBIT 9.2 Value of a $100-Strike Put at Maturity

Exhibit 9.2 shows the value at maturity of a $100-strike put option as a function of the underlying stock price. Observe that, while the value of the call option can increase without limit, the value of a put option is limited to a maximum of K since the stock price S_t can never be negative.

Moneyness

At maturity, the value of a call or put option is completely determined by the difference between the strike price and the current stock price. In most cases, at any time t up to and including the maturity T, the difference between the current stock price and the strike price is the most important determinant of the option's value, regardless of whether the option can be exercised at that point. Options are classified according to this relationship in the following way:

- *In-the-money (ITM):* Options that would have a positive value if exercised immediately, regardless of their maturity. A call is in-the-money if $S_t > K$ and a put is in-the-money if $S_t < K$.
- *At-the-money (ATM):* Options where the current stock price is equal to the strike price ($S_t = K$).
- *Out-of-the-money (OTM):* Options that would have negative value if exercised right now. Calls are OTM when $S_t < K$ and puts when $S_t > K$.

The value an option would have if it could be exercised immediately is called its *intrinsic value*. The intrinsic value of an ITM call or put is equal to difference between the current stock price and the strike price in absolute value[3] (the intrinsic value can never be negative). OTM and ATM options have zero intrinsic value.

$$\text{Intrinisic value}_{ITM} = |S_t - K|$$

Short Option Positions

The payoff for a short call or put position is symmetric to that of the long position but with all values negative—whatever is profitable for the long option holder produces a loss to the short holder. Graphically the payoff diagram is the same as for the long option positions we have seen previously, but reflected through the x-axis. The payoffs of the four possible option positions (long call, short call, long put, short put) are shown in Exhibit 9.3.

Computing Profit or Loss

We must be careful to keep in mind that the graphs in Exhibit 9.3 only represent the payoff at maturity of the four possible option positions and not the profit or loss from a given trade; clearly, not all short option positions lose money or no one would trade them. The profit or loss on a position

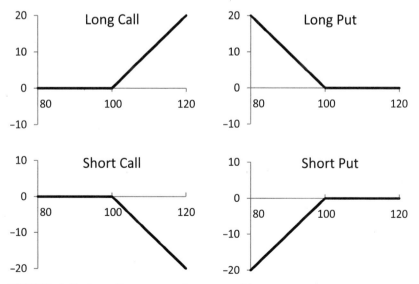

EXHIBIT 9.3 Payoff Diagrams of Four Possible Option Positions

is equal to the difference between the price at which the trade was initiated and the maturity value of the option (less frictions, carry costs, etc.). The graphs in Exhibit 9.3 only show this final value of the option for different levels of the underlying stock.

> *Example:* A call option with strike of $100 is purchased for $3.60 with the underlying stock at $98. At maturity the underlying stock is at $103 and the option expires in-the-money with a final value of $3. Unfortunately, the fact that the option expires in-the-money is small consolation to the investor who paid $3.60 to take on the position as it implies a total loss on the trade of $0.60.

This will become clearer when we look at the graphs of options prior to maturity in later sections.

Put-Call Combo

By combining a long call and a short put position with the same strike and maturity, we can create a synthetic long position in the underlying stock—effectively a forward. This is shown in Exhibit 9.4 using a graphical symbology based on the payoff diagrams at maturity.

The combination of these two options has created a position that no longer has optionality—we have removed the "kink" from the graph of the value at maturity and there is no longer uncertainty in the outcome.

- If the underlying stock is above $100 at maturity, we would exercise the long ITM call and buy the stock for $100 since it can be sold in the market for more than that. The short position in the OTM put expires worthless and would not be exercised against us.
- If the stock is below $100 at maturity, the short put is ITM and will be exercised against us, which means we will have to pay $100 for a stock that is trading below that price in the market. Our long position in the OTM call expires worthless.

Either way, we end up paying $100 for the stock, regardless of its price at maturity.[4]

This position is called a *put-call combo* and along with forwards, futures, and swaps, is another way to produce a "synthetic" stock position (i.e., something that is not stock but that moves one-for-one with the stock price). We can express this relationship formulaically as

$$C - P = S_{syn}$$

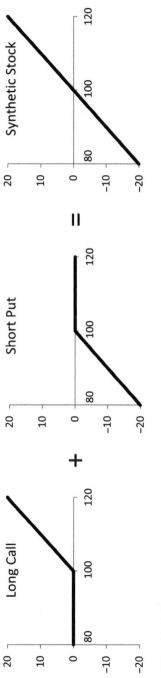

EXHIBIT 9.4 Combined Long Call + Short Put

Description	Formula	Graphically
Long Put + Short Call = Short Sock$_{syn}$	$P - C = {}^-S_{syn}$	
Long Stock$_{syn}$ + Long Put = Long Call	$S_{syn} + P = C$	
Short Stock$_{syn}$ + Long Call = Long Put	$-S_{syn} + C = P$	
Short Stock$_{syn}$ + Short Put = Short Call	$-S_{syn} - P = {}^-C$	
Long Stock$_{syn}$ + Short Call = Short Put	$S_{syn} - C = {}^-P$	

EXHIBIT 9.5 Combinations of Calls and Puts

where S_{syn} indicates "synthetic" stock. A synthetic short stock position via a put-call combo (short a call and long a put) with the same strike and maturity is known as a *conversion*. A synthetic long stock position (long a call and short a put) is called a *reversal* or *reverse conversion*.

We can rearrange the terms in this formula to create many other useful relationships, a few of which are shown in Exhibit 9.5. The graphical symbology is a useful way to visualize these formulas, all of which should be second nature to anyone who works with options.

Of particular interest is the second relationship from this list, which shows that a long call is equivalent to a long synthetic stock position plus a put. This highlights the fact that, from the perspective of a directional investor who views an options position as a substitute for a physical stock position, the asymmetric positive upside exposure that comes from owning a call is equivalent to what could be achieved through a purchase of the stock (which has symmetric exposure) and a put (which offsets the loss on the stock position below the strike). Based on this relationship, it will sometimes be convenient for us to refer to the put "implied" in a call vis-à-vis the long stock position. The third expression provides the corresponding expression for put as the sum of a short stock position and a call.

Put-Call Parity

We can now introduce one of the most fundamental relationships in options. As we have just seen, the combination of a long call and a short put in an underlier (with the same strike and maturity) creates a synthetic position in the underlying stock that is economically equivalent to a forward. At the maturity of the options, the holder of the long position in the combo will purchase—either because he wants to or because he is forced to—a share of stock at the options' strike price (in this case $100).

Let us now express the relationship between calls and puts in terms of the actual stock price S. We will make the simplifying assumption, here and in the rest of our discussion of options in this chapter and the next, that the dividends on the underlying stock are zero. (Options are complicated enough without them.) Ignoring noneconomic benefits, such as voting rights, the difference between a synthetic forward position via the put-call combo and a physical stock position is the question of payment; a physical stock position is paid for in full today, while the synthetic position does not require payment until the options mature. The holder of a share of stock worth $100 would be unwilling to exchange that share for a put-call combo made from 100-strike options because, while the exposure to the underlying stock is the same, at expiration the holder of the option combo must *pay* $100 for the share of stock, while the holder of the physical share has nothing additional to pay.

In order for the holder of a physical share to be indifferent to exchanging the stock for the put-call combo, he will require that we also give him the $100 to pay for the stock at maturity. Using continuously compounded interest,[5] the value today of $100 at maturity is $100e^{-rT}$, where r is the risk free rate of interest and T is the time until expiration measured in years. This allows us to express the relationship between calls and puts with the same strike and maturity in terms of the underlying stock, the time to maturity, and the risk-free rate of interest as:

$$C - P + Ke^{-rT} = S$$

The content of this formula can be expressed colloquially as:

> A long call and short put with the same maturity and strike, along with as much money as I need today to insure that I can pay the strike price of the options at maturity, is equivalent to holding the stock right now.

This important result, which is valid only for European options, is called *put-call parity*. It is usually written as:

$$C - P = S - Ke^{-rT}$$

An alternative, and particularly illustrative way to rewrite this relationship is to add and subtract K from the right-hand side and regroup the terms slightly to get:

$$C - P = (S - K) + (K - Ke^{-rT})$$

Examining each term independently:

- The left-hand side can be viewed as measuring the value of the put-call combo or, alternatively, as the difference in price between the call and the put.
- The first term on the right-hand side tells us how much higher or lower the current stock price is than the strike price. It measures the intrinsic value (subject to a possible change of sign) of the in-the-money option.
- The second term measures the carry costs on the strike price from now until maturity. If Ke^{-rT} is the present value of the strike price, then subtracting this from K gives the difference between the present value and the maturity value of the strike, which is equal to the interest carry on the money needed to pay the strike price at maturity.

As we will see later, there are many important properties of options that can be observed directly from this formula and we will use it extensively.

Arbitrage

If the put-call parity relationship is violated, there is an opportunity for a risk-free profit. Each side of the equation represents a way to buy a share of stock at the maturity date of the options for a price of K: The left-hand side of the equation is a synthetic forward contract to buy the underlying stock for the strike price, while the right-hand side is the price of buying a physical share of stock with an amount of borrowed funds equal to the present value of the strike price. The two identical cash flows in the future must cost the same today; if they do not, then there is an opportunity for an arbitrage profit.

Assume an investor wants to buy one share of stock and hold it for a year. The stock is currently trading at $107 and the risk-free rate of interest is 5 percent. (We will use simple interest in this calculation just to make the math easier.) He has two choices:

Scenario 1: Borrow $100 for one year and, with an investment of $7 of his own money, purchase a share of stock for $107. In one year's time, he will own a share of stock and owe $105 on the loan ($100 + $5 interest).

Scenario 2: Buy a one year, $105-strike put-call combo (buys call/sells put). In one year's time he will have either the option or obligation to buy one share of stock for $105.

The two scenarios result in identical payoffs—paying $105 in one year's time to own a share of stock. Put-call parity states that the price of each scenario today must be the same. Therefore, the price of the option combo in Scenario 2 must be equal to the $7 paid by the investor in Scenario 1. When this is violated there is an opportunity for an arbitrage.

- $C - P < \$7$: Assume the put-call combo can be purchased for $6. The investor sells a share of stock at $107 and with the cash raised buys the combo for $6. This leaves him with $101. Investing $100 at the risk free rate for one year will give him the $105 he needs to pay for the stock when the options are exercised at maturity, which will then be used to cover his short and complete the trade. The other $1 left over is the profit from the arbitrage.
- $C - P > \$7$: Assume the put-call combo is trading for $8. The investor borrows $100 and sells the combo (sells call/buys put) for $8, which gives him enough money to purchase a share of stock for $107 and still have $1 left over. When the options mature, he will sell his long stock for $105, which will give him the $105 he needs to pay off the loan and close out the position, leaving him with the same $1 profit.

In practice, arbitrages of this type rarely occur; option markets are very efficient and it is unusual to find an opportunity where the trading slippages and execution frictions do not completely consume the possible profit. In general, there aren't many free pennies left lying around on Wall Street.

OPTION VALUES PRIOR TO MATURITY

While the at-maturity payoff of calls and puts must be well understood before any more complicated characteristics are explored, the straight-line graphs give no indication of how complex and interesting the behavior of options actually is. Unfortunately, many people remember only the payoff graphs and believe they have an understanding of options. This is a huge mistake. Almost everything that an option trader or derivative salesperson needs to know about options is missing from the graphs at maturity.

Exhibit 9.6 shows the graph of a call option with a strike price of $100 and maturity in three months for various values of S_t. (We use the general subscript t to indicate an intermediate time between $t = 0$, when the trade is initiated, and $t = T$, the maturity of the option.) The kinked graph of the payout of the call at maturity is included as a reference. This kinked graph can also be viewed as the measure of the intrinsic value of the option at any time up to and including expiration. While the graph is rather simple, we

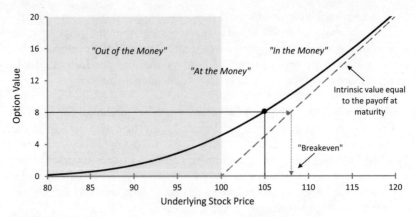

EXHIBIT 9.6   Value of a $100-Strike Call with 3 Months to Maturity

will spend quite a lot of time looking at it and examining how changes in the variables that impact options prices cause changes in the shape of this curve. It is possible to develop a fairly sophisticated understanding of option sensitivities and risk management just by studying this graph.

While the straight line graph from the previous section told us the payoff at maturity of the option, the curved line in Exhibit 9.6 tells us the fair market price for a call option that still has 90 days until maturity, across a range of prices for the underlying stock. For example, with the stock at $105, the $100-strike call is worth $8.

We also use this figure to introduce the concept of a *breakeven level*, which is the price that the underlying stock must attain at maturity in order for a given position to produce a profit. For example, if we pay $8 for the $100-strike call and hold the position to maturity, we will only make a profit if the underlying stock price is above $108. So long as the option expires in-the-money it will have value, but in order for our trade to be profitable, we need it to end up at least $8 in-the-money. For a plain-vanilla call option, the breakeven level is equal to the strike price plus the premium paid for the option.

It is also apparent from the graph that a call option expresses a bullish view on the underlying stock since the payoff diagram is positively sloped (it increases as you move from left to right) for all values of S; other things being equal, an increase in the stock price always increases the value of the call.

The equivalent graph for a $100-strike put option with three months until maturity is shown in Exhibit 9.7. Observe that the in-the-money and out-of-the-money regions have switched sides and that the put option expresses a bearish view on the stock; the value of the put increases as the stock price decreases.

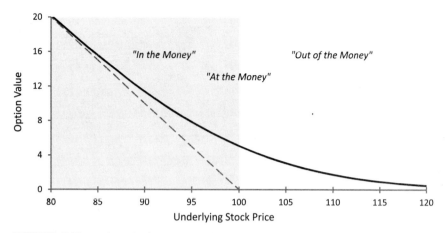

EXHIBIT 9.7 Value of a $100 Put with 3 Months to Maturity

To keep the explanations from becoming overly lengthy and repetitive, in the derivations and descriptions that follow, only the call option will be discussed. The corresponding properties of the put option follow by direct analogy or parity arguments. Where the put has a markedly different behavior or property, this will be mentioned.

Time Value

We can observe from Exhibits 9.6 and 9.7 that the value of an option prior to maturity is greater than its intrinsic value for all levels of the stock price S_t. Graphically this means that the curved line representing the value of the call option price is above the kinked line, which represents its intrinsic value (or alternatively, the value at maturity) for all values of the underlying stock price S_t. This additional value, above intrinsic, is called *time value* and is (almost) always positive.[6] We can express the value of an option at any time as the sum of these two parts:

$$\text{Option value} = \text{Intrinsic value} + \text{Time value}$$

The graph and table in Exhibit 9.8 show the separation of the option's total value into these two component parts as well as some numerical values for specific levels of the underlying stock price.

Considering that the payoff at maturity of the call option is greater than or equal to zero for all levels of the stock price, it becomes clear that an option that still has time left until maturity must be worth more

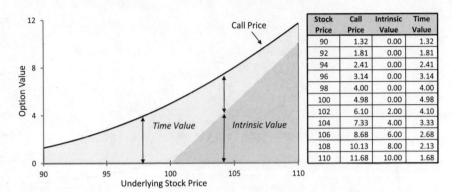

Stock Price	Call Price	Intrinsic Value	Time Value
90	1.32	0.00	1.32
92	1.81	0.00	1.81
94	2.41	0.00	2.41
96	3.14	0.00	3.14
98	4.00	0.00	4.00
100	4.98	0.00	4.98
102	6.10	2.00	4.10
104	7.33	4.00	3.33
106	8.68	6.00	2.68
108	10.13	8.00	2.13
110	11.68	10.00	1.68

EXHIBIT 9.8 Decomposition of the Call Value into Intrinsic and Time Value

than its intrinsic value. Consider a $100-strike call, with three months to maturity, on a stock currently trading at $98. Because the option is OTM it has no intrinsic value, but it is clearly not worthless. The easiest way to see this is to ask the question: Would an investor give the option away for free? The seller of the option assumes the risk that the stock price rises above the strike price by maturity, at which he will begin to lose money. Given that maturity is still three months away and the strike price is only 2 percent above the current market price, there is a significant possibility of this occurring and the seller would need to be compensated for taking on that risk.

There are several factors that give an option time value. The unique characteristic of options is the difference in behavior of the option on either side of the strike at maturity. While forwards, futures, and swaps behave consistently for all levels of the underlying stock, an option's behavior changes. At maturity, for stock prices above the strike price, an option price moves one-for-one with the stock price—it is economically equivalent to holding shares. Below the strike, the option loses its sensitivity to the stock price and expires worthless, but can never become negative. The time value of an option is the premium paid, above intrinsic value, to be exposed to this change in behavior.

For an OTM call option, the time value comes from the potential participation in the appreciation of the underlier, should it rise above the strike price. It is the price paid for the opportunity be "in the game" should the stock move favorably. For an ITM call option the time value comes from the protection offered below the strike. An ITM option already provides exposure to the underlying stock but, by put-call parity, also contains an implied put option that protects the call holder in the event the stock goes below the strike. Rearranging the terms in the put-call parity relationship we can write:

$$C = (S - Ke^{-rT}) + P$$

The parenthetical term is the intrinsic value $S - K$, with an adjustment on K for the cost of funding the position until maturity.[7] Thus, the value of the call is simply the intrinsic value of the option, plus the value of the OTM put, which itself must be worth something by the same argument we used for the OTM call. (An investor would not give it away for free, would he?)

If the time value of an option comes from the change in behavior as the stock crosses the strike, the amount of time value is directly proportional to the probability that the holder will benefit from this change in behavior—that is, the probability that S crosses K—and by how much. There are three principal factors that determine this probability:

1. How far is the current stock price from the strike? (*Moneyness*)
2. How much does the stock "bounce around"? (*Volatility*)
3. How long does it have to get there? (*Time*)

We examine the impact of each of these in turn. To facilitate our discussions going forward, let us introduce a bit of notation. Given the stock price S at any point in time, we will denote by $C(S)$, the value of the call option on S. The curved graph in Exhibit 9.6 is the graph of $C(S)$ across values of S from 80 to 120. The corresponding notation for a put option would be $P(S)$.

Moneyness

It is logical that the closer the current stock price is to the strike price, the greater the probability that the stock price crosses the strike and therefore the greater the time value. This is most easily seen by graphing the time value of the option as a function of the stock price (i.e., the spread between the graph of $C(S)$ and the kinked line of the final payoff).

When options are deep OTM or deep ITM, the stock price is far from the strike and the investor has very little chance of ever benefiting from the change in behavior that occurs when the stock price crosses the strike. These options therefore have very little time value. Close to the strike, however, the probability of benefiting from the change in behavior increases, as does the magnitude of the potential benefit. If a $100-strike call has time value when the stock is at $95 due to the possibility that the stock rallies above $100 before maturity and begins to participate in the upward movement of the stock price, then surely that same call has even greater value with the

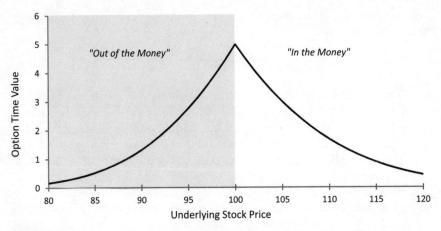

EXHIBIT 9.9 Time Value of a $100-Strike Call with 3 Months to Maturity

stock at $99 since the investor will start to benefit as soon as the stock rallies 1 percent. The maximum time value occurs right at the strike price, since this is the point of greatest uncertainty as well as greatest benefit, should the stock perform favorably.[8]

Observe that at the extremes, a slight asymmetry is evident in the graph. This is because, starting from 80, the stock needs to rally 25 percent to get to 100 and end up in-the-money, while starting from 120, the stock only needs to fall 16.67 percent to go through the strike on the downside. From the perspective of the two extremes, although the absolute distance is the same, the percentage change in the stock price necessary to cross the strike is not.

Changes in moneyness represent movements *along the curve* of the graph of $C(S)$ in Exhibit 9.6. We now look at changes in the other two variables that result in upward or downward *shifts* in the curve of $C(S)$, either closer to or further from intrinsic value.

Volatility

Volatility is defined more precisely later in the chapter. For the moment, it suffices to understand volatility conceptually as a measure of variability or uncertainty in the movements of the underlying stock, and know that it is expressed as percentage change in the stock price. If an investor is trying to guess a likely level for a stock's price in one week's time, with a low volatility stock he might comfortably assume that it will be within a range of ±2 percent from its current price, while with a highly volatile stock he might only be confident enough to say it will be within ±10 percent.

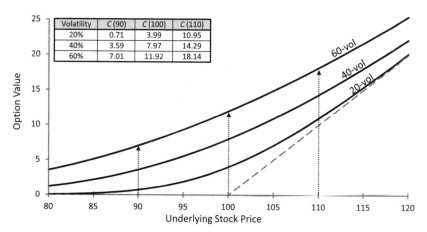

Volatility	C (90)	C (100)	C (110)
20%	0.71	3.99	10.95
40%	3.59	7.97	14.29
60%	7.01	11.92	18.14

EXHIBIT 9.10   Value of a $100-Strike Call Option with 90 Days to Maturity for Different Levels of Volatility

Volatility is a measure of the size of this range of confidence, calculated on an annualized basis. The volatility of a stock is usually denoted by the Greek letter sigma (σ).

Clearly the degree of variability in the stock's price directly impacts the probability that it crosses the strike price, and therefore the potential value in owning the option. A one-month call on a very low volatility stock that is 10 percent out-of-the-money may be worth next to nothing due to the small possibility that the stock price crosses the strike before maturity. The same option on a high volatility stock would be much more expensive given the greater probability of its crossing the strike and the risk the writer of the option assumes by selling it.

Exhibit 9.10 shows the graph of the price of a $100-strike call option with three months to maturity for three different levels of volatility in the underlying stock. For all values of the stock price, the impact of an increase in volatility is an increase in the time value of the option. As we can see from the table, the impact is not insignificant. With the underlying stock at $90, the increase in the value of the call caused by changing the volatility from 20 percent to 40 percent is roughly the same as that caused by the underlying stock rallying 11 percent from $90 to $100.

Time

In options pricing, time acts as a sort of sister concept to volatility. The probability of crossing the strike is a combined function of *how much* the

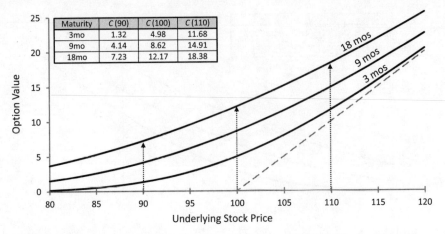

Maturity	$C(90)$	$C(100)$	$C(110)$
3mo	1.32	4.98	11.68
9mo	4.14	8.62	14.91
18mo	7.23	12.17	18.38

EXHIBIT 9.11 Value of a $100-Strike Call Option with 30 Percent to Maturity for Different times to Maturity

stock bounces around and *how long* is has to bounce around. Exhibit 9.11 shows the graph of a stock with volatility of 25 percent for maturities of 3 months, 9 months, and 18 months.

As can be seen from the graph, an increase in the time to maturity has a positive impact on the value of the call for all levels of the stock price. In fact, changes in the time to maturity have a very similar impact on the value of the call as do changes in the volatility. The similarity with Exhibit 9.10 is apparent. We will see in the next section that the quantity of relevance in the pricing of an option is actually the product of squared volatility and time, $\sigma^2 t$. If we price an option with one year to maturity and a 20 percent volatility we get exactly the same price for all values of S, as an option with three months to maturity and 40 percent volatility because they both give the same value for the combined quantity $\sigma^2 t$:

$$\sigma^2 t = (0.2)^2(1) = (0.4)^2(0.25) = 0.04$$

One important difference between time and volatility is that the time to maturity can only decrease while volatility can move up or down. Therefore, on a given option contract, the passage of time will only ever have a negative effect. This can be visualized intuitively from the graph—the stock price at maturity is the kinked payoff diagram, which is everywhere below the value of a call prior to maturity. With the passage of time, the curved line should "settle down" to the kinked line.

To an investor looking to express a directional view on a stock via options, the determination of the appropriate maturity contract to use to express that view is an important one. Unlike stock, which has an "infinite" life, options contracts expire in a fixed time. If the anticipated move in the underlying stock occurs too late—even one day after the contract has expired—the holder of the option will not benefit; with options the investor needs to make a correct assessment of not only direction but timing. Buying longer dated options gives the investor a greater chance of capturing the anticipated move, but this comes at a cost. From the graphs in Exhibits 9.10 and 9.11 we can see clearly how the greater time value of the longer-dated option implies a higher breakeven level at maturity. The trade-off for giving the stock more time to move around is the higher up-front cost of the option and greater risk of loss (if the stock does not reach the breakeven level by maturity).

Delta

Although more sophisticated strategies will be discussed later in this chapter and the next, at this point we are looking at options purely as a directional investment—that is, as a substitute for an outright long or short position in the underlier.

Immediately prior to maturity, when the graph of $C(S)$ is almost identical to the kinked final payoff, the relationship between changes in the underlying stock price and the price of the call is quite simple; movements of the stock have no impact if the option is out-of-the-money and a one-for-one impact if the option is in-the-money (and a weighted combination of the two if the stock price crosses the strike). While there is still time prior to maturity, the situation is more complicated. Using the 100-strike call with three months to expiry as shown in Exhibit 9.6 as an example, we calculate the change in the option price for successive $5 movements in the underlying stock price. We also compute the proportional sensitivity of the call to the stock, that is, how much the call price moves compared to the stock? The results are shown in Exhibit 9.12.

Rather than a distinct change in behavior between the in-the-money and out-of-the-money cases, the sensitivity of $C(S)$ to the stock price S changes gradually from close to zero, for low values of the stock price, to nearly one-for-one when the stock price is well above the strike price.

We can express this sensitivity of $C(S)$ to S in terms of the equivalent number of fractional shares that a call option represents (i.e., how many shares does the call option behave like?). For example, as the stock price rises $5 from $85 to $90, the long holder of a single physical share of the stock shows a profit of $5, while the holder of the call option sees a profit

S	C(S)	Change in C(S)	Change in C(S) / Change in S
80	0.17	-	-
85	0.52	0.36	0.07
90	1.32	0.80	0.16
95	2.76	1.44	0.29
100	4.98	2.22	0.44
105	7.99	3.01	0.60
110	11.68	3.69	0.74
115	15.89	4.21	0.84
120	20.44	4.55	0.91

EXHIBIT 9.12   Sensitivity of Call Price to Changes in Underlying Share Price

of $0.80. This $0.80 profit is equivalent to holding 0.16 shares of stock since 0.16 shares × $5 price change = $0.80 profit. When the stock price moves from $110 to $115, the value of the call increases by $4.21, making the call economically equivalent to a position in approximately 0.84 shares (0.84 shs × $5 = $4.20).

We can express this sensitivity of the option price to changes in the underlier more precisely as the mathematical derivative[9] of the call price with respect to S. We call this the *delta* of the option and denote it by Δ.

$$\Delta = \frac{\partial C}{\partial S}$$

The delta of a call ranges from zero (no sensitivity of the call price to the stock price), when the option is deep out-of-the-money, to one (one-for-one price sensitivity) when it is deep in-the-money. It is customary to refer to option deltas without the decimal, that is, if a call has a delta of 0.36 we say it is a "36-delta call."

The delta measures the "instantaneous" sensitivity of the call price to changes in S. That is, for a particular price S_1 in the underlying stock, the value of the delta evaluated at that point tells us how many shares of stock would need to be held to replicate the change in value of the option position for movements in the stock price S very near to that point. If the delta of the call option computed at S_1 is 0.36, then stock price movements around S_1 should produce changes in the option price that are approximately 0.36 times the size. Because the graph of $C(S)$ is curved, this *delta-equivalent* number of shares is only valid close to S_1. As the stock price moves, the delta will change: the delta computed at S_1 will not be an accurate measure of the sensitivity of $C(S)$ to changes in S at another point, S_2. As we will see later, the ability to replicate the changes in the price of an option locally by holding a delta-equivalent number of shares is fundamental to the valuation of options.

An easy way to visualize this concept of delta is via the geometric interpretation of the derivative as the slope of the tangent line to a graph. Recall that the slope of a line is the measure of the vertical change caused by a given horizontal displacement (the "rise over the run"). A horizontal line has slope zero and a 45 degree angle has a slope of one (equivalent horizontal and vertical changes). We can represent a position in x shares of the underlying stock by a straight line with slope of x (see accompanying Graphic Concepts), which allows us to express graphically how the delta-equivalent number of shares changes as the stock price increases.

Exhibit 9.13 shows the tangent lines to $C(S)$ for three different values of S. The slope of each is suggested by a triangle below the graph, which we can see is an accurate approximation to the slope of the curve, but only locally. The accompanying table contains the calculated values of the delta at each $5 interval in the underlying stock prices. We can see that the approximation of the delta based on the change over each $5 interval as calculated in Exhibit 9.12 is roughly equal to the average of the calculated deltas of each endpoint in Exhibit 9.13. For example, the delta approximation based on the difference between $C(90)$ and $C(95)$ is 0.29, which equals the average of the deltas when $S = 90$, equal to 0.22, and when $S = 95$ equal to 0.36.

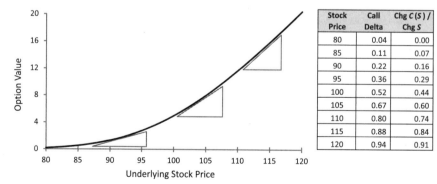

Stock Price	Call Delta	Chg C(S) / Chg S
80	0.04	0.00
85	0.11	0.07
90	0.22	0.16
95	0.36	0.29
100	0.52	0.44
105	0.67	0.60
110	0.80	0.74
115	0.88	0.84
120	0.94	0.91

EXHIBIT 9.13 Representation of the Delta as a Tangent Line to $C(S)$

GRAPHING CONCEPTS

In this chapter and the next, we use graphical representations of option values and stock positions extensively to facilitate the understanding of many concepts. Therefore, it is important to ensure that the graphs are well understood.

We can represent a stock position graphically by a straight line with slope equal to the number of (fractional or multiple) shares. For example, the value of a position in one-half a share of stock will increase by $1 for each $2 increase in the underlying stock price. If we graph the value of this position as a function of the stock price it would be a diagonal line with slope 0.5, which will change by $1 vertically for each $2 move horizontally.

The difficulty with showing stock and option positions on the same graph is the difference in scale: the value of an at-the-money, $100-strike call worth $3, and a $100 stock position cannot be easily compared on the same set of axes because there is a $97 gap between the two. Fortunately for our purposes, we are primarily concerned with the *change* in value of the stock position and this is entirely captured by the slope. In order to facilitate the visualization of the relationships between stock and option positions, we "detach" the graphs of the stock positions from the axes and instead overlay them on those portions of the graph to which they are being compared. In this way, a straight line with a slope of 0.5 represents a position of one-half a share of stock regardless of where it lies on the axes. This juxtaposition of the two graphs greatly simplifies the visualization of the relative movements of the stock and option positions.

Preliminary Observations

The addition of time value gives the option's price a much more complex behavior than would be suspected from the simple graph of the payoff at maturity. As the stock price moves, the value of the option changes, even while it still remains out-of-the-money. Additionally, we have seen that the option's sensitivity to changes in the price of the underlier, as measured by the delta, is a function of the underlying stock price itself—not only does the option price $C(S)$ depend on S, its sensitivity to changes in S is a function of the level of S itself. We have also introduced two other factors—the volatility of the underlying stock and time to maturity—which contribute to the time value to the option and can cause changes in the value of the option even when there is no movement in the stock price. Examining the graphs in Exhibits 9.10 and 9.11, we can see that changes in the volatility and time to maturity also impact the slope of the graph of $C(S)$. This indicates that the delta of the option is also affected by changes in the volatility and time to maturity.

For an options market-maker, who generally does not hold positions until maturity but rather trades in and out of positions continually, the risk management of all these sensitivities (and those that are still to be explored) is much more important that the simple in- or out-of-the-money viewpoint implied by the payoff diagram at maturity.

In order to further develop our understanding of the factors that influence option prices and their interrelationships it will be necessary to develop a more rigorous approach to option pricing and analysis than we have so far, which is the focus of the next section.

QUANTITATIVE CONSIDERATIONS

What follows is a brief overview of the standard mathematical model for valuing options. As discussed in the introduction to this chapter, I have stripped down the presentation to only those concepts that would potentially be of practical use to a trader or salesperson. For this reason, I would suggest the reader make every effort to understand these concepts well. That said, it is *not* important to memorize the formulas presented in of the Black-Scholes derivation, which is included to establish the necessary framework for options valuation. While mathematics provides the most convenient and precise language with which to express the relationships between option prices and the values of the underlying inputs, our focus is on conceptual understanding and the reader should not become too bogged-down in the mathematical details.

Volatility

Before we can develop a mathematical model for pricing options we need a more precise definition of volatility than "bounciness." As an input into our option pricing model, the volatility is defined as the "annualized standard deviation of continually compounded returns." As discussed in the Appendix, continuous compounding is a theoretical limit and the best we can do in practice is to estimate the volatility using observable price data from the market. Given a series of closing prices for a stock $\{X_0, X_1, \ldots X_n\}$

on $n + 1$ consecutive trading days, the process for estimating the volatility consists of the following steps:

1. We calculate the series of n one-day returns $\{u_1, u_2, \ldots, u_n\}$ where $u_i = \ln(x_i/x_{i-1})$ is the continuously compounded[10] one day return on day i $(i = 1, 2, \ldots, n)$
2. The average daily return, denoted by μ_1, is calculated as:

$$\mu_1 = \frac{1}{n} \sum_{i=1}^{n} \mu_i$$

The subscript "1" indicates that while n observations are used in its calculation, μ_1 is a measure of the one-day average return.
3. Given the one-day mean return, the standard deviation of the one-day returns, σ_1, can then be computed as:

$$\sigma_1 = \sqrt{\frac{1}{n-1} \sum_{i=1}^{n} (u_i - \mu_1)^2}$$

This value, σ_1, measures the average one-day volatility of the stock.[11]
4. We defined volatility as the "annualized standard deviation." To convert a one-day volatility σ_1 to an annualized volatility σ_{annual} we make use of the fact that the volatility scales with the square root of time (we will see why later). Given that there are approximately 255 trading days per year, the annualized volatility should be $\sigma_{annual} = \sqrt{255}\sigma_1$.

More generally, given observations taken every j trading days, we can compute the j-day volatility, σ_j, as above, and then convert this to an annualized volatility by multiplying by the number of j-day periods per year according to the formula:

$$\sigma_{annual} = \sqrt{\frac{255}{j}}\sigma_j$$

The volatility of a stock can be estimated using any number of observations of data, recorded at any regular intervals. We can use the 20 consecutive trading days (one month of daily price observations), or 52 observations of the weekly closing price. Both calculations will produce an estimate of the "annualized standard deviation of continually compounded returns," but they may not be equal. While the theoretical pricing models we will develop shortly assume that volatility is a constant value—which would imply that the number of observations and their frequency should not matter—in practice this is not the case. Volatility changes with time and there is a certain amount of subjectivity in deciding the number and frequency of observations to use.

It is also important to keep in mind that the standard deviation does not tell us anything about expected return or whether the stock is trending up or down—it is purely a measure of variability. Any trend in the stock's price is lost in the calculation of the volatility because the price deviation is calculated relative to the mean and not in absolute terms. Therefore, a stock that goes up every day between 1 percent and 1.2 percent has much lower volatility than a stock that moves horizontally but bounces up and down 0.50 percent per day. Observe also that volatility is a measure of the variability in the *percentage* change, not the absolute size of the change. A $20 stock that jumps around $1 per day is much more volatile than a $100 stock that jumps around $3.

Trader Trick The fourth step in our calculation of volatility provides the basis for a common trick used by traders to assess the risk of a position. The annualized volatility measures the one-standard deviation percentage move in a stock price on a one-year basis. Using the fact that volatility scales with the square root of time, and that the square root of 255 is almost exactly 16, traders divide the annualized volatility numbers by 16 to get a rough estimate of what a one-standard deviation move in the stock price would be on a one-day basis.

For example, if a stock has an annualized volatility of 24 percent, then a one-standard deviation move on a one-day basis is 1.5 percent $(= \frac{24\%}{16})$. The trader can then conclude that, about two-thirds of the time, his one-day profit or loss on a hypothetical $10 million position would be less than $150,000. A two standard deviation move ($300,000) has a probability of roughly 5 percent and should therefore occur in one out of every 20 trading sessions (approximately once a month). This gives the trader a general sense of how the position will compare with other risks in his trading book and allows him to size his position based on his level of conviction and risk tolerance. The important caveat in all this (and it is a big one) is that the trader is making the assumption of normally distributed stocks returns, which is a *big*—and frequently incorrect—assumption when dealing with stock price movements. Therefore, while he may be comfortable with a statistically estimated 2.5 percent chance of a loss greater than $300,000, he must also consider *how much greater* than $300,000 the loss could be and size his position accordingly.

An alternative approach to assessing the risk of a position is with the Bloomberg **HRH** (*Historical Return Histogram*) function, which computes the percentage change over a given time interval (daily, weekly, or other interval) during a historical time frame and produces a histogram showing the distribution of performance along with some basic statistical analyses of the data.

THE BLACK-SCHOLES DERIVATION

One of the most significant accomplishments of modern finance has been the development of the formula for valuing options, initially published by Fischer Black and Myron Scholes in 1973, with a nearly simultaneous publication of an alternative approach to the same result by their colleague, Robert Merton. For this work, Merton and Scholes shared the 1997 Nobel Prize for Economics (Fischer Black died in 1995). While the Black-Scholes formula is itself relatively simple (apart from a bit of messy notation) and can be easily calculated in a spreadsheet, the derivation of the formula is mathematically quite sophisticated and a thorough treatment involves concepts well beyond the scope of this book. Nevertheless, there are important insights to be gained from reading through the derivation and it would be a glaring omission not to include at least a sketch of it here. Fortunately, the fact is that in practice a trader or salesperson would never calculate by hand (let alone re-derive) the formula himself, which means that we can be rather loose and conceptual with the derivation and skip over the mathematical details that are not relevant for our purposes.

Note: The language and notation used in the explanation that follows is deliberately informal. In particular, there is a fluidity between the concepts of a small interval of time dt (which should properly be denoted Δt) and the mathematical differential dt. Also, we have assumed (correctly but without proof) that the standard operations of the calculus are also applicable to stochastic variables. This informality greatly simplifies the exposition without leading to any incorrect conclusions.

Derivation of the Black-Scholes Formula: Six Steps to a Nobel Prize

We now sketch the derivation of the Black-Scholes formula for pricing a European call option on a non-dividend paying stock.

Step 1: Make Some Assumptions To model the complexity of real-world finance we need first to make some simplifying assumptions. None of these assumptions is, in fact, accurate and some are clearly unreasonable. However, what we are developing is a theoretical model for options that will then guide our real-world actions and to do that, some simplification of the complexities of modern finance is necessary.

Assumptions

- All stocks can be sold short and there are no costs to borrow shares.
- There do not exist any arbitrage opportunities.
- Trading takes place continuously (markets never close and there are no gaps in trading or liquidity).
- There are no transaction costs or taxes.
- All securities are perfectly divisible (i.e., we can trade fractional shares).
- We can borrow and lend cash at the risk free rate (i.e., no funding spreads).
- There are no dividends.

Some of the more unrealistic of these assumptions can be relaxed (most obviously, the restriction on dividends) and models subsequent to Black-Scholes have produced pricing formulas that more closely approximate real-world trading conditions.

Step 2: Model the Stock Price In order to model options prices we first need to model stocks. The standard model treats stock prices as increasing at a steady "trend" rate of growth but subject to a random "noise" component that causes the price to fluctuate around the trend.

This model is not unreasonable. The underlying growth trend can be observed in historical data series of stock prices and, at a more conceptual level, stocks represent ownership of the companies that produce the goods and services that make up the GDP, which itself shows a relatively steady trend rate of growth (see Exhibits 12.1 and 12.2). Similarly, that stocks should exhibit volatility is obvious enough—we have already mentioned volatility as the measure of how much stocks "bounce around" and anyone who has ever looked at a stock chart can confirm, stock prices do not move in a straight line.

The question is how to model this volatility. For this, we need to introduce the concept of a stochastic process. A *stochastic process* is a random variable, which we denote by z, whose value evolves with time. While we generally think of random variables as taking on a single particular value (i.e., "I rolled two dice and got double fours"), a stochastic process is a continuous equivalent—a variable that is constantly evolving and changing in unpredictable ways. (As a physical analogy we can think of a variable that measures the position of a leaf blowing in turbulent wind.) The key is that a stochastic random variable is a continuous variable, rather than a discrete one (like a coin toss or series of tosses).

The particular type of stochastic process that we will use to model stock prices is called a *Weiner process* and has two important properties:

1. Over a small time interval dt, the change dz, of our stochastic random variable z is proportional to the square root of the length of the time interval according to:

$$dz = \varepsilon \sqrt{dt}$$

   where ε is a normally distributed random variable with mean 0 and standard deviation of 1.

2. The movements dz_1 and dz_2 during any two time intervals dt_1 and dt_2 are independent (zero correlation). This means that whatever the evolution has been of z prior to a given time has no impact on what z does in the future. The process is "memoryless." (This is called the *Markov property*.)

Given this definition of a stochastic process, our model for the stock price S then says that over an interval of time dt, the *percentage change* in the stock price, dS/S, is the sum of a steady upward drift and a random noise term described by a Weiner process. We express this mathematically as:

$$\frac{dS}{S} = \mu dt + \sigma dz$$

where μ is called the drift rate and σ is the volatility of the stock, which can be thought of as a scaling factor that acts on the Weiner process dz to determine how much noise there is around the trend rate of growth. Both μ and σ are assumed to be constant.

One important feature of this model is that the distribution of stock prices is *lognormal*—that is, the natural logarithm of the stock price, $\ln(S)$, is normally distributed. (Equivalently, this means that the continuously compounded returns of the stock price are normally distributed.) Without proving this explicitly, we can roughly "see" this fact from the formula. If we integrate both sides of the equation with respect to time, on the left we get $\ln(S)$, while on the right-hand side we get the sum of two terms: the deterministic growth term μt (which tells us the mean of the distribution—roughly where to expect to find the stock) and a second term involving σz, which is normally distributed with mean zero and standard deviation $\sigma \sqrt{t}$. The sum of the two terms is therefore normally distributed. Observe as well that the lognormal distribution can never be negative, which is a reasonable property for modeling stock prices.

WHY DOES VOLATILITY GROW WITH THE SQUARE ROOT OF TIME?

The natural question arises as to why we model stocks as having a standard deviation that grows with the square root of time. At first glance this is a bizarre assumption to make, but in reality it is a very natural consequence of our initial assumptions and some simple properties of probability.

Specifically, we assumed that the movements of the stock in any two time periods are unrelated—what we called the "memorylessness" property. Consider the move in a stock on two consecutive trading days $d1$ and $d2$. Using the definition of the standard deviation of a sum, the standard deviation of the movement over the two-day period is given in terms of the one-day standard deviations according to:

$$\sigma_{d1+d2} = \sqrt{\sigma_{d1}^2 + \sigma_{d2}^2 + 2\rho\sigma_{d1}\sigma_{d2}}$$

Where ρ is the correlation between the returns on $d1$ and $d2$. However, by assumption $\sigma_{d1}^2 = \sigma_{d2}^2$ (the volatility is constant) and $\rho = 0$ (since they are uncorrelated). Therefore the equation reduces to:

$$\sigma_{d1+d2} = \sqrt{2\sigma_{d1}^2} = \sqrt{2}\sigma_{d1}$$

If we extend this logic to n days which all have the same volatility and zero cross-correlations with each other, the general result is that the standard deviation over n days is $\sqrt{n}$ times the standard deviation of one day.

$$\sigma_n = \sqrt{n}\sigma_1$$

This is the result we quoted in our computation of annualized volatility. The structure of our stock model is the continuous time analog to this.

Step 3: Apply Itô's Lemma   Given our model for the stock price, we can now look to model the price of a call option, which we now denote by $C(S, t)$ to emphasize its dependence on the two variable terms: stock price S and time t. (We have assumed volatility is a constant so it is not included.) If we rewrite our stock model in the form $dS = \mu S dt + \sigma S dz$ we can apply an important mathematical result known as *Itô's Lemma* to produce the following expression for dC.

$$dC = \left(\frac{\partial C}{\partial S}\mu S + \frac{\partial C}{\partial t} + \frac{1}{2}\frac{\partial^2 C}{\partial S^2}\sigma^2 S^2 \right) dt + \left(\frac{\partial C}{\partial S}\sigma S \right) dz$$

The details of this formula are not important for our purposes—what we need to know is that Itô's Lemma allows us to move directly from our expression for a small change in the stock price, dS, to an expression for the corresponding change in the option price, dC.[12]

Step 4: Construct the Delta-Neutral Portfolio   As we have seen previously, the sensitivity of the option price to movements in the stock price can be approximated by a position in the underlying shares. The number of shares that must be held to replicate the option price movements is given by the delta (Δ) of the option, which can be viewed as either the first derivative of the option price with respect to the stock price ($\frac{\partial C}{\partial S}$) or alternatively as the slope of the tangent line to the graph of the option price, as shown in Exhibit 9.14.

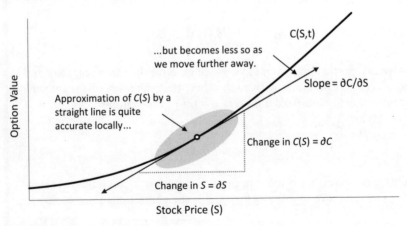

EXHIBIT 9.14   Delta as the Slope of the Tangent Line

If we calculate the value of the delta at a point S_0 then, for values of S close to S_0 the changes in the option price can be approximated by a position in a number of shares given by the delta, In the context of Exhibit 9.14 we are saying that movements along with the straight line of the triangle that touches the graph are roughly the same as movements along the curve of $C(S, t)$. An option position can therefore be hedged against movements in the underlying stock through the addition of an offsetting short position of $\partial C / \partial S$ shares of the underlier. This offsetting stock position, called the *delta hedge* is only effective locally and must be continuously updated as the stock price S changes. (While in practice this is unreasonable, it is possible in our theoretical framework given our assumptions from Step 1.)

We can therefore construct a *delta neutral* portfolio, V, consisting of a long position in the option and a short position of $\Delta = \partial C / \partial S$ shares of stock:

$$V = C - \frac{\partial C}{\partial S} S$$

Which is unaffected by changes in the stock price. We can then express the change dV in the value of the portfolio by:

$$dV = dC - \frac{\partial C}{\partial S} dS$$

That is, the change in the value of the portfolio is equal to the change in the value of the call (dC) minus the change in the value of the stock position (dS), applied to a number of shares given by the delta $\Delta = \partial C / \partial S$.

We can plug into this expression the value for dC provided by Itô's Lemma as well as our model for dS to arrive at the following expression for the change in the value of the portfolio:

$$dV = \left(\frac{\partial C}{\partial t} + \frac{1}{2} \frac{\partial^2 C}{\partial S^2} \sigma^2 S^2 \right) dt$$

Observe that, because the portfolio V is delta hedged, it is insensitive to small movements in the stock price. As a result, the expression for the change in the value of the portfolio dV does not contain the stochastic variable z, If there is no randomness in the movement of the portfolio then there is no risk. A key insight of Black and Scholes was that, if this portfolio is riskless, it must earn the same rate as all other riskless assets—the risk-free rate r.

The percentage change in the value of the portfolio over a time dt must be therefore be equal to the return on a riskless asset in that time:

$$\frac{dV}{V} = r\,dt$$

Step 5: Set up the PDE   Rewriting this last expression as $dV = rV dt$, and substituting the previously established expressions for V and dV we arrive at the Black-Scholes partial differential equation for the value of a call option $C(S,t)$:

$$\frac{\partial C}{\partial t} + rS\frac{\partial C}{\partial S} + \frac{1}{2}\sigma^2 S^2 \frac{\partial^2 C}{\partial S^2} = rC$$

This *partial differential equation* (PDE) has an infinite family of possible solutions[13] and, in order to specify the solution fully it is necessary to define its "*boundary conditions.*" In our case, the boundary is the expiration of the option and the limiting conditions are the terms of the payoff at expiry:

$$C(S, T) = Max(S_t - X, 0)$$

Step 6: Solve the PDE   Fortunately for Black and Scholes, the partial differential equation with these boundary conditions can be solved analytically, that is, for any combination of stock price, strike price, time to maturity, volatility, and interest rates, there exists a function involving all of these $C(S,\ K,\ t,\ \sigma,\ r)$ that solves the PDE.[14] This is actually a rare treat for much of applied finance—most things cannot be solved by a closed formula and a solution must be approximated via numerical methods.

The solution to the PDE is the famous Black-Scholes option pricing formula. For an initial stock price of S_0 and time to maturity of T, the formula for the call option price is given by:

$$C = S_0 N(d_1) - Ke^{-rT} N(d_2)$$

where d_1 and d_2 are defined as:

$$d_1 = \frac{\ln(S_0/K) + (r + \sigma^2/2)\,T}{\sigma\sqrt{T}}$$

$$d_2 = \frac{\ln(S_0/K) + (r - \sigma^2/2)\,T}{\sigma\sqrt{T}} = d_1 - \sigma\sqrt{T}$$

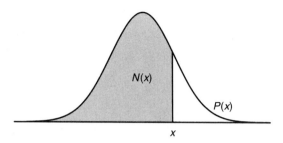

EXHIBIT 9.15 The Normal *P(x)* and Cumulative Normal *N(x)* Distribution Functions

Here, $N(x)$ is the cumulative probability distribution function for a standard normal distribution. Given the standard normal distribution function $P(x)$ (the familiar "bell curve") defined as:

$$P(x) = \frac{1}{\sqrt{2\pi}} e^{-\frac{x^2}{2}}$$

The cumulative probability distribution function $N(x)$ measures the probability of the normally distributed variable taking on a value *less than* x. For any value of a, $N(a)$ is the area under the bell curve from $-\infty$ to a as depicted in Exhibit 9.15.

$$N(a) = \int_{-\infty}^{a} P(x)dx$$

The Derivation for Puts

The function $C(S, t)$, which we interpreted to be the price of a call option, is actually much more general than that. We did not mention the particular characteristics of the call option until the last step, when we specified the boundary conditions for the solution of the PDE. For this reason, the entire derivation just presented can be used to solve for the value of a put option simply by changing the boundary conditions that we apply in the final step to those of a put option at maturity $P_T = Max(K - S_T, 0)$. The formula for the put is very similar to that of the call with just a few sign changes:

$$P = -S_0 N(-d_1) + Ke^{-rT} N(-d_2)$$

Where d_1 and d_2 are defined as before. It is actually not necessary to re-derive the expression for a value of a put option since we already know it by the put-call parity relationship. Given the formula for the price of a call, the value of the put option is simply:

$$P = C - S + Ke^{-rT}$$

American Options

The preceding derivation is only valid for European options. Because of the possibility of early exercise, the American option's price is path dependent—it not only matters where the option ends up but how it gets there—and can only be computed by numerical methods.[15]

As it turns out, the possibility of early exercise does not add a lot of value to an American option since it is rarely economically efficient to exercise early. The reason for this is intuitive enough. The possibility of early exercise is only interesting to the holder of an in-the-money option since an out-of-the-money option will not be exercised under any circumstances. For an in-the-money option, the act of exercising is equivalent to selling the option for its intrinsic value only (giving up all remaining time value). If the holder of a call wants to exchange the option for the stock he should sell the call in the market for its full value—intrinsic plus time value—and buy the stock separately, but not exercise.

It would only be attractive to exercise an option early if its market price were below its intrinsic value, in which case the ability to sell it for intrinsic would produce a profit. One situation where this occurs is with a deep ITM American put. Compared with an outright short stock position, the holder of a put has the benefit of the implied call option that protects him in the event of an upward move in the stock price above the strike. In return for this, however, he gives up the interest carry that could be earned on the funds raised from an actual short stock position.

If we slightly rearrange our alternative expression for put-call parity to isolate the value of the put we arrive at the following expression:

$$P = (K - S) + C - K(1 - e^{-rT})$$

This formula says that the value of an ITM put is equal to its intrinsic value $(K - S)$, plus the value of the implied call (C), minus the interest carry that could be earned between now and time T on the proceeds from a sale of the underlying stock at the strike price, $K(1 - e^{-rT})$. To determine whether early exercise would be optimal we compare the second and third terms: if the value of the foregone interest carry is greater than the value of the

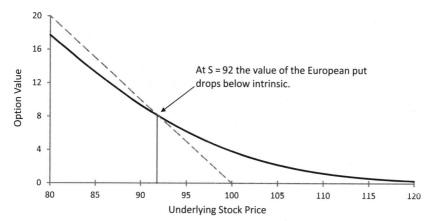

EXHIBIT 9.16 Deep ITM European Put Value below Intrinsic Value (K = 100, T = 3 Months)
Note: Interest rate assumed is 10 percent.

implied call option, the European put will be worth less than intrinsic value. This occurs when the put is deep ITM, which means that the implied call is deep OTM and therefore worth little. Exhibit 9.16 shows the value of a deep in-the-money European put.

The European put can trade below intrinsic because there is no mechanism for extracting the intrinsic value since the option cannot be exercised until maturity. The American put, however, can be exercised immediately to realize its intrinsic value (pay S in the market to buy a share of stock and then exercise the put and sell that share at K) and therefore will never trade below its intrinsic value. Using the example of Exhibit 9.16, for $S < 92$, the value of the American put would coincide with the straight line graph of the intrinsic value, which means that equivalent deep in-the-money American and European puts will trade at different prices with the American put being worth more.

Observations on the Black-Scholes Formula

We know that, as a whole, the price of a call option is the cost of holding leveraged long exposure to the underlier with loss protection below the strike price. At first glance, however, the Black-Scholes formula can be intimidating due to the notation. We can now look at the various components of the formula to develop a sense for what they tell us.

- The $\ln(S_0/K)$ terms tell us how far the strike is from the current price. Because our formula is developed in a continuous time framework, the distance between S and K is expressed as a natural logarithm. However, for values of S and K sufficiently close to each other, $\ln(S_0/K)$ can be approximated quite accurately by $(S - K)/K$, which is what we would typically think of as the "distance" (in percentage terms) from S to K. (For example, for $S_0 = 105$ and $K = 100$, the value of $\ln(105/100)$ is 4.88% versus 5% for the $(105-100)/100$ calculation.)

- The $\sigma^2 T$ (or $\sigma\sqrt{T}$) terms combine the "bounciness" of the stock, as measured by the annualized volatility σ, and the time it has to bounce around, T, to estimate how far the stock can be expected to move in the time remaining until maturity.

- The terms involving the risk free rate r can be interpreted as coming dually from the leveraging aspect of the option (it provides exposure to a larger notional amount with only a minimal initial investment) and from the fact that the riskless portfolio created by a delta-hedged option position must earn the risk-free rate.

- All of these terms are combined via the cumulative normal distribution function $N(x)$ which tells us the probability that a normally distributed random variable takes on a value below x. It is not surprising that this function should pop up given that our model for the stock price assumes normally distributed returns and that, due to the asymmetry in the payoff, we are only interested in the cases where the option ends in-the-money (i.e., one side of the distribution).

An important observation is that neither the Black-Scholes partial differential equation nor its solution depends on μ, the drift term that measures the expected growth rate from our stock price model. The price of a call has nothing to do with how much the investor thinks the stock will go up because this should already be implied in the stock price, on a risk-adjusted basis. The value of an option comes from what makes it different from stock—the kinked payoff and leverage—and not from what makes it similar to a stock—the long exposure to the underlier. This is underscored by the fact that in the Black-Scholes derivation we specifically eliminated the stock sensitivity with the delta-hedge.

The Important Take-Aways

We have presented the derivation of the Black-Scholes formula because it illustrates several important characteristics of option prices and how we model them. The reality is that in practice no one on a trading floor will ever calculate an option price themselves; firms will provide much more robust and sophisticated option price models for traders to use. Even lacking that, Bloomberg offers a very flexible option pricing function **OV** (*Option Valuation*), which is sufficient for most purposes. Readers should be careful, however, not to confuse familiarity with the notation with actually understanding the concepts. Salespeople and traders need to understand the *implications* of the Black-Scholes formula, its assumptions and what it tells us about options and how they behave. The formulas and terminology are simply a means to this end.

The important facts to remember from the Black-Scholes derivation are:

- The price of an option depends on the asymmetry in the payoff at maturity and the probability that the investor will benefit from it. It does not depend on the expected return of the stock.
- The value of the "kink" depends on how far it is from the current stock price $\ln(S_0/K)$ and the combination of squared volatility and time $\sigma^2 t$ that determines how far the stock is likely to go.
- The combination of a long call and short delta-equivalent number of shares produces a locally riskless portfolio that must grow at the risk-free rate.
- The delta-hedge is only accurate for a given value of the underlying stock price and must be adjusted with changes in the underlying stock price S.
- Stock prices are modeled by a lognormal distribution that says that the (continually compounded) percentage change in the stock price is normally distributed.
- The importance of Itô's Lemma is that it allows us to express the option price as a function of our model for the stock price.
- The volatility of a stock grows with the square root of time because of the "memorylessness" of the stock price process. The future movements of the stock are completely independent of the past movements.
- We made *huge* simplifying assumptions at the beginning of the derivation that are clearly not accurate in practice. The Black-Sholes formula is an effective guideline for real life pricing but there are many other factors that must be taken into consideration.

TYPES OF VOLATILITY

Of the variables that influence the price of an option, two are given (K and T), and two are observable in the market (S and r). The remaining variable—the volatility σ—must be estimated, and it is the difficulty in determining this value that gives the uncertainty, risk, and complexity to the pricing and trading of options. There are two measures of volatility that are of interest in the pricing and risk management of options: *historical volatility* and *implied volatility*.

Historical Volatility

In the section on Quantitative Considerations we showed how to calculate *historical volatility* using regularly sampled market price data over a given time period. This provides a starting point for estimating the likely future volatility. What is not clear is over what time interval, and with what frequency of data, the historical volatility should be computed. For short-dated options, a calculation based on the most recent 30 or 60 days of historical closing price data may provide a timely and accurate estimate of likely future volatility, while for longer-dated options, daily or even weekly data over several years may be preferable. There is the possibility, however, that data from several years ago may no longer be relevant if the size, structure, or other characteristics of the company (or the market conditions in general) have changed significantly since that time. Additionally, if there is a specific catalyst in the future, such as an earnings announcement or legal ruling, then the historical data may be of little or no relevance to the future volatility.

In our Black-Scholes derivation we assumed that the volatility σ is a constant over the life of the option. This was a necessary but impractical assumption as a historical analysis of stock prices quickly shows. The Bloomberg function **HVG** (*Historical Volatility Graph*) computes the historical price volatility on a rolling basis over a given time frame. (For example, the annualized volatility calculated based on the previous 30 trading sessions for each day in the last year) and then graphs these data. Applying this function to virtually any underlying asset shows clearly that volatility is far from constant and can, in fact, vary widely.

Traders frequently use the term *realized volatility,* as opposed to historical volatility. When speaking of a time period that has already passed, the terms are interchangeable: traders will say that a stock "is realizing a 30 vol" to say that the historical volatility in recent trading has been 30 percent. However, when referring to the volatility that will be experienced in a future time period, the term "realized" volatility is always used, to avoid ambiguity. For example, a trader might say he expects a stock "to realize a 25 vol over the next three months." That is, he expects that the historical volatility, computed three months in the future using the then-preceding 90 days, will be 25 percent.

Implied Volatility

An alternative approach to estimating the likely future volatility of the underlier is to "ask the market." Assuming there is active trading in the options of a given stock, the prices of these options will reflect the average of all participants' expectations of the future volatility of the underlier. Given the market prices of the option, C, and the other observable variables S, r and T, we can run the Black-Scholes formula in reverse to determine the value of the volatility σ that corresponds to the market price of the option. This is called the *implied volatility* of a stock.

Calculation	Inputs	Output
Black-Scholes Price	S, K, σ, t, r	C or P
Implied Volatility	S, K, t, C or P, r	σ

We can define implied volatility as the market's expectation of future realized volatility. Given the values of the known variables, every option price can be converted into a corresponding value for the implied volatility.

In the actual day-to-day activities of an options trader, the implied volatility is a far more important piece of information than any individual option price or even the realized volatility. There are several reasons for this.

Firstly, consider that a stock with an active options market will have both calls and puts with perhaps 10 or 15 different strike prices and six or seven different maturities (from one month to two years away) trading at any point in time, each with a bid and offer price. An options trader's book can contain tens of thousands of contracts long and short across dozens of different maturities and strikes, as well as a position in the underlying stock and potentially OTC products as well. With each movement in the underlier, every one of these hundreds of prices will update. It would be an impossible challenge to stay on top of every one of them.

However, every one of those prices can be converted to an implied volatility for the underlying stock. While the implied volatility for an option will vary across strikes and maturities (as we will see later) and can change as movements in the underlying stock or news events impact market participants' expectations of future realized volatility, the overall level is far more stable, and the changes far less abrupt, than the level of the underlying stock price. An options trader will generally know at what levels of implied volatility options are trading on the stocks he covers across a range of strikes and maturities.

Secondly, and more importantly, as we will see in the next section, an options trader will eliminate most, if not all, of his directional risk in the underlying security by delta-hedging the position. As a result, his trading book will be relatively unaffected by small moves in the underlying stock price. However, he is still exposed to changes in the implied volatility. A position held by the trader will be continually marked-to-market to reflect the current levels at which the option is trading. If the market's expectation of future volatility changes, this will affect the level of implied volatility in the market and therefore the level of option prices. This results in a change in the value of the trader's position even with no move in the underlying stock price.

As a result, while a move in the underlying stock and a change in the implied volatility will both affect the price of every option in the portfolio, it is easier for the trader to structure his book in such a way that the exposure to the stock price is minimal. Due to the relative ease and liquidity of stock trading, exposure to the underlier can be quickly eliminated. However, the only way to hedge exposure to the level of implied volatility is by trading options, which are far less liquid, making it much more difficult to run an active options trading book without taking on some directional exposure to the level of implied volatility.

An alternative viewpoint on implied volatility that may be appealing for the more technically inclined, is to think of the Black-Scholes formula as a transformation between the space of option prices—what we will call *price space*—to a much more stable *implied volatility space*. In price space we look at the value of the call and put on the stock for each combination of strike and maturity, every one of which will "tick" with each movement in the stock price. In implied volatility space we look at the level of volatility implied by every one of option prices in price space, given the level of the underlying stock. Though implied volatility is not constant across all strikes and maturities, it varies much less than option prices. What makes implied volatility space attractive as a means of visualizing the options market is the fact that changes in the option price caused by movements of the underlying stock—which are the most frequent source of change in the option price—do not cause changes in the implied volatility, which makes implied volatility space much more stable. For example, if the stock price has moved up by $1 and the value of a 0.20 delta option has experienced the commensurate $0.20 increase then, from the perspective of implied volatility space *nothing has happened* because the stock and option prices are still related by the same level of implied volatility.

There is no closed formula for the implied volatility and it must be calculated via numerical methods. Fortunately implied volatility information is readily available on Bloomberg.

- The **OMON** (*Options Monitor*) function provides a multi-page customizable summary of options trading activity in a given underlier across all strikes and maturities with real-time market information (last sale, bid, offer) expressed both in price terms and as a corresponding implied volatility. There are also the corresponding **CALL** (*Calls*) and **PUT** (*Puts*) functions that provide similar data for only one type of contract.

- The **HIVG** (*Historical Implied Volatility Graph*) computes the implied volatility of the most actively traded contracts and provides a historical comparison of the implied volatility, the realized volatility, and the level of the underlying stock price.

SUMMARY

The long holder of an option contract has the right, but not the obligation, to buy or sell an underlying asset at an agreed-upon price, called the *strike*. Options to buy are called *calls* and options to sell are called *puts*. *European options* can only be exercised at maturity while *American options* can be exercised at any point up to and including maturity, though early exercise is rarely optimal. The optionality of the contract creates a "kink" in the payoff diagram of the option at maturity—on one side of the strike price it behaves like stock (where there is an economic benefit to holding the option) while on the other side it loses its sensitivity to the stock and expires worthless. It never goes below zero, however. The relationship between the stock price and the strike price leads us to a classification of options as either *in-the-money* (those that would have value if exercised today), *at-the-money* (those where the strike price is equal to the current stock price), or *out-of-the-money* (those that would have no value if exercised today).

By combining a long position in a call and a short position in a put, with the same strike and maturity, it is possible to create a synthetic forward in the underlier, called a *put-call combo*. This brings us to one of the most fundamental relationships in options: *put-call parity*, which expresses the relationship between the prices of a call and put with the same strike and maturity in terms of the stock price, the strike price, the time to maturity, and the risk-free interest rate.

While the kinked payoff diagram gives us a picture of the maturity value, also known as the *intrinsic value* of an option, at any point prior to expiration an option also has *time value*, which comes from the possibility of benefiting from the change in behavior of the option when the stock price crosses the strike. For an OTM option, this is the possibility that the option ends up ITM, while for an ITM option this is the fact that, if the stock price crosses the strike, the option may expire worthless, but will never take on a negative value. The amount of time value is a function of three factors: how far the stock price is from the strike (*moneyness*), how much the stock "bounces around" (*volatility*), and how long it has to bounce (*time*).

The curved graph of the option price as a function of time produces a varying sensitivity of the option to the price of the underlying stock. This sensitivity is called the *delta*, which measures the change in the option price for a given change in the underlying stock price. By holding an offsetting position in a number of shares equal to the delta, called a *delta hedge*, the option's exposure to the underlying stock price can be neutralized, resulting in a *delta neutral* portfolio.

The Black-Scholes option pricing formula is one of the most significant accomplishments of modern finance. The price of a stock is modeled as a random variable, which is the sum of a steady upward drift and a "noise" term driven by a special type of random variable called a stochastic process. An important mathematical result known as Itô's Lemma allows us to convert our model for the stock price into a model for the option price. We then construct a delta-neutral portfolio and use the fact that it is riskless—and must therefore earn the risk-free rate—to set up the Black-Scholes partial differential equation. Applying the terms of the payoff at maturity as a boundary condition we can derive a closed formula for the price of a European call or put.

The Black-Scholes formula takes as inputs the stock price (S), the time to maturity (T), volatility of the underlier (σ), the risk-free rate (r) and the strike price (K) to produce a price for the option. All of these are readily observable in the market except for the volatility of the underlier—which represents a future realized variability that cannot be known a priori. To determine the market's view of the likely future volatility of the underlier, we can run the Black-Scholes formula in reverse by inputting the observable variables and the market price of the option to determine the corresponding level of implied volatility. The implied volatility of an option is one of the most important pieces of information for an options trader.

CHAPTER 10

Options (Part 2)

VOLATILITY TRADING

Up to this point, we have looked at options as a tool for expressing a directional view in the underlier. We have made some qualitative observations about the sensitivity of options to changes in volatility (σ) and time (t), which take on a more formal structure in the derivation of the Black-Scholes formula. We have also encountered the concept of a delta hedge and how the combination of an option and an offsetting position in a delta-equivalent number of shares creates a delta neutral portfolio that is locally unaffected by changes in the underlying stock price, but does retain its sensitivity to changes in volatility and time.

In this chapter we introduce a new way of looking at options and a new type of trader—the *volatility ("vol") trader*. A vol trader uses delta-neutral options positions to express directional views on the level of volatility in the underlying stock. Vol traders are not betting on the *direction* of the movement of the stock, but rather on the *quantity* of movement, whether up or down. The options market makers at Wall Street investment banks are volatility traders and on many trading floors they are not actually referred to as the options desk but rather the *vol desk*. While a vol trader will frequently have a directional view on the stocks he covers and bias his delta exposures accordingly, his primary focus is on volatility and his book will tend toward delta neutrality.

A First Look at Options Market Making

The majority of clients of Wall Street investment banks use options as a directional investment, either for hedging purposes or to structure views on particular stocks. As we will see, the fact that an option position can be viewed and traded from either a directional or volatility perspective is essential to the functioning of the options markets. The ability to strip out the directional view on the underlying stock via a delta hedge means that a directional investor looking to express a bullish view on the underlying stock can trade with a vol trader who has a similarly bullish view, a bearish view, or no particular view on the stock at all, as long as the level of implied volatility priced in the option is attractive. This is particularly important because, among directional investors, there tend to accumulate significant imbalances in the supply and demand for options of certain strikes and maturities. For example, there is persistent demand by hedgers for out-of-the-money puts to protect against downward moves in markets. Without the intermediation of vol traders, these imbalances would result in stalled or illiquid options markets.

The role of an options market maker in facilitating clients who use options to express directional views is analogous to that of the ETF market maker. As described in Chapter 6, when there is insufficient liquidity to complete a client order in the actual ETF shares, the trader sources the liquidity in the underlying stock portfolio via a program trade, and then uses the ETF creation and redemption process, to pass that liquidity through to the client order. The easy (and riskless) convertibility between ETF shares and stock portfolios allows the broker to transfer the liquidity of the underlying cash basket to the ETF and greatly facilitates trading.

An options market maker provides a similar service to clients by intermediating between the two types of option traders—the directional traders and the vol traders. In general, the most significant risk of an option position is the directional exposure to the underlying stock. While the level of volatility does change, and can do so abruptly, the impact of directional moves on the option price are much greater and a delta-hedged position carries much less risk than an outright long or short position. The less liquid options market is the trading among directional players, where clients tend to cluster on the same side of the market and the risks of the positions are too large for the broker to take the other side of the trade himself. The more liquid market is in the trading of volatility views, where interest is not so concentrated in specific contracts and larger positions can be held with much lower risk. By delta hedging, the vol trader intermediates between the two markets and converts a very large directional view on a stock or index into a much more manageable view on its volatility. In so doing, he passes the liquidity available among volatility traders through to the directional traders.

Pricing an Option Trade   In this chapter, we will look at some of the many factors that influence how a vol trader prices and risk manages a trade. At the most basic level, however, when asked by a client for a risk price on an option, a vol trader will need to answer two questions:

1. At what level of implied volatility should he buy (sell) the option?
2. At what price can he execute his delta hedge?

The first question is, to a vol trader, the equivalent of asking for a risk price in a single stock from a cash trader. The vol trader makes a bid or offer in the level of implied volatility based on his knowledge of the volatility currently being priced into other options on the same underlier as well as recent historical volatility, the details of the company itself, the relationship with the client, and many other factors. While the asset is volatility, instead of stock price, the vol trader's job is the same: buy low and sell high.

The second question asks what it will cost to convert the directional trade into a volatility trade. A vol trader views options from the perspective of delta-neutrality. Therefore, his interest is not in what the option is worth now, but what it will be worth once he has executed his delta-hedge. The trader estimates the market impact of the stock execution and then computes the option price that corresponds to this (using his desired level of implied volatility).

As we have discussed, the sensitivity of the option price to movements in the stock is measured by the delta. If, for example, in executing his delta hedge, the vol trader expects to have $0.20 impact on the price of the stock (i.e., his execution price will be $0.20 worse than current levels), and the delta of the option is 0.40, then he would adjust his option price by 0.40 × $0.20 = $0.08. He has no interest in holding the options on an unhedged basis so, based on the assumption that he will delta hedge the position immediately, he *delta adjusts*[1] the option price to reflect what the stock price will be when he is done hedging.

Not all clients are directional options traders. If the client is also a vol trader, then when he trades with the options market maker, he will have an equal and opposite delta hedge to execute in the market. In this case, the trade can be executed *delta-neutral*: the broker not only trades the options with the client, but crosses the delta hedge as well, removing the need for either side to execute stock in the market. A delta neutral options trade is quoted relative to a reference stock price at which the shares will be crossed. If the actual cross price of the delta to the client is different (i.e., if there are exchange rules which prevent the delta from being crossed at the agreed-upon price), then the option price will be delta-adjusted accordingly, as described above, to reproduce the originally agreed economics.

How Does a Vol Trader Trade Vol?

In this section we examine the two principal ways vol traders can make money from volatility: either from a change in the level of implied volatility or a mispricing of implied volatility relative to realized volatility.

Change in Implied Volatility Implied volatility represents the market's *expectation* of the future volatility in the underlying asset. Investors use the facts available to them (pending news announcements, overall market conditions, historical volatility) to arrive at their best estimate of what the realized volatility will be during the life of the option but, as it depends on the stock's reaction to unforeseeable events in the future, there is no "right" level. A consequence of this is that implied volatility is highly sensitive to investor sentiment and changes constantly. A vol trader will make a directional bet on the level of implied volatility when he feels the market's expectations of future conditions are incorrect—either excessively complacent or overly fearful—*and that these expectations will change.*

A delta-hedged options position is unaffected by small changes in the stock price, but retains its exposure to changes in the implied volatility. By establishing and maintaining a delta-neutral position (i.e., continuously updating his delta hedge as it changes), a trader can take a view on the direction of future changes in implied volatility. If the vol trader is long the option (either a call or a put) and the implied volatility increases, all other things being equal, the value of that option will increase, resulting in a profit. (Higher volatility increases the value of the optionality in the contract, which benefits the long holder.) A long position in an option is therefore said to be "long volatility." By the same logic, a short position in an option will benefit from a decrease in implied volatility and is therefore a "short volatility" position.

It does not matter whether the trader holds a long position in a call or put—the two positions, when delta hedged, have equivalent sensitivities (assuming same strike and maturity). We can see this by put-call parity: assuming the market is in equilibrium prior to the change in volatility (i.e., no arbitrage opportunity exists), then put-call parity must hold:

$$C - P = S - Ke^{-rT}$$

The right-hand side of the equation is unaffected by changes in implied volatility. This means that any change in implied volatility must have no net effect on the left-hand side as well, or else the parity relationship would be violated, creating the opportunity for an arbitrage. Therefore, the change in price of the call and put must be the same.

Difference between Implied and Realized Volatility   Another way of trading volatility is to express a view on the difference between the levels of implied and realized volatility. The trader locks in the level of implied volatility by either buying or selling an option (depending on whether he wants to go long or short implied volatility) and then attempts to capture the realized volatility through delta hedging. To understand the mechanism by which this is achieved, and the risks to the broker in implementing the strategy, we will require a more detailed explanation of the delta-hedging process, which we provide in the next few pages. Readers should give careful attention to this section to ensure it is well understood as delta hedging is what provides the conceptual link between implied and realized volatility and our explanation will illustrate many of the most fundamental considerations in the day-to-day work of an institutional options trader.

The derivation of the Black-Scholes pricing formula is based on the fact that the market exposures of an option can be replicated through a delta hedge, and that by continuously updating this hedge, it is theoretically possible (subject to certain assumptions) to replicate the payoff of the option across all levels of the stock price. Exhibit 10.1 shows the graph of a call option $C(S)$ and the delta hedge at a point $S = 100$. (In keeping with the notation introduced previous to our derivation of the Black-Scholes formula, we will denote the price of an option by $C(S)$ rather than the more precise, but much more clumsy notation $C(S, K, T, \sigma, r)$.) We can observe that, due to the curvature of the graph of $C(S)$, for an upward move in the stock price above 100, the value of the call increases more than the value of the delta hedge. At the same time, for a downward move in the stock, the loss suffered on the call is less what is made on the short stock position. Exhibit 10.2 shows the payoff of the sum of a long call and short delta-equivalent number of shares. As we can see, the change in value of the combined position is positive *regardless of what direction the stock moves.*

An investor holding this position does not care if the stock moves up or down—he just wants it to move. The position benefits not only from an

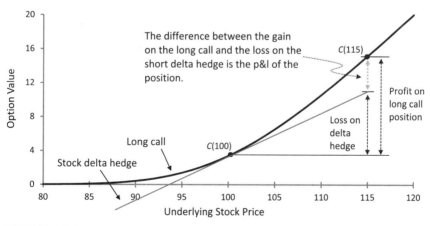

EXHIBIT 10.1   Analysis of Combined Long Call/Short Delta Hedge Position

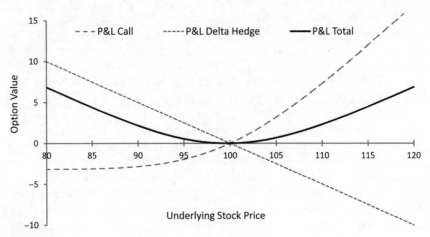

EXHIBIT 10.2 Net Profit or Loss on Combined Long Call/Short Delta Hedge Position

increase in implied volatility (due to the long calls) but also from the actual realized volatility caused by movements in the market.

Let us now examine these two figures in detail. As we have previously shown, the delta of an option changes as the underlying stock moves: for a call option, the delta increases as the stock price goes up and decreases as the stock price goes down. Therefore, with each incremental move higher in the stock price S, the call option behaves like a progressively larger stock position and benefits more from each subsequent increase in price than does the delta hedge, which has a constant linear sensitivity. As a result of the increasing delta of the call, the previously delta-neutral long call/short ΔS position develops a long market exposure, causing it to benefit from the upward movement of the stock price. Conversely, as the stock price decreases, the call's sensitivity to those changes (its delta) decreases and the call behaves like a smaller amount of stock, while the delta hedge retains its constant sensitivity, resulting in a net short position. In a sense it is the perfect position—it gets long when the market is going up and gets short as the market goes down.

What we need is a way to capture these profits. The delta-hedged portfolio produces a profit as the stock price moves up or down from $S = 100$ but will give back that profit if the stock price reverses direction and returns back to its original position. The way in which the vol trader captures this opportunity is by updating the delta hedge.

We can use option price and delta hedge ratio data from the option in Exhibit 10.1 (a $100-strike call with three months to expiry) to compute an example.

Stock Price	Call Price	Call Delta
95.0	1.20	27%
97.5	2.02	39%
100.0	3.15	52%
102.5	4.60	64%
105.0	6.33	74%

We assume that with the stock at $100, a vol trader pays $3.15 for one call and delta hedges the portfolio by shorting 0.52 shares against it. If the stock price increases from $100 to $105, we will show a profit on the long call position of $6.33 – $3.15 = $3.18 and a loss on the short stock position of 0.52 × $5 = ($2.60). The net mark-to-market gain on the combined position is $0.58. However, no profit has been captured yet—if the stock were now to drop back to $100 that gain would evaporate.

The reason we would lose money if the market went down is because the position is long. The delta on our call has increased from 52 percent to 74 percent while our short stock position is still only 0.52 shares. This leaves us with a net implied long delta of 0.22 shares. To correct this, we need to rehedge the position by shorting 0.22 shares at $105. We are now long a call worth $6.33 and short 0.74 shares of stock against it; this reestablishes our delta-neutral position.

If the stock now drops back to $100, the value of the call position will decrease from $6.33 back to $3.15 for a loss of ($3.18). However, because our short stock position is larger, we will make more money back on the delta hedge than we lose on the option. The short stock position of 0.74 shares will yield a gain of 0.74 × $5 = $3.70 for a net profit of $0.52. If we now re-adjust our delta hedge a second time, buying back the 0.22 shares we shorted up at $105, we get back to a short position of 0.52 and a delta-neutral position. In all of this, we have not touched our option position and its starting and ending value is the same. However, the exposures produced by the option gave us the reason to short 0.22 shares at $105 and buy them back at $100 for a net profit of $1.10 (= $0.58 + $0.52). The long call option can be seen as an asset that gives the trader a reason to sell stock high and buy low risklessly via delta hedging.

So far a long option position sounds like a miraculous invention. It produces exactly the conditions to trade profitably. It also seems inconceivable that anyone would ever sell an option and delta hedge as it would appear to result in a guaranteed loss. (For the short call / long delta hedge position the graph in Exhibit 10.2 would be flipped vertically, resulting in curve opening downward with its highest point at the x-axis.) This is almost true, but there are two very important caveats. The first is that the delta-hedged option position provides an opportunity to make money—but only if the markets move. If the underlying stock price does not move, then there is no way to capitalize on the opportunity provided by the delta-hedged option position. The second is that while the trader is waiting for the markets to do something, he is losing money. As we saw in Exhibit 9.11, for all values of the underlying stock price, the value of the call decreases with the passage of time—the curved profile of the option price prior to expiration drifts slowly toward the kinked graph of the intrinsic value. The daily loss of time value in the option is the cost of owning this "miracle" asset.

Of the three factors that influence the time value of an option (moneyness, time to maturity, and volatility), the first two can be observed objectively and would be applied uniformly by all investors. If these were the only inputs, the price of an option would be a simple deterministic function of the level of the stock price and time to maturity. In practice, however, there is considerable variability in option prices, even in the absence of movements in the underlying stock. This variability is a result of market participants' differing views of the appropriate level of volatility to price into the contract.

For a given strike and maturity, a high level of implied volatility indicates that the market expects the movement of the underlying stock to provide a considerable revenue opportunity for the delta-hedger. The trade-off is that the higher implied volatility also means that the option will have a greater time value (i.e., cost more). Because all time value is lost by maturity, the higher time value implies a greater daily cost of holding the position, which means that the vol trader needs to earn more each day through delta rehedging just to break even. If the realized volatility during the life of the option is lower than the level of implied volatility he paid for in the option price, the delta-hedging opportunities will be insufficient to cover the cost of the option and the position will result in a loss. If the realized volatility is greater than the implied volatility, the trader will recognize a profit (assuming he delta hedges appropriately, as we will see shortly).

We can now see how the vol trader is able to trade implied volatility versus realized volatility. The trader pays the price of implied volatility in the option premium for the opportunity to capture realized volatility.[2] If he believes the implied volatility is below what will actually be realized (i.e., market participants are overly complacent about future market movements and "vol is cheap"), he will buy the option and delta hedge. If he thinks implied vol is overpriced (i.e., investors are excessively fearful about future price movements), he can sell the options and delta hedge his position in the hope that the daily loss in value of the option (which would produce a profit on the short option position) will be sufficient to cover the daily losses accumulated through delta hedging.

Given the implied volatility, we can estimate the average daily movement that must be captured through delta-hedging for a delta-hedged option position to be profitable. As we saw in Chapter 9, an annualized volatility can be converted into an average daily move by dividing by the square root of the number of trading days, or roughly 16. Therefore, when a vol trader pays a 24 percent implied volatility on an option, he is betting that the average daily movement over the life of the option will be greater than 1.5 percent.[3]

The task of updating the delta hedge ("trading around your delta") to capture the realized volatility can be quite tricky. In the derivation of the Black-Scholes formula, the assumption was that the delta hedge was continuously updated. In practice, however, this is not feasible. A trader will generally set a threshold, either expressed as a percentage change in the delta or an absolute notional amount of delta exposure and will rehedge once the delta reaches that threshold. The challenge is that the further the trader allows the stock to move before rehedging, the greater the profit from the position. (The further the stock goes, the larger the delta exposure becomes and the greater the profit from each subsequent move.) However, by waiting longer before rehedging the trader runs the risk of the stock reversing and losing the opportunity to capture the delta-hedging profits at all.

If we recompute our example using a more conservative delta-hedging strategy, we can see the effect of letting the position run versus locking in profits. When the underlying stock reaches $102.50, the correct delta hedge is a short position of 0.64 shares. If the trader wants to update his hedge at this point he will need to sell 0.12 shares of stock. If the stock then continues to rally up to $105 then he will wish he had not rehedged since by doing so he will be shorter by 0.12 shares from $102.50 up to $105, which will cost him $0.12 × $2.50 = $0.30. If we assume he makes the same trade on the way down, reducing his delta hedge from 0.74 to 0.64 when the stock drops from $105 down to $102.50, the intermediate rebalancing trades will cost him an additional $0.25 (=0.10 shares × $2.50) for a total of $0.55, reducing the profitability of the trade by half.

Clearly there is the temptation to allow the delta to accumulate and try to maximize the profit on the movement. In doing so, the trader takes a view on the delta—he stays long because he thinks the stock will go even further up—rather than just trying to capture the volatility. If the stock swings back down to $100, and he has not captured any of the move, he will likely wish he had taken the middle road and at least locked in part of the profits. The decision of when to rehedge is a delicate one and an important part of a vol trader's responsibilities. If the delta hedging is not done correctly, some or all of the opportunity it presents may be lost. In the end it comes down to a subjective assessment by the trader of whether he thinks the market is trending, and the stock movement is likely to continue (in which case he tries to ride the delta as far as possible) or more likely to revert (in which case he will lock in profits). Traders may also have internal risk controls that limit the net delta exposures they are permitted to accumulate.

Observe, too, that the opportunity in the trade came from the fact that the delta changed. The profit or loss from a delta rehedging strategy comes from the slippage between the curved profile of $C(S)$ and the straight line of the delta hedge S, as shown in Exhibits 10.1 and 10.2. Flat parts of the graph (deep ITM and OTM options) provide little opportunity for generating profits through delta rehedging. Correspondingly, in these parts of the graph there is little time premium and therefore only a small daily loss due to the passage of time.

Short Option Positions   In practice, it is very often the client who wishes to purchase options, leaving the broker with the short position. A vol trader with a hedged short option position has the opposite economics to what we have just described: with each move in the stock price the delta-hedged position loses money because as the stock rallies, the position gets short while the position gets longer as the stock falls. (It is also negatively impacted by an increase in *implied* volatility.) Even if he has sold the options at a level of implied volatility he considers attractive, he must still work to capture the difference between implied and realized volatility through delta hedging.

When holding a short volatility position, a market maker will look to hedge more quickly if the market is trending (or potentially even over-hedge slightly in anticipation of further moves) and hold off on re-hedging if he feels the stock is likely to retrace its move. Rehedging a short option position locks in a loss, which is always a painful decision. However, by not taking the loss, the trader leaves himself with a large delta exposure and puts himself at risk for additional losses. This is a difficult balance to negotiate and requires a great deal of discipline on the part of the trader.

An additional danger of a short position is that it leaves the market maker exposed to *gap risk*. One of the assumptions in the Black-Scholes derivation is that stock trading is continuous, meaning that the delta-hedger can update his position at every price level. In reality, stocks often "gap"—jumping instantaneously from one price to another, much higher or lower price. Because the movement is instantaneous, nothing actually trades at any of the intermediate price levels which means that the trader cannot rehedge his delta along the way and will suffer an immediate and more substantial loss than would be considered possible in the theoretical framework. A simple example of this is the change between a stock's closing and opening price. Stocks can also gap intraday; bids and offers are not available at every price and if a news announcement causes a sudden rush of orders on one side of the market (and the orders on the other side to be pulled) the stock price can jump very discontinuously, particularly in stocks with thin liquidity. Gap risk is a significant concern to a trader with a short volatility position because not only is it potentially costly, but it cannot be effectively hedged.

In return for taking on this position, which loses money whether the stock moves up or down, the market maker earns a daily profit from the decrease in the value of the options (which he is short). In general, if the implied volatility of the options is greater than the realized volatility in the market, the vol trader will make more from the daily capture of time value than he will lose from delta rehedging. There is no guarantee however; a stock can show a low realized volatility on a closing price-to-closing price basis and still experience large gaps or violent intraday swings. A single large movement, if crystallized through a rehedge of the delta, can easily cost a market maker more than what he will earn from the total loss of time value on the option.

VOL TRADER MEETS DIRECTIONAL TRADER: HOW DID WE BOTH LOSE MONEY?

Investors who use options to express directional views are often confused when speaking with vol traders that run delta-hedged positions. A typical situation is as follows:

A client buys a $100-strike at-the-money call option expiring in two weeks on a biotech company that will be making a news announcement the next day about the result of a clinical trial. The client expects the result to be favorable and wants to participate in the upside of the stock but with protection on the downside in the event the announcement is negative. Due to the pending news and anticipation of volatility around the announcement the implied volatility is quite high and despite the short maturity the calls cost $5. The vol trader sells the calls and delta hedges by buying 0.5 shares of stock (the calls have a 50-delta).

The next day the news is announced that the trials of the drug were unsuccessful and the stock plummets 25 percent. The calls are now worthless, much to the client's frustration. In a conversation with

(Continued)

(Continued)

his broker he complains about the premium he lost and makes an off-hand comment that "You guys did well selling me those calls." To his surprise, the broker replies that his trader lost even more than the client did. While the $5 premium he took in for the options will soften the blow, the long position in 0.5 shares purchased to hedge the delta of the position has cost him $12.50 for a net loss of $7.5 per share.

The client was willing to pay a 5 percent premium for the calls because he thought it was likely that the stock would rally significantly. The trader was willing to sell the calls at a 5 percent premium because the implied volatility was attractive. In the end they were both wrong and they both lost money. The question is then: Who made money?

The important fact to remember is that when one party is expressing a directional view, and the other party is expressing a volatility view, there will always be a third party involved—the person who sold the trader his delta hedge. If the client and broker both take a directional view, or both express a vol view (and trade delta neutral), then the trade only involves two people with equal and offsetting positions, and the gain of one is the loss of the other. However, if the client is trading a directional view and the broker takes the other side on a volatility view, as in this case, then the positions held by each party are different: the client is long the calls and the broker is short the calls and long stock. It is the third party, who sold 0.5 shares to the trader for his delta hedge who has made a profit of $12.50 from the drop in the stock price, exactly offsetting both the client's loss of $5 and the trader's loss of $7.50.

OPTION SENSITIVITIES: THE "GREEKS"

The Black-Scholes formula shows how the option price is a function of five variables: the stock price (S), the strike price (K), the volatility of the underlying stock price (σ), the time to maturity (T) and the risk-free interest rate (r). In our analysis thus far we have focused on examining the impact of changes in some of these variables on an individual option position, either in isolation or combined with a delta hedge.

In practice, however, a vol trader may hold tens of thousands of contracts in a given underlier with long and short positions in calls and puts across many different strikes and maturities. Given the complex, nonlinear sensitivities of option prices to the various inputs in the pricing model, it is difficult to see how a single trader could appropriately aggregate and organize all the information necessary to properly risk manage such a large and complex portfolio.

This brings us to the concept of the *Greeks*. By taking the partial derivative of the option price with respect to one of the variable inputs (S, t, σ or r), we can measure the sensitivity of the option price to a change in that variable. To each of these partial derivatives we assign a Greek (or pseudo-Greek) letter (hence the name). The values of these "Greeks" can be calculated for each position and then summed to compute the aggregate exposure of the portfolio to changes in each input. For the non-stock-specific factors of time and interest rates the portfolio-level exposures can be aggregated across multiple underliers or even the desk as a whole. A vol trader then "sees" his book as a whole in terms of its exposures in each of the Greeks which is clearly a much more manageable task than individually monitoring the risks of each individual contract. The Greeks are also an invaluable tool for the risk managers who oversee the trading businesses and need a highly reduced summary of aggregate exposures.

While unquestionably an improvement over the contract-by-contract approach, analysis of an option portfolio via the Greeks remains a complex task. Each of the Greeks measures the sensitivity of the option to changes in one of the underlying variables that determine option prices. However, as we will see, the Greeks themselves are functions of these same underlying variables and are therefore affected by changes in them: a change in one of the variable inputs not only causes a change in the option price, it also changes the sensitivity of the option to subsequent changes in all of the variables.

As we have seen from the Black-Scholes derivation, the relevant variable in option valuation is $\sigma^2 T$. We can therefore simplify much of our analysis by looking at the impact of changes in this combined "volatility and time" variable rather than the two factors in isolation. In doing this we must keep in mind that the individual effects of the two variables are not equal—changes in volatility can be either positive or negative, while time is only in one direction, and the effect of changes in volatility are squared, which makes them more significant. Changes can also offset each other; an increase in volatility can be offset by the passage of time.

We will use a number of graphs in our analysis of the Greeks and their sensitivities, all of which are based on the three call options shown in Exhibit 10.3. This is an important exhibit and we will refer back to it several times. The value of $\sigma^2 T$ gets progressively smaller as the graph approaches the kinked payoff at maturity (corresponding to the progressively heavier lines). The accompanying table shows two sets of values for σ and T that

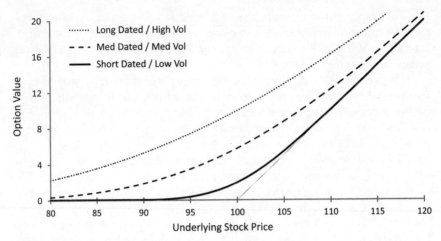

EXHIBIT 10.3 $100-Strike Call Options for Three Different Values of $\sigma^2 T$

can be used to create these graphs—one with constant volatility and varying times to maturity, and the second with constant time to maturity and varying levels of volatility. Depending on the circumstances we may prefer to view the movement between the three curves as the result of changes in one variable or the other.

	Fixed Volatility		Fixed Maturity	
Curve	σ	T	σ	T
Light	25%	2 wk	10%	3 mo
Medium	25%	4 mo	30%	3 mo
Heavy	25%	1 yr	50%	3 mo

Note: Because our focus is conceptual and not technical, we will not include the formulas for the option Greeks. The omission is a small one; the formulas are complex, of little practical value, and for most readers offer little insight beyond what can be observed graphically.

Delta

We have already encountered the first and most fundamental of the Greeks; the delta (Δ) measures the sensitivity of the option price to changes in the underlying stock price. Mathematically, it is the partial derivative of the price C with respect to S:

$$\Delta = \frac{\partial C}{\partial S}$$

The delta measures the most significant risk to the holder of an option. Movements in the underlier happen more quickly, and have greater impact on the option price, than changes in any of the other variables. For a vol trader looking to express a view on either the direction of implied volatility, or the difference between implied and realized volatility, the elimination of the delta exposure through an offsetting position in the underlying stock is the first and most important step.

The value of the delta can be interpreted in several ways, each of which provides a different insight into the behavior of option prices.

1. The sensitivity of $C(S)$ to changes in S.
2. The slope of the tangent line to $C(S)$.
3. The locally equivalent number of shares of the underlier.
4. A measure of the probability of the option expiring in-the-money (in absolute value).

We have already encountered the first three interpretations in our discussion of option prices. The fourth interpretation of the delta—as a measure of the probability that the stock price ends in-the-money—is a new and intuitively attractive viewpoint. Like a probability, the delta is between zero and one, and it takes on its extreme values—zero for deep out-of-the-money calls and one for deep in-the-money calls, in those situations where there is the least ambiguity in the outcome at maturity. For at-the-money calls, which have a roughly equal probability of ending in- or out-of-the-money, the delta is close to 0.50. (For put options, which have a negative delta, we can take the absolute value of the delta.)

It is worth pointing out that this interpretation is not mathematically rigorous. The option delta, computed using the Black-Scholes pricing model, provides only an approximation of the likelihood that the option expires in-the-money, and is not a precise measurement of probability. However, as long as this is understood, and the interpretation is used only qualitatively, as a tool to help visualize how options prices behave, the lack of mathematical precision is unlikely to cause any problems.

We can now look at how an option's delta is affected by changes in the other underlying variables. Observe that up to this point in our discussion of options we have looked primarily at one type of option graph—the call price $C(S)$ as a function of the underlying stock price S. We will now be looking at different types of graphs as we examine the sensitivities of each of the Greeks to changes in the underlying variables. It is worthwhile to double-check the descriptions of the graphs and understand what each of the axes represents to make clear what is being shown. In all cases we will present only the graph for a call option; it is left to the reader to explore the equivalent analysis for puts.

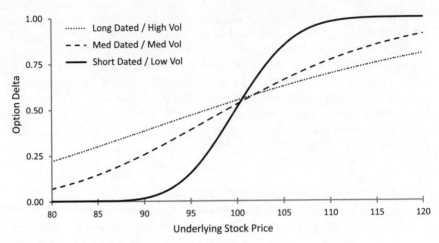

EXHIBIT 10.4   Option Delta as a Function of Price

We begin by looking at the sensitivity of the call option delta to changes in the underlying stock price. In Exhibit 10.4 we plot the graph of the call delta $\Delta(S)$ as a function of the underlying stock price S under each of the same three combinations of volatility and time shown in Exhibit 10.3. Using our interpretation of delta as the slope of the tangent line to the curve of $C(S)$, we can see that the height of the graph of the delta $\Delta(S)$ in Exhibit 10.4 is equal to the slope of the corresponding curve of $C(S)$ in Exhibit 10.3. The delta starts very close to zero for low values of S—corresponding to deep OTM calls whose sensitivity to the stock price is nearly zero—and increases to one, for high values of S, where the call is deep ITM and moves one-for-one with the stock.

We have seen how, as the combined quantity $\sigma^2 T$ decreases, the smooth curve of $C(S)$ in Exhibit 10.3 approaches the kinked graph of the payoff at maturity. In Exhibit 10.4 we can see how this impacts the delta. Using the interpretation of the delta as a measure of the probability that the option expires in-the-money, the impact on the delta of changes in the time to maturity or implied volatility is intuitive. The less volatile the stock, and the closer the option is to maturity, the nearer we expect to find the stock to its current level when the option expires. This then pushes the delta toward the two values associated with certainty: zero for options that are currently out-of-the-money options, and one for in-the-money options. If the underlying stock is at 95, a 100-strike call expiring in three months on even a moderately volatile stock, will have a reasonable chance of ending in-the-money. If the option only has one week before it expires, it is much more likely to end out-of-the-money and therefore has a much lower delta.

The graph of the delta at maturity poses an interesting problem. What do we do for the option that is precisely at-the-money ($S_T = K$)? The delta is zero for all $S < K$ and one for all $S > K$, but undefined at $S = K$. The mathematical reason for this is due to the "kink" in the payoff at maturity, which causes a discontinuity in the graph of the delta. (Calculus does not deal well with sharp corners.)

In practice, this mathematical subtlety has very significant implications for delta-hedged short positions in physically settled options (such as options on single stocks) at maturity. When an option expires, the holder of a short position knows, with a high degree of certainty, that an in-the-money option will be exercised against him while an out-of-the-money option will not. This allows him to fine-tune his delta hedge just prior to expiry to ensure he has the appropriate position to hedge the physical settlement. While there is always the possibility of a surprise, the clarity in the in-the-money and out-of-the-money cases comes from the fact that there is an economically optional action. The difficulty when an option expires at-the-money is that there is no economic reason why the long holder should choose to exercise or not. The decision depends on the specific circumstances of the long holder (their desire to hold the stock, any offsetting hedges that may or may not have been unwound, etc.), which cannot be known. The result may be a partial or complete exercise, or no exercise at all.

For a market maker, this uncertainty is problematic. If a short option position expires at-the-money, he cannot know for certain what the appropriate delta hedge is, since he does not know the number of contracts that will be exercised against him. Any mismatch between the number of shares held to hedge the position and the number of contracts exercised will result in an unhedged position in the underlying stock that will need to be unwound after expiry.

This is called *pin risk* and is a very real concern for an institutional market maker. The risk is exacerbated by the fact that exchange-traded equity options expire at the close of trading on a Friday and the market maker will not be advised of the number of contracts exercised against him until the weekend, and therefore will not be able to trade out of any residual exposure until Monday. Because delta hedging eliminates the directional exposure from an options position, and therefore greatly reduces the total risk of the position, market makers can accumulate very large positions in the options of a particular underlier, often corresponding to delta exposures of millions of shares and tens of millions of dollars. So long as the delta hedges are maintained, the risk of the position is manageable. If the appropriate delta hedge suddenly becomes ambiguous, due to the stock being pinned to a strike on expiration, the risks can be very significant.

Looking again at Exhibit 10.4, observe also that the rate at which the delta changes over time is not constant and depends on the moneyness of the option. For slightly in- and out-of-the-money calls (say, 5 percent ITM or OTM), the change in the curve of $\Delta(S)$ in the eight months between the first two graphs (one year to maturity and four months, assuming 25 percent volatility) is significantly less than the change in the curve of $\Delta(S)$ between the second and third graphs (four months and two weeks to maturity). And even with two weeks to maturity, the curve still has a fair way to go to reach the disconnected 0-or-1 shape it will have at maturity. This is consistent with our intuitive interpretation of delta as a measure of the probability of the option expiring in-the-money—for a near-the-money option this does not become clear until very close to maturity. For the deep ITM and OTM options, the sensitivity is greater earlier on, when things are still a bit less clear, while in the last weeks and months the result (the call expiring ITM or OTM) is virtually guaranteed and the delta settles down more quickly to either zero or one. Viewing the difference between the curves as a function of volatility (instead of time) we see that a change in the volatility has a greater impact on the deep ITM and OTM options, where the results are less clear, than it does on the near-the-money options, where the result will be ambiguous until the last moments anyway. For the ATM options, the passage of time or a change in volatility has no impact since the stock is already sitting right at the point of maximum uncertainty.

Gamma

The next Greek is *gamma* (Γ), which measures the sensitivity of the option's delta to changes in the underlying stock price. We can express Γ mathematically as either the derivative of Δ with respect to the stock price, or, since Δ is itself the derivative of C with respect to S, as the second derivative:

$$\Gamma = \frac{\partial \Delta}{\partial S} = \frac{\partial^2 C}{\partial S^2}$$

The Γ tells us, for a given movement in the stock price, by how much the delta changes. In terms of the graph of $C(S)$, the Γ tells us how curved the graph is. From our analysis of how a volatility trader captures the difference between implied and realized volatility we saw that although the graph of $C(S)$ is curved, in delta-hedging, the trader approximates this curve with a straight line. The profit or loss from the maintenance of a delta-hedged position was a direct function of the slippage between the curved option graph and the straight line approximation via the delta hedge. The more curved $C(S)$ is, the more slippage there will be between the profit or

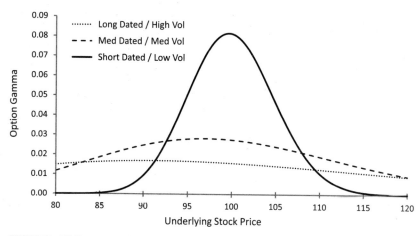

EXHIBIT 10.5   Option Gamma as a Function of Underlying Stock Price

loss on the option position and the stock hedge. The act of adjusting the delta hedge to maintain delta-neutrality—the process we described in our analysis of how to trade realized versus implied volatility—is called *gamma trading* and is the bread and butter of the institutional market-maker's job. Exhibit 10.5 shows the graph of $\Gamma(S)$.

We can now make some observations about which types of options have high or low gamma. From Exhibit 10.3 it is clear that the graph of $C(S)$ is most curved close to the strike price for short-dated options. Exhibit 10.5 confirms that, while gamma increases close to the strike price for all three options, the short-dated, at-the-money options have by far the highest gamma. In the deep in- and out-of-the-money ranges, or when there is still a long time until maturity or a high level of volatility, the graph of $C(S)$ is quite straight. In these cases, $C(S)$ can be accurately approximated by a straight line and the delta does not need to be updated frequently, implying a low gamma. With the passage of time (or a decrease in volatility), the smoothly curved profile of the graph of $C(S)$ approaches the kinked payoff at maturity. As the straight portions of the graph extend closer to $S = K$, the transition from $\Delta = 0$ to $\Delta = 1$ (i.e., the curve of $C(S)$ changing from a flat line to the 45° slope) is compressed into a smaller interval where the curvature becomes greater.

We can also see from the graph how the sensitivity of the gamma to changes in volatility and time is much more complex than what we have seen previously with the option price or the delta. The impact of changes in $\sigma^2 t$ is a function not only of the moneyness of the option but also of the absolute level of $\sigma^2 t$ itself. As $\sigma^2 t$ decreases (with the passage of time, for example), the gamma of the deep in- and out-of-the-money options decreases fairly quickly to zero as the curve of $C(S)$ flattens out and the delta becomes either one or zero. At the same time, the ATM option's gamma increases. A much more interesting behavior, however, is seen in the near-the-money options: for example, the case where $S = \$90$. Initially, as the curvature of the tails of $C(S)$ flattens to zero, this causes an increase in the gamma (the finely dotted line moves up to the heavier dashed line). However, as more time passes, and it becomes more clear that with the stock at $90, the option is very likely to expire worthless, the flat portion of the curve of $C(S)$ extends closer to $S = K$ and the gamma of the near-the-money option goes to zero (the dashed line drops down to the solid line).

As a general rule, short-dated at-the-money options have high gamma because the appropriate delta hedge changes rapidly: for an at-the-money option just about to expire, the delta will jump between zero and one each time the stock price crosses the strike, making the delta hedge only accurate for a one-tick interval. Longer-dated and further-from-the-money options have gently curved profiles, which means that the delta hedge is more accurate over a wider range of values of S and therefore have correspondingly lower Γ.

ON GAMMA

We defined gamma as the partial derivative of delta with respect to the underlying stock price:

$$\Gamma = \frac{\partial \Delta}{\partial S}$$

This means:

$$\int_{-\infty}^{\infty} \Gamma \, dS = \Delta_{\infty} - \Delta_{-\infty} = 1 - 0 = 1$$

That is, the area under the curve of $\Gamma(S)$ must always be equal to one. As the graph of gamma as a function of the stock price gets "squeezed together," (as the flat portions of the graph $C(S)$ in Exhibit 10.3 get closer to the strike with the passage of time) the area under the curve must remain the same, which causes the peak of the graph of $\Gamma(S)$ in Exhibit 10.5 to rise progressively higher.

For options market makers, who are frequently asked to facilitate client purchases of options by going short, options with very high gamma pose a significant risk. As we mentioned previously, despite the assumption in the Black-Scholes derivation that trading is continuous, real-life markets are susceptible to gaps. With a high-gamma option, the delta hedge is only effective within a very small neighborhood of the current stock price and in the event of a sudden, large move, the hedge is ineffective in mitigating the directional risk of the option. The higher the gamma, the greater the risk the trader takes in shorting it to the client. Other things being equal, the market maker will show a smaller offer, at a higher level of implied volatility, on an option with a lot of gamma as compared with a lower gamma alternative.

If the trader has sold options and hedged his delta he is *short gamma*. He earns the daily time decay of the option premium but will lose money every time he has to update his delta hedge. A short gamma position is particularly problematic when the size of the position is large relative to the liquidity in the underlier. In this case, he has to buy when the stock goes up and sell when it goes down, which will tend to exacerbate the moves in the stock price, which are already costing him money. It is occasionally the case that in a particular stock, there is a very high demand for options by directional traders. This results in the community of market makers ("the Street") being generally short gamma and leads to "whippy" trading in which even small moves are quickly exaggerated by the act of delta-rebalancing. When the Street is long gamma, this tends to reduce volatility in the underlier because when prices rise (fall), the market makers need to sell (buy) to lock in their profits. (This poses a problem for the market makers, who need the stock to move as much as possible to generate trading profits to cover their daily time decay.) There is ample evidence, both anecdotal and academic, of the impact of delta-hedging activity on the price movements in the underlying stock, particularly in the days immediately prior to maturity when the stock price is close to a strike with a large open interest set to expire (the highest gamma case).

Theta

As we saw previously in Exhibit 10.2, a delta-hedged long option is the "perfect" position because it makes money regardless of the direction of the move in the underlying stock. The profit from the position is the result of the slippage between the gain or loss on the option position and the delta hedge, which is a function of how well or poorly the curved graph of $C(S)$ can be approximated by the linear delta-hedge. The option gamma is the measure of this curvature—higher gamma means more curvature and, for the delta-hedger, more opportunity.

This opportunity does not come for free. The time value of an option is due to the optionality in the contract—the opportunity to benefit from the change in behavior as the stock crosses the strike price. With each passing day, the value of this optionality decreases as the uncertainty in the stock's position at maturity decreases. The daily loss in value of an option is the cost of holding a position that makes money regardless of the market's direction. Equivalently, for an options market maker who is holding a delta-hedged short position, the time decay is the payoff for taking such an undesirable position.

Theta measures the sensitivity of the option price (C) to a change in time (t). It is usually quoted on a per-day basis.

$$\theta = \frac{\partial C}{\partial t}$$

Theta is also known as *time decay* and is one of the more intuitive of the Greeks. It is not surprising that a contract that gives the holder the right to buy or sell an underlier at a given price will lose value as the time remaining before the expiry of the contract decreases. The passage of time will never increase the value of an option, so theta is always negative.

Theta is the sister concept to gamma. Where gamma is high, there is significant opportunity to make money by trading around a delta hedged option position (assuming the market moves) and the daily cost of holding the position is similarly high (which is what incentivizes the market maker to take the other side of the position). Similarly, an option with low gamma provides little opportunity to generate trading profits (but also low risk) and the daily time decay of the position is similarly small.

From the perspective of the maintenance of a delta hedged position to express a volatility view, the gamma measures the opportunity for trading profits (or losses) from capturing realized volatility, and theta is the daily cost of the implied volatility. The symmetric relationship between gamma and theta is apparent from a comparison of the graphs in Exhibits 10.5 and 10.6. Exhibit 10.6 shows the value of $\theta(S)$ for each of our three options across a range of values of S. As expected, high values of gamma are associated with large negative values of theta. The graphs look very similar, but reflected through the x-axis.

Regardless of whether an option is held to express a volatility view or a directional view, the daily loss of value due to time decay is clearly an important characteristic of options. However, particularly for investors who are using options as a directional investment, and may be less attentive

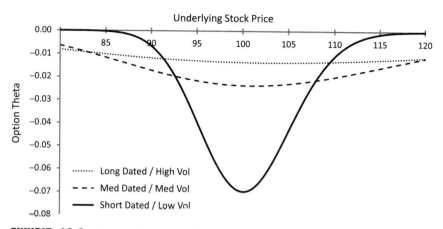

EXHIBIT 10.6 Option Theta as a Function of Underlying Stock Price

to the Greeks in their portfolio, it is important to be aware of the high theta of short-dated ATM options. Exhibit 10.7 shows the daily loss due to time decay of our $100-strike call when it is out-of-the-money ($S = \$110$), near-the-money ($S = \$104$) and at-the-money ($S = \$100$). So long as the underlying stock price is sufficiently far away from the strike, the daily loss due to time decay is small and relatively consistent from one day to the next. However, if the option is at or very close to the money, the option will retain a much larger amount of time value for much longer. This value is then rapidly lost in the last days before expiration, making the position

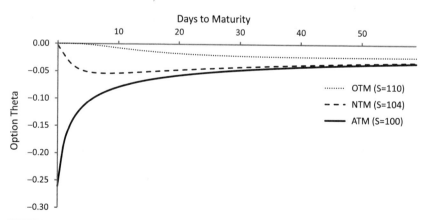

EXHIBIT 10.7 Theta Decay as a Function of Moneyness and Time to Maturity

potentially very expensive. Unless there is a specific reason why the view needs to be expressed via the soon-to-expire contract, it is often advisable to roll the option out to the next maturity and reduce the daily cost of time decay rather than concentrating such a large bet into such a small window of time. The very high theta decay of the at-the-money option in the final days before maturity is an offset to the very high gamma and the opportunity for delta-hedging gains in these contracts. However, if the position is held to express a directional view, the high price tag, in theta terms, may not be worth paying.

Premium Sellers and Premium Buyers The relationship between gamma and theta allows us to divide vol traders into two broad camps: *premium sellers* and *premium buyers*. This is by no means a rigid classification and smart traders will alternate between camps as circumstances dictate. It is common, however, for traders to have a preference for one side or the other, and some high-profile options traders have made a name for themselves in their adherence to, and avocation of, one approach or the other.

- *Premium sellers (Long θ/Short Γ):* "Premium sellers" are traders who prefer to sell options and take in the premium as profit, on the expectation that the losses they will accumulate through delta hedging will be less than what they were paid to take on the position. The idea behind the approach is that directional investors who use options (particularly puts) to hedge their portfolio against adverse market moves pay too much for these options—that there is a "fear premium" above the fair price for the option that investors are willing to pay to sleep easily, knowing their losses are limited. The premium seller acts like an insurance company, selling protection for a small premium. The long θ position means that the strategy provides a daily drip of positive P&L into the trader's book through the loss of time value. The short Γ, however, means that they are exposed to potentially catastrophic losses in the event of a sudden large move in the underlier (gap risk). When these large market disruptions occur, traders with short Γ positions risk "blowing up," that is, losing more money in a single event than was made over a long period of successful trading.
- *Premium buyers (Long Γ/Short θ):* The alternative approach is the trader who pays out premium to buy options and then has to "work for his pay" to recover the daily loss due to time decay through delta hedging. While the risk of a short gamma position is blowing up, the risk of a long gamma position is that the trader "bleeds to death" because the daily theta-related losses are not offset by sufficient trading-related gains from delta rehedging, either due to poor trading or a

low-volatility, trendless market. The challenge of starting each new day with a loss due to time decay and the potential for these losses to accumulate while nothing happens in the market can make a long gamma/short theta position mentally and emotionally draining (particularly while the premium sellers on the other side of the trade are making money just for showing up to work each day). The payoff comes when something finally happens. The long gamma position benefits most from sudden, large market moves, both for the delta-hedging opportunities they provide, as well as for inevitable increase in the level of implied volatility. Because market disruptions are usually followed by periods of higher-than-average volatility, the long gamma position can provide significant opportunity for additional profits in subsequent days of trading. When big moves happen, the short gamma positions start blowing up while the long gamma positions reap the rewards of patience and hard work.

While the premium seller's view is that directional traders and hedgers overestimate the risk of loss, the premium buyers' view is that the statistical estimates of risk are inaccurate and the real risk in the market is greater than commonly believed. There is convincing evidence that this is the case. Most standard risk models assume that the movements of stock prices and other financial assets are normally distributed (this was a central assumption of the Black-Scholes derivation). However, under this assumption, most of the major financial crises of the last 20 years are so fantastically impossible, that they simply could not have all happened. The stock market crash of October 1987, for example, when viewed in the context of the previous 1,000 trading days, was a 19 standard deviation move. Under the assumption that the returns on stocks are normally distributed, this is not something that needs to be planned for because probabilistically, it is a nearly impossible event—but it did happen.

A more recent example occurred in the summer of 2007. Many hedge funds and proprietary trading desks ran very large long-short stock portfolios based on statistical stock selection strategies. These *"quant funds"* had produced attractive returns with very low volatility during many years. Due to the diversification of these portfolios, the strategies were considered very low risk: the probability that all of the hundreds of long positions would go down simultaneously while the similarly numerous shorts went up was—under statistical assumptions of normally distributed returns—extraordinarily remote. This low risk profile gave traders confidence to leverage the positions heavily to multiply the returns generated.

However, as traders moved between employers and similar-thinking traders performed similar analyses, many funds were coming up to the same conclusions and taking on the same positions. The result was inevitable—the only question was what would be the trigger event. In this case, it was the tightening of the credit markets that decreased the availability of borrowable funds, which forced some of the funds to unwind their positions. With many funds holding the same positions, one fund's unwinding put pressure on other funds' positions, which suddenly began to lose money. As nervous traders hurried to unwind what were, in many cases, very large and illiquid positions, the effect snowballed. Suddenly, funds were seeing *all* their long positions going down (because other funds were selling them) and *all* their shorts going up (because other funds were covering their shorts in the same names). The assumptions of the underlying statistical models—that returns were normally distributed and that historical correlations between stock price movements would persist in the future—were no longer valid because there was now a powerful force in the market causing all of the positions to move together. As a result, some funds suffered spectacular losses, which were, under the statistical assumptions of their analysis, almost impossible.

In the midst of the chaos, one comment was particularly telling. In a conference call in August 2007 to discuss the losses in its Global Alpha fund, which had dropped nearly 30 percent in one month after years of consistent returns, Goldman Sachs CFO David Viniar commented that the fund's positions had experienced 25-standard deviation moves "several days in a row." Mathematically, a 25-standard deviation event should occur in 1 in every 10^{137} observations. To give a sense of magnitude, 10^{137} is equal to the number of atoms in the universe (10^{79}) multiplied by the nanoseconds since the big bang (10^{26}) times all the cells in the bodies of all the people on earth (10^{23}) ... times a billion (more or less). Given that this fund employed some of the brightest quant fund traders on the street, there is no question that the statistical analyses performed were correct; it was the assumptions about normally distributed returns and historical correlations—and the underestimation of how crowded the trades had become—that undid them.

THETA AND GAMMA—KICKING THE DEAD HORSE

Given the degree to which we have repeated the point, it should be clear that the relationship between gamma and theta—the measure of the risk (or opportunity) in a delta-hedge position due to the curvature of the graph of $C(S)$ and the daily cost, via time-decay, of holding that position—is an important one. It is, in fact, perhaps the most fundamental risk consideration for a vol trader and what distinguishes the vol trader's view of options from that of a directional trader.

To fully batter the point into submission we will make one final observation. Recall that, in our derivation of the Black-Scholes partial differential equation we made no mention of the specific characteristics of the derivative until the last step when we applied the boundary condition $C = Max(S - K, 0)$ to find the particular solution. This means that the relationship expressed by the partial differential equation must be satisfied by *any* derivative security or portfolio that meets our initial requirements (e.g., no arbitrage opportunities). Therefore, if we create a portfolio Π consisting of a delta-hedged long option position:

$$\Pi = C - \Delta S$$

The value of this portfolio must also satisfy the partial differential equation. Therefore:

$$\frac{\partial \Pi}{\partial t} + rS\frac{\partial \Pi}{\partial S} + \frac{1}{2}\sigma^2 S^2 \frac{\partial^2 \Pi}{\partial S^2} = r\Pi$$

Each of these partial derivatives is one of the Greeks we have just developed. Substituting:

$$\theta = \frac{\partial \Pi}{\partial t} \qquad \Delta = \frac{\partial \Pi}{\partial S} \qquad \Gamma = \frac{\partial^2 \Pi}{\partial S^2}$$

we can arrive at:

$$\theta + rS\Delta + \frac{1}{2}\sigma^2 S^2 \Gamma = r\Pi$$

However, by assumption the portfolio was delta neutral, therefore $\Delta = 0$ and we are left with:

$$\theta + \frac{1}{2}\sigma^2 S^2 \Gamma = r\Pi$$

From this, we can see the inverse relationship between Γ and θ—for a given value of the portfolio Π, a large positive gamma must be offset by a large negative theta, and vice versa. If we make the simplifying assumption that interest rates are zero, we get an even

(*Continued*)

(*Continued*)

clearer expression of the inverse relationship between these two factors:

$$\theta = -\frac{1}{2}\sigma^2 S^2 \Gamma$$

Vega

As we have mentioned before, all of the inputs into the Black-Scholes formula are either constants (K, t) or can be observed in the market (S, r), with the exception of the volatility, σ. Conceptually, the "correct" value of σ is the realized volatility of the underlier between the time of pricing and maturity. While an individual trader's estimate of the appropriate value to use would likely be a function of the historical volatility of the stock and any known upcoming events or catalysts, the implied volatility at which the option trades in the market is determined by supply and demand and is therefore as much a function of rational analysis as of fear, greed, emotion, and other subjective factors.

There can also be structural factors in the market that can impact the price of options and therefore their implied volatility. For example, the lack of availability of stock borrow can make it expensive (or impossible) to hold a short stock position. This will increase the price of put options since market makers will find it difficult and costly to delta hedge the position. Since the implied borrow cost cannot be easily separated from the market price of the option,[4] the increased cost of the put option would appear as a higher implied volatility.

As a result, although our Black-Scholes model assumes that actual stock volatility is constant, the market's expectation of what that future volatility will be—the implied volatility—is constantly changing as new participants enter the market and new information comes to light that requires a repricing of risk.

The sensitivity of the option price to changes in implied volatility is called vega (V) and is defined as:

$$V = \frac{\partial C}{\partial \sigma}$$

Vega is generally quoted as the change in the value of the option per one vol point change in the underlying stocks.[5]

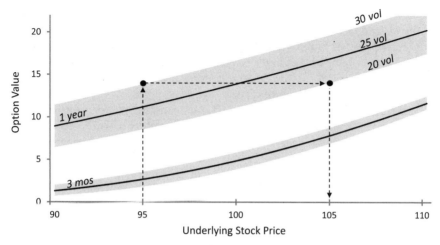

EXHIBIT 10.8 Impact of ± 5 Vol Point Shift on Call Options with One Year and Three Months to Maturity

As observed previously, the relevant quantity in option valuation is the product of squared volatility and time ($\sigma^2 t$). Squaring magnifies the impact of changes in the volatility while the time to maturity acts as a scaling factor that increases the impact on long-dated options and reduces it for short maturities. Exhibit 10.8 shows the impact of a ±5 vol move on a 25-vol call when it has one year and three months to maturity. The heavy line indicates the 25-vol option price and the grey band indicates the spread between the 20-vol and 30-vol cases.

We can see that the grey band is wider around the one year options, indicating higher vega in the long-dated maturity (i.e., the same 5 point change in volatility causes a much larger change in the option price). Though not easily visible from the exhibit, the width of the band also varies along the length of the curve with the at-the-money contracts having a higher sensitivity than the deeper in- or out-of-the-money contracts. These properties of vega are consistent with our intuitive ideas about the time value in an option. Long-dated options have higher vega because the more time the stock has to "bounce around," the greater the potential benefit from an increase in volatility. Near-to-the-money options are affected more by changes in implied volatility than when the stock price is very far from the strike since it is very unlikely that it will cross the strike under all but the most extreme conditions.

As suggested by the $\sigma^2 t$ that appears throughout the Black-Scholes formula, there is a direct relationship between vega and theta. Since all time value is lost by maturity, a vega-related increase in the time value of an option (due to an increase in implied volatility) will produce an increased daily loss due to theta decay going forward.

A vol trader looking to express a view on implied volatility would measure the size of his bet in terms of vega. A trader who is "long $250,000 of vega" will make or lose $250,000 for each one-vol point increase or decrease in the implied volatility.

While the vega of an option is a fundamental consideration for a vol trader, it is a common mistake by directional traders to underestimate (or ignore entirely) this sensitivity. This can be particularly problematic when trading in long-dated options where the profits from a correct view on the directional move in the underlier can be quickly lost if the move is accompanied by an adverse move in volatility. An example would be a long call position in a stock that has just received a favorable ruling in a court decision. Due to the significant vega sensitivity of long-dated options, the upside move in the stock price due to the positive outcome is offset by the decreased uncertainty—lower implied volatility—in the future prospects of the stock. This effect is not insignificant. As indicated in Exhibit 10.8, the loss on the call with one year to maturity caused by a 10 point drop in implied volatility (from 30 percent to 20 percent) would completely wipe out the gains from a $10 increase in the underlying stock price (from $95 to $105).

Rho

The last of the Greeks considered here is rho (ρ), which measures the sensitivity of the option price to changes in the interest rate, r.

$$\rho = \frac{\partial C}{\partial r}$$

Compared with the other Greeks, rho has historically been viewed as having very much secondary importance because the magnitude of the impact caused by changes in rates, as well as the volatility of interest rates themselves, is so much lower. However, in the aftermath of the financial crisis that began in the summer of 2007, the size of the movements in the interest rate markets has increased so drastically that traders are being forced to look much more closely at their interest rate exposures across all books, particularly volatility. While the interest rate exposure on an individual position is generally of relatively small importance, a market-making desk can, in aggregate, accumulate a significant interest rate exposure.

A call option provides leveraged long exposure to the underlier. If interest rates rise, the value of that leverage (the implied cost of borrowing funds to buy the long stock position) increases, which raises the price of the call. Call options therefore have positive rho. Holding a put option, on the other hand, is like being short the underlier. While a short sale of physical stock raises cash, which then earns interest, the put does not and the value of the put is reduced by the cost of this foregone interest carry. (We saw this when we looked at the European put trading below intrinsic value.) If interest rates rise, a larger discount for interest costs must be applied, which lowers the value of the put. Put options, therefore, have negative rho.

While we are on the subject of interest rates, and, in the interest of full disclosure, it should be pointed out that all of the option graphs presented so far have been constructed assuming an interest rate of zero (with the exception of the illustration of the deep-in-the-money put trading below intrinsic). To a certain degree this is misleading, since interest rates are almost never zero and therefore, relevant information has been excluded from the graphs. However, the introduction of a non-zero interest rate creates small asymmetries in the graphs, which have the potential to distract the reader from the insights the graphs are intended to communicate. Since interest rate considerations are of much smaller magnitude than any of the other option sensitivities, the simplification introduces little error.

The Greeks: Putting It All Together

The analysis of the sensitivity of an option to changes in the underlying variables that determine its price is an extremely complicated, multivariable problem in which movements in each variable affect not only the option's price but its subsequent sensitivity to changes in the others. The Greeks give us a framework for simplifying these risks to make them more easily understood. By decomposing each contract into its delta, gamma, theta, vega, and rho, we can easily compare the risks of options with very different characteristics. The Greeks for a given underlier are additive, which allows traders to analyze the aggregate exposures of a large, complex portfolio of listed and OTC options in terms of a set of relatively simple measurements.[6]

In pricing a trade, a vol trader will consider how the Greeks of the new position fit in with the existing exposures of his portfolio, and the price he gives the customer can be more or less aggressive depending on the degree to which the new position offsets existing risks.

As important as it is to understand the significance of the Greeks and how they can be used as a risk management tool, it is just as important to be aware of their limitations. The Greeks are a snapshot of the sensitivities of an option portfolio under a particular set of market conditions at a specific point in time. All of the Greeks vary in nonlinear ways with changes in the other variables and even a relatively "flat" portfolio (one with no significant exposures in any of the Greeks) can quickly develop a much riskier profile if market conditions change due to the different reactions of various positions. To compensate for the limitations of analysis of the Greeks, most vol desks will *stress-test* their portfolio to see the impact of movements in the underlier, volatility, time, and rates. Stress testing is essentially a formalized process for analyzing a variety of different "what if" scenarios. What if the market drops by 10 percent? What if volatility increases substantially? What if volatility decreases and the market does nothing for a month? Vol traders constantly analyze their portfolio to look for the risks that Greeks do not show.

IMPLIED VOLATILITY REVISITED

We now have enough vocabulary and understanding to revisit implied volatility and examine some of the more important concepts for a vol trader.

The first, and most important fact, is that we cannot speak of "the implied volatility" for a stock as though it were a single number. For each combination of strike and maturity, the market price of the option contract will imply a particular level of volatility in the underlier, which can vary significantly across time and strike. If we graph the implied volatility as a function of strike and maturity, we get something that options traders refer to as the *volatility surface*—a sort of three-dimensional landscape that describes much more completely the implied volatility of a stock.

For each strike and maturity there will be both a call and put trading. By put-call parity, the implied volatility of the two will be kept in line (with some margin for slippage due to trading costs, etc.). However, because directional investors tend to use puts for downside protection and calls for upside participation, these will be the more actively traded contracts and provide more current and accurate data. Therefore, the convention when computing implied volatility is to use the data for puts for all strikes below the current stock price and calls for all strikes above the stock price (i.e., use the out-of-the-money contracts).

To develop an understanding for what the vol surface tells us, we will look at it in each of the two dimensions independently: a single strike across multiple maturities (the term structure) and the range of strikes for a given maturity (skew).[7]

Term Structure

The *term structure* of volatility refers to the shape of the graph of implied volatility for a given strike as we extend out to progressively further maturities. The term structure can take on many different shapes though generally it will be described as one of the following:

- *Upward-sloping:* Higher implied volatility in longer-dated options.
- *Flat:* Similar levels of implied vol across all maturities.
- *Downward-sloping:* Longer-dated options trading at lower implied volatilities than short-dated contracts.

The shape of the term structure can have many different causes and the interpretation will depend heavily on market conditions and sentiment. An upward sloping term structure during a period of low realized volatility can indicate that the market views the current low levels of volatility as anomalous and expects a pick-up in the future. The same upward sloping term structure in a period of higher volatility may not indicate a genuine view that conditions will get more turbulent, but simply an increased risk premium, expressed via a higher level of implied volatility, being priced into longer-dated options due to customer demand for longer-dated portfolio protection via options. Active volatility traders will be able to draw more concrete conclusions about the reasons for the shape of the term structure based on the types of order flow they are seeing in the market.

Skew

When we look at options with the same underlier and maturity across a range of strikes, there is a recurring pattern in the variation in implied volatility. In general, out-of-the-money (*downside*) puts trade at a higher implied volatility than at-the-money options, with the level of implied volatility increasing the further the contract is from the at-the-money. Out-of-the-money (*upside*) calls have a less predictable relationship and can trade either at the same levels of implied volatility as the at-the-money options or at a higher or lower level, depending on which of several different forces is dominating at the time. If we take a slice through the volatility surface along a given maturity, we can see how the implied volatility varies across strikes. This variation in implied volatility as a function of strike is referred to as the *volatility smile*.

The fact that the implied volatilities of downside puts are higher than at-the-money options (and generally also higher than the equivalent upside calls) implies that the market is pricing an asymmetry in the distribution of stock returns in which the probability of large downward moves is greater than what would be predicted by the assumption of normal returns. In statistical terms, the measure of the asymmetry in a distribution is called *skew* (see definition in the Appendix).

Skewness was not always a property of the distribution of implied volatilities. It was only after the stock market crash of 1987 that market participants started to price in the risk of extreme non-normal market moves to the downside. The desire of investors to hedge their portfolios against these potentially devastating crash scenarios leads to increased demand for deep out-of-the-money puts, which raises their price and is then reflected as a higher implied volatility. In reality, the higher implied volatility of the downside puts is not a consequence of the market perceiving a downward move as more probable, but of the fact that, given that investors are generally long, a market sell-off is more painful to them than an explosive move to the upside and therefore they are willing to pay more for the protection.

The standard measure of skewness is to compare the implied volatilities of the 25-delta put and call:

$$\text{Skew} = \text{ImpVol}(\text{Put}_{25\Delta}) - \text{ImpVol}(\text{Call}_{25\Delta})$$

By referring to a specific delta for the put and call, this measurement of skewness automatically adjusts for the different absolute levels of volatility and price of different stocks (and of the same stock at different points in time.) Viewing the delta as an assessment of the probability of the option expiring in-the-money, the 25-delta put-call spread gives a clear measurement of the market's pricing of the relative probabilities of what should (at least theoretically) be roughly equally probable events. There will not, in general, be a strike with precisely a 25-delta, however a hypothetical 25-delta option can be interpolated from existing datapoints.

Volatility traders watch the changing value of the skew carefully as an indication of other participants' view on the risk in the market. Not only is the absolute level of the skew important, but so too is how the skewness is changing and what is causing those changes, all of which must be viewed within the framework provided by existing market conditions. In a rising market, an increase in skew due to higher demand for downside puts can indicate investors are generally quite long (i.e., fully invested or leveraged to the upside) and concerned about whether the rally is sustainable and want to buy protection. The same rally accompanied by a decrease in skew due to increased demand for upside calls can indicate that investors are underinvested and not benefitting from the rally as much as they should be and are looking for leveraged exposure to the upside to "catch up" with a rally that is leaving them behind. The change in the skew provides useful color on the drivers of the market rally, as well as investor positioning, sentiment, and the likely reaction to subsequent changes in market conditions.

The demand for downside protection causes out-of-the-money puts to have a higher implied volatility than their at-the-money equivalents. On the upside, the situation is reversed: out-of-the-money calls trade at a lower implied volatility than the at-the-money strikes. This is primarily due to a strategy known as *call overwriting* in which a long holder of a stock sells upside calls against his position as a means of generating additional income. The breakeven level on an overwritten position is equal to the strike price plus the premium taken in on the sale of the call. So long as the stock remains below that level until the maturity of the option, the investor remains fully exposed to the stock and keeps all or at least part of the premium from the short call position as additional performance. If the stock price rises above the strike, the investor stops participating in the upward movement in the price because the long physical position is cancelled out by the short call. In no case does a call overwrite produce a loss, since it is hedged 100 percent with a long physical position—it can only result in decreased gain in the event of a significant upward move in the stock price. Many large institutional funds have regular overwriting programs in which upside calls are sold against any long positions where they feel the stock has limited upside potential in the near term, or where the implied volatility of the upside calls make for an attractive risk-reward opportunity.

Two useful Bloomberg functions for analyzing options and their Greeks are **SKEW** (*Skew*), which compares implied volatility across the full range of strikes for multiple different maturities and graphs the results; and **OSA** (*Option Scenario Analysis*), which allows the user to explore sensitivities of an individual position or portfolio of options by "stress testing" then to analyze not only the current sensitivities (as shown by the Greeks) but how those sensitivities will change with shifts in the underlying variables.

OTC AND EXOTIC OPTIONS

So far in this chapter we have only considered the "plain-vanilla" options— calls and puts—and the assumption has been that these are exchange-listed contracts with standardized terms. There is also a large market for over-the-counter options with complex terms and more varied payoff structures. Trading in OTC options shares many of the same characteristics that were discussed in our discussion of swaps in Chapter 8: each trade is a unique agreement between two parties, each of whom takes on the credit risk of the other; all terms must be spelled out in detail, though this can be considerably simplified if both parties have signed an ISDA; there is no secondary market other than with the original counterparty and the transfer of the position to a third party is a complicated process.

There are three common reasons why options are traded over-the-counter:

1. *Plain-vanilla product with customized terms:* Clients may want a simple call or put structure but require specific terms—maturity date, notional amount, strike price, underlier—that do not match those of the standardized, exchange-listed contracts.

2. *Listed lookalikes:* The trading rules enforced by the options exchanges are designed to ensure that the greatest possible amount of options trading is executed through the exchange floor so that other traders and market makers have the opportunity to participate. While good in theory, these rules can often be counterproductive. A simple example is when a broker makes a risk price to a client on a trade requiring a large delta hedge that is likely to impact the stock price. Some exchanges prohibit the broker from crossing the options versus the client until the trade has been shown on the exchange floor, to give other market participants the opportunity to show a better price or participate in the trade. Until the broker has done this, he is forbidden from hedging his delta (*pre-hedging*). The problem is that, by showing the trade on the floor, the broker is advertising to the world the position he is about to take and, by implication, the delta he will need to trade. This makes him vulnerable to being front-run by other brokers looking to benefit from the market impact of the delta hedge. This can be costly for the broker, who will have more difficultly executing his delta hedge, as well as the client, who will be charged a wider bid-offer spread on the option as the broker factors in the greater impact of the delta hedge (his own trading plus that of others who jump in front of him).

   In this case the broker may offer the client an OTC *listed-lookalike*—an over-the-counter option with precisely the same terms as the listed option the client has requested. If the option is traded OTC, it is no longer subject to the exchange trading rules and the delta hedge can be done more discreetly. The broker can work his delta carefully in the market and then fill the client trade based on his hedge price or, if the client requires a risk price, he can price the trade more aggressively knowing that he will not be required to advertise his position to the market. If the client has the ability to trade OTC derivatives easily (i.e., sufficient middle office support) the listed lookalike can often be a cheaper and much more attractive alternative to an exchange-listed option.

3. *Exotic options:* All exchange-listed options are plain-vanilla—either calls or puts with European or American exercise. With OTC products, however, there are an infinite variety of possible payouts that can

be designed and within most large investment banks there will be a dedicated group of *financial engineers* who focus on the pricing, structuring, and risk management of *exotic options.* These unusual payoffs are particularly popular in Europe where they are used to create complex capital guaranteed structures (i.e., the worst-case scenario is that the investor only gets back what they invested) that are sold through retail banks to individual investors.[8]

Exotic Options

Exotic derivatives are a tremendously broad and complex field and a proper explanation requires a level of mathematical sophistication far above what is necessary for most salespeople and traders or appropriate to this book. For this reason, we will examine only superficially some of the more common types of exotics and their more important characteristics and relevant terminology. A tremendous amount has been written on all aspects of the exotic derivatives businesses and interested readers will have little difficulty finding other books that provide a more complete treatment.

While the number of possible payout structures that can be created with exotic options is unlimited, there are certain characteristics—either relating to the payoff structure or the risks in reproducing that payoff—that recur in many different options. We will utilize these common properties to structure our presentation of the exotic structures described below. This not only assists the reader in learning and remembering the different types of payoffs, but also provides a useful framework for understanding the structure of other exotic options that the reader may encounter later.

Discontinuous Payoffs Plain-vanilla options have a "kinked" payoff in which the behavior above and below the strike price is different. The line, however, is still continuous—it can be drawn without lifting the pencil. Some exotic options have payoffs that are discontinuous and instantaneously jump from one price to another.

- *Binary option* (also known as a *digital* or *all-or-nothing* option): Pays either a fixed amount or zero depending on whether the option expires in- or out-of-the-money. The payoff is constant no matter how far the option expires in the money (unlike a regular option that moves one-for-one when the option is in the money).

Path Dependence Path dependence is one of the more common characteristics of exotic options. Path dependent options are those in which the payoff depends not just on where the stock price ends up, but on how it got there.

- *Look-back option:* The payoff at maturity depends on the high or low price achieved by the underlying stock during the life of the option. The long holder gets the benefit of exercising at the best possible price during the life of the option.[9]
- *Barrier option:* Barrier options are plain-vanilla calls or puts that specify a *trigger level* (the *barrier*) at which the option either comes to life (*knocks-in*) or is cancelled (*knocks-out*). Depending on whether the trigger level is above or below the spot price, the option receives either an "*up*" or "*down*" prefix. For example, an at-the-money call that starts life switched off but has a trigger level 5 percent below the spot price that causes the option to come to life would be a *down-and-in* call. If the same call were initially "alive" and had a 5 percent out-of-the-money trigger that caused it to be cancelled, it would be a *down-and-out* call. Note that, because it is immediately activated or extinguished upon hitting the trigger, a barrier option also has a potential discontinuity in the payoff.
- *Asian option:* A call or put where the payoff at maturity is based on the average price of the stock over the period (measured at some pre-defined observation intervals) rather than just the stock price at maturity. Asian options, though more complex, are less risky because the sensitivity of the option to changes in the price of the underlier decreases with time as more and more price averaging observations are made.

"Vol of Vol"   In order to price some options, it is necessary to estimate not only the volatility of the underlying stock between today and a future date (i.e., how far is the stock likely to go?) but also the volatility of the implied volatility at which the options on that stock will trade (i.e., how much is the implied volatility likely to change?) The fact that we are looking to price the volatility of volatility ("vol of vol") indicates we are clearly not in a Black-Scholes framework anymore.

- *Forward-starting option:* The client buys an option that is struck based on the level of the market at some point in the future. For example, the client pays today for a three-month at-the-money call that will not be struck until two months in the future. The broker must determine what stock price is likely to define at-the-money in two months' time, as well as what the level of implied volatility is likely to be at that time.
- *Cliquet:* A cliquet option is made up of a series of prepaid forward starting options. For example, rather than buying a one-year, at-the-money

call, the client pays up-front for a series of four, successive three-month at-the-money options, each one struck at the expiration of the previous contract. Because the strike price is reset to the current market price at each observation, the client captures a rally in the stock price over any one of the three-month periods, even if the final stock price is lower than the initial stock price.

Cross-Currency   As we saw with swaps and single stocks, the effect of currency is a complicating factor for international investment. The same holds true for options. A call or put option on a foreign stock will carry similar currency exposures to a forward or swap. If the client wishes to eliminate this (i.e., buy a call on the Nikkei and ignore the fact that it prices in JPY and not USD) he can buy a *quanto option*, which, like a quanto swap, locks in a fixed exchange rate for the life of the option.

Correlation   When the payoff of an option depends on the performance of a group of underliers, the pricing of the option will depend on the degree of correlation in their movements. A simple case of this is a plain-vanilla call or put on a basket of stocks. If the underliers are highly correlated, the volatility of the basket as a whole will be close to the weighted average of the volatilities of the individual underliers. If the correlation is very low, there will be a significant amount of cancellation among the movements of the underlying stocks (some go down while others go up) and the overall basket will experience a lower volatility as a result.

- *Best-of/Worst-of options:* An option whose payout depends on the best- or worst-performing stock from within a group. The pricing of the structure—and the uses for it—depend on the degree of correlation between the movements of the stocks in the group. For example, if the client believes there will be significant dispersion in the returns of the stocks in the basket, the structure can be used to capture the return under the best possible scenario. For example, in a winner-take-all scenario involving competition for a contract among multiple companies, the winning stock is likely to perform very well, while the other stocks perform poorly. A client can capture the return of the best performing stock without knowing which company will actually win. The greater the dispersion of returns, the more the broker may potentially have to pay to the client, resulting in a higher price of the option. The broker is, in this case, long correlation—he wants all the stocks to perform similarly. The premium for a best-of call on a basket with very low correlation will therefore be very high because of the risk that a one-off event poses to the broker.

Alternatively, a worst-of call can be used to reduce the premium paid in the case where the client is of the view that all stocks will perform well—the "rising tide lifts all boats" scenario. For example, if the client believes that the market is going to fundamentally reconsider the future prospects for an entire industry, leading to an upward move in all stocks, he can buy a worst-of call. If all stocks perform generally well, he will still earn an attractive return but have paid a much lower premium for it. However, if one stock performs badly, and loses money, he will receive nothing. In this case, it is the client who is long correlation—he not only wants stocks to go up—because he owns a call—but he wants them all to go up.

In addition to trading correlation as a part of the facilitation of client orders in exotics, many firms will have a dedicated trader or group of traders who focus exclusively on trading correlation from a proprietary perspective. One way in which this is done is with a special type of volatility trading book called a *dispersion book*. In very simplified terms, the trader on a dispersion book will use single-stock and index derivatives, both listed and over-the-counter, to express a view on the difference between the average volatility of the constituent stocks of an index and the volatility of the index as a whole. The difference between mean single stock vol and index vol will increase as the dispersion of returns of the constituent stocks increases (due to cancelling) and decrease as stocks become more correlated (and all move as one). While at first glance, correlation may seem like a rather obscure "asset" to trade, it is actually an integral part of the movements of markets. A significant correction in a broad benchmark index is often composed of many relatively unexceptional single stock moves that just happen to all occur at the same time. What makes the market movement special is not the magnitude of the move in any particular stock but the high degree of correlation in the movements of all stocks.

Variance Swaps (Volatility Swaps)   Options provide a means of expressing a view on the future level of volatility in a given underlier. Unfortunately, while this is an attractive trade for many investors, the means by which it can be implemented—the continual hedging of a delta-neutral position in an option—is very labor-intensive and subject to significant slippages. *Variance swaps* and *volatility swaps* provide a means of expressing a pure bet on the level of realized volatility over a time period. In practice, variance swaps (swaps on squared volatility) are much more popular than volatility swaps because they are much easier to hedge. However, the two structures are conceptually identical and since readers will be more familiar with volatility than variance we will frame our explanation in terms of a volatility swap.

As is usually the case with swaps, the structure is simple; based on an agreed-upon notional value per percentage point of volatility, the long holder of the swap pays a "fixed" level of volatility and receives the realized level of volatility over the period. The long swap holder is the one paying a fixed rate to receive actual volatility—he benefits from increased volatility.

Consider an example in which, with current levels of realized volatility of 20 percent, an investor decides that markets are too complacent about the risks to the economy and that there will be a significant increase in market volatility in the next three months. He asks a broker for an offer on an SPX volatility swap for $100,000 vega—that is, at what price is the broker willing to "go short volatility" based on a notional payment of $100,000 per 1 percent difference between the broker's offer level and the level of realized volatility over the period. The broker offers three month SPX vol at 21.5 percent and the client agrees to trade for $100,000 notional. The client has now agreed to make a fixed payment of $100,000 × 21.5 = $2,150,000 at the maturity of the swap, and will receive in return $100,000 per percentage point of realized volatility during the time period. At the maturity of the swap in three months' time, the realized volatility (in annualized terms) during the period is calculated to be 26 percent. The broker must now pay to the client $100,000 × 26 = $2.6 million, resulting in a net payment to the client of $450,000 or $100,000 on 4.5 points of vega.

The popularity of variance and volatility swaps is largely due to the fact that they are pure bets on volatility—the client in the above example is long $100,000 of vega with no other Greek exposures to hedge and that they are "easy" to trade: the options market maker deals with the complex and time-consuming delta-hedging work while the client gets a simple swap structure.

SUMMARY

One of the key components of an option's price is the market's expectation of the future volatility of the underlying asset. A volatility trader uses delta-hedged option positions to express views on the level of volatility of the underlier. There are two ways he can profit from the delta-neutral position: through a change in the level of implied volatility, which immediately impacts the value of the option position, or by capturing the difference between the implied volatility of the option and the realized volatility of the underlier through the continuous re-hedging of the delta-neutral position. The slippage between the curved profile of the option price $C(S)$ and the straight-line approximation of the delta hedge is what allows the trader to capitalize on the difference between implied and realized volatility.

In order to risk manage large portfolios of option positions, a trader must be able to decompose the risks of each option position (and stock or other derivatives) and aggregate them across the whole book. This is done by computing the partial derivative with respect to each of the underlying variables that determine the option price. Each partial derivative is assigned a Greek letter: delta (Δ) measures the option sensitivity to changes in the price of the underlier; gamma (Γ) measures the sensitivity of the delta to changes in the underlier; theta (θ) measures the loss of value of the option with the passage of time; the pseudo-Greek letter "vega" (V) measures the sensitivity to changes in implied volatility; and rho (ρ) measures the sensitivity to changes in interest rates. Each of the Greeks is itself a function of the same five underlying variables that determine the option price. Changes in these variables not only affect the option price but also its subsequent sensitivity to changes in these same variables.

While the coverage of options has been primarily focused on plain-vanilla calls and puts, there is an extensive market for more complex exotic payoffs. Common characteristics of exotic derivatives are path dependence, discontinuous jumps in the payout, sensitivity to the volatility of volatility, or the correlation among assets.

CHAPTER 11

The Trading Floor

INTRODUCTION

One of the most exciting parts of working in the sales and trading business of an investment bank is sitting on the trading floor. Most trading floors are structured with large open floor plans and long desks where traders or salespeople sit side by side, surrounded by computer monitors, televisions, risk reports, research articles, newspapers, telephones, and a mishmash of personal items (family photos, food, candy, toys, aspirin, coffee cups, and just about anything else). There are no cubicles or other delineations of private space and even the management offices that generally surround the periphery of the floor have glass walls. Shouting across the floor is not only permitted, but encouraged, as this is often the quickest way to communicate information either across a distance or to a large group of people. Traders and salespeople tend to thrive on the buzz of the trading floor and the worst thing, both for morale and as an indicator of activity, is a trading floor that sounds like a library. The trading floor banter is challenging and aggressive—it is not a genteel place. The most successful traders and salespeople tend not only to be good at their jobs, but have a quick wit, personality, and presence. It is a unique work environment and for those who enjoy it, the transition off the floor can be a difficult one.

To a new arrival, "the floor" can appear extremely chaotic, with the sort of noise level one might expect to find in a factory but not inside a global investment bank. In reality, management gives a tremendous amount of thought to the layout of the trading floor and its apparently disorganized structure is, in fact, the deliberate result of a long evolutionary process driven by the joint pressures of ever-increasing client demands and the firm's own relentless pursuit of profits.

ORGANIZATION OF THE SALES AND TRADING BUSINESSES

The primary focus in the design of the trading floor is the maximization of the efficiency with which information is transmitted. The nature of that information, and the benefits of proper communication depend on the groups involved but all contribute in one form or another to the goals of minimizing risk, maximizing profitability, and providing the best possible client service.

The urgency of information flow varies greatly from product to product: a client asking for a risk price on a single stock or listed option trade would reasonably expect the broker to make a market on the wire while a client looking to price a complex, long-dated structured derivative will understand that this sort of product requires much longer to price and has a very different expectation for the appropriate turnaround time for the broker to respond.

An equally important challenge is the need to *prevent* information from flowing between particular groups. There is a great deal of confidential information inside an investment bank that must be treated properly, whether because it is "material, nonpublic" information, whose misuse by traders or salespeople can result in federal legal action, or simply because it relates to the trading activity or positions of clients that would quickly pull business away from any broker suspected of treating it with insufficient confidentiality. In order to prevent the misuse—or even the suspicion or perception of misuse—of confidential information, certain groups, such as Equities Research, Prime Brokerage, Electronic Trading (DMA), and Investment Banking, are separated physically from the trading floor, either by locked doors with limited access or by placing the entire group on a different floor or building.

Trading floors have been historically divided according first by function (sales or trading) and then by product (stock, options, program trading, etc.). While it is both natural and beneficial for people who perform the same function to sit next to each other, over time many firms have seen the advantage of distributing the floor based on other criteria.

Trading

Today, it is common to see cash trading and vol trading intermixed and broken down by sector rather than product. This allows for the quick transmission of information about flows in particular groups of stocks between the traders who operate in them. There is an obvious logic to this approach: if a cash trader is asked to provide a bid for a stock, he will determine his price based on where he believes he can sell out of the stock given his knowledge of the current market conditions and liquidity. If at the same time the vol trader is asked to provide an offer in a large number of at-the-money puts, he will need to assess where he can sell stock as a delta-hedge. Both traders are making a price based on an assessment of the likely short-term direction and liquidity of the stock. If they price the trades independently, their assessments of their ability to sell stock to hedge the position will be excessively optimistic. If each knows what the other is quoting, and the likely market impact of the other's actions, they will both make a more accurate price and better manage the risk to the firm.

Sales Trading

In general, sales-traders specialize in a particular product (derivatives, cash, program trading) but also cover a particular client base, which may be defined by client (e.g., hedge fund, pension fund) or the client's regional location (this is particularly common in Europe). This poses a problem: clearly it is easier for a group of sales-traders sitting close together to provide a consistently high level of client service to a particular group of clients, but should the priority be given to the type of client covered, or the type of product? If our goal is that the best backup to each sales trader is sitting beside him, who should we place next to a sales trader who specializes in selling derivatives to hedge funds? One option would be another hedge fund sales trader whose expertise is in cash trading. This person will certainly be aware of the type of response time and interaction that the client will expect, but may be unable to properly service client inquiries if he does not understand the product terminology and concepts. Alternatively, it could be a specialist in derivatives that is more accustomed to dealing with pension funds. Here the issue is not one of comprehension but of style: a trader accustomed to pricing longer-dated exotic structures over several hours will be unaccustomed to the urgency and demanding style typical of hedge fund traders.

There is no consensus among Wall Street firms as to which is the best structure for the sales trading desks and different firms use different models. In the end, what matters is that the necessary level of service is provided to clients. Many large clients have direct lines to multiple brokers and a phone that rings three times without being picked up, or is picked up and poorly attended to, can lead to a lost trade and the next phone call going to a more attentive and capable sales trader at another firm.

One group that is almost always seated separately is international program sales trading. Global portfolio trading requires very specific knowledge of trading systems and global markets that other cash or derivative salespeople would be unable to provide. Additionally, the client base that trades international program trades is more homogeneous than in other products, making it easier for one program trading salesperson to cover for another.

Sales

The generalist salesforce, who do not take client orders but are there to provide information, research, and other services, usually sits separately from both the traders and the sales traders. The appropriate servicing of client orders depends on the urgent flow of information between sales traders and traders, which is facilitated by close physical proximity. The interspersing of generalist salespeople into the parts of the floor where client orders are managed would create unnecessary interruptions in the flow of information and increased separation between traders and salespeople. It is also more difficult for a salesperson to have a relaxed conversation with a portfolio manager about news events and market flows when they are surrounded by traders and salespeople shouting at each other.

The positioning of the specialist salespeople differs from firm to firm. At some investment banks, the specialist sales force is separated off similarly to the generalist sales force in order to focus on client coverage. Other firms stress the specialist salesperson's role as floor authority in the goings-on of a particular sector and therefore intersperse them among the traders so that the authority on the stock is sitting next to the person who is being asked to work orders, commit capital, and take proprietary positions. The correct answer depends on the culture of the firm and the personalities of the specialist salespeople and how they view their role: some very much enjoy the close interaction with trading while others do not.

Portfolio Trading and ETFs

With the increase in program trading (PT) activity in recent years there has been a gradual recognition that, frequently, the largest orders in a particular stock may not be executed through the cash desk but through the program trading desk. Because program trading activity crosses all sectors, it has become common to place the program trading desk centrally on the trading floor to ensure that information about flows in different sectors can be rapidly transferred to all the relevant sector traders. This is particularly important at firms with an active program trading risk book. Additionally, this layout maximizes any opportunities for crossing of flows between the PT desk and the other cash traders.

The ETF trading desk is generally located directly beside program trading for similar reasons. ETF trading desks source the liquidity of the underlying cash markets in order to facilitate client flows. A consequence of the massive increases in trading activity is that much of the movement in the underlying stocks can be attributed to the activity in the sector ETFs. By placing the ETF trading desk in the middle of the floor, surrounded by the cash traders, the information about these trading flows is disseminated to the relevant trading desks more quickly. While a sector-specific cash trader can report on the presence or absence of activity in their sector, unless this information is aggregated across all sectors it gives a limited picture of what is going on in the market. The PT or ETF trader can report on what is happening in all sectors because he is involved in all of them.

Equity Finance/Swaps Trading

Equity finance is a broad term covering many different types of products, all of which provides one-delta (i.e., no volatility) exposure to equity underliers. This includes trading in swaps as well as certificates, put-call combos and zero-strike calls.[1] The type of trading and business mix of the equity finance desk varies significantly between Wall Street firms. At some, the focus is on structured transactions where almost no directional risk or execution is taken and the interaction with sales and trading is quite limited. At other firms, the equity finance desk is an integral part of the flow business and the swap is used simply as a convenient wrapper that facilitates directional trading in the underliers.

Because these very different types of business lines are all captured under the broad heading of equity finance, it is often difficult to determine where the group should sit on the floor. The right answer depends very much on the focus of the business mix of the particular desk. If the focus is primarily on structured trades, the desk can be comfortably located around the periphery of the trading floor since the traders neither require nor particularly benefit from the rapid flow of information with the other trading groups. For desks with a significant component of flow-related trading, the proximity to the other trading businesses will be more essential. It is generally the case that the swaps desk is placed closely to the program trading and ETF desks given the large percentage of swap flow that is index-related.

Futures Execution

The futures execution desk provides agency execution services for futures orders. While many clients trade their futures directly on the exchange there is a large component of the client base of a typical Wall Street investment bank that understands investing and stock selection well, but has a very limited understanding of execution. These clients benefit greatly from having a broker who understands the trading mechanics and structure of the futures and roll markets and can work their orders for them to achieve the best possible execution.

Index Options and Exotics

While the single name option traders are often intermixed with the cash traders, the index option traders exist as a separate group. Although our discussion of index products have been primarily been from the viewpoint of a replicating stock portfolio, in practice virtually all of the hedging on the index options desk is done at the index level, via futures or ETFs. In terms of information flow, the index options desks benefits most from proximity to the ETF and futures execution desks, where other index products are traded and offsetting flows can be encountered. Due to the high percentage of exotic derivatives that are based on indices, the exotic derivatives desk is usually located directly beside the index vol desk, though closer to the periphery, due to the less flow-like nature of the product.

OTHER GROUPS

There are other groups either seated on the trading floor or closely associated to it that provide services which are not strictly part of the front office sales and trading business but are nevertheless essential to its success. In what follows we present a brief overview of what these groups do and how they interact with the activities of the trading floor.

Quantitative/Derivative Strategies

It is common to find on the trading floor a group that is neither trading nor sales, and whose responsibility it is to provide quantitative analytics of various types to traders, salespeople, and clients. The analytics provided may be done on a reactive basis, in response to an inquiry, or proactively pushed out to clients via publications. Common types of analysis include:

- Calculation of index add/deletes and rebalance trades with estimates of expected inflows and outflows and resulting liquidity imbalances.
- Historical comparisons of the level of implied volatility, term structure (e.g., spread between 3 and 12 month implied vols), skewness, and correlation across broad indices and sectors.
- Analysis of the risks and factor exposures (market capitalization, sector, style) of client portfolios and the estimation of expected execution costs, market impact, liquidity limitations, and tracking risk.
- Construction of tracking portfolios and alternative hedging strategies for benchmark indices with estimations of expected and historical tracking error.

- Explanation of the structure, risks, and trading mechanics of derivative products, both in written publications and direct client presentations.
- Recommendations of trading ideas based on directional and volatility views.

While the role of the derivatives strategist could colloquially be described as that of a research analyst focusing on derivative and portfolio products, there is an important legal distinction between what can be called "Research" and other types of analysis. For this reason, these quantitative groups generally use the more loosely defined term "Strategy" when they are located on the trading floor and are only called "Research" if they sit on the other side of the Chinese wall from Sales and Trading.

Securities Lending (Stock Loan)

Throughout the book we have considered trading strategies that require the sale of borrowed stock. The Securities Lending group (commonly referred to as *stock loan*) exists to facilitate this process by acting as an intermediary, finding long holders willing to lend their shares and providing these shares to both external clients and internal trading desks to cover short sales.

The short sale of borrowed stock is a somewhat curious concept that many people find confusing initially because it does not really exist in the market for nonfinancial assets. In most cases you cannot sell something you do not already own. An important first step is to understand that the meanings of "loan" and "borrow" in a securities lending context are different from their colloquial use. A loan of shares is actually a complete transfer of beneficial ownership; the party that borrows the shares takes on all the rights and benefits of actual ownership as though they had purchased them in the market, including being the recipient of dividends and voting rights. The difference between a physical sale in the market and a loan is that the loan is governed by a stock loan agreement, signed by both the lender and borrower, which stipulates that:

- The loan is collateralized, either with cash or other securities, to protect against loss.
- The lender has the right to recall the shares at any time and the borrower is obliged to return those shares, either buying them back in the market or finding another lender.
- During the time the borrower holds the shares, he must make payments back to the lender that replicate all of the economic benefits of holding the long stock.

Economically, the only difference the long holder experiences between holding the long shares and having lent them out is the fee received for the loan. The economics of price movements, dividends, and corporate actions are all recreated in the long holders' account and charged against the borrower. Legally, however, the ownership of the shares has been transferred to the borrower and the long holder is no longer actually long but synthetically long. The most important difference between being physically and synthetically long is the right to vote. The stock borrower can manufacture back economic benefits but cannot guarantee that the shares will be voted in accordance with the wishes of the original long holder because once those shares are sold short in the market, the fractional ownership in the corporation that they represent is passed to the buyer, who does not know whether stock was sold short or not, and does not need to care. The purchase of shares brings with it the right to vote those shares. The new buyer and the original lender cannot both vote because there are only as many votes as there are shares. (Otherwise the lending of shares would dilute the voting rights of all shareholders.)

This does not mean that lenders of shares cannot vote or attend the *annual general meeting* (AGM). As per the stock loan agreement, they have the right to recall their lent shares at any time and by doing so, regain ownership and with it, voting rights. This is a risk to the borrower since, if the borrow cannot be covered by another lender for whom the right to vote is not important,[2] the shares will need to be repurchased in the market, even if the price is economically unattractive. If the borrower refuses to do so, the position will be *bought in* by the broker and his account charged.

When an investor wishes to take a short position she must first *get a locate*, that is, find someone who will lend her the shares by contacting the stock loan desk and indicating the particular security and the number of shares she wants to borrow. In general, the borrower will not specify for what length of time the shares will be needed since she herself will usually not know. (It depends on the stock's performance.) Stock loan desks will usually offer, for an additional fee, the option to receive *term borrow,* in which the borrower is guaranteed to not be recalled on the shares for a certain period of time. The higher fee compensates the stock loan desk for the fact that, in the event that borrow is lost before the term period is up, the shares will need to be bought in the market to cover the loan, which would expose it to market risk. Term borrow is most common in structured transactions where the parties involved wish to remove the borrow risk from the equation and request a term commitment.

When a client requests a locate, the stock loan desk removes the requested quantity of shares from the pool of available inventory that will be shown to other clients for the rest of that day. The client can then choose at what times, and at what prices during the day he wants to short stock. The locate is only good for one day; if the client decides to wait longer before selling the shares, he will need to get a fresh locate when he decides to trade and runs the risk that the borrow is no longer available. If the client is interested in shorting a very hard-to-borrow name but is unsure of precisely when he wants to sell the shares (or if he needs several days to execute the order due to poor liquidity), he may request that the broker deliver the shares to his account and begin paying for the borrow before he has actually sold anything. While this incurs a small additional cost, it allows the client more flexibility in how they execute the trade.

The short sale of stock raises cash in the borrower's account, which is then posted to the lender as collateral to secure the loan of shares. This cash carns interest while sitting with the lender, which is paid back to the borrower minus a small spread. This spread, called the *borrow rate*, is the payment to the lender for lending the stock and is generally in the range of 40 to 50 basis points per annum for easy to borrow stocks. When a stock becomes hard-to-borrow, rates can increase to several percent or even as high as 10 to 20 percent in extreme situations. The borrow rate is a function of the supply and demand in the stock loan market and higher rates can be the result of either increased demand (due to negative news or poor stock price performance) or decreased supply (just before the AGM when long holders recall shares to vote or because a previous source of borrow recalls their shares) or both.

When a client requests a locate, the stock loan desk will indicate whether there are shares available and if so, how many, and at what rate. In names that are difficult to borrow, the desk will also give an indication of the stability of the borrow—whether it can be sourced from multiple lenders or a single holder, and whether the lenders are long-term holders or short-term traders who are likely to sell out of their position—so that the client has appropriate expectations about the likelihood of recall. In the language of the stock loan desk, an easy-to-borrow stock is *cold* or *gc* (an abbreviation for *general collateral*), whereas a hard-to-borrow stock is *hot* or *special* (for *special collateral*).

The ability to borrow and lend shares is an essential component of the efficient functioning of the equity market. An investor can always buy a stock he thinks will go up and wait to sell it at a higher price in the future. However, if the investor believes the stock is overpriced and will correct, unless he has the ability to sell now and buy back later, he cannot profit from the mispricing. This creates an asymmetry in the views market participants can express and prevents the market price of stocks for properly reflecting all available information about the company. While most developed markets allow for stock lending, the exchange rules in many emerging markets prevent it, though in these cases, the economics of short-selling can be, to some degree, replicated via equity swaps.

The lack of a stock lending market also prevents the proper functioning of the market for equity derivatives. Without the ability to sell short, brokers are limited in the degree to which they can facilitate option trades (a client purchase of puts or sale of calls) or implement a long futures vs. short stock index arbitrage.

An issue that has received particular attention in the United States in recent years is *naked short selling,* that is, short sales undertaken without securing a borrow. Due to the massive size and transaction volumes in the United States, there are thousands of trades every day that fail to settle on time. Most of these are due to small operational frictions (misbooked trades, price discrepancies, and the like) that are late to be amended, and are cleared up quickly. However, there are some trades that are deliberate short sales where there is no possibility of covering the borrow. Since brokers are reluctant to take the confrontational step of buying-in a client on a failed share delivery, there will usually be a period of time—from a few days to a couple weeks—during which the broker tries to help the client resolve the issue.[3] In a naked short, the seller hopes that the delays in buying-in the uncovered position will be sufficient that a profit can be made on the short position without ever finding a lender.

In 2005 the SEC enacted Regulation SHO, which created new regulations for the stock loan market, some of them designed specifically to target naked short sales. Despite ample media coverage and a great deal of complaining by the managements of companies whose stock prices had declined sharply, deliberate and persistent naked shorting for the purpose of manipulating stock prices is a very rare occurrence.

While a client request for a locate is by no means a guarantee that he will sell shares short, it does at least indicate that the client is thinking about the possibility and will, in some percentage of cases, lead to a sale. This information can be sensitive, particularly when the quantity requested is large in relation to the liquidity in the stock, knowledge of which would encourage other clients or traders to make sales in anticipation of the sustained downward pressure on the stock price from a short sale. For this reason, there are information barriers between the sales and trading businesses and the stock loan desk is very careful to ensure that no information regarding client positions or inquiries is leaked either externally or to the firm's own traders.

Prime Brokerage

Prime brokerage (PB) is an umbrella term covering a broad range of client services, including securities lending, custodial services (booking, clearing, settlement, position management), financing, operational and technological support offered by broker dealers to hedge funds and other institutional clients. Compared with some of the "sexier" businesses of sales and trading, many of the services offered by the prime brokerage business can appear relatively unglamorous, however, they are integral to client firms' ability to function effectively, manage risk, and maximize efficiency. As a consequence of the rapid expansion of the hedge fund industry in recent years, the prime brokerage business has become one of the most important growth areas at many firms and an extraordinarily important component of the client relationship.

In general, most small investment firms have only one prime broker who manages all of their positions and accounts. They may have executing relationships with multiple brokers but the final position clearing, settlement, and payment is all coordinated through a single prime broker. When a new fund is being launched with high expectations for future success, multiple investment banks will try to win the prime brokerage mandate for the new fund. Later, when funds are larger, they will often have relationships with multiple prime brokers.

There are many ways in which a particular firm can differentiate its prime brokerage product including:

- *Superior client reporting:* Although it is expected that all firms will keep accurate track of positions, clients will prefer those brokers who provide more detailed, transparent, and intelligently structured reporting tools (usually web-based) for use in position reconciliation. The clarity with which corporate actions are processed is a key component.
- *Lower prices:* Prime brokers earn financing spreads on funds loaned to clients to increase leverage, as well as on stocks lent to facilitate short sales. While firms will generally prefer to differentiate themselves based on the quality of their product, new entrants into the prime brokerage business often find the easiest way to attract business is by competing on price.
- *Margin and collateral:* Many clients will look to leverage their ideas as much as possible to extract the maximum value from their trades. The lower the margin and collateral rates required by the prime broker, the higher the leverage that can be attained, which is attractive to clients. This must be balanced with the increased risk to the firm from lower margin requirements in the event of an inability to pay by the client. Many brokers will calculate margin requirements for clients based on the combined exposure of all of their holdings, taking into account the offsetting risks of different positions to reduce the total amount of collateral that must be posted.

- *Capital introduction:* Investment banks have an extensive network of relationships with institutional investors, corporations, and private families. This allows them to play an important matchmaking role for funds looking to increase their assets under management. Capital introduction refers to the act of connecting the management of funds looking for assets with potential investors.

While the maintenance of a positive and productive relationship with clients is extremely important for the sales and trading division, the nature of the interaction is such that, in many cases, the economic interests of the broker and client are opposed—what one makes, the other loses—and both parties are reluctant to disclose any information that could be used against them by the other. Many clients trade with multiple brokers simply to ensure that no broker has sufficient information to infer what their positions are.

The prime brokerage relationship is very different: The client not only discloses all of his positions to his prime broker, but passes over the responsibility for maintaining and monitoring those positions. In order for this relationship to work, clients must have total confidence in the integrity of the information barriers between PB and the sales and trading businesses. Fortunately, this is a case where both the broker and client interests are aligned. Prime brokerage is a multibillion dollar business for Wall Street and investment banks have much more to lose from a loss of client faith in the confidentiality of their positions than could ever be gained through improper trading based on that information. For this reason, there are strictly enforced and well-respected Chinese walls between the prime brokerage and sales and trading businesses.

Legal and Compliance

While the work of both the legal and compliance divisions are concerned with ensuring that the activities of the firm comply with the letter and spirit of the laws that govern the financial services industry, the specific roles and responsibilities of the two groups are quite different.

The *Compliance Department* (*"Compliance"*), as its name implies, is concerned with ensuring that the day-to-day activities of the sales and trading business comply with the relevant laws, exchange regulations and industry best practices. Compliance is responsible for making sure that traders and salespeople are properly licensed, have received the required training, and are sufficiently knowledgeable of the rules and regulations that govern their behavior and the consequences for breaches of those rules. There will usually be one or more members of Compliance who sit on the trading floor to provide quick answers to any questions that arise. A large part of the oversight responsibilities of the compliance groups is related to exchange rules and regulations that, while not laws, must be observed to avoid fines, sanctions, or loss of permission to trade on the exchange.

The *Legal Department* (*"Legal"*) of a global investment bank is a massive operation that touches on almost every part of firm activity—from investment banking to sales and trading to human resources. The Legal Department has specialists with detailed knowledge of not only the laws, but also the court rulings and legal precedents that shape the interpretation of the rules and regulations that govern activities in each part of the firm's business. In relation to the sales and trading business, Legal will sometimes act as a backup to the Compliance Division for situations where the appropriate approach to a particular trade or structure is unclear and requires clarification. Other areas where the Legal Department will become involved include specification of contract terms on derivatives that involve a novel structure or the approval of new structured trades that are designed to provide a particular legal or fiscal benefit.

LICENSING AND REGISTRATION: REGULATION OF THE FINANCIAL SERVICES INDUSTRY

The securities industry in the United States is subjected to a tremendous amount of regulatory scrutiny, both from the federal government as well as other nongovernmental organizations. The reasons for this are obvious enough; an efficiently run, transparent, and fair securities market is essential to the long-run financial success of American businesses and investors, and it is in the national interest that the government plays an oversight role to prevent abuses and ensure investors have confidence in the system.

While a certain level of government involvement is undoubtedly warranted, it is becoming increasingly clear that the level of regulatory intervention in the United States has become excessively burdensome and is actually driving away investment to less onerous regulatory environments, particularly Europe. Many of the investor protection rules developed in recent years, while no doubt well-intentioned, have imposed restrictions on brokers that are so limiting that they eventually hurt investors. One of the primary difficulties with recent trends in regulation has been the lack of differentiation between the level of

(Continued)

(Continued)

protection required for financially naïve "mom-and-pop" investors, and the protections necessary for a highly sophisticated, multibillion dollar hedge fund pushing a broker to provide capital commitment on trades worth tens of millions of dollars.

The primary governmental body responsible for the oversight of the securities industry is the Securities and Exchange Commission (SEC), which was created by the Securities Act of 1934. While the SEC has the final word on most issues, the pace of innovation is such that the day-to-day monitoring of trading activity is best left to parties much closer to the action. The SEC therefore endows certain *self-regulatory organizations (SRO)* with the oversight responsibility for their local markets. The largest of these is the Financial Industry Regulatory Authority (FINRA), which was created in 2007 through the merger of the regulatory arm of the NYSE and the National Association of Securities Dealers (NASD). FINRA has supervisory responsibility over all securities firms doing business in the United States. Other SROs include the Commodity Futures Trading Commission (CFTC), which has oversight for all futures trading, and the regional stock exchanges as well as the options and futures exchanges, each of which is responsible for the regulation of their own activities.

Exams

To ensure that professionals working in the financial services industry have a sufficient understanding of the rules and regulations that guide trading activity in the various products, FINRA has created a system of exams that must be passed by employees in the financial services industry before they can execute trades or take orders for customers. The five most common exams are as follows:

1. *Series 7 (General Securities Representative licensing exam):* All salespeople and traders must pass the Series 7 before they can handle client orders. It is a large exam consisting of 250 multiple-choice questions administered over six hours and requiring substantial preparation. Because the same exam is required of all finance professionals, the breadth of material covered is tremendous. As a result, a new trader or salesperson in the equities division who is still in the process of learning how his own business works must unfortunately study hundreds of pages of notes on the trading of municipal bonds, credit products, and other aspects of

the business that are, at least for the moment, entirely irrelevant to him.

2. *Series 63 (State licensing exam):* This is usually completed shortly after the Series 7 and is, by comparison, a quick and easy exam covering state-level securities regulation.

3. *Series 3 (National Commodity Futures Exam):* Required to trade futures or options in any asset class (not just commodities).

4. *Series 55 (Equity Trader Limited Representative):* Required of anyone who will have the ability to trade equities on an agency or principal basis (print trades to the tape).

5. *Series 24 (General Securities Principal):* It is a good sign if you are asked to take the Series 24 as this is the exam that must be passed in order to take on managerial responsibilities.

Back Office

The *back office* refers generally to the part of the investment bank or broker-dealer that is responsible for ensuring the timely settlement of trades in listed products such as stock, futures, or options and the reconciliation of firm positions. Given the massive volumes that are executed each day, the majority of trade clearing and settlement is automated and requires little or no manual intervention—referred to as *straight-through processing* (STP). The back-office employees are primarily involved with analyzing and resolving mismatched positions and trades that fail to settle properly, called *breaks*.

When a client executes an order over the course of the day, there may be hundreds of separate executions on the exchange that are combined to produce a single average price for the client. This results in two different types of trades being booked; the individual *street-side* executions between the broker and the exchange, and the *customer* trade between the broker and the client. In general, unless there is a technical error by the broker, street-side executions settle easily.

The client trades are far more likely to cause difficulties. When a broker executes a trade, the fill price is provided either verbally or electronically to the client, along with details of the commission rate, trade date, settlement date, and any taxes or exchange fees that must be paid. The client then instructs his prime broker (or custodian) to expect this trade to be charged against his account by the executing broker. The executing broker sends the same trade details to the client's prime broker to be matched off. In order for the trade to settle, all of the trade details must match exactly. Where the trade details alleged by the executing broker do not match those provided by the client, the trade will be rejected with a "*DK*" (short for "don't know"). The three-day settlement cycle for equity trades ensures that the back office has sufficient time to resolve most disputes and guarantees that the trades settle on time. Timely settlement is important not only to keep order in the markets but because one failure to deliver shares on settlement date can trigger a chain of subsequent failures as the sale of those shares by the buyer (or another short seller that has borrowed those shares from the buyer) cannot be delivered upon because the shares have not yet been received.

While the convention is that trades are settled three days after trade date ($T + 3$), it is possible to settle them anywhere from same day ($T + 0$, called *cash settlement*) to $T + 5$. If the settlement date is extended beyond $T + 5$ then the trade is considered to be a forward sale and not a standard equity market transaction. It should be pointed out that, while the language suggests an actual physical delivery of securities, today's securities market is completely electronic and physical share certificates have disappeared entirely.

Virtually all equity trading in the United States is cleared through the *Depository Trust and Clearing Corporation* (DTCC), a holding company whose subsidiaries include the *National Securities Clearing Corporation* (NSCC), which provides clearing and settlement services, and the *Depository Trust Company* (DTC), a member of the Federal Reserve System that acts as custodian and warehouses the positions on behalf of client companies. The other important clearing agent for U.S. securities business is the *Options Clearing Corporation* (OCC), which clears all exchange-listed single name and equity index options.

Clearing, settlement, and custody are businesses where economies of scale produce massive increases in efficiency and reductions in cost. This has driven a great deal of consolidation in the industry since the 1960s. As a result, the size and scope of the operations of DTCC today are staggering: below are a few statistics[4] from 2006:

- Notional value of securities transactions cleared: $1.5 quadrillion ($1,500,000,000,000,000).[5]
- Notional value of securities held in custody at DTCC: $36 trillion (36,000,000,000,000).
- Number of securities held in custody at DTCC: 2.8 million from 108 countries.
- Transactions cleared: 8.5 billion (Highest volume day: 50.1 million transactions).

One of the key efficiencies that results from centralization of transactions through a single clearing house is the netting down of payments across transactions. In 2006 the NSCC reduced the number of transactions requiring payment by 98 percent.

With a stock, once the shares are purchased or sold, the trade is complete and there is nothing more to do until the position is liquidated. For derivatives, while the volumes are much lower, the process is more complicated; the initial execution begins the trade and the unwind terminates it, but during the interim period there is a continued relationship between the holder of the position and the exchange. In both futures and options, there are issues of margin and collateral due to the leverage of the contracts, as well as the final payments that must be made at settlement, be it physical or cash settlement. For single name options, which have American exercise, there is the additional issue of *assignment,* which occurs when an option is exercised early and a short holder is chosen at random by the exchange to be the counterparty with whom the delivery of shares will be settled.

Middle Office

The *Middle Office* is responsible for management of the life cycle of over-the-counter derivatives such as swaps and options. This includes the calculation of payments at reset, the fixing of new interest rates, and any other changes, updates, or adjustments that need to be made. The Middle Office is also responsible for producing confirmations for client trades, which are then delivered to the trading desk for sign-off before being sent to the client. It is also the responsibility of the Middle Office to follow up with clients to ensure that confirmations are signed and returned in a timely fashion as a trade is not formally completed until it has been signed by both parties. If there is a disagreement on any of the details of the swap, no matter how apparently small or apparently insignificant, the Middle Office cannot change the terms unless it is approved by the trading desk as an amendment to the terms and could potentially result in the unintended assumption of a risk that the trading desk has not priced in or agreed to.

Risk Management, Controllers, and Credit

The *Firmwide Risk* division is responsible for assessing, monitoring, and controlling the level of risk taken by the firm across all products. In a global financial services firm this is an extraordinarily complex undertaking involving the analysis and control of many different types of risk, including:

- *Market risk:* The potential for adverse movements in the value of assets held on firm trading books either as proprietary bets or as the result of a client facilitation.

- *Operational risk:* The risk of loss or the assumption of unwanted market risk as a result of operational failures (trades booked incorrectly, miscalculated payments on OTC derivatives, etc.).
- *Systems/Technological risk:* In today's electronic markets, traders are entirely reliant on technology to do their jobs. All software applications are put through rigorous testing before being deployed to the trading desks. Furthermore, back-up trading and risk-management systems must be in place in the event of hardware failure.
- *Model risk:* Unlike stocks or liquid derivative products (index futures) that can be marked to an easily verifiable market price, the pricing and marking-to-market of complex derivatives is done through valuation models that must be carefully checked for accuracy.
- *Pricing controls:* Where inputs in valuation models are not observable in the market, these must be estimated by the trading desk. Clearly there is the potential for manipulation of the inputs by the traders, either to hide losses or produce false gains. Control groups are responsible for ensuring that traders can rigorously justify their markets and, wherever possible, to compare these marks to other more objectively verifiable quantities to assure they are consistent.
- *Compliance risk:* The potential for traders' actions to be in violation of securities law or exchange rules (front-running client orders, insider trading).
- *Reputational risk:* The potential for the firm's reputation to be damaged by the inappropriate actions of traders or salespeople.

From within the sales and trading division, the most prominent of these risks is market risk. The general concept is quite simple: traders' compensation is tied to the profits they make for the firm, and to make a profit, traders must take risk. The desire to limit and control the total risk taken by the firm goes against the individual trader's desire to maximize his book's profits by taking on as much risk as possible. In order to ensure that the total risk taken by the firm is managed appropriately, there is an independent oversight group, whose compensation is not tied to the performance of any particular trading book, which monitors the quantity and types of risk taken by the traders and provides this information to firm management. To guarantee objectivity, the risk management division is separate from the trading division and the risk managers who work on the trading floor do not report to trading floor managers.

The most commonly used metric for quantifying market risk is *value at risk (VaR),* which measures the maximum expected loss for a given level of confidence. For example, a firm might estimate its one-day VaR at $25 million with a 95 percent confidence. That is to say, the firm expects to sustain a one-day trading loss greater than $25 million in only one of every 20 trading days (about once a month).

Obviously a single number can only tell us a limited amount of information about the real risk profile of the firm. One of the common criticisms of VaR is that it indicates nothing about the potential loss in the other 5 percent of cases. To use a crude comparison, Russian roulette has roughly an 83 percent chance of winning you a bit of money ... it's the other 17 percent that causes a few difficulties.

This highlights two common, necessary but demonstrably incorrect assumptions used in the modeling of financial assets. The first is that the returns of asset prices are normally distributed. As we saw in our discussion of options, the existence of fat tails in the distribution of returns (kurtosis) means that events considered very improbable, under the assumption of normality, have a way of occurring with surprisingly high frequency.

The second source of error is the assumption that the historical correlations between assets will remain more or less the same. In practice, hedge fund traders, prop desks, and brokers all talk to each other and frequently end up putting on very similar positions. The problem, from a risk management perspective is that, even if the assets were not correlated in the past, their movements can suddenly become highly synchronized if tens of billions of dollars of hedge fund money become concentrated in these positions and a random trigger event sends everyone running for the door at the same time. It has been seen time and time again that, in periods of market stress, historically uncorrelated assets can suddenly begin moving in lockstep as funds with similar strategies begin aggressively unwinding positions.

Even where valuation models are correct, the business of finance is done by very fallible human beings and there will always be a certain component of risk that results from human error. While the mantra of "double, triple, quadruple check" is drilled into the heads of newly hired junior traders and salespeople by more senior staff, who have seen far too much hard-earned revenue lost through sloppiness, there are also multiple checks and balances built into the firm's systems and processes to catch as many of these inevitable mistakes before too much damage is done.

One of the most important of these checks is provided by the firm's accountants or *controllers*. While each trading desk will produce an end-of-day estimate of their profits of loss on the day, the official P&L is produced on a $T+1$ basis by an independent group whose responsibility it is to mark-to-market all desk positions and compute a daily report of the P&L and how it is attributed across the various trading books, strategies, and positions. The controllers compare their calculation of the P&L with the desk's estimate to ensure consistency. Any significant discrepancies are investigated to determine why the desk thought it made more or less than it really did. Where these deviations are due to demonstrable errors (e.g., an incorrect price used to value a particular asset) the controller can adjust the reported P&L for this. The month-end and quarter-end P&Ls receive particular scrutiny and may be audited by external accountants for accuracy.

Another component of risk management is the assessment of counterparty credit risk. When a client leverages a position by partially funding a position with borrowed funds, whether on a margined stock purchase or the purchase of a future, swap, or option (all of which provide leverage), the broker takes on the credit risk associated with the client's ability to meet margin requirements in the event that the trades move against him. The determination of counterparty credit risk and margin requirements is managed by a separate group from the sales and trading businesses, which is primarily focused on bringing in new business and therefore likely to be excessively optimistic about clients' credit prospects. The job of the *credit risk management* group is made much easier if the firm is the client's only prime broker as this allows the credit group to analyze all of the client's positions to assess more accurately the aggregate risk profile of their investments. If the credit risk assessment is to be computed based on an analysis of only a portion of a client's assets (because the rest are held by another prime broker), then the margin terms are likely to be somewhat more conservative to protect against any potential surprises lurking in the unseen positions.

SUMMARY

The layout of the trading floor is designed to maximize the efficiency with which traders and salespeople communicate, both within their respective groups and with each other, so as to best service client orders and manage risk. The two primary factors in determining the distribution of the sales force are the type of product they specialize in (flow versus structured, cash versus derivative) and the type of client covered.

There are a number of other groups that are outside of the trading floor but that provide services essential to the sales and trading businesses. Some of these groups, such as derivatives strategy or compliance, may have a physical presence on the floor to ensure that traders and salespeople have ready access to their expertise, while others, such as stock loan and prime brokerage, are deliberately separated to ensure that information flow can be strictly controlled.

PART Three

Economics

CHAPTER 12

Macroeconomics for Trading and Sales

INTRODUCTION

The price of a stock, and by implication the value of derivatives on that stock, is a complex and highly unstable function of two principal factors:

1. *Company-specific characteristics:* These are the microeconomic factors that we looked at in the first two chapters on fundamental valuation. (Is the business well run? Do they offer an attractive product?)
2. *Broader macroeconomic conditions:* While a well-run company offering an attractive product can be expected to produce superior returns to a poorly run company selling a low-quality product, neither company will do well if the economy as a whole goes into a downturn. Individuals will only consume if they have the money and confidence to do so, and high levels of unemployment, rising inflation, and low consumer confidence will negatively impact all companies. Though the impact is by no means equal across all businesses, no matter how appealing the specific characteristics of the company, the broader macroeconomic trend will usually dominate and even the best companies will suffer in a downturn.

As a result to properly understand (or better yet, anticipate) the movements of the equity market, an investor must have at least a general knowledge of the structure and functioning of the economy as a whole.

In the first part of the book, we looked at various methods for analyzing the fundamental characteristics of a particular company in order to determine whether its stock represents an attractive investment opportunity. In this final section of the book, we will first examine the overall structure of the economy and then look in more detail at some of the economic data releases that provide investors with information about the macroeconomic forces that impact their investment decisions.

CAPITAL ASSET PRICING MODEL (CAPM)

Economists have developed various models to explain the relationship between the performance of individual stocks and the fluctuations of larger market factors. By far the most popular of these is the *Capital Asset Pricing Model* (CAPM) which, because of its simple, intuitive structure and broad applicability, has become one of the most fundamental concepts in modern finance and serves as the lens through which traders, salespeople, investors, analysts, and economists alike view the market.

In simplified terms, the CAPM decomposes the return (R_S) of a single stock (or portfolio of stocks) into the sum of a market component and a stock-specific component. The market component consists of a multiplier, beta (β), that is applied to the excess return of the market as a whole (R_M) over and above the risk-free rate of return (r_f). The stock-specific return, based on the idiosyncratic characteristics of the particular company (or group of companies) is denoted by alpha (α). The return of the stock is therefore expressed as:

$$R_S = \alpha + \beta(R_M - r_f)$$

The CAPM is ubiquitous in the language of modern finance. Traders, investors, and economists alike refer to a stock's sensitivity to the general market as its "beta"[1] and the excess return earned on a position (above the market return) as "alpha." A stock picker is said to "extract alpha" through his stock selection decisions while an investor who hedges out the broad market sensitivity of his portfolio is said to be "eliminating the beta exposure." The adjustment of the size of a hedge portfolio to accommodate the different market sensitivities of different assets is called "beta-adjusting" a hedge. (Tailing futures is an example of this.)

OVERVIEW OF MACROECONOMICS

In this section we present the macroeconomic concepts, terminology, and relationships most relevant to traders and salespeople in the equities division. We will make no pretenses in this presentation: this is not intended as a formal or rigorous development of the fundamentals of macroeconomics—there are plenty of other books that provide that. Our focus here will be on those aspects of the economy that are most easily observed and whose changes have the greatest impact on financial markets, specifically equities. Our goal is to establish a sufficiently complete macroeconomic framework so that readers can understand the language used in the financial press and the significance of the daily economic data announcements and their impact on the markets.

To this end, we have purposely used colloquial terms in our presentation ("people buy more goods") in lieu of more formal economics language ("an incremental increase in real aggregate consumption"). The approach is also deliberately nonquantitative and focuses on developing an intuitive understanding of what economic data tell us. How much information is lost by this approach depends on whom you ask. Between professional economists and market practitioners there are sharply differing viewpoints about the benefits of applying rigorous mathematical analysis to something as slippery as economic data.

Most professional macroeconomists find themselves employed by one of the three main consumers of economists: academia, government, or Wall Street. When reading any economic analysis, it is important to keep in mind its origin (who wrote it), its audience, and the differences in the viewpoints, motivations, and goals of these groups:

- *Academia:* As Steven Levitt observes in his book *Freakonomics*, if morality is the way people would like the world to work, then economics is the study of how things actually do work. An academic economist's job is to model and understand interrelationships in the economy. Their goal is to answer the question: "What is?"
- *Government:* Economists employed by the government try to determine the appropriate policy actions to keep the economy on a path of stable growth, maximizing total wealth and insuring that it is distributed in the most equitable way possible. Their goal is to turn "What is" into "What should be."
- *Wall Street:* Economists employed on Wall Street are not interested in abstract theories but in the immensely practical and tangible world of markets. Their job is to anticipate the likely future actions of government regulators, consumers, producers, and foreign central banks (among others) and advise the firms that employ them and their clients so that they can position themselves accordingly. Their goal is to determine "What will be" before anyone else.

To compare these three viewpoints, we can consider the following example. Academics theorize what would happen *if* the Fed were to raise rates, policymakers decide whether they *should* raise rates and Wall Street tries to figure out whether the government *will* raise rates (so they can get short the market before it happens).

The Big Three: GDP, Employment, and Inflation

Underlying our study of macroeconomics are three central ideas: the Gross Domestic Product (GDP), which is the core concept around which all of macroeconomics is based; employment; and inflation. While GDP is the most fundamental of the three, employment and inflation are generally more tangible for the average investor given that he can feel their effects directly.

Gross Domestic Product (GDP)   The Gross Domestic Product (GDP) measures the market value of all goods and services produced domestically.[2] In 2007, the U.S. GDP was equal to approximately \$11.7 trillion.[3] The definition of GDP focuses on the location of the production, not the nationality of the producer and therefore includes the value of the croissants produced by a nonresident French baker in New York City but does not include the English classes taught by an American ex-pat living in Beijing. The calculation of GDP is a massive undertaking and is the responsibility of the *Bureau of Economic Analysis* (BEA), an agency of the U.S. government's Department of Commerce. It is released as part of the quarterly *National Income and Product Accounts* (NIPA) report, which contains comprehensive data on all aspects of national economic activity along with regional and sector breakdowns.

While the GDP is a measure of production, the most common method for computing it is actually based on a calculation of the total value of all things consumed and is expressed as:

$$GDP = C + I + G + (X - M)$$

Where the five variables are defined as follows:

1. *Consumer purchases (C):* All goods (both durable and nondurable) and services purchased by households. This includes clothing, food, medicine and transportation but excludes housing.
2. *Fixed investment (I).*[4] Fixed investment by corporations, which consists of purchases of capital goods—the sort of things that would be included on the Plant, Property and Equipment line of the balance sheet—plus any increases in inventory. The inclusion of inventory ensures that all goods that have been produced are accounted for, even if they have not yet been sold. Residential housing is included here.
3. *Government expenditure (G):* Money spent by the government on defense, infrastructure, schools, and so on.
4. *Net exports = Exports – Imports (X-M):* The last component that must be added to our calculation of GDP is net exports, which is the value

of all items produced domestically but sold abroad (exports) less those items purchased domestically that were produced abroad (imports). As mentioned previously, our computation of GDP, which measures the total value of all goods produced, is based on an analysis of the total value of all things purchased. However, purchases and production are equal only in a closed economy that has no net trade with the outside world. If the country is a net exporter (exports more than it imports) then the sum of all domestic purchases will be less than the sum of everything produced. This is because many items produced domestically were sold abroad, making a purchases-based estimate of the GDP too low. The reverse holds true for a country that is a net importer (imports more than it exports)—such as the United States.

The Business Cycle   Exhibit 12.1 shows growth in the real gross domestic product from 1929 through 2007. By "real" we mean that all dollar values have been adjusted for inflation and are expressed in terms of the purchasing power of a dollar at a single point in time (in this case, the year 2000). This adjustment ensures that the growth in the GDP that we see in the graph is indicative of an actual increase in production and not simply a result of increases in the prices being charged for the same items over time. (We will discuss inflation in more detail shortly.)

Looking at the graph we can observe that, while the absolute size of the economy has grown at an exponential rate since 1929, that growth has not always been steady; the graph has a slight wiggle to it. If we compute the annual rate of growth (the percentage change in GDP from one year

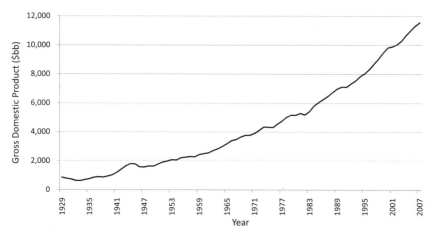

EXHIBIT 12.1   Real GDP in Chained 2000 Dollars: 1929–2007 ($ billions)
Source: U.S. Bureau of Economic Analysis data (www.bea.gov), June 13, 2008.

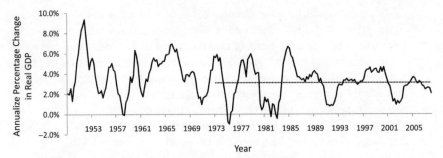

EXHIBIT 12.2   Real GDP Growth 1949–2008
Note: Two year moving average based on quarterly data.
Source: U.S. Bureau of Economic Analysis data (www.bea.gov), June 13, 2008.

to the next), as shown in the graph in Exhibit 12.2, we can see that GDP growth oscillates cyclically around a general trend rate, which has averaged 3.1 percent over the last 35 years (as indicated by the straight line).[5]

The *business cycle* is the name given to the socioeconomic phenomenon that causes this wiggle around the trend rate of GDP growth and is the primary focus in the analysis of GDP. It can be divided into four distinct phases based on how the current level of GDP growth compares to the trend level, and whether it is moving away from the trend or toward it.

- *Boom:* An economic boom is when the economy is at its most robust—GDP growth is not only above trend but accelerating. This corresponds to points in Exhibit 12.2 where the graph is above the straight line indicating the general trend and moving further above it. The economy is in full swing with lots of activity, new factories are being built, and job creation is robust.

- *Slowdown:* The economy enters a slowdown when the annual rate of GDP growth levels off and begins to decrease. This is the point on the graph where the curve has reached a local maximum—a peak above the trend rate of GDP growth—and begins to move back down toward the trend rate of growth. While the economy is still in an expansionary mode, growing faster than trend, the clouds are beginning to form—factories begin to see fewer orders and workers start having to make an effort to look busy.

- *Contraction:* The economy begins contracting when the rate of GDP growth drops below the trend level and continues to slow even further. This is where the graph has dropped below the trend line and is still negatively sloped (pointing downward). In a contraction, companies realize they were a bit overzealous in the boom phase and now have more capacity to produce than they have demand and begin closing factories and laying off workers. If GDP growth becomes negative—the actual production in the economy decreases—the economy is said to be in a recession. This corresponds to points in Exhibit 12.2 where the line is below the *x*-axis. The Great Depression of the 1930s was the worst recession in recent U.S. history. This can be seen from the graph in Exhibit 12.1 where, in the nine years between 1929 and 1938, the total growth in GDP was 1.7 percent, with an average of 7.3 percent negative GDP growth between 1930 and 1934.

- *Recovery:* At some point the business cycle reaches a low point and begins to turn upward. Economic conditions can still be poor: the recovery begins when GDP growth is at its lowest point relative to trend, which may be negative. However, the economy has begun to accelerate and the direction of change in GDP growth is positive (the line is upward sloping). The worst is past; the economy has stabilized and activity is beginning to pick back up toward "normal" levels and companies can begin to think about hiring workers, expanding production, or developing new products.

Given the hardship suffered during economic contractions and recessions, it is reasonable to ask why there is a business cycle in the first place. Why doesn't the economy stick to trend? Why can't regulators control it? This is one of the big, unanswered questions in macroeconomics. From the graph in Exhibit 12.2, it is clear that, while the business cycle is still a very real phenomenon, policymakers have learned from mistakes of the past and become much better at controlling the magnitude of the swings in economic activity. GDP growth since the late 1980s has been more consistently at or around trend, and much less volatile, than at any point in history.

One of the greatest challenges for policymakers is the fact that changes in economic conditions can take a long time to manifest themselves. By the time they have picked up on the changes in the economy, it may be too late to prevent the unwanted consequences of those changes and the actions they take may actually be counterproductive. The formation of economic policy based on economic data has been compared to driving while looking out the rear window: by the time you see the change you've already gone too far. This same challenge applies to Wall Street economists and traders trying to take positions based on the likely future course of economic conditions.

In the end, the business cycle is a relatively unsurprising consequence of human nature. All economic activity is the consequence of human decisions and, as the fields of behavioral finance and psychology demonstrate, humans display many characteristics that make us poorly suited to the task of keeping the economy on an even keel: we have very selective memories, are poor judges of the future, show a gross overconfidence in our own abilities, and have a tendency to make emotionally driven and irrational choices, particularly where money is involved. Corporations are run by human beings and inherit many of these same flaws. The business cycle occurs in much the same way that traffic jams form on otherwise uninterrupted freeways. While we could all travel along comfortably, in practice, we overshoot a bit, drive too fast and then have to pull back abruptly. This leads to congestion behind us as other drivers see us braking and overreact until traffic is at a standstill. Then, at some magic moment that no one can quite pinpoint, things start to open up, and traffic begins flowing smoothly again. It is hard to predict when, but eventually it does happen.

Employment   GDP growth measures the total economic activity of a country and gives us a means of observing the business cycle. It is, however, a very incomplete picture of the state of the economy because it gives no indication as to what percentage of the population is participating in that economic activity.

Employment statistics are based on a very specific definition of "unemployed." In order to be considered unemployed, a person must not only be jobless, but be actively looking for, and available to work. A person who is not working and has no intention to work (a retiree, for example), is not considered to be part of the *labor force* and is therefore not counted as unemployed. The *unemployment rate* measures the percentage of the labor force that is unemployed. The *participation rate* measures the percentage of the total population that is part of the labor force.

It is important to keep these definitions in mind when analyzing employment statistics. For example, in the midst of a protracted economic downturn, a decrease in the unemployment rate, which we would be inclined to interpret as a positive cyclical indicator, must be analyzed closely to determine whether it is actually such a good sign. If it is the result of a real pickup in employment—new job creation and hiring—then this is clearly very positive. However, the same decrease in the unemployment rate can be the result of a decrease in the participation rate—unemployed workers simply "giving up" and dropping out of the labor force—which is a unquestionably a very negative indicator for the economy. Unemployment statistics are also clouded by the existence of *underground economies*—illegal workers who are not counted in any measurements of employment, participation, or even population. In some countries, or specific regions within them, the exclusion of these workers from employment statistics can significantly distort the actual picture of the economy.

Insofar as it can be assessed with accuracy (a caveat that applies to every economic statistic and will therefore be taken as implied in all subsequent discussions), the level of employment is an enormously important cyclical indicator. During boom periods unemployment tends to be below average as companies expand and hire new workers. When the boom economy shifts into a slowdown, unemployment rates will still be below average but start to stabilize and potentially increase, particularly as new entrants to the workforce find it more difficult to find work. As business conditions continue to deteriorate and the economy moves into a contraction, unemployment rates increase to above-average levels as factories are closed and workers are laid off. While above-average unemployment rates can persist well into a recovery, they will begin to show signs of improvement as companies look to pick up talented workers left idle in the downturn.

Changes in the level of unemployment are also closely tied with consumption, both for the obvious reason that newly unemployed workers will quickly scale back on nonessential purchases, but also for the follow-on effect this has on those who are still employed. While you are no doubt smarter, harder-working, and more attractive than your colleague who just got laid off, you might still decide to put off any extravagant purchases until conditions seem more stable (just to be safe).

For government economists and policymakers, employment has a dual significance: aside from its importance as an economic indicator, one of the fundamental social obligations of the government is to keep the unemployment rate low so that, insofar as possible, anyone willing and able to work has the opportunity to do so. And if economics and ethics are insufficient, politicians have a third, unbeatable motivation: self-preservation—a high unemployment rate is a great way to lose an election.

Inflation　Inflation is the economic term that describes the tendency of prices to rise over time. Alternatively, it can be viewed as the decrease in the purchasing power of a dollar (or any currency) over time. Inflation is one of the reasons we discount the value of future cash flows to the present, whether in an NPV calculation for a derivative or in a discounted cash flow valuation of a stock.

While it is probably the economic measurement of which the average person is most acutely aware, it is also one of the most difficult to measure. Conceptually, the calculation is straightforward: We determine the basket of goods that best approximates the consumption of an "average" American and then compute the change in the price of that basket of goods from one year to the next. However, the operational and statistical challenges involved in its production are daunting. Aside from the sheer magnitude of the data that must be sampled and processed, there is the fact that, not only does the composition of the basket change from year to year, but there are also changes in the character of the goods consumed. A particularly simple example is technology: in the span of 20 years, the brick-sized mobile phones that were once considered a luxury item for the rich have evolved into the five ounce combination phone/camera/web browser/Mp3 players that can be found dangling from the back pocket of an average adolescent. The changes made to reflect consumers' changing expectations of quality and functionality, while maintaining continuity in the level of the price index, are called *hedonic adjustments* and are a highly contentious area of applied statistics due to the subjective nature of the analysis.

Inflation is a vitally important economic variable for several reasons. To begin with, the rate of inflation measures the decrease in value of a fixed amount of currency with the passage of time. For this reason, inflation is sometimes referred to as the "bogeyman" of the bond market because it directly erodes the value of the fixed interest payments made in the future.

The *real* return on any asset is defined as the nominal return less the rate of inflation:

$$\text{Real return} = \text{Nominal return} - \text{Inflation}$$

If an investment of \$100 returns \$6 at the end of one year, the nominal return is 6 percent. However, if inflation is 4 percent, then in terms of the real change in purchasing power, the investment has only returned 2 percent. For any investment or project, the inflation rate is the hurdle rate to real profitability. A project that returns less than the inflation rate has actually produced a reduction in purchasing power, even if it has produced a positive nominal return. High rates of inflation therefore act as a drag on the economy because only the most profitable projects will actually produce sufficient return to be worth undertaking.

The inflation rate is also extremely important in international trade. Holding all other things constant,[6] an increase in inflation causes the value of a currency to decrease, which will make imports more expensive. Eventually, in an extreme case of hyperinflation, the currency is no longer perceived as a means of storing value and becomes worthless. The opposite extreme is deflation, in which the purchasing power of the currency increases with time. This is similarly problematic; in a deflationary environment, the price of goods decreases with time, which encourages saving at the expense of consumption—an attitude of "don't buy now, it'll be cheaper tomorrow." As the last 20 years of experience in Japan have shown, once an economy is in a deflationary scenario, the efficacy of the standard tools of monetary policy is greatly decreased and restimulating the economy can become very difficult.

Government policy decisions are designed to keep the economy advancing at a healthy trend rate of growth with moderate inflation. A typical goal would be to have 5 percent nominal growth based on 3 percent real GDP growth and 2 percent inflation.

Inflation in the price of goods can come from three primary sources. The first is *cost push inflation*, in which the price of the raw goods of production increase and producers must increase their prices to maintain the same profit margins. Alternatively, they can look for ways to increase productivity or efficiency to compensate for the higher input costs. The second source is *demand pull inflation*, in which consumer demand exceeds supply, which leads producers to increase their prices and earn higher margins. A third cause is an increase in the money supply. As with any asset, an increase in supply leads to a decrease in price and an economy flooded with new currency will see the value of that currency depreciate. Money is a store of wealth and the act of printing new bills does not create wealth, just paper. While the increased availability of money may be a short-term stimulus to economic activity, in the medium- and long-term the impact is inflationary.

The theoretical relationship between inflation and the business cycle would indicate that, in periods of rapid expansion, the rate of inflation would run above its trend level as aggressive consumption encourages demand-push inflation. In periods of slowing consumption and economic contraction, inflation would drop below trend as producers fought aggressively for scarce consumer dollars by cutting prices. In practice, changes in inflation can be more difficult to predict and in the last decade the economy has experienced both above-trend growth with low inflation (largely attributed to the disinflationary effects of globalization and wide availability of easy credit) as well as a contracting economy with above-target inflation (as emerged in late 2007). This latter scenario is a worst-possible-case for the economy because the typical tools of economic policy that are used to stimulate growth (described later in the chapter) often produce inflation as a by-product. If the economy is already inflationary, a "damned if you do, damned if you don't" scenario emerges in which policy-makers must choose between the lesser of two evils—economic contraction and worsening of an already high level of inflation.

THE FED

The most basic component of a successful economy is a safe, reliable, and well-run banking system. The central bank of the United States is the *Federal Reserve System*, founded in 1913 by the U.S. Congress. The system consists of the Board of Governors in Washington, D.C. and 12 regional Federal Reserve Banks, each with responsibility for a particular section of the country. The Chairman of the Board of Governors of the Federal Reserve is currently Ben Bernanke, who replaced Alan Greenspan in February 2006.

The primary responsibilities of the Federal Reserve ("the Fed") are the determination and implementation of monetary policy, the regulation of the banking system, and the maintenance of the stability of the financial system in general, so as to "promote effectively the goals of maximum employment, stable prices, and moderate long-term interest rates."[7] If the economy is the ship then the central bankers (the Fed and Ben Bernanke) are at the helm.

It is the first of these responsibilities that is of greatest interest to us. *Monetary policy* refers to those actions taken by the Federal Reserve to influence the level of interest rates (the cost of borrowed money) and the availability of credit (money available to be borrowed). Monetary policy is set by the *Federal Open Market Committee* (FOMC), which consists of the seven members of the Board of Governors, the President of the Federal Reserve Bank of New York, and four of the other regional bank presidents who serve one-year terms on a rotating basis. The Chairman of the Federal Reserve is also chosen as the Chairman of the FOMC.

The Federal Reserve can implement monetary policy in three ways. The primary mechanism is via *open market operations*—the buying and selling of U.S. Treasuries—which are overseen by the FOMC. Depository institutions (e.g., banks) are required to maintain a fractional portion of their deposits on reserve with the Fed. The daily fluctuations in the balance of loans and deposits at each institution causes changes in their depository requirements. This results in an active market in which banks borrow and lend each other the excess funds they have deposited with the Fed on an overnight basis. The FOMC participates in this market in order to ensure that the supply and demand for balances meet at an equilibrium level that is in line with the *Fed Funds target rate,* which is set by the FOMC at its regular meetings. If demand for borrowing of overnight funds increases, the Fed can provide additional liquidity (lending) to keep rates from increasing above the target, while if there is excess supply the Fed will act as a buyer of balances to keep rates from falling.

A second mechanism for implementing monetary policy is through the control of the *discount rate,* which is the price at which banks can borrow additional funds from the Federal Reserve. While changes in the discount rate are usually a direct consequence of a change in the Fed Funds target rate, the discount rate can be adjusted independently. Compared with the market for Fed Funds overnight balances, there is much less borrowing by banks at the discount rate given that it is much higher than the Fed Funds target rate and banks can usually borrow more cheaply in the interbank lending market (i.e., from each other). Additionally, there has historically been a stigma attached to borrowing at the Fed's "discount window" as the need to "pay up" for cash by going to the Fed was perceived as a negative indication of a bank's financial health.

In times of market instability, however, the availability of funds from the discount window can be an important stabilizing force. In August of 2007, at the beginning of the credit crisis that would reach its peak in the autumn of 2008, concerns over the solvency of many financial institutions resulted in near paralysis of the interbank overnight and short-term lending markets. This lack of liquidity jeopardized many companies' ability to meet their short-term financing needs. As a first attempt to bring some order to the market—which would be followed in 2008 by unprecedented interventions in coordination with the Treasury Department—the Fed reduced the discount rate and increased the amount of available funds, acting as the lender of last resort to ensure that companies had the necessary funds to continue operating.

The least frequently used mechanism, but the one that can have the most immediate and draconian consequences, is a change in the *reserve requirements* for depositary institutions. To understand the significance of the reserve requirement we first need a brief explanation of the concept of *fractional reserve banking.*

Under fractional reserve banking, banks are not obliged to retain all the money that customers deposit with them. Instead, a fractional amount—the reserve requirement—is retained to ensure the bank can meet the day-to-day liquidity needs (to service withdrawals, payments, etc.) while the rest is loaned out to other clients (home mortgages, auto loans, etc.). A consequence of this is that there is much more "effective" money in circulation than what has actually been printed by the Treasury.

For example, assuming a reserve requirement of 10 percent, a bank receiving a $100 deposit would keep $10 in reserve and loan out the other $90. Eventually the $90 that was loaned out (e.g., as part of a home mortgage) makes its way back into the banking system somewhere (e.g., the construction workers deposit their paycheck in the bank). However, that bank will only need to hold $9 in reserve of the $90 deposited and can loan out the other $81 again. When this money makes its way back into the system, $8.10 will be held in reserve and $71.90 loaned out, and so forth.

The result is what is called the *money multiplier* effect. The $100 actually in circulation will continue to be deposited, fractionally reserved, and then loaned out again until a total of $1,000 is effectively circulating in the economy. The money multiplier—in this case 10x—measures the ratio of "effective" money to actual currency, and is calculated simply as one divided by the reserve requirement percentage.[8]

$$\text{Money multiplier} = \frac{1}{\% \text{ Reserve requirement}}$$

The impact of even small changes in the reserve requirement is significant. For example, an increase from 4 percent to 5 percent would reduce the money multiplier from 25 times to 20 times—effectively removing 20 percent of the liquidity in the market.

In the United States, the reserve requirement on *time deposits* (i.e., deposits that are expected to remain untouched for a given period of time, such as certificates of deposit) is currently 0 percent—the entire amount can be loaned out—while for *transaction accounts* (i.e., checking accounts and other deposits that provide continuous liquidity) it is 10 percent. Clearly, a precondition for fractional reserve banking to work is a general confidence in the solvency of the banking system. If too many depositors fear that a bank will "go under" and all withdraw their money at once (a "run on the bank"), the system breaks down as there is not enough currency in the system for all of the effective money ($1,000 in the previous example) to be withdrawn. The somewhat surprising reality is that the vast majority of the money each of us holds is not backed by hard currency in circulation but by credit extended by banks and investors to homeowners, businesses, or the government.[9]

Clearly, the risk to the financial system of a loss of investor confidence (a credit crisis) is tremendous. To promote investor confidence, at most banks, deposits below $100,000 are guaranteed by the *Federal Depositary Insurance Company* (FDIC), an independent agency of the federal government that was founded in 1933 in response to the thousands of bank failures during the Great Depression. FDIC insurance guarantees that, in the event of a bank failure, the government will intervene to protect individual's savings.

Due to their potentially violent impact, changes in the reserve requirement by central banks are quite infrequent—there has not been a significant change in U.S. reserve requirements since 1992 and it has been decades since there was an increase. One exception to this is the People's Bank of China, which increased the reserve requirement 16 times since the beginning of 2007 alone, from a low of 9.0 percent to a high of 17.5 percent, in an effort to slow an overheating economy (real GDP growth averaging 11.3 percent) and cool inflation (averaging over 5 percent with a peak of over 8 percent in the first quarter of 2008).

A fourth, "unofficial" means of implementing monetary policy that is available to the Fed goes by the pleasant-sounding name of *moral suasion*. This refers to ability of the Federal Reserve Board of Governors to influence the financial industry simply by speaking. One example of this occurred in December 1996 when then Chairman of the Federal Reserve, Alan Greenspan, commented on the market's "irrational exuberance"—lightly suggesting that investors had gotten a bit ahead of themselves and the Fed might need to react through more restrictive monetary policy. Whether intentional or not, the effect of the comments was an immediate drop in global equity markets of between 2 percent and 4 percent.

Moral suasion can be implemented via public announcements or private meetings between the Fed Board of Governors and the heads of major investment banks and depositary institutions. While the use of the word "moral" reinforces the fact that the Fed's goal is to do what is best for the economy and ensure the stability of the financial system, given the enormous power of the Fed, these closed-door meetings conjure up the image of the soft-spoken, elderly Mafia don gently reminding the shop owner that "We don't want any problems now . . . do we?" The bailout of the hedge fund Long-Term Capital Management (LTCM) in 1998 by a consortium of 14 investment banks was a classic example of the application of moral suasion in a private setting by the Fed. Everyone went into a room, and when they came out, Wall Street banks were suddenly willing to lend $3.6 billion to bail them out.

Impact of Monetary Policy

As mentioned earlier, the role of the Federal Reserve is to provide the monetary conditions necessary to promote long-term GDP growth, stable prices, and maximum employment. While its actions must be viewed within the larger framework of governmental policy, including fiscal policy (taxation) and other types of government stimulus, we will briefly consider the ways in which the Fed can achieve the rather lofty goals with which it is charged through monetary policy.

In the simplest terms, monetary policy acts as a throttle on the growth of the economy. We can consider two simple "textbook" cases to illustrate how, at least in a theoretical setting, the standard tools of monetary policy can be an effective means of directing the course of the economy.

The first is the case where the economy is stagnant and not operating at its potential—GDP growth and inflation are low and unemployment is high. The market needs a "kick" to get it moving and monetary policy can provide precisely the right sort of stimulus. By reducing the Fed Funds target rate, the Fed lowers the cost of borrowed money, which in turn reduces the hurdle-rate to profitability of projects financed with borrowed funds. This makes projects that were previously not economically viable look attractive, which stimulates corporate spending, as well as entrepreneurial startups, in turn creating jobs and reducing unemployment.

Spending in the private sector is also encouraged as the interest costs on financed purchases (e.g., new homes or cars) are reduced. In particular, the housing market is stimulated as the money previously factored into interest expense on the mortgage can now be used to pay for a more expensive home, which tends to push up prices. These house price increases, in turn, stimulate additional consumption through what is called the *wealth effect*: homeowners see the increased value of their property as an additional source of wealth and decide to save less from their incomes and consume more. ("Why save money from my paycheck when I just made a bundle on my house?")

The stock market benefits both as a result of the greater profitability of companies coming from increased consumption and lower financing costs, as well as from the fact that, given the relatively lower yield on fixed income securities due to lower government rates, the stock market becomes a relatively more attractive source of return, causing an asset allocation out of bonds and into equities. The "fair" price of equities will also rise as discounted cash flow valuations apply lower discounting rates to future cash flows, resulting in a higher present value. The U.S. dollar will generally weaken versus other currencies given that the interest earned on USD deposits is lower, making USD holdings less attractive. A weaker USD makes foreign imports more expensive (biasing consumption toward domestically produced goods) and makes U.S. goods cheaper to foreigners (further stimulating the demand for domestically produced goods). All of these forces contribute to increased GDP growth and employment and, while inflation will increase, given its current low level, this is not much of a concern.

The opposite scenario is the overheated economy in which, as a consequence of above-trend GDP growth and low unemployment, inflation is running at an unacceptably high level. In this case the monetary policy reaction is to raise the Fed Funds target (or the discount rate, or reserve requirements) to put the brakes on the economy. The impact is the reverse of the previous example; funding for new projects becomes more expensive, hurdle rates to profitability are higher, business expansion and consumption are slowed, savings increases, and the stock market reacts negatively. All of these factors—particularly the decrease in consumption—will tend to reduce inflationary pressures. The knock-on effects of slower GDP growth and higher unemployment, while they remain controlled, are acceptable as both of these are at above-trend levels.

In these highly stylized cases, the appropriate monetary policy action to correct the stated economic imbalances is clear. However, life is seldom so clean cut. Even in these simplified examples there are many questions that arise, such as:

- *How does the FOMC know how far to move rates?* Changes in monetary policy can take months to impact the economy during which time the Fed must decide whether enough has already been done to correct the imbalance or if additional steps are necessary. Is it necessary to swing the pendulum too far to achieve the appropriate balance?
- *What if the economy slips below trend when rates are already very low and cannot be cut more?* Rates cannot go negative and, in real dollar terms, any rate below the inflation rate is effectively negative.

In practice, economic conditions are rarely so clearly aligned to a particular monetary policy action. If, for example, GDP growth slips below trend while inflation is running at an undesirably high level, the choice of appropriate monetary policy becomes more difficult. Stimulating the economy will tend to push the GDP up but will also increase inflation, while inflation-fighting measures will tend to cool an already below-trend economy.

The theoretical impact of monetary policy changes can also be undone by changes in consumer sentiment—a reduction in the Fed Funds target can be interpreted by investors as an indication that the Fed is worried about the state of the economy and lead to a decrease in consumption as consumers brace for the worst. The evolution of the structure of the global economy can also mean that historical relationships between macroeconomic variables may need to be reconsidered. Over the last 20 years, the disinflationary forces of technological change and globalization have produced significant changes in the global economy to which the FOMC has needed to adapt.

Humphrey-Hawkins Twice a year, the Chairman of the Fed makes a presentation before members of both the House and Senate detailing the Fed's current stance on monetary policy and views on the economy. This presentation is known as the "Humphrey-Hawkins testimony" after the Humphrey-Hawkins Full Employment Act of 1978 that mandates it. Economists and traders alike listen carefully to the prepared speech, as it is much longer and comprehensive than the post-meeting press releases of the FOMC, and gives a more complete picture of the Fed's view on the state of the economy. The prepared presentation is followed by a question and answer period that is, in many ways, the more interesting part of the testimony as the Chairman must provide unscripted answers to the questions posed and is more likely to "slip-up" and divulge new information about the Fed's current thinking than what was deliberately included in the official presentation.

MOVING BEYOND THE BIG THREE: OTHER MACROECONOMIC CONCEPTS

Our focus thus far has been on the "big picture" ideas in macroeconomics: GDP, the business cycle, and the joint concepts of employment and inflation that guide the Fed's decision making. We now focus on some more specific aspects of the economy, their characteristics and relationship to the business cycle.

In the rest of this chapter and the next it is important that the reader keep in mind that economic concepts are intertwined and interrelated in many complicated ways. Each has its own independent characteristics but is also influenced by, and influences, others. Economics is full of many self-reinforcing, circular relationships, and chicken-and-egg paradoxes. As an example, what happens when unemployment increases? When people lose their jobs, they buy less "stuff" (a decrease in consumption), which means businesses make less money (a reduction in corporate profits), which will lead them to slow production and lay off more workers (even higher unemployment), which further reduces consumption, and so forth. If we take this logic to the extreme, we all end up unemployed and nobody buys anything. Clearly, this reasoning is flawed. The key is that these cycles do not exist in isolation and the interaction with other factors usually prevents them from spiraling to extremes. There are also many exogenous factors (bad harvests, flu epidemics, exceptionally inclement winter weather) that can play a significant role in shaping the economy but that are beyond our ability to predict or model accurately.

The Components of GDP

We have already presented the decomposition of GDP into its five contributing factors: consumer purchases, business investment, government expenditure, exports, and imports. We will begin by looking more closely at the composition of each of these items to see what information about the state of the economy can be derived from the changing composition of the GDP, even in the absence of a change in its absolute level.

- *Consumer purchases:* Individual household consumption is by far the largest contributor to the GDP, making up about 70 percent of the total figure.[10] It is divided roughly equally between retail sales—the purchase of physical goods—and services. Retail sales can then be further divided into purchases of durable goods (about 1/3) and nondurable goods (2/3). One of the challenges in forecasting changes in GDP growth comes from the difficulty in anticipating changes in household consumption patterns, which are heavily influenced by subjective and noneconomic factors, particularly as this refers to purchases of discretionary goods. (Things you buy because you want them, not because you need them.) While such subjectively defined measurements as "consumer confidence" will be influenced by changes in more traditional economic quantities such as housing prices, unemployment, or inflation, the impact of more subtle exogenous factors such as abnormal weather conditions, news events, or social contagions, can be very significant.

- *Fixed investment:* Capital spending by corporations makes up approximately 15 percent of GDP. Investment in new factories and equipment is a strong indicator that corporations are bullish on the prospects for the economy on a medium time horizon. (You don't build a new factory if you think the economy is going to turn downward in six months. Or at least you shouldn't.) An important component of the Fixed Investment portion of GDP is the change in the level of inventories. Increases in the level of inventories indicate a weakness in demand relative to expectations, resulting in an accumulation of finished goods in warehouses.

- *Government expenditure:* Government spending makes up the last 15 percent of GDP and is heavily concentrated in the industrial sector, most notably in aerospace and defense. Government spending is a highly politicized topic and, with the exception of a sudden demand for military supplies because of war, rarely changes quickly.

- *Net exports:* The U.S. imports between 30 and 45 percent more than what it exports, resulting in a negative *trade balance* (a *trade deficit*) of over $700 billion per year. The negative value of net exports reduces the $C + I + G$ computation of the GDP by around 6 percent. While it may not be immediately apparent, the trade balance is an extremely important economic variable in assessing the health of the economy. It is frequently viewed in the broader context of the *current account,* which adds to the trade balance the return earned on foreign assets owned by Americans. The current account can be thought of as the net amount of foreign currency that must be purchased or sold each year, either to fund foreign trade or to convert foreign income back into dollars.

Despite a partial offset to the trade deficit by income earned on foreign assets, the United States runs a massive current account deficit. This means that that there are many more dollars leaving the country then there is foreign currency entering.[11] As a result, there is a net accumulation of USD by foreigners who should, at least in theory, sell these dollars and purchase their local currency. This would tend to push down the value of the USD, making imported goods more expensive for U.S. consumers and U.S. goods cheaper for foreign consumers, which would, in turn, decrease the trade deficit by shifting consumption toward U.S. goods.

In practice, it has not worked like that. Many foreign economies are heavily dependent on the export of goods to the United States. The central banks of these countries are very concerned about their local currency appreciating, as this would make their goods more expensive to U.S. consumers, resulting in decreased demand, which would hurt their economy. As a result, these foreign central banks have chosen not to sell their accumulated USD and instead have built up vast reserves of USD. In some countries this is formalized via a currency peg, in which the government enforces a fixed exchange rate between the local currency and the dollar. This prevents the foreign currency from appreciating naturally and keeps foreign goods unnaturally inexpensive.

Foreign central banks have, in turn, invested these USD holdings in U.S. government debt, which we have been issuing in tremendous quantities to fund the budget deficit. As a result, the central banks of exporter nations are now the largest holders of U.S. government long-term debt (China and Japan alone hold nearly $1.1 trillion between them[12]), and the United States is, by far, the world's largest debtor nation. This imbalance has been a source of great debate and consternation among global policymakers and one of the significant points of friction in U.S.-China relations.

In the long run, a large trade deficit cannot be sustained indefinitely. At some point it has to correct and the longer the imbalance is sustained, the more violent and disruptive the correction has the potential to be. In the event that the Chinese renminbi were to appreciate substantially, low cost retailers such as Walmart, that operate on extremely narrow margins would have no option but to pass these price increases on to their customers, resulting in significant price inflation hitting millions of lower income Americans.

OTHER VARIABLES

There are many other variables that give information on the health of the economy and are used by economists to make predictions about the likely future direction of the economy, inflation, employment, and stock prices.

- *Production:* While our standard computation of GDP is based on measurements of consumption, production data are also watched very closely as an alternative level of determining the level of activity in the economy. Particular interest is paid to indicators of efficiency and costs—average weekly hours, wages, worker productivity—which are closely linked to inflation. For instance, if businesses are not being run efficiently, then demand increases can be met through greater productivity, rather than through price increases (inflation).
- *Interest rates:* The Fed's monetary policy is one of the principal drivers of the economy: a badly timed interest rate increase can tip the economy into contraction or hobble a nascent recovery while excessively lax policy can lead to inflation. Professional economists and traders scrutinize public comments by members of the Fed for possible indications of future changes in policy.
- *Money supply:* The monetarist school of economics, of which Milton Friedman is perhaps the most famous advocate, attributes changes in inflation to changes in the money supply. While monetarism rests on some sound theoretical arguments, in recent years the role of the money supply in monetary policy decisions has decreased in response to the increasing complexity of the financial markets which has made it progressively more difficult to properly measure the actual amount of money in circulation. Though monetarism is no longer a central component of Fed monetary policy decisions, the analysis of changes in monetary aggregates and their impact on the economy has regained some focus in light of the massive amount of new liquidity provided by global central banks in response to the financial crisis of 2008.

    The *monetary aggregates* are a series of measurements of the total supply of money based on four progressively more expansive definitions of what constitutes "money." They can be defined as follows:
- *M0:* The dollar value of all physical currency in circulation.
- *M1:* Sometimes referred to as "narrow money," M1 is equal to the sum of M0 plus demand deposits (immediately available cash deposits, such as checking accounts).
- *M2:* Add to M1 all savings deposits and money market accounts and small denomination (less than $100,000) time deposits. (Time deposits are funds that are deposited for a fixed period of time and are generally redeemable prior to maturity but may carry a penalty for early withdrawal.)
- *M3:* Referred to as "broad money," M3 is the sum of M2 plus large time deposits as well as institutional money-market funds and eurodollar deposits. M3 measures the total amount of currency and currency equivalents available in the economy.

- *Shipping and transportation:* Economists watch changes in the lease rates for cargo ships and oil tankers for indications of the volume of trade activity. *The Baltic Dry Index (BDI),* published by the Baltic Exchange in London, is a commonly used benchmark for measuring the cost of moving major raw materials by sea. Demand for air, road, and rail transport as well as package handling services such as UPS, FedEx, or DHL, can also give insight into activity levels in the economy.
- *Commodity prices:* Changes in the price of commodities—the raw inputs to production—have an impact on almost all aspects of the economy and all consumers. Economists watched with concern as the prices of oil, base metals (iron, steel, copper), and agricultural commodities (wheat, corn, rice) skyrocketed in recent years as this was viewed as a clear harbinger of inflation at the consumer level. Equally concerning was the precipitous drop in commodity prices in the summer and fall of 2008 for what this said about the state of global demand.
- *Weather:* Unusual weather conditions can be an important determinant of consumption and the price or agricultural commodities. Particularly cold or unseasonably warm weather during the winter holiday shopping season is often cited as a significant contributing factor in December retail sales data.
- *Geopolitical events:* In an increasingly interconnected economy, global political events take on a greater economic significance. Although much of the attention is focused on acute events—terrorist activity, epidemics (SARS, avian flu), oil supply disruptions caused by civil unrest, and the like—many longer-term social, political, demographic, and even environmental trends can play an important role in determining the future shape of the economy.
- *... and everything else:* In the end, every form of human endeavor contributes in some way to the economy. As the structure of the economy evolves, some historically relevant indicators will lose importance and be replaced by new measurements that are more useful to the analysis of today's economy.

A FINAL OBSERVATION

In our analysis of macroeconomics and the interpretation of economic data releases, it is important not to lose our focus. Our interest is, first and foremost, to understand the movements of the financial markets, specifically stock prices. Economics and the analysis of economic data releases are important tools in this process. We must be careful, however, not to confuse markets and the economy. While in the long-term markets are guided by underlying economic relationships, in the short- and medium-term they are driven in large part by the not-always-completely rational decisions of individual investors. The combination of fear and greed and the often irrational behavior of crowds make markets highly susceptible to panics, manias, and speculative bubbles. As John Maynard Keynes put it, "Markets can remain irrational longer than you can remain solvent."

As a very simplistic example of this, consider the scenario in which consumers decide to forgo present consumption and invest all their disposable income in the stock market. The underlying economic reality is that the economy has slipped into a massive contraction; household consumption—the largest component of the GDP—has been cut dramatically. Over the coming months, companies will cut back on production and decrease fixed investment and, eventually, lay off workers. In the meantime, however, the massive inflow of new funds will produce a major bull market for equities. While in time, the underlying economic reality will win out, not everyone is in a position to take the long-term view of a professional economist. To quote Keynes again, "In the long run, we are all dead." Economics may suggest a likely course for the market, but you make or lose money depending on what the market actually does.

SUMMARY

The fair price to pay for a share of stock is a function of both the specific characteristics of the company in question and the broader economic conditions in general. In the first two chapters, we looked at the tools of fundamental analysis used by financial analysts to assess the financial characteristics and risks of a specific company in order to determine its attractiveness as an investment. In this chapter, we have looked at the tools of macroeconomics, which are used to measure the financial condition of the economy at large.

The fundamental concept around which all of macroeconomics is built is the concept of the business cycle, used to describe how the level of activity in the economy oscillates around its long-term trend, passing through four phases: expansion, slowdown, contraction, and recovery. Our method for determining the economy's place in the business cycle is by measuring the rate of growth of the Gross Domestic Product (GDP), the broadest measure of domestic economic activity. GDP can be broken down into four components: household consumption, business investment, government spending, and net exports (exports minus imports). The largest of these is consumption, which accounts for approximately 70 percent of all economic activity.

Also crucial to the analysis of the economy are the level of employment, which measures the percentage of the labor force that is actually employed (and is important for both economic and social reasons), and inflation, which describes the rate at which the prices for the same goods increase over time. These three fundamental macroeconomic variables are brought together in the mandate of the Federal Reserve System (the U.S. central bank), whose responsibility it is to set monetary policy for the United States in order to "promote effectively the goals of maximum employment, stable prices, and moderate long-term interest rates." The actual monetary policy decisions, and the mechanisms chosen to implement them, are made by the Federal Open Market Committee (FOMC). The degree to which the deviations from the trend rate of GDP growth have become less severe in recent years is an indication of the successful application of monetary policy.

CHAPTER 13

Economic Data Releases

INTRODUCTION

In this chapter we look at the major economic data releases that are used by economists, investors, and traders to assess the current state, and likely future direction of the overall economy. In keeping with our practical focus, we restrict our attention to those data releases of greatest relevance and impact on the markets and deliberately limit the level of detail provided that are necessary to allow readers to properly assess the significance of each announcement. We then look at some of the specific factors that influence how markets react to unexpected outcomes in these data (the market's *reaction function*). Given this picture of how information about the state of the economy impacts the financial markets, in the last section of the chapter, we reverse the inference and look at some equity market indicators that are commonly used as indicators of the state of the underlying economy.

There is a great diversity to the economic statistics of interest to market practitioners. Many are produced by agencies of the federal government while others come from professional associations, universities, and independent statistical organizations. Depending on what is being measured, and the organization performing the analysis, the data may be gathered from a variety of sources including direct reporting by the corporations and individuals themselves, either voluntarily or by legal obligation (i.e., tax declarations) or collected via phone or mail surveys of sample populations.

Due to the significant impact they can have on markets, economic data releases are carefully controlled and leaks are extraordinarily rare. Three factors determine the importance of an economic data announcement to the market:

1. *Timeliness:* Economic releases tell us about the state of the economy at some point in the past. The closer that point is to today the more relevant the information is, which makes it of greater interest to the market.

2. *Accuracy:* Many economic statistics are revised after their publication. If these revisions tend to be large, this undermines the information content and level of interest in the initially published number.
3. *Relevance:* Due to the overwhelming volume of information, much of which is of little practical use, market practitioners focus on those data points that give the greatest amount of information about the broadest segment of the economy. Relevance is determined not only by the theoretical connection (i.e., how important *should* this information be for the economy) but also by the degree to which the data can be correlated with changes in the market—a convincing theoretical relationship is of no use if it has no predictive ability.

For a statistic to be of significant interest to the market it must score reasonably well on all three of these metrics and a poor rating on any of them will greatly reduce market focus. An easy example of this is the quarterly GDP calculation from the Bureau of Economic Analysis (BEA). GDP is the most central concept of macroeconomics and the National Income and Product Accounts (NIPA) report, which contains the official statement of the quarterly GDP and provides extensive detail on economic activity in all sectors of the domestic economy. In terms of accuracy and relevance, it could not score higher. Unfortunately, the price of accuracy and detail is time: the final revised data are not available for nearly three months after the end of the quarter under observation. As a result, by the time the data are published, markets already have a pretty good idea what the report will say and this information is already reflected in asset prices, making the announcement a relative nonevent. To compensate, the BEA publishes an "advance" GDP estimate toward the end of the first month following the quarter end, consisting of a top-line calculation of the GDP and some limited details on the various components. Though frequently subject to revisions, this statistic has a better balance between accuracy and timeliness and, as a result, is one of the most closely watched economic statistics in the world.

In advance of the release to the public, professional economists will publish their estimates of the likely outcome of most major economic data releases. These estimates are collected by market data providers and combined to form a consensus expectation for the number. The Bloomberg function **ECO** (*Economics*) provides a list of upcoming and historical economic data releases with details of the most recently published value and economists' expectations for the upcoming release. The page is immediately updated with new data as soon as they are released and also includes revisions to previous data. Each economic data point is assigned a ticker whose historical values can be analyzed with the same graphing functions available for standard indices. The **ECOS** (*Economist Estimates*) function provides more detailed information about the historical level of the statistic and its revisions, as well as an analysis of the dispersion of economists' estimates and their accuracy.

The size of the market reaction to an economic announcement depends on a combination of the importance of the statistic—as determined by the aforementioned three factors—and the magnitude of the deviation between the actual announcement and the consensus expectation. The larger the deviation, the greater the number of investors whose market positioning is based on misguided expectations and the greater the number of positions that need to be adjusted.

Economic statistics generally contain a headline number—for example, the nationwide unemployment rate—and then a more detailed report that breaks that headline statistic down into various subcategories. The headline number attracts the majority of the attention and has the greatest impact on the market, however, there can be hidden gems of information in the details of the report that reward the diligence of the careful analyst. One role of Wall Street economists is to comb through these data and assemble the relevant data into a more accurate picture of the economy.

PRELIMINARY DEFINITIONS

Leading, Lagging, and Coincident Indicators

Economic data releases are useful because of what they tell us about the current state and future direction of the economy as a whole and our position in the business cycle. For example, the average lease cost of a cargo ship between Hong Kong and Los Angeles is not, in itself, a particularly interesting piece of information. However, if that cost has dramatically increased over the past few months, then we have a *potentially* interesting piece of information. If we can further clarify whether the higher costs are due to increased demand for large-scale oceanic transport or skyrocketing fuel costs, we now have a very interesting piece of information with implications for the level of economic activity, consumer demand, and cost-push inflation.

An important question is: What is the relationship between the timing of the change in the indicator and the change in the underlying variable of interest? Increased attendance at soup kitchens says a lot about the state of the economy, but by the time people need to queue up for free food, we would probably already be pretty well aware that the economy was not at its most robust. Economic indicators are therefore classified as either *leading* (the indicator signals an upcoming change in the underlying variable), *coincident* (they change at the same time), or *lagging* (the indicator changes after the underlying economic reality has shifted). For Wall Street economists looking to anticipate changes in the economy, leading indicators are generally of greatest interest though the confirmation of changes in the underlying state of the economy—or lack thereof—from coincident and lagging indicators can also provide useful information.

Seasonal Adjustments and Base Effects

In many cases, the GDP being an obvious example, the absolute level of a particular economic data release is not of such interest as the percentage change in the data. This raises the immediate question—percentage change since when? Most economic statistics will be labeled as indicating either a *month-on-month* (MoM), *quarter-on-quarter* (QoQ), or *year-on-year* (YoY) change. That is, the percent change in the underlying statistic as compared with its value in the previous month, previous quarter, or the same period of the previous year.

This brings us to the concept of *seasonal adjustments*. When analyzing data over monthly or quarterly periods, it is important to recognize that activity in most sectors of the economy is not evenly distributed over the year. A particular percentage change in MoM or QoQ data cannot be interpreted as a positive or negative indicator without knowing what the typical change is between the two months of quarters in question.

As an example. Exhibit 13.1 shows the gross monthly sales data for Walmart, the world's largest retailer, for the 10-year period of January

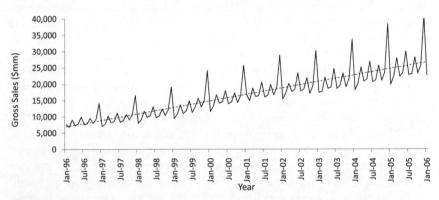

EXHIBIT 13.1 Walmart Monthly Sales ($ millions): 1996–2006
Source: Walmart press releases on PRNewswire

1996 to January 2006. The data show clear seasonal effects, most notably a massive spike up in sales in December (on average +57 percent), when holiday shopping kicks in, and subsequent drop off in January (on average –46 percent), when the credit card bills arrive and the hangover from the holidays really hits. The magnitude of these moves is so great that, without knowing the historical trend or the month in which it occurs, we cannot say a priori whether a 40 percent increase or decrease in MoM sales is a good or bad thing.

Seasonal adjustments is the term for the (highly imperfect) process of normalizing seasonal effects in monthly or quarterly data to capture the underlying trend (as shown by the dotted line in Exhibit 13.1). Using seasonally adjusted data, a MoM or QoQ increase is always indicative of a real increase in sales and can be compared to the underlying trend to determine whether the news is positive or negative. The challenge in determining how data should be adjusted for seasonal effects comes from the fact that, several years' worth of data is needed to make an appropriate assessment of the seasonal shift, during which time the seasonal variation may have changed. For example, the increased use of gift certificates as holiday gifts has shifted the recognition of a portion of holiday consumption from December to January. (Revenue from the purchase of a gift certificate is not recognized until the gift certificate is redeemed, not when it is initially purchased.) This is a slow but significant trend. A seasonal adjustment based on data from several years ago would not capture this shift.

While year-on-year data will not suffer from seasonal effects, since by definition they correspond to the same time of the year, they do suffer from so-called *base effects*. When a one-off occurrence in a particular year results in a particularly high (low) value for a statistic, the following year's data will look unusually low (high) in comparison. If base effects are not properly adjusted for, a generally positive result can be misperceived as a poor one, just because the data for the previous year were particularly spectacular. Individual companies account for this through the recognition of extraordinary items, which are then removed from the following year's YoY comparison.

Diffusion Indices

Some of the most important economic data releases are based on survey data taken from sample populations, either by phone or mail. To maximize the number of potential participants who actually complete the survey, the questions are kept deliberately simple and frequently limited to two- or three-option multiple-choice responses. These responses are then converted into a single statistic through *diffusion indices,* which compute the difference between the quantity of "high" and "low" responses, sometimes including an adjustment for the number of "middle" responses (if there are three options). For example, participants might be asked whether they expect job opportunities to be "more plentiful," "less plentiful," or "about the same" in six months' time. A diffusion index can then be computed as the percentage of "more plentiful" responses less the number of "less plentiful" responses, in which case potential index values would be distributed symmetrically between −100 and 100. Alternatively, the index might be equal to the difference between the "more plentiful" and "less plentiful" responses, plus one half the number of "about the same" responses. While this gives the same potential range of −100 to 100, the distribution is no longer symmetric but is skewed toward positive values. For example, under this methodology, if 100 percent of the respondents were to reply that job availability would be "about the same," the index level would be 50 while under the previous case it would be zero.

PRINCIPAL U.S. ECONOMIC INDICATORS

We have looked at the economic interrelationships between GDP, inflation, unemployment, and other factors, but we still have not provided any indications as where investors can get information about the current state of these macroeconomic variables. In this section we will look at 19 of the most popular indicators of economic conditions. These data are usually published between 8:30 A.M. and 10:00 A.M. Eastern Time and broadly disseminated via the financial news media. While the short-term market reaction is generally a function of the deviation between the actual result and expectation, it is also important to look at the long-term trend in the statistic. For example, in a weak housing market, a not-quite-as-terrible-as-expected housing sales number may cause a brief upward blip in the market as traders adjust positions, but for the longer-term investor, the more important information is in the general trend (terrible housing sales) and what that means for the economy.

To help structure and organize the presentation, the economic statistics are divided into four categories as shown in the following table. Given the complex interrelationships between economic forces, many of these statistics could be easily assigned to multiple categories. The division is purely to facilitate understanding and is not intended to be rigid or exclusive.

GDP and Contributors	Inflation
Advance GDP	CPI
Advance Retail Sales	PPI
ISM Manufacturing Survey	ECI
Housing Starts and Building Permits	GDP Price Deflator
Durable Goods Orders	Productivity and Costs Report
Industrial Production and Capacity Utilization	
Trade Balance	**Other**
	Consumer Confidence
Employment	Michigan Consumer Sentiment
	Conference Board Index of Leading Indicators
Employment Report	DOE Inventory Data
Unemployment Insurance Claims	FOMC Announcements

A summary of a wide variety of economic data for over a hundred countries can be found on Bloomberg using the *ECST* (*economic statistics*) feature.

GDP and Contributors

Advance GDP Estimate: U.S. Department of Commerce, Bureau of Economic Analysis Released approximately one month after the end of the quarter, the *advance estimate* of the GDP is the first preliminary estimate of aggregate national production provided by the Bureau of Economic Analysis, the federal agency responsible for compiling these data. While other data releases will have already provided economists with sufficient information to start forming estimates of the likely level of GDP growth, the advance estimate is the first "official" statement.

Given the limited amount of time in which it must be prepared, the advance report contains little more than a top-line estimate for the GDP and has none of the detailed regional or sector breakdowns provided later in the full National Income and Products Accounts (NIPA) report, which will not be available for another two months. About a month after the advance, GDP estimate (that is, two months after the end of the quarter) the BEA publishes an updated *preliminary estimate,* which, similar to the advance estimate, focuses primarily on the top line GDP estimate though some additional details are provided.

Advance Retail Sales: U.S. Department of Commerce, Bureau of the Census
Each month, the Bureau of the Census performs a survey by mail of 5,000

companies across the country (1,300 of which are fixed, the other 3,700 are chosen at random), who provide data on the dollar value of sales in the month. Surveys are mailed five working days before month-end and must be received back by the third business day of the next month. The advance estimate of the total value of retail sales is then disseminated during the second week of the new month. While the data in the advance report are preliminary, and therefore subject to significant subsequent revisions, the timeliness of the report makes it one of the most closely watched data releases of each month. The report also receives a great deal of attention because it provides information on the largest component of GDP, household consumption, of which retail purchases of goods (as opposed to services, a notable exclusion from the report) makes up approximately 50 percent. The data are adjusted for the large seasonal variation in consumption but can be significantly influenced by weather and other one-off factors. Due to the significant weight and high volatility of automobile sales, an "ex-autos" retail sales number is also computed and can be more indicative of the underlying trends in consumption.

Survey of Manufacturing: Institute for Supply Management (ISM) The first piece of new economic data, received on the first business day of each month, is the Institute for Supply Management's *Report on Business*. While limited only to manufacturing, the report is timely and well correlated to changes in GDP growth and therefore is widely considered one of the best indicators of current and near-term future economic conditions. A less closely watched sister statistic is the report on non-manufacturing activity, which is published two days later and usually echoes the tone of the manufacturing report.

The ISM indices are based on anonymous survey data received from over 300 supply management professionals[1] across the country who are asked to rank the activity and price levels in various aspects of their business as either "better," "the same," or "worse" than the previous period. Diffusion indices for each component are then calculated as the percentage reporting "better" plus half the percentage of those reporting "same." The *Prices Paid* index, a useful gauge of inflation, is the first of two closely watched components of the report. The second is the *Purchasing Managers' Index* (PMI), which is an aggregate diffusion index based on a weighted average of the seasonally adjusted responses on activity levels in five categories: new orders, production, employment, supplier deliveries, and inventories. A PMI level above 50 is indicative of growth and expansion in the economy (i.e., more respondents seeing "better" activity levels than "worse"), while below 50 indicates contraction.

Housing Starts and Building Permits: U.S. Department of Commerce, Bureau of the Census The economic relevance of changes in the housing market has increased dramatically in the past decade. (See "Housing, Credit, and the Fed" for a brief explanation.) The most commonly used indicator of residential housing activity—the part that most directly influences retail consumption and, therefore, the GDP—is the monthly construction data published by the Bureau of the Census. The report is published approximately three weeks after month-end and contains information on the construction of new, privately owned homes. The most closely watched components of the report are the data on the number of new houses started (*housing starts*) and the number of permits approved for the construction of new homes.

HOUSING, CREDIT, AND THE FED

In the market collapse[2] that followed the bursting of the Internet bubble in 2000, the Federal Reserve aggressively reduced the Fed Funds target rate, eventually reaching a low of 1 percent, where it stayed for one year, starting in June 2003. However, by mid-2003 the economy was already beginning to regain its footing and was shifting into a period of accelerating growth. As inflation began to pick up, the unusually low Fed target rate resulted in negative real rates of interest—the situation where the interest rate is below the inflation rate such that, in real terms, the amount of money paid back on a loan is less than what was originally borrowed.

Unsurprisingly, the availability of cheap money acted as a massive stimulus to the housing market, a home being the biggest and most highly leveraged purchase most people ever make. Lower interest costs effectively made houses cheaper because, for the same monthly mortgage payment, people could afford to buy a more expensive house. This resulted in an increase in demand and a decrease in price sensitivity, both of which helped push house prices higher.

Meanwhile, existing homeowners perceived the increased value of their property as a type of savings (the *wealth effect*) and began to spend more and save less from their current sources of income. On top of this, money lenders aggressively promoted home-equity lines of credit (money borrowed against the portion of the house that is not already mortgaged), which allowed homeowners to "equitize" the

(*Continued*)

(*Continued*)

paper profits on their homes and effectively treat their home as a giant cash machine. Homeowners borrowed against the increased market value of their property and used this borrowing to further fund current consumption, effectively paying for the family vacation by selling off part of their house. Operating in a robust, consumption-driven economy, lenders had little difficulty finding buyers for increasingly complex mortgaged-backed securities with which they were able to sell-off existing risks and fund new loans.

House prices increased at unprecedented rates between 2001 and 2005, as did the level of indebtedness of American consumers. As savings from current income actually became negative (consumers spending more than they earned), aggressive home-equity withdrawals actually resulted in a *decrease* in the average equity, in percentage terms, in American homes. That is to say, despite massive price increases, homeowners actually owned a smaller percentage of their homes than before, the difference having been withdrawn to fund current consumption. Lending excesses in the market for new homes were particularly concentrated at the low end of the credit spectrum, the now infamous "subprime" lending market, where high-risk borrowers with poor credit were lent sums that, under more sober analysis, they should never have been offered.

Economists were quite vocal about the risks of these imbalances and since the early part of the decade had watched the conditions of the housing market with increasing concern. Though clearly unsustainable in the long term, the party could continue, so long as house prices continued to trend higher and easy credit was widely available. In 2006, however, the record started to skip, and in 2007 the music officially stopped.

Beginning in late 2006, the economy began to suffer the consequences of lax lending practices, overconsumption, and speculative excesses in the housing markets—default rates on mortgages started to increase and the inability to find investors interested in purchasing mortgage-backed securities began to limit the availability of easy credit. By the summer of 2007 the economy was slipping rapidly into a severe contraction as the global banking system experienced the worst liquidity and confidence crisis since the Great Depression. As investment banks were forced to write-down the value of positions in mortgage backed securities by tens of billions of dollars, and market-wide lending conditions deteriorated dramatically, the Fed took aggressive action. Between September 2007 and October 2008 the Fed target rate was cut from 5.25 percent to 1.00 percent, including two un-precedented 75 bps rate cuts, one of which was done between FOMC meetings, a particularly rare event. Emergency federal credit facilities were established to relieve the short-term stresses on traditional banks, as well as investment banks and broker-dealers. This led to the passage of the Emergency Economic Stabilization Act of 2008 and the creation of the Office of Financial Stability (part of the Treasury Department) whose responsibility is implementation of the $700 billion Troubled Asset Relief Program (TARP) bailout package.[3]

As of late 2008, the housing and credit markets show few signs of improving. Another useful indicator of housing market activity is the *NAHB/Wells Fargo Housing Market Index*, a diffusion index based on a monthly survey of homebuilders of single family, detached homes regarding present sales and expectations for sales activity in six months' time. Conditions are rated as either "good," "fair," or "poor" and a seasonally adjusted index is produced such that any score over 50 indicates that more builders view conditions as good than poor. The index, shown in Exhibit 13.2, has been published continuously since January 1985. Prior to 2007, the index had only touched a low of 20 on one occasion, in January 1991 after which it quickly rebounded, reaching 41 by April of that year. The index hit 20 again in September 2007 but this time has failed to rebound, remaining continuously at or below 20 for more than a year (as of the time of writing) and reaching a new low of 9 in November 2008.

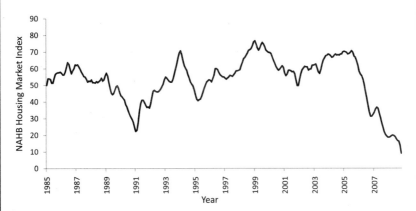

EXHIBIT 13.2 NAHB/Wells Fargo Housing Market Index
Source: National Association of Homebuilders (www.nahb.org) data as of December 8, 2008.

Durable Goods[4] Orders: U.S. Department of Commerce, Bureau of the Census Published about four weeks after each month-end, the *Advance Report on Durable Goods Manufacturers' Shipments, Inventories, and Orders* contains survey data on new orders, shipments, order backlogs, and inventories collected from 4,200 industrial manufacturers, most with annual shipments of at least $500 million. Though rather volatile and subject to significant revisions (a revised report is published one week later) the "durable goods report," as it is known, serves as a key indicator of the level of manufacturing activity, which is an important contributor to the GDP: purchases of durable goods make up approximately 15 percent of household consumption and also contribute to the fixed investment and government spending components.

Besides the headline number on total new orders for manufactured goods, significant attention is paid to the inventory and unfilled orders data released with the report. Order backlogs (demand greater than supply) and inventory build-ups (production greater than demand) can provide important leading indications of future production levels.

Industrial Production and Capacity Utilization: Federal Reserve Board Interest in industrial production data is very much dependent on the economy is in the business cycle. It receives particular attention at the bottom of the cycle, when market participants are looking for early indications that the economy is beginning to "turn the corner" and start the next upswing. At the peak of the cycle, when the economy has been growing at an above-trend rate for some time and is beginning to show signs of slowing, few companies are likely to undertake major industrial project; the expectation is that broad production and manufacturing indicators will be weak (so there is no new news in a low number) and the market will tend to write-off surprisingly high values as being due to one-off effects and not indicative of real expansion (so there's no news in a high number, either).

The Federal Reserve publishes a monthly index of industrial production and capacity utilization rates for manufacturing, mining, and utility companies approximately two weeks after month-end. The concept of capacity utilization is based on a comparison of current levels of production with an estimate of a maximum sustainable level of production. It can be thought of as the "slack" in the economy. The historic trend in capacity utilization is around 81 percent with levels above 85 percent considered inflationary (greater than 90 percent has only been achieved in wartime.) The *output gap* is the measure of how much additional production would be possible if the economy were operating at full capacity. Increasing doubts about the ability to accurately measure capacity and the output gap, due to the impact of globalization and the continued outsourcing of manufacturing jobs overseas, has removed some of the focus from this statistic.

Trade Balance: U.S. Department of Commerce, Bureau of the Census

Over many years, the combination of an unnaturally strong U.S. dollar, the insatiability of the American consumer (we have one of the lowest savings rates and highest consumption rates in the world), and the gradual shift of U.S. manufacturing overseas resulted in a massive imbalance in the amount of goods brought into the United States versus what is manufactured domestically and shipped abroad. During 2004–2007 this trade deficit averaged $60 billion *each month*.

The trade balance is computed by the Department of Commerce from data collected by the U.S. Customs offices on the flow of goods between the United States (and territories) and other countries. The monthly report, published six weeks after month-end, contains an extensive breakdown by product category and country and provides some very interesting insights into the interrelationships in the global economy. The short-term trading impact for equities is mitigated somewhat by the delays in publication and the fact that changes in the trade balance, and their consequences, are slow to evolve.

Even a quick look through the report highlights issues many issues that have received considerable media attention as well as some lesser-known facts about our trading partners:

- *China:* The trade deficit with China for 2007 was $256.2 billion or approximately one-third of the total deficit of $794.5 billion. This is more than three times the next-largest single country trade deficit (Japan: $82.8 billion) and twice the deficit with the whole of Europe ($121.1 billion).
- *Oil:* The trade deficit with the OPEC countries was $113.0 billion (16 percent of the total). In 2007, the United States imported a total of $237.2 billion of crude oil or an average of 10.1 million barrels per day.
- *United States as a consumer nation:* Total trading volume with the top 50 trading partners (based on the sum of absolute exports and imports) makes up 94.9 percent of the United States' total foreign trade. Of these 50 counterparties, the United States has a trade surplus with 12 of them for a total value of $75.1 billion. With the other 38 it has a deficit of $862.0 billion.

- *The Big Three:* While most people are generally aware of the massive volume of goods imported from China, it comes as a surprise to many that they are also the third largest destination for U.S. exports. More surprising still, the other two largest trading counterparties are Canada (#1 for exports, #2 for imports) and Mexico (#2 for exports, #3 for imports).[5]

Inflation

We will now look at five of the most commonly used measures of inflation, each of which has a slightly different focus:

- *Consumer Price Index (CPI):* Inflation as experienced by individual consumers.
- *Producer Price Index (PPI):* Inflation at the point of manufacture— increases in the costs paid by retailers for the products they sell.
- *GDP Price Deflator:* An aggregate measure of inflation effects across all sectors and products, including the influence of government spending.
- *Employment Costs Index (ECI):* Measures the impact of labor costs.
- *Productivity and Costs Report:* Examines how much the current workforce is producing, and how much it costs.

Consumer Price Index: U.S. Department of Labor, Bureau of Labor Statistics The *Consumer Price Index* (CPI) is probably the most commonly cited indicator of inflation, and certainly the one with the most direct impact on the "man on the street." Published monthly by the U.S. Bureau of Labor Statistics (BLS), the CPI measures the cost of a fixed basket of goods whose composition is intended to represent the consumption habits of a typical urban consumer. (Notably, this includes imports.) The constituents of the basket are reviewed every few years to reflect the changing consumption habits of individuals, as well as the "average" consumer's changing expectations of quality and functionality (the previously mentioned hedonic adjustments). The price of this basket of goods is determined by a monthly survey of approximately 80,000 items across the country. The breakdown of the individual constituent weights in the CPI is shown in Exhibit 13.3.

According to the Bureau of Labor Statistics, 80 million Americans' income is affected by the CPI, which is used to make cost-of-living adjustments to payments of Social Security, food stamps, and military wages, as well as the allowance for some 28 million school lunches.

Total		100.0%
Food & Beverages		14.9%
Housing		42.4%
Shelter	*32.6%*	
Owner's Equivalent Rent	*23.9%*	
Fuel & Utilities	*5.1%*	
Household Furniture & Operations	*4.7%*	
Apparel		3.7%
Transportation		17.7%
Medical Care		6.2%
Recreation		5.6%
Education & Communication		6.1%
Other		3.3%

EXHIBIT 13.3 Composition of CPI by Category
Source: U.S. Bureau of Labor Statistics (www.bls.gov) relative weights as of December 2007.

Given the impact of changes in the CPI to the incomes of so many Americans, it is extremely important that the index accurately and objectively reflect real changes in the level of prices. As a result, there is a significant amount of controversy surrounding the measure of *Owner's Equivalent Rent* (OER), which is the largest single component of the CPI. The OER is calculated by asking the homeowners themselves to estimate the monthly rental price for an unfurnished property identical to their own. Given the difficulty in making this assessment, even for an experienced assessor of property prices—much less through the biased eyes of the homeowners themselves—it is not hard to see how inaccuracies might enter into this estimate.

Due to the high volatility of food and energy prices, a separate *CPI ex-Food and Energy* is often used as a more a accurate measurement of the general underlying trend. In recent years, however, as the prices of crude oil and agricultural commodities have increased dramatically, many economists have begun to question whether the exclusion of food and energy prices has led to a persistent underestimation of inflation pressures.

As an aside, it is actually quite entertaining to look through the composition and relative sizes of the hundreds of different categories within the CPI. A few select observations:

- *Unsurprising:* "Women's apparel" (1.35 percent) is nearly twice "men's apparel" (0.70 percent).
- *Slightly odd:* "Uncooked ground beef" (0.23 percent) is greater than "personal computers and peripherals" (0.20 percent).
- *Somewhat disturbing:* "Pets, pet products, and services" (0.65 percent) is three times greater than the sum of "Nursing homes" and "Elderly home care" (0.20 percent).

Producer Price Index: U.S. Department of Labor, Bureau of Labor Statistics   While the CPI measures inflation from the perspective of the final consumer, the *Producer Price Index* (PPI) measures the changes in the price level of all domestically manufactured goods produced for sale either to retail or industrial clients and is based on a sample of nearly 100,000 prices. While many individual sector indices are calculated, the headline number is the *Finished Goods PPI,* which measures the price level for manufactured products that are ready to be shipped to retailers, effectively a measurement of the inflation experienced by retailers in the price level of the goods they sell. Increases in retailer mark-ups will therefore not impact the PPI but will affect the CPI. Because PPI weights are based on total domestic production, and not consumption, they include goods produced for export. Due to its greater impact on individual consumers, the CPI generally receives significantly more attention than the PPI.

GDP Price Deflator: U.S. Department of Commerce, Bureau of Economic Analysis   The GDP price deflator is published quarterly by the U.S. Bureau of Economic Analysis (BEA) together with the advance, preliminary, and final GDP estimates. Given the nominal value of GDP, it is important to know how much of the change in GDP from one period to the next is due to a real change in output and how much is due to simply a change in the price level (i.e., inflation). While most people tend to think of real GDP as the nominal GDP after adjusting for inflation, in practice, the BEA has methods for calculating both the real and nominal values of GDP directly, and the GDP deflator is then defined as the ratio of one to the other:

$$\text{GDP deflator} = \frac{\text{Nominal GDP}}{\text{Real GDP}}$$

The change in the GDP deflator from one period to the next measures the portion of the change in nominal GDP that can be attributed to inflation. For example, in a hypothetical economy in which actual production (real

GDP) increased 3 percent (from 100 to 103) while nominal GDP increased by 5 percent (150 to 157.5), the change in the GDP deflator would be roughly 2 percent.

	Nominal GDP	Real GDP	GDP Deflator
Period 1	150.0	100.00	1.5000
Period 2	157.5	103.00	1.5291
% Change	**5.00%**	**3.00%**	**1.94%**

Deflators are produced for the GDP as a whole as well as many different subcomponents. One of the most closely watched of these is the deflator on the *Personal Consumption Expenditure* (PCE), that portion of GDP composed of spending on goods and services by private individuals, as this is the Fed's preferred measure of inflation (having replaced the CPI in 2000).

Though much less timely than the CPI, the PCE deflator is a preferable measure of inflation for several reasons. The most significant is because, compared with a static basket such as is used for the CPI, a GDP-based measurement dynamically adapts to the changing composition of consumption and therefore incorporates the effects of substitution between similar items. If a particular item becomes too costly (i.e., pasta), consumers will decrease their consumption of that item and increase consumption of a cheaper substitute (i.e., rice or bread). Because a static basket assumes that the composition remains constant, it will tend to overstate the level of inflation by including too much of the higher priced item relative to what is actually being consumed. One shortcoming of the PCE deflator is the fact that, because it is based on the GDP, it only measures price changes in domestically produced goods and therefore does not capture changes in the cost of imported goods. In a period of dollar weakness, this can lead to an underestimation of the level of price increases actually experienced by consumers.

Employment Cost Index (ECI): U.S. Department of Labor, Bureau of Labor Statistics The *Employment Cost Index* (ECI), which is published quarterly with a one-month delay, provides an extremely accurate and complete picture of trends in costs related to employment and is, as a result, one of the statistics most closely watched by the Fed. A key feature of the ECI is that it includes information not only on wages and salaries, but also on expenditures on employee benefits, which can be as much as 30 percent of total employment costs. The report is constructed based on survey data collected by BLS economists from thousands of employers across the country. While the full report contains extensive detail on the trends in different regions, industries, and the like, the headline number is what receives the most attention from the market, particularly during the latter part of upswing of the business cycle when wage inflation is a greater concern.

Another important feature is the fact that the ECI is based on a fixed "basket of jobs," similar to the CPI. While we view this rigidity as a shortcoming of the CPI, because it does not allow for the effect of substitution, in the ECI it is an advantage because it prevents changes in the *composition* of the workforce from causing the appearance in changes in employment costs. If growth in a high-wage industry leads to increased hiring of those workers relative to lower-wage workers in other sectors, this is not indicative of increased wage pressure, simply a change in the type of labor needed.[6]

Productivity and Costs Report: U.S. Department of Labor, Bureau of Labor Statistics   One last indicator of inflation is the *Productivity and Costs Report*. This report receives somewhat less attention than other releases as it is quite volatile and subject to significant revisions and also not particularly timely. (It is published quarterly with a one-month lag for the preliminary estimate and an additional month for the revised version.) Despite this, it contains information on two important concepts with which the reader should be familiar: productivity and unit labor costs.

Productivity is simply the measure of the amount of actual output (real work done) divided by the time required to do it. If we were to define a theoretical "unit" of labor consisting of a task that should take one hour for a single worker to complete, then if productivity is running at 80 percent, this means that, in practice, actual workers are (on average) only completing 80 percent of that unit of labor in one hour, and the whole job in an hour and a quarter.

The measurement of *unit labor costs* (ULCs) combines the productivity data with information on wages to compute a dollar price per unit of labor. In our simplified example, if the employee is paid $10 per hour, then the cost of a unit of labor would be the price of an hour and a quarter of work, or $12.50. Unit labor costs capture the balance between increases in productivity and the price of achieving them.

The two headline numbers from the Productivity and Costs Report that receive the majority of the attention are the change in unit labor costs and the *nonfarm productivity* estimate, which, as its name suggests, measures the productivity of workers not employed in the agricultural sector.

Employment

Employment Report: U.S. Department of Labor, Bureau of Labor Statistics

The Bureau of Labor Statistics produces a monthly report called the *Current*

Employment Statistics (CES) survey based on a sample of 400,000 businesses nationwide. There are several key data points provided by this report:

- *Change in nonfarm payrolls:* This is the highlight figure and is widely used as a proxy for the results of the entire report. The change in manufacturing payrolls is also provided, though this receives less attention.
- *Unemployment rate:* While the unemployment rate is the definitive measure of employment, it is generally a lagging indicator of the economy as companies will usually make significant efforts to adjust to changes in demand through alternative means before hiring or firing employees.
- *Average hourly earnings:* Changes in hourly earnings are a useful measure of wage pressures, which, depending on the state of the economy and manufacturers' ability to pass on cost increases, can lead either to inflation (if costs are passed on to consumers) or margin pressure (if companies absorb them).
- *Average weekly hours:* Changes in the hours worked can be an early indicator of future changes in employment levels. Due to the many incidental costs associated with hiring a new employee (medical insurance, administrative costs, etc.), when faced with increased demand, employers will generally look to get more hours out of existing workers before increasing the size of the workforce (hiring). Similarly, as demand softens, employers will require fewer hours of existing workers before incurring the costs (and negative publicity) associated with layoffs.

Unemployment Insurance Claims: U.S. Department of Labor A more frequent (and therefore less significant) measure of employment conditions is the weekly report on claims for unemployment benefits, released each Thursday by the Department of Labor. There are two components to the report: the number of new applications for unemployment benefits (*initial jobless claims*) and the number of people already receiving support (*continuing claims*). The data can be quite volatile and the true trend can only be seen with several weeks' data. However, the higher frequency allows trends to be spotted more quickly.

Other Statistics

Consumer Confidence Survey: The Conference Board In general, economic theory is constructed around the concept of a *homo economicus*—the perfectly rational agent who reacts in logical, consistent, and predictable ways (at least in aggregate) to changes in income, price levels, employment, and so on. Outside of the nascent field of behavioral economics, the impact of emotions and other irrational factors have been ignored as too difficult to model and quantify. While from an academic perspective this may make sense, in practice, actual consumers are irrational, inconsistent, unpredictable and emotional and while Wall Street may use economic theory as a guideline, in the end what matters is what actually happens—profits and losses are marked to market, not to theory.

For this reason, indicators of market sentiment—how consumers *feel* about the economy in general and their personal situation in particular—play an important role in anticipating the likely short-term direction of markets. While it can take many months for changes in the economy to be felt by individuals, the mood of the man on the street is a key determinant of today's consumption. Given that household consumption comprises roughly 70 percent of GDP, in the short-term, sentiment will drive economics. (Though in the long run it is probably the other way around.)

One of the most important indicators of consumer sentiment is the report on consumer confidence published by the Conference Board, an independent business research organization. The report is released on the last Tuesday of the month in which the survey was conducted, which makes it an extremely timely indicator of how consumers feel *right now*. The data, collected monthly since 1969 through a telephone survey of roughly 5,000 households around the country, contain survey respondents' assessment of their personal circumstances as well as the state of national economic conditions, and their expectations for these in six months' time. Diffusion indices are computed based on participants' views on:

- *Business conditions:* Are they good, bad, or normal?
- *Employment:* Are jobs plentiful, not so plentiful, or hard to get?
- *Business conditions in six months' time:* Will they be better, worse, or the same?
- *Employment in six months' time:* Will there be more, fewer, or the same number of jobs available?
- *Income:* Do you expect your income in six months to increase, decrease or stay the same?
- *Major purchases:* Do you plan to purchase a home, car, or major appliance or to take a vacation in the next six months?
- *Economic outlook:* What are your expectations of the inflation rate, interest rates, and stock prices in 12 months' time?

Consumers' perceptions of market conditions are significantly influenced by the recent past, which makes it difficult to draw specific inferences about the actual state of the economy from the way consumers feel about them. After a prolonged contraction, investors may feel very positive amidst poor economic conditions if they perceive a recovery beginning to materialize. Similarly, the significantly above-trend conditions that still persist just as an economic bubble is beginning to deflate can feel very negative to consumers who had not counted on the party ever coming to an end. As a result, the absolute level of the index is less significant than the direction of changes in the index level.

Consumer Sentiment Survey: University of Michigan Survey Research Center Another consumer sentiment survey is conducted twice monthly by the University of Michigan and based on a sample of 500 men and women from across the country. Similar to the Conference Board survey, participants are asked to provide information on their household finances and their expectations for the national economy and inflation both presently and over the next one year and five years. Three separate indices are then published measuring consumer sentiment, the assessment of current conditions, and the expectations for the future. While the questions are almost naïvely simple (i.e., "Will you be better off, worse off, or the same 12 months from now?"), the statistic, which has been published since the 1950s, has shown to be a surprisingly useful barometer of consumer sentiment and leading indicator of economic conditions.

Composite Index of Leading Economic Indicators: The Conference Board The *Index of Leading Economic Indicators* is a composite statistic published monthly by the Conference Board (usually about three weeks after month end), and is computed as a weighted average of 10 of the most significant leading economic indicators. The values of the individual components that make up the index are known in advance of its publication and the dissemination of the index level generally has little impact on markets since, for the most part, it presents what is already old news. The index has shown to be quite accurate as an indicator of impending turns in the business cycle, though its usefulness is somewhat reduced by the fact that changes in the index do not anticipate shifts in the economy by a consistent amount, making it difficult to use the index as the basis for trading decisions.

The constituents of the index, along with the source for each one, are listed below. Most of these we have already discussed individually:

1. Average weekly hours (Employment Report, Bureau of Labor Statistics).
2. Average weekly initial claims for unemployment insurance (Unemployment Insurance Claims: Department of Labor).
3. Manufacturers' new orders for consumer goods and materials (ISM Manufacturing Survey).

4. Vendor performance (diffusion index of slower deliveries) (ISM Manufacturing Survey).
5. Manufacturers' new orders for nondefense capital goods (ISM Manufacturing Survey).
6. Building permits (Housing Report, Bureau of the Census).
7. Stock prices (The level of the Standard and Poor's 500 Index).
8. Money supply (M2 as published by the Federal Reserve).
9. Interest rate spread (Yield differential between 10 year Treasury notes and the Fed Funds overnight rate).
10. Index of Consumer Expectations (University of Michigan Consumer Survey).

The weights applied to each factor are inversely proportional to the volatility of the statistic. In this way, the contribution of each component to the volatility of the aggregate index is, on average, the same.

Crude Oil, Distillate, and Gasoline Inventory Data: U.S. Department of Energy

The multiyear rally in oil prices—from a low of $17.45 per barrel in November 2001 to a peak above $145 in mid-2008—produced a massive bull market for the energy sector. Many of the "super-major" oil companies[7] now rank among the largest companies in the world and their shares currently occupy the top places in many U.S. and foreign market cap-weighted indices.

Due to their dramatically increased market capitalization, the impact of movements in the oil sector on the broad market aggregates is much greater today than it was just a few years ago. As a result of this, the weekly inventory data published by the *U.S. Department of Energy* (DOE) have become a statistic of significant interest, to the point where the announcement is often broadcast on financial news networks live from the floor of the New York Mercantile Exchange, where futures on crude oil—and many other commodities—are traded.

On Wednesday of each week, the DOE disseminates its estimates of the change in the total inventories of crude oil, distillates (such as airplane fuel and heating oil), and gasoline held nationwide. Excluded from the inventory data is the federal government's *Strategic Petroleum Reserve* (SPR), a stockpile of crude oil that can be released into the market in the event of a disruption in the oil supply. Increases in reserves are negative for oil prices (and therefore oil shares) since it suggests increased supply in the future, due to the inventory of stored products being above the expected level and potentially being released into the market. Decreases in inventories suggest increased future demand (and are therefore bullish for the price of crude and therefore oil companies) as these stores are increased up to target levels.

Among the three components (crude, distillates, and gasoline), the market's focus shifts due to seasonal factors: more attention is paid to distillates (heating oil) in winter and gasoline during the summer driving season. While the market will react whenever actual changes in inventory differ from the anticipated amounts, there are some questions about the accuracy of the statistics and the actual impact changes in inventories have on the price of oil.

FOMC Policy Announcement

While other data points are suggestive of the *probable* course of future economic conditions, the FOMC decision on the Fed Funds target rate effectively *defines* the price of overnight Fed deposits, which acts as the primary reference point for all short-term borrowing of U.S. dollars. In terms of timeliness, relevance, and accuracy, the FOMC policy decision gets top marks in all three and is therefore the most closely watched of all the U.S. economic announcements.

The Federal Open Market Committee holds meetings approximately every six weeks to review economic and market conditions and to decide on the future direction of monetary policy. Six of the meetings are single-day events while the other two last two days. At the completion of the meetings the FOMC issues a press release that announces the new target for the Fed Funds rate and provides a summary of the FOMC's view of economic conditions and the balance of risks to the economy, as well as an indication of which way the committee is biased regarding potential future changes in the target rate. The relative infrequency of these meetings adds to the significance of the announcement.

With regard to the balance between the desire for growth and the threat of inflation, the tone of the statement, and the view of individual Fed governors and regional bank presidents themselves, is described as either *hawkish* or *dovish*. Inflation "hawks" are more concerned with the threat of inflation than with encouraging growth and are therefore more likely to prefer higher rates. Inflation "doves" prefer to run a more stimulative monetary policy, by keeping rates lower, and wait for concrete indications of above-target inflation before raising rates. Because of the various ways in which the Fed can enact monetary policy, the bias stated in the press release does not refer specifically to raising or lowering rates but instead to a "tightening" or "loosening" of economic conditions (though changes in the Fed target rate are by far the most common means of enacting policy changes).

Due to the brevity of the press release, which occupies only about a half page of text, economists have limited information about the specific issues in the market that are of concern to the Fed and the relative importance applied to each of these. As a result, the precise wording of the press release is scrutinized to the point that it has taken on a code-like quality in which the addition or deletion of a single word (i.e., Did they say the housing market has experienced "a significant deterioration" or just "a deterioration"?) is analyzed for significance as an indication of possible future policy decisions. The minutes of the meeting are not released until three weeks after the announcement and the full transcript is not available for five years.

While uncommon, there are occasionally changes in the target rate between meetings. Because of the consequences of changes in Fed policy, an unexpected announcement will almost always have tremendous market impact as it will surprise the market and trigger the immediate repricing of many fixed-income assets as well as having a significant impact on the equity markets. In terms of timeliness, accuracy, and relevance, an inter-meeting change in the target rate wins top place in all three. The most recent inter-meeting policy change was in January 2008 when the target rate was cut by 75 bps, followed by an additional 50 bps cut at the regularly scheduled meeting eight days later.

Fed Funds Futures In the equity markets, the impact of a change in the Fed Funds target rate is significant but indirect; changes in the cost of money have an impact on equities but so do many other factors and even an increase in the Fed Funds rate, if interpreted as an indication that the Fed is confident about future growth prospects, can result in an equity market rally, despite its undeniably negative impact on corporate financing expense.

In the fixed income markets, the impact is more direct as the Fed funds rate represents the overnight return on a "riskless" deposit and therefore acts as the reference point for all other interest rates, particularly those with shorter maturities. Nowhere is the impact of the Fed rate decision more direct than in the pricing of the Fed Funds futures contracts traded on the *Chicago Board of Trade* (CBOT).

Fed Funds futures are financing agreements covering a single calendar month whose value at maturity is equal to 100 minus the realized average Fed Funds overnight rate during that month (i.e., if the average rate during the month is 4.50 percent, the contract matures at 95.50).[8] Contracts carry a notional amount of $5mm and there are 24 consecutive monthly contracts trading at any time. Liquidity is tremendous with a notional value of contacts outstanding at any one time of roughly one trillion dollars.

Because the settlement value of the futures contract is a direct function of the realized Fed Funds overnight rate during the month, the value of the contract prior to maturity is the market's expected level of the Fed Funds rate during that month. If in June 2008, the price of a March 2009 Fed Funds future is 96.0, this suggests that the consensus market view is that the Fed Funds rate in nine months' time will be 4.0 percent. If the rate is higher, the value of the future will decline, while if the rate is lower, the future will gain in value. This allows investors not only to express a view on the future level of the Fed Funds rate, but also to hedge funding liabilities up to two years in the future.

Fed Funds Implied Probabilities The Fed Funds futures provide a useful means of determining the market's view of the future course of interest rates. For a simplified example, consider a Fed Funds future for a month in which there is no FOMC meeting. Assuming no surprise changes to the target rate between meetings, the value of the contract will be entirely determined by the target rate announced at the FOMC meeting immediately preceding the month in question. If the market is 100 percent in agreement that the target rate announced at the meeting will be 4.00 percent then the future will trade at 96.0 prior to the announcement.

However, if some market participants believe the Fed will raise rates to 4.25 percent, they will sell Fed Funds futures at 96.0 since, assuming a 4.25 percent rate, the fair price for the futures is 95.75. If the market is split evenly between those expecting 4 percent and those expecting 4.25 percent, then the futures contract will reach an equilibrium level of 95.875, implying a probability-weighted average rate of 4.125 percent. However, if 60 percent of investors expect 4.00 percent while only 40 percent expect 4.25 percent then the market price of the future will be biased 60/40 in favor of a 4.00 percent rate. This produces an equilibrium price of 95.90, implying a 4.10 percent rate. We would say in this case that the market is assigning a 40 percent probability to a rate hike of 25 bps. Visually, we can think of the "distance" between the market equilibrium price and the two possible rates as measuring the implied probability of each outcome—starting from 4.00 percent and "walking" toward 4.25 percent; by the time we reach 4.10 percent we have gone 40 percent of the way. Therefore, the market is assigning a 40 percent probability to a 25 bps rate hike.

The problem becomes more complicated when there is an FOMC announcement mid-month in which case the Fed Funds' future is a weighted average, based on the number of days before and after the announcement, of the current known rate and the probability-weighted average of the possible new target rates announced at the meeting. Still more complicated is the case where there are multiple possible outcomes (i.e., no change, 25 bps cut or a 50 bps cut). Fortunately, we do not have to do the calculation ourselves: Bloomberg offers an excellent function **FFIP** (*Fed Funds Implied Probability*), which measures the implied FOMC rate change probabilities implied by the market price of the Fed Funds' futures.

REST OF THE WORLD ECONOMICS

We now look briefly at economic data outside of the United States. In general, with the exception of globally focused investors or those particularly interested in macroeconomic trends, U.S. investors give relatively little attention to foreign economic data releases. In contrast, foreign investors give a great deal of attention to U.S. data releases—in many cases more even than their own domestic announcements. This imbalanced interest toward U.S. data as a global market indicator is neither surprising nor unjustified. U.S. economic data releases have a much greater impact on global markets, both in the trading immediately after the announcement as well as the longer-term trend, for several reasons:

- *Size:* The United States has the largest single economy in the world, accounting for approximately one-fifth of the global GDP and approximately one-third of all global consumption. The single most important external factor impacting many foreign markets is the evolution of the U.S. economy. It has only been in recent years that the possibility of global markets—particularly emerging economies—"decoupling" from U.S. growth has even come into consideration. As it stands, the United States remains, as it has been for several decades, the primary driving force in the global economy.
- *Globalization:* Most of the largest companies in foreign markets derive a significant percentage of their sales from foreign markets, particularly the United States (as demonstrated by the trade deficit). Due to the smaller size of their local economies, there was even greater benefit to be realized through international expansion. As a result, foreign manufacturers have a greater sensitivity to a decrease in U.S. demand than a comparable U.S. manufacturer would have to a slackening in demand in any single foreign market.
- *Data quality and timeliness:* As discussed previously, the market impact of an economic data announcement is directly proportional to its timeliness, accuracy, and relevance. In general, the United States produces more accurate statistics, and produces them earlier, than what is available in most other parts of the world.

- *Reliability:* The United States has the benefit of being a generally orderly and transparent economy. In many countries, the ability to produce statistics that accurately assess the GDP, hours worked, retail sales, or other broad measures of economic activity is much lower due to inefficient means of data collection and a larger component of the economy operating unofficially (undocumented labor, payments occurring "under the table," etc.).
- *Timing of release:* The market impact of a data announcement that occurs outside of trading hours can be difficult to measure—if investors have had several hours to digest the data, the reaction can be significantly muted by the time markets open. Asian and European economic announcements take place when only their local markets are open. U.S. economic announcements, on the other hand, are usually released between 8:30 A.M. and 10:00 A.M. Eastern Time. At this time, U.S. institutional investors are at their desks and Europe is in the middle of its trading session. The impact of the news announcement is felt immediately in live trading in the world's two largest equity markets.

This is not to suggest that European and Asian economic data are without significance. The first market information available in the morning is the overnight performance of the Asian and European markets and economic data releases are an important element to understanding these movements. We will look at some of the more important statistics in Europe and the more significant economies of Asia. While each country or region will have its own focus—depending on the particular structure of the economy, its strengths and weaknesses and the current situation in which it finds itself—the overall framework of economics is the same and the focus is what has been discussed already: GDP, employment, inflation, and interest rates, along with the other indicators that help us predict future changes in these factors (consumer confidence, retail sales, industrial production, etc.).

An important fact to keep in consideration is that it is often not possible to compare the absolute levels of economic data releases between different economies due to different calculation methodologies and the fact that the level of development and particular circumstances of each economy will dictate the appropriate levels for various economic variables.

EUROPE

For the purposes of our discussion, by "Europe" we are referring to the 17 western European countries: Austria, Belgium, Denmark, Finland,

France, Germany, Greece, Ireland, Italy, Luxembourg, Netherlands, Norway, Portugal, Spain, Sweden, Switzerland, and the United Kingdom.

Political and Economic Overview

The establishment of the *European Political and Monetary Union* and the adoption of the euro as the primary currency for many of these countries is arguably the most significant change in the structure of the European economy in the last half-century. While the seeds of European unification were laid with the signing of the Treaty of Paris in 1951, it was not until 42 years later, in November 1993 when the Maastricht Treaty went into effect, that the European Union was established as a formal political body in Europe.

The process of monetary unification followed soon after, with the establishment of the *European Central Bank* (ECB) in June 1998 and the official fixing of the exchange rates between the legacy currencies (French franc, Spanish peseta, German mark, etc.) with the euro at the end of that year. On January 1, 1999, the euro was adopted as the official currency of trade throughout the newly established *Eurozone* of Belgium, Germany, Greece,[9] Spain, France, Ireland, Italy, Luxembourg, Netherlands, Austria, Portugal, and Finland, and exactly three years later, on January 1, 2002, the legacy currencies were abandoned and euro notes and coins went into circulation as the official currency for more than 300 million European citizens.[10]

Given the scope of the undertaking—not to mention the fact that 50 years earlier many of these same countries were rather more focused on bombing each other than on harmonizing monetary policy—it is truly a remarkable accomplishment that the euro was ever launched at all, much less that is should, in the short span of 10 years, begin to threaten the hegemony of the U.S. dollar as the international currency of choice.

The integration and consolidation of the European economies has had a tremendous impact on trading in the European equity markets, which have undergone something of a revolution in the past 15 years. While there is no question that, even without the impetus of the establishment of the European Union, the financial services industry would have evolved during this time as the result of technological advances and innovations, the pace of change could not possibly have been so fast.

As recently as the mid-1990s, Europe was still a fragmented market of very independent countries with autonomous economic and monetary policies, different currencies, and local stock and derivative exchanges. Notwithstanding some cross-border economic agreements between specific countries, the economic focus was strongly national with a high degree of government involvement in "national champion" companies, many of which had only recently been privatized. While there was a significant amount of economic activity between countries, cross-border mergers, particularly in politically sensitive sectors such as utilities, energy, and banking, were extremely rare. In general, the economic focus of most companies was domestic, particularly among small- and mid-sized companies for whom the multiple currencies and administrative hurdles of cross-border activity were excessively burdensome.

Comparing this with markets post-Union, the contrasts are stark. Cross-border activity has been greatly facilitated by the more homogeneous legal frameworks, the common currency, and the free movement of workers between member states. The privatization of many sectors, and the "integrationist" viewpoint of the European commission, has facilitated mergers and acquisitions across national borders (though admittedly some countries still show strong protectionist sentiments). Of particular importance for equity investors has been the rapid pace at which independent national stock exchanges have begun to consolidate into larger regional entities covering multiple countries.

Economic Data

At the same time, it is important to recognize that while the establishment of the European Union led to harmonization of legislation in many areas including competition, trade, and intra-European emigration, we are not dealing with the United States of Europe. The individual member countries retain a great deal of autonomy in many important areas of economic policy including labor market regulations, taxation, and, most importantly for our purposes, the collection and dissemination of economic data.

Each country in Europe computes economic data independently, using its own methodology, and releases the results according to its own schedule. *Eurostat,* the statistical office of the European Community, produces aggregate statistics for the European Union and the Eurozone based on the individual national releases. As a result there is a very large volume of statistics to consider. While in the United States it is rare for more than three or four independent economic announcements to be made in any particular day, across Europe there can easily be 20 or 30. The analysis of European economic data therefore requires a combination of two apparently contradictory acts: *filtering,* to see through the mass of data and pinpoint those statistics of greatest relevance, and *aggregating,* to pull together the many disparate announcements to get a composite picture of the general trends in the economy. For example, the Belgian Business Confidence Survey is not a market-moving data point in its own right (the economy of Belgium being slightly smaller than that of New Jersey), and therefore not something that requires great attention by investors. However, when combined with similar statistics from France, Germany, and Italy it begins to give a more complete picture of pan-European sentiment. To give some sense of global perspective, Exhibit 13.4 contains a comparison of the relative size of the European countries and their economies.

While the European economy is, in aggregate, larger than that of the United States, this lack of homogeneity or coordination in the computation

	Market Cap ($mm)	GDP ($bb)	Population (mm)
World	53,116.36	65,610.0	6,677.56
United States	16,014.91	13,840.0	303.82
European Union	13,970.27	13,516.6	399.31
Eurozone	7,951.95	10,293.7	311.61
United Kingdom	3,627.51	2,137.0	60.94
France	2,282.74	2,047.0	64.06
Germany	1,943.15	2,810.0	82.37
Switzerland†	1,180.61	300.2	7.58
Italy	946.53	1,786.0	58.15
Spain	955.34	1,352.0	40.49
Sweden†	520.04	334.6	9.05
Netherlands	454.07	639.5	16.65
Belgium	370.69	376	10.40
Norway†	409.92	247.4	4.64
Finland	290.02	185.5	5.24
Denmark†	280.24	203.7	5.48
Austria	230.76	317.8	8.21
Greece	199.64	324.6	10.72
Ireland	112.38	186.2	4.16
Portugal	134.07	230.5	10.68
Luxembourg	32.56	38.6	0.49

EXHIBIT 13.4 Relative Size of European Economies[a]
[a]Based on the original definition of the European Union (the 17 listed countries). Using the current definition of the numbers would be (roughly) 20 percent larger.
Note: A dagger (†) denotes countries that have not adopted the euro.
Source: Bloomberg, Market Capitalization and Population (July 18, 2008); and U.S. GDP, *CIA World Factbook*, 2007 (www.cia.gov).

and dissemination of economic data is one of the primary reasons why U.S. economic releases have greater impact on European markets than European data itself. In the United States the information available about the state of the entire economy emerges in discrete steps with each new economic announcement, which makes these announcements significant, while in Europe there is a gradual unfolding of information about economic conditions, which reduces the impact of each new release.

While there are certain unique characteristics of the United States that give greater global significance to its economic data releases, prompt aggregate data for any other economic body that produced or consumed as much as the United States would have similar impact and importance as U.S. economic data. One can imagine a reversed scenario in which the EU published a single, consolidated statistic in a timely manner while the United States published staggered, heterogeneously defined statistics by region (North-East, Mid-Atlantic, South, etc.) over several weeks. One would expect the market would react much more to EU data under this scenario.

Central Banks and Monetary Policy

By adopting the euro, each participating country gave up the control of monetary policy from their national central banks to the European Central Bank. Sweden, Switzerland, Denmark, Norway and, most significantly, the United Kingdom chose not to join the monetary union and retained their national currencies and the independence of their monetary policy. As a result of the relative sizes of these economies, monetary policy in Europe is now essentially a two-player game, with the ECB responsible for 76 percent of pan-European GDP and the Bank of England (BoE), the central bank of the United Kingdom, overseeing 16 percent. The remaining 8 percent is divided fairly evenly between Switzerland and the three nonparticipating Nordic countries.[11]

The European Central Bank (ECB)   The Board of Governors of the European Central Bank, consisting of the six member governing council plus the governors of the 12 national central banks, meets every second Thursday in Frankfurt. Monetary policy is discussed at the first meeting of each month and a decision on interest rates is then announced at approximately 1:45 P.M. (Central European Time). The ECB President, currently Jean-Claude Trichet, then holds a press conference at 2:30 P.M. While the most significant reaction is to the interest rate decision, markets are very sensitive anytime a central bank governor speaks, particularly during the question-and-answer period when the responses are unscripted. The minutes of the meetings are not published.

The ECB's stated goal for monetary policy is the maintenance of price stability in the Eurozone over the medium term. "Price stability" is defined as an annual increase in the *Harmonized Index of Consumer Prices* (HICP) (the benchmark European inflation indicator) of "below but close to 2.0 percent." To achieve this, the ECB employs a *"two-pillar"* strategy, which seeks to balance short-term and longer-term economic indicators. The first pillar includes an analysis of a broad range of economic indicators to assess the outlook for price stability in the short to medium term. The second pillar focuses on identifying long-run inflation risks through the relationship between money supply and prices. The ECB has a specific target for the growth of the broad money supply (M3) of 4.5 percent per year, which is based on an expected long-term GDP growth rate of between 2.0 percent and 2.5 percent and inflation of 2 percent. The ECB is a bit of an outlier among central banks in including an analysis of the money supply in their monetary policy decisions; while there is general consensus within the academic community that the total amount of money available is a key determinant of long-term inflation, there is significant disagreement about what role this analysis should play in monetary policy given the increasing complexity of the modern financial systems and the difficulty of accurately assessing the money supply.

The Bank of England (BoE)   Monetary policy for the United Kingdom is determined by the *Bank of England* (BOE), which meets monthly to discuss monetary policy and make a decision on interest rates. The BoE shares the same two-percent inflation target as the ECB but looks to achieve that rate on a two-year time horizon. Bank of England decisions are therefore more affected by factors that will impact the future course of inflation rather than simply on current conditions. The meetings of the Bank of England's *Monetary Policy Committee* (MPC) are frequently scheduled within a few days or even on the same day as the ECB meetings, with the MPC announcement released about one hour earlier.

EUROPEAN ECONOMIC STATISTICS

What follows below is a brief overview of the most significant economic statistics published in Europe. As with the U.S. economic announcements discussed previously, the factors that determine the importance, and with it the market impact of a given data point are timeliness, relevance, accuracy, and deviation from expectation. As a result, many of the most significant European economic statistics are from Germany, which is the largest economy in Europe (as well as the world's largest exporter nation) and tends to produce higher-quality statistics relatively more quickly than other European countries.

Due to the staggered release of similar data by different countries, timeliness is an even greater determinant of significance in European data. Once a consumer price index or confidence survey has been published by one country, investors will already form a view on the likely outcome of the equivalent statistic from other European countries. The publication of the second or third consumer price index or confidence survey for a given month will not be viewed so much as new information but merely as supporting (or potentially contradicting) evidence to the view established by the first release. For this reason, several of the most important European statistics are diffusion indices as these require less work to collect and compute and are therefore timelier and less likely to require significant revisions.

While the United Kingdom is a very significant part of the European economy, because it retains an independent monetary policy, the significance of economic data is more limited as it will not impact the decisions of the ECB. In general, the only data point that receives significant attention outside the United Kingdom is the BoE policy announcement. Other statistics (inflation, retail sales, etc.) will generally only have a noticeable impact on the U.K. domestic market and potentially a small knock-on effect in the broader European market if they are significantly away from consensus.

While the economic statistics presented are the primary tools used by investors and policymakers to assess the current state of economic conditions in Europe, particularly the Eurozone, their announcement do not, in general, have significant short-term impact on equity markets. A greater impact is generally recognized in the fixed income and currency markets, which may then have a follow-through effect on equities.

GDP

German, French, Italian, and Euroland "Flash" GDP Estimates
The first indicative data on quarterly GDP begin to appear in about six weeks after quarter end, when the federal statistical offices of Germany, France, and Italy[12] publish their "flash" estimates of quarterly GDP. These estimates are akin to those in the U.S. advance GDP estimate but contain less information—usually just a headline GDP growth estimate—and are published somewhat later. The more complete "preliminary" GDP estimates for these countries are anywhere from one week to a month later.

Shortly after the data from these three countries are released, Eurostat publishes an advance estimate of Euroland GDP growth. While this is little more than a simple extrapolation of the German, French, and Italian flash estimates, and therefore subject to revision as the individual country data are revised and new countries publish their results, it receives attention from the market as it is the first official estimate of GDP for the Eurozone.

Survey Data

IFO Business Survey Probably the most closely watched of all Euroland economic indicators is the *Business Climate Survey* published by the IFO Institute. The survey is published during the last week of the month and is based on survey responses received from nearly 7,000 German businesses operating in manufacturing, construction, wholesaling, and retailing. The data are extremely timely and includes responses received up to the day before publication—the calculation of the index is done on the morning of the day the data are published.

The structure of the survey is similar to the consumer confidence surveys of the Conference Board and University of Michigan Confidence. Participants are asked to provide their assessment of the current business situation ("good," "satisfactory," or "poor") and their expectations for the next six months ("more favorable," "unchanged," or "more unfavorable"). Diffusion indices are then calculated as the difference between the number of positive and negative responses. The headline index level is the average of the present and future expectations subindices. Details of the subindices, as well as the decomposition of responses between different sectors, are also published.

ZEW Financial Market Report In the second week of each month the Centre for Economic Research (ZEW) at Manheim University publishes the results of a monthly survey of approximately 400 finance professionals, including academics as well as fund managers and traders on their views and outlook of the German economy as a whole. (As financial institutions are not included in the IFO survey, the ZEW acts as a useful sister statistic.) A diffusion index is computed based on the difference between the percentages of respondents whose six-month view of the economy is "optimistic" versus "pessimistic." While the IFO has shown to be a more reliable, and less volatile, indicator of turning points in the economy, the ZEW receives considerable attention because it serves as a leading indicator of the IFO due to the fact that it is published a week earlier.

Industrial Production

Euroland Manufacturing Purchasing Managers Index (PMI) Published on the first business day of each month by Reuters-NTC, the *Euroland Manufacturing PMI* is one of the very few economic statistics for the full

Eurozone that is published in a timely manner, which makes it one of the most closely watched data releases in Europe. Its popularity is enhanced by the fact that the structure of the survey is similar to that of the ISM Manufacturing Survey, allowing the comparison of economic conditions between the United States and Europe.

Approximately 2,500 survey participants in manufacturing, construction, and service industries across eight Eurozone countries[13] provide information on various aspects of business activity including new orders, output, employment, inventory levels, and suppliers' delivery times. Diffusion indices are then computed based on the change in activity from the previous month and normalized such that a level of 50 indicates no growth, while higher levels indicate expansion and lower levels indicate contraction. While a number of different diffusion indices are published, the primary focus is on the overall Eurozone PMI, which is computed as a weighted average of five factors: new orders (30 percent), output (25 percent), employment (20 percent), delivery times (15 percent), and inventory (10 percent).

Consumer Prices and Inflation

Preliminary German CPI and German States' CPI   Around the 22nd of each month, the Federal Statistics Bureau of the German Bundesbank publishes the preliminary estimate of the German CPI for the month in progress. This estimate is based on the data published by six of the German states, which are released 30 minutes earlier. As the conversion of the six individual states' data to an estimate for the whole of Germany are a relatively simply econometric calculation, it is possible to estimate the preliminary German CPI quite accurately before it is released. As a result, despite their seemingly narrow scope, the announcement of the German states' CPIs is actually the more significant event from the perspective of market impact.

Euroland HICP   The inflation metric used by the ECB in monetary policy decisions is the *Harmonized Index of Consumer Prices*, published by Eurostat three weeks after the end of the month under observation. Given that the ECB has an explicit inflation target of "close to, but less than 2 percent," the announcement of the HICP is an important statistic, even though it arrives some four weeks after the German states' CPIs. The raw data for the calculation of the HICP are the individual CPI calculations produced by the statistical agencies of each of the member countries who have responsibility for determining the composition of the basket of goods used in their country. HICP then computes a weighted average based on the percentage of total consumption of each country.

While the Eurozone HICP shares many similarities with the U.S. CPI, one very important difference is that the HICP does not include an estimate of "Owner's Equivalent Rent" and is therefore less sensitive to house price inflation.

Employment

German Unemployment (Labor Report)   The first piece of employment data received each month is the German Unemployment Report, published by the Federal Labor Office in the first week of the next month. The report measures the number of unemployed as a percentage of the total labor force. The statistic must be interpreted with care as the German definition of unemployed (a person registered with the unemployment office) is more liberal than the measure used in most other unemployment analyses (a person registered with the unemployment office and actively seeking employment) and therefore registers significantly higher level of unemployment (about 1 to 2 percent). Employment data are released one month later but generally have relatively little market impact due to time lag in publication.

Other

Euroland M3   As discussed previously, the ECB is unusual among central banks in its inclusion of changes in the money supply (M3) in its policy decisions. While in the United States, monetarism has lost importance in economic analysis, the ECB includes it as an integral part of its monetary policy as one of the two "pillars" of ECB strategy. While the relevance of monetary aggregates to economic policy may be debatable, so long as changes in the money supply are used to guide ECB decisions, information on Euroland M3 will continue to be an economic statistic to be aware of.

ASIA

Because of the small size and limited global influence of many of the smaller Asian economies, the market impact of most Asian economic data releases is quite small. Even with the most significant announcements, it is difficult to measure the impact on markets outside of the region due to the limited overlap between the market hours of European and Asian exchanges. At the open of European trading, investors have to digest the information in the last four hours of the previous day's trading in the United States as well as any after-hours earnings announcements from U.S. companies and other overnight news events. Amidst this mass of information, only the most globally significant economic data from Asia will have any discernible effect.

The economic data releases that do have global significance are those that relate to Asia's unique role in the global economy, as either a source of inexpensive financing (Japan) or the provider of inexpensive manufacturing and production (China, South Korea).

Japan

While Japan is the second largest economy in the world (third if the Eurozone is considered as a single economy), the economic stagnation that has prevailed in its economy for the better part of the last 20 years has greatly reduced the significance of Japanese economic data announcements. Despite its size, the lack of growth means that Japan behaves, in many ways, like a much smaller economy, and therefore receives relatively less focus than many smaller but more rapidly expanding economies.

While true in all markets, it is particularly the case in Japan that, in order to properly understand the economy, and particularly the stock market today, it is necessary to understand where it has been. There was some excitement, in December 2005, when the Nikkei-225 hit 15,000, having nearly doubled in the two-and-a-half years since reaching a low of 7,600 in April 2003. While this was a significant accomplishment, it must be viewed in the proper historical context: the Nikkei had touched 15,000 10 years earlier in June 1995 and 10 years before that, when it crossed it for the first time, in March 1986. In between these two dates it reached a peak of nearly 39,000 in December 1989. The excitement of reaching 15,000 in 2005 was not one of historic accomplishment, but of a potential reawakening of the generally dormant Japanese market from an extended downward (or at best horizontal) trend. In the end, despite the brief flurry of activity, sustained growth failed to materialize and the Japanese stock market slipped lower as the global economy began to slow in 2007.

Another important characteristic of the Japanese economy is the extraordinarily low level of interest rates. During the 1980s the Japanese economy entered a period of spectacular growth, culminating in a massive stock market and property price bubble. When this bubble finally burst in 1989, the economy entered into a sustained period of economic stagnation characterized by very low inflation (and actually deflation), high household savings rates, and low levels of consumption. In an effort to stimulate economic growth and consumption and inflation, the Bank of Japan (BoJ) cut interest rates aggressively, eventually reaching a *zero interest rate policy* (ZIRP).

Monetary policy cannot get more stimulative than that, but the Japanese economy did not move.

But the rest of the world did. As a result of these extraordinarily low rates of interest, many investors globally used Japan as the source of cheap funding with which to leverage up their exposure to more attractive investments elsewhere. While this required the assumption of exchange rate risk between the Japanese yen (JPY) and the currency where they were investing, the interest rate differential was so significant that it was worthwhile to assume the risk. In one particularly popular trade, known as the *carry trade,* investors would borrow in JPY and then lend (buy bonds) in high-yielding countries such as New Zealand and Brazil. While far from a risk-free strategy, the 16 percent interest rate differential between the low-growth Japanese economy and the high-growth Brazilian economy compensated for the risk. In the end, the strengthening Brazilian economy (as well as lots of other investors putting on the same position) led to a strengthening Brazilian real (BRL) and the carry trade paid a double benefit—a huge interest rate differential plus positive currency appreciation. This trade was very popular with global investors for many years until the credit crisis of 2007–2008 forced the liquidations of highly leveraged positions causing violent currency movements between the JPY and many other currencies.

While investors have long viewed the Japanese economy as a "sleeping dragon" that would one day reawaken and begin to show signs of real growth and inflation, the primary importance of Japanese economic data for global investors has less to do with what they imply for the Japanese stock market, and more to do with what they imply about the global availability of cheap financing. As a result, the Japanese economic data announcements that receive greatest international attention are those that indicate signs of inflation, which, if sustained, would give the BoJ the room to increase interest rates. The two primary inflation measures in Japan are the *Consumer Price Index* (CPI), published by the Ministry of Public Management, Home Affairs, Posts, and Telecommunications, and the *Corporate Goods Price Survey* (CGPS) published by the BoJ (starting in 1887!).

The monetary policy meetings of the BoJ, which occur about every four weeks, do not receive particular international attention due to the fact that for so long there has been very little uncertainty in the outcome of the meeting. An exception to this was in 2006 when the Japanese economy showed sufficient indications of recovery to allow the BoJ to raise interest rates by 50 bps, the first time in five years that the ZIRP was lifted.

During periods when interest in the Japanese economy is heightened, one of the best summaries of the overall state of the economy is the quarterly *TANKAN* survey performed by the BoJ. The report is based on responses from approximately 10,000 companies across 30 different industries and contains both subjective judgments of the state of the economy and future economic developments, as well as more rigorously quantitative assessments of sales, fixed investment, and hiring. The survey, which is similar in many ways to the IFO or ISM, has been published since 1951.

While Japan's economy is heavily export-based, one of the key components to any real, sustained economic expansion in Japan is an increase in domestic consumption. For this reason, investors give considerable attention to the *Tertiary Industry Activity Index* (TIAI), published monthly by the Ministry of Economy, Trade and Industry (METI), which provides a summary of activity in the services sector, which is primarily domestically focused and therefore provides a useful indicator of domestic demand.

Asia ex-Japan (AeJ)

By Asia ex-Japan (AeJ), also referred to as non-Japan Asia (NJA), we are generally referring to the countries of China, India, Singapore, Indonesia, Thailand, Malaysia, Hong Kong, South Korea, Taiwan, Australia, and New Zealand. With the exception of Hong Kong, Singapore, Australia, and New Zealand, these are all generally considered emerging markets. China and India are often considered separately and are more frequently viewed in the context of the BRIC countries (Brazil, Russia, India, and China), which, due to the combination of their size, population, natural resources, and rapid growth and industrialization, are considered to have the greatest potential to significantly alter the global economic landscape over the next 50 years.

In order to properly appreciate the markets of non-Japan Asia, it is important to get some sense of perspective on the region. Perhaps the two most noteworthy characteristics are its size and diversity. In terms of size, AeJ spans eight time zones and is home to half of the world's population. In the same time it takes for a Hong Kong-based salesperson to visit one of her clients in Auckland, New Zealand, she could have flown to London or Los Angeles.

The contrasts in the ability to do business are no less striking. While Singapore, Hong Kong, Australia, and New Zealand possess open, highly developed and well-regulated markets, the regional behemoths of China and India, as well as most of the smaller economies, are still very much emerging markets with significant restrictions on capital flows, opaque trading, and structural advantages for local investors. *Transparency International*, a global anti-corruption organization, produces an annual *Corruption Perceptions Index* (also called the "CPI") measuring the degree to which corruption is perceived to exist among public officials and politicians in countries around the world. The report is based on survey data taken from experts and businesses and institutions operating around the world. The results for AeJ, shown in Exhibit 13.5, are illustrative of the diversity of the business climates in this region.

For investors whose activity is focused on these markets, the economic statistics of relevance are the same as what is important in any economy: GDP, employment, and inflation, though in emerging markets one must also assess many more basic factors such as political stability or the risk of currency devaluation. Due to the significant dependence of most of the economies of AeJ on demand from developed market consumers, many globally focused investors look at the performance of the Southeast Asian economies as much for their own intrinsic investment potential as for their value as an economic indicator for the level of activity in western countries. AeJ's contribution to global consumption is quite small, while its

	Market Cap ($mm)	GDP ($bb)	Population (mm)	Transparency Score[a]	Rank[b]
World	53,116.36	65,610.0	6,677.56	4	67
United States	16,014.91	13,840.0	303.82	7.2	20
Eurozone	7,951.95	10,293.7	311.61	7.3	19
Japan	4,428.53	4,290.0	127.29	7.5	17
China	2,587.89	6,991.0	1,330.04	3.5	72
India	1,165.86	2,989.0	1,148.00	3.5	72
Singapore	462.03	228.1	4.61	9.3	4
Indonesia	192.28	837.8	237.51	2.3	143
Thailand	169.18	519.4	65.49	3.3	84
Malaysia	273.42	357.4	25.27	5.1	43
Hong Kong	2,216.39	292.8	7.02	8.3	14
South Korea	943.93	1,201.0	49.23	5.1	43
Taiwan	756.35	695.4	22.92	5.7	34
Australia	1,364.95	760.8	20.60	8.6	11
New Zealand	35.84	111.7	4.17	9.4	1

EXHIBIT 13.5 Relative Size of Asian Economies
[a]Score out of 10.
[b]Rank out of 180.
Source: Bloomberg, Market Capitalization and Population (July 18, 2008); U.S. GDP, CIA World Factbook, 2007 (www.cia.gov); and Transparency International, Corruption Perceptions Index for 2007 (www.transparency.org).

contribution to global production is significantly larger. While the economic cycles of some of the larger economies (i.e., China) have begun to attract interest in their own right, many Asian economies tell us more by what they are doing—what are they making for the rest of the world to consume—than by what they themselves are consuming.

THE MARKET'S REACTION FUNCTION

We now look at some of the factors that shape the way in which the market reacts to announcements of economic data—what is often referred to as the market's *reaction function*. While we use the term "function," we must be careful not to imply a level of determinism and predictability that is not warranted. The market's reaction to economic data is highly unpredictable and depends on a mixture of some objectively observable economic conditions as well as a wide range of highly subjective, unobservable, and at times irrational factors. In our discussion of exotic options in Chapter 10, we introduced the term "path dependence" to describe derivatives whose value depended not just on the value of the underlying asset at maturity, but on how it got there. The reaction to economic data is very much the same: the absolute level of the particular statistic has only partial relevance—what matters just as much are the surrounding circumstances in which that event occurs and how it impacts investors' expectations for the future.

We must also keep in mind that just because it happened after the announcement, does not mean it was caused by the announcement. Particularly with regards to more significant data announcements, even if the decision has already been made to trade, many investors will wait until after the announcement to actually execute, just in case the data make them reconsider their decision. As a result, a certain part of the post-announcement market movements is actually attributable to pre-announcement decisions whose execution has simply been withheld.

There are three levels at which we might look to measure the market's reaction to an economic data announcement:

1. *Trading immediately after the number is announced:* How do the markets react to the news? This may include futures trading in U.S. markets or intra-day stock price action in Europe, as well as movements in the fixed income and currency markets. This is usually the impact most directly observable and easily attributable to the announcement.
2. *Trading on the day:* The morning economic announcements can have a significant impact on the general "feel" of trading during the full

day. Are traders talking about the numbers? Does the market seem to care about the news? This can actually be quite difficult to assess as the impact of previously made decisions cannot be easily separated from the trading initiated based on the announcement. One or two large orders that may have nothing to do with the announcement can significantly bias the tone of the day's trading.

3. *Relationship with other numbers:* Does the number provide information that is consistent with other recent releases? Does the number reinforce or disprove a general theme in the market? In the larger context of recent economic announcements, the significance of a particular data point can generally be determined by the frequency with which economists and traders use it as a contributing factor in their arguments for the likely direction of markets.

The reaction to news flow differs dramatically between different types of investors. A useful analogy is to consider the significance of waves on the ocean. To the short-term traders who focus on flows, the market movements immediately following the announcement may provide significant opportunity to move quickly in and out of positions and capture a profit; these are the surfers who try to capture the most from every wave. For pension funds, endowments, and other investors who take a much longer view of markets, the impact of a single announcement may be relatively small; these are the cruise ships that focus their attention on the general conditions of the sea rather than on any single wave. For statistical arbitrage and other model-driven strategies, the news announcement may have little significance at all; these are the submarines who are more interested in what can be found under the surface than on the superficial conditions the rest of the market is watching. Institutional traders and salespeople, whose job requires a significant focus on the intra-day management of order flow, are probably best viewed as small boats.

What then, are the primary factors that influence the market's reaction to economic numbers? A comprehensive list would have to include everything from economics to politics to news events to the weather. Our interest here will be simply to focus attention on a few of the factors that receive most attention and are the basis for the largest proportion of trading floor "chatter," both before and after the number is released.

The first level of analysis is on the fundamental economic interpretation of the number. This is based on the combination of the three factors we have discussed (timelines, accuracy, and relevance), which determine how much actual information content there is in the announcement, and the "classical" interpretation of the underlying information. While most traders have at least a passing familiarity with macroeconomics, the market's reaction is heavily influenced by the published estimates of professional economists, who have the more subtle understanding of both the statistical methods used in the computation of the number, as well as the overall economic conditions of the market in which to frame their views.

While formal economics provides the framework for understanding the significance of a number, trader positioning, and psychology have a much greater relevance to the actual market impact of the announcement. Depending on the current mind-set of the investing community, the potential reaction to a particular economic data release can become highly imbalanced. If most traders are looking for a very strong result, above and beyond what economists are predicting, then even if the results are significantly above published expectations, the reaction can be fairly muted since this is not really a surprise but an in-line result (relative to heightened trader expectations), while a result consistent with or below expectations will be seen as a big miss and received very negatively. There will often be an informal *whisper number* that represents the result the market is hoping for and it is the performance versus this number that matters—as this is what traders' positions will be based on. In the language of Wall Street, the whisper number is what is "priced into the market" before the announcement and the trading reaction will depend on how the announced data compare with the what is priced in, rather than on the average of the surveyed economists' expectations.

Market reaction to news can often be counterintuitive. Traders are often said to "buy the rumor and sell the news." That is, in anticipation of what is expected to be a very positive economic data release, traders will build up long positions that they will then look to sell into the expected spike in the markets upon release of the data. While this may sometimes work, if too many traders try to execute the same trade, the flow of sell orders into the markets upon release of the news is greater than the demand from those who waited to buy until the data were released, and markets end up going down. Another similar phenomenon in a market dominated by negative economic announcements is the "It's so bad it must be good!" view. When an economic data release is very much worse than expected, traders will usually react negatively. However, due to the backward-looking nature of economic data releases, there is occasionally the view—particularly when faced with a particularly awful result—that the worst must be behind us, in which case markets will soon start to look better, and the trading impact can actually be positive.

Traders will also watch recent market trends to determine how they think other investors are positioned for the number. If the street expects the data to be more positive than economists are predicting, then the risks are actually biased toward traders being disappointed by an insufficiently excellent result. In this case, even though everyone thinks it is going to be a really good number, maybe it would be better to be set up for a negative reaction. Unless, of course, *everyone* thinks the rest of the street is long, in which case everyone is actually going to be set up to the short side and you should be long. Traders are experts at second, third, and fourth-guessing the positioning of other traders and some statistics become so over-analyzed that it becomes anyone's guess what will happen when the number is actually released.

In the end, the reaction to any particular announcement is a combination of so many factors that it can be extremely difficult to anticipate how markets will perform when the announcement is made. As a guideline for understanding, and eventually anticipating, the market's reaction, it can be helpful to work through the following questions:

- *Is the statistic important?* How well does it score in terms of timeliness, accuracy, and relevance? There is no point wasting precious time analyzing meaningless statistics.
- *What is the fundamental economic interpretation of the data?* What does it tell us about the economy, inflation, unemployment, or the business cycle? Is it a leading, coincident, or lagging indicator?
- *What are the economists' expectations?* Many traders will react based solely on the difference between the average expectation and actual outcome. It is important to know what the average expectation is as well as to have a sense of how widely distributed estimates were. If economists are in consensus, traders probably are as well, and a deviation from the expectation will be a bigger surprise to the market and elicit a greater reaction.
- *What is the general economic trend?* Where are we and where have we been? What does that say about where we are probably going? It is impossible to assess the significance of a statistic without knowing where it has been in the recent past.
- *How is the street positioned?* Does recent asset price action suggest anything about how traders are positioned? What is the market chatter? Is there a whisper number? This last, subjective assessment can be very important to the actual market reaction. However, particularly for new arrivals to Wall Street, it is also the most difficult to determine.

A Real-World Example

As a useful illustration of the many factors that can contribute impact of a given data release, we will analyze the market reaction to the Advance

Retail Sales announcement from Friday, October 13, 2006. As discussed previously, the Advance Retail Sales report, released at 8:00 A.M. Eastern Time, is one of the most important and timely indicators of consumption and therefore GDP.

At the time of the announcement, the U.S. economy had enjoyed several years of above-trend economic growth and was widely considered to be in the late states of an extended economic expansion. To prevent the economy from overheating, the Federal Reserve had raised the Fed Funds' target rate 17 times in the last 24 months from a 2004 low of 1.00 percent to the then-current level of 5.25 percent. Rate increases had only recently been stopped as inflation risks appeared controlled and the concern turned to preparing for a slowdown in economic growth. The highlight question of the moment was whether the inevitable slowdown would be a "soft landing" (a gradual economic deceleration but with non-negative GDP growth) or a "hard landing" (a full-blown recession with negative GDP growth).

The primary factors in the hard versus soft landing debate were housing prices and oil. By mid-2006, the U.S. housing bubble was already rapidly deflating and there was significant concern about the impact this would have on consumer spending. In addition, commodity prices were exploding, particularly crude oil, which had risen over 400 percent in the previous five years from a 2001 low of $17.45/barrel, to a mid-2006 high of $77.03. Despite a recent pull-back, dropping to $62.90 at the end of September, the dramatic increases in gasoline prices and approaching concerns about winter heating fuel prices were perceived by economists as a significant threat to the continued strength of the American consumer.

Given the huge international importance of the U.S. consumer, this was not just a local concern. Markets globally were watching to see if American consumers could weather the storm and keep on buying or if the dual frictions of lower housing and higher oil prices would force them to pull back the throttle on spending, which would likely trigger a hard-landing scenario. The number would set the tone not only for the day but for how traders went into their weekend. Expectation was for a 0.2 percent month-on-month increase in sales.

At 8:30 A.M. the data are released and the actual report is a 0.4 percent *decrease*—a disastrous result. In the previous 24 months there had only been five negative prints, all of which were relatively small and due to base effects following months with very strong sales. The initial roar on the trading floor is *extremely* negative: the consumer is dead, the hard-landing scenario looms large, and the market immediately begins to react with equities moving quickly to the downside.

But wait! There's something brewing beneath the surface. Newswires immediately publish a crucial piece of information: due to the decrease in oil prices, gasoline station revenues dropped 9.6 percent in the month of September. If these are removed from the calculation, the month-on-month change in retail sales is actually a 0.6 percent *increase* significantly higher than expected. It would seem that the consumer is not so badly off and that the difference between the expected and actual numbers was due primarily to economists' inability to accurately assess the impact of gasoline price decreases on spending.

Investors anxiously digest this information and the market opens without significant activity as traders wait for the other economic statistic to be published that day—the Michigan Consumer Confidence survey at 10:30 A.M. Given the mixed message of the Advance Retail Sales report, focus has now shifted to consumer confidence for guidance, where expectations are for a reasonably positive result of 86.5—weaker than recent levels, but still strong given current conditions.

At 10:30 A.M. the Michigan Survey is released and shows a stunning 92.3, a 5.8 point outperformance versus expectations (2.2 standard deviations). The impact of the relief at the gas pump on consumers' view of the economy had been dramatically underestimated by professional economists, whose most optimistic estimate (of the 57 economists surveyed by Bloomberg) was for a report of 90.0.

Unsurprisingly, markets love it and rally sharply through the morning: the consumer is alive and well and seems to be saying, as Mark Twain put it, "The reports of my death have been greatly exaggerated."

Over the rest of the session, however, the euphoria fades as doubts begin to return that the hard landing can actually be avoided. Crude oil futures imply higher gasoline prices will return in the future and this year's heating bills will be significantly larger than last year's. Given the uncertainty, traders who are reluctant to go home long over the weekend begin selling out of their positions. In the end, the session closes with markets virtually unchanged.

WHAT THE MARKET TELLS US ABOUT THE ECONOMY

So far we have looked at economic data and how it can be used to make trading decisions about the likely future direction of the market. However, due to the infrequency and delays in the publication of economic data, the inference is often performed in reverse—investors look at the movements of the market to see what they can infer about the state of the economy (or at least other investors' view of it).

There are two general approaches to this. The first is to isolate distinct subsets of the market—sectors, market capitalization ranges, countries—and try to identify and interpret the trends in their relative performances. The second alternative is to use much more sophisticated statistical analysis in an attempt to isolate more subtle characteristics that might lead one group of stocks to outperform another. This is the general approach of many so-called "quant funds" and involves extensive historical and out-of-sample testing to insure that the patterns that are perceived are real and not spurious correlations.

We will focus on the first approach since it is what the majority of market practitioners can actually do (most are not statisticians). The fact that it is not as rigorously quantitative an approach does not mean that it is easy. To detect true patterns in the market, a trader needs a broad understanding of finance, trading, and economics as well as the ability to filter out a great deal of noise and focus on what is actually meaningful. The key is not just to perceive correlations, which do not necessarily imply causal relationships, but to find coherent logical explanations that explain the price action in different parts of the market and tie this in with the known economic data.

It takes years to develop the breadth of understanding needed to properly construct a framework for understanding the mass of market information and see in it a coherent picture of the economy as a whole. There are, however, some general trends commonly used as building blocks in these sorts of analyses that it will be worth our while to introduce. This list is by no means comprehensive but is intended to give the reader a basic working vocabulary in some of the more common thematic relationships that are used to draw conclusions about the economy and the view of investors about the economy.

- *Market capitalization:* The relative performance of large-cap versus small-cap stocks is a useful indication of investors' appetite for risk and view on the future prospects for the economy. Small-cap companies are a higher-risk investment than large-cap companies due to the greater possibility that they will not survive a downturn in the economy. The trade-off for their increased risk is a much higher potential return on investment. As a result, in a general economic up-trend, small-cap indices tend to outperform large-cap indices as investors shift into riskier assets to capture the greatest benefit from the economic expansion. If investors begin shifting out of small cap and into large cap, this indicates a decreased confidence in the future prospects for the economy. It is worth keeping in mind that the same notional amount shifted between large- and small-cap indices will have much greater market impact on the small-cap index, where liquidity is much lower.

- *Style:* As their name would suggest, growth stocks are much more leveraged to an economic expansion than value stocks. While the precise definitions will differ from one analyst to another, the general characteristics are the same: Growth stocks are those whose business activities or industries are expected to expand, resulting in higher sales and increased EPS. These stocks trade on higher price-to-earnings (PE) ratios as the expectation is that the "E" (earnings) will grow. Value stocks are related to stable, dividend-producing stocks with low P/E ratios. Outperformance of growth over value generally indicates a more positive stance on the future of the economy.

- *Cyclical versus defensives:* The performance of certain sectors tends to be highly correlated with the business cycle, while others are less affected. The relative performance of cyclical versus defensive sectors gives an indication of the market's view of the economy's position in the cycle. A shift out of cyclical and into defensives would indicate a view that the peak of the cycle had passed, which the reverse shift would indicate a view on the beginning of an economic recovery.

"Cyclicals"—industries and sectors that move with the cycles:
- Consumer discretionary: retailing, media, homebuilding
- Financials
- Industrials: machinery, transportation
- Technology
- Materials: chemicals, metals, and mining

"Defensives"—industries and sectors relatively unaffected by the cycle:
- Consumer staples: food staples, tobacco, household and personal products
- Energy
- Healthcare: pharmaceuticals, biotechnology, healthcare equipment and services
- Telecommunications services
- Utilities

- *Bellwether companies:* In many cases the earnings announcements of the largest companies in the sector are used as indications of the overall performance of the sector. Companies like Walmart (retail), FedEx (transportation), Intel (technology) are taken as "bellwether" stocks whose earnings are indicative not only of the conditions of the company but of the market as a whole.

- *Specific sectors:* The performance of certain sectors is often used as an indication of the health of different parts of the economy and as an advance indication for upcoming data announcements. Weakness in consumption will eventually show up in the performance of retail and consumer products companies, though this is generally a lagging indicator as earnings are only announced quarterly. Weakness in homebuilders and other companies leveraged to the housing market can provide early indications of potential softening of consumption, though the time it takes for that weakness to manifest itself can be difficult to predict. The "deep" cyclical sectors such as mining and steel, give a very early heads-up of softening of demand at the level of production.

- *Korea and commodities:* South Korea's economy is highly export-driven and strongly cyclical with significant concentrations in commodities, base metals, and semiconductors. Because these "deep" cyclical industries are among the first to feel the effects of a decrease in demand, the performance of the South Korean economy is a useful leading indicator for the global business cycle. A similar inference can be drawn at an even earlier stage of the production cycle, by analyzing changes in the demand for the raw materials of production, particularly base metals such as steel, copper, or iron. (Copper is sometimes referred to as "Dr. Copper" in recognition of its ability—rare among professional economists—to accurately predict shifts in the business cycle.)

- *Emerging markets(EM):* The shift between large-cap and small-cap in domestic equities can be expressed globally as either a large-cap versus small-cap trade or, alternatively, a developed-market versus emerging market trade. Emerging markets are inherently riskier and more volatile than developed markets. As a result, they tend to outperform in a strong economy and suffer more in a slowdown. Certain ones of the more liquid emerging markets, particularly Brazil, are often used as a proxy for the performance of EM as a whole.

- *VIX (volatility index):* The Chicago Board Options Exchange *Volatility Index* (VIX) calculates a weighted average implied volatility for short-dated SPX options across a number of strikes. Implied volatility tends to increase when markets move down. As such, a heightened level in the VIX can indicate a greater uncertainty about the future direction of the economy and of markets in general. (As an indication of the severity of the market conditions of September and October of 2008, the VIX, which had oscillated between 20 and 30 for most of the previous 18 months as the credit crisis was unfolding, suddenly spiked up to close above 80 on October 27, having traded above 90 intraday).

Across most of these market-based indicators, the general theme is one of shifting between risky assets and less risky assets based on the expected future direction of the market and of the economy. The shift into "safer" assets (more defensive) and out of riskier assets is often referred to as the "flight to quality." This is a broad description of a risk-averse trend across many asset classes and may include shifts between asset classes (out of equities and into bonds) as well as within equities, credit, and fixed income.

SUMMARY

Investors, economists, policymakers, and Wall Street traders use various economic data releases to make assessments about the state of the economy. The three general characteristics that determine whether a particular economic data announcement will have significant market impact are timeliness, accuracy, and relevance. All economic statistics tell us about activity in the past, the closer time period to which the data relate is to the present (timeliness), the more relevant the data. Investors will be reluctant to make trading decisions based on data if there is a strong likelihood that data will be subsequently revised (accuracy). Finally the broader the segment of the market to which the particular data apply, the greater the informational content of the announcement and the greater the impact of the announcement (relevance).

In this chapter we surveyed 19 of the most significant economic data releases in the United States, with details of what these statistics tell us, how they are calculated, why they are significant, and the professional or governmental body that disseminates them. We then expanded this analysis to look at the economies of Europe and Asia and the economic data of relevance in each of these regions. A variety of factors shape the way in which the market reacts to announcements of economic data (the market's reaction function) including economic theory, investor positioning, and overall market conditions.

Due to the infrequency and delays of economic data releases, it is often useful to reverse the direction of the inference between economics and markets and look at how changes in market conditions can give indications of shifts in the state of the underlying economy long before these manifest themselves through traditional economic indicators.

Mathematical Review

INTRODUCTION

What follows is a brief review of the mathematical and statistical concepts with which the reader must be familiar in order to fully understand the material presented in this book. The assumption is that this material has already been encountered in elementary mathematics, statistics, or finance classes and that this presentation is simply a refresher. If this is not the case, I highly recommend picking up an introductory calculus or statistics text. These concepts are not only fundamental to an understanding of modern finance, but an essential part of the set of intellectual tools that should be available to any educated adult: innumeracy is no less a shortcoming than illiteracy.

In keeping with the "practical" objectives of the book, our presentation is deliberately informal and includes no derivations or proofs. Our goal is to make as clear as possible the *meaning* of the mathematical concepts so that the reader is able to see through the symbology to the underlying significance of the formulas and in doing so, better understand the characteristics of the products and markets discussed. The fact is that mathematics provides an incredibly concise and clear way to explain the structure of financial instruments, determine their value, and understand their risks. Unfortunately the teaching of mathematics too often focuses on the mechanical manipulation of formulas rather than on the underlying significance of the operations—like learning to spell words without knowing their meaning. Concepts learned in this way are not only of little use, but are quickly forgotten.

For readers who typically find mathematics anxiety-producing, please relax: loosen your tensing neck muscles and shake out your hands and arms. We will not be doing any calculations and there are no problem sets, quizzes, or exams. For our purposes here, calculation is not important since in practice, a trader or salesperson would never actually compute a partial derivative of an option price or the standard deviation of an asset's returns: there are specially designed systems provided that do this and highly trained engineers, physicists, and mathematicians, known as *quants*, whose job it is to ensure that these calculations are done correctly. What *is* important is to understand intuitively what a partial derivative or standard deviation tells us. Fortunately, this is much simpler. The best advice is simply to approach the material with an open mind and try to forget that this is "math" and just take the ideas for what they are: you are likely to be surprised how easy they are.

FUNCTIONS

Given a variable x, a function $f()$ is an operator that manipulates the variable x in some way to produce a new value called $f(x)$. Depending on your preference, feel free to think of a function as an operator, a manipulator, a make-over, a transformation, a mapping, or any other similar image. We can think of $f()$ as a machine that takes a value of x in and spits out something called $f(x)$. We may choose to associate another variable y with the transformed value of x, that is $y = f(x)$. See Exhibit A.1.

If our variable x represents a young man who has just enlisted for military service, $f()$ could be the operation of shaving his head and assigning him a military uniform. Given a recruit x, the $f()$ process produces a standard-issue soldier $f(x)$. To use a more standard mathematical example, given a number x, the function $f(x) = x^2$ produces its square.

To visualize the relationship between x and $f(x)$, we can graph the function on an x and y coordinate axis as $y = f(x)$. For example, for the case where $y = f(x) = x^2$, the plot of the graph is shown in Exhibit A.2.

If the function $f()$ is a function of more than one variable, say x, y, and t, we say $f()$ is a multivariable function and write $y = f(x, t)$. The graph of a function of two variables can be represented as a surface in space. Functions of three or more variables can be more difficult to visualize. The standard approach to understanding the interrelationships between the variables in a multivariable function is to hold all but one variable constant and then analyze the sensitivity of the overall function to movements in just that variable. This process is then repeated for each of the other variables to

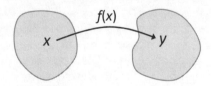

EXHIBIT A.1

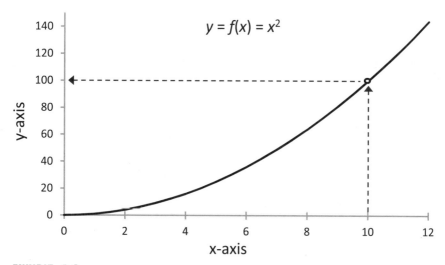

EXHIBIT A.2

assemble a full picture of the sensitivities of the function and the interactions among the individual variables.

COMPOUND INTEREST AND EXPONENTIAL GROWTH

Simple Interest

Suppose an investment pays a guaranteed yield of 6 percent per annum. For an amount x invested, after one year you will have an amount V equal to your original investment plus an additional $0.06x$. Expressed formulaically, $V = x(1 + 0.06)$. This is called *simple interest*. It has the property that it scales linearly with time—if you stay invested only six months you get 3 percent while if you stay invested for two years you get 12 percent, and so forth. The general function $V(x, r, t)$ that gives the value of an amount x invested for time t (expressed in years or fraction thereof) at an annual simple interest rate r is therefore:

$$V(x, r, t) = x(1 + rt)$$

In other words, the value of the original investment x is scaled (increases) by a *growth factor* $g(r, t) = (1 + rt)$. It is this growth function $g(r, t)$ that we will focus on.

Compound Interest

One feature of simple interest is that the investor receives no benefit from the interest income that is accruing until it is withdrawn. Specifically, this interest income does not, itself, earn interest. However, if the rate is guaranteed for the full year (and any subset of the year), then an investor can improve his returns in the following way: he deposits an amount x at a simple interest rate of 6 percent but withdraws it after six months ($t = 0.5$ years), at which time his investment will have grown by a factor of $g(6\%, 0.5) = 1 + 0.06 \times 0.5 = 1.03$ (he has earned 3% interest). If he then reinvests the $1.03x$ funds for the rest of the year, they will grow by the same factor resulting in a year-end value of $1.03 \times 1.03x = 1.0609x$, equivalent to an annual interest rate of 6.09 percent. This higher annual rate is due to the fact that for the second six months of the year, the investor received additional interest on the 3 percent interest earned in the first six months. This process of realizing accrued interest and immediately reinvesting it is called *compounding* and many types of investments (debt instruments like bonds, mortgages, loans, etc.) do it automatically.

If compounding once was good, then why not do it more frequently? If our investor withdraws and reinvests his money after the first quarter, then for the second quarter he will be earning interest on $1.015x$ of invested money, as opposed to the previous case where for the entire first half of the year he was only earning interest on his initial investment of x. In this case, he ends the first half-year with $1.015 \times 1.015x = 1.03225x$, as opposed to just $1.03x$ and, compounding again after the third quarter, will end the year with $1.06136x$. If we divide the investment period t into n equal compounding intervals, the value of the investment will grow by the factor $g(r, {}^t/_n) = (1 + {}^{rt}/_n)$ in each period. The compound growth factor over the n periods $G(r, t, n)$ can be expressed as:

$$G(r, t, n) = \left(1 + \frac{rt}{n}\right)^n$$

Continuous Compounding

The table that follows shows values of $G(1, 1, n)$, which would be the compound interest growth factor for 100 percent interest over one year, as calculated for different values of n. (See Exhibit A.3.)

As n becomes large (and the interval of time between each compounding reduces to zero) we approach the limiting case of what is called *continuous compounding* and the growth factor $G()$ approaches a limit. This value is called e and is one of the most important constants in all of mathematics.

Frequency	n	G(1,1, n)
Annual	1	2
Semiannual	2	2.25
Quarterly	4	2.441406
Monthly	12	2.613035
Daily	365	2.714567
Hourly	8,760	2.718127
Minute	525,600	2.718279
Second	31,536,000	2.718282

EXHIBIT A.3

The value of e is defined as:

$$e = \lim_{n \to \infty} \left(1 + \frac{1}{n}\right)^n$$

For readers less familiar with the notation, this equation can be read as "the variable e is equal to the limit, as the variable n goes to infinity of the function $\left(1 + \frac{1}{n}\right)^n$." As we have shown, it is roughly[1] equal to 2.718282.

Observe that our choice of the variable n was arbitrary—it does not have any particular significance in itself, it is simply the counter of the number of times we compound our interest calculation and we eventually increase it to become arbitrarily large. This allows us to do a substitution and replace n with n/rt where r and t are the rate and time (both positive).

$$e = \lim_{\frac{n}{rt} \to \infty} \left(1 + \frac{1}{n/rt}\right)^{\frac{n}{rt}}$$

Since r and t are constants, the only way that n/rt goes to infinity is if n goes to infinity. This allows us to rewrite the equation taking the limit as $n \to \infty$. If we now raise both sides of the equation to the power rt, we get the expression:

$$e^{rt} = \lim_{n \to \infty} \left(1 + \frac{rt}{n}\right)^n$$

This formula says that the growth factor, under continuous compounding, of an interest rate r over a time t can be expressed as e^{rt}. Raising e to a power x is called "taking the exponential of x" and a process whose

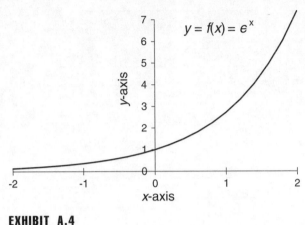

EXHIBIT A.4

growth is expressed in terms of powers of e is said to experience *exponential growth*. The graph of $y = e^x$ is shown in Exhibit A.4.

Discounting

If x grows at a continuously compounded rate of r, its value y after time t will be $y = xe^{rt}$. The value of x is scaled by the exponential growth factor e^{rt}. Dividing both sides of this equation by e^{rt} yields the formula $x = ye^{-rt}$. This tells us the amount x necessary today such that, if x grows at a continuously compounded rate r it will be worth y after time t. This value x is called the *present value* of y.

Natural Logarithms

We can also run the exponential operation in reverse. For a given value of y (must be a positive number), we might wish to determine the value of x such that $y = e^x$. The inverse function to the exponential $y = e^x$ is called the *natural logarithm* function and is defined as $x = \ln(y)$ ("x is the natural log of y").

The natural log function is often used to scale the graph of functions or data that exhibit an exponential growth in order to see changes more clearly. In a graph with a *log-scaling*, exponential growth looks like a straight line. The graph in Exhibit A.5 shows growth in U.S. GDP (the same data as Exhibit 12.1) using a linear scale on the left axis and a logarithmic scale on the right axis. Observe that in the log scaling each equally spaced line

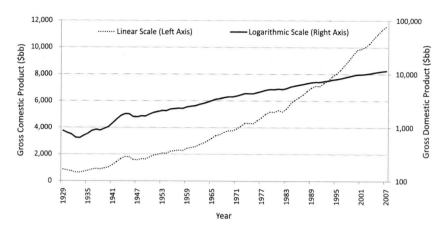

EXHIBIT A.5 U.S. Real GDP Growth 1949–2007 (linear and log scaling)

represents a change of an order of magnitude (10 times in this case) rather than an equally sized step.

CALCULUS

There are two fundamental concepts from calculus that are essential for finance: the *derivative* and the *integral*. In what follows all references to "the derivative," refer to the precise mathematical definition and not the concept of a financial derivative security.

Derivative

The mathematical derivative measures the rate of change of one variable with respect to another. Alternatively, it can also be thought of as the sensitivity of one variable to changes in another. In either case, these are familiar concepts—the derivative is simply the formal, mathematical expression of what is often a perfectly simple colloquial expressions. Exhibit A.6 provides several examples.

There are two common ways to denote the derivative symbolically. If $y = f(x)$ is a function of x, then the derivative of $f()$ with respect to x is denoted by any one of the following:

$$y' = \frac{dy}{dx} \quad \text{or} \quad f'(x) = \frac{df}{dx}$$

Colloquial Expression	Mathematical Expression
How does the temperature change as you climb a mountain?	What is the derivative of temperature with respect to altitude?
How fast are we going?	What is the rate of change of position with respect to time?
Lowering the thermostat a few degrees can save you a lot on your energy bill.	What is the sensitivity of the heating cost to changes in the level of the thermostat?

EXHIBIT A.6

The act of taking the derivative with respect to x can be thought of as an operation applied to the function $f(x)$, in much the same way that $f()$ performed an operation on the variable x. Because of this, it is common to separate the operator d/dx from the function $f(x)$ notationally as:

$$\frac{d}{dx} f(x)$$

What Is the Derivative?

In each of the three colloquial examples, we are looking for a function $f(x)$ that describes the relationship between an independent variable x and a dependent variable, y. For example, x is altitude and y is temperature and $f(x)$ describes the temperature as a function of the altitude. To understand the relationship between the independent and dependent variables, we want to calculate the change Δy in y for a given change Δx in x. To do this, we calculate the value of y for two points x and $x + \Delta x$. The change, Δy, is equal to the difference between the two:

$$\Delta y = f(x + \Delta x) - f(x)$$

We can now divide this by the change Δx to derive a ratio $\Delta y/\Delta x$, which tells us how much y changed as a portion of the change in x. For large values of Δx, this indicates the *average* change in y per change in x over the interval Δx, but as we let Δx get very small, we get a progressively more accurate estimate of the "instantaneous" rate of change of y with respect to x.

This derivation of the rate of change is most easily visualized graphically, as shown in Exhibit A.7. Recall that the *slope* of a line is the "rise over the

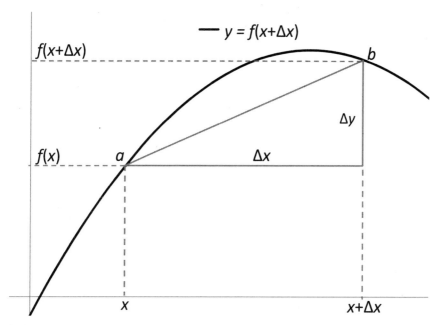

EXHIBIT A.7   Change in $y = f(x)$ between x and $x + \Delta x$

run," that is, the change in y divided by the change in x. A horizontal line (zero rise for any run) has a slope of zero, a 45° angle has a slope of 1 (rise = run) and the slope approaches infinity as the line approaches the vertical (rise divided by a run that is going to zero). Based on this definition, the rate of change of y with respect to x over the interval Δx is approximated by $\Delta y / \Delta x$, which is the slope of the line $\overline{ab}$. The slope of this line can be expressed as:

$$\frac{\Delta y}{\Delta x} = \frac{f(x + \Delta x) - f(x)}{\Delta x}$$

The definition of the derivative *is* simply the limiting case of this expression where we let the value Δx become arbitrarily small ($\Delta x \to 0$):

$$\frac{dy}{dx} = \lim_{\Delta x \to 0} \frac{f(x + \Delta x) - f(x)}{\Delta x}$$

This is shown in Exhibit A.8 where the limit as the interval Δx goes to zero ($\Delta x \to 0$) is represented by a series of points $b_1, b_2 \ldots b_t$, each of which is

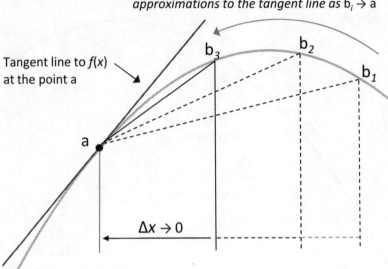

Slope of line a-b$_i$ becomes a more accurate approximations to the tangent line as b$_i$ → a

Tangent line to $f(x)$ at the point a

b$_3$

b$_2$

b$_1$

a

$\Delta x \to 0$

EXHIBIT A.8 Derivatives as the Limiting Case Where $\Delta x \to 0$

closer to a. The slope of the line $\overline{ab_i}$ approaches the tangent line to $f(x)$ at the point a.

It is important to remember that, although the derivation of the concept of derivative involves the slope of the tangent line to the graph $f(x)$ at a particular point, the derivative $f'(x)$ is a *function*, not a single value—the slope of the tangent line to the graph depends on the value of x you choose. The function $f'(x)$ gives an expression that can be evaluated at any point x to derive the slope of the tangent to $f(x)$ at that point. To illustrate this, Exhibit A.9 shows the graph of a function $f(x)$ in the upper box and compares it to the graph of its derivative $f'(x)$, which is shown in the lower box. The value of $f'(x)$ for any value x is equal to the slope of the tangent line to the graph of $f(x)$ at that point.

Since derivative $f'(x)$ is itself a function, we can also take its derivative— the second derivative of $f(x)$ with respect to x. We denote this by

$$y'' = \frac{d^2 y}{dx^2} \quad \text{or alternatively} \quad f''(x) = \frac{d^2 f}{dx^2}$$

Higher-order derivatives (third, fourth, n^{th}) are denoted similarly.

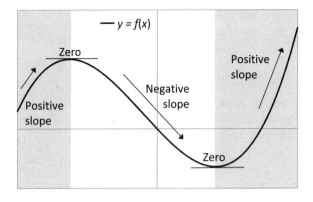

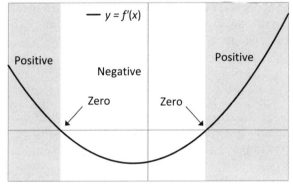

EXHIBIT A.9 A Function $f(x)$ and the Graph of its Derivative $f'(x)$

Partial Derivatives

For functions of more than one variable the concept of derivative is similar. Given a function $f(x, z)$, we calculate the "partial derivative of f with respect to x" by calculating the derivative with respect to x while treating y constant. This is the familiar idea of "all other things constant, how does $f()$ depend on x." To use the previously mentioned example of the change in temperature as one climbs a mountain, it is implicit in the question that all other variables are being held constant. The temperature at any point on the mountain is a function of the weather, time of day, season, and many other factors. It makes no sense to measure the temperature at the base at night and at the summit at midday and conclude that the temperature increases with altitude. The partial derivative of temperature with respect to altitude is precisely what the question is asking for. We indicate a partial derivative with a script ∂ to distinguish it from a total derivative of a single-variable function. The two possible partial derivatives of $f(x, z)$ are:

$$\frac{\partial f}{\partial x} \qquad \frac{\partial f}{\partial z}$$

Higher-order partial derivatives are designated similarly to derivatives of a single variable function. There are three possible second partial derivatives of $f(x, z)$, the two second order partials:

$$\frac{\partial^2 f}{\partial x^2} \qquad \frac{\partial^2 f}{\partial z^2}$$

and the "mixed" second order partial, which is the partial with respect to x of the partial with respect to z of $f()$ (i.e., we differentiate with respect to z first, and then differentiate the result of that with respect to x).

$$\frac{\partial}{\partial x} \left(\frac{\partial f}{\partial z} \right) = \frac{\partial^2 f}{\partial x \partial z}$$

A *differential equation* is an equation involving a function and its derivatives. An *ordinary differential equation* (ODE) is a differential equation involving a function of a single variable. For example:

$$f'(x) - 2xf(x) = 0$$

A *partial differential equation* (PDE) is a differential equation involving a multi-variable function and its partial derivatives. An example is the Black-Scholes PDE from Chapter 9.

The function e^x has the interesting property that it is its own derivative:

$$\frac{d}{dx} e^x = e^x$$

The second, third and n^{th} derivatives are also all equal to e^x. This means that for any value of x, the slope of the graph of e^x is equal to the value of the function e^x. Functions of e^x appear frequently in solutions to differential equations.

Integration

The other fundamental concept from calculus is that of the *integral*. The concept of integration arises from the desire to calculate the area under a curve $y = f(x)$. See Exhibit A.10.

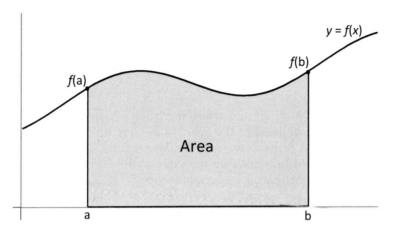

EXHIBIT A.10   An Area Defined by a Function $f(x)$

   This is done by dividing the interval from a to b into a series of small increments of width Δx, as shown in Exhibit A.11. The area a under the curve can then be approximated by summing the areas of the rectangles—each with height $f(x_i)$ and width Δx.

$$A \approx \sum_{i=1}^{n} f(x_i)\Delta x$$

We can produce progressively more accurate results by reducing the width of the interval Δx. This leads us to the limiting case where $\Delta x \to 0$ where we

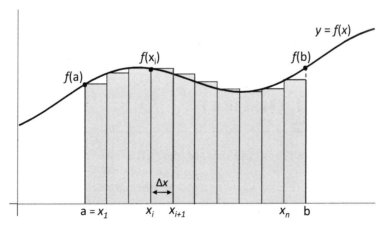

EXHIBIT A.11   Geometric Interpretation of Integration

denote the "infinitesimal" Δx by dx and write the summation as an *integral* from points a to b, of the function $f(x)$:

$$A = \int_a^b f(x)\,dx$$

A *definite integral* is one in which the limits a and b have been specified, and the value of the definite integral is equal to the area between the graph of $f(x)$ and the x-axis between the specified limits. For each new pair of points a and b we need to recalculate the value of the definite integral. It would be convenient if we had an "integral function," which we will denote by $F(x)$ such that, for any a and b we could determine the area between the limits by simply subtracting $F(b) - F(a)$. This function $F(x)$ is called the *indefinite integral* of $f(x)$ and we denote it by:

$$F(x) = \int f(x)\,dx$$

Notice that the right hand side no longer specifies the limits of integration—it is now a function of x.

This brings us to the pleasing (and surprising) result that there is, in fact, just such a function $F(x)$ for every sufficiently nice function $f(x)$. (By "sufficiently nice" we mean no discontinuities (jumps) or sharp corners.) In fact, there is not just one, but an infinite number of functions that do the job—any function $F(x)$ such that derivative $F'(x) = f(x)$ will work and provide the solution to:

$$\int_a^b f(x)\,dx = F(b) - F(a)$$

This is not a minor result. In fact, it is known as the Fundamental Theorem of Calculus.

RANDOM VARIABLES, PROBABILITY, AND STATISTICS

Probability and statistics rank comfortably among the least-enjoyed subjects for many students. They are, however, quite possibly two of the most important. Given the option of studying more mathematics (above the level of calculus or differential equations) or learning some probability and/or statistics, I would highly recommend the latter. Much of the phenomena we encounter in real world experimentation (and nearly every observable financial variable) is not deterministic—we do not know the underlying relationships that govern its behavior and we cannot anticipate future values with certainty. Learning to think in correct probabilistic and statistical terms is an invaluable aid in understanding the world around us. Unfortunately, there is ample evidence that our brains have not evolved to think in correct probabilistic terms—we are deterministic creatures and understanding the noise, chaos, and randomness around us is not always easy. Probability and statistics can be an enormous help.

Random Variable

A random variable x, is a variable whose value is not known with certainty. Random variables can be broken into two categories:

1. A *discrete* random variable is one that can take on a finite number of distinct values. For example, let x equal the value that comes up on a roll of a six-sided die.
2. A *continuous* random variable can take on any value from within a range, and therefore has an infinite number of possible values. For example, let x equal a number randomly chosen between 0 and 1.

Probability

Pinpointing a strict definition of probability can be slippery—an intuitive understanding will be sufficient for our purposes. Given a random variable x, we denote by Prob[a] the probability that x takes on value a. A few interpretations of the meaning of Prob[a] are:

1. Prob[a] is a numerical measure of the "likelihood" of the event $x = a$ occuring, which ranges between 0 (impossibility) to 1 (certainty).
2. For a variable x that can experimentally observed, given a large number of repetitions of particular action in which x can take on a certain number of outcomes, Prob[a] is the fraction of the total number of trials in which the outcome $x = a$ occurs.
3. Given all possible future states of the world, Prob[a] is the percentage of those states in which the random variable x takes on the value a.

The first definition is a bit philosophical and not mathematically rigorous; the second is experimental and requires that the experiment be capable of repetition, and the third requires us to specify "all possible states of the world," which is a bit of a vague concept. No definition is perfectly satisfactory but, between the three, we get an intuitive understanding of the meaning of Prob[a]. Although colloquially it is common to refer to probabilities as percentages, we will generally express them as decimals.

Probability versus Statistics

A common confusion is the difference between probability and statistics:

- In probability we know the underlying forces that determine the likelihood of the various possible outcomes of a random variable x. Based on this, we derive conclusions about the distributions of those outcomes, the likelihood of particular combinations of events, and so on.
- In statistics, we have a set of observed values of a random variable $x = x_1, x_2, \ldots, x_n$, which we try to fit to a probabilistic model in order to make statements about the likelihood of future outcomes of x.

In general it is more natural to present the concepts of probability first and then introduce the statistical methods for discovering these patterns in data based on those probabilistic models.

For our purposes in this book, we focus primarily on probability and the few statistical concepts we do need are introduced alongside their probabilistic equivalents. This should not be misinterpreted as a suggestion of the relative importance of probability to statistics: they are both hugely important and inextricably intertwined.

Probability

There are two fundamental rules that apply to probabilities:

1. For any event a, Prob[a] ≥ 0 (there are no negative probabilities).
2. The sum of the probabilities of all possible outcomes must equal 1.

Discrete: Given a discrete random variable x that can take on any of a finite number of values $\{x_1, x_2, \ldots, x_n\}$, we can assign a corresponding set of probabilities $\{P_1, P_2, \ldots, P_n\}$ to each outcome x_i such that Prob[x_i] $= P_i$ and $\sum_{\text{all } i} P_i = 1$.

Continuous: For a continuous random variable things work a bit differently. Consider the example where x is a number randomly chosen between 0 and 1 with all numbers equally probable. Since the random variable x can assume any one of an infinite number of equally possible values, then the probability that x takes on a particular value x_i must be zero since, using the third definition of probability:

$$\text{Prob}[x_i] = \frac{\text{States where } x = x_i}{\text{Total \# of states}} = \frac{1}{\infty} = 0$$

This yields the counterintuitive result that while the probability of any given value is zero, by definition the sum of the probabilities is equal to 1.

This difficulty is resolved through the concept of a *probability density function* (PDF). A probability density function $P(x)$ is a function such that, when we calculate the area under the graph $P(x)$ between points a and b we get the probability that x falls in that interval. That is:

$$\int_a^b P(x)\, dx = \text{Prob}[a < x < b]$$

A probability density function must satisfy the following two analogous conditions to those for discrete probabilities:

1. $P(x) \geq 0$ for all x (Positive probabilities)
2. $\int_{-\infty}^{\infty} P(x)dx = 1$ (Probabilities must sum to 1)

By far, the most commonly known probability density function is the Gaussian standard normal distribution that produces the bell curve. The normal distribution is so prevalent in so many fields of study that it has become a part of the vernacular of everyday speech and a fundamental part of our way of seeing the world. We speak of professors who "grade on a curve" or read books about "six-sigma" performance in industry. Both these concepts have their origins in the normal distribution. (In reality, we tend to overuse the normal distribution. Many observed phenomena are not normally distributed and our tendency to assume normality is actually the cause of many errors.) The probability density function for the standard normal distribution is:

$$P(x) = \frac{1}{\sqrt{2\pi}} e^{\frac{-x^2}{2}}$$

Mean, Variance and Standard Deviation

There are several ways that we can summarize the general properties of a distribution without going into the details of the likelihood of every possible scenario. In many cases, if the structure of the distribution matches one of the standard models (for example, the normal distribution), then the specific values of a few of these aggregate characteristics are sufficient to precisely describe the entire structure of the distribution. In each case we present the formula for the discrete and continuous time cases.

Probabilistic Mean   The mean μ_x of a random variable x is the average outcome we expect to achieve if we take a large sample of values of x. It is calculated as the sum across all possible states of the world i, of the value of x in each state i multiplied by the probability of state i occurring and is sometimes referred to as the *expected value* of the random variable. Said otherwise, it is a probability-weighted average of all possible outcomes. The calculation of the mean μ_x of a discrete random variable x can be expressed as:

$$\mu_x = \sum_i P_i x_i$$

In the continuous case we use the analogous operation to summation, which is integration. The discrete x_i are replaced by the continuous variable x and the discrete probability P_i of state i occurring, by $P(x)dx$, where $P(x)$ is the probability density function and $P(x)\,dx$ is the likelihood of x taking on a value in some small interval dx:

$$\mu_x = \int_{-\infty}^{\infty} P(x)x\,dx$$

As a discrete example we calculate the expected value of rolling a six-sided die. Assuming the die is fair, all outcomes are equally probable and therefore the mean μ_x is:

$$\mu_x = \sum_{i=1}^{6} \frac{1}{6}i = \frac{1}{6}(1+2+3+4+5+6) = \frac{21}{6} = 3.5$$

Notice that the expected value of x is not one of the possible outcomes. The mean does not measure the most common or most likely outcome: it is the probability-weighted average of all possible outcomes.

Statistical Mean   In statistics we start from a sample of data $\{x_1, x_2, \ldots, x_n\}$ and calculate the mean as:

$$\mu_x = \frac{1}{n}\sum_{i=1}^{n} x_i$$

We no longer have a P_i term because we do not know the probability distribution. However, the frequency with which a particular value of x occurs in the data will already be determined by the probability of that event so the equally weighted average of the observations will already include the probability of each outcome occurring. If these x_i are only a small subset of a large population, the $1/n$ term is replaced by $1/(n-1)$, which gives a more accurate estimate of the mean of the entire population (versus the sample mean).

Variance and Standard Deviation   The mean tells us what the average result of a distribution will be. We now want a measure of how widely dispersed the x_i are around that mean—are they tightly bunched up or does x take on a wide range of values? The standard measure of this is the *variance*, which is defined as the expected value of the square of the distance between x and its mean μ_x. The expected value is calculated in the same way as the mean—by summing the value of $(x_i - \mu_x)^2$ in all possible states of the world i multiplied by the probability of that state of the world occurring. We denote the variance of a random variable x by σ_x^2. The formulas for the discrete and continuous cases are respectively:

$$\text{Discrete} \quad \sigma_x^2 = \sum_{\text{all } i} P_i (x_i - \mu_x)^2$$

$$\text{Continuous} \quad \sigma_x^2 = \int_{-\infty}^{\infty} P(x)(x - \mu_x)^2 \, dx$$

The variance is a product of squared distances and positive probabilities so it will always be a positive number and we can therefore confidently assign it the value σ^2. The reason for this unusual notation for variance is because we are generally more interested in the square root of the variance $\sqrt{\sigma^2} = \sigma$, which is called the *standard deviation*. The standard deviation is the most common measure of how widely the distribution of possible outcomes is spread around its mean. The higher the standard deviation, the greater the dispersion of outcomes and the further from the mean you are likely to find values of x. A standard deviation of zero means that all values are equal to the mean (no dispersion).

In statistics, given the sample data, we compute the variance as:

$$\sigma_x^2 = \frac{1}{n} \sum_{i=1}^{n} (x_i - \mu_x)^2$$

We use the same substitution of $1/(n-1)$ as before for samples from large populations. The standard deviation is simply the square root of this, σ_x.

Normal Distributions   The normal distribution mentioned previously was the "standard" normal distribution, which has mean zero and standard deviation of 1. Clearly not all normally distributed phenomena have the same mean and standard deviation. The probability density function for a normally distributed random variable x with mean μ and standard deviation σ is:

$$P(x) = \frac{1}{\sigma\sqrt{2\pi}}e^{-\frac{(x-\mu)^2}{2\sigma^2}}$$

All we have done here is substitute $x - \mu/\sigma$ for x in the standard normal formula presented previously. This is an important concept. All normally distributed data "looks" the same—the only difference is that the center of the distribution has been shifted by the mean μ and the width of the distribution is multiplied by a scaling factor of σ. These two parameters completely describe the structure of all normal distributions. A normal distribution with mean μ and standard deviation σ is denoted by $\Phi(\mu, \sigma^2)$. Exhibit A.12 shows three different normal distributions, each with a slightly different mean and standard deviation.

As we can see from the figure, as the standard deviation of the distribution is reduced the likelihood of events around the mean increases. As has been mentioned, one of the fundamental properties of a probability distribution is that the area under the curve must always sum to 1. Therefore, as the width is squeezed the height of the peak must increase.

Because the structure of normally distributed data is always the same (just shifted by μ and stretched by σ), we can make a general statement about how far observations are likely to be found from the mean in terms

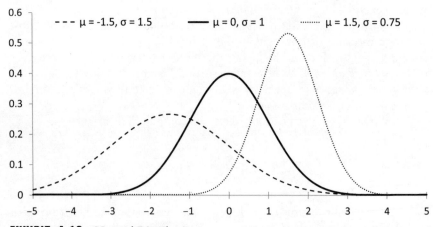

EXHIBIT A.12   Normal Distributions

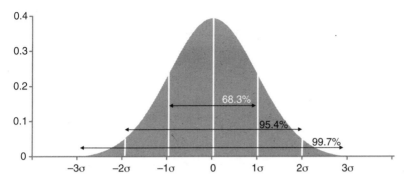

EXHIBIT A.13 Standard Deviations of the Normal Distribution

of the standard deviation—units of σ, so to speak. In a normal distribution, approximately 68.3 percent of the data falls within 1 standard deviation of the mean. (That is, the area under the curve from $-\sigma$ to $+\sigma$ is 0.683.) Exhibit A.13 shows the percentages for other values of σ.

Skew and Kurtosis There are two other characteristics of distributions that can be helpful. The first is *skew*, which is the expected value of $((x - \mu)/\sigma)^3$. Because the cube retains the same sign as the original, the skew can be either positive or negative. A symmetric distribution, like the normal distribution, has a skew of zero because all the positive and negative values cancel. If the skew is positive the "tail" on the right hand side of the distribution is thicker and longer than on the left. Negative skew has a longer left tail.

The other characteristic is called *kurtosis,* which is the expected value of $((x - \mu)/\sigma)^4 - 3$. This "minus 3" term ensures that the kurtosis of the standard normal distribution is equal to zero. Because of the fourth power, the kurtosis is extremely sensitive to events far from the mean. If the kurtosis is positive it means that the distribution has *fat tails*—that is, the probability of events far from the mean is greater.

In practice, the observed behavior of the movements of stock prices (and other financial assets) displays positive kurtosis—extreme events occur with greater frequency than they ought to under probabilistic assumptions.

Correlation The concept of correlation has taken on significantly greater importance in recent years as financial innovations in derivatives have allowed investors to trade products that are sensitive to the correlation of various assets. It remains, however, an often misunderstood concept and for that we will provide a bit more careful analysis.

We will consider only the discrete case, since that is sufficient to understand the conceptual basis of correlation and I do not want to lose people in excessive notation by presenting both the discrete and continuous cases.

Consider two random variables, x and y, each of which has its own probability distribution. We wish to calculate the mean and standard deviation for the sum of the two variables. We begin with the mean. If we apply the discrete formula for the mean developed to the combined variable $x + y$ we get:

$$\mu_{x+y} = \sum_i P_i(x+y)_i$$

Since $(x + y)$ is simply the value of the sum of x and y in the ith state of the world, we can rewrite $(x + y)_i$ as $(x_i + y_i)$. This gives us:

$$= \sum_i P_i(x_i + y_i) = \sum_i P_i x_i + \sum_i P_i y_i = \mu_x + \mu_y$$

Therefore the mean of the sum is equal to the sum of the means—which is what we would expect.

We now calculate the variance of the sum by applying the single variable formula stated to the sum of $x + y$:

$$\sigma^2_{x+y} = \sum_i P_i((x+y)_i - \mu_{x+y})^2$$

Making the same substitutions of $(x + y)i = (x_i + y_i)$ and $\mu_{x+y} = \mu_x + \mu_y$ as and with a little algebra, we can rewrite this expression as:

$$= \sigma^2_x + \sigma^2_y + 2\sum_i P_i(x_i - \mu_x)(y_i - \mu_y)$$

So the variance of the sum is equal to the sum of the individual variances plus an additional term. This last term (not including the 2) is called the *covariance* of x and y and denoted by $\text{Cov}(x, y)$:

$$\text{Cov}(x, y) = \sum_i P_i(x_i - \mu_x)(y_i - \mu_y)$$

Let us consider what the formula is saying and try to gain some intuition about what covariance measures. In each possible state of the world i, we are calculating the product of the deviation of x_i from its mean μ_x and of y_i from its mean μ_y. Both of these terms, $(x_i - \mu_x)$ and $(y_i - \mu_y)$, can be either positive or negative, depending on which side of the mean each variable finds itself in the given state of the world. We therefore have four possible cases to consider: where both terms are positive, both negative and the two cases of one positive and one negative. We denote these four cases by PP, NN, PN, and NP. The product is positive in the first two cases, and negative in the latter two.

If we assume that there is no relationship whatsoever between x and y, then in any state of the world, these four cases are equally probable (let us assume x and y have symmetric distributions for simplicity). When we take the sum of all possible cases we would expect the positives and negatives to cancel each other out and we would end up with $Cov(x, y) = 0$.

Now consider the situation where the instances in which x is above its mean $(x_i > \mu_x)$ tend generally to coincide with instances where y is above its mean $(y_i > \mu_y)$, and alternatively, $x_i > \mu_x$ tends to coincide with $y_i > \mu_y$. In this situation, we will have more occurrences of PP or NN (positive values) and fewer NP and PN (negative values) and the covariance will be positive $(Cov(x, y) > 0)$. Similarly, if $x_i < \mu_x$ tends generally to coincide with $y_i > \mu_y$ and, $x_i < \mu_x$ tends to coincide with $y_i > \mu_y$, we will have more occurrences of NP and PN (negative values) than PP or NN and $Cov(x, y) < 0$.

The covariance tells us to what degree the movements of the two variables are related and in what way—positively covariant means they go up and down together, while negatively covariant means one goes up when the other goes down.

While the sign of the covariance tells us generally about the relationship between x and y, we cannot compare the degree of "relatedness" of the two variables with that of any two other variables p and q, because they are not on a consistent scale—variables that take on large values can have a much larger covariance than two closely related variables that happen to have small magnitude. To get around this problem, we normalize the deviations $(x_i - \mu_x)$ and $(y_i - \mu_y)$ by dividing each one by the standard deviation of the random variable, σ_x and σ_y respectively.

$$\rho = \frac{Cov(x, y)}{\sigma_x \sigma_y} = \sum_i P_i \frac{(x_i - \mu_x)}{\sigma_x} \frac{(y_i - \mu_y)}{\sigma_y}$$

We call this new value ρ the *correlation*.

The benefit of the correlation is that it is a pure measure of "relatedness" without the effect of size. The correlation of x and y is always between -1 and 1. To see this, consider the case where x and y are perfectly correlated. By this we mean that the degree of deviation of x from its mean, measured in standard deviations of x, that is $(x_i - \mu_x)/\sigma_x$ is always identical to the deviation of y from its mean, as measured in standard deviations of y,

$(y_i - \mu_y)/\sigma_y$. In this case, we could substitute one for the other and our formula becomes:

$$\rho = \sum_i P_i \frac{(x_i - \mu_x)}{\sigma_x} \frac{(x_i - \mu_x)}{\sigma_x} = \frac{1}{\sigma_x^2} \sum_i P_i (x_i - \mu_x)^2 = \frac{1}{\sigma_x^2} \sigma_x^2 = 1$$

If the deviations from the mean are always the same, the correlation is said to be 1. Similarly, if the deviations from the mean of each variable are inverse, $(x_i - \mu_x)/\sigma_x = -(y_i - \mu_y/\sigma_y)$, then the correlation $\rho = -1$. We can now measure the correlation between any two variables in a consistent manner using the correlation.

Returning to our calculation of the variance of the sum of x and y we can write:

$$\sigma_{x+y}^2 = \sigma_x^2 + \sigma_x^2 + 2\rho\sigma_x\sigma_y$$

The variance of the sum is equal to the sum of the variances plus twice the product of the standard deviations and the correlation. By natural extension the formula for the standard deviation of $x + y$ is:

$$\sigma_{x+y} = \sqrt{\sigma_x^2 + \sigma_y^2 + 2\rho\sigma_x\sigma_y}$$

A few observations on correlation:

1. If the correlation is zero the variance of the sum is the sum of the variances. Standard deviation, however, is never directly additive (i.e., $\sigma_{x+y} \neq \sigma_x + \sigma_y$) because of the square root.
2. A positive correlation increases the variance of the sum, while a negative correlation dampens it.
3. Correlation says nothing about the size of the move in absolute terms—we have normalized that out. The correlation of x and $2x$ is exactly 1 but that does not mean you can hedge x with $2x$ and have a riskless portfolio. Correlation is about direction and relative magnitude of movements only.

Cumulative Distribution Function

Given a probability density function $P(x)$, the *cumulative density function* $F(x)$ is equal to the area under the curve $P(x)$ from $-\infty$ to x. That is:

$$F(a) = \int_{-\infty}^{a} P(x)dx$$

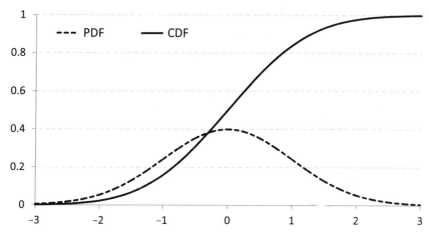

EXHIBIT A.14 Normal Distribution and Cumulative Normal Distribution

The cumulative density (or distribution) function for the normal distribution is denoted by $N(x)$ and appears in the Black-Scholes formula in Chapter 8. Its graph is shown in Exhibit A.14. Observe that the cumulative distribution function increases from nearly zero, on the far left, to one, on the far right. Also notice that because the probability density function is the derivative of the cumulative density function, the value of the PDF is equal to the slope of the CDF for all values of x.

SUMMARY

1. The exponential is a continually compounded rate of growth and is denoted by the mathematical constant e. Continuous compounding can be thought of the limiting case in which the investor is receiving a simple interest rate but withdraws the earned interest and reinvests it "continuously" (imagine compounding every second).
2. The natural logarithm function $\ln(x)$ is the inverse of the exponential. It is often useful to visualize exponentially growing data via a graph with a log-scale, where it will appear as a straight line.
3. The slope is a measure of steepness and is calculated as the "rise over the run" (change in y divided by the change in x). A horizontal line has a zero slope and a $45°$ angle has a slope of 1.
4. Given a function $y = f(x)$, the derivative $y' = dy/dx$ measures how fast y changes with respect to x, or alternatively as the sensitivity of y to a change in x. Graphically, the derivative measures the slope of the graph of $f(x)$.

5. The definite integral of a function $\int_a^b f(x)dx$ between two points a and b, measures the area under the graph $y = f(x)$ between these two points. It was derived as the limiting case of an approximation to the area by rectangles of width Δx. The indefinite integral $F(x) = \int f(x)dx$ is any function such that $F'(x) = f(x)$. The Fundamental Theorem of Calculus says that $\int_a^b f(x)dx = F(b) - F(a)$.

6. Probability measures the "likelihood" of an event. We describe the likelihood of a particular outcome by a probability distribution, which assigns to each possible outcome a positive value (between 0 and 1) such that the sum of the probabilities of all possible events is equal to one. For continuous variables, which can assume any of an infinite number of values, we refer to the distribution as a probability density function that can be used to describe the probability of the value of the random variable falling in a particular interval. The most popular probability density function is the normal distribution.

7. The mean of a distribution describes the "average" outcome of the random variable x, and is computed by summing the product of the value of the random variable in each possible states of the world with the probability of that state of the world occurring. The mean does not have to be a possible outcome of the random variable. We denote the mean of x by μ_x.

8. The variance measures how far around the mean the values of x are likely to be found and is computed as the average of the squared deviations of x from μ_x. Variance is always positive and is denoted by σ_x^2. The more commonly used measure of the breadth of the distribution is the standard deviation, which is the square root of the variance σ_x. The skew (mean of cubed deviations) is the standard measure of symmetry of a distribution while the kurtosis (mean of deviations raised to the fourth power) measures the likelihood of extreme outcomes (the "fatness" of the tails of the distribution).

9. The correlation between two random variables describes the degree to which their movements are related and whether the relationship is positive (both increase or decrease at the same time) or negative (their moves are opposite—one increases when the other decreases).

Notes

Preface

1. The analysis of execution costs, non-continuous trading, and many other real-world market inefficiencies is a significant area of interest in academic finance. However, research in this area is predominantly at an advanced level and out of reach of most undergraduates and MBAs.

Chapter 1   Equity Fundamentals (Part 1): Introduction to Financial Statements

1. *Company*, *corporation*, and *firm* are used interchangeably throughout the text. However, while *company* and *firm* are general terms, *corporation* has a specific legal definition. All publicly traded companies are corporations.
2. There are many ways to do this. The most common is *straight-line depreciation*, in which an equal amount is written off each year over the life of the asset. Depreciation can also be front-loaded to recognize more of the loss of value of the asset in the first few years, which is sometimes more consistent with the actual resale value of many goods.
3. The method for constructing the statement of cash flows presented here—in which the starting point for determining the net cash to the firm is to use the net income from the income statement—is called the *indirect method* and is by far the most common in practice. There is another method called the *direct method* in which actual cash receipts and payments are itemized starting from cash payments received from customers. Both methods must, by definition, arrive at the same final result.

Chapter 2   Equity Fundamentals (Part 2): Financial Ratios, Valuation, and Corporate Actions

1. This ratio assumes the majority of COGS is raw materials. This clearly is not meaningful for all companies (i.e., a management consultancy or investment bank that provides a service and not a manufactured good). The average inventory (and all other "average" values) are computed as the simple average of the value in the current and previous accounting periods.

2. A single user license starts at $1,800 per month per terminal ($1,500 for multiple user clients). Additional charges for real-time data (15 minute delayed data are available free of charge for most products), full order book depth, index constituent information, and other supplementary services can easily add another thousand dollars or more per month to this cost. See: http://about. bloomberg.com/contactus/factsheets/profservice.pdf.

3. If all companies grow slower than the economy, then how is the economy growing so fast?

4. PE ratios are commonly written as "15x" rather than just "15" to indicate that the stock price is "15 times" earnings. A stock is then said to be trading "on a PE of 15."

5. In fact, if anything there is an operational cost related to the processing of the new share issuance and delivery to all existing shareholders.

6. Some markets operate on a shorter settlement cycle, which moves the ex-dividend date forward. In Germany, trades settle on a T+2 basis (making the ex-date one day before the record date) and in Taiwan trades settle on a T+1 basis (making the ex-date and record date the same).

7. For simplicity, we will pretend shares are divisible into fractional units. Prices will always be quoted on a per share basis.

8. While this may seem like a fairly meager return, if the deal has a very high probability of completion then the 2.3 percent nearly riskless return over two months is equivalent to a 13.9 percent annual return, which compares very favorably with the 4 percent annual risk-free rate. If the arbitrageur can use borrowed funds to leverage his position, the 2.3 percent return can be magnified several times.

Chapter 3   Cash Market

1. The ticker symbol is a mnemonic, usually consisting of between one and five letters, which is used to identify the stock without needing to spell out the entire name. An alternative to ticker symbols is the Reuters Instrument Code (RIC), which consists of a similar three- or four-digit mnemonic followed by a ."N" or ".Q" depending on whether the stock trades on the New York Stock Exchange (NYSE) or the NASDAQ, respectively. While tickers and RICs are quite similar in the United States, they can often differ significantly for foreign stocks. There exist other identifiers, such as the CUSIP, SEDOL, or ISIN, which consist of long, unmemorable combinations of letters and numbers and are used primarily for back-office processing purposes.

2. A few extremely high-priced stocks trade in round lots of one share. Orders for quantities below 100 shares are called *odd lots* and are treated differently by the exchange.

3. Read the letters of the acronym individually—don't make a cow sound.

4. The *volume smile* refers to the fact that volumes are higher at the open and close of trading and lower midday. As a result, the graph of the volume profile has a smile shape.

5. There exist information barriers—commonly referred to as *Chinese walls*—between the investment banking and sales and trading divisions to ensure that material, non-public information about upcoming corporate activity is not leaked to the traders who could be tempted to trade on it (which would be illegal). When a salesperson is given potentially sensitive information he is said to be "over the wall." Wall crossings are carefully documented and overseen by compliance.

6. Investment funds, pension plans, mutual funds, hedge funds, and other clients of the sales and trading division are considered to be on the "buy side" (they pay the commission) while the investment bank or broker-dealer is the "sell side" (they sell their service).

7. Recall that in the percent-of-volume instruction, one-third of the volume was considered aggressive.

8. For simplicity, we ignore the financing costs on the borrowed euros. While this is certainly an important consideration in international investing, their inclusion here would unnecessarily complicate the explanation.

Chapter 4   Equity Indices

1. The Bloomberg **HDS** (*Holders*) function provides information about all publicly disclosed holders of stock, including details of the timing and quantity of purchases and sales by corporate insiders.

2. Based on Bloomberg weightings as of July 28, 2008.

3. For readers that are paying close attention, this actually means that not all the shares received are sold—the percentage of additional shares kept is equal to the new percentage weight of the post-split stock in the index.

4. More precisely, the percentage rally and sell-off of the winning and losing subsets are inversely proportional to their weights in the index.

5. Because the index share quantities represent millions of shares in free float, the market capitalization of NTI is therefore equal to $43.5 billion. The scaling of the share quantities by 1 million makes the numbers more manageable and, because it is applied equally to all stocks, does not introduce any error in the calculations and can be ignored.

6. It comes down to a question of your frame of reference. Recalling the standard presentation from introductory physics class—or the typical scene from a romance movie—from the perspective of the woman on the train, the man on the platform is moving backwards, even as he runs toward her shouting and waving. He's moving in the right direction, just not fast enough.

7. We are ignoring for the moment the possibility of replicating an index by trading an ETF or futures contract because we have not introduced those concepts yet.

8. This turns out to be very important for index futures that expire at the opening price of the index. It is usually several hours until the final opening print is agreed upon.

9. If we think of the index as a portfolio itself, then the act of hedging the return of the index via a basket of stock is simply a question of making sure that the

prices at which the index "portfolio" is rebalanced are the same as where the hedge portfolio is rebalanced. If the index adds LNA to its "portfolio" at a price of 20.70 and the broker buys it into his portfolio at 20.71, he will underperform relative to the index. Similarly, if he sells out of his MTT position at 60.75 while the index removes it at 63.70, he will outperform.

10. The divisor is not included on the **MEMB** or **WGT** pages of Bloomberg, though it is sometimes included on the **DES** page for the index.

11. All specific figures and details of the methodology are taken from Standard & Poor's data (www.standardandpoors.com) on July 10, 2008.

12. Bloomberg data as of July 14, 2008.

13. Information on methodology is taken from the NASDAQ (www.nasdaq.com); all specific numerical data are from Bloomberg as of July 14, 2008.

14. Information on methodology is taken from Russell (www.russell.com) and Bloomberg data as of July 28, 2008.

15. The equivalent indices based on the S&P 1500 Composite index have the same ticker with the prefix "S15" replacing "S5."

16. MSCI Barra (www.mscibarra.com) data as of July 31, 2008.

17. Pronounced "ee-fah."

18. Based on nominal GDP from the *CIA World Factbook 2007* (www.cia.gov) retrieved July 17, 2008; and 2007 individual state gross domestic product data from the U.S. Bureau of Economic analysis (www.bea.gov) on June 5, 2008.

19. There is a 20 percent cap on the weight of any single security in the STOXX 600 as well as each of the three size indices and the Eurozone equivalents of each of these. The STOXX 50 and Euro STOXX 50 apply a 10 percent cap. Currently, the market cap weightings of all of the indices discussed are sufficiently distributed that none of these caps actually affects the weight of any stock.

20. "Europe" is defined by STOXX as Austria, Belgium, Denmark, Finland, France, Germany, Greece, Iceland, Ireland, Italy, Luxembourg, the Netherlands, Norway, Portugal, Spain, Sweden, Switzerland, and the United Kingdom.

21. Cyclical companies are those that are heavily influenced by the changes in the economic cycle. See Chapter 13 for a more complete description.

Chapter 5   Program Trading

1. It is impossible to discuss either program trading or equity index futures without making reference to the other, due to the many overlaps between the trading and pricing of the two products. As a result, this chapter contains several references to futures contracts, despite the fact that this product is not introduced until Chapter 7. For readers who are completely unfamiliar with the product, it is sufficient to understand, for the purposes of this chapter, that an equity index future is an exchange-traded product that replicates the returns of a broad benchmark index, such as the SPX.

2. "But didn't he say that automated trading strategies make up only a small percentage of volume?" This is still true, but requires clarification. The automated

trading strategies that draw particular concern from the public and regulators are those that involve the coordinated execution of baskets of stock without regard for the individual stocks. For example: selling a basket of 400 stocks "at market." Algorithmic strategies are different from the basket-level strategies because they work on a stock-by-stock basis. Once a wave of orders is in the algorithmic trading engines system, they do not work together anymore—their execution is governed by stock-specific variables.

3. We will encounter another definition of *strike price* in Chapter 9 on options. The two are unrelated.

4. This is usually done by trading index futures to increase or decrease exposure as necessary. Alternatively, if there is a significant sector bias between the two sides of the portfolio, sector ETFs may be used to balance the exposures. These products will be explained in more detail in Chapters 6 and 7.

5. Colloquially, volatility can be thought of as a measurement of how much the price of an asset jumps around. It is defined more precisely in Chapter 9 on options.

Chapter 6   Exchange Traded Funds (ETFs)

1. The net asset value of a fund is the per-share value of the fund assets and is computed as the value of all positions as of the closing prices of the day, plus any cash held by the fund, divided by the number of shares outstanding.

2. ETF management fees depend on the complexity and costs of replicating the benchmark. In highly commoditized indices this can be below 10 bps, while for more complex indices it can 70 bps or higher. Complex ETF structures with embedded derivatives can charge fees of more than 100 bps.

3. When a stock is purchased on margin, the broker lends the investor money to buy the shares, up to 50 percent of the purchase price.

4. If the cash held in the fund is insufficient to cover the management fee, a small portion of the shares may be sold off to cover expenses.

5. This and all other market values are taken from Bloomberg as of July 31, 2008.

6. *Exchange traded commodities* (ETC), are not technically ETFs because they are not funds but listed securities. The mechanics of trading and the ability to source the underlying liquidity are the same as for ETFs and colloquially they are usually referred to as *commodity ETFs*.

7. Cash inflows and outflows from mutual funds are paid out on a $T + 1$ basis, versus the $T + 3$ settlement convention for stocks. Some cash needs to be held on hand to ensure that customer redemption requests can be met.

8. BGI is the world's largest ETF issuer with approximately 50 percent market share.

Chapter 7   Forwards and Futures

1. Among market practitioners, the term "fair value" is alternatively used to refer to the fair forward price and the fair value of the basis. The specific meaning will generally be clear from the context.

2. *Over the counter* (OTC) is a general term to describe products which are not traded on the exchange. We will discuss OTC agreements in more detail in Chapter 8.

3. There also exists a market for single stock futures, but this is a small fraction of the size of the index futures market.

4. From the perspective of valuation and fundamental analysis, the price of a stock is equal to the market's best assessment of the present value of the future cash flows the company will produce. However, as these are generally very difficult to quantify with any precision, within the sales and trading business the price of a stock is generally perceived as an independent variable in derivative pricing.

5. Source: CME website. Calculation based on SPX index level of approximately 1,320 as of June 20, 2008.

6. We will, for the moment, continue to ignore frictional costs, such as execution costs, bid-offer spreads or stock borrow fees, in our analysis.

7. An exception to this is when the position becomes so large, compared to the liquidity of the futures roll market, that the act of rolling the position itself will have significant impact on the pricing of the futures roll.

8. There is a small amount of directional exposure created when trading equal quantities of futures with different maturities, due to the difference in the financing costs of each position to maturity and the dependence of this on the level of the index. This is explained more clearly later in the discussion of "tailing" futures.

9. Although the basis for the EFP is quoted relative to the prior night's closing index level, it is not yesterday's fair value. The basis is for today and is calculated using today's dividends, interest rate, and days to maturity. The market convention is to use yesterday's closing level simply because it is a convenient reference.

10. In order to remove the potentially distracting slippages caused by rounding errors, calculations are done including fractional contracts where they arise.

Chapter 8   Swaps

1. This would more accurately be described as a spectrum from most advantaged to most disadvantaged but the division into two groups simplifies the argument. As long as one investor is better off than another, the concepts hold.

2. From the perspective of the trading desk the "Bank" in Figure 8.1 is the firm's internal treasury group that manages all funds for the company.

3. As we will see later, for brokers and clients who trade actively, there can be a significant amount of standardization in the terms of their business. However, for our purposes here we will assume this is a one-off transaction and unique.

4. Our treatment here of the mechanics of borrowing stock is a deliberate over-simplification. Stock loan is covered in more detail in Chapter 11.

5. In order to prevent small investors (precisely those that Regulation T is meant to protect) from using swaps to leverage their positions excessively, investment banks will impose a set of requirements to ensure that only sophisticated investors who fully understand the risks of derivatives are allowed to trade

swaps. It is not in the broker's interest to let a client over-leverage himself as this creates the potential for the broker to be stuck with the client's trading losses in the event of insolvency.

6. Total return swap on the SPX index swaps are frequently written as price return swaps on the total return index, SPTR. The swap is documented as price return since, by definition, the SPTR has no dividends. Because an SPX swap can be hedged via futures, which are much less expensive to hold than a stock portfolio, the funding spread is much tighter.

7. While *index* and *basket* are often used interchangeably, there is an important difference. A basket is considered to be a static collection of securities with updates occurring infrequently, either at the discretion of the client or to adjust for corporate actions. An index is assumed to have regular updates (i.e., quarterly rebalances) and must have a clearly defined stock selection and weighting methodology.

8. A zero correlation does not mean that the quanto price will be the same as that of a currency-exposed swap. No correlation simply means the broker has no expectation that he will make a gain or a loss. He still has the risk of a loss, however, and will need to make an assessment of how much he thinks he could reasonably lose and will charge for that.

Chapter 9   Options 1

1. As with futures, index options are cash settled due to the impossibility of physically settling an index position.

2. This is simply a naming convention and has nothing to do with where the options trade.

3. Recall that the absolute value of a number x, denoted $|X|$ is the positive value of a number. If $x > 0$, $|X| = X$ (i.e., $|3| = 3$), and if $X < 0$, $|X| = -1 \times X$ (i.e., the same number without the negative sign, $|-3| = 3$).

4. The curious reader may be asking "What if the stock is at exactly 100 at expiration?" This is a subtle but important concept in the risk management of an option portfolio called *pin risk* that we will explore later. It is also worth observing that while we say that the put-call combo "no longer has optionality," we must be clear what we mean by this. While for our purposes we will not consider the cases where an investor acts in an economically inefficient manner, there is nothing that prevents a long option holder from exercising an out-of-the-money option or not exercising an in-the-money option. It just doesn't happen very often.

5. Throughout our presentation we will use interest calculations based on continuous compounding, as opposed to simple interest, as we have done previously, as this is the standard for options calculations. For an explanation of continuous compounding, see the Appendix.

6. We will explore the exceptions to this later.

7. If we make the simplifying assumption that interest rates are zero the formula reduces to $C = (S - K) + P$.

8. This is not exactly correct. The precise statement is actually that the maximum time value occurs at the present value of the strike price. However, in order to avoid potentially small, distracting asymmetries in the graphs caused by the interest rate considerations, all exhibits are prepared based on interest rates of zero and therefore the point of maximum time value lines up with the strike price. We will discuss the impact of interest rates on option prices in more detail in the next chapter.

9. While at this point, we are only examining the sensitivity of the call price to changes in the underlying stock price, we will see more clearly later that there are other variables that influence option prices. For this reason, we introduce the correct notation from the start and use partial derivatives as opposed to single variable formulations (i.e., using ∂C as opposed to dC).

10. The term $\mu_i = \ln(x_i/x_{i-1})$ is frequently replaced by the simple return $\mu_i = (x_i - x_{i-1})/x_{i-1}$. The error in this approximation is very small for daily returns.

11. For those who noticed and are wondering why we use $n-1$ in the denominator, as opposed to n, this is a standard statistical adjustment to account for the difference between the standard deviation of the sample (i.e., the data points we used to compute the volatility) and the standard deviation of the full population (all price movements). We are interested in computing the stock's real volatility, not just the volatility realized in our sample of data. Therefore, we use the $n-1$ formulation.

12. Kyoshi Itô published this important property of stochastic variables in 1951. Considering that calculus and probability have been around since the late seventeenth century, this is a very recent result. It would have been unlikely for Black and Scholes to have produced their result had they attempted it 25 years earlier, before the result was available.

13. Curiously, the PDE can be converted, via a change of variable, into the one-dimensional heat diffusion equation from thermodynamics.

14. With the exception of the strike price, K, which is static except where a corporate action requires it to be changed, the other four inputs $(S, t, \sigma,$ and $r)$ are all variable and we will look at the sensitivity of the option price to movements in all of these in Chapter 10. While for convenience we commonly abbreviate the notation for the call price as $C(S)$, $C(S, t)$ or simply C, the more correct expression is $C(S, K, t, \sigma, r)$ which recognizes the full scope of the sensitivities of the call price to each of the underlying variables.

15. If an algebraic formula cannot be found that gives a general solution to the problem, the best that can be done is to find a numerical approximation to the solution for a particular case. The branch of mathematics that develops methods for quickly finding these sorts of numerical approximations is called *numerical analysis*.

Chapter 10 Options 2

1. While at some level analogous, this use of the term "delta adjust" should not be confused with the delta adjustment of the futures basis.

2. In the Black-Scholes framework, where hedging is continuous, the option's time value can be viewed as the expected value of the trading-related gains from delta-hedging.

3. This conversion of a level of implied volatility into an estimate of the average daily percent movement in the underlying stock price is intended only as a guideline. The realities of delta-hedging are much more complex and the impact of factors such as intraday movements which revert (e.g., the stock rallies until midday and then sells off back to its original level by the close) or discontinuous jumps (e.g., overnight newsflow causing large moves in the stock price at the market opening) can have significant impact on the profits or losses from delta-hedging that are not captured in the simplistic "divide by 16" estimate.

4. If the borrow costs are known then an adjustment can be made to the interest rate to account for them, which would allow the true level of implied volatility to be known.

5. Vega is not actually a Greek letter and is sometimes replaced by kappa (κ).

6. Delta, gamma, and vega are only strictly additive for a single underlier, while theta and rho can be summed across multiple underliers to produce a picture of the aggregate exposure to the passage of time or rates. Notwithstanding, it is common to aggregate delta, gamma, and vega across different underliers (with, perhaps, an adjustment for individual stock betas) to produce an estimate of the aggregate market exposure of the whole desk.

7. We are effectively taking the partial derivatives of the implied volatility with respect to maturity and strike.

8. Given the extremely conservative investor protection laws in the United States, I still find it refreshing and somewhat amusing to see the relaxed way in which highly complex, long-dated exotic derivatives are embedded into capital-protected structures that are then sold to retail investors at local bank branch offices (and even post offices) across Europe.

9. Another type of exotic option that has a similar look-back feature (but is not path-dependent) is a *chooser option*, which allows the holder to decide at maturity whether the option was a call or a put.

Chapter 11   The Trading Floor

1. By lowering the strike price to zero, the option is always deep in-the-money and has zero probability of ending out-of-the-money (the option to buy something for nothing is always worth something). It therefore has no curvature or volatility sensitivity and is a pure one-delta product.

2. The large stock positions held by passively indexed ETFs, mutual, and pension funds, whose managers do not choose the stocks based on their particular fundamentals but simply to replicate the performance of a benchmark index, are an immensely useful pool of long positions that can be sourced by stock lending desks to provide short access to more dynamic traders. For the index fund manager, the pick-up from lending stock is a welcome source of additional revenue, which improves their performance versus the benchmark.

3. The assumption is that the broker is not aware that the uncovered short was deliberate, in which case the position would be bought-in immediately.
4. Depository Trust & Clearing Corporation data (www.dtcc.com).
5. At current levels, this is approximately 120 years of U.S. GDP.

Chapter 12   Macroeconomics for Trading and Sales

1. This is not strictly correct. Beta measures the sensitivity to the *excess* return over the risk-free rate. However, over short periods, the difference is minimal and is generally ignored within the trading floor environment.
2. Our discussion of macroeconomics will be from a U.S.-centric viewpoint, though the general concepts can be applied to any country. We will also allow the occasional imprecise use of "American" as the adjective for things pertaining to the United States, with apologies to our neighbors to the north and south for the linguistic arrogance.
3. Bureau of Economic Analysis data (www.bea.gov) as of July 31, 2008.
4. "Investment," in the computation of GDP, has nothing to do with financial investments (purchases of stocks or bonds) as these do not represent actual production of goods or services.
5. To be specific, the graph shows the rolling eight-quarter moving average of the annualized rate of real GDP growth based on seasonally adjusted data in constant, year 2000 dollars. (Is anyone surprised I decided to hide this lovely bit of detail in a footnote?) The graph starts in 1949 because quarterly data were not available before then.
6. In economics literature this is often replaced by the Latin *ceteris paribus*.
7. The Federal Reserve Act of 1913.
8. This formula comes from the same infinite series we used in Chapter 2 on Valuation and Chapter 7 on Futures.
9. These concepts are central to one of the key scenes in the holiday classic film *It's a Wonderful Life* (1946). While George Bailey (played by Jimmy Stewart) never actually uses the term "fractional reserve banking," when a mob of customers storm into his family-owned building and loan (a type of savings bank that specializes in mortgages) demanding their money, he desperately tries to explain it to them:

> "No, but you ... you ... you're thinking of this place all wrong! As if I had the money back in a safe. The money's not here. Your money's in Joe's house ... right next to yours ... and in the Kennedy house, and Mrs. Macklin's house, and a hundred others! Why, you're lending them the money to build, and then they're going to pay it back to you as best they can. Now what are you going to do? Foreclose on them?"
> (Quote transcribed by the author)

This sort of panicked withdrawal of deposits was, until very recently thought of as a depression-era phenomenon. However, since the onset of the credit crisis in August of 2007, it has recurred numerous times around the world, triggering a wave of bankruptcies, capital injections, bail-outs, and, in some cases, nationalizations of what were previously considered perfectly sound banks.

10. For simplicity, percentages are expressed of GDP excluding net trade, which, in the case of the United States, is actually a negative contribution.

11. We will make the simplifying assumption that all foreign companies are kind enough to allow U.S. consumers to pay in USD. While this is not generally true—with the notable exception of oil and other commodities that trade in dollars globally—it greatly simplifies the explanation.

12. U.S. Treasury Department data (www.treas.gov) as of July 31, 2008.

Chapter 13   Economic Data Releases

1. The Institute for Supply Management was formerly known as the National Association of Purchasing Managers and the Survey of Manufacturing is still occasionally referred to as the NAPM survey. According to its website (www.ism.ws), ISM defines supply management as "the identification, acquisition, access, positioning and management of resources and related capabilities the organization needs or potentially needs in the attainment of its strategic objectives." This definition is effectively a generalized and more formal version of the intuitive notion of a purchasing manager as "the guy in charge of buying all the stuff."

2. Between March 2000 and October 2002, the SPX dropped nearly 49 percent and the NDX more than 83 percent.

3. The months of September and October of 2008 were arguably the most tumultuous to the global economic system since the Great Depression. In the span of fewer than eight weeks, the two largest mortgage lenders in the United States, Fannie Mae and Freddie Mac, were nationalized; Lehman Brothers declared bankruptcy; Merrill Lynch was acquired by Bank of America; American Insurance Group (AIG) received a $150 billion bailout from the Treasury; Morgan Stanley and Goldman Sachs became bank holding companies; Washington Mutual Bank was seized by the FDIC; Fortis Bank was partially nationalized by the Benelux governments; Iceland nationalized all the major banks and suspended trading in the Icelandic krona; the Treasury made equity investments worth $125 billion in nine major banks; short-selling was partially or completely suspended in more than a dozen countries and trading in many emerging markets was halted as global equity markets dropped an average of between 30 and 40 percent from what were already depressed levels. These were truly unbelievable days to be working in the financial services industry, the consequences of which will not be fully understood for many years.

4. *Durable goods* are generally defined as items with a life expectancy of at least three years.

5. U.S. International Trade in Goods and Services—Annual Revision for 2007, June 10, 2008 (www.census.gov).
6. From the perspective of a given industry, each employer "consumes" (hires) only a single type of employee and there is, in general, little potential for substitution. A hospital can't fire a highly trained anesthesiologist and replace her with the local Starbucks barista just because he requires a lower wage.
7. Companies such as ExxonMobil, Royal Dutch-Shell, Total and British Petroleum that are involved in all aspects of the exploration, extraction, refinement, and distribution of crude oil and distillates.
8. Note that the average is computed using the actual overnight rates as reported by the New York Fed, not the target rate, though outside of times of significant stress in the markets, of which there was much in 2008, these will usually not differ significantly.
9. Greece did not adopt the euro until January 1, 2001.
10. In recent years, more countries have joined the European Union, bringing current membership to 27 countries. Three of these, Cyprus, Malta, and Slovenia have adopted the euro as their official currency. However, by convention, the Eurozone is still used to refer only to the 11 countries (plus Greece) that adopted the euro at inception.
11. Due to the large size and global diversification of many U.K. companies, the significance of the Bank of England is somewhat greater than these statistics would suggest. Weighing each country by stock market capitalization, the Bank of England oversees 28 percent of the European market cap while the ECB oversees 56 percent.
12. The three largest economies in Euroland, responsible for approximately 65 percent of the Eurozone GDP.
13. Belgium, Finland, Portugal, and Luxembourg are not included. However, the included countries account for more than 92 percent of the Eurozone GDP.

Appendix: Mathematical Review

1. The number e is irrational—a nonterminating, nonrepeating decimal, and therefore can never be written precisely as a decimal or fraction. It is also a transcendental number (cannot be expressed as the solution to a polynomial equation), which sounds even cooler.

About the Author

Matthew Tagliani, CFA, has more than 10 years trading and risk management experience in delta-one products including equity swaps, ETFs, futures, and program trading. He has worked at Morgan Stanley, Goldman Sachs, Credit Suisse, and Banco Santander in New York, London, and Madrid. Prior to his professional career, he received a master's degree in Applied Mathematics from the University of Massachusetts at Amherst. He lives in London with his wife and two children.

Index